Praise for other *Head First books*

"I received the book yesterday and started to read it...and I couldn't stop. This is definitely très 'cool.' It is fun, but they cover a lot of ground and they are right to the point. I'm really impressed."

— **Erich Gamma, IBM Distinguished Engineer, and co-author of *Design Patterns***

"One of the funniest and smartest books on software design I've ever read."

— **Aaron LaBerge, VP Technology, ESPN.com**

"What used to be a long trial and error learning process has now been reduced neatly into an engaging paperback."

— **Mike Davidson, CEO, Newsvine, Inc.**

"Elegant design is at the core of every chapter here, each concept conveyed with equal doses of pragmatism and wit."

— **Ken Goldstein, Executive Vice President, Disney Online**

"I ♥ Head First HTML with CSS & XHTML—it teaches you everything you need to learn in a 'fun coated' format."

— **Sally Applin, UI Designer and Artist**

"Usually when reading through a book or article on design patterns, I'd have to occasionally stick myself in the eye with something just to make sure I was paying attention. Not with this book. Odd as it may sound, this book makes learning about design patterns fun.

"While other books on design patterns are saying 'Buehler… Buehler… Buehler…' this book is on the float belting out 'Shake it up, baby!'"

— **Eric Wuehler**

"I literally love this book. In fact, I kissed this book in front of my wife."

— **Satish Kumar**

Other related books from O'Reilly

Programming C# 3.0

C# 3.0 in a Nutshell

C# 3.0 Cookbook™

C# 3.0 Design Patterns

C# Essentials

C# Language Pocket Reference

Other books in O'Reilly's *Head First* series

Head First Java

Head First Object-Oriented Analysis and Design (OOA&D)

Head Rush Ajax

Head First HTML with CSS and XHTML

Head First Design Patterns

Head First Servlets and JSP

Head First EJB

Head First PMP

Head First SQL

Head First Software Development

Head First JavaScript

Advance Praise for *Head First C#*

"I've never read a computer book cover to cover, but this one held my interest from the first page to the last. If you want to learn C# in depth and have fun doing it, this is THE book for you."

> — **Andy Parker, fledgling C# programmer**

"Head First C# is a great book for hobbyist programmers. It provides examples and guidance on a majority of the things [those] programmers are likely to encounter writing applications in C#."

> —**Peter Ritchie, Microsoft MVP (2006-2007), Visual Developer, C#**

"With Head First C#, Andrew and Jenny have presented an excellent tutorial on learning C#. It is very approachable while covering a great amount of detail in a unique style. If you've been turned off by more conventional books on C#, you'll love this one."

> —**Jay Hilyard, Software Developer, co-author of *C# 3.0 Cookbook***

"Head First C# is perfect blend of unique and interesting ways covering most of the concepts of programming. Fun excercises, bullet points, and even comic strips are some of the catchy and awesome works that this book has. The game-based labs are something that you really don't want to miss. [This book is] a great work... the novice as [well as the] well-experienced will love this book. GREAT JOB!"

> —**Aayam Singh, .NET professional**

"Head First C# is a highly enjoyable tutorial, full of memorable examples and entertaining exercises. Its lively style is sure to captivate readers—from the humorously annotated examples, to the Fireside Chats, where the abstract class and interface butt heads in a heated argument! For anyone new to programming, there's no better way to dive in."

> —**Joseph Albahari, C# Design Architect at Egton Medical Information Systems, the UK's largest primary healthcare software supplier, co-author of *C# 3.0 in a Nutshell***

"[Head First C#] was an easy book to read and understand. I will recommend this book to any developer wanting to jump into the C# waters. I will recommend it to the advanced developer that wants to understand better what is happening with their code. [I will recommend it to developers who] want to find a better way to explain how C# works to their less-seasoned developer friends."

> —**Giuseppe Turitto, C# and ASP.NET developer for Cornwall Consulting Group**

"Andrew and Jenny have crafted another stimulating Head First learning experience. Grab a pencil, a computer, and enjoy the ride as you engage your left brain, right brain, and funny bone."

> —**Bill Mietelski, Software Engineer**

"Going through this Head First C# book was a great experience. I have not come across a book series which actually teaches you so well…This is a book I would definitely recommend to people wanting to learn C#"

> —**Krishna Pala, MCP**

Head First C#

> Wouldn't it be dreamy if there was a C# book that was more fun than endlessly debugging code? It's probably nothing but a fantasy...

Andrew Stellman
Jennifer Greene

O'REILLY®

Beijing • Cambridge • Köln • Paris • Sebastopol • Taipei • Tokyo

SHROFF PUBLISHERS & DISTRIBUTORS PVT. LTD.
Mumbai   Bangalore   Chennai   Kolkata   New Delhi

Head First C#

by Andrew Stellman and Jennifer Greene

Copyright © 2008 O'Reilly Media, Inc. All rights reserved. ISBN-10: 0-596-51482-4, ISBN-13: 978-0-596-51482-2
Originally Printed in the United States of America.

Published by O'Reilly Media, Inc., 1005 Gravenstein Highway North, Sebastopol, CA 95472.

O'Reilly books may be purchased for educational, business, or sales promotional use.
Online editions are also available for most titles *(safari.oreilly.com)*. For more information, contact our corporate/
institutional sales department: (800) 998-9938 or *corporate@oreilly.com*.

Series Creators:	Kathy Sierra, Bert Bates
Series Editor:	Brett D. McLaughlin
Design Editor:	Louise Barr
Cover Designers:	Louise Barr, Steve Fehler
Production Editor:	Sanders Kleinfeld
Proofreader:	Colleen Gorman
Indexer:	Julie Hawks
Page Viewers:	Quentin the whippet and Tequila the pomeranian

Printing History:

November 2007:   First Edition.

First Indian Reprint: December 2007

ISBN 10: 81-8404-419-4
ISBN 13: 978-81-8404-419-5

Published by **Shroff Publishers and Distributors Pvt. Ltd.** C-103, MIDC, TTC Industrial Area, Pawane, Navi Mumbai 400 701, Tel: (91 22) 2763 4290, Fax: (91 22) 2768 3337, e-mail: spdorders@shroffpublishers.com. Printed at Decora Printers, Mumbai.

This book is dedicated to the loving memory of Sludgie the Whale, who swam to Brooklyn on April 17, 2007.

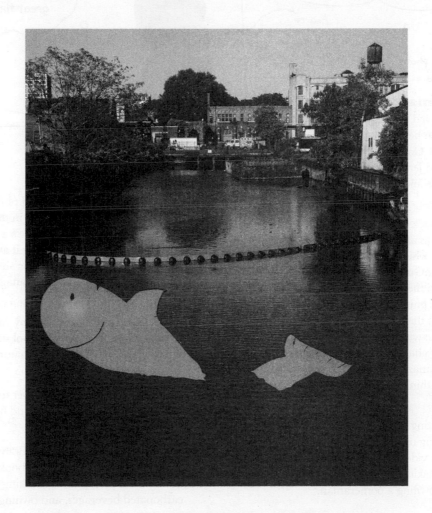

You were only in our canal for a day, but you'll be in our hearts forever.

Thanks for buying our book! We really love writing about this stuff, and we hope you get a kick out of reading it...

Andrew

... because we know you're going to have a great time learning C#.

Jenny

This photo (and the photo of the Gowanus Canal) by Nisha Sondhe

Andrew Stellman, despite being raised a New Yorker, has lived in Pittsburgh *twice*. The first time was when he graduated from Carnegie Mellon's School of Computer Science, and then again when he and Jenny were starting their consulting business and writing their first book for O'Reilly.

When he moved back to his hometown, his first job after college was as a programmer at EMI-Capitol Records—which actually made sense, since he went to LaGuardia High School of Music and Art and the Performing Arts to study cello and jazz bass guitar. He and Jenny first worked together at that same financial software company, where he was managing a team of programmers. He's had the privilege of working with some pretty amazing programmers over the years, and likes to think that he's learned a few things from them.

When he's not writing books, Andrew keeps himself busy writing useless (but fun) software, playing music (but video games even more), studying taiji and aikido, having a girlfriend named Lisa, and owning a pomeranian.

Jennifer Greene studied philosophy in college but, like everyone else in the field, couldn't find a job doing it. Luckily, she's a great software tester, so she started out doing it at an online service, and that's the first time she really got a good sense of what project management was.

She moved to New York in 1998 to test software at a financial software company. She managed a team of testers at a really cool startup that did artificial intelligence and natural language processing.

Since then, she's traveled all over the world to work with different software teams and build all kinds of cool projects.

She loves traveling, watching Bollywood movies, reading the occasional comic book, waiting for her Xbox to be repaired, drinking carloads of carbonated beverages, and owning a whippet.

Jenny and Andrew have been building software and writing about software engineering together since they first met in 1998. Their first book, *Applied Software Project Management*, was published by O'Reilly in 2005. They published their first book in the Head First series, *Head First PMP*, in 2007.

They founded Stellman & Greene Consulting in 2003 to build a really neat software project for scientists studying herbicide exposure in Vietnam vets. When they're not building software or writing books, they do a lot of speaking at conferences and meetings of software engineers, architects and project managers.

Check out their blog, *Building Better Software*: http://www.stellman-greene.com

Table of Contents (Summary)

	Intro	xxix
1	Get productive with C#: *Visual Applications, in 10 minutes or less*	1
2	It's All Just Code: *Under the hood*	43
3	Objects Get Oriented: *Making code make sense*	85
4	Types and References: *It's 10:00. Do you know where your data is?*	123
	C# Lab 1: *A Day at the Races*	163
5	Encapsulation: *Keep your privates… private*	173
6	Inheritance: *Your object's family tree*	205
7	Interfaces and abstract classes: *Making classes keep their promises*	251
8	enums and collections: *Storing lots of data*	309
	C# Lab 2: *The Quest*	363
9	Reading and writing files: *Save the byte array, save the world*	385
10	Exception handling: *Putting Out Fires Gets Old*	439
11	events and delegates: *What Your Code Does When You're Not Looking*	483
12	Review and preview: *Knowledge, Power, and Building Cool Stuff*	515
13	Controls and graphics: *Make it pretty*	563
14	Captain Amazing: *The Death of the Object*	621
15	LINQ: *Get control of your data*	653
	C# Lab 3: *Invaders*	681

Table of Contents (the real thing)

Intro

Your brain on C#. You're sitting around trying to *learn* something, but your *brain* keeps telling you all that learning *isn't important.* Your brain's saying, "Better leave room for more important things, like which wild animals to avoid and whether nude archery is a bad idea." So how *do* you trick your brain into thinking that your life really depends on learning C#?

Who is this book for?	xxx
We know what you're thinking	xxxi
Metacognition	xxxiii
Bend your brain into submission	xxxv
What you need for this book	xxxvi
Read me	xxxvii
The technical review team	xxxviii
Acknowledgments	xxxix

get productive with C#

Visual Applications, in 10 minutes or less

Want to build great programs really fast?

With C#, you've got a **powerful programming language** and a **valuable tool** at your fingertips. With the **Visual Studio IDE**, you'll never have to spend hours writing obscure code to get a button working again. Even better, you'll be able to **focus on getting your work done**, rather than remembering which method parameter was for the *name* for a button, and which one was for its *label*. Sound appealing? Turn the page, and let's get programming.

Why you should learn C#	2
C# and the Visual Studio IDE make lots of things easy	3
Help the CEO go paperless	4
Get to know your users' needs before you startbuilding your program	5
Here's what you're going to build	6
What you do in Visual Studio…	8
What Visual Studio does for you…	8
Develop the user interface	12
Visual Studio, behind the scenes	14
Add to the auto-generated code	15
You can already run your application	16
We need a database to store our information	18
Creating the table for the Contact List	20
The blanks on contact card are columns in our People table	22
Finish building the table	25
Diagram your data so your application can access it	26
Insert your card data into the database	28
Connect your form to your database objects with a data source	30
Add database-driven controls to your form	32
Good apps are intuitive to use	34
How to turn YOUR application into EVERYONE'S application	37
Give your users the application	38
You're NOT done: test your installation	39
You built a complete data-driven application	40

it's all just code
Under the Hood

2

You're a programmer, not just an IDE-user.

You can get a lot of work done using the IDE. But there's only so far it can take you. Sure, there are a lot of **repetitive tasks** that you do when you build an application. And the IDE is great at doing those things for you. But working with the IDE is *only the beginning*. You can get your programs to do so much more—and **writing C# code** is how you do it. Once you get the hang of coding, there's *nothing* your programs can't do.

When you're doing this...	44
...the IDE does this	45
Where programs come from	46
The IDE helps you code	48
When you change things in the IDE, you're also changing your code	50
Anatomy of a program	52
Your program knows where to start	54
You can change your program's entry point	56
Two classes can be in the same namespace	61
Your programs use variables to work with data	62
C# uses familiar math symbols	64
Loops perform an action over and over again	65
Time to start coding	66
if/else statements make decisions	67
Set up conditions and see if they're true	68

Build this form →

Every time you make a new program, you define a namespace for it so that its code is separate from the .NET Framework classes.

A class contains a **piece** of your program (although some very small programs can have just one class). →

A class has one or more methods. Your methods always have to live **inside a class**. And methods are made up of statements — like the ones you've already seen. →

objects get oriented
Making Code Make Sense

3

Every program you write solves a problem.

When you're building a program, it's always a good idea to start by thinking about what *problem* your program's supposed to solve. That's why **objects** are really useful. They let you structure your code based on the problem it's solving, so that you can spend your time *thinking about the problem* you need to work on rather than getting bogged down in the mechanics of writing code. When you use objects right, you end up with code that's *intuitive* to write, and easy to read and change.

Navigator

SetDestination()
ModifyRouteToAvoid()
ModifyRouteToInclude()
GetRoute()
GetTimeToDestination()
TotalDistance()

new Navigator()

navigator1
Navigator object

new Navigator()

navigator2
Navigator object

new Navigator()

navigator3
Navigator object

When you define a class, you define its methods, just like a blueprint defines the layout of the house.

You can use one blueprint to make any number of houses, and you can use one class to make any number of objects.

How Mike thinks about his problems	86
How Mike's car navigation system thinks about his problems	87
Mike's Navigator class has methods to set and modify routes	88
Use what you've learned to build a simple application	89
Mike gets an idea	90
Mike can use objects to solve his problem	91
You use a class to build an object	92
When you create a new object from a class, it's called an instance of that class	93
A better solution… brought to you by objects!	94
An instance uses fields to keep track of things	98
Let's create some instances!	99
Thanks for the memory	100
What's on your program's mind	101
You can use class and method names to make your code intuitive	102
Give your classes a natural structure	104
Class diagrams help you organize your classes so they make sense	106
Build a class to work with some guys	110
Create a project for your guys	111
Build a form to interact with the guys	112
There's an even easier way to initialize objects	115
A few ideas for designing intuitive classes	116

types and references

It's 10:00. Do you know where your data is?

4

**Data type, database, Lieutenant Commander Data...
it's all important stuff.** Without data, your programs are useless. You need **information** from your users, and you use that to look up or produce new information, to give back to them. In fact, almost everything you do in programming involves **working with data** in one way or another. In this chapter, you'll learn the ins and outs of C#'s **data types**, how to work with data in your program, and even figure out a few dirty secrets about **objects** (*psstt... objects are data, too*).

The variable's type determines what kind of data it can store	124
A variable is like a data to-go cup	126
10 pounds of data in a 5 pound bag	127
Even when a number is the right size, you can't just assign it to any variable	128
When you cast a value that's too big, C# will adjust it automatically	129
C# does some casting automatically	130
When you call a method, the variables must match the types of the parameters	131
Combining = with an operator	136
Objects are variables, too	137
Refer to your objects with reference variables	138
References are like labels for your object	139
If there aren't any more references, your object gets garbage collected	140
Multiple references and their side effects	142
Two references means TWO ways to change an object's data	147
A special case: arrays	148
Arrays can contain a bunch of reference variables, too	149
Welcome to Sloppy Joe's Budget House o' Discount Sandwiches!	150
Objects use references to talk to each other	152
Where no object has gone before	153

```
Dog fido;
Dog lucky = new Dog();
```

```
fido = new Dog();
```

```
lucky = null;
```

C# Lab 1

A Day at the Races

Joe, Bob, and Al love going to the track, but they're tired of losing all their money. They need you to build a simulator for them so they can figure out winners before they lay their money down. And, if you do a good job, they'll cut you in on their profits.

The Spec: Build a Racetrack Simulator   164

The Finished Product   172

5 encapsulation

Keep your privates... private

Ever wished for a little more privacy?

Sometimes your objects feel the same way. Just like you don't want anybody you don't trust reading your journal, or paging through your bank statements, good objects don't let *other* objects go poking around their properties. In this chapter, you're going to learn about the power of **encapsulation**. You'll **make your object's data private**, add methods to **protect how that data is accessed**.

ciaAgent

kgbAgent

mi5Agent

Kathleen is an event planner	174
What does the estimator do?	175
Kathleen's Test Drive	180
Each option should be calculated individually	182
It's easy to accidentally misuse your objects	184
Encapsulation means keeping some of the data in a class private	185
Use encapsulation to control access to your class's methods and fields	186
But is the realName field REALLY protected?	187
Private fields and methods can only be accessed from inside the class	188
A few ideas for encapsulating classes	191
Encapsulation keeps your data pristine	192
Properties make encapsulation easier	193
Build an application to test the Farmer class	194
Use automatic properties to finish the class	195
What if we want to change the feed multiplier?	196
Use a constructor to initialize private fields	197

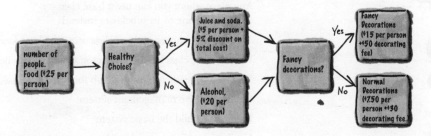

inheritance

Your object's family tree

Sometimes you *DO* want to be just like your parents.

6

Ever run across an object that *almost* does exactly what you want *your* object to do? Found yourself wishing that if you could just *change a few things*, that object would be perfect? Well that's just one reason that **inheritance** is one of the most powerful concepts and techniques in the C# language. Before you're through this chapter, you'll learn how to **subclass** an object to get its behavior, but keep the **flexibility** to make changes to that behavior. You'll **avoid duplicate code**, **model the real world** more closely, and end up with code that's **easier to maintain**.

Kathleen does birthday parties, too	206
We need a BirthdayParty class	207
One more thing... can you add a $100 fee for parties over 12?	213
When your classes use inheritance, you only need to write your code once	214
Build up your class model by starting general and getting more specific	215
How would you design a zoo simulator?	216
Use inheritance to avoid duplicate code in subclasses	217
Different animals make different noises	218
Think about how to group the animals	219
Create the class hierarchy	220
Every subclass extends its base class	221
Use a colon to inherit from a base class	222
We know that inheritance adds the base class fields, properties, and methods to the subclass...	225
A subclass can override methods to change or replace methods it inherited	226
Any place where you can use a base class, you can use one of its subclasses instead	227
A subclass can access its base class using the base keyword	232
When a base class has a constructor, your subclass needs one too	233
Now you're ready to finish the job for Kathleen!	234
Build a beehive management system	239
First you'll build the basic system	240
Use inheritance to extend the bee management system	245

interfaces and abstract classes

Making classes keep their promises

7

Actions speak louder than words.

Sometimes you need to group your objects together based on the **things they can do** rather than the classes they inherit from. That's where **interfaces** come in—they let you work with any class that can do the job. But with **great power comes great responsibility**, and any class that implements an interface must promise to **fulfill all of its obligations**... or the compiler will break their kneecaps, see?

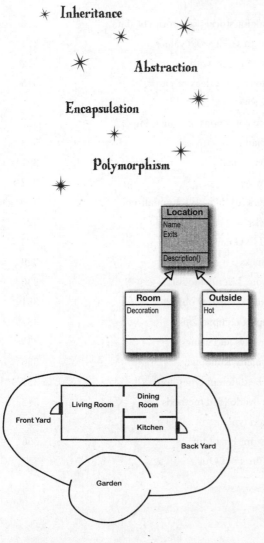

✳ Inheritance

Abstraction

Encapsulation

Polymorphism

Let's get back to bee-sics	252
We can use inheritance to create classes for different types of bees	253
An interface tells a class that it must implement certain methods and properties	254
Use the interface keyword to define an interface	255
Now you can create an instance of NectarStinger that does both jobs	256
Classes that implement interfaces have to include ALL of the interface's methods	257
Get a little practice using interface	258
You can't instantiate an interface, but you can reference an interface	260
Interface references work just like object references	261
You can find out if a class implements a certain interface with "is"	262
Interfaces can inherit from other interfaces	263
The RoboBee 4000 can do a worker bee's job without using valuable honey	264
is tells you what an object implements, as tells the compiler how to treat your object	265
A CoffeeMaker is also an Appliance	266
Upcasting works with both objects and interfaces	267
Downcasting lets you turn your appliance back into a coffee maker	268
Upcasting and downcasting work with interfaces, too	269
There's more than just public and private	273
Access modifiers change scope	274
Some classes should never be instantiated	277
An abstract class is like a cross between a class and an interface	278
Some classes should never be instantiated	280
An abstract method doesn't have a body	281
Polymorphism means that one object can take many different forms	289

enums and collections

Storing lots of data

When it rains, it pours.

In the real world, you don't get to handle your data in tiny little bits and pieces. No, your data's going to come at you in **loads, piles and bunches**. You'll need some pretty powerful tools to organize all of it, and that's where **collections** come in. They let you **store, sort and manage** all the data that your programs need to pore through. That way you can think about writing programs to work with your data, and let the collections worry about keeping track of it for you.

Strings don't always work for storing categories of data	310
Enums let you enumerate a set of valid values	311
Enums let you represent numbers with names	312
We could use an array to create a deck of cards...	315
Arrays are hard to work with	316
Lists make it easy to store collections of... anything	317
Lists are more flexible than arrays	318
Lists shrink and grow dynamically	321
List objects can store any type	322
Collection initializers work just like object initializers	326
Let's create a list of Ducks	327
Lists are easy, but SORTING can be tricky	328
Two ways to sort your ducks	329
Use IComparer to tell your List how to sort	330
Create an instance of your comparer object	331
IComparer can do complex comparisons	332
Use a dictionary to store keys and values	335
The Dictionary Functionality Rundown	336
Your key and value can be different types, too	337
You can build your own overloaded methods	343
And yet MORE collection types...	355
A queue is FIFO — First In, First Out	356
A stack is LIFO — Last In, First Out	357

poof!

C# Lab 2

The Quest

Your job is to build an adventure game where a mighty adventurer is on a quest to defeat level after level of deadly enemies. You'll build a turn-based system, which means the player makes one move and then the enemies make one move. The player can move or attack, and then each enemy gets a chance to move and attack. The game keeps going until the player either defeats all the enemies on all seven levels or dies.

The spec: build an adventure game   364

The fun's just beginning!   384

reading and writing files

Save the byte array, save the world

Sometimes it pays to be a little persistent.

So far, all of your programs have been pretty short-lived. They fire up, run for a while, and shut down. But that's not always enough, especially when you're dealing with important information. You need to be able to **save your work**. In this chapter, we'll look at how to **write data to a file**, and then how to **read that information back in** from a file. You'll learn about the .NET **stream classes**, and also take a look at the mysteries of **hexadecimal** and **binary**.

C# uses streams to read and write data	386
Different streams read and write different things	387
A FileStream writes bytes to a file	388
Reading and writing takes two objects	393
Data can go through more than one stream	394
Use built-in objects to pop up standard dialog boxes	397
Dialog boxes are objects, too	399
Use the built-in File and Directory classes to work with files and directories	400
Use File Dialogs to open and save files	403
IDisposable makes sure your objects are disposed properly	405
Avoid file system errors with using statements	406
Writing files usually involves making a lot of decisions	412
Use a switch statement to choose the right option	413
Add an overloaded Deck() constructor that reads a deck of cards in from a file	415
What happens to an object when it's serialized?	417
But what exactly IS an object's state? What needs to be saved?	418
When an object is serialized, all of the objects it refers to get serialized too...	419
Serialization lets you read or write a whole object all at once	420
If you want your class to be serializable, mark it with the [Serializable] attribute	421
.NET converts text to Unicode automatically	425
C# can use byte arrays to move data around	426
Use a BinaryWriter to write binary data	427
You can read and write serialized files manually, too	429
StreamReader and StreamWriter will do just fine	433

Eureka! ➡ 69 117 114 101 107 97 33

exception handling

Putting out fires gets old

Programmers aren't meant to be firefighters.

You've worked your tail off, waded through technical manuals and a few engaging Head First books, and you've reached the pinnacle of your profession: **master programmer**. But you're still getting pages from work because **your program crashes**, or **doesn't behave like it's supposed to**. Nothing pulls you out of the programming groove like having to fix a strange bug . . . but with **exception handling**, you can write code to **deal with problems** that come up. Better yet, you can even react to those problems, and **keep things running**.

10

Brian needs his excuses to be mobile	440
When your program throws an exception, .NET generates an Exception object.	444
Brian's code did something unexpected	446
All exception objects inherit from Exception	448
The debugger helps you track down and prevent exceptions in your code	449
Use the IDE's debugger to ferret out exactly what went wrong in the excuse manager	450
Uh-oh—the code's still got problems...	453
Handle exceptions with try and catch	455
What happens when a method you want to call is risky?	456
Use the debugger to follow the try/catch flow	458
If you have code that ALWAYS should run, use a finally block	460
Use the Exception object to get information about the problem	465
Use more than one catch block to handle multiple types of exceptions	466
One class throws an exception, another class catches the exception	467
Bees need an OutOfHoney exception	468
An easy way to avoid a lot of problems: using gives you try and finally for free	471
Exception avoidance: implement IDisposable to do your own clean up	472
The worst catch block EVER: comments	474
Temporary solutions are okay (temporarily)	475
A few simple ideas for exception handling	476
Brian finally gets his vacation...	481

Work's boring today. I want to go scuba diving. Time to fire up the Excuse generator.

events and delegates

What your code does when you're not looking

11

Your objects are starting to think for themselves.

You can't always control what your objects are doing. Sometimes things... happen. And when they do, you want your objects to be smart enough to **respond to anything** that pops up. And that's what events are all about. One object *publishes* an event, other objects *subscibe*, and everyone works together to keep things moving. Which is great, until you've got too many objects responding to the same event. And that's when **callbacks** will come in handy.

Ever wish your objects could think for themselves?	484
But how does an object KNOW to respond?	484
When an EVENT occurs... objects listen	485
One object raises its event, others listen for it...	486
Then, the other objects handle the event	487
Connecting the dots	488
The IDE creates event handlers for you automatically	492
The forms you've been building all use events	498
Connecting event senders with event receivers	500
A delegate STANDS IN for an actual method	501
Delegates in action	502
Any object can subscribe to a public event...	505
Use a callback instead of an event to hook up exactly one object to a delegate	507
Callbacks use delegates, but NOT events	508

When the ball gets hit, BallHasBeenHit() gets called.

The ball was hit with a 70 degree trajectory from homeplate, and it's going to travel 82 feet.

`Ball.OnBallInPlay(70, 82)`

We want the Pitcher to catch this ball.

Ball object

The pitcher can handle the angle the ball was hit, and the distance (90 is greater than 82).

Pitcher object

`Pitcher.CatchBall(70, 90)`

review and preview

Knowledge, power, and building cool stuff

Learning's no good until you BUILD something.

Until you've actually written working code, it's hard to be sure if you really *get* some of the tougher concepts in C#. In this chapter, we're going to learn about some new odds and ends: **timers** and dealing with collections using **LINQ** (to name a couple). We're also going to build phase I of a **really complex application**, and make sure you've got a good handle on what you've already learned from earlier chapters. So buckle up... it's time to build some **cool software**.

12

You've come a long way, baby	516
We've also become beekeepers	517
The beehive simulator architecture	518
Building the beehive simulator	519
Life and death of a flower	523
Now we need a Bee class	524
Filling out the Hive class	532
The hive's Go() method	533
We're ready for the World	534
We're building a turn-based system	535
Giving the bees behavior	542
The main form tells the world to Go()	544
We can use World to get statistics	545
Timers fire events over and over again	546
The timer's using a delegate behind the scenes	547
Let's work with groups of bees	554
A collection collects... DATA	555
LINQ makes working with data in collections and databases easy	557

Life and death of a flower

age = 0
nectar = 1.5
Flower object

age = 17809
nectar = 3.2
Flower object

age = 30291
nectar = .83
alive = false
DEAD
Flower object

controls and graphics
Make it pretty

13

Sometimes you have to take graphics into your own hands.

We've spent a lot of time on relying on controls to handle everything visual in our applications. But sometimes that's not enough—like when you want to **animate a picture**. And once you get into animation, you'll end up **creating your own controls** for your .NET programs, maybe adding a little **double buffering**, and even **drawing directly onto your forms**. It all begins with the **Graphics** object, **Bitmap**s, and a determination to not accept the graphics status quo.

You've been using controls all along to interact with your programs	564
Form controls are just objects	565
Add a renderer to your architecture	568
Controls are well-suited for visual display elements	570
Build your first animated control	573
Your controls need to dispose their controls, too!	577
A UserControl is an easy way to build a control	578
Add the hive and field forms to the project	582
Build the Renderer	583
Let's take a closer look at those performance issues	590
You resized your Bitmaps using a Graphics object	592
Your image resources are stored in Bitmap objects	593
Use System.Drawing to TAKE CONTROL of graphics yourself	594
A 30-second tour of GDI+ graphics	595
Use graphics to draw a picture on a form	596
Graphics can fix our transparency problem...	601
Use the Paint event to make your graphics stick	602
A closer look at how forms and controls repaint themselves	605
Double buffering makes animation look a lot smoother	608
Double buffering is built into forms and controls	609
Use a Graphics object and an event handler for printing	614
PrintDocument works with the print dialog and print preview window objects	615

14 CAPTAIN AMAZING
THE DEATH
OF THE OBJECT

Captain Amazing, Objectville's most amazing object
pursues his arch-nemesis...   622

Your last chance to DO something... your object's finalizer   628

When EXACTLY does a finalizer run?   629

Dispose() works with using, finalizers work with garbage collection 630

Finalizers can't depend on stability   632

Make an object serialize itself in its Dispose()   633

Meanwhile, on the streets of Objectville...   636

A struct *looks* like an object...   637

..but *isn't* on the heap   637

Values get copied, references get assigned   638

Structs are value types; objects are reference types   639

The stack vs. the heap: more on memory   641

Captain Amazing... not so much   645

Extension methods add new behavior to EXISTING classes   646

Extending a fundamental type: string   648

Welcome to
Objectville
Home of *Polymorphism*

LINQ
Get control of your data

15

It's a data-driven world... you better know how to live in it.

Gone are the days when you could program for days, even weeks, without dealing with **loads of data**. But today, *everything is about data*. In fact, you'll often have to work with data from **more than one place**... and in more than one format. Databases, XML, collections from other programs... it's all part of the job of a good C# programmer. And that's where **LINQ** comes in. LINQ not only lets you **query data** in a simple, intuitive way, but it lets you **group data**, and **merge data from different data sources**.

An easy project...	654
...but the data's all over the place	655
LINQ can pull data from multiple sources	656
.NET collections are already set up for LINQ	657
LINQ makes queries easy	658
LINQ is simple, but your queries don't have to be	659
LINQ is versatile	662
LINQ can combine your results into groups	667
Combine Jimmy's values into groups	668
Use join to combine two collections into one query	671
Jimmy saved a bunch of dough	672
Connect LINQ to a SQL database	674
Use a join query to connect Starbuzz and Objectville	678

C# Lab 3

Invaders

In this lab you'll pay homage to one of the most popular, revered and replicated icons in video game history, a game that needs no further introduction. It's time to build Invaders.

The grandfather of video games	682
And yet there's more to do...	701

leftovers

The top 5 things we wanted to include in this book

The fun's just beginning!

We've shown you a lot of great tools to build some really **powerful software** with C#. But there's no way that we could include **every single tool, technology or technique** in this book—there just aren't enough pages. We had to make some *really tough choices* about what to include and what to leave out. Here are some of the topics that didn't make the cut. But even though we couldn't get to them, we still think that they're **important and useful**, and we wanted to give you a small head start with them.

#1 LINQ to XML	704
#2 Refactoring	706
#3 Some of our favorite Toolbox components	708
#4 Console Applications	710
5 Windows Presentation Framework	712
Did you know that C# and the .NET Framework can...	714

how to use this book

Intro

In this section, we answer the burning question:
"So why <u>DID</u> they put that in a C# programming book?"

Who is this book for?

If you can answer "yes" to all of these:

1. Do you want to **learn** C#?

2. Do you like to tinker—do you learn by doing, rather than just reading?

3. Do you prefer **stimulating dinner party conversation** to **dry, dull, academic lectures**?

this book is for you.

Who should probably back away from this book?

If you can answer "yes" to any of these:

1. Does the idea of writing a lot of code make you bored and a little twitchy?

2. Are you a kick-butt C++ or Java programmer looking for a reference book?

3. Are you **afraid to try something different**? Would you rather have a root canal than mix stripes with plaid? Do you believe that a technical book can't be serious if C# concepts are anthropomorphized?

this book is not for you.

[Note from marketing: this book is for anyone with a credit card.]

We know what you're thinking.

"How can *this* be a serious C# programming book?"

"What's with all the graphics?"

"Can I actually *learn* it this way?"

And we know what your *brain* is thinking.

Your brain craves novelty. It's always searching, scanning, *waiting* for something unusual. It was built that way, and it helps you stay alive.

So what does your brain do with all the routine, ordinary, normal things you encounter? Everything it *can* to stop them from interfering with the brain's *real* job—recording things that *matter*. It doesn't bother saving the boring things; they never make it past the "this is obviously not important" filter.

How does your brain *know* what's important? Suppose you're out for a day hike and a tiger jumps in front of you, what happens inside your head and body?

Neurons fire. Emotions crank up. *Chemicals surge.*

And that's how your brain knows...

This must be important! Don't forget it!

But imagine you're at home, or in a library. It's a safe, warm, tiger-free zone. You're studying. Getting ready for an exam. Or trying to learn some tough technical topic your boss thinks will take a week, ten days at the most.

Just one problem. Your brain's trying to do you a big favor. It's trying to make sure that this *obviously* non-important content doesn't clutter up scarce resources. Resources that are better spent storing the really *big* things. Like tigers. Like the danger of fire. Like how you should never have posted those "party" photos on your Facebook page.

And there's no simple way to tell your brain, "Hey brain, thank you very much, but no matter how dull this book is, and how little I'm registering on the emotional Richter scale right now, I really *do* want you to keep this stuff around."

Your brain thinks THIS is important.

Your brain thinks THIS isn't worth saving.

Great. Only 700 more dull, dry, boring pages.

We think of a "Head First" reader as a <u>learner</u>.

So what does it take to *learn* something? First, you have to *get* it, then make sure you don't *forget* it. It's not about pushing facts into your head. Based on the latest research in cognitive science, neurobiology, and educational psychology, *learning* takes a lot more than text on a page. We know what turns your brain on.

Some of the Head First learning principles:

Make it visual. Images are far more memorable than words alone, and make learning much more effective (up to 89% improvement in recall and transfer studies). It also makes things more understandable. **Put the words within or near the graphics** they relate to, rather than on the bottom or on another page, and learners will be up to *twice* as likely to solve problems related to the content.

Use a conversational and personalized style. In recent studies, students performed up to 40% better on post-learning tests if the content spoke directly to the reader, using a first-person, conversational style rather than taking a formal tone. Tell stories instead of lecturing. Use casual language. Don't take yourself too seriously. Which would *you* pay more attention to: a stimulating dinner party companion, or a lecture?

Get the learner to think more deeply. In other words, unless you actively flex your neurons, nothing much happens in your head. A reader has to be motivated, engaged, curious, and inspired to solve problems, draw conclusions, and generate new knowledge. And for that, you need challenges, exercises, and thought-provoking questions, and activities that involve both sides of the brain and multiple senses.

Get—and keep—the reader's attention. We've all had the "I really want to learn this but I can't stay awake past page one" experience. Your brain pays attention to things that are out of the ordinary, interesting, strange, eye-catching, unexpected. Learning a new, tough, technical topic doesn't have to be boring. Your brain will learn much more quickly if it's not.

Touch their emotions. We now know that your ability to remember something is largely dependent on its emotional content. You remember what you care about. You remember when you *feel* something. No, we're not talking heart-wrenching stories about a boy and his dog. We're talking emotions like surprise, curiosity, fun, "what the...?", and the feeling of "I Rule!" that comes when you solve a puzzle, learn something everybody else thinks is hard, or realize you know something that "I'm more technical than thou" Bob from engineering *doesn't*.

Metacognition: thinking about thinking

If you really want to learn, and you want to learn more quickly and more deeply, pay attention to how you pay attention. Think about how you think. Learn how you learn.

Most of us did not take courses on metacognition or learning theory when we were growing up. We were *expected* to learn, but rarely *taught* to learn.

I wonder how I can trick my brain into remembering this stuff...

But we assume that if you're holding this book, you really want to learn how to build programs in C#. And you probably don't want to spend a lot of time. If you want to use what you read in this book, you need to *remember* what you read. And for that, you've got to *understand* it. To get the most from this book, or *any* book or learning experience, take responsibility for your brain. Your brain on *this* content.

The trick is to get your brain to see the new material you're learning as Really Important. Crucial to your well-being. As important as a tiger. Otherwise, you're in for a constant battle, with your brain doing its best to keep the new content from sticking.

So just how *DO* you get your brain to treat C# like it was a hungry tiger?

There's the slow, tedious way, or the faster, more effective way. The slow way is about sheer repetition. You obviously know that you *are* able to learn and remember even the dullest of topics if you keep pounding the same thing into your brain. With enough repetition, your brain says, "This doesn't *feel* important to him, but he keeps looking at the same thing *over* and *over* and *over*, so I suppose it must be."

The faster way is to do **anything that increases brain activity,** especially different *types* of brain activity. The things on the previous page are a big part of the solution, and they're all things that have been proven to help your brain work in your favor. For example, studies show that putting words *within* the pictures they describe (as opposed to somewhere else in the page, like a caption or in the body text) causes your brain to try to makes sense of how the words and picture relate, and this causes more neurons to fire. More neurons firing = more chances for your brain to *get* that this is something worth paying attention to, and possibly recording.

A conversational style helps because people tend to pay more attention when they perceive that they're in a conversation, since they're expected to follow along and hold up their end. The amazing thing is, your brain doesn't necessarily *care* that the "conversation" is between you and a book! On the other hand, if the writing style is formal and dry, your brain perceives it the same way you experience being lectured to while sitting in a roomful of passive attendees. No need to stay awake.

But pictures and conversational style are just the beginning.

Here's what WE did:

We used *pictures*, because your brain is tuned for visuals, not text. As far as your brain's concerned, a picture really *is* worth a thousand words. And when text and pictures work together, we embedded the text *in* the pictures because your brain works more effectively when the text is *within* the thing the text refers to, as opposed to in a caption or buried in the text somewhere.

We used *redundancy*, saying the same thing in *different* ways and with different media types, and *multiple senses*, to increase the chance that the content gets coded into more than one area of your brain.

We used concepts and pictures in *unexpected* ways because your brain is tuned for novelty, and we used pictures and ideas with at least *some* *emotional* content, because your brain is tuned to pay attention to the biochemistry of emotions. That which causes you to *feel* something is more likely to be remembered, even if that feeling is nothing more than a little *humor*, *surprise*, or *interest*.

We used a personalized, *conversational style*, because your brain is tuned to pay more attention when it believes you're in a conversation than if it thinks you're passively listening to a presentation. Your brain does this even when you're *reading*.

We included more than 80 *activities*, because your brain is tuned to learn and remember more when you *do* things than when you *read* about things. And we made the exercises challenging-yet-do-able, because that's what most people prefer.

We used *multiple learning styles*, because *you* might prefer step-by-step procedures, while someone else wants to understand the big picture first, and someone else just wants to see an example. But regardless of your own learning preference, *everyone* benefits from seeing the same content represented in multiple ways.

BULLET POINTS

We include content for *both sides of your brain*, because the more of your brain you engage, the more likely you are to learn and remember, and the longer you can stay focused. Since working one side of the brain often means giving the other side a chance to rest, you can be more productive at learning for a longer period of time.

Fireside Chats

And we included *stories* and exercises that present *more than one point of view,* because your brain is tuned to learn more deeply when it's forced to make evaluations and judgments.

We included *challenges*, with exercises, and by asking *questions* that don't always have a straight answer, because your brain is tuned to learn and remember when it has to *work* at something. Think about it—you can't get your *body* in shape just by *watching* people at the gym. But we did our best to make sure that when you're working hard, it's on the *right* things. That *you're not spending one extra dendrite* processing a hard-to-understand example, or parsing difficult, jargon-laden, or overly terse text.

We used *people*. In stories, examples, pictures, etc., because, well, because *you're* a person. And your brain pays more attention to *people* than it does to *things*.

Cut this out and stick it on your refrigerator.

Here's what YOU can do to bend your brain into submission

So, we did our part. The rest is up to you. These tips are a starting point; listen to your brain and figure out what works for you and what doesn't. Try new things.

- -

(1) Slow down. The more you understand, the less you have to memorize.

Don't just *read*. Stop and think. When the book asks you a question, don't just skip to the answer. Imagine that someone really *is* asking the question. The more deeply you force your brain to think, the better chance you have of learning and remembering.

(2) Do the exercises. Write your own notes.

We put them in, but if we did them for you, that would be like having someone else do your workouts for you. And don't just *look* at the exercises. **Use a pencil.** There's plenty of evidence that physical activity *while* learning can increase the learning.

(3) Read the "There are No Dumb Questions"

That means all of them. They're not optional sidebars—*they're part of the core content!* Don't skip them.

(4) Make this the last thing you read before bed. Or at least the last challenging thing.

Part of the learning (especially the transfer to long-term memory) happens *after* you put the book down. Your brain needs time on its own, to do more processing. If you put in something new during that processing time, some of what you just learned will be lost.

(5) Drink water. Lots of it.

Your brain works best in a nice bath of fluid. Dehydration (which can happen before you ever feel thirsty) decreases cognitive function.

(6) Talk about it. Out loud.

Speaking activates a different part of the brain. If you're trying to understand something, or increase your chance of remembering it later, say it out loud. Better still, try to explain it out loud to someone else. You'll learn more quickly, and you might uncover ideas you hadn't known were there when you were reading about it.

(7) Listen to your brain.

Pay attention to whether your brain is getting overloaded. If you find yourself starting to skim the surface or forget what you just read, it's time for a break. Once you go past a certain point, you won't learn faster by trying to shove more in, and you might even hurt the process.

(8) Feel something.

Your brain needs to know that this *matters*. Get involved with the stories. Make up your own captions for the photos. Groaning over a bad joke is *still* better than feeling nothing at all.

(9) Write a lot of software!

There's only one way to learn to program: **writing a lot of code**. And that's what you're going to do throughout this book. Coding is a skill, and the only way to get good at it is to practice. We're going to give you a lot of practice: every chapter has exercises that pose a problem for you to solve. Don't just skip over them—a lot of the learning happens when you solve the exercises. We included a solution to each exercise—don't be afraid to **peek at the solution** if you get stuck! (It's easy to get snagged on something small.) But try to solve the problem before you look at the solution. And definitely get it working before you move on to the next part of the book.

What you need for this book:

We wrote this book using Visual Studio 2008 Express Edition. That means we used C# 3.0 and the .NET Framework 3.5. The thing is, when we wrote this book, Visual Studio 2008 was still in beta, and it won't be released until after the first printing. But we know that every single exercise and piece of code in the book works 100% with the current beta version of Visual Studio 2008 Express. So we recommend that you download it from Microsoft's website—it's free to download and use.

SETTING UP VISUAL STUDIO 2008 EXPRESS EDITION

- Before you start, keep in mind that if you bought this book in the first few months after it was released, you're probably going to be using a beta version of Visual Studio 2008 Express Edition, so the usual beta version warnings apply. We did that because there have been some really amazing improvements to C# and .NET, and we wanted to make sure that you learned about them. And just so you know, we haven't had a single problem using the VS2008 beta.

- It's easy enough to download and install Visual C# 2008 Express Edition. Here's the link to the Visual Studio 2008 Express Edition download page:

  ```
  http://msdn2.microsoft.com/en-us/express/future/bb421473.aspx
  ```

  Make sure that you check all of the options when you install it.

  If you absolutely must use an older version of Visual Studio, C# or the .NET Framework, then please keep in mind that you'll come across topics in this book that won't be compatible with your version. The C# team at Microsoft has added some pretty cool features to the language. We'll give you warnings when we talk about any of these topics. But definitely keep in mind that if you're not using the latest version, there will be some code in this book that won't work.

- Download the installation package for Visual C# 2008 Express Edition. Make sure you do a complete installation That should install everything that you need: the IDE (which you'll learn about), SQL Server Express Edition, and .NET Framework 3.5.

- Once you've got it installed, you'll have a new Start menu option: ***Microsoft Visual C# 2008 Express Edition***. Click on it to bring up the IDE, and you're all set.

Read me

This is a learning experience, not a reference book. We deliberately stripped out everything that might get in the way of learning whatever it is we're working on at that point in the book. And the first time through, you need to begin at the beginning, because the book makes assumptions about what you've already seen and learned.

We use a lot of diagrams to make tough concepts easier to understand.

ciaAgent

mi5Agent

The activities are NOT optional.

The exercises and activities are not add-ons; they're part of the core content of the book. Some of them are to help with memory, some for understanding, and some to help you apply what you've learned. ***Don't skip the exercises.*** The crossword puzzles are the only things you don't *have* to do, but they're good for giving your brain a chance to think about the words from a different context.

The redundancy is intentional and important.

One distinct difference in a Head First book is that we want you to *really* get it. And we want you to finish the book remembering what you've learned. Most reference books don't have retention and recall as a goal, but this book is about *learning*, so you'll see some of the same concepts come up more than once.

You should do ALL of the "Sharpen your pencil" activities

Sharpen your pencil

Do all the exercises!

The one big assumption that we made when we wrote this book is that you want to learn how to program in C#. So we know you want to get your hands dirty right away, and dig right into the code. We gave you a lot of opportunities to sharpen your skills by putting exercises in every chapter. We've labeled some of them "Do this!"—when you see that, it means that we'll walk you through all of the steps to solve a particular problem. But when you see the Exercise logo with the running shoes, then we've left a big portion of the problem up to you to solve, and we gave you the solution that we came up with. Don't be afraid to peek at the solution—**it's not cheating**! But you'll learn the most if you try to solve the problem first.

Activities marked with the Exercise (running shoe) logo are really important! Don't skip them if you're serious about learning C#.

Exercise

We've also placed all the exercise solutions' source code on the web so you can download it. You'll find it at `http://www.headfirstlabs.com/books/hfcsharp/`

If you see the Pool Puzzle logo, the activity is optional, and if you don't like twisty logic, you won't like these either.

The "Brain Power" exercises don't have answers.

For some of them, there is no right answer, and for others, part of the learning experience of the Brain Power activities is for you to decide if and when your answers are right. In some of the Brain Power exercises you will find hints to point you in the right direction.

The technical review team

Lisa Kellner   Joe Albahari   Jay Hilyard   Daniel Kinnaer

Not pictured (but just as awesome): Wayne Bradney, Dave Murdoch, and Bridgette Julie Landers

Aayam Singh   Theodore Casser   Andy Parker   Peter Ritchie   Bill Mietelski

Krishna Pala

Technical Reviewers:

When we wrote this book, it had a bunch of mistakes, issues, problems, typos, and terrible arithmetic errors. Okay, it wasn't quite that bad. But we're still really grateful for the work that our technical reviewers did for the book. We would have gone to press with errors (including one or two big ones) had it not been for the most kick-ass review team EVER...

First of all, we really want to thank **Joe Albahari** for the enormous amount of technical guidance. He really set us straight on a few really important things, and if it weren't for him you'd be learning incorrect stuff. We also want to thank **Lisa Kellner**—this is our third book that she's reviewed for us, and she made a huge difference in the readability of the final product. Thanks, Lisa! And special thanks to **Jay Hilyard** and **Daniel Kinnaer** for catching and fixing a whole lot of our mistakes, and **Aayam Singh** for actually going through and doing every one of these execises **before** we fixed them and corrected their problems. Aayam, you're really dedicated. Thanks!

Giuseppe Turitto

Acknowledgments

Our editor:

We want to thank our editor, **Brett McLaughlin**, for editing this book. He helped with a lot of the narrative, and the comic idea in Chapter 14 was completely his, and we think it turned out really well. Thanks, Brett!

Brett McLaughlin

The O'Reilly team:

Lou Barr

Lou Barr is an amazing graphic designer who went above and beyond on this one, putting in unbelievable hours and coming up with some pretty amazing visuals. If you see anything in this book that looks fantastic, you can thank her (and her mad InDesign skillz) for it. She did all of the monster and alien graphics for the labs, and the entire comic book. Thanks so much, Lou! You are our hero, and you're awesome to work with.

There are so many people at O'Reilly we want to thank that we hope we don't forget anyone. First of all, the Head First team rocks—**Laurie Petrycki**, **Catherine Nolan**, **Sanders Kleinfeld** (the most super production editor ever!), **Caitrin McCullough**, and **Keith McNamara**. Special thanks to **Colleen Gorman** for her sharp proofread, **Ron Bilodeau** for volunteering his time and preflighting expertise, and **Adam Witwer** for offering one last sanity check—all of whom helped get this book from production to press in record time. And as always, we love **Mary Treseler**, and can't wait to work with her again! And a big shout out to our other friends and editors, **Andy Oram**, **Isabel Kunkle**, and **Mike Hendrickson**. And if you're reading this book right now, then you can thank the greatest publicity team in the industry: **Marsee Henon**, **Sara Peyton**, **Mary Rotman**, **Jessica Boyd**, and the rest of the folks at Sebastopol.

Catherine Nolan

Safari® Books Online

 When you see a Safari® icon on the cover of your favorite technology book that means the book is available online through the O'Reilly Network Safari Bookshelf.

Safari offers a solution that's better than e-books. It's a virtual library that lets you easily search thousands of top tech books, cut and paste code samples, download chapters, and find quick answers when you need the most accurate, current information. Try it for free at `http://safari.oreilly.com`.

1 get productive with c#

Visual Applications, in 10 minutes or less

> Don't worry, Mother. With Visual Studio and C#, you'll be able to program so fast that you'll never burn the pot roast again.

Want to build great programs really fast?

With C#, you've got a **powerful programming language** and a **valuable tool** at your fingertips. With the **Visual Studio IDE**, you'll never have to spend hours writing obscure code to get a button working again. Even better, you'll be able to **focus on getting your work done**, rather than remembering which method parameter was for the *name* for a button, and which one was for its *label*. Sound appealing? Turn the page, and let's get programming.

Why you should learn C#

C# and the Visual Studio IDE make it easy for you to get to the business of writing code, and writing it fast. When you're working with C#, the IDE is your best friend and constant companion.

The IDE—or Visual Studio Integrated Development Environment—is an important part of working in C#. It's a program that helps you edit your code, manage your files, and publish your projects.

Here's what the IDE automates for you...

Every time you want to get started writing a program, or just putting a button on a form, your program needs a whole bunch of repetitive code.

```
using System;
using System.Collections.Generic;
using System.Windows.Forms;
namespace A_New_Program
{
    static class Program
    {
        /// <summary>
        /// The main entry point for the application.
        /// </summary>
        [STAThread]
        static void Main()
        {
            Application.EnableVisualStyles();
            Application.SetCompatibleTextRenderingDefault(false);
            Application.Run(new Form1());
        }
    }
}
```

```
private void InitializeComponent()
{
    this.button1 = new System.Windows.Forms.Button();
    this.SuspendLayout();
    //
    // button1
    //
    this.button1.Location = new System.Drawing.Point(105, 56);
    this.button1.Name = "button1";
    this.button1.Size = new System.Drawing.Size(75, 23);
    this.button1.TabIndex = 0;
    this.button1.Text = "button1";
    this.button1.UseVisualStyleBackColor = true;
    this.button1.Click += new System.EventHandler(this.button1_Click);
    //
    // Form1
    //
    this.AutoScaleDimensions = new System.Drawing.SizeF(8F, 16F);
    this.AutoScaleMode = System.Windows.Forms.AutoScaleMode.Font;
    this.ClientSize = new System.Drawing.Size(292, 267);
    this.Controls.Add(this.button1);
    this.Name = "Form1";
    this.Text = "Form1";
    this.ResumeLayout(false);
}
```

It takes all this code just to draw a button on a form. Adding a few more visual elements to the form could take ten times as much code.

What you get with Visual Studio and C#...

With a language like C#, tuned for Windows programming, and the Visual Studio IDE, you can focus on what your program is supposed to **do** immediately:

The result is a better looking application that takes less time to write.

Form Objects

.NET Framework solutions

Data access

C# and the Visual Studio IDE have pre-built structures that handle the tedious code that's part of most programming tasks.

Your Program

Input   Let's get started!

How good?   ○ Good   ○ Better   ● Best

Value

Do it now

All right!

C# and the Visual Studio IDE make lots of things easy

When you use C# and Visual Studio, you get all of these great features, without having to do any extra work. Together, they let you:

① **Build an application, FAST.** Creating programs in C# is a snap. The language is powerful and easy to learn, and the Visual Studio IDE does a lot of work for you automatically. You can leave mundane coding tasks to the IDE and focus on what your code should accomplish.

② **Design a great looking user interface.** The Form Designer in the Visual Studio IDE is one of the easiest design tools to use out there. It does so much for you that you'll find that making stunning user interfaces is one of the most satisfying parts of developing a C# application. You can build full-featured professional programs without having to spend hours writing a graphical user interface entirely from scratch.

③ **Create and interact with databases.** The IDE includes a simple interface for building databases, and integrates seamlessly with SQL Server Express, as well as several other popular database systems.

④ **Focus on solving your REAL problems.** The IDE does a lot for you, but *you* are still in control of what you build with C#. The IDE just lets you focus on your program, your work (or fun!), and your customers. But the IDE handles all the grunt work, such as:

- ★ Keeping track of all of your projects
- ★ Making it easy to edit your project's code
- ★ Keeping track of your project's graphics, audio, icons, and other resources
- ★ Managing and interacting with databases

All this means you'll have all the time you would've spent doing this routine programming to put into **building killer programs**.

You're going to see exactly what we mean next.

Help the CEO go paperless

The Objectville Paper Company just hired a new CEO. He loves hiking, coffee, and nature... and he's decided that to help save forests. He wants to become a paperless executive, starting with his contacts. He's heading to Aspen to go ski for the weekend, and expects a new address book program by the time he gets back. Otherwise... well... it won't be just the old CEO who's looking for a job.

You'd better find a way to get this data onto the CEO's laptop quick.

Get to know your users' needs <u>before</u> you start building your program

Before we can start writing the address book application—or *any* application—we need to take a minute and think about **who's going to be using it**, and **what they need** from the application.

(1)   The CEO needs to be able to run his address book program at work and on his laptop too. He'll need an installer to make sure that all of the right files get onto each machine.

Windows installer

> The CEO wants to be able to run his program on his desktop and laptop, so an installer is a must.

(2)   The Objectville Paper company sales team wants to access his address book, too. They can use his data to build mailing lists and get client leads for more paper sales.

The CEO figures a database would be the best way that everyone in the company to see his data, and then he can just keep up with one copy of all his contacts.

We already know that Visual C# makes working with databases easy. Having contacts in a database lets the CEO and the sales team all access the information, even though there's only one copy of the data.

SQL Database

Here's what you're going to build

You're going to need an application with a graphical user interface, objects to talk to a database, the database itself, and an installer. It sounds like a lot of work, but you'll build all of this over the next few pages.

Here's the structure of the program we're going to create:

You'll be building a Windows form with a bunch of visual controls on it.

The application has a separate data layer that interacts with the database.

.NET Visual Objects

.NET Database Objects

SELECT command
INSERT command
UPDATE command
DELETE command

System.Windows.Form object

data entry objects

PictureBox object

ToolBar object

BindingSource object

TableAdapter object

BindingNavigator object

DataSet object

Database diagram

Each of these objects represents a control on the address book form we'll create.

We'll need objects to talk to our tables, a diagram to let our application know what the database structure is, and more.

The data is all stored in a table in a SQL Server Express database.

Once the program's built, it'll be packaged up into a Windows installer.

Data Storage

Deployment Package

Table

DB diagram support objects

SQL Database

Database

.exe

Program file

The sales department will just need to point and click to install and then use his program.

Windows installer

Here's the database itself, which Visual Studio will help us create and maintain.

What you do in Visual Studio...

Go ahead and start up Visual Studio, if you haven't already. Skip over the start page and select New Project from the **File** menu. Name your project "Contacts" and click OK.

Watch it!

Things may look a bit different in your IDE.

This is what the "New Project" window looks like in Visual Studio 2008 Express Edition. If you're using the Professional or Team Foundation edition, it might be a bit different. But don't worry, everything still works exactly the same.

What Visual Studio does for you...

As soon as you save the project, the IDE creates a Form1.cs, Form1.Designer.cs, and Program.cs file when you create a new project. It adds these to the Solution Explorer window, and by default, puts those files in My Documents\Visual Studio 2008\Projects\Contacts\.

Make sure that you save your project as soon as you create it by selecting "Save All" from the File menu—that'll save all of the project files out to the folder. If you select "Save", it just saves the one you're working on.

This file contains the C# code that defines the behavior of the form.

This has the code that starts up the program and displays the form.

The code that defines the form and its objects lives here.

Form1.cs

Program.cs

Form1.Designer.cs

Visual Studio creates all three of these files automatically.

Sharpen your pencil

Below is what your screen probably looks like right now. You should be able to figure out what most of these windows and files are based on what you already know. In each of the blanks, try and fill in an annotation saying what that part of the IDE does. We've done one to get you started.

This toolbar has buttons that apply to what you're currently doing in the IDE.

If your IDE doesn't look exactly like this picure, you can select "Reset Window Layout" from the Window menu.

We've blown up this window below so you have more room.

Form1 Gui which helps creating design of the form

Displays error or warning messages

properties window shows props of each control

Defines the behavior of the form. C# code

displays all the files in the directory and the relevant properties & refs

Sharpen your pencil
Solution

We've filled in the annotations about the different sections of the Visual Studio C# IDE. You may have some different things written down, but you should have been able to figure out the basics of what each window and section of the IDE is used for.

This toolbar has buttons that apply to what you're currently doing in the IDE.

We've blown up this window below so you have more room.

This is the toolbox. It has a bunch of visual controls that you can drag onto your form.

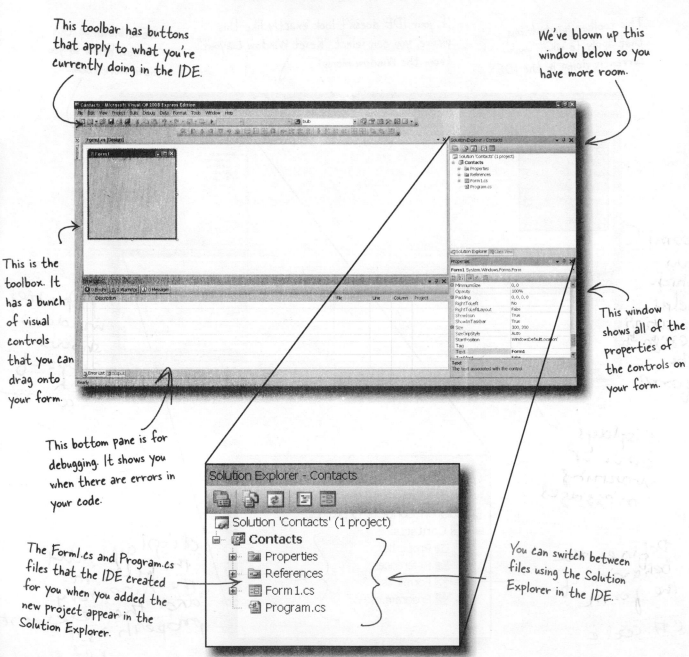

This window shows all of the properties of the controls on your form.

This bottom pane is for debugging. It shows you when there are errors in your code.

The Form1.cs and Program.cs files that the IDE created for you when you added the new project appear in the Solution Explorer.

You can switch between files using the Solution Explorer in the IDE.

Dumb Questions

Q: So if the IDE writes all this code for me, is learning C# just a matter of learning how to use the IDE?

A: No. The IDE is great at automatically generating some code for you, but it can only do so much. There are some things it's really good at, like setting up good starting points for you, and automatically changing properties of controls on your forms. But the hard part of programming—figuring what your program needs to do and making it do it—is something that no IDE can do for you. Even though the Visual Studio IDE is one of the most advanced development environments out there, it can only go so far. It's **you**—not the IDE—who writes the **action code**, or the code that does the work.

Q: I created a new project in Visual Studio, but when I went into the "Projects" folder under My Documents, I didn't see it there. What gives?

A: First of all, you must be using Visual Studio 2008—in 2005, this doesn't happen. When you first create a new project in Visual Studio 2008, the IDE creates the project in your `Local Settings\ Application Data\Temporary Projects` folder. When you save the project for the first time, it will prompt you for a new filename, and save it in the `My Documents\Visual Studio 2008\Projects` folder. If you try to open a new project or close the temporary one, you'll be prompted to either save or discard the temporary project.

Q: What if the IDE creates code I don't want in my project?

A: You can change it. The IDE is set up to create code based on the way the element you dragged or added is most commonly used. But sometimes that's not exactly what you wanted. Everything the IDE does for you—every line of code it creates, every file it adds—can be changed, either manually by editing the files directly or through an easy-to-use interface in the IDE.

Q: Is it OK that I downloaded and installed Visual Studio Express? Or do I need to use one of the versions of Visual Studio that isn't free in order to do everything in this book?

A: There's nothing in this book that you can't do with the free version of Visual Studio (which you can download from Microsoft's website). The main differences between Express and the other editions (Professional and Team Foundation) aren't going to get in the way of writing C# and creating fully functional, complete applications.

Q: Can I change the names of files the IDE generates for me?

A: Absolutely, you can change any aspect of your program. But the IDE is set up to name your files sensibly. When you add a file to your project, the filename you choose affects the way the code is generated, and the code it generates will include that name. In some cases, if you rename the file you'll either have to go through and change other parts of the code, or live with the difference between the filename and the code inside it. Since that's a bit of a pain, we recommend you don't change filenames unless you've got a really good reason to.

Q: I'm looking at the IDE right now, but my screen doesn't look like yours! It's missing some of the windows, and others are in the wrong place. What gives?

A: If you click on the "Reset Window Layout" command under the "Window" menu, the IDE will restore the default window layout for you. Then your screen will look just like the ones in this chapter.

Visual Studio will generate code you can use as a starting point for your applications.

Making sure the application does what it's supposed to do is still up to you.

Develop the user interface

Adding controls and polishing the user interface is as easy as dragging and dropping with the Visual Studio IDE. Let's add a logo to the form:

1 **Use the PictureBox control to add a picture.**

Click on the PictureBox control in the Toolbox, and drag it onto your form. In the background, the IDE added code to `Form1.Designer.cs` for a new picture control.

> If you don't see the toolbox, try hovering over the word "Toolbox" that shows up in the upper left-hand corner of the IDE. If it's not there, select "Toolbox" from the View menu to make it appear.

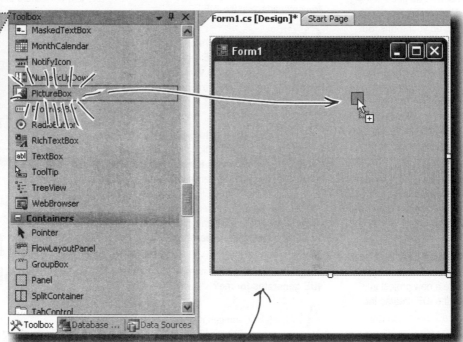

Every time you make a change to a control's properties on the form, the code in Form1. Designer.cs is getting changed by the IDE.

Form1.Designer.cs

It's OK if you're not a pro at user interface design.

We'll talk a lot more about designing good user interfaces later on. For now, just get the logo and other controls on your form, and worry about *behavior*. We'll add some style later.

You are Here ➜

.NET Visual Objects   .NET Database Objects   Data Storage   Deployment Package

2 **Set the PictureBox to Zoom mode.**
Every control on your form has properties that you can
set. Click the little black arrow for a control to access
these properties. Change the PictureBox's Size property
to "Zoom" to see how this works:

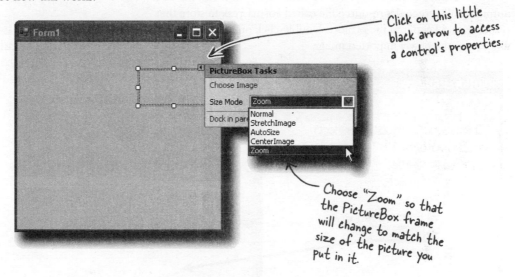

Click on this little
black arrow to access
a control's properties.

Choose "Zoom" so that
the PictureBox frame
will change to match the
size of the picture you
put in it.

3 **Download the Objectville Paper Company logo.**
Download the Objectville Paper Co. logo from Head First Labs
(**http://www.headfirstlabs.com/books/hfcsharp**)
and save it to your hard drive. Then click the PictureBox properties
arrow, and select Choose Image. Click Import, find your logo, and
you're all set:

Here's the OPC logo,
and the PictureBox
zooms to get the size
just right.

Visual Studio, behind the scenes

Every time you do something in the Visual Studio IDE, the IDE is *writing code for you*. When you created the logo and told Visual Studio to use the image you downloaded, Visual Studio created a resource and associated it with your application. A **resource** is any graphics file, audio file, icon, or other kind of data file that gets bundled with your application. The graphic file gets integrated into the program, so that when it's installed on another computer, the graphic is installed along with it and the PictureBox can use it.

When you dragged the PictureBox control onto your form, the IDE automatically created a resource file called Form1.resx to store that resource and keep it in the project. Double-click on this file, and you'll be able to see the newly imported image.

This image is now a resource of the Contact List application.

If you click on Form1.resx in the Solution Explorer, you can see the logo that you imported. That file is what links it to the PictureBox, and the IDE added code to do the linking.

Here are the files Visual Studio created earlier.

When you imported the image, the IDE created this file for you. It contains all of the resources (graphics, video, audio and other stored data) associated with Form1.

Add to the auto-generated code

The IDE creates lots of code for you, but you'll still want to get into this code and add to it. Let's set the logo up to show an About message when the users double-click on it.

Make sure you've got your form showing in the IDE, and double-click on the PictureBox control. You should see some code pop up that looks like this:

```csharp
public partial class Form1 : Form
{
    public Form1()
    {
        InitializeComponent();
    }
    private void pictureBox1_Click(object sender, EventArgs e)
    {
        MessageBox.Show("Contact List 1.0.\nWritten by: Your Name", "About");
    }
}
```

When you double-clicked on the PictureBox control, the IDE created *this* method. It will run every time a user clicks on the logo in the running application.

This method name gives you a good idea about when it runs: when someone clicks on this PictureBox control.

When you double-click on the PictureBox, it will open this code up with a cursor blinking right here. Ignore any windows the IDE pops up as you type; it's trying to help you, but we don't need that right now.

Type in this line of code. It causes a message box to popup with the text you provide. The box will be titled "About".

Once you've typed in the line of code, save it using the Save icon on the IDE toolbar or by selecting "Save" from the File menu. Get in the habit of doing "Save All" regularly!

there are no Dumb Questions

Q: What's a method?

A: A **method** is just a *named block of code*. We'll talk a lot more about methods in Chapter 2.

Q: What does that \n thing do?

A: That's a line break. It tells C# to put "Contact List 1.0." on one line, and then start a new line for "Written by:".

You can <u>already</u> run your application

Press the F5 key on your keyboard, or click the green
arrow button (▶) on the toolbar to check out what you've
done so far. (This is called "Debugging", which just means
running your program using the IDE.) You can stop
debugging by selecting "Stop Debugging" from the Debug
menu or clicking this toolbar button: ▣

All three of these buttons work—and you didn't have to write any code to make them work.

Clicking on the OPC logo brings up the About box you just coded.

Where are my files?

When you run your program, Visual Studio copies
all of your files to `My Documents\Visual
Studio 2008\Projects\Contacts\
Contacts\bin\debug`. You can even hop over
to that directory and run your program by double-
clicking on the .exe file the IDE creates.

C# turns your program into a file that you can run, called an executable. You'll find it in here, in the debug folder.

Program.cs

Form1.cs

Form1.
Designer.cs

Form1.resx

Contacts.csproj

Properties

bin

This isn't a mistake; there are two levels of folders. The inner folder has the actual C# code files.

Dumb Questions

Q: In my IDE, the green arrow is marked as "Debug". Is that a problem?

A: No. Debugging, at least for our purposes right now, just means running your application inside the IDE. We'll talk a lot more about debugging later, but for now, you can simply think about it as a way to run your program.

Q: I don't see the Stop Debugging button on my toolbar. What gives?

A: The Stop Debugging button only shows up in a special toolbar that **only shows up** when your program is running. Try starting the application again, and see if it appears.

Here's what we've done so far

We've built a form and created a PictureBox object that pops up a message box when it's clicked on. Next, we need to add all the other fields from the card, like the contact's name and phone number.

Let's store that information in a database. Visual Studio can connect fields directly to that database for us, which means we don't have to mess with lots of database access code (which is good). But for that to work, we need to create our database so that the controls on the form can hook up to it. So we're going to jump from the .NET Visual Objects straight to the Data Storage section.

Here's what we've already done...

...but we still need some objects to interact with the data we'll put in our database.

This step is about connecting our form to the database, so we're not ready for it yet, since we don't <u>have</u> a database.

So we need to focus on this step next: creating our database, and putting some initial data into it.

Visual Studio can generate code to connect your form to a database, but you need to have the database in place <u>**BEFORE**</u> generating that code.

We need a database to store our information

Before we add the rest of the fields to the form, we need to create a database to hook the form up to. The IDE can create lots of the code for connecting our form to our data, but we need to define the database itself first.

Make sure you've stopped debugging before you continue.

1 **Add a new SQL database to your project.**
In the Solution Explorer, **right-click the Contacts project**, select Add, and then choose New Item. Choose the SQL Database icon, and name it ContactDB.mdf.

This file is our new database.

ContactDB.mdf

Pick the right icon for the version you're using. Choose **SQL Database** *if you're using Visual Studio Express 2005 and* **Service-Based Database** *if you're using 2008.*

The SQL Database icon only works if you have SQL Server Express installed. Flip back to the README if you're not sure how to do this.

2 **Cancel the Data Source Configuration Wizard.**
For now, we want to skip configuring a data source, so click the Cancel button. We'll come back to this once we've set up our database structure.

Watch it!

If you're not using the Express edition, you'll see "Server Explorer" instead of "Database Explorer".

The Visual Studio 2008 Professional and Team Foundation editions don't have a Database Explorer window. Instead, they have a Server Explorer window, which does everything the Database Explorer does, but also lets you explore data on your network.

3 **View your database in the Solution Explorer.**
Go to the Solution Explorer, and you'll see that ContactDB has been added to the file list. Double click ContactDB.mdf in the Solution Explorer and look at the left side of your screen. The Toolbox has changed to a Database Explorer.

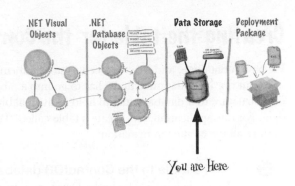

You are Here

The IDE created a database

When you told the IDE to add a new SQL database to your project, the IDE created a new database for you. A **SQL database** is a system that stores data for you in an organized, interrelated way. The IDE gives you all the tools you need to maintain your data and databases.

Data in a SQL database lives in tables. For now, you can think of a table like a spreadsheet. It organizes your information into columns and rows. The columns are the data categories, like a contact's name and phone number, and each row is the data for one contact card.

A SQL database stores your data, and has information about how it's structured and SQL code to help you access it.

Your data's stored in a table with columns and rows, like in a spreadsheet.

Tables

SQL Database

Stored Procedures

Stored procedures are statements that let you work with your data easily.

SQL is its own language

SQL stands for **Structured Query Language**. It's a programming language for accessing data in databases. It's got its own syntax, keywords, and structure. SQL code takes the form of **statements** and **queries**, which access and retrieve the data. A SQL database can hold **stored procedures**, which are a bunch of SQL statements and queries that you are stored in the database and can be run at any time. The IDE generates SQL statements and stored procedures for you automatically to let your program access the data in the database.

← [note from marketing: Can we get a plug for 'Head First SQL' in here?]

SQL

ContactDB.mdf

The SQL database is in this file. We're just about to define tables and data for it, and all of that will be stored in here too.

Creating the table for the Contact List

We have a database, and now we need to store information in it. But our information actually has to go into a table, the data structure that databases use to hold individual bits of data. For our application, let's create a table called "People" to store all the contact information:

❶ Add a table to the ContactDB database.
Right click on Tables in the Database Explorer, and select Add New Table. This will open up a window where you can define the columns in the table you just created.

Now we need to add columns to our table. First, let's add a column called ContactID to our new People table, so that each Contact record has its own unique ID.

❷ Add a ContactID column to the People table.
Type "ContactID" in the Column Name field, and select Int from the Data Type dropdown box. Be sure to uncheck the Allow Nulls checkbox.

Finally, let's make this the primary key of our table. Highlight the ContactID column you just created, and click the Primary Key button. This tells the database that each entry will have a unique primary key entry.

This is the Primary Key button. A primary key helps your database look up records quickly.

---

there are no Dumb Questions

Q: What's a column again?

A: A column is one field of a table. So in a People table, you might have a FirstName and LastName column. It will always have a data type, too, like String or Date or Bool.

Q: Why do we need this ContactID column?

A: It helps to have a unique ID for each record in most database tables. Since we're storing contact information for individual people, we decided to create a column for that, and call it ContactID.

Q: What's that Int from Data Type mean?

A: The data type tells the database what type of information to expect for a column. Int stands for integer, which is just a whole number. So the ContactID column will have whole numbers in it.

Q: This is a lot of stuff. Should I be getting all of this?

A: No, it's OK if you don't understand everything right now. Focus on the basic steps, and we'll spend a lot more time on databases in the later chapters of the book. And if you're dying to know more right away, you can always pick up **Head First SQL** to read along with this book.

.NET Visual Objects   .NET Database Objects   Data Storage   Deployment Package

You are Here

3 Tell the database to auto-generate IDs.

Since ContactID is a number for the database, and not our users, we can tell our database to handle creating and assigning IDs for us automatically. That way, we don't have to worry about writing any code to do this.

In the properties below your table, scroll down to Identity Specification, click the + button, and select Yes next to the (Is Identity) property.

This window is what you use to define your table and the data it will store.

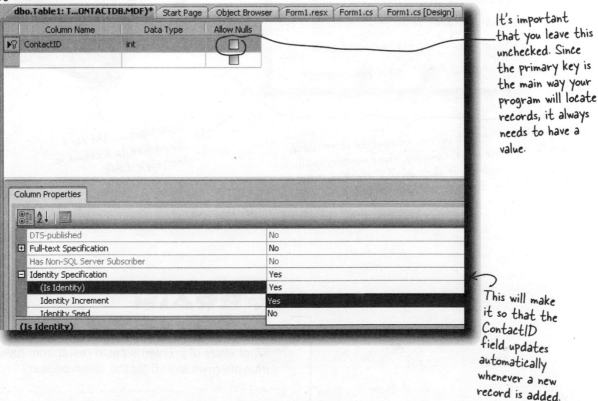

It's important that you leave this unchecked. Since the primary key is the main way your program will locate records, it always needs to have a value.

This will make it so that the ContactID field updates automatically whenever a new record is added.

The blanks on contact card are columns in our People table

Now that you've created a primary key for the table, you need to define all of the fields your going to track in the database. Each field on our written contact card should become a column in the People table.

Name: Laverne Smith   Objectville Paper company

Company: XYZ Industries

Telephone: (212)555-8129

Email: Laverne.Smith@xyzindustries.com

Client: Yes   **Last call:** 05/26/07

People

For each person, we want to store data, her name, company, phone number, email address, if she's an OPC client, and date of the last time she was called.

Each blank on the card should map to a column in the People table.

BRAIN POWER

What kinds of problems could result from having multiple rows stored for the same person?

WHO DOES WHAT?

Now that you've created a People table and a primary key column, you need to add columns for all of the data fields. See if you can work out which data type goes with each of the columns in your table, and also match the data type to the right description.

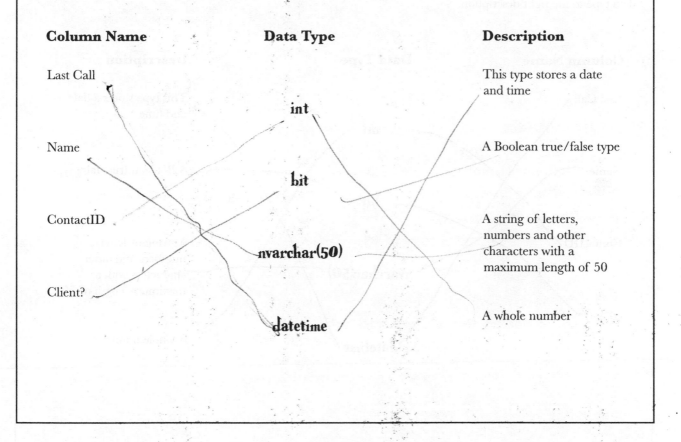

Column Name	Data Type	Description
Last Call		This type stores a date and time
	int	
Name		A Boolean true/false type
	bit	
ContactID		A string of letters, numbers and other characters with a maximum length of 50
	nvarchar(50)	
Client?		A whole number
	datetime	

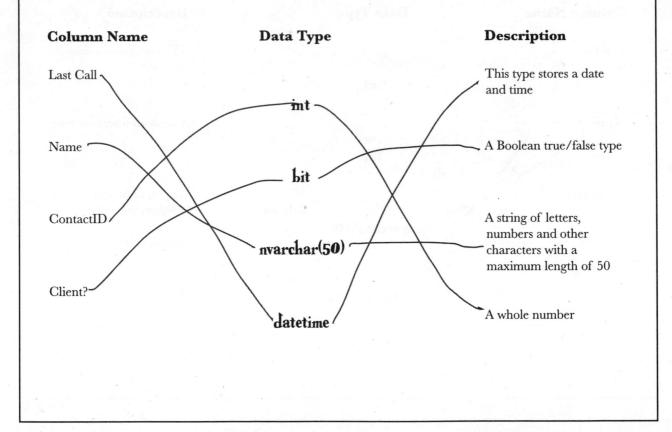

WHO DOES WHAT?

Now that you've created a People table and a primary key column, you need to add columns for all of the data fields. See if you can work out which data type goes with each of the columns in your table, and also match the data type to the right description.

Column Name	Data Type	Description

Last Call

Name

ContactID

Client?

int

bit

nvarchar(50)

datetime

This type stores a date and time

A Boolean true/false type

A string of letters, numbers and other characters with a maximum length of 50

A whole number

.NET Visual Objects .NET Database Objects Data Storage Deployment Package

You are Here

Finish building the table

Go back to where you entered the ContactID column and add the other five columns from the contact card. Here's what your database table should look like when you're done:

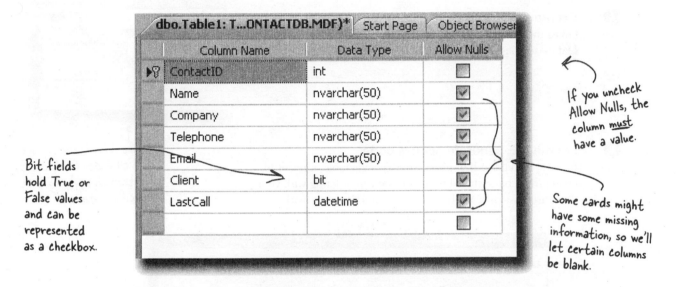

dbo.Table1: T...ONTACTDB.MDF)* | Start Page | Object Browser

Column Name	Data Type	Allow Nulls
ContactID	int	☐
Name	nvarchar(50)	☑
Company	nvarchar(50)	☑
Telephone	nvarchar(50)	☑
Email	nvarchar(50)	☑
Client	bit	☑
LastCall	datetime	☑
		☐

Bit fields hold True or False values and can be represented as a checkbox.

If you uncheck Allow Nulls, the column <u>must</u> have a value.

Some cards might have some missing information, so we'll let certain columns be blank.

Click on the Save button on the toolbar to save your new table. You'll be asked for a name. Call it "People" and click OK.

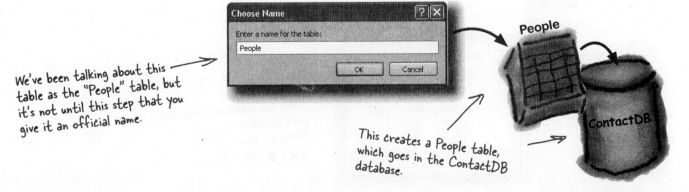

Choose Name

Enter a name for the table:

People

OK   Cancel

People

ContactDB

We've been talking about this table as the "People" table, but it's not until this step that you give it an official name.

This creates a People table, which goes in the ContactDB database.

Diagram your data so your application can access it

Once you've created your database and tables, you have to let your application know about it. That's where a database diagram comes in. A **database diagram** is a simple description of your table that the Visual Studio IDE can use to work with the table. It also lets the IDE automatically generate SQL statements to add, change, and delete rows in the table.

① **Create a new database diagram.**
Go to the Database Explorer window and right-click on the Database Diagrams node. Select Add New Diagram.

Remember, these options are all under ContactDB, so they all apply to that specific database.

② **Let the IDE generate access code.**
Before you tell the IDE about your specific table, it needs to create some basic stored procedures for interacting with your database. Just click Yes here, and let the IDE go to work.

The IDE creates several stored procedures that allow your code to interact with the database you created.

③ **Select the tables you want to work with.**
Select the People table from the window that pops up, and click Add. Now the IDE is ready to generate code specific to your table.

When you have databases with multiple tables, each table will show up as an entry on this window.

.NET Visual Objects   .NET Database Objects   Data Storage   Deployment Package

You are Here

❹ Name your diagram PeopleDiagram.
Select File>Save Diagram. You'll be asked to name your new database diagram. Call it PeopleDiagram, and you're all set.

If you're using Visual Studio 2005, select File>Save All instead.

The database diagram is shown here visually. It's a very simple representation of your table.

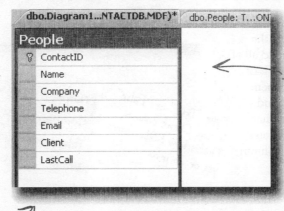

dbo.Diagram1...NTACTDB.MDF)*   dbo.People: T...ON

People

ContactID
Name
Company
Telephone
Email
Client
LastCall

This is just a picture of the database design you've just done. It marks the ContactID field as your primary key and lists off all of the columns in the table.

If you had any other tables in the database you wanted diagrammed, they would appear here, too.

A database diagram describes your tables to the Visual Studio IDE. The IDE then uses the database diagram to auto-generate code to work with your database.

Insert your card data into the database

Now you're ready to start entering cards into the database.
Here are some of the boss's contacts—we'll use those to
set up the database with a few records.

① Expand Tables and then right click
on the People Table in the Database
Explorer (or Server Explorer) and
select Show Table Data.

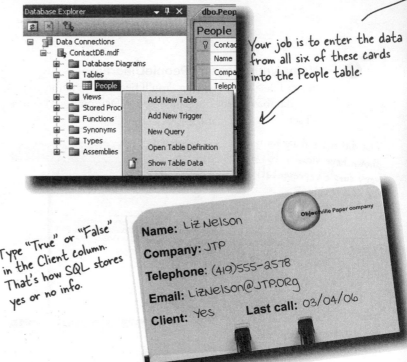

*Your job is to enter the data
from all six of these cards
into the People table.*

② Once you see the Table grid in the
main window, go ahead and add all of
the data below. (You'll see all NULL
values at first—just type over them
when you add your first row. And
ignore the exclamation points that
appear next to the data.) You don't
need to fill in the ContactID column,
that happens automatically.

*Type "True" or "False"
in the Client column.
That's how SQL stores
yes or no info.*

Name: Liz Nelson
Company: JTP
Telephone: (419)555-2578
Email: LizNelson@JTP.org
Client: Yes   **Last call:** 03/04/06

Name: Lucinda Ericson
Company: Ericson Events
Telephone: (212)555-9523
Email: Lucy@EricsonEvents.info
Client: No   **Last call:** 05/17/07

Name: Lloyd Jones
Company: Black Box inc.
Telephone: (718)555-5638
Email: LJones@xblackboxinc.com
Client: Yes   **Last call:** 05/26/07

Name: matt Franks
Company: XYZ Industries
Telephone: (212)555-8112
Email: matt.Franks@xyzindustriescom
Client: Yes   **Last call:** 05/26/07

Name: Sarah Kalter
Company: Kalter, Riddle, and Stoft
Telephone: (614)555-5641
Email: Sarah@kRS.org
Client: no   **Last call:** 12/10/05

Name: Laverne Smith
Company: XYZ Industries
Telephone: (212)555-8129
Email: Laverne.Smith@xyzindustriescom
Client: Yes   **Last call:** 05/26/07

③ Once you've entered all six records, select Save All from the File menu again. That should save the records to the database.

"Save All" tells the IDE to save everything in your application. That's different from "Save", which just saves the file you're working on.

there are no
Dumb Questions

Q: So what happened to the data after I entered it? Where did it go?

A: The IDE automatically stored the data you entered into the People table in your database. The table, its columns, the data types, and all of the data inside it is all stored in the SQL Server Express file, ContactDB.mdf. That file is stored as part of your project, and the IDE updates it just like it updates your code files when you change them.

Q: Okay, I entered these six records. Will they be part of my program forever?

A: Yes, they're as much a part of the program as the code that you write and the form that you're building. The difference is that instead of being compiled into an executable program, the ContactDB.mdf file is copied and stored along with the executable. When your application needs to access data, it reads and writes to ContactDB.mdf, in the program's output directory.

This file is actually a SQL database, and your program can use it with the code the IDE generated for you.

ContactDB.mdf

Connect your form to your database objects with a data source

We're finally ready to build the .NET database objects that our form will use to talk to your database. We need a **data source**, which is really just a collection of SQL statements your program will use to talk to the ContactDB database.

① Go back to your application's form.

Close out the People table and the ContactDB database diagram. You should now have the Form1.cs [Design] tab visible.

> You need to close both the data grid and the diagram to get back to your form.

ContactID	Name	Company	Telephone	Email	Client	LastCall
1	Lloyd Jones	Black Box Inc	718555638	ljones@blackbox...	True	5/26/2007 12:0...
2	Lucinda Ericson	Ericson Events	2125559523	Lucy@ericsonev...	False	5/17/2007 12:0...
3	Liz Nelson	JTP	4195552578	liznelson@jtp.org	True	3/4/2006 12:00:...
4	Matt Franks	XYZ Industries	2125558125	matt.franks@xy...	True	5/26/2007 12:0...
5	Sarah Kalter	Kalter, Riddle, a...	6145555641	sarah.kalter@K...	False	12/10/2006 12:...
6	Laverne Smith	XYX Industries	2125558129	Laverne.Smitth...	True	5/26/2007 12:0...
NULL	NULL	NULL	NULL	NULL	NULL	NULL

People: Query...ONTACTDB.MDF) | dbo.PeopleDi...ONTACTDB.MDF) | dbo.People: T...ONTACTDB.MDF) | Start Page | Object Browser

② Add a new data source to your application.

This should be easy by now. Click the Data menu, and then select Add New Data Source... from the drop down.

> The data source you're creating will handle all the interactions between your form and your database.

.NET Visual Objects .NET Database Objects Data Storage Deployment Package

You are Here

3 **Configure your new data source.**

Now you need to setup your data source to use the ContactDB database. Here's what to do:

★ Select Database and click the Next button.

★ Click Next in the "Choose your Data Connection" screen.

★ Make sure the Save the connection checkbox is checked in the "Save the Connection" screen that follows and click Next.

★ In the "Choose Your Objects" screen, click the Table checkbox.

★ In the Dataset Name field, make sure it says "ContactDBDataSet" and click Finish.

These steps connect your new data source with the People table in the ContactDB database.

Now your form can use the data source to interact with the ContactDB database.

ContactDBDataSet.

XML

C#

SQL

ContactDB.mdf

ContactDBDataSet. Designer.cs

Here's your existing form.

These files are what's generated by the data source you just setup.

This file is your database.

Form1

About
Contact List 1.0
Written by: Your Name
OK

Add database-driven controls to your form

Now we can go back to our form, and add some more controls. But these aren't just any controls, they are controls that are *bound* to our database, and the columns in the People table. That just means that a change to the data in one of the controls on the form automatically changes the data in the matching column in the database.

← *It took a little work, but now we're back to creating form objects that interact with our data storage.*

Here's how to create several database-driven controls:

❶ Select the data source you want to use.
Select Show Data Sources from the Data pull down menu. This will bring up the Data Sources window, showing the sources you have setup for your application.

If you don't see this tab, select "Show Data Sources" from the Data menu.

🛠 Toolbox	🗄 Database ...	🗐 Data Sources

This window shows you all your data sources. We've only got one setup, but you could have more for different tables or databases.

You can also look for, and click on, the Data Sources tab along the bottom of your Database Explorer window.

❷ Select the People table.
Under the ContactDBDataSet, you should see the People table and all of the columns in it. If you don't see the columns, click the arrow for the drop down menu, and select Details.

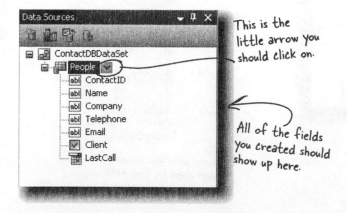

This is the little arrow you should click on.

All of the fields you created should show up here.

You are Here

③ Create controls that bind to the People table.
Drag and drop the People table onto your form. You should see
controls appear for each column in your database. Don't worry
too much about how they look right now; just make sure that
they all appear on the form.

> If you accidentally click out of the form you're working on, you
> can always get back to it by clicking the "Form1.cs [Design]"
> tab, or opening Form1.cs from the Solution Explorer.

The IDE
creates this
toolbar for
navigating
through the
People table.

When you dragged
the People table
onto the form, a
control was created
for each column in
the table.

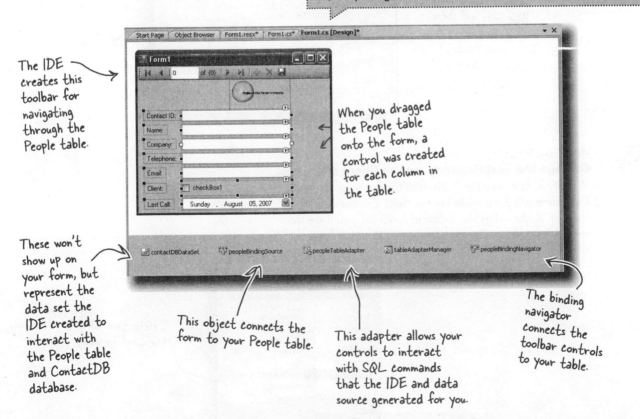

These won't
show up on
your form, but
represent the
data set the
IDE created to
interact with
the People table
and ContactDB
database.

This object connects the
form to your People table.

This adapter allows your
controls to interact
with SQL commands
that the IDE and data
source generated for you.

The binding
navigator
connects the
toolbar controls
to your table.

Good programs are <u>intuitive</u> to use

Right now, the form works. But it doesn't look that great. Your application has to do more than be functional. It should be easy to use. With just a few simple steps, you can make the form look a lot more like the paper cards we were using at the beginning of the chapter.

Our form would be more intuitive if it looked a lot like the contact card.

Name: Laverne Smith
Company: XYZ Industries   Objectville Paper company
Telephone: (212)555-8129
Email: Laverne.smith@xyzindustries.com
Client: Yes   **Last call:** 05/26/07

① **Line up your fields and labels.**
Line up your fields and labels along the left edge of the form. Your form will look like other applications, and make your users feel more comfortable using it.

Blue lines will show up on the form as you drag controls around. They're there to help you line the fields up.

② **Change the Text Property on the Client checkbox.**
When you first drag the fields onto the form your Client Checkbox will have a label to the right that needs to be deleted. Right below the Solution Explorer, you'll see the properties window. Scroll down to the Text property and delete the "checkbox1" label.

Delete this word to make the label go away.

You are Here →

③ Make the application look professional.

You can change the name of the form by clicking on any space within the form, and finding the Text property in the Properties window of your IDE. Change the name of the form to "Objectville Paper Co. - Contact List."

You can also turn off the Maximize and Minimize buttons in this same window, by looking for the MaximizeBox and MinimizeBox properties. Set these both to False.

> The reason you want to turn off the Maximize button is that maximizing your form won't change the positions of the controls, so it'll look weird.

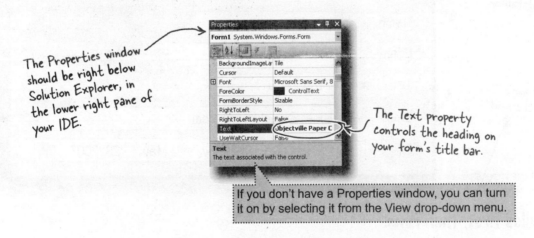

> The Properties window should be right below Solution Explorer, in the lower right pane of your IDE.

> The Text property controls the heading on your form's title bar.

If you don't have a Properties window, you can turn it on by selecting it from the View drop-down menu.

A good application not only works, but is easy to use. It's always a good idea to make sure it behaves as a typical user would expect it to.

Test drive

Okay, just one more thing to do… run your program and make sure it works the way you think it should! Do it the same way you did before—press the F5 key on your keyboard, or click the green arrow button ▶ on the toolbar (or choose "Run" from the Debug menu).

You can always run your programs at any time, even when they're not done—although if there's an error in the code, the IDE will tell you and stop you from executing it.

Click the X box in the corner to stop the program so you can move on to the next step.

These controls let you page through the different records in the database.

We'll spend more time on this in the next chapter.

The IDE builds first, then runs.

When you run your program in the IDE it actually does two things. First it **builds** your program, then it **executes** it. This involves a few distinct parts. It **compiles** the code, or turns it into an executable file. Then it places the compiled code, along with any resources and other files, into a subdirectory underneath the bin folder.

In this case, you'll find the executable and SQL database file in `bin/debug`. Since it copies the database out each time, any changes you make will be lost the next time you run inside the IDE. But if you run the executable from Windows, it'll save your data—until you build again, at which point the IDE will overwrite the SQL database with a new copy that contains the data you set up from inside the Database Explorer.

Building your program overwrites the data in your database.

How to turn YOUR application into EVERYONE'S application

You are Here

At this point, you've got a great program. But it only runs on your machine. That means that nobody else can use the app, pay you for it, see how great you are and hire you… and your boss and customers can't see the reports you're generating from the database.

C# makes it easy to take an application you've created, and **deploy** it. Deployment is taking an application and installing it onto other machines. And with the Visual C# IDE, you can set up a deployment with just two steps.

1 Select *Publish Contacts* from the Build menu.

Building the solution just copies the files to your local machine. Publish creates a Setup executable and a configuration file so that any machine could install your program.

2 Just accept all of the defaults in the Publish Wizard by clicking Finish. You'll see it package up your application and then show you a folder that has your Setup.exe in it.

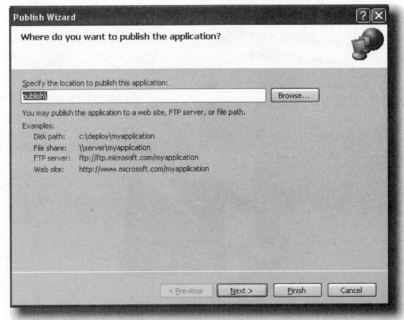

Give your users the application

Once you've created a deployment, you'll have a new folder called `publish/`. That folder has several things in it, all used for installation. The most important for your users is `setup`, a program that will let them install your program on their own computers.

This is where all of the supporting files for the installer are stored.

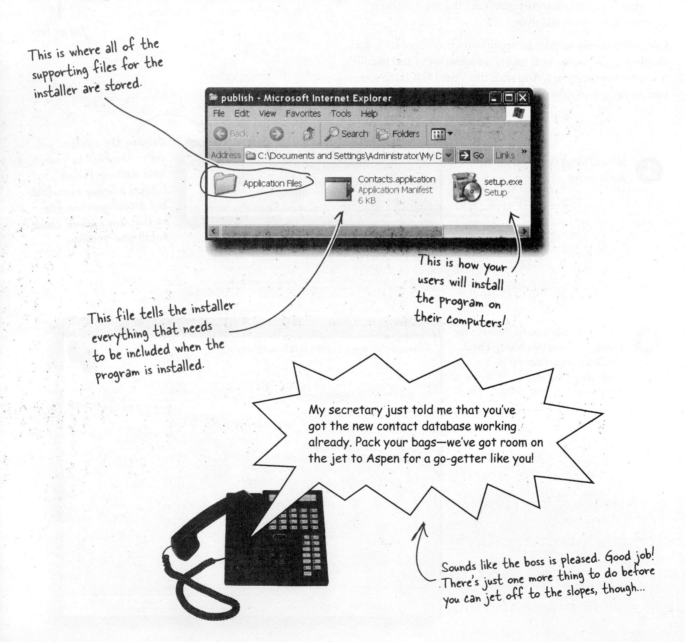

This file tells the installer everything that needs to be included when the program is installed.

This is how your users will install the program on their computers!

My secretary just told me that you've got the new contact database working already. Pack your bags—we've got room on the jet to Aspen for a go-getter like you!

Sounds like the boss is pleased. Good job! There's just one more thing to do before you can jet off to the slopes, though...

You're NOT done: test your installation

Before you pop the cork on any champagne bottles, you need to test your deployment and installation. You wouldn't give anyone your program without running it first, would you?

Close the Visual Studio IDE. Click the setup program, and select a location on your own computer to install the program. Now run it from there, and make sure it works like you expect. You can add and change records, too, and they'll be saved to the database.

You are Here

Now you can add, change, and delete records, and they'll get saved to the database.

You can use the arrows and the text field to switch between records.

Objectville Paper Co. - Contact List

| ◁◁ | ◁ | 1 | of 6 | ▷ | ▷▷| | ⊕ | ✕ | 🖫 |

Contact ID: 1

Name: Lloyd Jones

Company: Black Box Inc

Telephone: 718555638

Email: ljones@blackboxinc.com

Client: ☑   Last Call: Saturday   May   26, 2007 ▼

Objectville Paper company

Go ahead... make some changes. You've deployed it so this time, they'll stick.

The six records you initially entered are all there.

TEST EVERYTHING!
Test your program, test your deployment, test the data in your application.

You built a complete data-driven application

The Visual Studio IDE made it pretty easy to create a Windows application, create and design a database, and hook the two together. You even were able to build an installer with a few extra clicks.

From this

Name: Lloyd Jones

Company: Black Box inc.

Telephone: (718)555-5638

Email: LJones@xblackboxinc.com

Client: Yes   **Last call:** 05/26/07

to this

Objectville Paper Co. - Contact List

|◄ ◄ 1 of 6 ► ►| ✛ ✕ 🖫

Contact ID: 1

Name: Lloyd Jones

Company: Black Box Inc

Telephone: 718555638

Email: ljones@blackboxinc.com

Client: ☑   Last Call: Saturday, May 26, 2007 ▼

in no time flat.

The power of Visual C# is that you can quickly get up and running, and then focus on your what your <u>program's supposed to do</u>... not lots of windows, buttons, and SQL access code.

CSharpcross

Take some time to sit back and exercise your C# vocabulary with this crossword; all of the solution words are from this chapter.

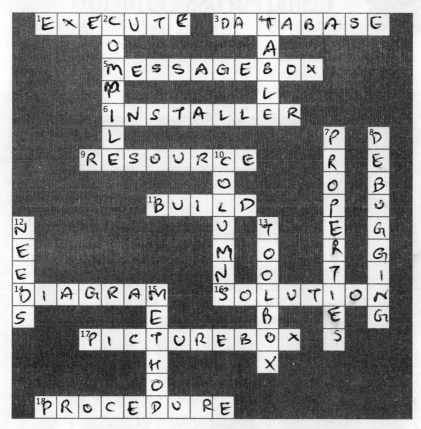

Across

1. When you do this from inside the IDE, it's called "debugging".
3. The _____ explorer is where you edit the contents of your SQL tables and bind them to your program.
5. The "About" box in the Contact List program was one of these
6. You build one of these so you can deploy your program to another computer.
9. An image, sound, icon or file that's attached to your project in a way that your objects can access easily.
11. Before you can run your program, the IDE does this to create the executable and move files to the output directory.
14. The database _____ gives the IDE information about your database so it can generate SQL statements automatically.
16. The _____ explorer in the IDE is where you'll find the files in your project.
17. Drag one of these objects onto your form to display an image.
18. A stored _____ is a way for a SQL database to save queries and statements that you can reuse later.

Down

2. What's happening when code is turned into an executable.
4. A SQL database can use many of these to store its data.
7. What you change to alter the appearance or behavior of objects on your form.
8. What you're doing to your program when you run it from inside the IDE.
10. Every row in a database contains several of these, and all of them can have different data types.
12. Before you start building any application, always think about the users and their _____.
13. You drag objects out of this and onto your form.
15. When you double-clicked on a visual control, the IDE created this for you and you added code to it.

CSharpcross Solution

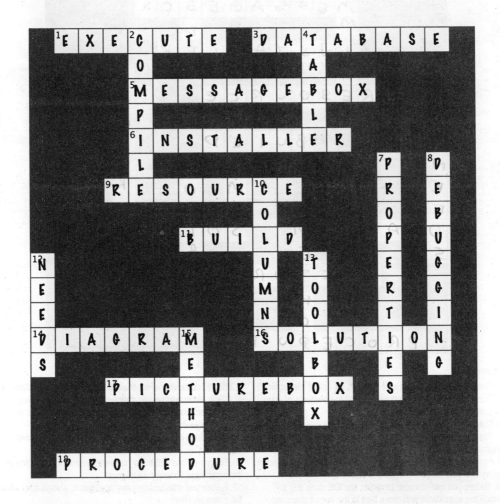

Across:
1. EXECUTE
3. DATABASE
5. MESSAGEBOX
6. INSTALLER
9. RESOURCE
11. BUILD
14. DIAGRAM
16. SOLUTION
17. PICTUREBOX
18. PROCEDURE

Down:
2. COMPILE
4. TABLE
7. PROPERTIES
8. DEBUGGING
10. COLUMN
12. NEEDS
13. TOOLBOX
15. METHOD

2 it's all just code

Under the Hood

One of these days I'll figure out what's going on under there...

You're a programmer, not just an IDE-user.

You can get a lot of work done using the IDE. But there's only so far it can take you. Sure, there are a lot of **repetitive tasks** that you do when you build an application. And the IDE is great at doing those things for you. But working with the IDE is *only the beginning*. You can get your programs to do so much more—and **writing C# code** is how you do it. Once you get the hang of coding, there's *nothing* your programs can't do.

When you're doing this...

The IDE is a powerful tool—but that's all it is, a *tool* for you to use. Every time you change your project or drag and drop something in the IDE, it creates code automatically. It's really good at writing **boilerplate** code, or code that can be reused easily without requiring much customization.

Let's look at what the IDE does in typical application development, when you're...

> All of these tasks have to do with standard actions, and boilerplate code. Those are the things the IDE is great for helping with.

1 **Creating a new Windows Application solution**
There are several kinds of applications the IDE lets you build, but we'll be concentrating on Windows applications for now. Those are programs that have visual elements, like forms and buttons.

> Make sure you always create a Windows Forms Application project—that tells the IDE to create an empty form and add it to your new project.

2 **Dragging a button out of the toolbox and onto your form, and then double-clicking it**
Buttons are how you make things happen in your form. We'll use a lot of buttons to explore various parts of the C# language. They're also a part of almost every C# application you'll write.

3 **Setting a property on your form**
The **Properties window** in the IDE is a really powerful tool that you can use to change attributes of just about everything in your program: all visual and functional properties for the controls on your form, attributes of your databases, and even options on your project itself.

> The Properties window in the IDE is just a really easy way to edit a specific chunk of code in Form1.Designer.cs automatically. It would take a lot longer to do it by hand.

...the IDE does this

Every time you make a change in the IDE, it makes a
change to the code, which means it changes the files that
contain that code. Sometimes it just modifies a few lines,
but other times it adds entire files to your project.

These files are created from
a predefined template that
contains the basic code to
create and display a form.

1   ... the IDE creates the files and
folders for the project.

| WindowsApplication1 .csproj | Form1.cs | Form1.Designer.cs | Program.cs | Properties |

2   ... the IDE adds code to the Form1.Designer.cs file that adds
the button to the form, and then adds code to the Form1.cs
file to handle the button click.

```
private void button1_Click(object sender, EventArgs e)
{

}
```

The IDE knows how to add an empty method
to handle a button click. But it doesn't know
what to put inside it—that's your job.

This code
gets added to
Form1.cs.

Form1.Designer.cs

Form1.cs

3   ... the IDE opens the Form1.Designer.cs file and
updates a line of code.

The IDE went into this file...

```
partial class Form1
{
    ⋮
        this.Text = "Contacts";
    ⋮
}
```

Form1.Designer.cs

...and updated this line of code.

Where programs come from

A C# program may start out as statements in a bunch of
files, but it ends up as a program running in your computer.
Here's how it gets there.

Every program starts out as source code files

You've already seen how to edit a program, and how the IDE saves your program
to files in a folder. Those files **are** your program—you can copy them to a new
folder and open them up, and everything will be there: forms, resources, code, and
anything else you added to your project.

You can think of the IDE as a kind of fancy file editor. It automatically does the
indenting for you, changes the colors of the keywords, matches up brackets for you,
and even suggests what words might come next. But in the end, all the IDE does is
edit the files that contain your program.

There's no reason you
couldn't build your
programs in Notepad,
but it'd be a lot
more time-consuming.

The IDE bundles all of the files for your program into a **solution** by creating a
solution (.sln) file and a folder that contains all of the other files for the program.
The solution file has a list of the project files (which end in .csproj) in the solution,
and the project files contain lists of all the other files associated with the program.
In this book, you'll be building solutions that only have one project in them, but
you can easily add other projects to your solution using the IDE's Solution Explorer.

The .NET Framework gives you the right tools for the job

C# is just a language—by itself, it can't actually **do** anything. And that's where
the **.NET Framework** comes in. Remember that Maximize button you turned
off for the Contacts form? When you click the Maximize button on a window,
there's code that tells the window how to maximize itself and take up the whole
screen. That code is part of the .NET Framework. Buttons, checkboxes, lists...
those are all pieces of the .NET framework. So are the internal bits that hooked
your form up to the database. It's got tools to draw graphics, read and write files,
manage collections of things... all sorts of tools for a lot of jobs that programmers
have to do every day.

The tools in the .NET Framework are divided up into **namespaces**. You've
seen these namespaces before, at the top of your code in the "using" lines. One
namespace is called System.Windows.Forms—it's where your buttons, checkboxes,
and forms come from. Whenever you create a new Windows Forms Application
project, the IDE will add the necessary files so that your project contains a form,
and those files have the line "using System.Windows.Forms;" at the top.

Build the program to create an executable

When you select "Build Solution" from the Build menu, the IDE **compiles** your program. It does this by running the **compiler**, which is a tool that reads your program's source code and turns it into an **executable**. The executable is a file on your disk that ends in `.exe`—that's what you double-click on to run your program. When you build the program, it creates the executable inside the `bin` folder, which is inside the project folder. When you publish your solution, it copies the executable (and any other files necessary) into the folder you're publishing to.

When you select "Start Debugging" from the Debug menu, the IDE compiles your program and runs the executable. It's got some more advanced tools for **debugging** your program, which just means running it and being able to pause (or "break") it so you can figure out what's going on.

Your program runs inside the CLR

When you double-click on the executable, Windows runs your program. But there's an extra "layer" between Windows and your program called the **Common Language Runtime**, or CLR. Once upon a time, not so long ago (but before C# was around), writing programs was harder, because you had to deal with hardware and low-level machine stuff. You never knew exactly how someone was going to configure his computer. The CLR—often referred to as a **virtual machine**—takes care of all that for you by doing a sort of "translation" between your program and the computer running it.

You don't really have to worry about the CLR much right now. It's enough to know it's there, and takes care of running your program for you automatically. You'll learn more about it as you go.

You'll learn about all sorts of things the CLR does for you. For example, it tightly manages your computer's memory by figuring out when your program is finished with certain pieces of data and getting rid of them for you. That's something programmers used to have to do themselves, and it's something that you don't have to be bothered with. You won't know it at the time, but the CLR will make your job of learning C# a whole lot easier.

The IDE helps you code

You've already seen a few of the things that the IDE can do.
Let's take a closer look at some of the tools it gives you.

⭐ **The Solution Explorer shows you everything in your project**
You'll spend a lot of time going back and forth between classes, and the easiest
way to do that is to use the solution explorer. It's got two views: a Solution
Explorer view (which shows you the files in your project) and a Class View
(which shows you how your code logically breaks down into classes).

The Solution Explorer shows you how the different files in the solution folder.

You'll learn more about classes in a minute.

⭐ **Use the tabs to switch between open files**
Since your program is split up into more than one file, you'll usually have several
code files open at once. When you do, each one will be in its own tab in the code
editor. The IDE displays an asterisk (*) next to a filename if it hasn't been saved yet.

Here's the form's resource file that you added the Objectville Paper Company logo to.

When you're working on a form, you can have two tabs for
it at the same time—one for the form designer, and one
to view the form's code.

The IDE helps you write code

Did you notice little windows popping up as you typed code into the IDE? That's a feature called IntelliSense, and it's really useful. One thing it does is show you possible ways to complete your current line of code. If you type `MessageBox` and then a period, it knows that there are three valid ways to complete that line:

> The IDE knows that MessageBox has three methods called Equals, ReferenceEquals, and Show. If you type S, it selects Show. Press the tab or enter key to select it. That can be a real timesaver if you're typing a lot of really long method names.

If you select Show and type **(**, the IDE's IntelliSense will show you information about how you can complete the line:

> This means that there are 21 different ways that you can call the MessageBox's Show method (like ways to display different buttons or icons).

```
MessageBox.Show(
```
◄ 3 of 21 ► DialogResult MessageBox.Show (**string text**, string caption)
text: The text to display in the message box.

The IDE also has shortcuts called **snippets** that let you type an abbreviation to tell it to fill in the rest of the code. Here's a useful one: type mbox and press the tab key twice, and the IDE will fill in the `MessageBox.Show` method for you:

```
MessageBox.Show("Test");
```

> When you use Start Debugging to run your program inside the IDE, the first thing it does is build your program. If it compiles, then your program runs. If not, it won't run, and will show you errors in the Error List.

 The Error List helps you troubleshoot compiler errors

If you haven't already discovered how easy it is to make typos in a C# program, you'll find out very soon! Luckily, the IDE gives you a great tool for troubleshooting them. When you build your solution, any problems that keep it from compiling will show up in the Error List window at the bottom of the IDE:

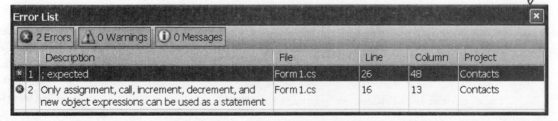

		Description	File	Line	Column	Project
✖	1	; expected	Form1.cs	26	48	Contacts
✖	2	Only assignment, call, increment, decrement, and new object expressions can be used as a statement	Form1.cs	16	13	Contacts

Error List — 2 Errors, 0 Warnings, 0 Messages

Double-click on an error, and the IDE will jump to the problem in the code:

```
private void pictureBox1_Click(object sender, EventArgs e)
{
    MessageBox.Show("Contact List 1.0")
}
```

> The IDE will show a red underscore where it finds you're missing a semicolon.

When you change things in the IDE, you're also changing your code

When you see a "Do this!", pop open the IDE and follow along. We'll tell you exactly what to do, and point out what to look for to get the most out of the example we show you.

Do this!

The IDE is great at writing visual code for you. But don't take our word for it. Open up Visual Studio, **create a new Windows Application project**, and see for yourself.

❶ Open up the designer code

Open the `Form1.Designer.cs` file in the IDE. But this time, instead of opening it in the Form Designer, open up its code by right-clicking on it in the Solution Explorer and selecting "View Code". Look for the `Form1` class declaration:

```
public partial class Form1 : Form
```

Notice how it's a partial class?

❷ Open up the Form designer and add a PictureBox to your form

Get used to working with more than one tab. Go to the Solution Explorer and open up the Form designer by double-clicking on `Form1.cs`. **Drag a new PictureBox** onto a new form.

❸ Find and expand the designer-generated code for the PictureBox control

Then go back to the `Form1.Designer.cs` tab in the IDE. Scroll down and look for this line in the code:

Click on the plus sign

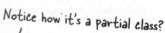

```
⊞    Windows Form Designer generated code
```

Click on the + on the left-hand side of the line to expand the code. Scroll down and find these lines:

```
//
// pictureBox1
//
this.pictureBox1.Location = new System.Drawing.Point(276, 28);

this.pictureBox1.Name = "pictureBox1";

this.pictureBox1.Size = new System.Drawing.Size(100, 50);

this.pictureBox1.TabIndex = 1;

this.pictureBox1.TabStop = false;
```

Don't worry if the numbers in your code for the Location and Size lines are a little different than these...

Wait, wait! What did that say?

Scroll back up for a minute. There it is, at the top of the Windows
Form Designer generated code section.

```
/// <summary>
/// Required method for Designer support - do not modify
/// the contents of this method with the code editor.
/// </summary>
```

*Most comments only start
with two slashes (//).
But the IDE sometimes
adds these three-slash
comments.*

There's nothing more attractive to a kid than a big sign that says, "Don't
touch this!" Come on, you know you're tempted… let's go modify the
contents of that method with the code editor! **Add a button** to your
form, and then go ahead and do this:

❶ **Change the code that sets the button1.Text property. What
do you think it will do to the Properties window in the IDE?**
Give it a shot—see what happens! Now go back to the form designer and
check the Text property. Did it change?

❷ **Stay in the designer, and use the Properties window to
change the Name property to something else.**
See if you can find a way to get the IDE to change the Name property. It's
in the Properties window at the very top, under "(Name)". What happened
to the code? What about the comment in the code?

❸ **Change the code that sets the Location property to (0,0) and
the Size property to make the button really big.**
Did it work?

❹ **Go back to the designer, and change the button's BackColor
property to something else.**
Look closely at the Form1.Designer.cs code. Were any lines added?

*You don't have to save the
form or run the program
to see the changes. Just
make the change in the
code editor, and then click
on the designer tab to flip
over to the form designer—
the changes should show up
immediately.*

It's always easier to use the IDE to change your form's
Designer-generated code. But when you do, any change you
make in the IDE ends up as a change to your projects' code.

Anatomy of a program

Every C# program's code is structured in exactly the same way. All programs use **namespaces**, **classes**, and **methods** to make your code easier to manage.

A class contains a piece of your program (although some very small programs can have just one class).

A class has one or more methods. Your methods always have to live inside a class. And methods are made up of statements—like the ones you've already seen.

Every time you make a new program, you define a namespace for it so that its code is separate from the .NET Framework classes.

Let's take a closer look at your code

Open up the code from your Contact project's `Form1.cs` so we can go through it piece by piece.

1 **The code file starts by using the .NET Framework tools**

You'll find a set of `using` lines at the top of every program file. They tell C# which parts of the .NET Framework to use. If you use other classes that are in other namespaces, then you'll add `using` lines for them too. Since forms often use a lot of different tools from the .NET Framework, the IDE automatically adds a bunch of `using` lines when it creates a form and adds it to your project.

```
using System;
using System.Collections.Generic;
using System.ComponentModel;
using System.Data;
using System.Drawing;
using System.Linq;
using System.Text;
using System.Windows.Forms;
```

These **using** lines are at the top of every code file. They tell C# to use all of those .NET Framework classes. Each one tells your program that the classes in this particular .cs file will use all of the classes in one specific .NET Framework namespace.

❷ C# programs are organized into classes

Every C# program is organized into **classes**. A class can do anything, but most classes do one specific thing. When you created the new program, the IDE added a class called Form1 that displays a form.

> When you called your program Contacts, the IDE created a namespace for it called Contacts by adding the namespace keyword at the top of your code file. Everything inside its pair of curly brackets is part of the Contacts namespace.

```
namespace Contacts
{
    public partial class Form1 : Form
    {
```

> This is a class called Form1. It contains all of the code to draw the form and the Toolbox controls on it. The IDE created it when you told it to create a new Windows Forms Application project.

❸ Classes contain methods that perform actions

When a class needs to do something, it uses a **method**. A method takes an input, performs some action, and sometimes produces an output. The way you pass input into a method is by using **parameters**. Methods can behave differently depending on what input they're given. Some methods produce output. When they do, it's called a **return value**. If you see the keyword void in front of a method, that means it doesn't return anything.

> Look for the matching pairs of brackets. Every { is eventually paired up with a }. Some pairs can be inside others.

```
    public Form1()
    {
        InitializeComponent();
    }
```

> This line calls a method named InitializeComponent(), which the IDE also created for you.

❹ A statement performs one single action

When you added the MessageBox.Show() line to your program, you were adding a **statement**. Every method is made up of statements. When your program calls a method, it executes the first statement in the method, then the next, then the next, etc. When the method runs out of statements or hits a return statement, it ends, and the program resumes after the statement that originally called the method.

> This is a method called pictureBox1_Click() that gets called when the user clicks on the picture box.

> This method has two parameters called sender and e.

```
    private void pictureBox1_Click(object sender, EventArgs e)
    {
        MessageBox.Show("Contact List 1.0", "About");
    }
}
```

> This is a statement. You already know what it does—it pops up a little message box window.

> Your statement called the Show() method, which is part of the MessageBox class, which is inside the System.Windows.Forms namespace.

> Your statement passed two parameters to the Show() method. The first one was a string of text to display in the message box, and the second one was a string to display in its title bar.

Your program knows where to start

When you created the new Windows Application solution, one of the files the IDE added was called **Program.cs**. Go to the Solution Explorer and double-click on it. It's got a class called Program, and inside that class is a method called Main(). That method is the **entry point**, which means that it's the very first thing that's run in your program.

> Every C# program can only have one entry point method, and it's always called Main(). That's how it knows where to start when you run it.

> Here's some code the IDE built for you automatically in the last chapter. You'll find it in Program.cs.

Y̌our C̆ǒde Up Clǒse

```csharp
❶ using System;
using System.Linq;
using System.Collections.Generic;
using System.Windows.Forms;

❷ namespace Contacts
{

    ❸ static class Program
    {

        /// <summary>
        /// The main entry point for the application.
        /// </summary>
        [STAThread]
        static void Main()
        ❺ {

            Application.EnableVisualStyles();
            ❹Application.SetCompatibleTextRenderingDefault(false);
            Application.Run(new Form1());

        }

    }
}
```

> The namespace for all this code is Contacts. We'll talk about namespaces more in a few pages.

> Lines that begin with slashes are comments, which you can add anywhere you want. The slashes tell C# to ignore them.

> Every time you run your program, it starts here, at the entry point.

> This statement creates and displays the Contacts form, and ends the program when the form's closed.

I do declare!

The first line of every class or method is called the <u>declaration</u>.

> Remember, this is just a starting point for you to dig into the code. But before you do, you'll need to know what you're looking at.

1 **C# and .NET have lots of built-in features.**
You'll find lines like this at the top of almost every C# class file. `System.Windows.Forms` is a **namespace**. The `using System.Windows.Forms` line makes everything ← in that namespace available to your program. In this case, that namespace has lots of visual elements in it like buttons and forms.

Your programs will use more and more namespaces like this one as you learn about C# and .NET's other built-in features throughout the book.

2 **The IDE chose a namespace for your code.**
Here's the namespace the IDE created for you—it chose `Contacts` based on your project's name. All of the code in your program lives in this namespace.

Namespaces let you use the same name in different programs, as long as those programs aren't also in the same namespace.

3 **Your code is stored in a class.**
This particular class is called `Program`. The IDE created it and added the code that starts the program and brings up the Contacts form.

You can have multiple classes in a single namespace.

4 **This code has one method, and it contains three statements.**
A namespace has classes in it, and classes have methods. Inside each method is a set of statements. In this program, the statements handle starting up the Contacts form. Methods are where the action happens—every method **does** something.

5 **Each program has a special kind of method called the entry point.**
Every C# program **must** have exactly one method called `Main`. Even though your program has a lot of methods, only one can be the first one that gets executed, and that's your `Main` method. C# checks every class in your code for a method that reads `static void Main()`. Then, when the program is run, the first statement in this method gets executed, and everything else follows from that first statement.

Every C# program must have exactly <u>one</u> method called Main. That method is the <u>entry</u> <u>point</u> for your code.

When you run your code, the code in your Main() method is executed FIRST.

You can change your program's entry point

As long as your program has an entry point, it doesn't matter which class your entry point method is in, or what that method does. Let's remove the Main method in Program.cs, and create a new entry point.

Do this!

Write down what happened when you changed the method name, and why you think that happened.

1 Go back to Program.cs and change the name of the Main method to NotMain. Now **try to build and run** the program. What happens?

_____

_____

Right-click on the project in Properties and select "Add" and "Class…"

2 Now let's create a new entry point. **Add a new class** called AnotherClass.cs. You add a class to your program by right-clicking on the project name in the Solution Explorer and selecting "Add>>Class…". Name your class file AnotherClass.cs. The IDE will add a class to your program called AnotherClass. Here's the file the IDE added:

```
using System;
using System.Linq;
using System.Collections.Generic;
using System.Text;

namespace Contacts
{
    class AnotherClass
    {
    }
}
```

These four standard **using** lines were added to the file.

This class is in the same Contacts namespace that the IDE added when you first created the Windows Application project.

The IDE automatically named the class based on the filename.

3 Add a new using line to the top of the file: **using System.Windows.Forms;** Don't forget to end the line with a semicolon!

4 Add this method to the **AnotherClass** class by typing it in between the curly brackets:

MessageBox is a class that lives in the System.Windows.Forms namespace, which is why you had to add the using line in step #3. Show() is a method that's part of the MessageBox class.

```
class AnotherClass
{
    public static void Main()
    {
        MessageBox.Show("Pow!");
    }
}
```

Now run it!

So what happened?

Instead of popping up the Contacts application, your program now shows this messagebox. When you made the new Main() method, you gave your program a new entry point. Now the first thing the program does is run the statements in that method—which means running that MessageBox.Show() statement. There's nothing else in that method, so once you click the OK button, the program runs out of statements to execute and then it ends.

5 Figure out how to fix your program so it pops up Contacts again.

Hint: you only have to change two lines in two files to do it.

Sharpen your pencil

Fill in the annotations so they describe the lines in this C# file that they're pointing to. We've filled in the first one for you.

```csharp
using System;
using System.Linq;
using System.Text;
using System.Windows.Forms;


namespace SomeNamespace
{

    class MyClass {

        public static void DoSomething() {

            MessageBox.Show("This is a message");

        }

    }

}
```

C# classes have these "using" lines to add methods from other namespaces

Class containing the main method

A method

show this message in the box

there are no
Dumb Questions

Q: What's with all the curly brackets?

A: C# uses curly brackets (or "braces") to group statements together into **blocks**. Curly brackets always come in pairs. You'll only see a closing curly bracket after you see an opening one. The IDE helps you match up curly brackets—just click on one, and you'll see it and its match get shaded darker.

Q: I don't quite get what the entry point is. Can you explain it one more time?

A: Your program has a whole lot of statements in it, but they're not all run at once. The program starts with the first statement in the program, executes it, and then goes on to the next one, and the next one, etc. Those statements are usually organized into a bunch of classes. So when you run your program, how does it know which statement to start with?

That's where the entry point comes in. The compiler will not build your code unless there is **exactly one method called Main()** which we call the entry point. The program starts running with the first statement in Main().

Q: How come I get errors in the Error List window when I try to run my program? I thought that only happened when I did "Build Solution."

A: Because the first thing that happens when you choose "Start Debugging" from the menu or press the toolbar button to start your program running is that it saves all the files in your solution and then tries to compile them. And when you compile your code—whether it's when you run it, or when you build the solution—if there are errors, the IDE will display them in the Error List instead of running your program.

Sharpen your pencil
Solution

Fill in the annotations so they describe the lines in this C# file that they're pointing to. We've filled in the first one for you.

```csharp
using System;
using System.Linq;
using System.Text;
using System.Windows.Forms;

namespace SomeNamespace
{

    class MyClass {

        public static void DoSomething() {

            MessageBox.Show("This is a message");

        }

    }

}
```

C# classes have these "using" lines to add methods from other namespaces.

All of the code lives in classes, so the program needs a class here.

This is a method. Every method in the program does something. Methods are used to group statements together.

This is a statement. When it's executed, it pops up a little window with a message inside of it.

WHAT'S MY PURPOSE?

Match each of these fragments of code generated by the IDE to what it does.
(Some of these are new—take a guess and see if you got it right!)

```
partial class Form1
{
  ⋮
  this.BackColor = Color.DarkViolet;
  ⋮
}
```

Set properties for a label

```
// This loop gets executed three times
```

Nothing—it's a comment that the programmer added to explain the code to anyone who's reading it

```
partial class Form1
{
  private void InitializeComponent()
  {
    ⋮
  }
}
```

Disable the maximize icon (⬚) in the title bar of the Form1 window

```
number_of_pit_stopsLabel.Name
        = "number_of_pit_stopsLabel";
number_of_pit_stopsLabel.Size
        = new System.Drawing.Size(135, 17);
number_of_pit_stopsLabel.Text
        = "Number of pit stops:";
```

A special kind of comment that the IDE uses to explain what an entire block of code does

```
/// <summary>
/// Bring up the picture of Rover when
/// the button is clicked
/// </summary>
```

Change the background color of the Form1 window

```
partial class Form1
{
  ⋮
  this.MaximizeBox = false;
  ⋮
}
```

A block of code that executes whenever a program opens up a Form1 window

WHAT'S MY PURPOSE?

Match each of these fragments of code generated by the IDE to what it does.
(Some of these are new—take a guess and see if you got it right!)

```
partial class Form1
{
   ⋮
   this.BackColor = Color.DarkViolet;
   ⋮
}
```

Set properties for a label

```
// This loop gets executed three times
```

Nothing—it's a comment that the programmer added to explain the code to anyone who's reading it

```
partial class Form1
{
   private void InitializeComponent()
   {
      ⋮
   }
}
```

Disable the maximize icon ( ) in the title bar of the Form1 window

```
number_of_pit_stopsLabel.Name
        = "number_of_pit_stopsLabel";
number_of_pit_stopsLabel.Size
        = new System.Drawing.Size(135, 17);
number_of_pit_stopsLabel.Text
        = "Number of pit stops:";
```

A special kind of comment that the IDE uses to explain what an entire block of code does

```
/// <summary>
/// Bring up the picture of Rover when
/// the button is clicked
/// </summary>
```

Change the background color of the Form1 window

```
partial class Form1
{
   ⋮
   this.MaximizeBox = false;
   ⋮
}
```

A block of code that executes whenever a program opens up a Form1 window

Two classes can be in the same namespace

Take a look at these two class files from a program called PetFiler2. They've got three classes: a Dog class, a Cat class, and a Fish class. Since they're all in the same PetFiler2 namespace, statements in the Dog.Bark() method can call Cat.Meow() and Fish.Swim(). It doesn't matter how the various namespaces and classes are divided up between files. They still act the same when they're run.

When a class is "public" it means every other class in the program can access its methods.

SomeClasses.cs

```
namespace PetFiler2 {

    public class Dog {

        public void Bark() {
            // statements go here
        }

    }

    public partial class Cat {

        public void Meow() {
            // more statements
        }

    }

}
```

MoreClasses.cs

```
namespace PetFiler2 {

    public class Fish {

        public void Swim() {
            // statements
        }

    }

    public partial class Cat {

        public void Purr() {
            // statements
        }

    }

}
```

Since these classes are in the same namespace, they can all "see" each other—even though they're in different files. A class can span multiple files too, but you need to use the "partial" keyword when you declare it.

You can only split a class up into different files if you use the **partial** keyword. You probably won't do that in any of the code you write in this book, but the IDE used it to split your form up into two files, Form1.cs and Form1.Designer.cs.

Your programs use <u>variables</u> to work with data

When you get right down to it, every program is basically a data cruncher. Sometimes the data is in the form of a document, or an image in a video game, or an instant message. But it's all just data. And that's where **variables** come in. A variable is what your program uses to store data.

Declare your variables

Whenever you **declare** a variable, you tell your program its *type* and its *name*. Once C# knows your variable's type, it'll keep your program from compiling if you make a mistake and try to do something that doesn't make sense, like subtract "Fido" from 48353.

These are the variable types.

These are the names of these variables.

```
int maxWeight;
string message;
bool boxChecked;
```

C# uses the variable type to limit what data these variables can hold.

These names are for YOU. Like methods and classes, use names that make sense and describe the variable's usage.

Variables vary

A variable is equal to different values at different times while your program runs. In other words, a variable's value *varies*. (Which is why "variable" is such a good name.) This is really important, because that idea is at the core of every program that you've written or will ever write. So if your program sets the variable myHeight equal to 63:

```
int myHeight = 63;
```

any time myHeight appears in the code, C# will replace it with its value, 63. Then, later on, if you change its value to 12:

```
myHeight = 12;
```

C# will replace myHeight with 12—but the variable is still called myHeight.

> **Whenever your program needs to work with numbers, text, true/false values, or any other kind of data, you'll use variables to keep track of them.**

You have to assign values to variables before you use them

Try putting these statements into a C# program:

```
int z;
MessageBox.Show("The answer is " + z);
```

Go ahead, give it a shot. You'll get an error, and the IDE will refuse to compile your code. That's because the IDE checks each variable to make sure that you've assigned it a value before you use it. The easiest way to make sure you don't forget to assign your variables values is to combine the statement that declares a variable with a statement that assigns its value:

These values are assigned to the variables.

```
int maxWeight = 25000;
string message = "Hi!";
bool boxChecked = true;
```

Each declaration has a type, exactly like before.

A few useful types

Every variable has a type that tells C# what kind of data it can hold. We'll go into a lot of detail about the many different types in C# in Chapter 4. In the meantime, we'll concentrate on the three most popular types. `int` holds integers (or whole numbers), `string` holds text, and `bool` holds Boolean true/false values.

> **var-i-a-ble, adjective.**
> able to be changed or adapted
> *the drill's **variable** speed bit let Bob change the drill speed from slow to fast based on the job he had to do.*

If you write code that uses a variable that hasn't been assigned a value, your code won't compile. It's easy to avoid that error by combining your variable declaration and assignment into a single statement.

Once you've assigned a value to your variable, that value can change. So there's no disadvantage to assigning a variable an initial value when you declare it.

C# uses familiar math symbols

Once you've got some data stored in a variable, what can you
do with it? Well, if it's a number, you'll probably want to add,
subtract, multiply, or divide it. And that's where **operators** come
in. You already know the basic ones. Let's talk about a few more.
Here's a block of code that uses operators to do some simple math:

We declared a new
int variable called
number and set it
to 15. Then we added
10 to it. After the
second statement,
number is equal to 25.

The third statement changes the
value of number, setting it equal
to 36 times 15, which is 540. Then
it resets it again, setting it equal
to 12 - (42 / 7), which is 6.

```csharp
int number = 15;

number = number + 10;

number = 36 * 15;

number = 12 - (42 / 7);

number += 10;

number *= 3;

number = 71 / 3;
```

This operator is a little different. +=
means take the value of number
and add 10 to it. Since number is
currently equal to 6, adding 10 to it
sets its value to 16.

The *= operator
is similar to +=,
except it multiplies
the current value of
number by 3, so it
ends up set to 48.

71 divided by 3 is 23.666666. Since number is an integer,
it can only store whole numbers, so it gets rounded to 23.

```csharp
int count = 0;

count ++;

count --;
```

You'll use int a lot for counting, and when you do the ++
and -- operators come in handy. ++ increments count
by adding one to the value, and -- decrements count
by subtracting one from it, so it ends up equal to zero.

This MessageBox
will pop up a box
that says "hello
again hello"

```csharp
string result = "hello";

result += " again " + result;

MessageBox.Show(result);

result = "the value is: " + count;

result = "";
```

When you use the + operator
with a string, it just puts
two strings together. It'll
automatically convert
numbers to strings for you.

The "" is an empty string.
It has no characters.
(It's kind of like a zero
for adding strings.)

A bool stores true
or false. The !
operator means NOT.
It flips true to
false, and vice versa.

```csharp
bool yesNo = false;

bool anotherBool = true;

yesNo = !anotherBool;
```

**Don't worry about
memorizing these
operators now.**

You'll get to know them
because you'll see 'em over and over again.

Loops perform an action over and over again

Here's a peculiar thing about most large programs: they almost always involve doing certain things over and over again. And that's what **loops** are for– they tell your program to keep executing a certain set of statements as long as some condition is true (or false!).

That's a big part of why booleans are so important. A loop uses a test to figure out if it should keep looping.

```
while (x > 5)
{
    x = x - 3;
}
```

In a while loop, all of the statements inside the curly brackets get executed as long as the condition in the parentheses is true.

Every for loop has three statements. The first sets up the loop. The statement will keep looping as long as the second one is true. And the third statement gets executed after each time through the loop.

```
for (i = 0; i < 8; i = i + 2)
{
    MessageBox.Show("I'll pop up 4 times");
}
```

Use a code snippet to write simple for loops

You'll be typing for loops in a just a minute, and the IDE can help speed up your coding a little. Type `for` followed by two tabs, and the IDE will automatically insert code for you. If you type a new variable, it'll automatically update the rest of the snippet. Press tab again, and the cursor will jump to the length.

Press tab to get the cursor to jump to the length. The number of times this loop runs is determined by whatever you set length to. You can change length to a number or a variable.

```
for (int i = 0; i < length; i++)
{

}
```

If you change the variable to something else, the snippet automatically changes the other two occurrences of it.

Time to start coding

The real work of any program is in its statements. But statements don't exist in a vacuum. So let's set the stage for digging in and getting some code written. **Create a new Windows Forms Application project**.

This will tell the IDE to create a new project with a blank form and an entry point. You might want to name it something like "Chapter 2 program 1"—you'll be building a whole lot of programs throughout the book.

✦ Build this form ➡

Syntax 101

✱ Each statement must end in a semicolon.

```
x = x + 1;
```

✱ A single-line comment begins with two forward slashes.

```
// this line is ignored
```

✱ Most white space doesn't matter.

```
x        =        3    ;
```

is the same as

```
x = 3;
```

✱ Variables are declared with a **name** and a **type** (there are plenty of types that you'll learn about in chapter 4).

```
int weight;
// weight is an integer
```

✱ Classes and methods must be defined within a pair of curly braces.

```
public void go() {
    // amazing code here
}
```

Add statements to show a message

Get started by double-clicking on the first button. Then add these 6 statements to the button1_Click() method. Look closely at the code, and the output it produces.

x is a variable. The "int" part tells C# that it's an integer, and the rest of the statement sets its value to 3.

```
private void button1_Click(object sender, EventArgs e)
{
    // this is a comment
    String name = "Quentin";
    int x = 3;
    x = x * 17;
    double d = Math.PI / 2;
    MessageBox.Show("name is " + name
        + "\nx is " + x
        + "\nd is " + d);
}
```

There's a built-in class called Math, and it's got a member called PI. Math lives in the System namespace, so the file this code came from needs to have a <u>using System;</u> line at the top.

The \n is an <u>escape sequence</u> to add a line break to the message box.

Output:
```
name is Quentin
x is 51
d is 1.5707963267949
```

if/else statements make decisions

Use **if/else statements** to tell your program to do certain things only when the **conditions** you set up are (or aren't) true. A lot of if/else statements check if two things are equal. That's when you use the == operator. That's different from the single equal sign (=) operator, which you use to set a value.

> *Every if statement starts with a conditional test.*

```
if (someValue == 24)
{
        MessageBox.Show("The value was 24.");
}
```

> *The statement inside the curly brackets is executed only if the test is true.*

> *Always use two equal signs to check if two things are equal to each other.*

```
if (someValue == 24)
{
    // You can have as many statements
    // as you want inside the brackets
    MessageBox.Show("The value was 24.");
} else {
    MessageBox.Show("The value wasn't 24.");
}
```

> *if/else statements are pretty straightforward. If the conditional test is true, the program executes the statements between the first set of brackets. Otherwise, it executes the statements between the second set.*

Watch it!

Don't confuse the two equal sign operators!

You use one equal sign (=) to set a variable's value, but two equal signs (==) to compare two variables. You won't believe how many bugs in programs—even ones made by experienced programmers!—were caused by using = instead of ==. If you see the IDE complain that you "cannot implicitly convert type 'int' to 'bool'", that's probably what happened.

Set up conditions and see if they're true

Use **if/else statements** to tell your program to do certain things only when the **conditions** you set up are (or aren't) true.

Use logical operators to check conditions

You've just looked at the == operator, which you use to test whether two variables are equal. There are a few other operators, too. Don't worry about memorizing them right now—you'll get to know them over the next few chapters:

★ The != operator works a lot like == except it's true if the two things you're comparing are **not equal**.

★ You can use > and < to compare numbers and see if one is bigger or smaller than the other.

★ The ==, !=, >, and < are called **conditional operators**. When you use them to test two variables or values, it's called performing a **conditional tests**.

★ You can combine individual conditional tests into one long test using the && operator for AND and the || operator for OR. So to check if i equals 3 or j is less than 5, do (i == 3) || (j < 5).

> **When you use a conditional operator to compare two numbers, it's called a conditional test.**

Set a variable and then check its value

Here's the code for the second button. It's an if/else statement that checks an integer **variable** called x to see if it's equal to 10.

> Make sure you stop your program before you do this—the IDE won't let you edit the code while the program's running. You can stop it by closing the window, using the stop button on the toolbar, or selecting "Stop Debugging" from the Debug menu.

```
private void button2_Click(object sender, EventArgs e)
{
    int x = 5;
    if (x == 10)
    {
        MessageBox.Show("x must be 10");
    }
    else
    {
        MessageBox.Show("x isn't 10");
    }
}
```

First we set up a variable called x and make it equal to 5. Then we check if it's equal to 10.

Here's the output. See if you can tweak one line of code and get it to say "x must be 10" instead.

Add another conditional test

The third button makes this output. Now make a change to two lines of code so that it pops up both message boxes.

This line checks someValue to see if it's less than 3, and then it checks to make sure name is "Joe".

this line runs no matter what

OK

```
private void button3_Click(object sender, EventArgs e)
{
    int someValue = 4;
    String name = "Bobbo Jr.";
    if ((someValue < 3) && (name.Equals("Joe")))
    {
        MessageBox.Show("x is 3 and the name is Joe");
    }
    MessageBox.Show("this line runs no matter what");
}
```

Add loops to your program

Here's the code for the last button. It's got two loops. The first is a **while** loop, which repeats the statements inside the brackets as long as the condition is true—do something *while* this is true. The second one is a **for** loop. Take a look and see how it works.

```
private void button4_Click(object sender, EventArgs e)
{
    int count = 0;
    while (count < 10)
    {
        count = count + 1;
    }

    for (int i = 0; i < 5; i++)
    {
        count = count - 1;
    }
    MessageBox.Show("The answer is " + count);
}
```

This loop keeps repeating as long as the count variable is less than 10.

The second part of the for statement is the test. It says "for as long as i is less than five the loop should keep on going".

This sets up the loop. It just assigns a value to the integer that'll be used in it.

This is where the loop actually does something. In this case, it adds one to i. So every time the loop executes, it will add 1 to i.

Before you click on the button, read through the code and try to figure out what the message box will show. Then click the button and see if you were right!

over and over and over and...

Sharpen your pencil

Let's get a little more practice with conditional tests and loops. Take a look at the code below. Circle the conditional tests, and fill in the blanks so that the comments correctly describe the code that's being run.

```
int result = 0; // this variable will hold the final result
```
We filled in the first one for you.

```
int x = 6; // declare a variable x and  set it to 6

while (x > 3) {

   // execute these statements as long as  x > 3

   result = result + x; // add x  to result

   x = x - 1; // subtract  1 from x
}

for (int z = 1; z < 3; z = z + 1) {

   // start the loop by  z = 1

   // keep looping as long as  z < 3

   // after each loop,  z = z + 1

   result = result + z; //  add z to result

}

// The next statement will pop up a message box that says
//  The result is  result

MessageBox.Show("The result is " + result);
```

More about conditional tests

You can do simple conditional tests by checking the value of a variable using a comparison operator. Here's how you compare two numbers, x and y:

```
x < y (less than)
x > y (greater than)
x == y (equals—and yes, with two equals signs)
```

These are the ones you'll use most often.

Wait up! There's a flaw in your logic. What happens to my loop if I write a conditional test that never becomes false?

Then your loop runs forever!

Every time your program runs a conditional test, the result is either **true** or **false**. If it's **true**, then your program goes through the loop one more time. Every loop should have code that, if it's run enough times, should cause the conditional test to eventually return **false**. But if it doesn't then the loop will keep running until you kill the program or turn the computer off!

Sometimes you call this an infinite loop.

Sharpen your pencil

Here are a few loops. Write down if each loop will repeat forever or eventually end. If it's going to end, how many times will it loop?

Loop #1
```
int count = 5;
while (count > 0) {
    count = count * 3;
    count = count * -1;
}
```
~~inf~~ once

Loop #2
```
int i = 0;
while (i == 0) {
    count = count * 3;
    count = count * -1;
}
```
inf

Loop #3
```
int j = 2;
for (int i = 1; i < 100;
    i = i * 2)
{
    j = j - i;
    while (j < 25)
    {
        j = j + 5;
    }
}
```
ends 7

Loop #4
```
while (true) { int i = 1;}
```
inf

Loop #5
```
int p = 2;
for (int q = 2; q < 32;
    q = q * 2)
{
    while (p < q)
    {
        p = p * 2;
    }
    q = p - q;
}
```
ends 8

BRAIN POWER

Can you think of a reason that you'd want to write a loop that never stops running?

Sharpen your pencil
Solution

Let's get a little more practice with conditional tests and loops. Take a look at the code below. Circle the conditional tests, and fill in the blanks so that the comments correctly describe the code that's being run.

```
int result = 0; // this variable will hold the final result
int x = 6; // declare a variable x and  set it to 6
while (x > 3) {
   // execute these statements as long as  x is greater than 3

   result = result + x; // add x  to the result variable

   x = x - 1; // subtract  1 from the value of x
}
for (int z = 1; (z < 3); z = z + 1) {
   // start the loop by  declaring a variable z and setting it to 1
   // keep looping as long as  z is less than 3
   // after each loop,  add 1 to z
   result = result + z; //  add the value of z to result
}
// The next statement will pop up a message box that says
//  The result is 18
MessageBox.Show("The result is " + result);
```

This loop runs twice—first with z set to 1, and then a second time with z set to 2. Once it hits 3, it's no longer less than 3, so the loop stops.

Sharpen your pencil
Solution

Here are a few loops. Write down if each loop will repeat forever or eventually end. If it's going to end, how many times will it loop?

Loop #1
```
This loop executes once
```

Loop #2
```
This loop runs forever
```

Loop #3
```
This loop executes 7 times
```

Loop #4
```
Another infinite loop
```

Loop #5
```
This loop
executes 8 times.
```

there are no
Dumb Questions

Q: Is every piece of code always in a class?

A: Yes. Any time a C# program does something, it's because statements were executed. Those statements are a part of classes, and those classes are a part of namespaces. Even when it looks like something is not a statement in a class—like when you use the designer to set a property on an object on your form—if you search through your code you'll find that the IDE added or changed statements inside a class somewhere.

Q: Are there any namespaces I'm not allowed to use? Are there any I *have* to use?

A: Yes, there are a few namespaces you're not allowed to use. Notice how all of the `using` lines at the top of your C# class files always said `System`? That's because there's a System namespace that's used by the .NET Framework. It's where you find all of your important tools to add power to your programs. Like `System.Data`, which lets you work with tables and databases, and `System.Math`, which has mathematical functions. But for the most part, you can choose any name you want for a namespace (as long as only has letters, numbers and underscores). When you create a new program, the IDE will automatically choose a namespace for you based on the program's name.

Q: I still don't get why I need this partial class stuff.

A: Partial classes are how you can spread the code for one class between more than one file. The IDE does that when it creates a form—it keeps the code you edit in one file (like Form1.cs), and the code it modifies automatically for you in another file (Form1.Designer.cs). You don't need to do that with a namespace, though. One namespace can span two, three or a dozen or more files. Just put the namespace declaration at the top of the file, and everything within the curly brackets after the declaration is inside the same namespace. One more thing: you can have more than one class in a file. And you can have more than one namespace in a file. You'll learn a lot more about classes in the next few chapters.

Q: Let's say I drag something onto my form, so the IDE generates a bunch of code automatically. What happens to that code if I click "Undo"?

A: The best way to answer this question is to try it! Give it a shot—do something where the IDE generates some code for you.

Drag a button on a form, change properties. Then try to undo it. What happens? Well, for simple things what you'll see is that the IDE is smart enough to undo it itself. But for more complex things, like adding a new SQL database to your project, you'll be given a warning message. It still knows how to undo the action, but it may not be able to redo it.

Q: So exactly how careful do I have to be with the code that's automatically generated by the IDE?

A: You should generally be pretty careful. It's really useful to know what the IDE is doing to your code, and once in a while you'll need to know what's in there in order to solve a serious problem. But in almost all cases, you'll be able to do everything you need to do through the IDE.

BULLET POINTS

- You tell your program to perform actions using statements. Statements are always part of classes, and every class is in a namespace.

- Every statement ends with a semicolon (`;`)

- When you use the visual tools in the Visual Studio IDE, it automatically adds or changes code in your program.

- Code blocks are surrounded by curly braces { }. Classes, while loops, if/else statements and lots of other kinds of statements use those blocks.

- A conditional test is either `true` or `false`. You use conditional tests to determine when a loop ends, and which block of code to execute in an if/else statement.

- Any time your program needs to store some data, you use a variable. Use = to assign a variable, and == to test if two variables are equal.

- A `while` loop runs everything within its block (defined by curly braces) as long as the *conditional test* is `true`.

- If the conditional test is `false`, the while loop code block won't run, and execution will move down to the code immediately after the loop block.

Code Magnets

Part of a C# program is all scrambled up on the fridge. Can you rearrange the code snippets to make a working C# program that produces the message box? Some of the curly braces fell on the floor and they were too small to pick up, so feel free to add as many of those as you need!

The "" is an empty string—it means Result has no characters in it yet.

This magnet didn't fall off the fridge...

```
string Result = "";
```

```
if (x == 1) {
Result = Result + "d";
x = x - 1;
}
```

```
if (x == 2) {
Result = Result + "b c";
}
```

```
if (x > 2) {
Result = Result + "a";
}
```

```
int x = 3;
```

```
x = x - 1;
Result = Result + "-";
```

```
while (x > 0) {
```

```
MessageBox.Show(Result);
```

Output:

a-b c-d

OK

Answers on page 82.

We'll give you a lot of exercises like this throughout the book. We'll give you the answer in a couple of pages. If you get stuck, don't be afraid to peek at the answer—it's not cheating!

Exercise

Time to get some practice using if/else statements. Can you build this program?

Here's the form.

Add this checkbox.
Drag it out of the toolbox and onto your form. Use the **Text** property to change the text that's next to it. (You also use the **Text** property to change the button and label text.)

This is a label.
You can use the properties to change the font size and make it boldface. Use the **BackColor** property to set to red—choose "**Red**" from the selection of web colors.

Pop up this message if the user clicks the button but the box IS NOT checked.
If your checkbox is named **checkBox1** (you can change the **Name** property if you want), then here's the conditional test to see if it's checked:

```
checkBox1.Checked == true
```

If the user clicks the button and the box IS checked, change the background color of the label.
If the label background color is red, change it to blue when the button is clicked. If it's blue, change it back to red. Here's a statement that sets the background color of a label called **label1**:

```
label1.BackColor = Color.Red;
```

(Hint: The conditional test to check whether a label's background color is red looks a lot like that statement—but with one important difference!)

Exercise

Let's build something **flashy**!

① **Here's the form to build** ⟶

Hint: If you declare a variable inside a for loop—for (int c = 0;
...)—then that variable's only valid inside the loop's curly brackets. So if
you have two for loops that both use the variable, you'll either declare
it in each loop or have one declaration outside the loop.

② **Make the form background go all psychedelic!**
When the button's clicked, make the form's background
color cycle through a whole lot of colors! Create a loop that
has a variable **c** go from 0 to 254. Here's the block of code
that goes inside the curly brackets:

```
this.BackColor = Color.FromArgb(c, 255 - c, c);

Application.DoEvents();
```

This line tells the program to let the operating system do
other things outside of your program. Without it, your
program will take up all the CPU cycles—and it won't
listen for events that happen (like the user clicking the X
box to close the window).

Color me impressed!
.NET has a bunch of predefined
colors like Blue and Red, but it also
lets you make your own colors using
the `Color.FromArgb()` method,
by specifying three numbers: a red
value, a green value, and a blue value.

③ **Make it slower**
Slow down the flashing by adding this line before
the `Application.DoEvents()` line:

```
System.Threading.Thread.Sleep(3);
```

This statement inserts a 3 millisecond
delay in the loop. It's a part of
the .NET library, and it's in the
`System.Threading` namespace.

You'll be creating a lot of applications throughout this book, and you'll need to give each one a different name. We recommend naming this one "2 Fun with if–else statements" based on the chapter number and the text in the title bar of the form.

④ Make it smoother

Let's make the colors cycle back to where they started. Add another loop that has **c** go from 254 down to 0. Use the same block of code inside the curly brackets.

⑤ Keep it going

Surround your two loops with another loop that continuously executes and doesn't stop, so that when the button is pressed, the background starts changing colors and then keeps doing it. (Hint: The while (true) loop will run forever!)

When one loop is inside another one, we call it a "nested" loop.

Uh-oh! The program doesn't stop!

Run your program in the IDE. Start it looping. Now close the window. Wait a minute—the IDE didn't go back into edit mode! It's acting like the program is still running. You need to actually stop the program using the square stop button in the IDE (or select "Stop Debugging" from the Debug menu).

---

⑥ Make it stop

Make the loop you added in step #5 stop when the program is closed. Change your outer loop to this:

```
while (Visible)
```

Now run the program and click the X box in the corner. The window closes, and then the program stops! Except… there's a delay of a few seconds before the IDE goes back to edit mode.

When you're checking a boolean value like Visible in an if statement or a loop, sometimes it's tempting to test for (Visible == true). You can leave off the "== true"—it's enough to include the boolean.

When you're working with a form or control, Visible is true as long as the form or control is being displayed. If you set it to false, it makes the form or control disappear.

Hint: The && operator means "AND". It's how you string a bunch of conditional tests together into one big test that's true only if the first test is true AND the second is true AND the third, etc. And it'll come in handy to solve this problem.

Can you figure out what's causing that delay? Can you fix it so the program ends immediately when you close the window?

Exercise Solution

Time to get some practice using if/else statements. Can you build this program?

Here's the entire Form1.cs file for the "Fun with If/Else Statements!" exercise. If we show you a lot of code in a file like this, we'll draw a grey box behind the part that you should add.

```csharp
usihg System;
using System.Collections.Generic;
using System.ComponentModel;
using System.Data;
using System.Drawing;
using System.Linq;
using System.Text;
using System.Windows.Forms;

namespace Fun_with_If_Else
{
    public partial class Form1 : Form
    {
        public Form1()
        {
            InitializeComponent();
        }

        private void button1_Click(object sender, EventArgs e)
        {
            if (checkBox1.Checked == true)
            {
                if (label1.BackColor == Color.Red)
                {
                    label1.BackColor = Color.Blue;
                }
                else
                {
                    label1.BackColor = Color.Red;
                }
            }
            else
            {
                MessageBox.Show("The box is not checked");
            }
        }
    }
}
```

Here's the code for the form. We named our solution "Fun with If Else", so the IDE made the namespace Fun_with_If_Else. If you gave your solution a different name, it'll have a different namespace.

The IDE added the method called button1_Click() to your form when you double-clicked on the button. The method gets run every time the button's clicked.

The inner if statement checks the label's color. If the label is currently red, it executes a statement to turn it blue.

The outer if statement checks the checkbox to see if it's been checked. Check!

This statement's run if the label's background color is not red to make it set back to red.

This MessageBox pops up if the checkbox isn't checked.

You can download the code for all of the exercise solutions in this book from www.headfirstlabs.com/books/hfcsharp/

Let's build something **flashy!**

Exercise Solution

Sometimes we won't show you the entire code in the solution, just the bits that changed. All of the logic in the FlashyThing project is in this button1_Click() method that the IDE added when you double-clicked the button in the form designer.

When the IDE added this method, it added an extra return before the curly bracket. Sometimes we'll put the bracket on the same line like this to save space—but C# doesn't care about extra space, so this is perfectly valid.

```csharp
private void button1_Click(object sender, EventArgs e) {
    while (Visible) {
        for (int c = 0; c < 254 && Visible; c++) {
            this.BackColor = Color.FromArgb(c, 255 - c, c);
            Application.DoEvents();
            System.Threading.Thread.Sleep(3);
        }

        for (int c = 254; c >= 0 && Visible; c--) {
            this.BackColor = Color.FromArgb(c, 255 - c, c);
            Application.DoEvents();
            System.Threading.Thread.Sleep(3);
        }
    }
}
```

The outer loop keeps running as long as the form is visible. As soon as it's closed, Visible is false, and the while will stop looping.

The first for loop makes the colors cycle one way, and the second for loop reverses them so they look smooth.

We fixed the extra delay by using the && operator to make each of the for loops also check Visible. That way the loop ends as soon as Visible turns false.

Can you figure out what's causing that delay? Can you fix it so the program ends immediately when you close the window?

The delay happens because the for loops need to finish before the while loop can check if Visible is still true. You can fix it by adding **&& Visible == true** to the conditional test in each for loop.

Was your code a little different than ours? There's more than one way to solve any programming problem—like you could have used while loops instead of for loops. If your program works, then you got the exercise right!

Pool Puzzle

Your *job* is to take code snippets from the pool and place them into the blank lines in the code. You may **not** use the same snippet more than once, and you won't need to use all the snippets. Your *goal* is to make a class that will compile and run. Don't be fooled—this one's harder than it looks.

Output

We included these "Pool Puzzle" exercises throughout the book to give your brain an extra-tough workout. If you're the kind of person who loves twisty little logic puzzles, then you'll love this one. If you're not, give it a shot anyway—but don't be afraid to look at the answer to figure out what's going on. And if you're stumped by a pool puzzle, definitely move on.

Note: each snippet from the pool can only be used once!

```csharp
using System;
using System.Windows.Forms;
namespace Chapter_2 {
  class Chapter2PoolPuzzle {
    public static void Main() {
      int x = 0;
      String Poem = "";

      while ( _____ ) {

        _____

        if ( x < 1 ) {

        _____

        }

        _____

        if ( _____ ) {

        _____

        _____

        }
        if ( x == 1 ) {

        _____

        }
        if ( _____ ) {

        _____

        }

        _____

      }

      _____

    }
  }
}
```

```
x > 0
x < 1          x = x + 1;
x > 1          x = x + 2;
x > 3          x = x - 2;
Poem = Poem + " ";    x < 4     x = x - 1;
Poem = Poem + "a ";
Poem = Poem + "n";
Poem = Poem + "an";   MessageBox.Show(Poem);
```

```
Poem = Poem + "noys ";
Poem = Poem + "oise ";
Poem = Poem + " oyster ";
Poem = Poem + "annoys";
Poem = Poem + "noise";
```

Answers on page 83.

Csharpcross

How does a crossword help you learn C#? Well, all the words are C#-related and from this chapter. The clues also provide mental twists and turns that will help you burn alternative routes to C# right into your brain

Across

3. You give information to a method using these
4. button1.Text and checkBox3.Name are examples of
8. Every statement ends with one of these
10. The name of every C# program's entry point
11. Contains methods
12. Your statements live here
14. A kind of variable that's either true or false
15. A special method that tells your program where to start
16. This kind of class spans multiple files

Down

1. The output of a method is its _____ value
2. System.Windows.Forms is an example of one of these
5. A tiny piece of a program that does something
6. A block of code is surrounded by
7. The kind of test that tells a loop when to end
9. You can call _____.Show() to pop up a simple Windows dialog box
13. The kind of variable that contains a whole number

Code Magnets Solution

Part of a C# program is all scrambled up on the fridge. Can you rearrange the code snippets to make a working C# program that produces the message box? Some of the curly braces fell on the floor and they were too small to pick up, so feel free to add as many of those as you need!

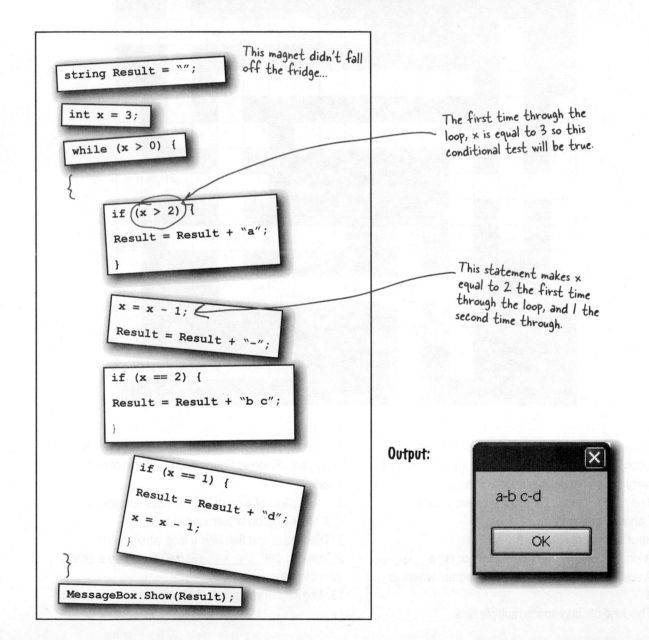

```
string Result = "";
```

```
int x = 3;
```

```
while (x > 0) {
```

This magnet didn't fall off the fridge...

The first time through the loop, x is equal to 3 so this conditional test will be true.

```
if (x > 2) {
Result = Result + "a";

}
```

```
x = x - 1;
Result = Result + "-";
```

This statement makes x equal to 2 the first time through the loop, and 1 the second time through.

```
if (x == 2) {
Result = Result + "b c";

}
```

```
if (x == 1) {
Result = Result + "d";
x = x - 1;
}
```

```
}
```

```
MessageBox.Show(Result);
```

Output:

a-b c-d

OK

Pool Puzzle Solution

Your *job* was to take code snippets from the pool and place them into the blank lines in the code. Your *goal* was to make a class that will compile and run.

```csharp
using System;
using System.Windows.Forms;
namespace Chapter_2 {
  class Chapter2PoolPuzzle {
    public static void Main() {
      int x = 0;
      String Poem = "";

      while ( x < 4 ) {

        Poem = Poem + "a";
        if ( x < 1 ) {
          Poem = Poem + " ";
        }
        Poem = Poem + "n";

        if ( x > 1 ) {

          Poem = Poem + " oyster";

          x = x + 2;
        }
        if ( x == 1 ) {

          Poem = Poem + "noys ";
        }
        if ( x < 1 ) {

          Poem = Poem + "oise ";
        }

        x = x + 1;
      }
      MessageBox.Show(Poem);
    }
  }
}
```

Csharpcross Solution

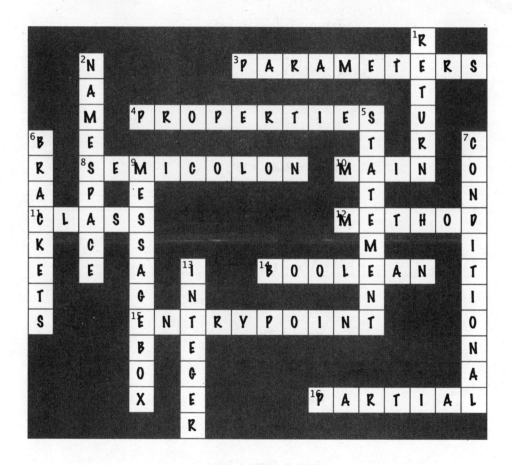

Across:
3. PARAMETERS
4. PROPERTIES
8. SEMICOLON
10. MAIN
11. CLASS
12. METHOD
14. BOOLEAN
15. ENTRYPOINT
16. PARTIAL

Down:
1. RETURN
2. NAMESPACE
5. STATEMENT
6. BRACKETS
7. CONDITIONAL
9. MESSAGEBOX
13. INTEGER

Making Code Make Sense

... and that's why my Husband class doesn't have a HelpOutAroundTheHouse() method or a PullHisOwnWeight() method.

Every program you write solves a problem.

When you're building a program, it's always a good idea to start by thinking about what *problem* your program's supposed to solve. That's why **objects** are really useful. They let you structure your code based on the problem it's solving, so that you can spend your time *thinking about the problem* you need to work on rather than getting bogged down in the mechanics of writing code. When you use objects right, you end up with code that's *intuitive* to write, and easy to read and change.

How Mike thinks about his problems

Mike's a programmer about to head out to a job interview. He can't wait to show off his C# skills, but first he has to get there—and he's running late!

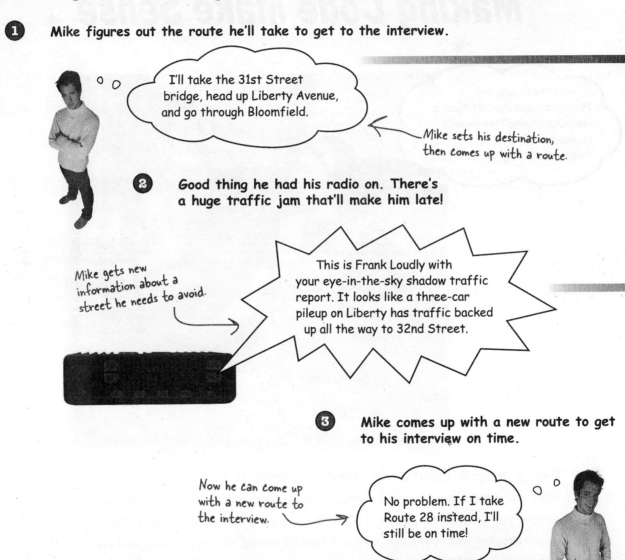

1 Mike figures out the route he'll take to get to the interview.

> I'll take the 31st Street bridge, head up Liberty Avenue, and go through Bloomfield.

Mike sets his destination, then comes up with a route.

2 Good thing he had his radio on. There's a huge traffic jam that'll make him late!

Mike gets new information about a street he needs to avoid.

> This is Frank Loudly with your eye-in-the-sky shadow traffic report. It looks like a three-car pileup on Liberty has traffic backed up all the way to 32nd Street.

3 Mike comes up with a new route to get to his interview on time.

Now he can come up with a new route to the interview.

> No problem. If I take Route 28 instead, I'll still be on time!

How Mike's car navigation system thinks about his problems

Mike built his own GPS navigation system, which he uses to help him get around town.

Here's a diagram of a class in Mike's program. It shows the name on top, and the methods on the bottom.

Navigator
SetDestination()
ModifyRouteToAvoid()
ModifyRouteToInclude()
GetRoute()
GetTimeToDestination()
TotalDistance()

```
SetDestination("Fifth Ave & Penn Ave");
string route;
route = GetRoute();
```

Here's the output from the GetRoute() method—it's a string that contains the directions Mike should follow.

The navigation system sets a destination and comes up with a route

"Take 31St Street Bridge to Liberty Avenue to Bloomfield"

The navigation system gets new information about a street it needs to avoid.

```
ModifyRouteToAvoid("Liberty Ave");
```

Now it can come up with a new route to the destination.

```
string route;
route = GetRoute();
```

"Take Route 28 to the Highland Park Bridge to Washington Blvd"

GetRoute() gives a new route that doesn't include the street Mike wants to avoid.

Mike's navigation system solves the street navigation problem the same way he does

Mike's Navigator class has methods to set and modify routes

Mike's Navigator class has methods, which are where the action happens. But unlike the `button_Click()` methods in the forms you've built, they're all focused around a single problem: navigating a route through a city. That's why Mike stuck them together into one class, and called that class `Navigator`.

Mike designed his Navigator class so that it's easy to create and modify routes. To get a route, Mike's program calls the `SetDestination()` method to set the destination, and then uses the `GetRoute()` method to put the route into a string. If he needs to change the route, his program calls the `ModifyRouteToAvoid()` method to change the route so that it avoids a certain street, and then calls the `GetRoute()` method to get the new directions.

Mike chose method names that would make sense to someone who was thinking about how to navigate a route through a city.

```
public class Navigator() {

    public void SetDestination(string destinationName) { ... };

    public void ModifyRouteToAvoid(string streetName) { ... };

    public string GetRoute() { ... };

}
```

This is the <u>return type</u> of the method. It means that the statement calling the GetRoute() method can use it to set a string variable that will contain the directions. When it's <u>void</u>, that means the method doesn't return anything.

```
string route;
route = GetRoute();
```

Some methods have a return value

Every method is made up of statements that do things. Some methods just execute their statements and then exit. But other methods have a **return value**, or a value that's calculated or generated inside the method, and sent back to the statement that called that method. The type of the return value (like `string` or `int`) is called the **return type**.

The **return** statement tells the method to immediately exit. If your method doesn't have a return value—which means it's declared with a return type of **void**—then the `return` statement just ends with a semicolon, and you don't always have to have one in your method. But if the method has a return type, then it must use the `return` statement.

Here's an example of a method that has a return type—it returns an int. The method uses the two parameters to calculate the result and uses the return statement to pass the value back to the statement that called it.

```
public int MultiplyTwoNumbers(int firstNumber, int secondNumber) {
    int result = firstNumber * secondNumber;
    return result;
}
```

Here's a statement that calls a method to multiply two numbers. It returns an int:

```
int myResult = MultiplyTwoNumbers(3, 5);
```

Methods can take values like 3 and 5. But you can also pass variables to them.

Use what you've learned to build a simple application

Let's hook up a form to a class, and make its button call a method inside that class.

Do this!

1   Create a new Windows Application project in the IDE. Then add a class file to it called `Talker.cs` by right-clicking on the project in the Solution Explorer and selecting "Class..." from the Add menu. When you name your new class file "Talker.cs", the IDE will automatically name the class in the new file Talker. Then it'll pop up the new file in a new tab inside the IDE.

2   Add using `System.Windows.Forms;` to the top of the class file. Then add code to the class:

```
class Talker {
    public static int BlahBlahBlah(string thingToSay, int numberOfTimes) {
        string finalString = "";
        for (int count = 1; count <= numberOfTimes; count++) {
            finalString = finalString + thingToSay + "\n";
        }
        MessageBox.Show(finalString);
        return finalString.Length;
    }
}
```

This statement declares a finalString variable and sets it equal to an empty string.

The BlahBlahBlah() method's return value is an integer that has the total length of the message it displayed. You can add ".Length" to any string to figure out how long it is.

The new class has one method called `BlahBlahBlah()` that takes two parameters. The first parameter is a string that tells it something to say, and the second is the number of times to say it. When it's called, it pops up a MessageBox with the message repated a number of times. Its return value is the length of the string. The method needs a string for its thingToSay parameter and a number of its numberOfTimes parameter. It'll get those parameters from a form that lets the user enter text using a **TextBox** control and a number using **NumericUpDown** control.

Set the default text of the TextBox to "Hello!" using its Text property.

3   Add this form to your project. ⟶

Then double-click on the button and have it run this code:

```
int len = Talker.BlahBlahBlah(textBox1.Text, (int) numericUpDown1.Value);
MessageBox.Show("The message length is " + len);
```

This is a NumericUpDown control. Set its Minimum property to 1, its Maximum property to 10, and its Value property to 3.

4   Now run your program! Click the button and watch it pop up two message boxes. The class pops up the first message box, and the form pops up the second one.

The BlahBlahBlah() method pops up this message box based on what's in its parameters.

When the method returns a value, the form pops it up in this message box.

Mike gets an idea

The interview went great! But the traffic jam this morning got Mike thinking about how he could improve his navigator.

It'd be great if I could compare a few routes and figure out which is fastest...

He could create three different Navigator classes...

Mike could copy the Navigator class code and paste it into two more classes. Then his program could store three routes at once.

This box is a **class diagram**. It lists all of the methods in a class, and it's an easy way to see everything that it does at a glance.

Navigator

SetDestination()
ModifyRouteToAvoid()
ModifyRouteToInclude()
GetRoute()
GetTimeToDestination()
TotalDistance()

Navigator2

SetDestination()
ModifyRouteToAvoid()
ModifyRouteToInclude()
GetRoute()
GetTimeToDestination()
TotalDistance()

Navigator3

SetDestination()
ModifyRouteToAvoid()
ModifyRouteToInclude()
GetRoute()
GetTimeToDestination()
TotalDistance()

Whoa, that can't be right! What if I want to change a method? Then I need to go back and fix it in three places.

Right! Maintaining three copies of the same code is really messy. A lot of problems you need to solve need a way to represent one *thing* a bunch of different times. In this case, it's a bunch of routes. But it could be a bunch of turbines, or dogs, or music files, or anything. All of those programs have one thing in common: they always need to treat the same kind of thing in the same way, no matter how many of the thing they're dealing with.

Mike can use <u>objects</u> to solve his problem

Objects are C#'s tool that you use to work with a bunch of similar things. Mike can use objects to program his Navigator class just once, but use it *as many times as he wants* in a program.

This is the Navigator class in Mike's program. It lists all of the methods that a Navigator object can use.

Navigator
SetDestination()
ModifyRouteToAvoid()
ModifyRouteToInclude()
GetRoute()
GetTimeToDestination()
TotalDistance()

new Navigator()

new Navigator()

new Navigator()

navigator1
Navigator object

navigator2
Navigator object

navigator3
Navigator object

Mike needed to compare three different routes at once, so he used three Navigator objects at the same time.

All you need to create an object is the new keyword and the name of a class.

```
Navigator navigator1 = new Navigator();
navigator1.SetDestination("Fifth Ave & Penn Ave");
string route;
route = navigator1.GetRoute();
```

Now you can use the object! When you create an object from a class, that object has all of the methods from that class.

You use a <u>class</u> to build an <u>object</u>

A class is like a blueprint for an object. If you wanted to build five identical houses in a suburban housing development, you wouldn't ask an architect to draw up five identical sets of blueprints. You'd just use one blueprint to build five houses.

When you define a class, you define its methods, just like a blueprint defines the layout of the house.

You can use one blueprint to make any number of houses, and you can use one class to make any number of objects.

An object gets its methods from its class

Once you build a class, you can create as many objects as you want from it using the new statement. When you do, every public method in your class becomes part of the object.

House

GiveShelter()
AppreciateInValue()
GrowLawn()
MailDelivered()
ClogDrainPipes()
AccruePropertyTaxes()
NeedRepairs()

26A Elm Lane
House object

38 Pine Street
House object

115 Maple Drive
House object

When you create a new object from a class, it's called an <u>instance</u> of that class.

Guess what… you already know this stuff! Everything in the toolbox is a class: there's a `Button` class, a `TextBox` class, a `Label` class, etc. When you drag a button out of the toolbox, the IDE automatically creates an instance of the `Button` class and calls it `button1`. When you drag another button out of the toolbox, it creates another instance called `button2`. Each instance of `Button` has its own properties and methods. But every button acts exactly the same way, because they're all instances of the same class.

Before: Here's a picture of your computer's memory when your program starts.

Your program executes a new statement.

```
House 115MapleDrive = new House();
```

After: Now it's got an instance of the House class in memory.

115 Maple Drive

House object

Check it out for yourself!

Do this!

Open any project that uses a button called `button1`, and use the IDE to search the entire project for the text "**new button1**". You'll find the code that the IDE added to the form designer to create the instance of the `Button` class.

in-stance, noun.
an example or one occurrence of something. *The IDE search-and-replace feature finds every **instance** of a word and changes it to another.*

A better solution... brought to you by objects!

Mike came up with a new route comparison program that uses objects to find the shortest of three different routes to the same destination. Here's how he built his program.

> GUI stands for Graphical User Interface, which is what you're building when you make a form in the form designer.

1 Mike set up a GUI with a text box—`textBox1` contains the **destination** for the three routes. Then he added `textBox2`, which has a street that one of the routes should **avoid**; and `textBox3`, which contains a different street that the third route has to **include**.

2 He created a Navigator object and set its destination.

> The navigator1 object is an instance of the Navigator class.

Navigator
SetDestination()
ModifyRouteToAvoid()
ModifyRouteToInclude()
GetRoute()
GetTimeToDestination()
TotalDistance()

navigator1
3.5 miles
Navigator object

```
String destination = textBox1.Text;

Navigator navigator1 = new Navigator()

navigator1.SetDestination(destination);

route = navigator1.GetRoute();
```

3 Then he added a second Navigator object called `navigator2`. He called its `SetDestination()` method to set the destination, and then he called its `ModifyRouteToAvoid()` method.

> The SetDestination(), ModifyRouteToAvoid() and ModifyRouteToInclude() methods all take a string as a parameter.

4 The third Navigator object is called `navigator3`. Mike set its destination, and then called its `ModifyRouteToInclude()` method.

navigator1 — 3.5 miles — *Navigator object*
navigator2 — 3.8 miles — *Navigator object*
navigator3 — 4.2 miles — *Navigator object*

Any time you create a new object from a class, it's called creating an instance of that class.

5 Now Mike can call each object's `TotalDistance()` method to figure out which route is the shortest. And he only had to write the code once, not three times!

Sharpen your pencil

Follow the same steps that Mike followed on the facing page to write the code to create Navigator objects and call their methods.

```
String destination = textBox1.Text;
String route2StreetToAvoid = textBox2.Text;
String route3StreetToInclude = textBox3.Text;
```

> We gave you a head start. Here's the code Mike wrote to get the destination and street names from the textboxes.

```
Navigator navigator1 = new Navigator()
navigator1.SetDestination(destination);
int distance1 = navigator1.TotalDistance();
```

> And here's the code to create the navigator object, set its destination, and get the distance.

---

1. Create the **navigator2** object, set its destination, call its **ModifyRouteToAvoid()** method, and use its **TotalDistance()** method to set an integer variable called **distance2**.

Navigator navigator2 = new Navigator();

navigator2. setDestination();

navigator2. ModifyRouteToAvoid(route2streetavoid)

int distance2 = TotalDistance();

---

2. Create the **navigator3** object, set its destination, call its **ModifyRouteToInclude()** method, and use its **TotalDistance()** method to set an integer variable called **distance3**.

Navigator navigator3 = new Navigator();

navigator3. setDestination();

navigator3. ModifyRouteToAvoid(route3streettoavoid);

int distance3 = Total Distance();

The built-in C# Math.Min() method compares two numbers and returns the smallest one. Mike used it to find the shortest distance to the destination.

```
int shortestDistance = Math.Min(distance1, Math.Min(distance2, distance3));
```

Sharpen your pencil
Solution

Follow the same steps that Mike followed on the facing page to write the code to create Navigator objects and call their methods.

```
String destination = textBox1.Text;
String route2StreetToAvoid = textBox2.Text;
String route3StreetToInclude = textBox3.Text;

Navigator navigator1 = new Navigator()
navigator1.SetDestination(destination);
int distance1 = navigator1.TotalDistance();
```

We gave you a head start. Here's the code to get the destination and street names, along with the code to create the first Navigator object, set its route, and get the distance.

---

1. Create the **navigator2** object, set its destination, call its **ModifyRouteToAvoid()** method, and use its **TotalDistance()** method to set an integer varable called **distance2**.

Navigator navigator2 = new Navigator()

navigator2. SetDestination(destination);

navigator2. ModifyRouteToAvoid(route2StreetToAvoid);

int distance2 = navigator2.TotalDistance();

---

2. Create the **navigator3** object, set its destination, call its **ModifyRouteToInclude()** method, and use its **TotalDistance()** method to set an integer varable called **distance3**.

Navigator navigator3 = new Navigator()

navigator3.SetDestination(destination);

navigator3.ModifyRouteToInclude(route3StreetToInclude);

int distance3 = navigator3.TotalDistance();

The built-in C# Math.Min() method compares two numbers and returns the smallest one. Mike used it to find the shortest distance to the destination.

```
int shortestDistance = Math.Min(distance1, Math.Min(distance2, distance3));
```

> Hold it! I've written a few classes now, but I haven't used "new" to create an instance yet! So does that means I can call methods without creating objects?

Yes! That's why you used the `static` keyword in your methods.

Take another look at the declaration for the `Talker` class you built a few pages ago:

```
class Talker
{
  public static int BlahBlahBlah(String thingToSay, int numberOfTimes)
  {
    string finalString = "";
```

When you called the method you didn't create a `new` instance of Talker. You just did this:

```
Talker.BlahBlahBlah("Hello hello hello", 5);
```

That's how you call `static` methods, and you've been doing that all along. If you take away the `static` keyword from the `BlahBlahBlah()` method declaration, then you'll have to create an instance of Talker() in order to call the method. Other than that distinction, static methods are just like object methods. You can pass parameters, they can return values, and they live in classes.

There's one more thing you can do with the `static` keyword. You can mark your **whole class** as static, and then all of its methods **must** be `static` too. If you try to add a non-static method to a static class, it won't compile.

---

there are no
Dumb Questions

Q: When I think of something that's "static", I think of something that doesn't change. Does that mean non-static methods can change, but static methods don't? Do they behave differently?

A: No, both static and non-static methods act exactly the same. The only difference is that static methods don't require an instance, while non-static methods do. A lot of people have trouble remembering that, because the word "static" isn't really all that intuitive.

Q: So I can't use my class until I create an instance of an object?

A: You can use its static methods. But if you have methods that aren't static, then you need an instance before you can use them.

Q: Then why would I want a method that needs an instance? Why wouldn't I make all my methods static?

A: Because if you have an object that's keeping track of certain data—like Mike's instances of his Navigator class that each kept track of a different route—then you can use each instance's methods to work with that data. So when Mike called his ModifyRouteToAvoid() method in the navigator2 instance, it only affected the route that was stored in that particular instance. It didn't affect the navigator1 or navigator3 objects. That's how he was able to work with three different routes at the same time—and his program could keep track of all of it.

Q: So how does an instance keep track of data?

A: Turn the page and find out!

An instance uses <u>fields</u> to keep track of things

You change the text on a button by setting its `Text` property in the
IDE. When you do, the IDE adds code like this to the designer:

```
button1.Text = "Text for the button";
```

Now you know that `button1` is an instance of the `Button` class.
What that code does is modify a **field** for the `button1` instance.
You can add fields to a class diagram—just draw a horizotal line in
the middle of it. Fields go above the line, methods go underneath it.

> Technically, it's setting a
> <u>property</u>. A property is a
> special kind of field—but
> we'll get into all that a
> little later on.

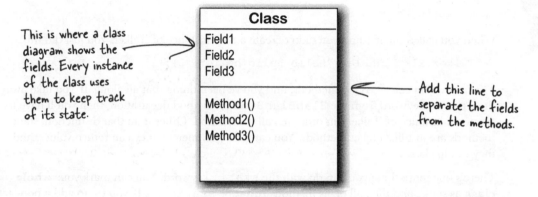

This is where a class
diagram shows the
fields. Every instance
of the class uses
them to keep track
of its state.

Class

Field1
Field2
Field3

Method1()
Method2()
Method3()

Add this line to
separate the fields
from the methods.

Methods are what an object <u>does</u>. Fields are what the object <u>knows</u>.

When Mike created three instances of `Navigator` classes, his program created three objects.
Each of those objects was used to keep track of a different route. When the program created the
`navigator2` instance and called its `SetDestination()` method, it set the destination for that
one instance. But it didn't affect the `navigator1` instance or the `navigator3` instance.

Navigator

Destination
Route

SetDestination()
ModifyRouteToAvoid()
ModifyRouteToInclude()
GetRoute()
GetTimeToDestination()
TotalDistance()

Every instance of Navigator knows
its destination and its route.

What a Navigator object does is
let you set a destination, modify
its route, and get information
about that route.

**An object's behavior is defined by its methods,
and it uses fields to keep track of its state.**

Let's create some instances!

It's easy to add fields to your class. Just declare variables outside of any methods. Now every instance gets its own copy of those variables.

> Remember, when you see "void" in front of a method, it means that it doesn't return any value.

```
public class Clown {
    public String Name;
    public int Height;

    public void TalkAboutYourself() {
        MessageBox.Show("My name is "
            + Name + " and I'm "
            + Height + " inches tall.");
    }
}
```

```
Clown
Name
Height

TalkAboutYourself()
```

When you want to create instances of your class, **don't use** the static keyword in either the class declaration or the method declaration.

> Remember, the *= operator tells C# to take whatever's on the left of the operator and multiply it by whatever's on the right.

Sharpen your pencil

Write down the contents of each message box that will be displayed after the statement next to it is executed.

```
Clown oneClown = new Clown();
oneClown.Name = "Boffo";
oneClown.Height = 14;

oneClown.TalkAboutYourself();
```
"My name is _Boffo_ and I'm _14_ inches tall."

```
Clown anotherClown = new Clown();
anotherClown.Name = "Biff";
anotherClown.Height = 16;

anotherClown.TalkAboutYourself();
```
"My name is _Biff_ and I'm _16_ inches tall."

```
Clown clown3 = new Clown();
clown3.Name = anotherClown.Name;
clown3.Height = oneClown.Height - 3;

clown3.TalkAboutYourself();
```
"My name is _Biff_ and I'm _11_ inches tall."

```
anotherClown.Height *= 2;
anotherClown.TalkAboutYourself();
```
"My name is _Biff_ and I'm _32_ inches tall."

Thanks for the memory

When your program creates an object, it lives in a part of the computer's memory called the **heap**. When your code creates an object with a new statement, C# immediately reserves space in the heap so it can store the data for that object.

Here's a picture of the heap before the project starts. Notice that it's empty.

Let's take a closer look at what happened here

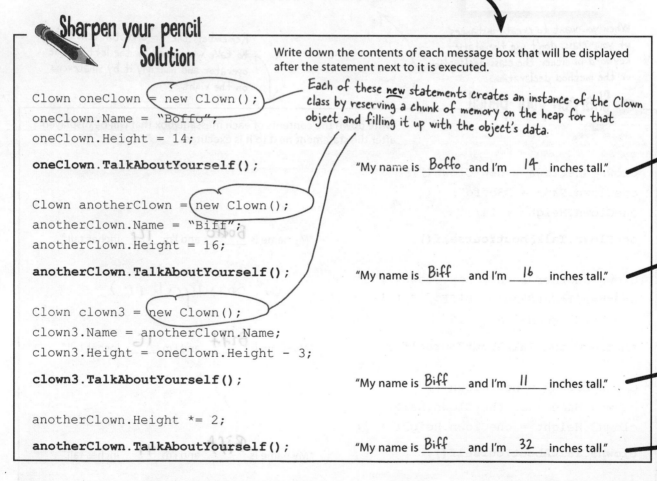

Sharpen your pencil
Solution

Write down the contents of each message box that will be displayed after the statement next to it is executed.

Each of these <u>new</u> statements creates an instance of the Clown class by reserving a chunk of memory on the heap for that object and filling it up with the object's data.

```
Clown oneClown = new Clown();
oneClown.Name = "Boffo";
oneClown.Height = 14;

oneClown.TalkAboutYourself();
```
"My name is ___Boffo___ and I'm ___14___ inches tall."

```
Clown anotherClown = new Clown();
anotherClown.Name = "Biff";
anotherClown.Height = 16;

anotherClown.TalkAboutYourself();
```
"My name is ___Biff___ and I'm ___16___ inches tall."

```
Clown clown3 = new Clown();
clown3.Name = anotherClown.Name;
clown3.Height = oneClown.Height - 3;

clown3.TalkAboutYourself();
```
"My name is ___Biff___ and I'm ___11___ inches tall."

```
anotherClown.Height *= 2;

anotherClown.TalkAboutYourself();
```
"My name is ___Biff___ and I'm ___32___ inches tall."

When your program creates a new object, it gets added to the heap.

What's on your program's mind

Here's how your program creates a new instance of the
Clown class:

```
Clown myInstance = new Clown();
```

That's actually two statements combined into one. The
first statement declares a variable of type Clown (Clown
myInstance;). The second statement creates a new
object and assigns it to the variable that was just created
(myInstance = new Clown();). Here's what the heap
looks like after each of these statements:

This object is an instance of the Clown class.

"Boffo"
14
Clown object #1

①
```
Clown oneClown = new Clown();
oneClown.Name = "Boffo";
oneClown.Height = 14;
oneClown.TalkAboutYourself();
```

The first object is created, and its fields are set.

"Boffo"
14
Clown object #1

"Biff"
16
Clown object #2

②
```
Clown anotherClown = new Clown();
anotherClown.Name = "Biff";
anotherClown.Height = 16;
anotherClown.TalkAboutYourself();
```

These statements create the second object and fill it with data.

"Boffo"
14
Clown object #1

"Biff"
11
Clown object #3

"Biff"
16
Clown object #2

③
```
Clown clown3 = new Clown();
clown3.Name = anotherClown.Name;
clown3.Height = oneClown.Height - 3;
clown3.TalkAboutYourself();
```

Then the third Clown object is created and populated.

"Boffo"
14
Clown object #1

"Biff"
16
Clown object #3

"Biff"
32
Clown object #2

④
```
anotherClown.Height *= 2;
anotherClown.TalkAboutYourself();
```

There's no new command, which means
these statements don't create a new
object. They're just modifying one
that's already in memory.

You can use class and method names to make your code intuitive

When you put code in a method, you're making a choice about how to structure your program. Do you use one method? Do you split it into more than one? Or do you even need a method at all? The choices you make about methods can make your code much more intuitive—or, if you're not careful, much more convoluted.

1 Here's a nice, compact chunk of code. It's from a control program that runs a machine that makes candy bars.

The chkTemp() method returns an integer... but what does it do?

```
int t = m.chkTemp();
if (t > 160) {
    T obj = new T();
    tb.clsTrpV(2);
    ics.Fill();
    ics.Vent();
    m.airsyschk();
}
```

"obj", "ics", and "m" are terrible names! We have no idea what they do. And what's that T() class for?

The clsTrpV() method has one parameter, but we don't know what it's supposed to be.

Take a second and look at that code. Can you figure out what it does?

2 Those statements don't give you any hints about why the code's doing what it's doing. In this case, the programmer was happy with the results because she was able to get it all into one method. But making your code as compact as possible isn't really useful! Let's break it up into methods to make it easier to read, and make sure the classes are given names that make sense. But we'll start by figuring out what the code is supposed to do.

How do you figure out what your code is supposed to do? Well, all code is written for a reason. So it's up to you to figure out that reason! In this case, we can look up the page in the specification manual that the programmer followed.

General Electronics Type 5 Candy Bar Maker Specification Manual

The nougat temperature must be checked every 3 minutes by an automated system. If the temperature **exceeds 160°C**, the candy is too hot, and the system must **perform the candy isolation cooling system (CICS) vent procedure**.

- Close the trip throttle valve on turbine #2

- Fill the isolation cooling system with a solid stream of water

- Vent the water

- Verify that there is no evidence of air in the system

---

3 That page from the manual made it a lot easier to understand the code. It also gave us some great hints about how to make our code easier to understand. Now we know why the conditional test checks the variable t against 160—the manual says that any temperature above 160°C means the nougat is too hot. And it turns out that "**m**" was a class that controlled the candy maker, with static methods to check the nougat temperature and check the air system. So let's put the temperature check into a method, and choose names for the class and the methods that make the purpose obvious.

The IsNougatTooHot() method's return type

```
public boolean IsNougatTooHot() {
    int temp = Maker.CheckNougatTemperature();
    if (temp > 160) {
        return true;
    } else {
        return false;
    }
}
```

By naming the class "Maker" and the method "CheckNougatTemperature", the code is a lot easier to understand.

This method's return type is boolean, which means it returns a true or false value.

4 What does the specification say to do if the nougat is too hot? It tells us to perform the candy isolation cooling system (or CICS) vent procedure. So let's make another method, and choose an obvious name for the "T" class (which turns out to control the turbine) and the "ics" class (which controls the isolation cooling system, and has two static methods to fill and vent the system):

A void return type means the method doesn't return any value at all.

```
public void DoCICSVentProcedure() {
    Turbine turbineController = new Turbine();
    turbineController.CloseTripValve(2);
    IsolationCoolingSystem.Fill();
    IsolationCoolingSystem.Vent();
    Maker.CheckAirSystem();
}
```

5 Now the code's a lot more intuitive! Even if you don't know that the CICS vent procedure needs to be run if the nougat is too hot, **it's a lot more obvious what this code is doing**:

```
if (IsNougatTooHot() == true) {
    DoCICSVentProcedure();
}
```

You can make your code easier to read and write by thinking about the problem your code was built to solve. If you choose names for your methods that make sense to someone who understands that problem, then your code will be a lot easier to decipher...and develop!

Give your classes a <u>natural</u> structure

Take a second and remind yourself why you want to make your methods intuitive: **because every program solves a problem or has a purpose.** It might not be a business problem—sometimes a program's purpose (like FlashyThing) is just to be cool or fun! But no matter what your program does, the more you can make your code resemble the problem you're trying to solve, the easier your program will be to write (and read, and repair, and maintain…).

Use class diagrams to plan out your classes

A class diagram is a simple way to draw your classes out on paper. It's a really valuable tool for designing your code BEFORE you start writing it.

Write the name of the class at the top of the diagram. Then write each method in the box at the bottom. Now you can see all of the parts of the class at a glance!

ClassName

Method()
Method()
Method()
⋮

Let's build a class diagram

Take another look at the `if` statement in #5 on the last page. You already know that statements always live inside methods, which always live inside classes, right? In this case, that `if` statement was in a method called `DoMaintenanceTests()`, which is part of the `CandyController` class. Now take a look at the code and the class diagram. See how they relate to each other?

```
public class CandyController {

  public void DoMaintenanceTests() {

    ...

    if (IsNougatTooHot() == true) {

      DoCICSVentProcedure();

    }

    ...

  }

  public void DoCICSVentProcedure() ...

  public boolean IsNougatTooHot() ...

}
```

CandyController

DoMaintenanceTests()
DoCICSVentProcedure()
IsNougatTooHot()

Sharpen your pencil

The code for the candy control system we built on the previous page called three other classes. Flip back and look through the code, and fill in their class diagrams.

Turbine

CloseTrigValve
(int number)

> We filled in this class name for this one. What method goes here?

IsolationCoolingSystem

Fill()

Isolation cooling system

Vent()

> One of the classes had a method called Fill(). Fill in its class name and its other method.

Maker

CheckTroughTemp()

IsNotTooHot();

Check(AirSystem)

> There was one other class in the code on the previous page. Fill in its name and method.

Class diagrams help you organize your classes so they make sense

Writing out class diagrams makes it a lot easier to spot potential problems in your classes **before** you write code. Thinking about your classes from a high level before you get into the details can help you come up with a class structure that will make sure your code addresses the problems it solves. It lets you step back and make sure that you're not planning on writing unnecessary or poorly structured classes or methods, and that the ones you do write will be intuitive and easy to use.

Dishwasher
CleanDishes()
AddDetergent()
SetWaterTemperature()
ParkTheCar()

The class is called "Dishwasher", so all the methods should be about washing dishes. But one method—ParkTheCar()—has nothing to do with dishes, so it should be taken out and put in another class.

Dishwasher
CleanDishes()
AddDetergent()
SetWaterTemperature()

Sharpen your pencil
Solution

The code for the candy control system we built on the previous page called three other classes. Flip back and look through the code, and fill in their class diagrams.

You could figure out that Maker is a class because it appears in front of a dot in Maker.CheckAirSystem().

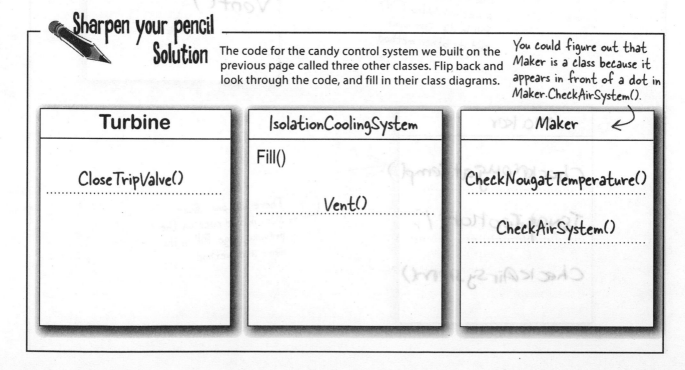

Turbine
CloseTripValve()

IsolationCoolingSystem
Fill()
Vent()

Maker
CheckNougatTemperature()
CheckAirSystem()

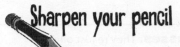
Sharpen your pencil

Each of these classes has a serious design flaw. Write down what you think is wrong with each class, and how you'd fix it.

Class23

CandyBarWeight()
PrintWrapper()
GenerateReport()
Go()

This class is part of the candy manufacturing system from earlier.

Name of class should be related to candy manufacture and not absurd.

DeliveryGuy

AddAPizza()
PizzaDelivered()
TotalCash()
ReturnTime()

DeliveryGirl

AddAPizza()
PizzaDelivered()
TotalCash()
ReturnTime()

These two classes are part of a system that a pizza parlor uses to track the pizzas that are out for delivery.

Instead of using two classes, both should be clubbed into a single class with a gender variable.

CashRegister

MakeSale()
NoSale()
PumpGas()
Refund()
TotalCashInRegister()
GetTransactionList()
AddCash()
RemoveCash()

The `CashRegister` class is part of a program that's used by an automated convenience store checkout system.

PumpGas() method does not have anything to do with a cash reg - placed in different class ✓

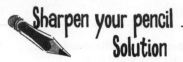

Sharpen your pencil
Solution

Here's how we corrected the classes. They're just one possible way to fix the problems—but there are plenty of other ways you could design these classes depending on how they'll be used.

This class is part of the candy manufacturing system from earlier.

The class name doesn't describe what the class does. A programmer who sees a line of code that calls Class23.Go() will have no idea what that line does. We'd also rename the method to something that's more descriptive—we chose MakeTheCandy(), but it could be anything.

ClassMaker

CandyBarWeight()
PrintWrapper()
GenerateReport()
MakeTheCandy()

These two classes are part of a system that a pizza parlor uses to track the pizzas that are out for delivery.

It looks like the DeliveryGuy class and the DeliveryGirl class both do the same thing—they track a delivery person who's out delivering pizzas to customers. A better design would replace them with a single class that adds a field for gender.

DeliveryPerson

Gender

AddAPizza()
PizzaDelivered()
TotalCash()
ReturnTime()

We added the Gender field because we assumed there was a reason to track both delivery guys and girls separately, and that's why there were two classes for them.

The `CashRegister` class is part of a program that's used by an automated convenience store checkout system.

All of the methods in the class do stuff that has to do with a cash register—making a sale, getting a list of transactions, adding cash... except for one: pumping gas. It's a good idea to pull that method out and stick it in another class.

CashRegister

MakeSale()
NoSale()
Refund()
TotalCashInRegister()
GetTransactionList()
AddCash()
RemoveCash()

```
public partial class Form1 : Form
{
  private void button1_Click(object sender, EventArgs e)
  {
    String result = "";
    Echo e1 = new Echo();
    Echo e2 = new Echo();
    int x = 0;
    while (  x < 4   ) {
      result = result + e1.hello() + "\n";
      e1.count = e1.count + 1;
      if (  x == 3  ) {
        e2.count = e2.count + 1;
      }
      if (  x > 0   ) {
        e2.count = e2.count + e1.count;
      }
      x = x + 1;
    }
    MessageBox.Show(result + "Count: " + e2.count);
  }

  public class Echo {
    public int count = 0;
    public string hello() {
      return "helloooo...";
    }
  }
}
```

Pool Puzzle

Your *job* is to take code snippets from the pool and place them into the blank lines in the code. You **may** use the same snippet more than once, and you won't need to use all the snippets. Your *goal* is to make classes that will compile and run and produce the output listed.

Output

```
helloooo...
helloooo...
helloooo...
helloooo...
Count: 10
```
OK

Bonus Question!

If the last line of output was **24** instead of **10** how would you complete the puzzle? You can do it by changing just one statement.

Make e2 = e1

Note: Each snippet from the pool can be used more than once!

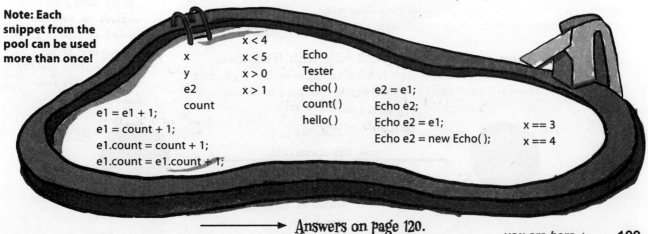

```
e1 = e1 + 1;             x            x < 4       Echo
e1 = count + 1;          y            x < 5       Tester
e1.count = count + 1;    e2           x > 0       echo()      e2 = e1;
e1.count = e1.count + 1; count        x > 1       count()     Echo e2;
                                                  hello()     Echo e2 = e1;           x == 3
                                                              Echo e2 = new Echo();   x == 4
```

→ **Answers on page 120.**

Build a class to work with some guys

Joe and Bob lend each other money all the
time. Let's build a class to keep track of them.

Guy
Name
Cash
GiveCash()
TakeCash()

1 **We'll create a Guy class and add two instances of it to a form**
The form will have two fields, one called `joe` (to keep track of the first object),
and the other called `bob` (to keep track of the second object).

The new statements
that create the two
instances lives in the
code that gets run as
soon as the form is
created. Here's what
the heap looks like
after the form is
loaded.

Guy object#1   Guy object#2

2 **We'll set each Guy object's cash and name**
The two objects represent different guys, so each one has its own name
and a different amount of cash in his pocket.

Each guy has a Name
field that keeps track of
his name, and a Cash field
that has the number of
bucks in his pocket.

"Joe"
100
Guy object#1

"Bob"
50
Guy object#2

When you take an
instance of Guy and
call its TakeCash()
method, you pass the
amount of cash to take
as a parameter. So
calling joe.TakeCash(25)
takes 25 bucks from
Joe.

3 **We'll give cash to the guys and take cash from them**
We'll use each guy's `GiveCash()` method to give cash to a guy, and
we'll use his `TakeCash()` method to take cash back from him.

The form calls the object's
TakeCash() method.

"Joe"
100
Guy object#1

```
joe.TakeCash(25);
```

The method returns the
number of bucks that
were taken.

"Joe"
75
Guy object#1

Create a project for your guys

Create a new Windows Forms Application project (because
we'll be using a form). Then use the Solution Explorer to add a
new class to it called Guy. Make sure to add "using System.
Windows.Forms;" to the top of the Guy class file. Then fill
in the Guy class. Here's the code for it:

Do this!

The Guy class has two fields. The Name field is
a string, and it'll contain the guy's name ("Joe").
And the Cash field is an int, which will keep
track of how many bucks are in his pocket.

```
public class Guy {
    public string Name;
    public int Cash;

    public int GiveCash(int amount) {
        if (amount <= Cash && amount > 0) {
            Cash -= amount;
            return amount;
        } else {
            MessageBox.Show(
             "I don't have enough cash to give you " + amount,
             Name + " says...");
            return 0;
        }
    }
```

The GiveCash() method has one parameter
called amount that you'll use to tell the
guy how much cash to give you.

He uses an if statement to check
whether he has enough cash—if he
does, he takes it out of his pocket and
returns it as the return value.

The Guy makes
sure that you're
asking him for a
positive amount
of cash, otherwise
he'd add to his
cash instead of
taking away from
it.

If the guy doesn't have enough cash, he'll
tell you so with a message box, and then
he'll make GiveCash() return 0.

```
    public int ReceiveCash(int amount) {
        if (amount > 0) {
            Cash += amount;
            return amount;
        } else {
            MessageBox.Show(amount + " isn't an amount I'll take",
                    Name + " says...");
            return 0;
        }
    }
}
```

The ReceiveCash() method works just like
the GiveCash() method. It's passed an
amount as a parameter, checks to make
sure that amount is greater than zero,
and then adds it to his cash.

If the amount was positive, then the
ReceiveCash() method returns the amount
added. If it was zero or negative, the guy
shows a message box and then returns 0.

Be careful with your curly brackets. It's easy to
have the wrong number—make sure that every opening
bracket has a matching closing bracket. When they're
all balanced, the IDE will automatically indent them
for you when you type the last closing bracket.

Build a form to interact with the guys

The Guy class is great, but it's just a start. Now put together
a form that uses two instances of the Guy class. It's got labels
that show you their names and how much cash they have, and
buttons to give and take cash from them.

Build this!

  Add two buttons and six labels to your form

The labels on the right-hand side of the form show how much cash each guy has. We'll also
add a variable called `bank` to the form—the third label on the right shows how much cash is in
it. We're going to have you name some of the labels that you drag onto the forms. You can do
that by **clicking on each label** that you want to name and **changing its "(Name)" row** in
the Properties window. That'll make your code a lot easier to read, because you'll be able to use
"joesCash" and "bobsCash" instead of "label4" and "label5".

This button will call the Joe
object's ReceiveCash() method,
passing it 10 as the amount, and
subtracting the cash it gives to
Joe from the bank variable.

Name the top label joesCash,
the label underneath it
bobsCash, and the bottom
label bankCash. You can leave
their Text properties alone,
we'll add a method to the
form to set them.

This button will call the Bob
object's GiveCash() method,
passing it 5 as the amount, and
adding the cash it receives
from Joe to the bank variable.

  Add variables to your form

Your form will need to keep track of the two guys, so you'll need a variable for each of them. Call
them `joe` and `bob`. Then add a variable to the form called `bank` to keep track of how much
money the form has to give to and receive from the guys.

Since we're using
Guy objects to
keep track of
Joe and Bob,
you declare
their variables
using Guy.

```
namespace Your_Project_Name {
    public partial class Form1 : Form {
        Guy joe;
        Guy bob;
        int bank = 100;

        public Form1() {
            InitializeComponent();
        }
    }
```

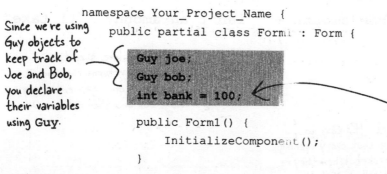

The amount of cash in
the bank goes up and
down depending on how
much money the form
gave to and received
from the Guy objects.

3 Add a method to the form to update the labels

The labels on the right-hand side of the form show how much cash each guy has and how much is in the bank variable. So add the UpdateForm() method to keep them up to date—**make sure the return type is void** to tell C# that the method doesn't return a value. Type this method into the form right underneath where you added the bank variable:

```
public void UpdateForm() {
    joesCash.Text = joe.Name + " has $" + joe.Cash;
    bobsCash.Text = bob.Name + " has $" + bob.Cash;
    bankCash.Text = "The bank has $" + bank;
}
```

Notice how the labels are updated using the Guy objects' Name and Cash fields.

This new method is simple. It just updates the three labels by setting their Text properties. You'll have each button call it to keep the labels up to date.

4 Double-click on each button and add the code to interact with the objects

Make sure the left-hand button is called button1, and the right-hand button is called button2. Then double-click each of the buttons—when you do, the IDE will add two methods called button1_Click() and button2_Click() to the form. Add this code to each of them:

```
private void button1_Click(object sender, EventArgs e) {
    if (bank >= 10) {
        bank -= joe.ReceiveCash(10);
        UpdateForm();
    } else {
        MessageBox.Show("The bank is out of money.");
    }
}
```

When the user clicks the "Give $10 to Joe" button, the form calls the Joe object's ReceiveCash() method—but only if the bank has enough money.

The bank needs at least $10 to give to Joe. If there's not enough, it'll pop up this message box.

```
private void button2_Click(object sender, EventArgs e) {
    bank += bob.GiveCash(5);
    UpdateForm();
}
```

The "Receive $5 from Bob" button doesn't need to check how much is in the bank, because it'll just add whatever Bob gives back.

If Bob's out of money, GiveCash() will return zero.

---

5 Start Joe out with $50 and start Bob out with $100

It's up to you to **figure out how to get Joe and Bob to start out with their Cash and Name fields set properly.** Put it right underneath InitializeComponent() in the form. That's part of a special method that gets run once, when the form is first initialized. Once you've done that, click both buttons a number of times—make sure that one button takes $10 from the bank and adds it to Joe, and the other takes $5 from Bob and adds it to the bank.

Exercise

```
public Form() {
    InitializeComponent();
    // Initialize joe and bob here!
}
```

Add the lines of code here to create the two objects and set their Name and Cash fields.

It's up to you to **figure out how to get Joe and Bob to start out with their Cash and Name fields set properly.** Put it right underneath `InitializeComponent()`

```
public Form1() {
    InitializeComponent();

    bob = new Guy();
    bob.Name = "Bob";
    bob.Cash = 100;

    joe = new Guy();
    joe.Name = "Joe";
    joe.Cash = 50;

    UpdateForm();
}
```

Here's where we set up the first instance of Guy. The first line creates the object, and the next two set its fields.

Then we do the same for the second instance of the Guy class.

Make sure you call UpdateForm() so the labels look right when the form first pops up.

there are no Dumb Questions

Make sure you save the project now—we'll come back to it in a few pages.

Q: Why doesn't the solution start with "Guy bob = new Guy()"? Why did you leave off the first "Guy"?

A: Because you already declared the bob variable at the top of the form. Remember how the statement "int i = 5;" is the same as the two statements "int i" and "i = 5;"? This is the same thing. You could try to declare the bob variable in one line like this: "Guy bob = new Guy();". But you already have the first part of that statement ("Guy bob;") at the top of your form. So you only need the second half of the line, the part that sets the bob variable to create a new instance of Guy().

Q: Okay, so then why not get rid of the "Guy bob;" line at the top of the form?

A: Then the bob variable will only exist inside that special "public Form1()" method. When you declare a variable inside a method, it's only valid inside the method—you can't access it from any other method. But when you declare it outside of your method but inside the form or a class that you added, then you can access it from *any other method* inside the form or class.

Q: What happens if I don't leave off that first "Guy"?

A: You'll run into problems—your form won't work, because it won't ever set the form's bob variable. Think about it for a minute, and you'll see why it works that way. If you have this code at the top of your form:

```
public partial class Form1 : Form {
    Guy bob;
```

and then you have this code later on, inside a method:

```
Guy bob = new Guy();
```

then you've declared *two* variables. It's a little confusing, because they both have the same name. But one of them is valid throughout the entire form, and the other one—the new one you added—is only valid inside the method. The next line (bob.Name = "Bob";) only updates that *local* variable, and doesn't touch the one in the form. So when you try to run your code, it'll give you a nasty error message ("NullReferenceException not handled"), which just means you tried to use an object before you created it with new.

There's an even easier way to initialize objects

Almost every object that you create needs to be initialized in some way. And the Guy object is no exception—it's useless until you set its Name and Cash fields. It's so common to have to initialize fields that C# gives you a shortcut for doing it called an **object initializer**. And the IDE's IntelliSense will help you do it.

Watch it!

> **Object initializers only work with C# 3.0.**
>
> *If you're running Visual Studio 2005, then this won't work. Definitely consider downloading Visual Studio 2008 Express Edition—it's free, and you can install it alongside your existing VS2005 installation.*

① Here's the original code that you wrote to initialize Joe's Guy object.

```
joe = new Guy();
joe.Name = "Joe";
joe.Cash = 50;
```

② Delete the second two lines, and the semicolon after "Guy()" and add a right curly bracket.

```
joe = new Guy() {
```

③ Press space. As soon as you do, the IDE pops up an IntelliSense window that shows you all of the fields that you're able to initialize.

```
joe = new Guy() {
```

④ Press tab to tell it to add the Cash field. Then set it equal to 50.

```
joe = new Guy() { Cash = 50
```

⑤ Type in a comma. As soon as you do, the other field shows up.

```
joe = new Guy() { Cash = 50,
```

⑤ Finish the object initializer. Now you've saved yourself two lines of code!

```
joe = new Guy() { Cash = 50, Name = "Joe" };
```

This new declaration does exactly the same thing as the three lines of code you wrote originally. It's just shorter and easier to read.

Object intializers save you time and make your code more compact and easier to read... and the IDE helps you write them.

A few ideas for designing intuitive classes

* ### You're building your program to solve a problem.
  Spend some time thinking about that problem. Does it break down into pieces easily? How would you explain that problem to someone else? These are good things to think about when designing your classes.

It'd be great if I could compare a few routes and figure out which is fastest...

* ### What real-world things will your program use?
  A program to help a zoo keeper track her animals' feeding schedules might have classes for different kinds of food and types of animals.

ROAD CLOSED
CHEMIN FERMÉ

* ### Use descriptive names for classes and methods.
  Someone should be able to figure out what your classes and methods do just by looking at their names.

myInst
obj Object

bestRoute
Navigator object

* ### Look for similarities between classes.
  Sometimes two classes can be combined into one if they're really similar. The candy manufacturing system might have three or four turbines, but there's only one method for closing the trip valve that takes the turbine number as a parameter.

BlockedRoad
Name
Duration

FindDetour()

ClosedRoad
StreetName
ReasonItsClosed

CalculateDelay()

Detour
Name
Duration
ReasonItsClosed

FindDetour()
CalculateDelay()

Add buttons to the "Fun with Joe and Bob" program to make the guys give each other cash.

Exercise

1 **Use an object initializer to initialize Bob's instance of Guy**
You've already done it with Joe. Now make Bob's instance work with an object initializer too.

If you already clicked the button, just delete it, add it back to your form, and rename it. Then delete the old button3_Click() method that the IDE added before, and use the new method it adds now.

2 **Add two more buttons to your form**
The first button tells Joe to give 10 bucks to Bob, and the second tells Bob to give 5 bucks back to Joe. **Before you double-click on the button,** go to the Properties window and change each button's name using the "(Name)" row—it's **at the top** of the list of properties. Name the first button **joeGivesToBob**, and the second one **bobGivesToJoe**.

This button tells Joe to give 10 bucks to Bob, so you should use the "(Name)" row in the Properties window to name it joeGivesToBob.

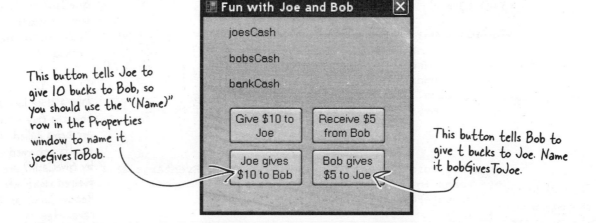

This button tells Bob to give t bucks to Joe. Name it bobGivesToJoe.

3 **Make the buttons work**
Double-click on the joeGivesToBob button in the designer. The IDE will add a method to the form called joeGivesToBob_Click() that gets run any time the button's clicked. Fill in that method to make Joe give 10 bucks to Bob. Then double-click on the other button and fill in the new bobGivesToJoe_Click() method that the IDE creates so that Bob gives five bucks to Joe. Make sure the form updates itself after the cash changes hands.

Exercise Solution

Add buttons to the "Fun with Joe and Bob" program to make the guys give each other cash.

```csharp
public partial class Form1 : Form {
    Guy joe;
    Guy bob;
    int bank = 100;

    public Form1() {
        InitializeComponent();
        bob = new Guy() { Cash = 100, Name = "Bob" };
        joe = new Guy() { Cash = 50, Name = "Joe" };
        UpdateForm();
    }

    public void UpdateForm() {
        joesCash.Text = joe.Name + " has $" + joe.Cash;
        bobsCash.Text = bob.Name + " has $" + bob.Cash;
        bankCash.Text = "The bank has $" + bank;
    }

    private void button1_Click(object sender, EventArgs e) {
        if (bank >= 10) {
            bank -= joe.ReceiveCash(10);
            UpdateForm();
        } else {
            MessageBox.Show("The bank is out of money.");
        }
    }

    private void button2_Click(object sender, EventArgs e) {
        bank += bob.GiveCash(5);
        UpdateForm();
    }

    private void joeGivesToBob_Click(object sender, EventArgs e) {
        bob.ReceiveCash(joe.GiveCash(10));
        UpdateForm();
    }

    private void bobGivesToJoe_Click(object sender, EventArgs e) {
        joe.ReceiveCash(bob.GiveCash(5));
        UpdateForm();
    }

}
```

Here are the object initializers for the two instances of the Guy class. Bob gets initialized with 100 bucks and his name.

To make Joe give cash to Bob, we call Joe's GiveCash() method and send its results into Bob's ReceiveCash() method.

Take a close look at how the Guy methods are being called. The results returned by GiveCash() are pumped right into ReceiveCash() as its parameter.

The trick here is thinking through who's giving the cash and who's receiving it.

Objectcross

It's time to give your left brain a break, and put that right brain to work: all the words are object-related and from this chapter.

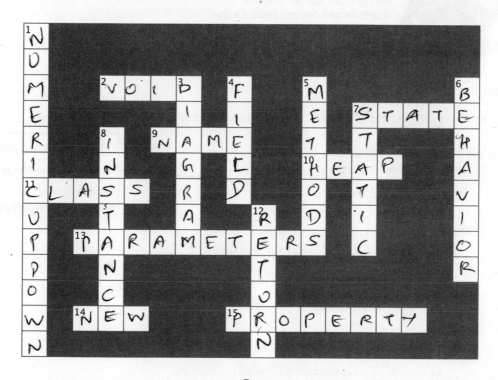

Across

2. If a method's return type is _____, it doesn't return anything

7. An object's fields define its _____

9. A good method _____ makes it clear what the method does

10. Where objects live

11. What you use to build an object

13. What you use to pass information into a method

14. The statement you use to create an object

15. A special kind of field that's used by the form controls

Down

1. This form control lets the user choose a number from a range you set

3. It's a great idea to create a class _____ on paper before you start writing code

4. What an object uses to keep track of what it knows

5. These define what an object does

6. An object's methods define its _____

7. Don't use this keyword in your class declaration if you want to be able to create instances of it

8. An object is an _____ of a class

12. This statement tells a method to immediately exit, and specifies the value that should be passed back to the statement that called the method

Pool Puzzle Solution

Your *job* was to take code snippets from the pool and place them into the blank lines in the code. Your *goal* was to make classes that will compile and run and produce the output listed.

```
public partial class Form1 : Form
{
    private void button1_Click(object sender, EventArgs e)
    {
        String result = "";
        Echo e1 = new Echo();
        Echo e2 = new Echo( );
        int x = 0;
        while (    x < 4    ) {
            result = result + e1.hello() + "\n";
            e1.count = e1.count + 1;
            if (    x == 3    ) {
                e2.count = e2.count + 1;
            }
            if (    x > 0    ) {
                e2.count = e2.count + e1.count;
            }
            x = x + 1;
        }
        MessageBox.Show(result + "Count: " + e2.count);
    }

    public class  Echo     {
        public int  count    = 0;
        public string  hello( )    {
            return "helloooo...";
        }
    }
}
```

> That's the correct answer.
> And here's the bonus answer!
> Echo e2 = e1;

Objectcross Solution

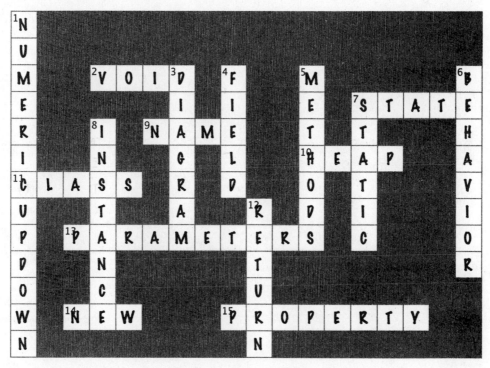

4 Types and References

It's 10:00.
Do you know where your data is?

This data just got garbage collected.

Data type, database, Lieutenant Commander Data...

it's all important stuff. Without data, your programs are useless. You

need **information** from your users, and you use that to look up or produce new

information, to give back to them. In fact, almost everything you do in programming

involves **working with data** in one way or another. In this chapter, you'll learn the

ins and outs of C#'s **data types**, how to work with data in your program, and even

figure out a few dirty secrets about **objects** (*psstt... objects are data, too*).

The variable's <u>type</u> determines what kind of data it can store

There are fifteen **value types** built into C#, and each one stores a different kind of data. You've already seen some of the most common ones, and you know how to use them. But there are a few that you haven't seen, and they can really come in handy, too.

Value types you'll use all the time

It shouldn't come as a surprise that `int`, `string`, `bool`, and `float` are the most common types.

A whole number doesn't have a decimal point.

★ `int` can store any **whole** number from -2,147,483,648 to 2,147,483,647.

★ `string` can hold text of any length (including the empty string "").

★ `bool` is a Boolean value—it's either `true` or `false`.

★ `float` can store any **decimal** number from $\pm 1.5 \times 10^{-45}$ to $\pm 3.4 \times 10^{38}$ with up to 7 significant figures. That range looks weird and complicated, but it's actually pretty simple. The "significant figures" part means the *precision* of the number: 35,048,410,000,000, 1,743,059, 14.43857, and 0.00004374155 all have seven significant figures. The 10^{38} thing means that you can store any number as large as 10^{38} (or 1 followed by 38 zeroes)—as long as it only has 7 or fewer significant figures. On the other end of the range, 10^{-45} means that you can store any number as small as 10^{-45} (or a decimal point followed by 45 zeroes followed by 1)... but, you guessed it, as long as it only has 7 or fewer significant figures.

"float" is short for "floating point"—as opposed to a "fixed point" number, which always has the same number of decimal places.

More types for whole numbers

The "u" in uint stands for "unsigned", which means it can't be negative (so there's no minus sign).

Once upon a time, computer memory was really expensive, and processors were really slow. And, believe it or not, if you used the wrong type, it could seriously slow down your program. Luckily, times have changed, and most of the time if you need to store a whole number you can just use an `int`. But sometimes you really need something bigger... and once in a while, you need something smaller, too. That's why C# gives you more options:

★ `byte` can store any **whole** number between 0 and 255.

★ `sbyte` can store any **whole** number from -127 to 128.

★ `short` can store any **whole** number from -32,767 to 32,768.

★ `ushort` can store any **whole** number from 0 to 65,535.

★ `uint` can store any **whole** number from 0 to 4,294,967,295.

★ `long` can store any number between minus and plus 9 billion billion.

★ `ulong` can store any number between 0 and about 18 billion billion.

The "u" stands for "unsigned"

A lot of times, if you're using these types it's because you're solving a problem where it really helps to have the "wrapping around" effect that you'll read about in a few minutes.

Types for storing *really* HUGE and *really* <small>tiny</small> numbers

Sometimes 7 significant figures just isn't precise enough. And, believe it or not, sometimes 10^{38} isn't big enough and 10^{-45} isn't small enough. A lot of programs written for finance or scientific research run into these problems all the time, so C# gives us two more types:

> The double type is actually <u>as common</u> as float. A lot of people use it all the time, and rarely use float.

- ★ double can store any number from $\pm 5.0 \times 10^{-324}$ to $\pm 1.7 \times 10^{308}$ with 15-16 significant digit.

- ★ decimal can store any number from $\pm 1.0 \times 10^{-28}$ to $\pm 7.9 \times 10^{28}$ with 28-29 significant digits.

> A literal just means a number that you type into your code. So when you type "int i = 5;", the 5 is a literal.

> When you used the Value property in your numericUpDown control, you were using a decimal.

Literals have types, too

When you type a number directly into your C# program, you're using a **literal**... and every literal is automatically assigned a type. You can see this for yourself—just enter this line of code that assigns the literal 14.7 to an int variable:

```
int myInt = 14.7;
```

Now try to build the program. You'll get this:

> ⊗ 1   Cannot implicitly convert type 'double' to 'int'. An explicit conversion exists (are you missing a cast?)

That's the same error you'll get if you try to set an int equal to a double variable. What the IDE is telling you is that the literal 14.7 has a type—it's a double. You can change its type to a float by sticking an F on the end (14.7F). And 14.7M is a decimal.

> If you try to assign a float literal to a double or a decimal literal to a float, the IDE will give you a helpful message reminding you to add the right suffix. Cool!

A few more useful built-in value types

Did you notice how the byte type has 256 possible values? Well, there's another type that also has 256 possible values: char. But it's not numeric; you use it to store a character. Literal values for char are always inside single quotes ('x', '3'). You can include **escape sequences** in the quotes, too ('\n' is a line break, '\t' is a tab).

And finally, there's one more important type: **object**. You've already seen how an object can inherit from another one, and that object can in turn inherit from yet a different object. At the top of every inheritance hierarchy is the object class—that's a special type that every other object inherits from. That's really useful, because it means that **you can assign any value, variable, or object to an object variable**.

> You'll learn a lot more about how char and byte relate to each other in Chapter 9.

BRAIN POWER

You can use the Windows calculator to convert between decimal (normal, base-10) numbers and binary numbers (base-2 numbers written with only ones and zeroes)—put it in Scientific mode, enter a number, and click the **Bin** radio button to convert to binary. Then click **Dec** to convert it back. Now **enter some of the upper and lower limits for the whole number types** (like -32,767 and 255) and convert them to binary. Can you figure out *why* C# gives you those particular limits?

A variable is like a data to-go cup

All of your data takes up space in memory. (Remember the heap from last chapter?) So part of your job is to think about how *much* space you're going to need whenever you use a string or a number in your program. That's one of the reasons you use variables. They let you set aside enough space in memory to store your data.

Think of a variable like a cup that you keep your data in. C# uses a bunch of different kinds of cups to hold different kinds of data. And just like the different sizes of cups at the coffee shop, there are different sizes of variables, too.

> int is commonly used for whole numbers. It holds numbers up to 2,147,483,647.

> A short will hold whole numbers up to 32,767.

> You'll use long for whole numbers that are going to be really big.

> byte holds numbers between zero and 255.

long   int   short   byte
 64   32   16   8

> These are the number of bits of memory set aside for the variable when you declare it.

Numbers that have decimal places are stored differently than whole numbers. You can handle most of your numbers that have decimal places using `float`, the smallest data type that stores decimals. If you need to be more accurate, use a `double`, and if you're writing a scientific application where the numbers need to be extremely accurate, the `decimal` type has the most precision.

float double decimal
 32   64   128

> These types are for fractions. Larger variables store more decimal places.

It's not always about numbers, though. (You wouldn't expect to get hot coffee in a plastic cup or cold coffee in a paper one.) The C# compiler also can handle characters and non-numeric types. The `char` type holds one character, and `string` is used for lots of characters "strung" together. There's no set size for a `string` variable, either. It expands to hold as much data as you need to store in it. The `bool` data type is used to store true or false values, like the ones you've used for your `if` statements.

bool   char   string
 8   16   depends on
                the size
                of the string

> string is pretty unique. It's the only data type without a set size, except for objects (think about that for a bit).

10 pounds of data in a 5 pound bag

When you declare your variable as one type, that's how your compiler looks at it. Even if the value is nowhere near the upper boundary of the type you've declared, the complier will see the cup it's in, not the number inside. So this won't work:

```
int leaguesUnderTheSea = 20000;

short smallerLeagues = leaguesUnderTheSea;
```

20,000 would fit into a short, no problem. But since **leaguesUnderTheSea** is declared as an int, the compiler sees it as int-sized and considers it too big to put in a short container. The compiler won't make those translations for you on the fly. You need to make sure that you're using the right type for the data you're working with.

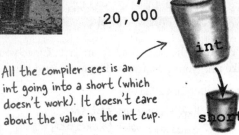

20,000

int

short

This makes sense. What if you later put a larger value in the int cup, that wouldn't fit into the short cup? The compiler is trying to protect you.

All the compiler sees is an int going into a short (which doesn't work). It doesn't care about the value in the int cup.

Sharpen your pencil

Three of these statements won't compile, either because they're trying to cram too much data into a small variable or because they're putting the wrong type of data in. Circle them.

```
int hours = 24;                        string taunt = "your mother";

short y = 78000;                       byte days = 365;

bool isDone = yes;                     long radius = 3;

short RPM = 33;                        char initial = 'S';

int balance = 345667 - 567;            string months = "12";
```

Even when a number is the right size, you can't just assign it to <u>any</u> variable

Let's see what happens when you try to assign a decimal value to an int variable.

Do this

1 Create a new project and add a button to it. Then add these lines to the button's **Click()** method:

```
decimal myDecimalValue = 10;
int myIntValue = myDecimalValue;

MessageBox.Show("The myIntValue is " + myIntValue);
```

2 Try building your program. Uh-oh—you got an error that looks like this:

Check out how the IDE figured out that you were probably missing a cast.

3 Make the error go away by **casting** the decimal to an int. Once you change the second line so it looks like this, your program will compile and run:

```
int myIntValue = (int) myDecimalValue;
```

Here's where you <u>cast</u> the decimal value to an int.

So what happened?

The compiler won't let you assign a value to a variable if it's the wrong type—even if that variable can hold the value just fine—because that's the underlying cause behind an enormous number of bugs. When you use casting, you're essentially making a promise to the compiler that you know the types are different, and that in this particular instance it's okay for C# to cram the data into the new variable.

Take a minute to flip back to the beginning of the last chapter and check out how you used casting when you passed the NumericUpDown.Value to the Talker Tester form.

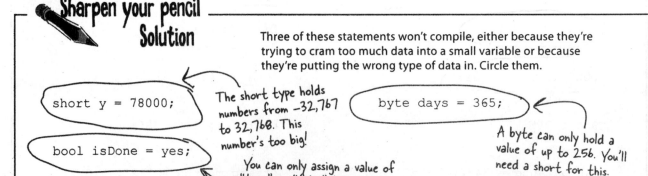

Sharpen your pencil
Solution

Three of these statements won't compile, either because they're trying to cram too much data into a small variable or because they're putting the wrong type of data in. Circle them.

```
short y = 78000;
```
The short type holds numbers from −32,767 to 32,768. This number's too big!

```
bool isDone = yes;
```
You can only assign a value of "true" or "false" to a bool.

```
byte days = 365;
```
A byte can only hold a value of up to 256. You'll need a short for this.

When you cast a value that's too big, C# will adjust it automatically

Wrap it yourself!

There's no mystery to how casting "wraps" the numbers—you can do it yourself. Just pop up the Windows calculator, switch it to Scientific mode, and calculate 365 Mod 256 (using the "Mod" button, which does a modulo calculation). You'll get 109.

You've already seen that a `decimal` can be cast to an `int`. It turns out that *any* number can be cast to *any other* number. But that doesn't mean the ***value*** stays intact through the casting. If you cast an `int` variable that's set to 365 to a `byte` variable, 365 is too big for the **byte**. But instead of giving you an error, the value will just **wrap around**: for example, 256 cast to a `byte` will have a value of 0. 257 would be converted to 1, 258 to 2, etc., up to 365, which will end up being **109**. And once you get back to 255 again, the conversion value "wraps" back to zero.

> Hey, I've been combining numbers and strings in my message boxes since I learned about loops in Chapter 2! Have I been casting this whole time?

Yes! The + operator casts for you.

What you've been doing is using the + operator, which **does a lot of casting for you automatically**—but it's especially smart about it. When you use + to add a number or boolean to a string, then it'll automatically convert that value to a string, too. If you use + (or *, / or −) with two different types, it **automatically casts the smaller type to the bigger one**. Here's an example:

When you're assigning a number value to a float, you need to add an F to the end of the number to tell the compiler that it's a float, and not a double.

```
int myInt = 36;
float myFloat = 16.4F;
myFloat = myInt + myFloat;
```

Since an `int` can fit into a `float` but a `float` can't fit into an `int`, the + operator casts `myInt` to a float before adding it to `myFloat`.

Sharpen your pencil

You can't always cast any type to any other type. Create a new project, drag a button onto a form, and type these statements into its method. Then build your program—it will give lots of errors. Cross out the ones that give errors. That'll help you figure out which types can be cast, and which can't!

```
int myInt = 10;

byte myByte = (byte)myInt;

double myDouble = (double)myByte;

bool myBool = (bool)myDouble;

string myString = "false";

myBool = (bool)myString;

myString = (string)myInt;

myString = myInt.ToString();

myBool = (bool)myByte;

myByte = (byte)myBool;

short myShort = (short)myInt;

char myChar = 'x';

myString = (string)myChar;

long myLong = (long)myInt;

decimal myDecimal = (decimal)myLong;

myString = myString + myInt + myByte
+ myDouble + myChar;
```

C# does some casting <u>automatically</u>

There are two important conversions that don't require you to do the casting. The first is done automatically any time you use arithmetic operators, like in this example:

```
long l = 139401930;

short s = 516;

double d = l - s;

d = d / 123.456;

MessageBox.Show("The answer is " + d);
```

The − operator subtracted the short from the long, and converted the result to a double.

This + operator is smart enough to convert the decimal to a string.

The other way C# converts types for you automatically is when you use the + operator to **concatenate** strings (which just means sticking one string on the end of another, like you've been doing with message boxes). When you use + to concatenate a string with something that's another type, it automatically converts the numbers to strings for you. Here's an example. The first two lines are fine, but the third one won't compile.

```
long x = 139401930;

MessageBox.Show("The answer is " + x);

MessageBox.Show(x);
```

The C# compiler spits out an error that mentions something about invalid arguments (an argument is another name for a method's parameter). That's because the parameter for **MessageBox.Show()** is a string, and this code passed a long, which is the wrong type for the method. But you can convert it to a string really easily by calling its **ToString()** method. That method is a member of every value type and object. (All of the classes you build yourself have a ToString() method that returns the class name.) That's how you can convert x to something that **MessageBox.Show()** can use:

```
MessageBox.Show(x.ToString());
```

Sharpen your pencil
Solution

You can't always cast any type to any other type. Create a new project, drag a button onto a form, and type these statements into its method. Then build your program—it will give lots of errors. Cross out the ones that give errors. That'll help you figure out which types can be cast, and which can't!

```
int myInt = 10;

byte myByte = (byte)myInt;

double myDouble = (double)myByte;

bool myBool = (bool)myDouble;

string myString = "false";

myBool = (bool)myString;

myString = (string)myInt;

myString = myInt.ToString();

myBool = (bool)myByte;

myByte = (byte)myBool;

short myShort = (short)myInt;

char myChar = 'x';

myString = (string)myChar;

long myLong = (long)myInt;

decimal myDecimal = (decimal)myLong;

myString = myString + myInt + myByte
+ myDouble + myChar;
```

When you call a method, the variables must match the types of the parameters

Try calling **MessageBox.Show(123)**—passing MessageBox.Show() a literal (123) instead of a string. The IDE won't let you build your program. Instead, it'll show you an error in the IDE: "Argument '1': cannot convert from 'int' to 'string'."

But MessageBox.Show() isn't the only method that will give you compiler errors if you try to pass it a variable whose type doesn't match the parameter. *All* methods will do that, even the ones you write yourself. Go ahead and try typing this completely valid method into a class:

```
public int MyMethod(bool yesNo) {

    if (yesNo) {
        return 45;
    } else {
        return 61;
    }

}
```

One reminder—the code that calls this parameter doesn't have to pass it a variable called yesNo. It just has to pass it a boolean value or variable. The only place it's called yesNo is inside the method's code.

It works just fine if you pass it what it expects (a `bool`)—call MyMethod(true) or MyMethod(false), and it compiles just fine.

But what happens if you pass it an integer or a string instead? The IDE gives you a similar error to the one that you got when you passed 123 to `MessageBox.Show()`. Now try passing it a boolean, but assigning the return value to a long or passing it on to **MessageBox.Show()**. That won't work, either—the method returns an int, not a long or the **string** that **MessageBox.Show()** expects.

> When the compiler gives you an "invalid arguments" error, it means that you tried to call a method with variables whose types didn't match the method's parameters.

You can assign anything to a variable, parameter, or field with the type object.

if statements always test to see if something's true

Did you notice how we wrote our if statement like this:

    if (yesNo) {

We didn't have to explicitly say "if (yesNo == true)". That's because an if statement always checks if something's true. You check if something's false using ! (an exclamation point, or the NOT operator). "if (!yesNo)" is the same thing as "if (yesNo == false)". In our code examples from now on, you'll usually just see us do "if (yesNo)" or "if (!yesNo)", and not explicitly check to see if a boolean is true or false.

this table reserved

Exercise

There are about 77 **reserved words** in C#. These are words reserved by the C# compiler; you can't use them for variable names. You'll know them all really well by the time you finish the book. Here are some you've already used. Write down what you think these words do in C#.

namespace

declares a namespace within which all the code for the program resides

for

Initiates the for loop

class

Declares a class

public

makes a class, variables or methods of the class available to all other classes.

else

executes if the "if condition" is not satisfied.

new

declares an object i.e. instance of a class.

using

Tells the compiler to use some header files containing different methods.

if

if decision.

while

while loop

———————▶ Answers on page 161.

Create a reimbursement calculator for a business trip. It should allow the user to enter a starting odometer reading and an ending odometer reading. From those two numbers, it will calculate how many miles she's travelled and figure out how much she should be reimbursed if her company pays her $.39 for every mile she puts on her car.

1 **Start with a new Windows project.**
Make the form look like this:

Get rid of the minimize and maximize buttons.

This label is 12 pt bold.

The range for these fields should be 1–999,999.

When you're done with the Form, double-click on the button to add some code to the project.

2 **Create the variables you'll need for the calculator.**
Put the variables in class definition at the top of `Form1`. You need two whole number variables to track the starting odometer reading and the ending odometer reading. Call them `startingMileage` and `endingMileage`. You need three numbers that can hold decimal places. Make them `doubles` and call them `milesTraveled`, `reimburseRate`, and `amountOwed`. Set the value for `reimburseRate` to .39.

3 **Make your calculator work.**
Add code in the `button1_Click()` method to:

★ Make sure that the number in the Starting Mileage field is smaller than the number in the Ending Mileage field. If not, show a messagebox that says "The starting mileage must be less than the ending mileage". Make the title for the message box "Cannot Calculate".

★ Subtract the starting number from the ending number and then multiply it by the reimburse rate using these lines:

```
milesTraveled = endingMileage -= startingMileage;

amountOwed = milesTraveled *= reimburseRate;

label4.Text = "$" + amountOwed;
```

4 **Run it.**
Make sure it's giving the right numbers. Try changing the starting value to be higher than the ending value and make sure it's giving you the message box.

Here's the code for the first part of the exercise.

```
public partial class Form1 : Form
{
    int startingMileage;
    int endingMileage;
    double milesTraveled;
    double reimburseRate = .39;
    double amountOwed;
    public Form1() {
        InitializeComponent();
    }
    private void button1_Click(object sender, EventArgs e){
        startingMileage = (int) numericUpDown1.Value;
        endingMileage = (int)numericUpDown2.Value;
        if (startingMileage <= endingMileage){
            milesTraveled = endingMileage -= startingMileage;
            amountOwed = milesTraveled *= reimburseRate;
            label4.Text = "$" + amountOwed;
        } else {
            MessageBox.Show(
        "The starting mileage must be less than the ending mileage",
                    "Cannot Calculate Mileage");
        }
    }
}
```

int works great for whole numbers. This number could go all the way up to 999,999. So a short or a byte won't cut it.

Did you remember that you have to change the decimal value from the numericUpDown control to an int?

This block is supposed to figure out how many miles were traveled and then multiply them by the reimbursement rate.

We used an alternate way of calling the MessageBox.Show() method here. We gave it two parameters: the first one is the message to display, and the second one goes in the title bar.

This button seems to work, but it has a pretty big problem. Can you spot it?

1 **Now add another button to the form.**
Make it so that the number of miles traveled is displayed
on the form after you've calculated the amount owed.

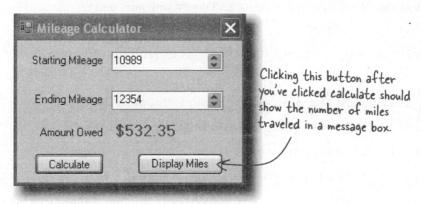

Clicking this button after
you've clicked calculate should
show the number of miles
traveled in a message box.

When you're done with the Form, double-click on the
Display Miles button to add some code to the project.

2 **One line should do it.**
All we need to do is get the form to display the `milesTraveled` variable, right? So this line
should do that:

```
private void button2_Click(object sender, EventArgs e) {
        Messagebox.Show(milesTraveled + " miles", "Miles Traveled");
}
```

3 **Run it**
Type in some values and see what happens.

4 **Um, something's not right...**
The number of miles always matches the amount owed. Why?

Combining = with an operator

Take a good look at the operator we used to subtract ending mileage from starting mileage (-=). The problem is it doesn't just subtract, it also assigns a value to the variable on the left side of the subtraction sign. The same thing happens in the line where we multiply number of miles traveled by the reimbursement rate. We should replace the -= and the *= with just - and *:

```
private void button1_Click(object sender, EventArgs e)
{
    startingMileage = (int) numericUpDown1.Value;

    endingMileage = (int)numericUpDown2.Value;

    if (startingMileage <= endingMileage){

        milesTraveled = endingMileage -= startingMileage;

        amountOwed = milesTraveled *= reimburseRate;

        label4.Text = "$" + amountOwed;

    } else {

        MessageBox.Show("The starting mileage number must
                        be less than the ending mileage number",
                        "Cannot Calculate Mileage");

    }
```

These are called compound operators. This one subtracts startingMileage from endingMileage but also assigns the new value to endingMileage and milesTraveled at the same time.

This is better—now your code won't modify endingMileage and milesTraveled.

```
milesTraveled = endingMileage - startingMileage;
amountOwed = milesTraveled * reimburseRate;
```

So can good variable names help you out here? Definitely! Take a close look at what each variable is supposed to do. You already get a lot of clues from the name milesTraveled—you know that's the variable that the form is displaying incorrectly, and you've got a good idea of how that value ought to be calculated. So you can take advantage of that when you're looking through your code to try to track down the bug. It'd be a whole lot harder to find the problem if the incorrect lines looked like this instead:

```
mT = eM -= sM;
aO = mT *= rR;
```

Variables named like this are essentially useless in telling you what their purpose might be.

Objects are variables, too

So far, we've looked at objects separate from other types. But
an object is just another data type. Your code treats objects
exactly like it treats numbers, strings, and booleans. It uses
variables to work with them:

Using an int

① Write a statement to declare the integer.

```
int myInt;
```

② Assign a value to the new variable.

```
myInt = 3761;
```

③ Use the integer in your code.

```
while (i < myInt) {
```

Using an object

① Write a statement to declare the object.

```
Dog spot;
```

When you have a class like Dog, you use it as the type in a variable declaration statement.

② Assign a value to the object.

```
spot = new Dog();
```

③ Check one of the object's fields.

```
while (spot.Happy) {
```

> So it doesn't matter if I'm
> working with an object or a value. If
> it's going into memory, and my program
> needs to use it, I use a variable.

Objects are just one more type of variable your program can use.

If your program needs to work with a whole
number that's really big, use a long. If it needs
a whole number that's small, use a short. If it
needs a yes/no value, use a boolean. And if it
needs something that barks and sits, use a Dog.
No matter what type of data your program
needs to work with, it'll use a variable.

Refer to your objects with reference variables

When you create a new object, you use code like **new Guy**. But that's not enough; even though that code creates a new **Guy** object on the heap, it doesn't give you a way to *access* that object. **You need a reference to the object**. So you create a **reference variable**: a variable of type **Guy** with a name, like **Joe**. So **Joe** is a reference to the new **Guy** object you created. Anytime you want to use that particular guy, you can reference it with the reference variable called **Joe**.

That's called instantiating the object.

So when you have a variable that is an object type, it's a reference variable: a reference to a particular object. Take a look:

Here's the heap before your code runs. Nothing there.

This variable is named Joe, and will reference an object of type Guy.

```
public partial class Form1 : Form
{
    Guy Joe;

    public Form1()
    {
        InitializeComponent();

        Joe = new Guy();
    }
}
```

This is the reference variable...

...and this is the object that Joe now refers to.

Creating a reference is like making a label with a label maker—instead of sticking it on your stuff, you're using it to label an object so you can refer to it later.

Here's the heap after this code runs. There's an object, with the variable Joe referring to it.

JOE

Guy object #1

The ONLY way to reference this guy object is through the reference variable called Joe.

References are like labels for your object

In your kitchen, you probably have a container of salt and sugar. If you switched their labels, it would make for a pretty disgusting meal—even though the labels changed, the contents of the containers stayed the same. *References are like labels.* You can move labels around, point them at different things, but it's the **object** that dictates what methods and data are available, not the reference itself.

> **When your code needs to work with an object in memory, it uses a reference, which is a variable whose type is a class of the object it's going to point to. A reference is like a label that your code uses to talk about a specific object.**

This object is of type Guy. It's a SINGLE object with MULTIPLE references.

Forml's buttonl_Click method has a variable called "Joe" that references this object.

An instance of the Guy class is keeping a reference to this object in a variable called "Dad".

Every one of these labels is reference variable, but they all point to the SAME Guy object.

There are lots of different references to this same Guy, because a lot of different methods use him for different things. Each reference has a different name that makes sense in its context.

You never refer to your object directly. For example, you can't write code like **Guy.GiveCash()** if **Guy** is your object type. The C# compiler doesn't know which **Guy** you're talking about, since you might have several instances of **Guy** on the heap. So you need a reference variable, like **joe**, that you assign to a specific instance, like **Guy joe = new Guy()**.

Now, you can call methods, like **joe.GiveCash()**. **joe** refers to a specific instance of the **Guy** class, and your C# compiler knows exactly which instance to use. And, as you saw above, you might have *multiple labels pointing to the same instance*. So you could say **Guy dad = joe**, and then call **dad.GiveCash()**. That's okay, too—that's what Joe's kid does every day.

If there aren't any more references, your object gets garbage collected

If all of the labels come off of an object, no programs can access that object anymore. That means C# can mark the object for **garbage collection**. That's when C# gets rid of any unreferenced objects, and reclaims the memory those objects took up for your program's use.

1 **Here's some code that creates an object.**

```
Guy joe = new Guy()
    { Name = "Joe", Cash = 50 };
```

The first line had a declaration that created the label. The second line created the object and slapped the label on it.

2 **Now let's create a second object.**

```
Guy bob = new Guy()
    { Name = "Bob", Cash = 75 };
```

Now we have two Guy object instances, and two reference variables: one for each Guy.

3 **Let's take the reference to the first object, and change it to point at the second object.**

```
joe = bob;
```

Now joe is pointing to the same object as bob.

For an object to stay in the heap, it has to be referenced. When the last reference to the object disappears, so does the object.

But there is no longer a reference to the first Guy object...

...so C# marks the object for garbage collection, and trashes it. It's gone!

Typecross

Take a break, and sit back and give your right brain something to do. It's your standard crossword; all of the solution words are from this chapter.

When you're done, turn the page, and take on the rest of the chapter.

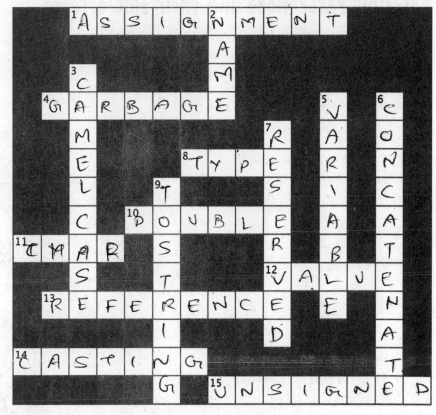

Across

1. You can combine the variable declaration and the _____ __ into one statement

4. When an object no longer has any references pointing to it, it's removed from the heap using _____ collection

8. A variable declaration always starts with this

10. The type that holds the biggest numbers

11. The type that stores a single letter or number

12. If you never set this for a variable, your program won't compile

13. A variable that points to an object

14. What (int) does in this line of code: x = (int) y;

15. The four whole number types that only hold positive numbers

Down

2. The second part of a variable declaration

3. Variable names like myBigNumber and bobTheDog use this style of capitalization

5. What your program uses to work with data that's in memory

6. What you're doing when you use the + operator to stick two strings together

7. "namespace", "for", "while", "using" and "new" are examples of _____ words

9. Every object has this method that converts it to a string

——————➤ Answers on page 162.

Multiple references and their side effects

You've got to be careful when you start moving around reference variables. Lots of times, it might seem like you're simply pointing a variable to a different object. But, you could end up removing all references to another object in the process. That's not a bad thing, but it may not be what you intended. Take a look:

1
```
Dog rover = new Dog();
rover.Breed = "Greyhound";
```

Objects: __1__

References: __1__

Rover is a Dog object with a Breed field called Greyhound.

2
```
Dog fido = new Dog();
fido.Breed = "Beagle";
Dog spot = rover;
```

Objects: __2__

References: __3__

Fido is another Dog object. But Spot is just another reference to the first object.

3
```
Dog lucky = new Dog();
lucky.Breed = "Dachshund";
fido = rover;
```

Objects: __2__

References: __4__

poof!

Lucky is a third object. But Fido is now pointing to Object #1. So, Object #2 has no references. It's done as far as the program is concerned.

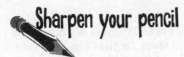

Sharpen your pencil

Now it's your turn. Here's one long block of code. Figure out how many objects and references there are at each stage. On the right-hand side, draw a picture of the objects and labels in the heap.

1
```
Dog rover = new Dog();
rover.Breed = "Greyhound";
Dog rinTinTin = new Dog();
Dog fido = new Dog();
Dog quentin = Fido;
```

Objects: 3

References: 4

2
```
Dog spot = new Dog();
spot.Breed = "Dachshund";
spot = rover;
```

Objects: 3

References: 5

3
```
Dog lucky = new Dog();
lucky.Breed = "Beagle";
Dog charlie = fido;
fido = rover;
```

Objects: 4

References: 7

4
```
rinTinTin = lucky;
Dog laverne = new Dog();
laverne.Breed = "pug";
```

Objects: 4

References: 8

5
```
charlie = laverne;
lucky = rinTinTin;
```

Objects: 4

References: 8

Sharpen your pencil
Solution

Now it's your turn. Here's one long block of code. Figure out how many objects and references there are at each stage. On the right-hand side, draw a picture of the objects and labels in the heap.

1
```
Dog rover = new Dog();
rover.Breed = "Greyhound";
Dog rinTinTin = new Dog();
Dog fido = new Dog();
Dog quentin = Fido;
```

Objects: ___3___

References: ___4___

One new Dog object is created but Spot is the only reference to it. When Spot is set = to Rover, that object goes away.

2
```
Dog spot = new Dog();
spot.Breed = "Dachshund";
spot = rover;
```

Objects: ___3___

References: ___5___

Here a new Dog object is created, but when Fido is set to Rover, Fido's object from #1 goes away.

3
```
Dog lucky = new Dog();
lucky.Breed = "Beagle";
Dog charlie = fido;
fido = rover;
```

Charlie was set to Fido when Fido was still on object #3. Then, after that, Fido moved to object #1, leaving Charlie behind.

Objects: ___4___

References: ___7___

Dog #2 lost its last reference, and it went away.

4
```
rinTinTin = lucky;
Dog laverne = new Dog();
laverne.Breed = "pug";
```

Objects: ___4___

References: ___8___

When Lucky moved to Rin Tin Tin's object, the old Lucky object disappeared.

5
```
charlie = laverne;
lucky = rinTinTin;
```

Objects: ___4___

References: ___8___

Here the references move around but no new objects are created. And setting Lucky to Rin Tin Tin did nothing because they already pointed to the same object.

poof!

Exercise

Create a program with an elephant class. Make two elephant instances and then have them switch properties, *without* getting any Elephant instances garbage collected.

①   Start with a new Windows Application project.
Make the form look like this:

Clicking on the "Lucinda" button calls lucinda.WhoAmI(), which displays this messagebox.

Here's the class diagram for the Elephant class you need to create.

Elephant
Name EarSize
WhoAmI()

This gives you a clue as to what WhoAmI() should return: a single string with this message.

②   Create the Elephant class.
Add an Elephant class to the project. Have a look at the Elephant class diagram—you'll need an int field called EarSize and a String field called Name. (Make sure both are public.) Then add a method called WhoAmI() that displays a messagebox that tells you the name and ear size of the elephant.

③   Create two elephant instances and a reference.
Add two Elephant fields to the Form1 class (in the area right below the class declaration) named Lloyd and Lucinda. Initialize them so they have the right name and ear size. Here are the **Elephant** object initializers to add to your form:

```
lucinda = new Elephant() { Name = "Lucinda", EarSize = 33 };
lloyd = new Elephant() { Name = "Lloyd", EarSize = 40 };
```

④   Make the "Lloyd" and "Lucinda" buttons work.
Have the Lloyd button call lloyd.WhoAmI() and the Lucinda button call lucinda.WhoAmI().

⑤   Hook up the swap button.
Here's the hard part. Make the Swap button *exchange* the two references, so that when you click Swap, the Lloyd and Lucinda variables swap objects and a "Objects swapped" box is displayed. Test out your program by clicking the Swap button and then clicking the other two buttons. The first time you click Swap, the Lloyd button should pop up Lucinda's messagebox, and the Lucinda button should pop up Lloyd's messagebox. If you click the Swap button again, everything should go back.

C# garbage collects any object with no references to it. So here's your hint: If you want to pour a glass of beer into another glass that's currently full of water, you'll need a third glass to pour the water into...

Exercise Solution

Create a program with an elephant class. Make two elephant instances and then have them switch properties, *without* getting any Elephant instances garbage collected.

```
using System.Windows.Forms;

class Elephant {

  public int EarSize;
  public String Name;

  public void WhoAmI() {
    MessageBox.Show("My ears are " + EarSize + " inches tall.",
      Name + " says…");
  }
}
```

This is the Elephant class definition code in the Elephant.cs file we added to the project. Don't forget the "using System.Windows.Forms;" line at the top of the class. Without it, the MessageBox statement won't work.

```
public partial class Form1 : Form {

    Elephant lucinda;
    Elephant lloyd;

    public Form1()
    {
        InitializeComponent();
        lucinda = new Elephant()
            { Name = "Lucinda", EarSize = 33 };
        lloyd = new Elephant()
            { Name = "Lloyd", EarSize = 40 };
    }

    private void button1_Click(object sender, EventArgs e) {
        lloyd.WhoAmI();
    }

    private void button2_Click(object sender, EventArgs e) {
        lucinda.WhoAmI();
    }

    private void button3_Click(object sender, EventArgs e) {
        Elephant holder;
        holder = lloyd;
        lloyd = lucinda;
        lucinda = holder;
        MessageBox.Show("Objects swapped");
    }
}
```

Here's the Form1 class code from Form1.cs.

If you just point Lloyd to Lucinda, there won't be any more references pointing to Lloyd and his object will be lost. That's why you need to have the Holder reference hold onto the Lloyd object until Lucinda can get there.

There's no new statement for the reference because we don't want to create another instance of Elephant.

BRAIN POWER

Why do you think we didn't add a Swap() method to the Elephant class?

Two references means TWO ways to change an object's data

Besides losing all the references to an object, when you have multiple references to an object, you can unintentionally change an object. In other words, one reference to an object may *change* that object, while another reference to that object has *no idea* that something has changed. Watch:

Do this

❶   Add another button to your form.

❷   Add this code for the button. Can you guess what's going to happen when you click it?

```
private void button4_Click(object sender, EventArgs e)
{
    lloyd = Lucinda;
    lloyd.EarSize = 4321;
    lloyd.WhoAmI();
}
```

This statement says to set EarSize to 4321 on whatever object the lloyd reference happens to point to.

You're calling the WhoAmI() method from the lloyd object.

After this code runs, both the lloyd and lucinda variables reference the SAME Elephant object.

But lloyd points at the same thing that lucinda does.

LLOYD
LUCINDA
Elephant Object

❸   OK, go ahead and click the new button. Wait a second, that's the Lucinda messagebox. Didn't we call the WhoAmI() method from Lloyd?

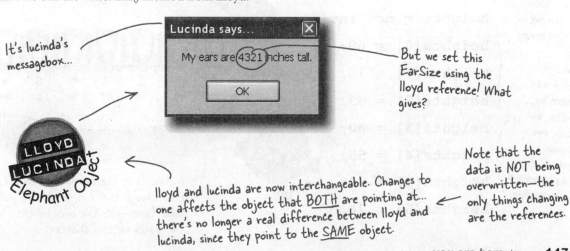

It's lucinda's messagebox...

Lucinda says...

My ears are (4321) inches tall.

OK

But we set this EarSize using the lloyd reference! What gives?

LLOYD
LUCINDA
Elephant Object

lloyd and lucinda are now interchangeable. Changes to one affects the object that BOTH are pointing at... there's no longer a real difference between lloyd and lucinda, since they point to the SAME object.

Note that the data is NOT being overwritten—the only things changing are the references.

A special case: <u>arrays</u>

If you have to keep track of a lot of data of the same type, like a list of heights or a group of dogs, you can do it in an **array**. What makes an array special is that it's a **group of variables** that's treated as one object. An array gives you a way of storing and changing more than one piece of data without having to keep track of each variable individually. When you create an array, you declare it just like any other variable, with a name and a type:

> You could combine the declaration of the myArray variable with its initialization—just like any other variable. Then it'd look like this:
>
> bool[] myArray = new bool[15];

You declare an array by specifying its type, followed by square brackets. ———>

```
bool[] myArray;

myArray = new bool[15];

myArray[4] = true;
```

This array has 15 elements within it.

You use the new keyword to create an array because it's an object. So an array variable is a kind of reference variable.

This line sets the value of the fifth element of myArray to true. It's the fifth one because the first is myArray[0], the second is myArray[1], etc.

Use each element in an array like it is a normal variable

Here's an example of code that declares and fills up an array—and what's happening on the heap when you do it. The first element in the array has an **index** of zero.

In memory, the array is stored as one chunk of memory, even though there are multiple int variables within it.

The type of each element in the array.

```
int[] heights;
heights = new int[7];
heights[0] = 68;
heights[1] = 70;
heights[2] = 63;
heights[3] = 60;
heights[4] = 58;
heights[5] = 72;
heights[6] = 74;
```

name

You reference these by index, but each one works essentially like a normal int variable.

7 int variables

| 0 | 1 | 2 | 3 | 4 | 5 | 6 |
| int | int | int | int | int | int | int |

HEIGHTS Array

Notice that the array is an object, even though the 7 elements are just value types—like the ones on the first two pages of this chapter.

Arrays can contain a bunch of reference variables, too

You can create an array of object references just like you create an array of numbers or strings. Arrays don't care what the type of variable is that they store; it's up to you. So you can have an array of ints, or an array of Duck objects, with no problem.

Here's code that creates an array of 7 **Dog** variables. The line that initializes the array only creates reference variables. Since there are only two new Dog() lines, only two actual instances of the **Dog** class) are created.

```
Dog[] dogs = new Dog[7];
dogs[5] = new Dog();
dogs[0] = new Dog();
```

This line declares a dogs variable to hold an array of references to Dog objects, and then creates a 7-element array.

These two lines create new instances of Dog() and put them at indexes 0 and 5.

When you set or retrieve an element from an array, the number inside the brackets is called the index. The first element in the array has an index of zero.

The first line of code only created the array, not the instances. The array is a list of seven Dog reference variables.

Dog Object

Dog Object

7 Dog variables

```
0    1    2    3    4    5    6
Dog  Dog  Dog  Dog  Dog  Dog  Dog
```

An array's length

You can find out how many elements are in an array using its Length field. So if you've got an array called heights, then you can use heights.Length to find out how long it is. If there are 7 elements in the array, that'll give you 7—which means the array elements are numbered 0 to 6.

Array

All of the elements in the array are references. The array itself is an object.

Welcome to Sloppy Joe's Budget House o' Discount Sandwiches!

Sloppy Joe has a pile of meat, a whole lotta bread, and more condiments than you can shake a stick at. But what he doesn't have is a menu! Can you build a program that makes a new *random* menu for him every day?

Do this

MenuMaker
Randomizer
Meats
Condiments
Breads
GetMenuItem()

① Start a new project and add a MenuMaker class

If you need to build a menu, you need ingredients. And arrays would be perfect for those lists. We'll also need some way of choosing random ingredients to combine together into a sandwich. Luckily, the .NET Framework has a built-in class called **Random** that generates random numbers. So we'll have four fields in our class: a Randomizer field that holds a reference to a Random object, and three arrays of `strings` to hold the meats, condiments, and breads.

The class has three fields to store three different arrays of strings. It'll use them to build the random menu items.

The field called Randomizer holds a reference to a Random object. Calling its Next() method will generate random numbers.

```
public class MenuMaker {
    public Random Randomizer;

    string[] Meats = { "Roast beef", "Salami", "Turkey", "Ham", "Pastrami" };
    string[] Condiments = { "yellow mustard", "brown mustard",
            "honey mustard", "mayo", "relish", "french dressing" };
    string[] Breads = { "rye", "white", "wheat", "pumpernickel",
            "italian bread", "a roll" };
}
```

Remember, use square brackets to access a member of an array. The value of Breads[2] is "wheat".

② Add a GetMenItem() method to generate a random sandwich to the class

The point of the class is to generate sandwiches, so let's add a method to do exactly that. It'll use the Random object's **Next()** method to choose a random meat, condiment and bread from each array. When you pass an `int` parameter to `Next()`, the method returns a random that's less than that parameter. So if your Random object is called Randomizer, then calling `Randomizer.Next(7)` will return a random number between 0 and 6.

So how do you know what parameter to pass into the `Next()` method? Well, that's easy—just pass in each array's Length. That will return the index of a random item in the array.

The GetMenuItem() method returns a string that contains a sandwich built from random elements in the three arrays.

```
public string GetMenuItem() {
    string randomMeat = Meats[Randomizer.Next(Meats.Length)];
    string randomCondiment = Condiments[Randomizer.Next(Condiments.Length)];
    string randomBread = Breads[Randomizer.Next(Breads.Length)];
    return randomMeat + " with " + randomCondiment + " on " + randomBread;
}
```

The method puts a random item from the Meats array into randomMeat by passing Meats.Length to the Random object's Next() method. Since there are 5 items in the Meats array, Meats.Length is 5, so Next(5) will return a random number between 0 and 4.

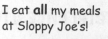

I eat **all** my meals at Sloppy Joe's!

How it works...

The randomizer.Next(7) method gets a random number that's less than 7. Meats.Length returns the number of elements in Meats. So `randomizer.Next(Meats.Length)` gives you a random number that's greater than or equal to zero, but less than the number of elements in the Meats array.

Meats[Randomizer.Next(Meats.Length)]

Meats is an array of strings. It's got five elements, numbered from zero to 4. So Meats[0] equals "Roast Beef", and Meats[3] equals "Ham".

③ Build your form

Add six labels to the form, `label1` through `lablel6`. Then add code to set each label's `Text` property using a `MenuMaker` object. You'll need to initialize the object using a new instance of the Random class. Here's the code:

Use an object initializer to set the MenuMaker object's Randomizer field to a new instance of the Random class.

```
public Form1() {
    InitializeComponent();

    MenuMaker menu = new MenuMaker() { Randomizer = new Random() };

    label1.Text = menu.GetMenuItem();
    label2.Text = menu.GetMenuItem();
    label3.Text = menu.GetMenuItem();
    label4.Text = menu.GetMenuItem();
    label5.Text = menu.GetMenuItem();
    label6.Text = menu.GetMenuItem();
}
```

Now you're all set to generate six different random sandwiches using the GetMenuItem() method.

When you run the program, the six labels show six different random sandwiches.

Sloppy Joe's Menu ☒

Roast beef with honey mustard on wheat
Turkey with mayo on italian bread
Ham with relish on white
Pastrami with yellow mustard on rye
Turkey with mayo on rye
Roast beef with brown mustard on white

Objects use references to talk to each other

So far, you've seen forms talk to objects by using reference variables to call their methods and check their fields. Objects can also call each others' methods using references, too. In fact, there's nothing that a form can do that your objects can't do, because **your form is just another object**. And when objects talk to each other, one useful keyword that they have is **this**. Any time an object uses the this keyword, it's referring to itself—it's a reference that points to the object that calls it.

1 **Here's a method to tell an elephant to speak**

Let's add a method to the Elephant class. Its first method is a message from an elephant. Its second method is the elephant that said it:

```
public void TellMe(string message, Elephant whoSaidIt) {
    MessageBox.Show(whoSaidIt.Name + " says: " + message);
}
```

Here's what it looks like when it's called:

```
Elephant lloyd = new Elephant() { Name = "Lloyd", EarSize = 40 };
Elephant lucinda = new Elephant() { Name = "Lucinda", EarSize = 33 };
lloyd.TellMe("Hi", lucinda);
```

We called Lloyd's TellMe() method, and passed it two parameters: "Hi" and a reference to Lucinda's object. The method uses its whoSaidIt parameter to access the Name parameter of whatever elephant was passed into TellMe() using its second parameter.

2 **Here's a method that calls another method**

Now let's this SpeakTo() method to the Elephant class. It uses a special keyword: **this**. That's a reference that **lets an object talk about itself**.

```
public void SpeakTo(Elephant talkTo, string message) {
    talkTo.TellMe(message, this);
}
```

← *This method in the Elephant class calls another elephant's TalkTo() method. It lets one elephant communicate with another one.*

Let's take a closer look at how this works.

```
lucinda.SpeakTo(lloyd, "Hello");
```

When Lucinda's SpeakTo() method is called, it uses its talkTo reference parameter to call Lloyd's TellMe() method.

```
talkTo.TellMe(message, this);
```

Lucinda uses talkTo (which has a reference to Lloyd) to call TellMe()

this is replaced with a reference to Lucinda's object

```
lloyd.TellMe(message, [a reference to Lucinda]);
```

So Lloyd acts as if he was called with ("Hello", lucinda), and shows this message:

Lucinda says: Hello

OK

Where no object has gone before

There's another important keyword that you'll use with objects. When you create a new reference and don't set it to anything, it has a value. It starts off set to **null**, which means it's not pointing to anything.

```
Dog fido;
```

Right now, there's only one object. The fido reference is set to null.

```
Dog lucky = new Dog();
```

LUCKY
Dog object #1

```
fido = new Dog();
```

Now that fido's pointing to an object, it's no longer equal to null.

LUCKY
Dog object #1

FIDO
Dog object #2

When we set lucky to null, it's no longer pointing at its object, so it gets garbage collected.

```
lucky = null;
```

poof!

FIDO
Dog object #2

there are no Dumb Questions

Q: One more time—my form is an object?

A: Yes! That's why your class code starts with a class declaration. Open up code for a form and see for yourself. Then open up Program.cs in any program you've written so far and look inside the InitializeComponent() method—you'll find "`new Form1()`".

Q: Why would I ever use `null`?

A: There are a few ways you see null used in typical programs. The most common way is testing for it:

```
if (lloyd == null) {
```

That test will return `true` if the `lloyd` reference is set to null.

Another way you'll see the `null` keyword used is when you *want* your object to get garbage collected. If you've got a reference to an object and you're finished with the object, setting the reference to `null` will immediately mark it for collection (unless there's another reference ot it somewhere.)

Q: You keep talking about garbage collecting, but what's actually doing the collecting?

A: Remember how we talked about the **Common Language Runtime (or CLR)** back in the beginning of the first chapter? That's the virtual machine that runs all .NET programs. A *virtual machine* is a way for to isolate running programs from the rest of the operating system. One thing that virtual machines do is manage the memory that they use. That means that it keeps track of all of your objects, figures out when the last reference to the object disappears, and frees up the memory that it was using.

there are no Dumb Questions

Q: I'm still not sure I get how references work.

A: References are the way you use all of the methods and fields in an object. If you create a reference to a Dog object you can then use that reference to access any methods you've created for the Dog object. If you have (non-static) a method called Dog.Bark() or Dog.Beg(), you can create a reference called spot. Then you can use that to access spot.Bark() or spot.Beg(). You could also change information in the fields for the object using the reference. So you could change a Breed field using spot.Breed.

Q: Wait, then doesn't that mean that every time a change a value through a reference I'm changing it for all of the other references to that object too?

A: Yes. If rover is a reference to the same object as spot, changing rover.Breed to "beagle" would make it so that spot.Breed was "beagle."

Q: Go back to that stuff about value types. Now, why can't I change a small number from a bigger type if it's small enough?

A: Okay. The thing about variables is they assign a size to your number no matter how big its value is. So if you name a variable and give it a long type even though the number is really small, (like, say, 5) C# sets aside enough memory for it to get really big. When you think about it, that's really useful. After all, they're called variables because they change all the time.

C# assumes you know what you're doing and you're not going to give a variable a type that you don't need. So even though the number might not be big now, there's a chance that after some math happens, it'll change and C# gives it enough memory to handle whatever type of number you call it.

Q: Remind me again—what does "this." do?

A: this is a special variable that you can only use inside an object. When you're inside a class, you use this to refer to any field or method of that particular instance. It's especially useful when you're working with an class whose methods call other classes. One object can use it to send **a reference to itself** to another object. So if Spot calls one of Rover's methods passing this as a parameter, he's giving Rover a reference to the Spot object.

> **Any time you've got code in an object that's going to be instantiated, the instance can use the special this variable that has a reference to itself.**

BULLET POINTS

- There are **value types** for numbers that hold different sizes of numbers. The biggest numbers should be of the type, long and the smallest ones (up to 128) can be declared as bytes.

- When you declare a variable you ALWAYS give a type. Sometimes you combine it with setting the value.

- Every value type has a size, and you can't put a value of a bigger type into a smaller variable, no matter what the actual size of the data is.

- When you're using literal values, use the F suffix to indicate a float (15.6F) and M for a decimal (36.12M).

- The compiler won't let you set a variable equal to a value of a different type unless you cast it.

- There are some words that are reserved by the language and you can't name your variables with them. They're words like, for, while, using, new, and others that do specific things in the language.

- References are like labels you can have as many references to an object as you want and they all refer to the same thing.

- If an object doesn't have a reference, it gets garbage collected.

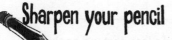

Sharpen your pencil

Here's an array of Elephant objects and a loop that will go through it and find the one with the biggest ears. What's the value of the biggestEars.Ears **after** each iteration of the `for` loop?

```
private void button1_Click(object sender, EventArgs e)
{
    Elephant[] elephants = new Elephant[7];                    We're creating an array of 7
                                                               Elephant() references.
    elephants[0] = new Elephant() { Name = "Lloyd", EarSize = 40 };
    elephants[1] = new Elephant() { Name = "Lucinda", EarSize = 33 };
    elephants[2] = new Elephant() { Name = "Larry", EarSize = 42 };     Every array
                                                                        starts with
    elephants[3] = new Elephant() { Name = "Lucille", EarSize = 32 };   index 0, so the
                                                                        first elephant
    elephants[4] = new Elephant() { Name = "Lars", EarSize = 44 };      in the array is
                                                                        Elephants[0].
    elephants[5] = new Elephant() { Name = "Linda", EarSize = 37 };

    elephants[6] = new Elephant() { Name = "Humphrey", EarSize = 45 };
```

Iteration #1 biggestEars.Earssize = _____

```
    Elephant biggestEars = elephants[0];

    for (int i = 1; i < elephants.Length; i++)
    {
```

Iteration #2 biggestEars.EarSize = _____

```
        if (elephants[i].EarSize > biggestEars.EarSize)
        {
            biggestEars = elephants[i];
```

Iteration #3 biggestEars.EarSize = _____

```
        }
    }
```

This line makes the biggestEars reference point at whatever elephant elephants[i] points to.

```
    MessageBox.Show(biggestEars.EarSize.ToString());
}
```

Iteration #4 biggestEars.EarSize = _____

Be careful—this loop starts with the second element of the array (at index 1) and iterates six times until i is equal to the length of the array.

Iteration #5 biggestEars.EarSize = _____

Iteration #6 biggestEars.EarSize = _____

Sharpen your pencil
Solution

Here's an array of Elephant objects and a loop that will go through it and find the one with the biggest ears. What's the value of the biggestEars.Ears **after** each iteration of the `for` loop?

```
private void button1_Click(object sender, EventArgs e)
{

    Elephant[] elephants = new Elephant[7];

    elephants[0] = new Elephant() { Name = "Lloyd", EarSize = 40 };

    elephants[1] = new Elephant() { Name = "Lucinda", EarSize = 33 };

    elephants[2] = new Elephant() { Name = "Larry", EarSize = 42 };

    elephants[3] = new Elephant() { Name = "Lucille", EarSize = 32 };

    elephants[4] = new Elephant() { Name = "Lars", EarSize = 44 };

    elephants[5] = new Elephant() { Name = "Linda", EarSize = 37 };

    elephants[6] = new Elephant() { Name = "Humphrey", EarSize = 45 };
```

Did you remember that the loop starts with the second element of the array? Why do you think that is?

Iteration #1 biggestEars.Earssize = **40**

```
    Elephant biggestEars = elephants[0];

    for (int i = 1; i < elephants.Length; i++)

    {
```

Iteration #2 biggestEars.EarSize = **42**

```
        if (elephants[i].EarSize > biggestEars.EarSize)
```

The `biggestEars` reference is used to keep track of which element we've seen while going through the `for` loop has the biggest ears so far.

```
        {

            biggestEars = elephants[i];

        }

    }
```

Iteration #3 biggestEars.EarSize = **42**

```
    MessageBox.Show(biggestEars.EarSize.ToString());
```

Iteration #4 biggestEars.EarSize = **44**

```
}
```

The `for` loop starts with the second elephant and compares it to whatever elephant `biggestEars` points to. If its ears are bigger, it points `biggestEars` at that elephant instead. Then it moves to the next one, then the next one... by the end of the loop `biggestEars` points to the one with the biggest ears.

Iteration #5 biggestEars.EarSize = **44**

Iteration #6 biggestEars.EarSize = **45**

Code Magnets

The code for a button is all scrambled up on the fridge. Can you reconstruct the code snippets to make a working method that produces the output listed below?

```
int y = 0;
```

```
refNum = index[y];
```

```
islands[0] = "Bermuda";
islands[1] = "Fiji";
islands[2] = "Azores";
islands[3] = "Cozumel";
```

```
int refNum;
while (y < 4) {
```

```
result += islands[refNum];
```

```
MessageBox.Show(result);
```

```
index[0] = 1;
index[1] = 3;
index[2] = 0;
index[3] = 2;
```

```
}
```

```
}
```

```
String[] islands = new String[4];
```

```
result += "\nisland = ";
```

```
int[] index = new int[4];
```

```
y = y + 1;
```

```
private void button1_Click (object sender, EventArgs e)
{
```

```
String result = "";
```

```
island = Fiji
island = Cozumel
island = Bermuda
island = Azores

      OK
```

Code Magnets Solution

The code for a button is all scrambled up on the fridge. Can you
reconstruct the code snippets to make a working method that
produces the output listed below?

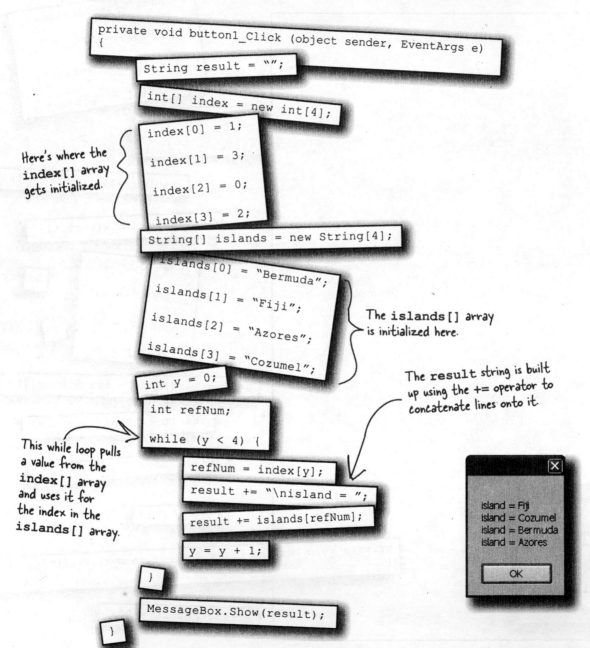

```
private void button1_Click (object sender, EventArgs e)
{
    String result = "";
    int[] index = new int[4];
    index[0] = 1;
    index[1] = 3;
    index[2] = 0;
    index[3] = 2;
    String[] islands = new String[4];
    islands[0] = "Bermuda";
    islands[1] = "Fiji";
    islands[2] = "Azores";
    islands[3] = "Cozumel";
    int y = 0;
    int refNum;
    while (y < 4) {
        refNum = index[y];
        result += "\nisland = ";
        result += islands[refNum];
        y = y + 1;
    }
    MessageBox.Show(result);
}
```

Here's where the **index[]** array gets initialized.

The **islands[]** array is initialized here.

The **result** string is built up using the += operator to concatenate lines onto it.

This while loop pulls a value from the **index[]** array and uses it for the index in the **islands[]** array.

island = Fiji
island = Cozumel
island = Bermuda
island = Azores

OK

Pool Puzzle

Your *job* is to take code snippets from the pool and place them into the blank lines in the code. You **may** use the same snippet more than once, and you won't need to use all the snippets. Your *goal* is to make a class that will compile and run and produce the output listed.

Output

```
triangle 0, area = 4
triangle 1, area = 10
triangle 2, area = 18
triangle 3, area= _____
y = _____

          OK
```

Bonus Question!

For extra bonus points, use snippets from the pool to fill in the two blanks missing from the output.

Note: Each snippet from the pool can be used more than once

```
class Triangle
{
    double area;
    int height;
    int length;
    public static void Main(String[] args)
    {
        string results = "";

        _____

        _____
        while ( _____ )
        {

            _____.height = (x + 1) * 2;
            _____.length = x + 4;

            results += "triangle " + x + ", area";
            results += " = " + _____.area + "\n";

            _____
        }

        _____
        x = 27;
        Triangle t5 = ta[2];
        ta[2].area = 343;
        results += "y = " + y;
        MessageBox.Show(results +
            ", t5 area = " + t5.area);
    }
    void setArea()
    {

        _____ = (height * length) / 2;
    }
}
```

Here's the entry point for the application. Assume it's in a file with the right "using" lines at the top.

Hint: SetArea() is NOT a static method. Flip back to Chapter 3 for a refresher on what the static keyword means.

Pool:

```
                4, t5 area = 18
    area        4, t5 area = 343
    ta.area     27, t5 area = 18        int x;
x   ta.x.area   27, t5 area = 343       int y;        x = x + 1;    ta.x
y   ta[x].area                          int x = 0;    x = x + 2;    ta(x)
                   ta[x] = setArea();   int x = 1;    x = x - 1;    ta[x]     x < 4
Triangle [ ] ta = new Triangle(4);      ta.x = setArea();   int y = x;                      x < 5
Triangle ta = new [ ] Triangle[4];      ta[x].setArea();        28        ta = new Triangle();
Triangle [ ] ta = new Triangle[4];                              30.0      ta[x] = new Triangle();
                                                                          ta.x = new Triangle();
```

Pool Puzzle Solution

Notice how this class contains the entry point, but it also creates an instance of itself? That's completely legal in C#.

```
class Triangle
{
    double area;
    int height;
    int length;
    public static void Main(String[] args)
    {
        string results = "";
        int x = 0;
        Triangle[] ta = new Triangle[4];
        while (  x < 4  )
        {
            ta[x] = new Triangle();
            ta[x].height = (x + 1) * 2;
            ta[x].length = x + 4;
            ta[x].setArea();
            results += "triangle " + x + ", area";
            results += " = " + ta[x].area + "\n";
            x = x + 1;
        }
        int y = x;
        x = 27;
        Triangle t5 = ta[2];
        ta[2].area = 343;
        results += "y = " + y;
        MessageBox.Show(results +
            ", t5 area = " + t5.area);
    }
    void setArea()
    {
        area            = (height * length) / 2;
    }
}
```

After this line, we've got an array of four Triangle references—but there aren't any Triangle objects yet!

The while loop creates the four instances of Triangle by calling the new statement four times.

Bonus Answer

triangle 0, area = 4
triangle 1, area = 10
triangle 2, area = 18
triangle 3, area= 28
y = 4, t5 area = 343

OK

The SetArea() method uses the height and length fields to set the area field. Since it's not a static method, it can only be called from inside an instance of Triangle.

Exercise Solution

There are about 77 **reserved words** in C#. These are words reserved by the C# compiler; you can't use them for variable names. You'll know them all really well by the time you finish the book. Here are some you've already used. Write down what you think these words do in C#.

namespace

Namespaces make sure that the names you are using in your program don't collide with the ones in the .NET Framework or other external classes you've used in your program. All of the classes and methods in a program are inside a namespace.

for

This lets you do a loop that executes three statements. First it declares the variable it's going to use, then there's the statement that evaluates the variable against a condition. The third statement does something to the value.

class

A class is how you define an object. Classes have properties and methods. Properties are what they know and methods are what they do.

public

A public class can be used by every other class in the project. When a variable or method is declared as public, it can be used by classes and called by methods that are outside of the one it's being declared in.

else

Code that starts with else will get executed if the if statement preceding it fails.

new

You use this to create a new instance of an object.

using

This is a way of listing off all of the namespaces you are using in your program. Using lets you use code from the .NET framework and pre-defined classes from third parties as well as classes you can make yourself.

if

One way of setting up a conditional statement in a program. It says if one thing is true, do one thing and if not do something else.

while

while loops are loops that keep on going as long as the condition in them is true.

Typecross Solution

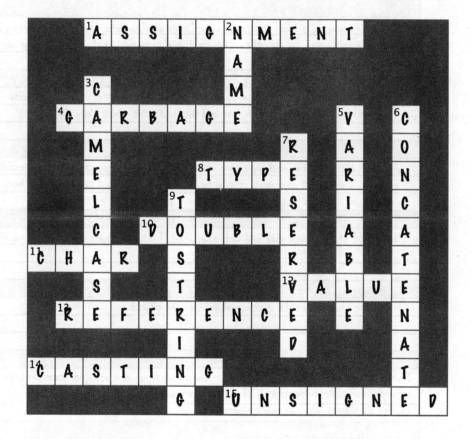

```
      ¹A S S I G N ²N M E N T
                    A
              ³C    M
      ⁴G A R B A G E        ⁵V    ⁶C
        M                ⁷R   A    O
        E            ⁸T Y P E  R   N
        L         ⁹T     S   I   C
        C      ¹⁰D O U B L E  A   A
      ¹¹C H A R S      R   B   T
        S         T     ¹²V A L U E
      ¹³R E F E R E N C E    E   N
              I     D       A
      ¹⁴C A S T I N G           T
              G  ¹⁵U N S I G N E D
```

C# Lab

A Day at the Races

This lab gives you a spec that describes a program for you to build, using the knowledge you've gained over the last few chapters.

This project is bigger than the ones you've seen so far. So read the whole thing before you get started, and give yourself a little time. And don't worry if you get stuck—there's nothing new in here, so you can move on in the book and come back to the lab later.

We've filled in a few design details for you, and we've made sure you've got all the pieces you need... and nothing else.

It's up to you to finish the job. You can download an executable for this lab from the website... but we won't give you the code for the answer.

The Spec: Build a Racetrack Simulator

Joe, Bob, and Al love going to the track, but they're tired of losing all their money. They need you to build a simulator for them so they can figure out winners *before* they lay their money down. And, if you do a good job, they'll cut you in on their profits.

Here's what you're going to build for them...

The Guys

Joe, Bob, and Al want to bet on a dog race. Joe starts with 50 bucks, Bob starts with 75 bucks, and Al starts with 45 bucks. Before each race, they'll each decide if they want to bet, and how much they want to put down. The guys can change their bets right up to the start of the race... but once the race starts, all bets are final.

The Betting Parlor

The betting parlor keeps track of how much cash each guy has, and what bet he's placed. There's a minimum bet of 5 bucks. The parlor only takes one bet per person for any one race.

The parlor checks to make sure that the guy who's betting has enough cash to cover his bet—so the guys can't place a bet if they don't have the cash to cover the bet.

Welcome to Curly's Betting Parlor
Minimum Bet: $5
One bet per person per race
Got enough cash?

Betting

Every bet is double-or-nothing—either the winner doubles his money, or he loses what he bet. There's a minimum bet of 5 bucks, and each guy can bet up to 15 bucks on a single dog. If the dog wins, the bettor ends up with twice the amount that he bets (after the race is complete). If he loses, that amount disappears from his pile.

Say a guy places a $10 bet at the window. At the end of the race, if his dog wins, his cash goes up by $10 (because he keeps the original $10 he bet, plus he gets $10 more from winning). If he loses, his cash goes down by $10.

> **All bets: double-or-nothing**
> **Minimum Bet: $5**
> **Up to $15 per dog**
> **Win: $$ added**
> **Lose: $$ removed**

The Race

There are four dogs that run on a straight track. The winner of the race is the first dog to cross the finish line. The race is totally random, there are no handicaps or odds, and a dog isn't more likely to win his next race based on his past performance.

If you want to build a handicap system, by all means do it! It'll be really good practice writing some fun code.

Sound fun? We've got more details coming up... ⟶

You'll need three classes and a form

You'll build three main classes in the project, as well as a GUI for the simulator. You should have an array of three Guy objects to keep track of the three guys and their winnings, and an array of four Greyhound objects that actually run the race. Also, each instance of Guy should have its own Bet object that keeps track of his bet and pays out (or takes back) cash at the end of the race.

We've gotten you started with class descriptions and some snippets of code to work from. You've got to finish everything up.

> You'll need to add "using System.Windows.Forms" to the top of the Greyhound and Guy classes.

> We've given you the skeleton of the class you need to build. Your job is to fill in the methods.

```
public class Greyhound {
    public int StartingPosition; // Where my PictureBox starts
    public int RacetrackLength; // How long the racetrack is
    public PictureBox MyPictureBox = null; // My PictureBox object
    public int Location = 0; // My Location on the racetrack
    public Random MyRandom; // An instance of Random

    public bool Run() {
        // Move forward either 1, 2, 3 or 4 spaces at random
        // Update the position of my PictureBox on the form
        // Return true if I won the race
    }

    public void TakeStartingPosition() {
        // Reset my location to the start line
    }
}
```

Greyhound

StartingLocation
RacetrackLength
MyPictureBox
Location
MyRandom

Run()
TakeStartingPosition()

> See how the class diagram matches up with the code?

> The Greyhound object initializer is pretty straightforward. Just make sure you pass a reference to the right PictureBox on the form to each Greyhound object.

> We've added comments to give you an idea of what to do.

> Don't overthink this... sometimes you just need to set a variable, and you're done.

Your object can control things on your form...

> You'll have to make sure the form passes the right picturebox into each Greyhound's object initializer.

The Greyhound class keeps track of its position on the racetrack during the race. It also updates the location of the PictureBox representing the dog to move down the race track. Each instance of Greyhound uses a field called MyPictureBox to reference the PictureBox control on the form that shows the picture of the dog. Suppose the distance variable contains the distance to move the dog forward. Then this code will update the location of MyPictureBox by adding distance to its X value:

```
Point p = MyPictureBox.Location;
p.X += distance;
MyPictureBox.Location = p;
```

> You get the current location of the picture...

> ...add the value to move forward to its X coordinate...

> ...and then update the picture box location on the form.

Guy
Name
MyBet
Cash
MyRadioButton
MyLabel
UpdateLabels()
PlaceBet()
ClearBet()
Collect()

```
public class Guy {
    public string Name; // The guy's name
    public Bet MyBet; // An instance of Bet() that has his bet
    public int Cash; // How much cash he has


    // The last two fields are the guy's GUI controls on the form
    public RadioButton MyRadioButton; // My RadioButton
    public Label MyLabel; // My Label

    public void UpdateLabels() {
        // Set my label to my bet's description, and the label on my
        // my radio button to show my cash ("Joe has 43 bucks")
    }

    public void ClearBet() { } // Reset my bet so it's zero

    public bool PlaceBet(int Amount, int Dog) {
        // Place a new bet and store it in my bet field
        // Return true if the guy had enough money to bet
    }

    public void Collect(int Winner) { } // Ask my bet to pay out
}
```

When you intialize the Guy object, make sure you set its MyBet field to null, and call its UpdateLabels() method as soon as it's initialized.

Add your code here.

Remember that bets are represented by instances of Bet.

The key here is to use the Bet object... let it do the work.

This is the object that Guy uses to represent bets in the application.

The object initializer for Bet just sets the amount, dog and bettor.

Bet
Amount
Dog
Bettor
GetDescription
PayOut

```
public class Bet {
    public int Amount; // The amount of cash that was bet
    public int Dog; // The number of the dog the bet is on
    public Guy Bettor; // The guy who placed the bet

    public string GetDescription() {
        // Return a string that says who placed the bet, how much
        // cash was bet, and which dog he bet on ("Joe bets 8 on
        // dog #4"). If the amount is zero, no bet was placed
        // ("Joe hasn't placed a bet").
    }

    public int PayOut(int Winner) {
        // The parameter is the winner of the race. If the dog won,
        // return the amount bet. Otherwise, return the negative of
        // the amount bet.
    }
}
```

Hint: You'll instantiate Bet in the Guy code. Guy willl use the this keyword to pass a reference to himself to the Bet's initializer.

This is a common programming task: assembling a string or message from several individual bits of data.

Here's your application architecture

Spend some time looking closely at the architecture. It looks pretty complicated at first, but there's nothing here you don't know. Your job is to recreate this architecture yourself, starting with the Greyhound and Guy arrays in your main form.

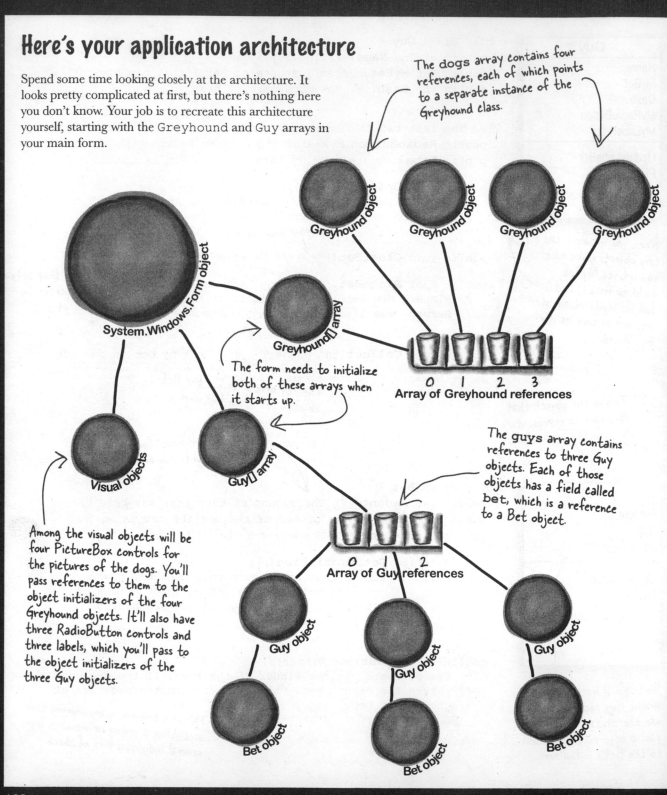

The dogs array contains four references, each of which points to a separate instance of the Greyhound class.

Greyhound object

Greyhound object

Greyhound object

Greyhound object

System.Windows.Form object

Greyhound[] array

The form needs to initialize both of these arrays when it starts up.

0 1 2 3
Array of Greyhound references

Visual objects

Guy[] array

The guys array contains references to three Guy objects. Each of those objects has a field called bet, which is a reference to a Bet object.

0 1 2
Array of Guy references

Among the visual objects will be four PictureBox controls for the pictures of the dogs. You'll pass references to them to the object initializers of the four Greyhound objects. It'll also have three RadioButton controls and three labels, which you'll pass to the object initializers of the three Guy objects.

Guy object

Guy object

Guy object

Bet object

Bet object

Bet object

When a Guy places a bet, he creates a new Bet object

First the form tells Guy #2 to place a bet for 7 bucks on dog #3...

`Guy[1].PlaceBet(7, 3)`

...so Guy #2 creates a new instance of Bet, using the `this` keyword to tell the Bet object that he's the bettor...

`MyBet = new Bet(7, 3, this)`

Form object   Guy object   Bet object

true

...and since the Guy had enough money to place the bet, PlaceBet() returns true.

The form tells the dogs to keep running until there's a winner

When the user tells the form to start the race, the form starts a loop to animate each dog running along the track.

Each dog's Run() method checks to see if that dog won the race, so the loops should end immediately as soon as one of the dog wins.

```
while ( there's no winner ) {
   for ( loop through each dog, making
          sure there's still no winner ) {
       have the dog run one pace
   }
}
```

System.Windows.Form object

Greyhound[] array

The Bet object figures out if it should pay out

The betting parlor in the form tells each Guy which dog won so he can collect any winnings from his bet.

`Guy[1].Collect(winningDog)`   `MyBet.PayOut(winningDog)`

Form object   Guy object   Bet object

The Guy will add the result of Bet.Payout() to his cash. So if the dog won, it should return Amount; otherwise, it'll return -Amount.

```
if ( my dog won ) {
   return Amount;
} else {
   return -Amount;
}
```

169

Here's what your GUI should look like

The graphical user interface for the "Day at the Races" application consists of a form that's divided into two sections. The top is the racetrack: a `PictureBox` control for the track, and four more for the dogs. The bottom half of the form shows the betting parlor, where three guys (Joe, Bob, and Al) can bet on the outcome of the race.

Each of the four dogs has its own PictureBox control. When you initialize each of the four Greyhound objects, each one's MyPicturebox field will have a reference to one of these objects. You'll pass the reference (along with the racetrack length and starting position) to the Greyhound's object initializer.

You'll use the Length property of the racetrack PictureBox control to set the racetrack length in the Greyhound object, which it'll use to figure out if it won the race.

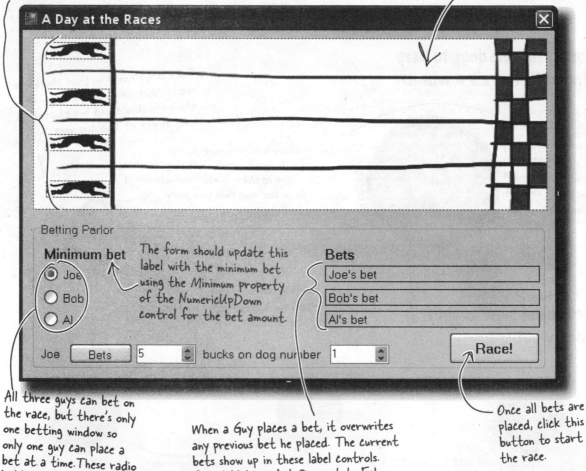

The form should update this label with the minimum bet using the Minimum property of the NumericUpDown control for the bet amount.

All three guys can bet on the race, but there's only one betting window so only one guy can place a bet at a time. These radio buttons are used to select which guy places the bet.

When a Guy places a bet, it overwrites any previous bet he placed. The current bets show up in these label controls. Each lablel has AutoSize set to False and BorderStyle set to FixedSingle.

Once all bets are placed, click this button to start the race.

You can download the graphics files from www.headfirstlabs.com/books/hfcsharp/

Placing bets

Use the controls in the Betting Parlor groupbox to place each guy's bet. There are three distinct stages here:

1. No bets have been placed yet

When the program first starts up, or if a race has just finished, no bets have been placed in the betting parlor. You'll see each guy's total cash next to his name on the left.

When a guy places a bet, his Guy object updates this label using the MyLabel reference. He also updates the cash he has using his MyRadioButton reference.

Each guy's cash shows up here.

2. Each guy places his bets

To place a bet, select the guy's radio button, select an amount and a dog, and click the Bets button. His `PlaceBet()` method will update the label and radio button.

Once Bob places his bet, his Guy object updates this label and the radio button text.

3. After the race, each guy collects his winnings (or pays up!)

Once the race is complete and there's a winner, each Guy object calls his `Collect()` method and adds his winnings or losses to his cash.

Since Al bet 12 bucks on the winning dog, his cash goes up by 12. The other two guys lose the money they bet.

The Finished Product

You'll know your "Day at the Races" application is done when your guys can place their bets and watch the dogs race.

During the race, the four dog images run across the racetrack until one of them wins the race.

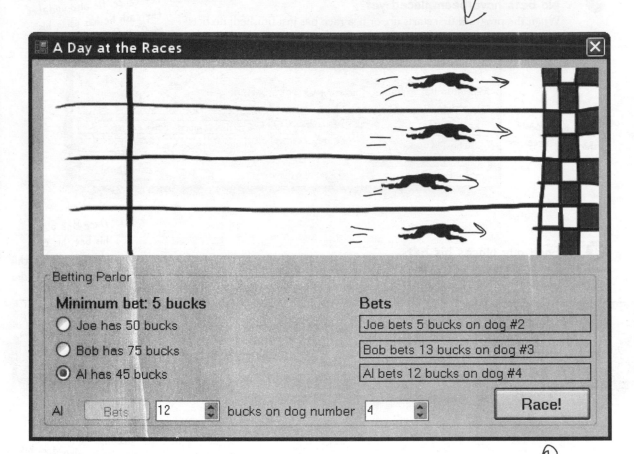

You can download a finished executable, as well as the graphics files for the four dogs and the racetrack, from the Head First labs website: www.headfirstlabs.com/books/hfcsharp

During the race, no bets can be placed... and make sure you can't start a new race while the dogs are running!

But you won't find the source code! In real life, you don't get a solution to your programming problems. Here's your chance to really test your C# knowledge and see just how much you've learned!

5 encapsulation

Keep your privates...
private

No peeking!

Ever wished for a little more privacy?

Sometimes your objects feel the same way. Just like you don't want anybody you don't trust reading your journal or paging through your bank statements, good objects don't let *other* objects go poking around their fields. In this chapter, you're going to learn about the power of **encapsulation**. You'll **make your object's data private**, and add methods to **protect how that data is accessed**.

Kathleen is an event planner

She's been planning dinner parties for
her clients and she's doing really well.
But lately she's been having a hard time
responding to clients fast enough with an
estimate for her services.

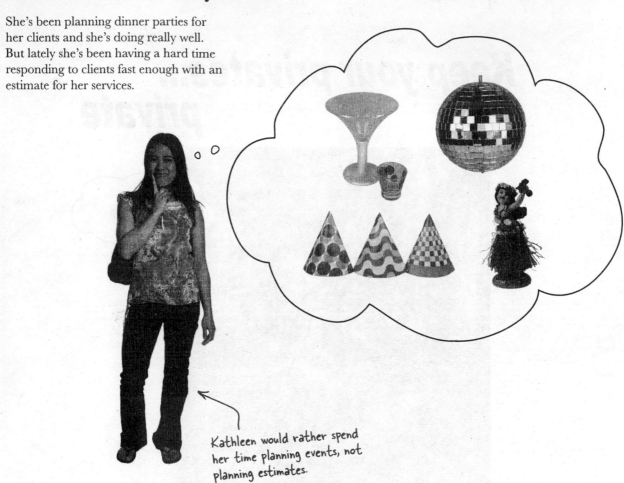

Kathleen would rather spend
her time planning events, not
planning estimates.

When a new client calls Kathleen to do a party, she needs to find
out the number of guests, what kind of drinks to serve, and what
decorations she should buy. Then she uses a pretty complicated
calculation to figure out the total cost, based on a flow chart she's
been using for years. The bad news is that it takes her a long time
to work through her chart, and while she's estimating, her potential
clients are checking out other event planners.

It's up to you to build her a C#-driven event estimator and save
her business. Imagine the party she'll throw you when you succeed!

What does the estimator do?

Kathleen runs down some of the basics of her system
for figuring out the costs of an event. Here's part of
what she came up with:

Kathleen's Party Planning Program—Cost Estimate for a Dinner Party

- For each person on the guest list there's a $25 food charge.

- Clients have a choice when it comes to drinks. Most parties serve alcohol, which costs $20 per person. But they can also choose to have a party without alcohol. Kathleen calls that the "Healthy Option," and it only costs $5 per person to have soda and juice instead of alcohol. Choosing the Healthy Option is a lot easier for her, so she gives the client a 5% discount on the entire party, too.

- There are two options for the cost of decorations. If a client goes with the normal decorations, it's $7.50 per person with a $30 decorating fee. A client can also upgrade the party decorations to the "Fancy Option"—that costs $15 per person with a $50 one-time decorating fee.

Here's another look at this same set of costs, broken
down into a little flow chart to help you see how it works:

Some of these choices involve a change to the final price of the event, as well as individual per-person costs.

While most choices affect the cost for each guest, there are also one-time fees to figure in.

Exercise

Build a program to solve Kathleen's party estimating problem.

1 Create a new Windows Application project and add a class file to it called `DinnerParty.cs`, and build the DinnerParty class using the class diagram to the left. It's got three methods: `CalculateCostOfDecorations()`, `SetHealthyOption()`, and `CalculateCost()`. For the fields, use `decimal` for the two costs, `int` for the number of people, and `bool` to keep track of whether or not the healthy option was selected. Make sure you **add an M after every literal** you assign to a decimal value (`10.0M`).

DinnerParty

NumberOfPeople
CostOfBeveragesPerPerson
CostOfDecorations
HealthyOption

SetHealthyOption()
CalculateCostOfDecorations()
CalculateCost()

Here's the class diagram for the DinnerParty class you'll need to create.

2 Here's a useful C# tool. Since the cost of food won't be changed by the program, you can declare it as a ***constant***, which is like a variable except that its value can never be changed. Here's the declaration to use:

```
public const int CostOfFoodPerPerson = 25;
```

3 Flip back to the previous page to be sure you've got all of the logic right for the methods. Only one of them returns a value (a `decimal`)—the other two are `void`. The `CalculateCostOfDecorations()` method figures out the cost of decorations for the number of people attending the party. Use the `CalculateCost()` method to figure out the total cost by adding up the cost of the decorations to the cost of drinks and food per person. If the client wants the Healthy Option, you can apply the discount inside the `CalculateCost()` method after you've figured out the total cost.

4 Add this code to your form:

```
DinnerParty dinnerParty;
public Form1() {
    InitializeComponent();
    dinnerParty = new DinnerParty() { NumberOfPeople = 5 };
    dinnerParty.SetHealthyOption(false);
    dinnerParty.CalculateCostOfDecorations(true);
    DisplayDinnerPartyCost();
}
```

You'll declare the dinnerParty field in the form, and then add these four lines below InitializeComponent().

The SetHealthyOption() method uses a bool parameter (healthyOption) to update the CostOfBeveragesPerPerson field based on whether or not the client wants the healthy option.

5 Here's what the form should look like. Use the NumericUpDown control's properties to set the maximum number of people to 20, the minimum to 1, and the default to 5. Get rid of the maximize and minimize buttons, too.

Set the default value to 5. The minimum should be 1 and the maximum should be 20.

The Fancy decorations box should have Checked set to true.

You don't need to add "using System.Windows.Forms;" to your DinnerParty class, because it doesn't use MessageBox.Show(), Point, or anything else from that .NET Framework namespace.

Party Planner

Number of People
5

☑ Fancy decorations
☐ Healthy Option

Cost $

This is just a label with the Text Property set to "", the BorderStyle property set to Fixed3D, and the AutoSize property set to false.

6 Instead of using a button to calculate the costs, this form will update the cost label automatically as soon as you use a checkbox or the NumericUpDown control. The first thing you need to do is create a method in the form that displays the cost.

This method will get called by all of the other methods you create on the form. It's how you update the cost label with the right value whenever anything changes.

Add this method to Form1(). It'll get called when the NumericUpDown control is clicked:

```
private void DisplayDinnerPartyCost()
{
    decimal Cost = dinnerParty.CalculateCost(checkBox2.Checked);
    costLabel.Text = Cost.ToString("c");
}
```

Add this method to the form—it'll recalculate the cost of the party and put it in the Cost label.

This is true if the checkbox for the Healthy Option is checked.

Change the name of the lablel that displays the cost to costLabel.

Passing "c" to ToString() tells it to format the cost as a currency value. If you're in a country that uses dollars, it'll add a dollar sign.

When you double-click on a button in the IDE to add code that gets run when the button is clicked, that's an event handler too.

7 Now hook up the NumericUpDown field to the NumberOfPeople variable you created in the DinnerParty class and display the cost in the form. Double-click on the NumericUpDown control—the IDE will add an *event handler* to your code. That's a method that gets run every time the control is changed. It'll reset the number of people in the party. Fill it in like this:

```
private void numericUpDown1_ValueChanged(
                            object sender, EventArgs e)
{
    dinnerParty.NumberOfPeople = (int) numericUpDown1.Value;
    DisplayDinnerPartyCost();
}
```

You need to cast numericUpDown.Value to an int because it's a Decimal property.

Uh-oh—there's a problem with this code. Can you spot it? Don't worry if you don't see it just yet. We'll dig into it in just a couple of minutes!

The value you send from the form to the method will be fancyBox.Checked. That will be passed as a boolean parameter to the method in the class.

These are just two-line methods. The first line will call the method you created in the class to figure out the costs and the second will display the total cost on the form.

8 Double-click on the Fancy Decorations checkbox on the form and make sure that it first calls CalculateCostOfDecorations(), and then DisplayDinnerPartyCost(). Next, double-click the Healthy Option checkbox and make sure that it calls the SetHealthyOption() method in the DinnerParty class and then calls the DisplayDinnerPartyCost() method.

Exercise Solution

Here's the code that goes into DinnerParty.cs.

Using a constant for CostOfFoodPerPerson ensures the value can't be changed. It also makes the code easier to read—it's clear that this value never changes.

When the form first creates the object, it uses the initializer to set NumberOfPeople. Then it calls SetHealthyOption() and CalculateCostOfDecorations() to set the other fields.

```csharp
public class DinnerParty {
    const int CostOfFoodPerPerson = 25;
    public int NumberOfPeople;
    public decimal CostOfBeveragesPerPerson;
    public decimal CostOfDecorations = 0;

    public void SetHealthyOption(bool healthyOption) {
        if (healthyOption) {
            CostOfBeveragesPerPerson = 5.00M;
        } else {
            CostOfBeveragesPerPerson = 20.00M;
        }
    }

    public void CalculateCostOfDecorations(bool fancy) {
        if (fancy)
        {
            CostOfDecorations = (NumberOfPeople * 15.00M) + 50M;
        } else {
            CostOfDecorations = (NumberOfPeople * 7.50M) + 30M;
        }
    }

    public decimal CalculateCost(bool healthyOption) {
        decimal totalCost = CostOfDecorations +
                ((CostOfBeveragesPerPerson + CostOfFoodPerPerson)
                    * NumberOfPeople);

        if (healthyOption) {
            return totalCost * .95M;
        } else {
            return totalCost;
        }
    }
}
```

We used "if (Fancy)" instead of typing "if (Fancy == true)" because the if statement always checks if the condition is true.

We used parentheses to make sure the math works out properly.

This applies the 5% discount to the overall event cost if the non-alcoholic option was chosen.

We had you use a `decimal` for the prices because it's designed for monetary values. Just make sure you always put an "M" after every literal—so if you want to store $35.26, make sure you write `35.26M`.

```
public partial class Form1 : Form {
    DinnerParty dinnerParty;
    public Form1() {
        InitializeComponent();
        dinnerParty = new DinnerParty() { NumberOfPeople = 5 };
        dinnerParty.CalculateCostOfDecorations(fancyBox.Checked);
        dinnerParty.SetHealthyOption(healthyBox.Checked);
        DisplayDinnerPartyCost();
    }

    private void fancyBox_CheckedChanged(object sender, EventArgs e) {
        dinnerParty.CalculateCostOfDecorations(fancyBox.Checked);
        DisplayDinnerPartyCost();
    }

    private void healthyBox_CheckedChanged(object sender, EventArgs e) {
        dinnerParty.SetHealthyOption(healthyBox.Checked);
        DisplayDinnerPartyCost();
    }

    private void numericUpDown1_ValueChanged(object sender, EventArgs e) {
        dinnerParty.NumberOfPeople = (int)numericUpDown1.Value;
        DisplayDinnerPartyCost();
    }

    private void DisplayDinnerPartyCost() {
        decimal Cost = dinnerParty.CalculateCost(healthyBox.Checked);
        costLabel.Text = Cost.ToString("c");
    }
}
```

We call DisplayDinnerPartyCost to initialize the label that shows the cost as soon as the form's loaded.

Changes to the checkboxes on the form set the healthyOption and Fancy booleans to true or false in the SetHealthyOption() and CalculateCostOfDecorations() methods.

We named our checkboxes "healthyBox" and "fancyBox" so you could see what's going on in their event handler methods.

The new dinner party cost needs to be recalculated and displayed any time the number changes or the checkboxes are checked.

String formatting

You've already seen how you can convert any variable to a string using its ToString() method. If you pass "c" to ToString(), it converts it to the local currency. You can also pass it "f3" to format it with as a decimal number with three decimal places, "0" (that's a zero) to convert to a whole number, "0%" for a whole number percentage, and "n" to display it as a number with a comma separator for thousands. Take a minute and see how each of these looks in your program!

Kathleen's Test Drive

This rocks! Estimating is about to get a whole lot easier.

Rob's one of Kathleen's favorite clients. She did his wedding last year, and now she's planning an important dinner party for him.

Rob (on phone): Hi Kathleen. How are the arrangements for my dinner party going?

Kathleen: Just great. We were out looking at decorations this morning and I think you'll love the way the party's going to look.

Rob: That's awesome. Listen, we just got a call from my wife's aunt. She and her husband are going to be visiting for the next couple of weeks. Can you tell me what it does to the estimate to move from 10 to 12 people on the guest list?

Kathleen: Sure! I'll have that for you in just one minute.

Changing the Number of People value from 10 to 12 and hitting enter shows $665 as the total cost. Hmm, that seems a little low...

Kathleen: OK. It looks like the total cost for the dinner will go from $575 to $665.

Rob: Only $90 difference? That sounds like a great deal! What if we decide to cut the fancy decorations? What's the cost then?

Turning off the Fancy Decorations checkbox only reduces the amount by $5. That can't be right!

Kathleen: Um, it looks like... um, $660.

Rob: $660? I thought the decorations were $15 per person. Did you change your pricing or something? If it's only $5 difference, we might as well go with the Fancy Decorations. I've gotta tell you though, this pricing is confusing.

Kathleen: We just had this new program written to do the estimation for us. But it looks like there might be a problem. Just one second while I add the fancy decorations back to the bill.

When you turn the Fancy Decorations back on, the number shoots up to $770. These numbers are just <u>wrong</u>.

Kathleen: Rob, I think there's been a mistake. It looks like the cost with the fancy decorations just shot up to $770. That does seem to make more sense. But I am beginning not to trust this application. I'm going to send it back for some bug fixes and work up your estimate by hand. Can I get back to you tomorrow?

Rob: I am not paying $770 just to add two people to the party. The price you quoted me before was a lot more reasonable. I'll pay you the $665 you quoted me in the first place, but I just can't go higher than that!

Why do you think the numbers are coming out wrong every time Kathleen makes a change?

Each option should be calculated <u>individually</u>

Even though we made sure to calculate all of the amounts according to what Kathleen said, we didn't think about what would happen when people made changes to just one of the options on the form.

When you launch the program, the form sets the number of people to 5 and Fancy Decorations to true. It leaves Healthy Option unchecked and it calculates the cost of the dinner party as $350. Here's how it comes up with the initial total cost:

Don't worry! This one wasn't your fault.

We built a nasty little bug into the code we gave you to show you just how easy it is to have problems with how objects use each others' fields... and just how hard those problems are to spot.

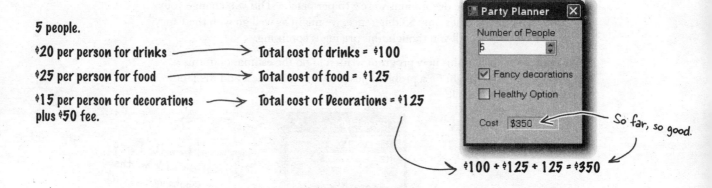

5 people.

$20 per person for drinks ⟶ Total cost of drinks = $100

$25 per person for food ⟶ Total cost of food = $125

$15 per person for decorations plus $50 fee. ⟶ Total cost of Decorations = $125

So far, so good.

$100 + $125 + 125 = $350

When you change the number of guests, the application should recalculate the total estimate the same way. But it doesn't:

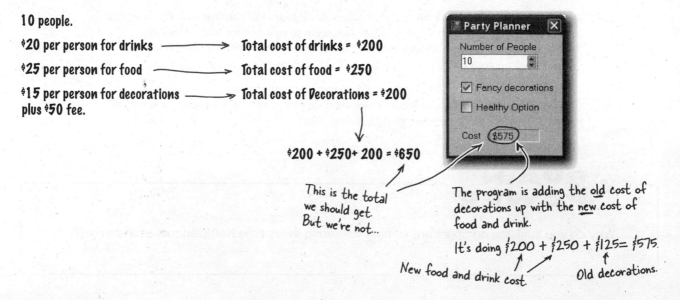

10 people.

$20 per person for drinks ⟶ Total cost of drinks = $200

$25 per person for food ⟶ Total cost of food = $250

$15 per person for decorations plus $50 fee. ⟶ Total cost of Decorations = $200

$200 + $250 + 200 = $650

This is the total we should get. But we're not...

The program is adding the <u>old</u> cost of decorations up with the <u>new</u> cost of food and drink.

It's doing $200 + $250 + $125 = $575.

New food and drink cost.   Old decorations.

The Problem Up

Take a look at the method that handles changes to the value in the `numericUpDown` control. It sets the value from the field to the `NumberofPeople` variable and then calls the `DisplayDinnerPartyCost()` method. Then it counts on that method to handle recalculating all the individual new costs.

```
private void numericUpDown1_ValueChanged(
                        object sender, EventArgs e) {
    dinnerParty.NumberOfPeople = (int)numericUpDown1.Value;
    DisplayDinnerPartyCost();
}
```

This line sets the value of NumberofPeople in this instance of DinnerParty to the value in the form.

This method calls the CalculateCost() method, but not the CalculateCostofDecorations() method.

So, when you make a change to the value in the NumberofPeople field, this method never gets called:

```
public void CalculateCostOfDecorations(bool Fancy) {
    if (Fancy) {
        CostOfDecorations = (NumberOfPeople * 15.00M) + 50M;
    } else {
        CostOfDecorations = (NumberOfPeople * 7.50M) + 30M;
    }
}
```

This variable is set to $125 from when the form first called it and, since this method doesn't get called again, it doesn't change.

That's why the number corrects itself when you turn fancy decorations back on. Clicking the checkbox makes the program run CalculateCostOf Decorations() again.

> Hold on! I assumed Kathleen would always set all three options at once!

People won't always use your programs in exactly the way you expect.

Luckily, C# gives you a powerful tool to make sure your program always works correctly—even when people do things you never thought of. It's called **encapsulation** and it's a really helpful technique for working with objects.

It's easy to accidentally misuse your objects

Kathleen ran into problems because her form ignored the
convenient `CalculateCostOfDecorations()` method that
you set up and instead went directly to the fields in the DinnerParty
class. So even though your DinnerParty class worked just fine, the
form called it in an unexpected way... and that caused problems.

① How the DinnerParty class expected to be called
The DinnerParty class gave the form a perfectly good method to calculate the
total cost of decorations. All it had to do was set the number of people and then
call `CalculateCostOfDecorations()`, and then `CalculateCost()`
will return the correct cost.

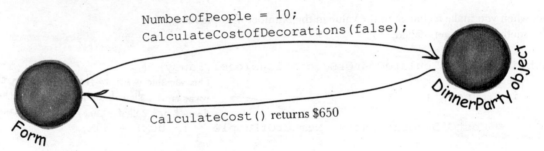

```
NumberOfPeople = 10;
CalculateCostOfDecorations(false);
```

`CalculateCost()` returns $650

② How the DinnerParty class was actually called
The form set the number of people, but just called the `CalculateCost()`
method without first recalculating the cost of the decorations. That threw off
the whole calculation, and Kathleen ended up giving Rob the wrong price.

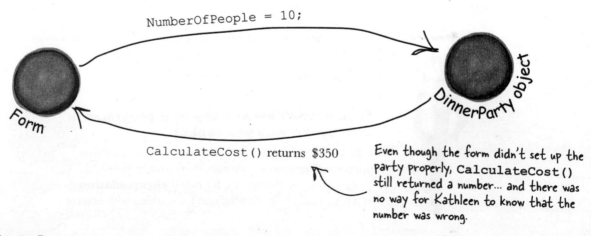

```
NumberOfPeople = 10;
```

`CalculateCost()` returns $350

Even though the form didn't set up the
party properly, `CalculateCost()`
still returned a number... and there was
no way for Kathleen to know that the
number was wrong.

Encapsulation means keeping some of the data in a class private

There's an easy way to avoid this kind of problem: make sure that there's only one way to use your class. Luckily, C# makes it easy to do that by letting you declare some of your fields as **private**. So far, you've only seen public fields. If you've got an object with a public field, any other object can read or change that field. But if you make it a private field, then **that field can only be accessed from inside that object** (or by another object *of the same class*).

Use your laziness to your own benefit—if you leave off the "private" or "public", then C# will just assume that your field is private.

```
public class DinnerParty {

    private int numberOfPeople;
```

If you want to make a field private, all you need to do is use the private keyword when you declare it. That tells C# that if you've got an instance of DinnerParty, its numberOfPeople field can only be read and written by that instance. Other objects won't even know it's there.

```
    ...

    public void SetPartyOptions(int people, bool fancy) {

        numberOfPeople = people;

        CalculateCostOfDecorations(fancy);

    }

    public void GetNumberOfPeople() {

        return numberOfPeople;

    }
```

Other objects still need a way to set the number of people for the dinner party. One good way to give them access to it is to add methods to set or get the number of people. That way you can make sure that the CalculateCostOfDecorations() method gets run every time the number of people is changed. That'll take care of that pesky bug.

By making the field that holds the number of party guests *private*, we only give the form one way to tell the DinnerParty class how many people are at the party—and we can make sure the cost of decorations is recalculated properly. When you make some data private and then write code to use that data, it's called *encapsulation*.

en-cap-su-la-ted, adj.
enclosed by a protective coating or membrane. *The divers were fully* **encapsulated** *by their submersible, and could only enter and exit through the airlock.*

Use encapsulation to control access to your class's methods and fields

When you make all of your fields and methods public, any other class can access them. Everything your class does and knows about becomes an open book for every other class in your program... and you just saw how that can cause your program to behave in ways you never expected. Encapsulation lets you control what you share and what you keep private inside your class. Let's see how this works:

SecretAgent
Alias
RealName
Password
AgentGreeting()

1 Super-spy Herb Jones is defending life, liberty, and the pursuit of happiness as an undercover agent in the USSR. His ciaAgent object is an instance of the SecretAgent class.

ciaAgent

```
RealName: "Herb Jones"
Alias: "Dash Martin"
Password: "the crow flies at midnight"
```

EnemyAgent
Borscht
Vodka
ContactComarades()
OverthrowCapitalists()

2 Agent Jones has a plan to help him evade the enemy KGB agents. He added an `AgentGreeting()` method that takes a password as its parameter. If he doesn't get the right password, he'll only reveal his alias, Dash Martin.

3 Seems like a foolproof way to protect the agent's identity, right? As long as the agent object that calls it doesn't have a the right password, the agent's name is safe.

The ciaAgent object is an instance of the SecretAgent class, while kgbAgent is an instance of EnemyAgent.

AgentGreeting("the jeep is parked outside")

The KGB agent uses the wrong password in his greeting.

"Dash Martin"

The KGB only gets the alias of the CIA agent. Perfect. Right?

kgbAgent

ciaAgent

But is the realName field __REALLY__ protected?

So as long as the KGB doesn't know any CIA agent passwords, the CIA's real names are safe. Right? But what about the field declaration for the realName field:

Setting your variables public means they can be accessed, and even changed, from outside the class.

→ `public string RealName;`

He left the field public... Why go through all of the trouble to guess his password? I can just get his name directly!

Setting your variables as public means they can be accessed, and even changed, from outside the class.

`string name = ciaAgent.RealName;`

kgbAgent

ciaAgent

There's no need to call any method. The realName field is wide open for everyone to see!

Agent Jones can use **private** fields to keep the his identity secret from enemy spy objects. Once he declares the realName field as private, the only way to get to it is ***by calling methods that have access to the private parts of the class***. So the KGB agent is foiled!

The kgbAgent object can't access the ciaAgent's private fields because they're instances of different classes.

Just replace public with private, and boom, your fields are now hidden from the world.

→ **private string realName;**

You'd also want to make sure that the field that stores the password is private, otherwise the enemy agent can get to it.

Keeping your fields and methods private makes sure no outside code is going to make changes to the values you're using when you don't expect it.

Private fields and methods can only be accessed from inside the class

There's only one way that an object can get at the data stored inside another object's private fields: by using the public fields and methods that return the data. But while KGB and MI5 agents need to use the AgentGreeting() method, friendly spies can see everything—any class can **see private fields in other instances of the same class**.

Now that the fields are private, this is pretty much the only way the mi5Agent can get the ciaAgent's real name.

mi5gent is an instance of the BritishAgent class, so it doesn't have access to ciaAgent's private fields either.

Only another ciaAgent object can see them.

`AgentGreeting("the crow flies at midnight")`

`"Herb Jones"`

mi5Agent

ciaAgent

there are no Dumb Questions

Q: Okay, so I need to access private data through public methods. But what happens if the class with the private field doesn't give me a way to get at that data, but my object needs to use it?

A: Then you can't access the data from outside the object. When you're writing a class, you should always make sure that you give other objects some way to get at the data they need. Private fields are a very important part of encapsulation, but they're only part of the story. Writing a class with good encapsulation means giving a sensible, easy-to-use way for other objects to get the data they need, without giving them access to hijack data your class needs.

Q: Why would I ever want to keep a field with no way for another class to access?

A: Sometimes a class needs to keep track of information that is necessary for it to operate, but which no other object really needs to see. Here's an example. When computers generate random numbers, they use special values called *seeds*. You don't need to know how they work, but every instance of

`Random` actually contains an array of several dozen numbers that it uses to make sure that `Next()` always gives you a random number. If you create an instance of `Random`, you won't be able to see that array. That's because you don't need it—but if you had access to it, you might be able to put values in it that would cause it to give non-random values. So the seeds have been completely encapsulated from you.

Q: Hey, I just noticed that all of the event handlers I've been using have the **private** keyword. Why are they private?

A: Because C# forms are set up so that only the controls on the forms can trigger event handlers. When you put the `private` keyword in front of any method, then that method can only be used from inside your class. When the IDE adds an event handler method to your program, it declares it as private so other forms or objects can't get to it. But there's no rule that says that an event handler must be private. In fact, you can check this out for yourself—double-click on a button, then change its event handler declaration to `public`. The code will still compile and run.

> **The only way that one object can get to data stored in a private field inside another object is by using public methods that return the data.**

Sharpen your pencil

Here's a class with some private fields. Circle the statements below that **won't compile** if they're run from outside the class using **an instance of the object called mySuperChef**.

```
public class SuperChef
{
      public string cookieRecipe;
      private string secretIngredient;
      private const int loyalCustomerOrderAmount = 60;
      public int Temperature;
      private string ingredientSupplier;

      public string GetRecipe (int orderAmount)
      {
            if (orderAmount >= loyalCustomerOrderAmount)
            {
                  return cookieRecipe + " " + secretIngredient;
            }
            else
            {
                  return cookieRecipe;
            }
      }
}
```

string

Int value

1. string ovenTemp = mySuperChef.Temperature;

2. string supplier = mySuperChef.ingredientSupplier;

3. int loyalCustomerOrderAmount = 94;

4. mySuperChef.secretIngredient = "cardamom";

5. mySuperChef.cookieRecipe = "get 3 eggs, 2 1/2 cup flour, 1 tsp salt, 1 tsp vanilla and 1.5 cups sugar and mix them together. Bake for 10 minutes at 375. Yum!";

6. string recipe = mySuperChef.GetRecipe(56);

7. After running all of the lines that will compile above, what's the value of recipe?

....

....

Sharpen your pencil
Solution

Here's a class with some private fields. Circle the statements below that **won't compile** if they're run from outside the class using **an instance of the object called mySuperChef**.

```
public class SuperChef
{
        public string cookieRecipe;
        private string secretIngredient;
        private const int loyalCustomerOrderAmount = 60;
        public int Temperature;
        private string ingredientSupplier;

        public string GetRecipe (int orderAmount)
        {
                if (orderAmount >= loyalCustomerOrderAmount)
                {
                        return cookieRecipe + " " + secretIngredient;
                }
                else
                {
                        return cookieRecipe;
                }
        }
}
```

(circled: const) This is a private constant. Its value can't be changed, and it can't be accessed outside of this class.

The only way to get the secret ingredient is to order a whole lot of cookies. Outside code can't access this field directly.

1. `string ovenTemp = mySuperChef.Temperature;`   #1 doesn't compile because you can't just assign an int to a string.

2. `string supplier = mySuperChef.ingredientSupplier;`

3. `int loyalCustomerOrderAmount = 94;`

#2 and #4 don't compile because ingredientSupplier and secretIngredient are private.

4. `mySuperChef.secretIngredient = "cardamom";`

5. `mySuperChef.cookieRecipe = "get 3 eggs, 2 1/2 cup flour, 1 tsp salt, 1 tsp vanilla and 1.5 cups sugar and mix them together. Bake for 10 minutes at 375. Yum!";`

6. `string recipe = mySuperChef.GetRecipe(56);`

7. After running all of the lines that will compile above, what's the value of recipe?

"Get 3 eggs, 2 1/2 cup flour, 1 tsp salt, 1 tsp vanilla and 1.5 cups sugar and mix them together. Bake for 10 minutes at 375. Yum!"

A few ideas for encapsulating classes

✦ Think about ways the fields can be misused.
What can go wrong if they're not set properly?

✦ Is everything in your class public?
If your class has nothing but public fields and methods, you probably need to spend a little more time thinking about encapsulation.

✦ What fields require some processing or calculation to happen when they're set?
Those are prime candidates for encapsulation. If someone writes a method later that changes the value in any one of them, it could cause problems for the work your program is trying to do.

> The cost of decorations needs to be figured out first. Once you know that, you can just add it up with the cost of the food and drink to get the total cost.

✦ Only make fields and methods public if you need to.
If you don't have a reason to declare something public, don't. You could make things really messy for yourself by making all of the fields in your program public—but don't just go making everything private, either. Spending a little time up front thinking about which fields really need to be public and which don't can save you a lot of time later.

Encapsulation keeps your data pristine

Sometimes the value in a field changes as your program does
what it's supposed to do. If you don't explicitly tell your program
to reset the value, you can do your calculations using the old
one. When this is the case, you want to have your program
execute some statements any time a field is changed—like
having Kathleen's program recalculate the cost every time
you change the number of people. We can avoid the problem
by encapsulating the data using private fields. We'll provide a
method to get the value of the field, and another method to set
the field and do all the necessary calculations.

A quick example of encapsulation

A Farmer class uses a field to store the number of cows, and
multiplies it by a number to figure out how many bags of cattle
feed are needed to feed the cows:

```
class Farmer
{
        private int numberOfCows;

}
```

> We'd better make this field private
> so nobody can change it without also
> changing bagsOfFeed—if they get
> out of sync, that'll create bugs!

When you create a form to let a user enter the number of cows into a numeric field,
you need to be able to change the value in the numberOfCows field. To do that, you
can create a method that returns the value of the field to the form object.

```
public int GetNumberOfCows()
{
        return numberOfCows;
}

public void SetNumberOfCows(int newNumberOfCows)
{
        numberOfCows = newNumberOfCows;
        BagsOfFeed = numberOfCows * FeedMultiplier;
}
```

> We'll add a method to give
> other classes a way to get
> the number of cows.

> These accomplish the same thing!

> We used camelCase for the private fields
> and PascalCase for the public ones.

> And here's a method to set the
> number of cows that makes sure
> the BagsOfFeed field is changed
> too. Now there's no way for the
> two to get out of sync.

Properties make encapsulation easier

C# has special kinds of methods that make it easy to encapsulate your data. You can use **properties**, methods that are executed every time a field is called to set or return the value of the field, which is called a **backing field**.

We'll rename the private field to numberOfCows (notice the lowercase "n"). This will become the backing field for the NumberOfCows property.

```
private int numberOfCows;
```

You use properties by combining them with a normal field declaration. Here's the declaration for NumberOfCows.

```
public int NumberOfCows
{
```

This is a get accessor. It's a method that's run any time the NumberOfCows field is read. It has a return value that matches the type of the variable—in this case it returns the value of the private numberOfCows field.

```
    get
    {
        return numberOfCows;
    }
```

This is a set accessor that's called every time the NumberOfCows field is set. Even though the method doesn't look like it has any parameters, it actually has one called value that contains whatever value the field was set to.

```
    set
    {
        numberOfCows = value;
        BagsOfFeed = numberOfCows * FeedMultiplier;
    }
}
```

You *use* get and set accessors exactly like fields. Here's code for a button that sets the numbers of cows and then gets the bags of feed:

```
private void button1_Click(object sender, EventArgs e) {
    Farmer myFarmer = new Farmer();
    myFarmer.NumberOfCows = 10;

    int howManyBags = myFarmer.BagsOfFeed;

    myFarmer.NumberOfCows = 20;
    howManyBags = myFarmer.BagsOfFeed;
}
```

When this line sets NumberOfCows to 10, the set accessor sets the private numberOfCows field and then updates the public BagsOfFeed field.

Since the NumberOfCows set accessor updated BagsOfFeed, now you can get its value.

Even though the code treats NumberOfCows like a field, it runs the set accessor, passing it 20. And when it queries the BagsOfFeed field it runs the get accessor, which returns 300.

Build an application to test the Farmer class

Create a new Windows Forms application that we can use to test the Farmer class and see properties in action. We'll use the **Console.WriteLine()** method to write the results to the output window in the IDE.

—Do this ✷

1 Add the Farmer class to your project:

```
public class Farmer {
    public int BagsOfFeed;
    public const int FeedMultiplier = 30;

    private int numberOfCows;
    public int NumberOfCows {
        (add the get and set accessors from the previous page)
    }
}
```

2 Build this form:

Name this button Calculate—it uses the public Farmer data to write a line to the output.

Set the NumericUpDown control's Value to 15, its Minimum to 5, and its Maximum to 300.

3 Here's the form for the code. It uses Console.WriteLine() to send its output to the Output window (which you can bring up by selecting "Output" from the View menu). You can pass several parameters to WriteLine()—the first one is the string to write. If you include "{0}" inside the string, then WriteLine() replaces it with the first parameter. It replaces "{1}" with the second parameter, "{2}" with the third, etc.

```
public partial class Form1 : Form {
    Farmer farmer;
    public Form1() {
        InitializeComponent();
        farmer = new Farmer() { NumberOfCows = 15 };
    }
    private void numericUpDown1_ValueChanged(object sender, EventArgs e) {
        farmer.NumberOfCows = (int)numericUpDown1.Value;
    }
    private void calculate_Click(object sender, EventArgs e) {
        Console.WriteLine("I need {0} bags of feed for {1} cows",
            farmer.BagsOfFeed, farmer.NumberOfCows);
    }
}
```

Use the Console.WriteLine() method to send a line of text to the IDE's Output window.

WriteLine() replaces "{0}" with value in the first parameter, and "{1}" with the second parameter.

Use automatic properties to finish the class

It looks like the Cow Calculator works really well. Give it a shot—run it and click the button. Then change the number of cows to 30 and click it again. Do the same for 5 cows and then 20 cows. Here's what your Output window should look like:

But there's a problem with the class. Add a button the form that executes this statement:

```
farmer.BagsOfFeed = 5;
```

Now run your program again. It works fine until you press the new button. But press that button and then press the Calculate button again. Now your ouput tells you that you need 5 bags of feed—<u>no matter how many cows you have</u>!

Fully encapsulate the Farmer class

The problem is that your class **isn't fully encapsulated**. You used properties to encapsulate NumberOfCows, but BagsOfFeed is still public. This is a common problem. In fact, it's so common that C# has a way of automatically fixing it. Just change the public BagsOfFeed field to an ***automatic property***. And the IDE makes it really easy for you to add automatic properties. Here's how:

Watch it!

Automatic properties are a C# 3.0 feature.

*If you're still using Visual Studio 2005 and C# 2.0, this code won't work. We highly recommend that you use Visual Studio 2008 Express. You can download it for **free**!*

> The prop-tab-tab code snippet adds an automatic property to your code.

① Remove the BagsOfFeed field from the Farmer class. Put your cursor where the field used to be, and then type **prop** and press the tab key twice. The IDE will add this line to your code:

```
public int MyProperty { get; set; }
```

② Press the tab key—the cursor jumps to MyProperty. Change its name to BagsOfFeed:

```
public int BagsOfFeed { get; set; }
```

Now you've got a property instead of a field. When C# sees this, it works exactly the same as if you used a backing field (like the private numberOfCows behind the public NumberOfCows property).

③ That hasn't fixed our problem yet. But there's an easy fix—just make it a **read-only property**:

```
public int BagsOfFeed { get; private set; }
```

Try to rebuild your code—you'll get an error on the line in the button that sets BagsOfFeed telling you that the **set accessor is private**. Now your Farmer class is better encapsulated!

What if we want to change the feed multiplier?

We built the Cow Calculator to use a `const` for the feed multiplier. But what if we want
to use the same Farmer class in different programs that need different feed multipliers?
You've seen how you poor encapsulation can cause problems when you make fields
in one class too accessible to other classes. That's why you should **only make fields
and methods public if you need to**. Since the Cow Calculator never updates
FeedMultiplier, there's no need to allow any other class to set it. So let's change it
to a read-only automatic property.

Do this!

1 Remove this line from your program:

```
public const int FeedMultiplier = 30;
```

Use `prop-tab-tab` to add a read-only automatic property:

```
public int FeedMultiplier { get; private set; }
```

2 Go ahead and make that change to your code. Then run it. Uh-oh—something's wrong!
BagsOfFeed **always returns 0 bags**!

Wait, that make sense. FeedMultiplier never got initialized. It starts out with the
default value of zero and never changes. When it's multiplied by the number of cows, it still
gives you zero. So add an object initializer:

```
public Form1() {
    InitializeComponent();
    farmer = new Farmer() { NumberOfCows = 15, FeedMultiplier = 30 };
```

Uh-oh—the program won't compile! You should get this error:

**You can only initialize <u>public</u> fields and properties inside an object initializer.
So how can you make sure your object gets initialized properly if some of
the fields that need to be initialized are <u>private</u>?**

Use a <u>constructor</u> to initialize private fields

If you need to initialize your object, but some of the fields that need to be initialized are private then an object initializer just won't do. Luckily, there's a special method that you can add to any class called a **constructor**. If a class has a constructor, then that constructor is the **very first thing that gets run** when the class is created with the new statement. You can pass parameters to the constructor to give it values that need to be initialized. But the constructor **does not have a return value**, because you don't actually call it directly. You pass its parameters to the new statement. And you already know that new returns the object—so there's no way for a constructor to return anything.

All you have to do to add a constructor to a class is add a method that has the same name as the class and no return value.

① **Add a constructor to your Farmer class**

This constructor only has two lines, but there's a lot going on here. So let's take it step by step. We already know that we need the number of cows and a feed multiplier for the class, so we'll add them as parameters to the constructor. Then we'll set the two properties.

Notice how there's no "void" or "int" or another type after "public". That's because constructors don't have a return value.

```
public Farmer(int numberOfCows, int feedMultiplier) {

    FeedMultiplier = feedMultiplier;

    this.NumberOfCows = numberOfCows;

}
```

The first thing we'll do is set the feed multiplier, because it needs to be set before we can call the NumberOfCows set accessor.

If we just set the private numberOfCows field, the NumberOfCows set accessor would never be called. Setting this.NumberOfCows makes sure it's called.

This is the error you'll get if your constructor takes parameters but your new() doesn't have any.

Error List   ✕

⊗ 1 Error	⚠ 0 Warnings	ⓘ 0 Messages			
	Description		File	Line	Column
⊗ 1	'__Cow_Calculator.Farmer' does not contain a constructor that takes '0' arguments		Form1.cs	18	22

② **Now change the form so that it uses the constructor**

The only thing you need to do now is change the form so that the new statement that creates the Farmer object uses the constructor instead of an object initializer.

```
public Form1() {

    InitializeComponent();

    farmer = new Farmer(15, 30);

}
```

Here's where the new statement calls the constructor. It looks just like any other new statement, except that it has parameters that it passes into the constructor method. When you type it in, watch for the IntelliSense pop-up—it looks just like any other method.

You already know that the form is an object. Well, it's got a constructor too! That's what this method is—notice how it's named Form1 (like the class) and it doesn't have a return value.

constructors deconstructed

Constructors Way Up Close

Let's take a closer look at the Farmer constructor so we can get a good sense of what's really going on.

Constructors don't return anything, so there's no return type.

This constructor has two parameters, which work just like ordinary parameters. The first one gives the number of cows, and the second one is the feed multiplier.

```
public Farmer(int numberOfCows, int feedMultiplier) {

    FeedMultiplier = feedMultiplier;

    this.NumberOfCows = numberOfCows;

}
```

We need to set the feed multiplier first, because the second statement calls the NumberOfCows set accessor, which needs FeedMultiplier to have a value in order to set BagsOfFeed.

You'll often see the this keyword a constructor. By calling this.NumberOfCows, we're telling C# to set the NumberOfCows property using its public set accessor.

If you leave off "this." then C# will call the private set accessor instead. Give it a shot—remove "this." and see for yourself.

there are no Dumb Questions

Q: Is it possible to have a constructor without any parameters?

A: Yes. It's actually very common for a class to have a constructor without a parameter. In fact, you've already seen an example of it—**your form's constructor**. Look inside a newly added Windows form and find its constructor's declaration:

```
public Form1() {
  InitializeComponent();
}
```

That's the constructor for your form object. It doesn't take any parameters, but it does have to do a lot. Take a minute and open up Form1.Designer.cs. Find the InitializeComponent() method by clicking on the plus symbol next to "Windows Form Designer generated code".

That method initializes all of the controls on the form and sets all of their properties. If you drag a new control onto your form in the IDE's form designer and set some of its properties in the Properties window, you'll see those changes reflected inside the InitializeComponent() method.

The InitializeComponent() method is called inside the form's constructor is so that the controls all get initialized as soon as the form object is created. (Remember, every form that gets displayed is just another object that happens to use methods that the .NET Framework provides in the System.Windows.Forms namespace to display windows, buttons and other controls.)

Watch it!

When a method's parameter has the same name as a field, then it masks the field.

Did you notice how the constructor's numberOfCows parameter looks just like the backing field behind the NumberOfCows property? If you wanted to use to the backing field in of the constructor, you'd use "this."—numberOfCows refers to the parameter, and this.numberOfCows is how you'd access the private field.

Q: Why would I need complicated logic in a get or set accessor? Isn't it just a way of creating a field?

A: Because sometimes you know that every time you set a field, you'll have to do some calculation or perform some action. Think about Kathleen's problem—she ran into trouble because the form didn't run the method to recalculate the cost of the decorations after setting the number of people in the DinnerParty class. If we replaced the field with a set accessor, then we could make sure that the set accessor recalculates the cost of the decorations. (In fact, you're about to do exactly that in just a couple of pages!)

Q: Wait a minute—so what's the difference between a method and a get or set accessor?

A: There is none! Get and set accessors are a special kind of method—one that's declared inside a field and called whenever that field is set. Get accessors always return a value that's the same type as the field, and set accessors always take exactly one parameter called value whose type is the same as the field. Oh, and by the way, you can just say "property" instead of "get and set accessor".

Q: So you can have ANY kind of statement in a property?

A: Absolutely. Anything you can do in a method, you can do in a property. They can call other methods, access other fields, even create objects and instances. But they only get called when a field gets accessed, so it doesn't make sense to have any statements in them that don't have to do with getting or setting the field.

Q: If a set accessor always takes a parameter called value, why doesn't its declaration have parentheses with "int value" in them, like you'd have with any other method that takes a parameter called value?

A: Because C# was built to keep you from having to type in extra information that the compiler doesn't need. The parameter gets declared without you having to explicitly type it in, which doesn't sound like much when you're only typing one or two—but when you have to type a few hundred, it can be a real time saver (not to mention a bug preventer).

Every set accessor *always* has exactly one parameter called value, and the type of that parameter *always* matches the type of the field. C# was designed to save you from writing redundant code. C# has all the information it needs about the type and parameter as soon as you type "get {". So there's no need for you to type any more, and the C# compiler isn't going to make you type more than you have to.

Q: Wait, a sec—is that why I don't add a return value to my constructor?

A: Exactly! Your constructor doesn't have a return value because *every* constructor is always void. It would be redundant to make you type "void" at the beginning of each constructor, so you don't have to.

Q: Can I have a get without a set or a set without a get?

A: Yes! When you have a get accessor but no set, you create a read-only field. For example, the SecretAgent class might have a ReadOnly field for the name:

```
string name = "Dash Martin";
public string Name {
   get { return name; }
```

And if you create a property with a set accessor but no get, then your field can only be written, but not read. The SecretAgent class could use that for a Password field that other spies could write to but not see:

```
public string Password {
 set {
   if (value == secretCode)
{
     name = "Herb Jones";
   }
}
```

Both of those techniques can come in really handy when you're doing encapsulation.

Properties (get and set accessors) are a special kind of method that's only run when another class reads or writes a property.

what's in a name?

Sharpen your pencil

Take a look at the get and set accessors here. The Form that is using this class has a new instance of CableBill called thisMonth and calls the GetThisMonthsBill () method with a button click. Write down the value of the amountOwed variable after the code below executed.

```
class CableBill
{
    private int payPerViewMovies;
    public int numberOfChannels;
    public const int serviceFee = 45;

    public int PayPerViewMovies
    {
        get
        {
            return payPerViewMovies;
        }
        set
        {
            payPerViewMovies = value;
        }
    }


    public int GetThisMonthsBill()
    {
        int payPerViewCost = PayPerViewMovies * 4;
        int channelCost = numberOfChannels * 2;
        int totalCost = payPerViewCost + channelCost + serviceFee;
        return totalCost;
    }
}
```

1. ```
   thisMonth.PayPerViewMovies = 5;
   thisMonth.numberOfChannels = 2;
   int amountOwed = thisMonth.GetThisMonthsBill();
   MessageBox.Show ("You Owe " + amountOwed);
   ```

What's the value of amountOwed?

[69]

2. ```
   thisMonth.payPerViewMovies = 5;
   thisMonth.numberOfChannels = 2;
   int amountOwed = thisMonth.GetThisMonthsBill();
   MessageBox.Show ("You Owe " + amountOwed);
   ```

What's the value of amountOwed?

[error!]

3. ```
   thisMonth.PayPerViewMovies = 5;
   int amountOwed = thisMonth.GetThisMonthsBill();
   MessageBox.Show ("You Owe " + amountOwed);
   ```

What's the value of amountOwed?

[65]
   ```

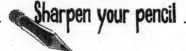

there are no Dumb Questions

Q: I noticed that you used uppercase names for some fields but lowercase ones for others. Does that matter?

A: Yes—it matters to you. But it doesn't matter to the compiler. C# doesn't care what you name your variables, but if you choose weird names then it makes your code hard to read. Sometimes it can get confusing when you have variables that are named the same, except one starts with an uppercase letter and the other starts with a lowercase one.

Here are a few tips about variable names to help you keep it straight. They're not hard-and-fast rules—the compiler doesn't care whether a variable is uppercase or lowercase—but they're good suggestions to help make your code easier to read).

1. When you declare a private field, it should be in camelCase and start with a lowercase letter.).

2. Public properties and methods are in PascalCase (they start with an uppercase letter).

3. Parameters to methods should be in camelCase.

4. Some methods, especially constructors, will have parameters with the same names as fields. When this happens, the parameter **masks** the field, which means statements in the method that use the name end up referring to the parameter, not the field. Use the `this` keyword to fix the problem—add it to the variable to tell the compiler you're talking about the field, not the parameter.

Sharpen your pencil

This code has problems. Write down what you think is wrong with the code, and what you'd change.

```
class GumballMachine {
        private int gumballs;

        private int price;
        public int Price
        {
           get
           {
             return price;
           }
        }
        public GumballMachine(int gumballs, int price)
        {
           gumballs = this.gumballs;
           price = Price;
        }
        public string DispenseOneGumball(int price, int coinsInserted)
        {
           if (this.coinsInserted >= price) { // check the field
             gumballs -= 1;
             return "Here's your gumball";
           } else {
             return "Please insert more coins";
           }
        }
}
```

(handwritten annotations)

this Price = price

this.gumballs = gumballs

masks a private field called price

this is on the wrong parameter

Sharpen your pencil
Solution

Write down the value of the amountOwed variable after the code below executed.

```
1. thisMonth.PayPerViewMovies = 5;
   thisMonth.numberOfChannels = 2;
   int amountOwed = thisMonth.GetThisMonthsBill();
   MessageBox.Show ("You Owe " + amountOwed);
```

What's the value of amountOwed?

69

```
2. thisMonth.payPerViewMovies = 5;
   thisMonth.numberOfChannels = 2;
   int amountOwed = thisMonth.GetThisMonthsBill();
   MessageBox.Show ("You Owe " + amountOwed);
```

What's the value of amountOwed?

won't compile

```
3. thisMonth.PayPerViewMovies = 5;
   int amountOwed = thisMonth.GetThisMonthsBill();
   MessageBox.Show ("You Owe " + amountOwed);
```

What's the value of amountOwed?

77

Sharpen your pencil
Solution

This code has problems. Write down what you think is wrong with the code, and what you'd change.

Lowercase price refers to the parameter to the constructor, not the field. This line sets the PARAMETER to the value returned by the Price get accessor, but Price hasn't even been set yet! So it doesn't do anything useful. If you change the constructor's parameter to uppercase Price, this line will work properly.

The "this" keyword is on the wrong "gumballs". this.gumballs refers to the property, while gumballs refers to the parameter.

This parameter masks the private field called Price, and the comment says the method is supposed to be checking the value of the price backing field.

```
public GumballMachine(int gumballs, int price)
{
    gumballs = this.gumballs;
    price = Price;
}

public string DispenseOneGumball(int price, int coinsInserted)
{
    if (this.coinsInserted >= price) { // check the field
        gumballs -= 1;
        return "Here's your gumball";
    } else {
        return "Please insert more coins";
    }
}
```

The "this" keyword is on a parameter, where it doesn't belong. It should be on price, because that field is masked by a parameter.

Use what you've learned about properties and constructors to fix Kathleen's Party Planner program.

ExeRcise

1 ### How to fix the Dinner Party calculator

If we want to fix the DinnerParty class, we'll need a way to make sure that the CalculateCostODecorations() method gets called every time that NumberOfPeople changes.

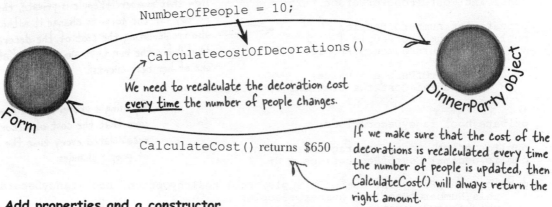

NumberOfPeople = 10;

CalculatecostOfDecorations()

We need to recalculate the decoration cost every time the number of people changes.

Form

DinnerParty object

CalculateCost() returns $650

If we make sure that the cost of the decorations is recalculated every time the number of people is updated, then CalculateCost() will always return the right amount.

2 ### Add properties and a constructor

All you need to do to fix Kathleen's problem is make sure the DinnerParty class is well-encapsulated. You'll start by **changing NumberOfPeople to a property** that always calls CalculateCostOfDecorations() any time it's called. Then you'll **add a constructor** that makes sure the instance is initialized properly. Finally, you'll **change the form** so it uses the new constructor. If you do this right, that's the only change you'll need to make to the form.

★ You'll need to create a new property for `NumberOfPeople` that has a set accessor which calls `CalculateCostOfDecorations()`. It'll need a backing field called `numberOfPeople`.

★ The `NumberOfPeople` set accessor needs to have a value to pass as the parameter to the `CalculateCostOfDecorations()` method. So add a private `bool` field called `fancyDecorations` that you set every time `CalculateCostOfDecorations()` is called.

★ Add a constructor that sets up the class. It needs to take three parameters for the Number of People, Healthy Option, and Fancy Decorations. The form currently calls two methods when it initializes the DinnerParty object—move them into the constructor.
```
dinnerParty.CalculateCostOfDecorations(fancyBox.Checked);
dinnerParty.SetHealthyOption(healthyBox.Checked);
```

★ Here's the constructor for the form—everything else in the form stays the same:
```
public Form1() {
    InitializeComponent();
    dinnerParty = new DinnerParty((int)numericUpDown1.Value,
                      healthyBox.Checked, fancyBox.Checked);
    DisplayDinnerPartyCost();
}
```

Use what you've learned about properties and constructors to fix Kathleen's Party Planner program.

```
public class DinnerParty {
    const int CostOfFoodPerPerson = 25;

    private int numberOfPeople;
    public int NumberOfPeople {
        get. { return numberOfPeople; }
        set {
            numberOfPeople = value;
            CalculateCostOfDecorations(fancyDecorations);
        }
    }
    private bool fancyDecorations;

    public decimal CostOfBeveragesPerPerson;
    public decimal CostOfDecorations = 0;

    public DinnerParty(int numberOfPeople, bool healthyOption, bool fancyDecorations) {
        this.NumberOfPeople = numberOfPeople;
        this.fancyDecorations = fancyDecorations;
        SetHealthyOption(healthyOption);
        CalculateCostOfDecorations(fancyDecorations);
    }

    public void SetHealthyOption(bool healthyOption) {
        if (healthyOption) {
            CostOfBeveragesPerPerson = 5.00M;
        } else {
            CostOfBeveragesPerPerson = 20.00M;
        }
    }

    public void CalculateCostOfDecorations(bool fancy) {
        fancyDecorations = fancy;
        if (fancy) {
            CostOfDecorations = (NumberOfPeople * 15.00M) + 50M;
        } else {
            CostOfDecorations = (NumberOfPeople * 7.50M) + 30M;
        }
    }

    public decimal CalculateCost(bool healthyOption) {
        decimal totalCost = CostOfDecorations
            + ((CostOfBeveragesPerPerson + CostOfFoodPerPerson) * NumberOfPeople);

        if (healthyOption) {
            return totalCost * .95M;
        } else {
            return totalCost;
        }
    }
}
```

Now that numberOfPeople is private, there's no way for the form to change it without also recalculating the cost of the decorations. That'll fix the bug that almost cost Kathleen one of her best clients!

By using a property, you can make sure that the cost of decorations is recalculated every time the number of people changes.

Be careful how you use "this.". Make sure you put it in front of NumberOfPeople so that it calls the set accessor.

Make sure you store the fancy decorations in a field so the NumberOfPeople set accessor can use it.

And you'll need to put it in front of "fancyDecorations" because the fancyDecorations parameter masks the private field with the same name.

6 inheritance

Your object's family tree

So there I was riding my bicycle object down dead man's curve when I realized it inherited from TwoWheeler and I forgot to add a Brakes() method...long story short, twenty-six stitches and Mom said I'm grounded for a month.

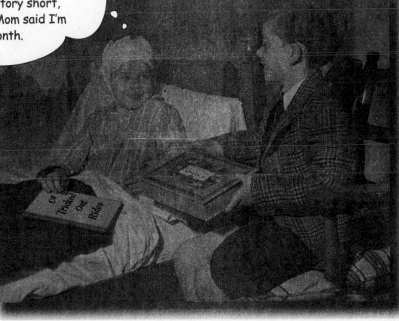

Sometimes you *DO* want to be just like your parents.

Ever run across an object that *almost* does exactly what you want *your* object to do? Found yourself wishing that if you could just *change a few things*, that object would be perfect? Well that's just one reason that **inheritance** is one of the most powerful concepts and techniques in the C# language. Before you're through this chapter, you'll learn how to **subclass** an object to get its behavior, but keep the **flexibility** to make changes to that behavior. You'll **avoid duplicate code**, **model the real world** more closely, and end up with code that's **easier to maintain**.

Kathleen does birthday parties, too

Now that you got your program working, Kathleen is using it all the
time. But she doesn't just handle dinner parties—she does birthdays
too, and they're priced a little differently. She'll need you to add
birthdays to her program.

> I just got a call for a
> birthday party for 10 people.
> Can your program handle that?

These are both the same as the dinner party.

Cost Estimate for a Birthday Party

- $25 per person.

- There are two options for the cost of decorations. If a client
  goes with the normal decorations, it's $7.50 per person with a $30
  decorating fee. A client can also upgrade the party decorations
  to the "Fancy Option"—that costs $15 per person with a $50 one-
  time decorating fee.

- When the party has four people or less, use an 8-inch cake ($40).
  Otherwise, she uses a 16-inch cake ($75).

- Writing on the cake costs $.25 for each letter. The 8-inch cake can
  have up to 16 letters of writing, and the 16-inch one can have up
  to 40 letters of writing.

The application should handle both types of parties. Use a tab control,
one tab for each kind of party.

Most of the changes have to do with cakes and writing.

We need a BirthdayParty class

Modifying your program to calculate the cost of Kathleen's birthday parties means adding a new class and changing the form to let you handle both kinds of parties.

You'll do all this in a minute—but first you'll need to get a sense of what the job involves.

BirthdayParty
NumberOfPeople
CostOfDecorations
CakeSize
CakeWriting
CalculateCostOfDecorations()
CalculateCost()

Here's what we need to do:

①　Create a new BirthdayParty class
Your new class will need to calculate the costs, deal with decorations, and check the size of the writing on the cake.

②　Add a TabControl to your form
Each tab on the form is a lot like the GroupBox control you used to show how much cash Joe and Bob had back in Chapter 3. Just click on the tab you want to display, and drag controls into it.

③　Label the first tab and move the Dinner Party controls onto it
You'll drag each of the controls that handle the dinner party into the new tab. They'll work exactly like before, but they'll only be displayed when the dinner party tab is selected.

④　Label the second tab and add new Birthday Party controls onto it
You'll design the interface for handling birthday parties just like you did for the dinner parties.

⑤　Wire your birthday party class up to the controls
Now all you need to do is add a BirthdayParty reference to the form's fields, and add the code to each of your new controls to so that it uses its methods and properties.

---

there are no
Dumb Questions

Q: Why can't we just create a new instance of DinnerParty, like Mike did when he wanted to compare three routes in his navigation program?

A: Because if you created another instance of the DinnerParty class, you'd only be able to use it to plan extra dinner parties. Two instances of the same class can be really useful if you need to manage two different pieces of the same kind of data. But if you need to store **different kinds of data**, you'll need **different classes** to do it.

Q: How do I know what to put in the new class?

A: Before you can start building a class, you need to know what problem it's supposed to solve. That's why you had to talk to Kathleen—she's going to be using the program. Good thing you took a lot of notes! You can come up with your class's methods, fields, and properties by thinking about its behavior (what it **needs to do**) and its state (what it **needs to know**).

Exercise

Add birthday parties to Kathleen's party planning program.

Make sure you use decimal as the type for the fields and properties that hold currency.

BirthdayParty

BirthdayParty
NumberOfPeople
CostOfDecorations
CakeSize
CakeWriting
CalculateCostOfDecorations()
CalculateCost()

❶ Add the new BirthdayParty class to your program

You already know how you'll handle the NumberOfPeople property and the CostOfDecorations methods—they're just like their counterparts in DinnerParty. Start by creating your new class and adding those. Then add the rest of the behavior:

If the cake writing is too long for the cake, the set accessor cuts the backing field down to size. So you'll need to make sure to reload the text into the text box every time the text changes or the number of people changes (in case there's a long string and she cuts down to a smaller cake).

★ Add a CakeSize integer property. Make a private method called CalculateCakeSize() that sets CakeSize to either 8 or 16 depending on the number of people. You'll need to call it from the constructor and the NumberOfPeople set accessor.

★ You'll need a CakeWriting string property to hold the writing on the cake. We'll give you the code for this one.

We don't want any other methods changing the value of CakeWriting.

★ The CakeWriting set accessor checks CakeSize because different sizes of cake can hold different numbers of letters. Then it uses `value.Length` to check how long the string is. If it's too long, instead of setting the private field, the set accessor pops up a message box that says, "Too many letters for a 16-inch cake" (or 8-inch cake).

★ Every string has a **Substring()** method that returns a portion of the string. CakeWriting uses it to cut the size of the cake writing down—if the number of people changes and reduces the cake size, you'll need to cut down the string, too.

★ Finally, add the CalculateCost() method. But instead of taking the decoration cost and adding the cost of beverages (which is what happens in DinnerParty), it'll add the cost of the cake.

Click on the tabs to switch between them. Use the TabCollection property to change the text for each tab. Click the "..." button next to it and select each tab's Text property.

❷ Update the form to add tabs

Drag a TabControl out of the toolbox and onto your form, and resize it so it takes up the entire form. Change the text of each tab using the TabPages property: a "..." button shows up in the Properties Window next to the property. When you click it, the IDE pops up a window that lets you edit the properties of each tab. Set the Text property of the tabs to "Dinner Party" and "Birthday Party".

❸ Name the first tab and move the Dinner Party controls onto it

You'll drag the each of the controls that handle the dinner party into the new tab. They'll work exactly like they do now, but they'll only be displayed when that tab is selected.

After you drag the Dinner Party controls onto the tab, they'll only be visible when the Dinner Party tab is selected.

4 Build the Birthday Party user interface

The Birthday Party GUI has a NumericUpDown control for the number of people, a CheckBox control for fancy decorations, and a Label control with a 3D border for the cost. Then you'll add a TextBox control for the cake writing.

This tab uses the NumericUpDown, CheckBox, and Label controls just like the Dinner Party tab does. Name them numberBirthday, fancyBirthday, and birthdayCost.

Click on the Birthday Party tab and add the new controls.

Add a TextBox control called cakeWriting for the writing on the cake (and a label above it so the user knows what it's for). Use its Text property to give it a default value of "Happy Birthday".

5 You'll need this property

Here's the code for the BirthdayParty.CakeWriting property—it'll come in handy:

```
private string cakeWriting = "";
public string CakeWriting {
    get { return this.cakeWriting; }
    set {
        int maxLength;
        if (CakeSize == 8)
            maxLength = 16;
        else
            maxLength = 40;
        if (value.Length > maxLength) {
            MessageBox.Show("Too many letters for a " + CakeSize + " inch cake");
            if (maxLength > this.cakeWriting.Length)
                maxLength = this.cakeWriting.Length;
            this.cakeWriting = cakeWriting.Substring(0, maxLength);
        }
        else
            this.cakeWriting = value;
    }
}
```

Did you notice how we left out some of the brackets? When you only have one statement in a code block, you don't need to add curly brackets around it.

This property is a little more complex than the ones you've seen before. It checks the cake size to see if it's too long for the cake, using the maxLength variable to store the maximum length. If it's too long, it gives an error message and then cuts the backing field down to the right size, so it can be reloaded into the text box.

Every string has a Substring() method that returns a portion of the string. This one cuts it down to the allowed length, so you'll need to reload the writing into the textbox when the text or cake size change.

6 Put it all together

All the pieces are there, now it's just a matter of writing a little code to make the controls work.

★ Add a BirthdayParty object to the form. Make sure you instantiate it.

★ Add code to the NumericUpDown control's event handler method to set the object's NumberOfPeople property.

★ Make the Fancy Decorations checkbox work.

★ Add a DisplayBirthdayPartyCost() method and add it to all of the event handlers so the cost label is updated automatically any time there's a change.

7 Run it

Make sure the program works the way it's supposed to. Check that it pops up a message box if the writing is too long for the cake. Make sure the price is always right. Once it's working, you're done!

Exercise Solution

Add birthday parties to Kathleen's party planning program.

```
public partial class Form1 : Form {
    DinnerParty dinnerParty;
    BirthdayParty birthdayParty;
    public Form1() {
        InitializeComponent();
        dinnerParty = new DinnerParty((int)numericUpDown1.Value,
                        healthyBox.Checked, fancyBox.Checked);
        DisplayDinnerPartyCost();

        birthdayParty = new BirthdayParty((int)numberBirthday.Value,
                        fancyBirthday.Checked, cakeWriting.Text);
        DisplayBirthdayPartyCost();
    }

    // The fancyBox, healthyBox, and numericUpDown1 event handlers and
    // the DisplayDinnerCost() method are identical to the ones in the
    // Dinner Party exercise at the end of Chapter 5.


    private void numberBirthday_ValueChanged(object sender, EventArgs e) {
        birthdayParty.NumberOfPeople = (int)numberBirthday.Value;
        DisplayBirthdayPartyCost();
    }

    private void fancyBirthday_CheckedChanged(object sender, EventArgs e) {
        birthdayParty.CalculateCostOfDecorations(fancyBirthday.Checked);
        DisplayBirthdayPartyCost();
    }


    private void cakeWriting_TextChanged(object sender, EventArgs e) {
        birthdayParty.CakeWriting = cakeWriting.Text;
        DisplayBirthdayPartyCost();
    }

    private void DisplayBirthdayPartyCost() {
        cakeWriting.Text = birthdayParty.CakeWriting;
        decimal cost = birthdayParty.CalculateCost();
        birthdayCost.Text = cost.ToString("c");
    }
}
```

The BirthdayParty instance is initialized in the form's constructor, just like the instance of DinnerParty.

The CheckBox and NumericUpDown controls' event handlers are just like the ones for the dinner party.

The way that the form handles the cake writing can be really simple because the BirthdayParty class is well encapsulated. All the form has to do is use its controls to set the properties on the object, and the object takes care of the rest.

All the intelligence for dealing with making sure the writing, the number of people, and the cake size are built into the NumberOfPeople and CakeWriting set accessors, so the form just has to set and display the values.

```
using System.Windows.Forms;

public class BirthdayParty {
    public const int CostOfFoodPerPerson = 25;

    public decimal CostOfDecorations = 0;
    private bool fancyDecorations;
    public int CakeSize;

    public BirthdayParty(int numberOfPeople, bool fancyDecorations, string cakeWriting) {
        this.numberOfPeople = numberOfPeople;
        this.fancyDecorations = fancyDecorations;
        CalculateCakeSize();
        this.CakeWriting = cakeWriting;
        CalculateCostOfDecorations(fancyDecorations);
    }

    private void CalculateCakeSize() {
        if (NumberOfPeople <= 4)
            CakeSize = 8;
        else
            CakeSize = 16;
    }

    private string cakeWriting = "";
    public string CakeWriting {
        get { return this.cakeWriting; }
        set {
            int maxLength;
            if (CakeSize == 8)
                maxLength = 16;
            else
                maxLength = 40;
            if (value.Length > maxLength) {
                MessageBox.Show("Too many letters for a " + CakeSize + " inch cake");
                if (maxLength > this.cakeWriting.Length)
                    maxLength = this.cakeWriting.Length;
                this.cakeWriting = cakeWriting.Substring(0, maxLength);
            }
            else
                this.cakeWriting = value;
        }
    }
}
```

When the BirthdayParty object is initialized, it needs to know the number of people, the fancy decorations and the writing on the cake, so it can start out with the right cake cost when CalculateCost() is called.

The constructor's calling the set accessor to set the cake writing, in case the parameter is too long for the cake, so it's got to calculate the cake size first.

The constructor sets the properties and then runs the calculations.

The CalculateCakeSize() method sets the CakeSize field. It's called by the NumberOfPeople set accessor and the CalculateCost() method.

The CakeWriting property makes sure that the cake's writing is never too long for the cake size. Its set accessor checks the cake size, then uses the backing fields Length property to make sure it's not too long. If it is, it cuts the string down to the right size.

Exercise Solution

Add birthday parties to Kathleen's party planning program.

We're using decimal because we're dealing with prices and currency.

```csharp
public decimal CalculateCost() {
    decimal TotalCost = CostOfDecorations + (CostOfFoodPerPerson * NumberOfPeople);
    decimal CakeCost;
    if (CakeSize == 8)
        CakeCost = 40M + CakeWriting.Length * .25M;
    else
        CakeCost = 75M + CakeWriting.Length * .25M;
    return TotalCost + CakeCost;
}
```

The CalculateCost() method is a lot like the one from DinnerParty, except that it adds the cost of the cake instead of the Healthy Choice option.

```csharp
private int numberOfPeople;
public int NumberOfPeople {
    get { return numberOfPeople; }
    set {
        numberOfPeople = value;
        CalculateCostOfDecorations(fancyDecorations);
        CalculateCakeSize();
        this.CakeWriting = cakeWriting;
    }
}
```

Making the CakeWriting method cut down the size of the cake is only half of the solution. The other half is making sure that the CakeWriting set accessor gets run every time the number of people changes.

So when the number of people changes, the class first recalculates the cake size, and then it uses its set accessor for CakeWriting to cut the text down—so if a 10-person party turns into a 4-person one, their 36-letter message will be cut down to one that'll fit on the smaller cake.

This method is just like the one in the DinnerParty class.

```csharp
public void CalculateCostOfDecorations(bool fancy) {
    fancyDecorations = fancy;
    if (fancy)
        CostOfDecorations = (NumberOfPeople * 15.00M) + 50M;
    else
        CostOfDecorations = (NumberOfPeople * 7.50M) + 30M;
}
```

Curly brackets are optional for single-line blocks

A lot of times you'll have an if statement or while loop that's just got a single statement inside its block. When that happens a lot, you can end up with a whole lot of curly brackets—and that can be a real eyesore! C# helps you avoid that problem by letting you drop the curly brackets if there's just one statement. So this is perfectly valid syntax for a loop and an if statement:

```csharp
for (int i = 0; i < 10; i++)
    DoTheJob(i);
```

```csharp
if (myValue == 36)
    myValue *= 5;
```

One more thing... can you add a $100 fee for parties over 12?

Kathleen's gotten so much business using your program that she can afford to charge a little more for some of her larger clients. So what would it take to change your program to add in the extra charge?

★ Change the DinnerParty.CalculateCost() to check NumberOfPeople and add $100 to the return value if it's over 12.

★ Do the exact same thing for BirthdayParty.CalculateCost().

Take a minute and think about how you'd add a fee to both the DinnerParty and BirthdayParty class. What code would you write? Where would it have to go?

Easy enough... but what happens if there are three similar classes? Or four? Or twelve? And what if you had to maintain that code and make more changes later? What if you had to make the *same exact change* to five or six *closely related* classes?

Wow, I'd have to write the same code over and over again. That's a really inefficient way to work. There's got to be a better way!

You're right! Having the same code repeated in different classes is inefficient and error-prone.

Lucky for us, C# gives us a better way to build classes that are related to each other, and share behavior: ___inheritance___.

When your classes use inheritance, you only need to write your code once

It's no coincidence that your DinnerParty and BirthdayParty classes have a lot of the same code. When you write C# programs, you often create classes that represent things in the real world—and those things are usually related to each other. Your classes have **similar code** because the things they represent in the real world—a birthday party and a dinner party—have **similar behaviors**.

A birthday party handles the number of people and the cost of decorations in almost the same way as a dinner party.

Kathleen needs to figure out the cost of her parties, no matter what kind of parties they are.

DinnerParty	BirthdayParty
NumberOfPeople	NumberOfPeople
CostOfDecorations	CostOfDecorations
HealthyOption	CakeSize
CostOfBeveragesPerPerson	CakeWriting
CalculateCostOfDecorations()	CalculateCostOfDecorations()
CalculateCost()	CalculateCost()
SetHealthyOption()	

Dinner parties and birthday parties are both parties

When you have two classes that are more specific cases of something more general, you can set them up to **inherit** from the same class. When you do that, each of them is a **subclass** of the same **base class**.

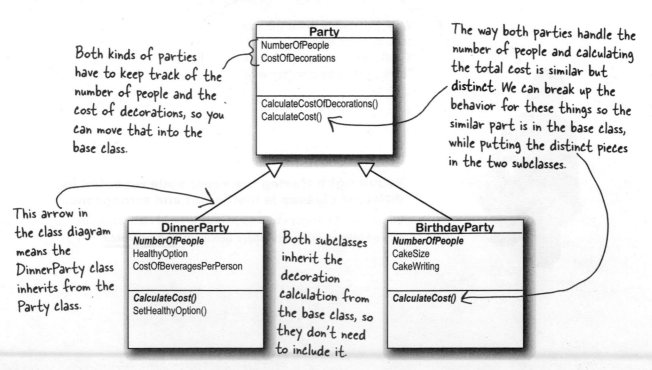

Both kinds of parties have to keep track of the number of people and the cost of decorations, so you can move that into the base class.

Party
NumberOfPeople
CostOfDecorations
CalculateCostOfDecorations()
CalculateCost()

The way both parties handle the number of people and calculating the total cost is similar but distinct. We can break up the behavior for these things so the similar part is in the base class, while putting the distinct pieces in the two subclasses.

This arrow in the class diagram means the DinnerParty class inherits from the Party class.

DinnerParty
NumberOfPeople
HealthyOption
CostOfBeveragesPerPerson
CalculateCost()
SetHealthyOption()

Both subclasses inherit the decoration calculation from the base class, so they don't need to include it.

BirthdayParty
NumberOfPeople
CakeSize
CakeWriting
CalculateCost()

Build up your class model by starting general and getting more specific

C# programs use inheritance because it mimics the relationship that the things they model have in the real world. Real-world things are often in a **hierarchy** that goes from more general to more specific, and your programs have their own **class hierarchy** that does the same thing. In your class model, classes further down in the hierarchy **inherit** from those above it.

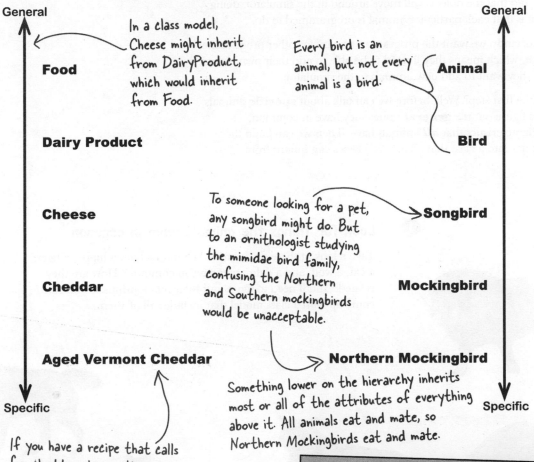

General

In a class model, Cheese might inherit from DairyProduct, which would inherit from Food.

Every bird is an animal, but not every animal is a bird.

General

Food

Animal

Dairy Product

Bird

Cheese

To someone looking for a pet, any songbird might do. But to an ornithologist studying the mimidae bird family, confusing the Northern and Southern mockingbirds would be unacceptable.

Songbird

Cheddar

Mockingbird

Aged Vermont Cheddar

Northern Mockingbird

Specific

Something lower on the hierarchy inherits most or all of the attributes of everything above it. All animals eat and mate, so Northern Mockingbirds eat and mate.

Specific

If you have a recipe that calls for cheddar cheese, then you can use aged Vermont cheddar. But if it specifically needs aged Vermont, then you can't just use any cheddar—you need that specific cheese.

in-her-it, verb.
to derive an attribute from one's parents or ancestors. *She wanted the baby to **inherit** her big brown eyes, and not her husband's beady blue ones.*

How would you design a zoo simulator?

Lions and tigers and bears... oh my! Also, hippos, wolves, and the occasional cat. Your job is to design a program that simulates a zoo. (Don't get too excited—we're not going to actually build the code, just design the classes to represent the animals.)

We've been given a list of some of the animals that will be in the program, but not all of them. We know that each animal will be represented by an object, and that the objects will move around in the simulator, doing whatever it is that each particular animal is programmed to do.

More importantly, we want the program to be easy for other programmers to maintain, which means they'll need to be able to add their own classes later on if they want to add new animals to the simulator.

So what's the first step? Well, before we can talk about **specific** animals, we need to figure out the **general** things they have in common, abstract characteristics that **all** animals have. Then we can build those characteristics into a class that all animal classes can inherit from.

1   ## Look for things the animals have in common

Take a look at these six animals. What do a lion, a hippo, a tiger, a cat, a wolf, and a dalmatian have in common? How are they related? You'll need to figure out their relationships so you can come up with a class model that includes all of them.

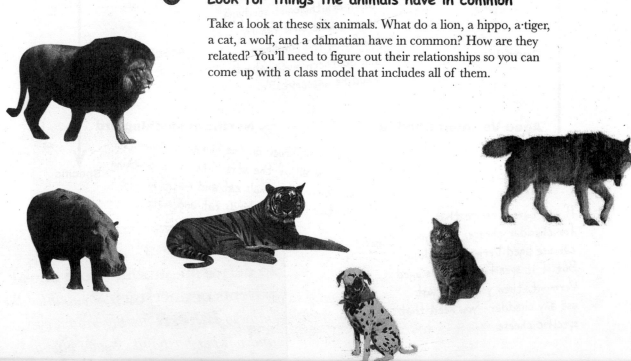

Use inheritance to avoid duplicate code in subclasses

You've already got a good idea that duplicate code sucks. It's hard to maintain, and always leads to headaches down the road. So let's choose fields and methods for an Animal base class that you **only have to write once**, so each of the animal subclasses can inherit from them. Let's start with the public fields:

★ Picture: an image that you can put into a PictureBox.

★ Food: the type of food this animal eats. Right now, there can be only two values: meat or grass.

★ Hunger: an int representing the hunger level of the animal. It changes depending on when (and how much) the animal eats.

★ Boundaries: a reference to a class that stores the height, width and location of the pen that the animal will roam around in.

★ Location: the X and Y coordinates where the animal's standing.

And the Animal class has four methods the animals can inherit:

★ MakeNoise(): a method to let the animal make a sound.

★ Eat(): behavior for when the animal encounters its preferred food.

★ Sleep(): a method to make the animal lie down and take a nap.

★ Roam(): the animals like to wander around their pens in the zoo.

❷ **Build a base class to give the animals everything they have in common**

The fields, properties, and methods in the base class will give all of the animals that inherit from it a common state and behavior. They're all animals, so it makes sense to call the base class Animal.

Animal
Picture
Food
Hunger
Boundaries
Location
MakeNoise()
Eat()
Sleep()
Roam()

Choosing a base class is about making choices. You could have decided to use a ZooOccupant class that defines the feed and maintenance costs, or an Attraction class with methods for how the animals entertain the zoo visitors. But we think Animal makes the most sense here. Do you agree?

Lion

Hippo

Tiger

Dog

Cat

Wolf

Different animals make different noises

Lions roar, dogs bark, and as far as *we* know hippos don't make any sound at all. Each of the classes that inherit from Animal will have a MakeNoise() method, but each of those methods will work a different way and will have different code. When a subclass changes the behavior of one of the methods that it inherited, we say that it **overrides** the method.

Think about what you need to override

When a subclass changes the behavior of a method it inherited, we call it **overriding**. Every animal needs to eat. But a dog might take little bites of meat, while a hippo eats huge mouthfuls of grass. So what would the code for that behavior look like? Both the dog and the hippo would override the Eat() method. The hippo's method would have it consume, say, 20 pounds of hay each time it was called. The dog's Eat() method, on the other hand, would reduce the zoo's food supply by one 12-ounce can of dog food.

So when you've got a subclass that inherits from a base class, it must inherit all of the base class's behaviors... but you can modify them in the subclass so they're not performed exactly the same way. That's what overriding is all about.

Just because a property or a method is in the Animal base class, that doesn't mean every subclass has to use it the same way... or at all!

3 **Figure out what each animal does that the Animal class does differently—or not at all**

What does each type of animal do that all the other animals don't? Dogs eat dog food, so the dog's Eat() method will need to override the Animal.Eat() method. Hippos swim, so a hippo will have a Swim() method that isn't in the Animal class at all.

Grass is yummy! I could go for a good pile of hay right now.

I beg to differ.

Animal
Picture
Food
Hunger
Boundaries
Location
MakeNoise()
Eat()
Sleep()
Roam()

☢ BRAIN POWER

We already know that some animals will override the **MakeNoise()** and **Eat()** methods. Which animals will override **Sleep()** or **Roam()**? Will any of them? What about the properties—which animals will override some properties?

Think about how to group the animals

Aged Vermont cheddar is a kind of cheese, which is a dairy product, which is a kind of food, and a good class model for food would represent that. Lucky for us, C# give us an easy way to do it. You can create a chain of classes that inherit from each other, starting with the topmost base class and working down. So you could have a Food class, with a subclass called DairyProduct that serves as the base class for Cheese, which has a subclass called Cheddar, which is what AgedVermontCheddar inherits from.

4 ## Look for classes that have a lot in common

Don't dogs and wolves seem pretty similar? They're both canines, and it's a good bet that if you look at their behavior they have a lot in common. They probably eat the same food and sleep the same way. What about domestic cats, tigers, and lions? It turns out all three of them move around their habitats in exactly the same way. It's a good bet that you'll be able to have a Feline class that lives between Animal and those three cat classes that can help prevent duplicate code between them.

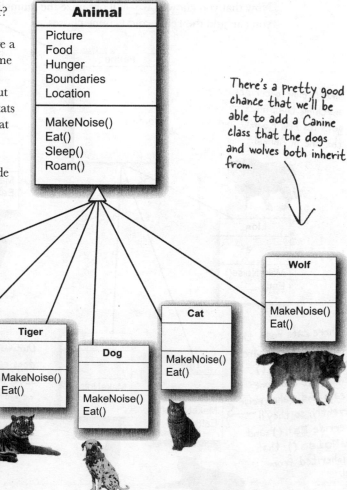

Animal
Picture Food Hunger Boundaries Location
MakeNoise() Eat() Sleep() Roam()

There's a pretty good chance that we'll be able to add a Canine class that the dogs and wolves both inherit from.

Lion
MakeNoise() Eat()

Wolf
MakeNoise() Eat()

The subclasses inherit all four methods from Animal, but we're only having them override MakeNoise() and Eat().

Hippo
MakeNoise() Eat()

Tiger
MakeNoise() Eat()

Dog
MakeNoise() Eat()

Cat
MakeNoise() Eat()

That's why we only show those two methods in the class diagrams.

Create the class hierarchy

When you create your classes so that there's a base class at the top with subclasses below it, and those subclasses have their own subclasses that inherit from them, what you've built is called a **class hierarchy**. This is about more than just avoiding duplicate code, although that is certainly a great benefit of a sensible hierarchy. But when it comes down to it, the biggest benefit you'll get is that your code becomes really easy to understand and maintain. When you're looking at the zoo simulator code, when you see a method or property defined in the Feline class, then you *immediately know* that you're looking at something that all of the cats share. Your hierarchy becomes a map that helps you find your way through your program.

Animal

Picture
Food
Hunger
Boundaries
Location

MakeNoise()
Eat()
Sleep()
Roam()

❺ **Finish your class hierarchy**

Now that you know how you'll organize the animals, you can add the Feline and Canine classes.

Feline

Roam()

Since Feline overrides Roam(), anything that inherits from it gets its new Roam() and not the one in Animal.

Canine

Eat()
Sleep()

Hippo

MakeNoise()
Eat()

Lion

MakeNoise()
Eat()

The three cats roam the same way, so they share an inherited Roam() method. But each one still eats and makes noise differently, so they'll all override Eat() and MakeNoise() that they inherited from Animal.

Cat

MakeNoise()
Eat()

Tiger

MakeNoise()
Eat()

Our wolves and dogs eat the same way, so we moved their common Eat() method up to the Canine class.

Wolf

MakeNoise()

Dog

MakeNoise()

Every subclass <u>extends</u> its base class

You're not limited to the methods that a subclass inherits from its base class... but you already know that! After all, you've been building your own classes all along. When you add inheritance to a class, what you're doing is taking the class you've already built and **extending** it by adding all of the fields, properties, and methods in the base class. So if you wanted to add a Fetch() method to the dog, that's perfectly normal. It won't inherit or override anything—only the dog will have that method, and it won't end up in Wolf, Canine, Animal, Hippo, or any other class.

> **hi-er-ar-chy, noun.**
> an arrangement or classification in which groups or things are ranked one above the other. *The president of Dynamco had worked his way up from the mailroom to the top of the corporate **hierarchy**.*

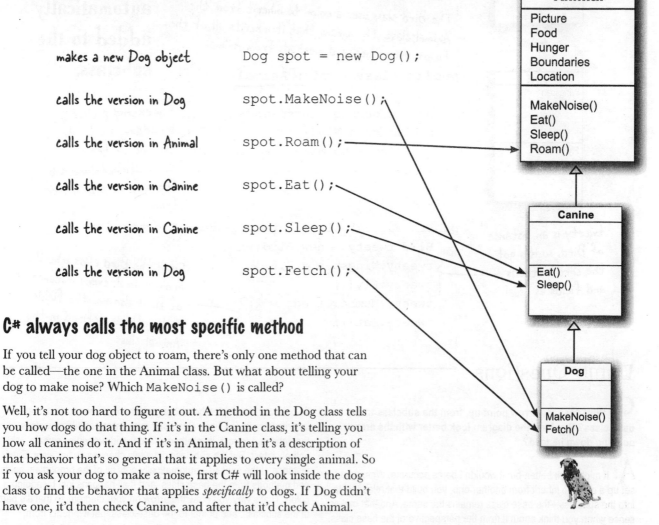

makes a new Dog object	`Dog spot = new Dog();`	
calls the version in Dog	`spot.MakeNoise();`	
calls the version in Animal	`spot.Roam();`	
calls the version in Canine	`spot.Eat();`	
calls the version in Canine	`spot.Sleep();`	
calls the version in Dog	`spot.Fetch();`	

Animal
Picture
Food
Hunger
Boundaries
Location

MakeNoise()
Eat()
Sleep()
Roam()

Canine

Eat()
Sleep()

Dog

MakeNoise()
Fetch()

C# always calls the most specific method

If you tell your dog object to roam, there's only one method that can be called—the one in the Animal class. But what about telling your dog to make noise? Which MakeNoise() is called?

Well, it's not too hard to figure it out. A method in the Dog class tells you how dogs do that thing. If it's in the Canine class, it's telling you how all canines do it. And if it's in Animal, then it's a description of that behavior that's so general that it applies to every single animal. So if you ask your dog to make a noise, first C# will look inside the dog class to find the behavior that applies *specifically* to dogs. If Dog didn't have one, it'd then check Canine, and after that it'd check Animal.

Use a colon to inherit from a base class

When you're writing a class, you use a **colon (:)** to have it inherit from a base class. That makes it a subclass, and gives it **all of the fields, properties, and methods** of the class it inherits from.

> When a subclass inherits from a base class, all of the fields, properties, and methods in the base class are automatically added to the subclass.

```
public class Animal
{
    public int NumberOfLegs;
    public void Eat() {
        // code to make the animal eat
    }
}
```

The Bird class uses a colon to inherit from the Animal class. This means that it inherits all of the fields, properties, and methods from Animal.

```
public class Bird : Animal
{
    public double Wingspan;
    public void Fly() {
        // code to make the bird fly
    }
}
```

You extend a class by adding a colon to the end of the class declaration, followed by the base class to inherit from.

tweety is an instance of Bird, so it's got the Bird methods and fields as usual.

```
public button1_Click(object sender, EventArgs e) {
    Bird tweety = new Bird();
    tweety.Wingspan = 7.5;
    tweety.Fly();
    tweety.NumberOfLegs = 2;
    tweety.Eat();
}
```

Since the Bird class inherits from Animal, every instance of Bird also has the fields and methods defined in the Animal class.

there are no Dumb Questions

Q: Why does the arrow point up, from the subclass to the base class? Wouldn't the diagram look better with the arrow pointing down instead?

A: It might look better, but it wouldn't be as accurate. When you set up a class to inherit from another one, you build that relationship into the subclass—the base class remains the same. And that makes sense when you think about it from the perspective of the base class.

Its behavior is completely unchanged when you add a class that inherits from it. The base class isn't even aware of this new class that inherited from it. Its methods, fields, and properties remain entirely intact. But the subclass definitely changes its behavior. Every instance of the subclass automatically gets all of the properties, fields, and methods from the base class, and it all happens just by adding a colon. That's why you draw the arrow on your diagram so that it's part of the subclass, and points to the base class that it inherits from.

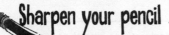
Sharpen your pencil

Take a look at these class models and declarations, and then circle the statements that won't work.

Aircraft
AirSpeed
Altitude

TakeOff()
Land()

```
public class Aircraft {
    public double AirSpeed;
    public double Altitude;
    public void TakeOff() { ... };
    public void Land() { ... };
}

public class FirePlane : Aircraft {
    public double BucketCapacity;
    public void FillBucket() { ... };
}

public void FireFightingMission() {
    FirePlane myFirePlane = new FirePlane();
    new FirePlane.BucketCapacity = 500;
    Aircraft.Altitude = 0;
    myFirePlane.TakeOff();
    myFirePlane.AirSpeed = 192.5;
    myFirePlane.FillBucket();
    Aircraft.Land();
}
```

FirePlane
BucketCapacity

FillBucket()

Sandwich
Toasted
SlicesOfBread

CountCalories()

```
public class Sandwich {
    public boolean Toasted;
    public int SlicesOfBread;
    public int CountCalories() { ... }
}

public class BLT : Sandwich {
    public int SlicesOfBacon;
    public int AmountOfLettuce;
    public int AddSideOfFries() { ... }
}
```

BLT
SlicesOfBacon
AmountOfLettuce

AddSideOfFries()

```
public BLT OrderMyBLT() {
    BLT mySandwich = new BLT();
    BLT.Toasted = true;
    Sandwich.SlicesOfBread = 3;
    mySandwich.AddSideOfFries();
    mySandwich.SlicesOfBacon += 5;
    MessageBox.Show("My sandwich has "
        + mySandwich.CountCalories + "calories".);
    return mySandwich;
}
```

i can think of one way to make a penguin fly...

Sharpen your pencil Solution

Take a look at these class models and declarations, and then circle the statements that won't work.

Aircraft
AirSpeed
Altitude

TakeOff()
Land()

```
public class Aircraft {
    public double AirSpeed;
    public double Altitude;
    public void TakeOff() { ... };
    public void Land() { ... };
}

public class FirePlane : Aircraft {
    public double BucketCapacity;
    public void FillBucket() { ... };
}

public void FireFightingMission() {
    FirePlane myFirePlane = new FirePlane();
    new FirePlane.BucketCapacity = 500;
    Aircraft.Altitude = 0;
    myFirePlane.TakeOff();
    myFirePlane.AirSpeed = 192.5;
    myFirePlane.FillBucket();
    Aircraft.Land();
}
```

FirePlane
BucketCapacity

FillBucket()

That's not how you use the new keyword.

These statements all use the class names instead of the name of the instance, myFirePlane.

Sandwich
Toasted
SlicesOfBread

CountCalories()

```
public class Sandwich {
    public boolean Toasted;
    public int SlicesOfBread;
    public int CountCalories() { ... }
}

public class BLT : Sandwich {
    public int SlicesOfBacon;
    public int AmountOfLettuce;
    public int AddSideOfFries() { ... }
}

public BLT OrderMyBLT() {
    BLT mySandwich = new BLT();
    BLT.Toasted = true;
    Sandwich.SlicesOfBread = 3;
    mySandwich.AddSideOfFries();
    mySandwich.SlicesOfBacon += 5;
    MessageBox.Show("My sandwich has "
        + mySandwich.CountCalories + "calories".);
    return mySandwich;
}
```

BLT
SlicesOfBacon
AmountOfLettuce

AddSideOfFries()

These properties are part of the instance, but the statements are trying to call them incorrectly using the class names.

CountCalories is a method, but this statement doesn't include the parentheses () after the call to the method.

We know that inheritance adds the base class fields, properties, and methods to the subclass...

Inheritance is simple when your subclass needs to inherit **all** of the base class methods, properties, and fields.

Bird
Fly()
LayEggs()
PreenFeathers()

Pigeon is a subclass of Bird, so any fields and methods in Bird are automatically part of Pigeon, too.

Pigeon
Coo()

```
public class Bird {
    public void Fly() {
      // here's the code to make the bird fly
    }

    public void LayEggs() { ... };
    public void PreenFeathers() { ... };
}


public class Pigeon : Bird {
    public void Coo() { ... }
}


public class Penguin : Bird {
    public void Swim() { ... }
}


public void BirdSimulator() {

    Pigeon Harriet = new Pigeon();

    Penguin Izzy = new Penguin();

    Harriet.Fly();

    Harriet.Coo();

    Izzy.Fly();

}
```

... but some birds don't fly!

What do you do if your base class has a method that your subclass needs to *modify*?

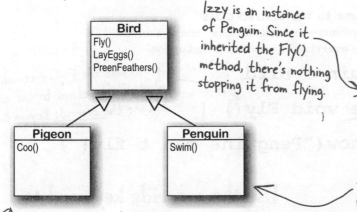

Bird
Fly()
LayEggs()
PreenFeathers()

Izzy is an instance of Penguin. Since it inherited the Fly() method, there's nothing stopping it from flying.

Pigeon
Coo()

Penguin
Swim()

Pigeons fly, lay eggs, and preen their feathers, so there's no problem with the Pigeon class inheriting from Bird.

Both Pigeon and Penguin inherit from Bird, so they both get the Fly(), LayEggs(), and PreenFeathers() methods.

Penguin objects shouldn't be able to fly! But if the Penguin class inherits from Bird, then you'll have penguins flying all over the place. So what do we do?

 BRAIN POWER

If this were your Bird Simulator code, what would you do to keep the penguins from flying?

A subclass can override methods to change or replace methods it inherited

Sometimes you've got a subclass that you'd like to inherit *most* of the behaviors from the base class, but *not all of them.* When you want to change the behaviors that a class has inherited, you can **override** the methods.

❶ Add the virtual keyword to the method in the base class

A subclass can only override a method if it's marked with the **virtual** keyword, which tells C# to allow the subclass to override methods.

```
public class Bird {
    public virtual void Fly() {
        // code to make the bird fly
    }
}
```

> Adding the virtual keyword to the Fly() method tells C# that a subclass is allowed to override it.

❷ Add a method with the same name to the derived class

You'll need to have exactly the same signature—meaning the same return value and parameters—and you'll need to use the **override** keyword in the declaration.

```
public class Penguin : Bird {
    public override void Fly() {
        MessageBox.Show("Penguins can't fly!")
    }
}
```

> To override the Fly() method, add an identical method to the subclass and use the override keyword.

> When you override a method, your new method needs to have exactly the same signature as the method in the base class it's overriding. In this case, that means it needs to be called Fly, return void, and have no parameters.

Use the override keyword to add a method to your subclass that replaces one that it inherited. Before you can override a method, you need to mark it virtual in the base class.

Sandwich
Toasted
SlicesOfBread
CountCalories()

△

BLT
SlicesOfBacon
AmountOfLettuce
AddSideOfFries()

Any place where you can use a base class, you can use one of its subclasses instead

One of the most useful things you can do with inheritance is use a subclass in place of the base class it inherits from. So if your `Recipe()` method takes a `Cheese` object and you've got an `AgedVermontCheddar` class that inherits from `Cheese`, then you can pass an instance of `AgedVermontCheddar` to the `Recipe()` method. `Recipe()` only has access to the fields, properties, and methods that are part of the `Cheese` class, though—it doesn't have access to anything specific to `AgedVermontCheddar`.

1 Let's say we have a method to analyze sandwich objects:

```
public void SandwichAnalyzer(Sandwich specimen) {
    int calories = specimen.CountCalories();
    UpdateDietPlan(calories);
    PerformBreadCalculations(specimen.SlicesOfBread, specimen.Toasted);
}
```

2 You could pass a sandwich to the method—but you could also pass a BLT. Since a BLT is a *kind* of sandwich, we set it up so that it inherits from the Sandwich class.

```
public button1_Click(object sender, EventArgs e) {
    BLT myBLT = new BLT();
    SandwichAnalyzer(myBLT);
}
```

We'll talk about this more in the next chapter!

3 You can always move ***down*** the class diagram—a reference variable can always be set equal to an instance of one of its subclasses. But you can't move ***up*** the class diagram.

```
public button2_Click(object sender, EventArgs e) {
    Sandwich mySandwich = new Sandwich();
    BLT myBLT = new BLT();
    Sandwich someRandomSandwich = myBLT;
    BLT anotherBLT = mySandwich;     // <--- THIS WON'T COMPILE!!!
}
```

You can assign myBLT to any Sandwich variable because a BLT is a kind of sandwich.

But you can't assign mySandwich to a BLT variable, because not every sandwich is a BLT! That's why this last line will cause an error.

MiXed MesSages

Exercise

```
a = 6;      56
b = 5;      11
a = 5;      65
```

A short C# program is listed below. One block of the program is missing! Your challenge is to match the candidate block of code (on the left), with the output—what's in the messagebox that the program pops up—that you'd see if the block were inserted. Not all the lines of output will be used, and some of the lines of output might be used more than once. Draw lines connecting the candidate blocks of code with their matching output.

Instructions:

1. Fill in the four blanks in the code.
2. Match the code candidates to the output.

```csharp
public class A {
  public int ivar = 7;
  public _____ string m1() {
    return "A's m1, ";
  }
  public string m2() {
    return "A's m2, ";
  }
  public _____ string m3() {
    return "A's m3, ";
  }
}

public class B : A {
  public _____ string m1() {
    return "B's m1, ";
  }
}
```

```csharp
public class C : B {
  public _____ string m3() {
    return "C's m3, " + (ivar + 6);
  }
}
```

Here's the entry point for the program—it doesn't show a form, it just pops up a messagebox.

```csharp
public class Mixed5 {
  public static void Main(string[] args) {
    A a = new A();
    B b = new B();
    C c = new C();
    A a2 = new C();
    string q = "";

    [              ]   candidate code
                       goes here
                       (three lines)

    System.Windows.Forms.MessageBox.Show(q);
  }
}
```

code candidates:

```
q += b.m1();  ⎫
q += c.m2();  ⎬
q += a.m3();  ⎭
_____

q += c.m1();  ⎫
q += c.m2();  ⎬
q += c.m3();  ⎭
_____

q += a.m1();  ⎫
q += b.m2();  ⎬
q += c.m3();  ⎭
_____

q += a2.m1();  ⎫
q += a2.m2();  ⎬
q += a2.m3();  ⎭
```

output:

A's m1, A's m2, C's m3, 6

B's m1, A's m2, A's m3,

A's m1, B's m2, A's m3,

B's m1, A's m2, C's m3, 13

B's m1, C's m2, A's m3,

B's m1, A's m2, C's m3, 6

A's m1, A's m2, C's m3, 13

(Don't just type this into the IDE—you'll learn a lot more if you figure this out on paper!)

Pool Puzzle

Your **job** is to take code snippets from the pool and place them into the blank lines in the code. You may use the same snippet more than once, and you might not need to use all the snippets. Your **goal** is to make a set of classes that will compile and run together as a program. Don't be fooled—this one's harder than it looks.

```
public class Rowboat ......................{

   public ............... rowTheBoat() {

      return "stroke natasha";

   }

}
```

```
public class ................ {

   private int ................ ;

   ............ void ...................... ( ............ ) {

      length = len;

   }

   public int getLength() {

      ..................... ;

   }

   public ...................... move() {

      return   "............... ";

   }

}
```

```
public class TestBoats {

   ...................... Main(){

   ............ xyz = "";

   ............. b1 = new Boat();

      Sailboat b2 = new ................ ();

      Rowboat ........... = new Rowboat();

      b2.setLength(32);

      xyz = b1. .......... ();

      xyz += b3. .......... ();

      xyz += .........move();

      System.Windows.Forms.MessageBox.Show(xyz);

   }

}
```

Hint: This is the entry point for the program.

```
public class ................ : Boat {

   public ............................... () {

      return "............... ";

   }

}
```

OUTPUT:

drift drift hoist sail

[OK]

Pool snippets:

Rowboat   subclasses
Sailboat   ;
Boat   Testboats   override
   int len   drift   hoist sail
return   virtual   stroke natasha   rowTheBoat
continue   int length   move
b1 .   break   :   int b1   string   setLength
b2 b3 length   int b2   int b3   void   public
   len   int b2   int   static   private   getLength

MiXed MessageS

```
a = 6;        56
b = 5;        11
a = 5;        65
```

EXercise Solution

```
public class A {
    public  virtual  string m1() {
    ...
    public  virtual  string m3() {
}
```

```
public class B : A {
    public  override  string m1() {
    ...
public class C : B {
    public  override  string m3() {
```

```
q += b.m1();
q += c.m2();  }
q += a.m3();
────────────
q += c.m1();
q += c.m2();  }
q += c.m3();

q += a.m1();
q += b.m2();  }
q += c.m3();
────────────
q += a2.m1();
q += a2.m2(); }
q += a2.m3();
```

A's m1, A's m2, C's m3, 6

B's m1, A's m2, A's m3,

A's m1, B's m2, C's m3, 6

B's m1, A's m2, C's m3, 13

B's m1, C's m2, A's m3,

A's m1, B's m2, A's m3,

B's m1, A's m2, C's m3, 6

A's m1, A's m2, C's m3, 13

Pool Puzzle Solution

```
public class Rowboat  Boat  {
    public  string  rowTheBoat() {
        return "stroke natasha";
    }
}
public class  Boat  {
    private int  length  ;
    public  void  setLength  ( int len ) {
        length = len;
    }
    public int getLength() {
        return length  ;
    }
    public  virtual string  move() {
        return "  drift  ";
    }
}
```

```
public class TestBoats {
    public static void Main(){
        string  xyz = "";
        Boat b1 = new Boat();
        Sailboat b2 = new  Sailboat  ();
        Rowboat  b3  = new Rowboat();
        b2.setLength(32);
        xyz = b1.  move  ();
        xyz += b3.  move  ();
        xyz +=  b2  .move();
        System.Windows.Forms.MessageBox.Show(xyz);
    }
}
public class  Sailboat  : Boat {
    public  override string move  () {
        return "  hoist sail  ";
    }
}
```

there are no
Dumb Questions

Q: About the entry point that you pointed out in the Pool Puzzle—does this mean I can have a program that doesn't have a Form1 form?

A: Yes. When you create a new Windows Application project, the IDE creates all the files for that project for you, including Program.cs (which contains a static class with an entry point) and Form1.cs (which contains an empty form called Form1).

Try this: instead of creating a new Windows Application project, create an empty project by selecting "Empty Project" instead of "Windows Application" when you create a new project in the IDE. Then add a class file to it in the Solution Explorer and type in everything in the Pool Puzzle solution. Since your program uses a messagebox, you need to add a **reference** by right-clicking on "References" in the Solution Explorer, selecting "Add Reference", and choosing System.Windows.Forms from the .NET tab. (That's another thing the IDE does for you automatically when you create a Windows Application.) Finally, select "Properties" from the Project menu and choose the "Windows Application" project type.

Now run it... you'll see the results! Congratulations, you just created a C# program from scratch.

↑
Flip back to the beginning of Chapter 2 if you need a refresher on Main() and the entry point!

Q: Can I inherit from the class that contains the entry point?

A: Yes. The entry point *must* be a static method, but that method *doesn't have to be* in a static class. (Remember, the static keyword means that the class can't be instantiated, but that its methods are available as soon as the program starts. So in the Pool Puzzle program, you can call TestBoats.Main() from any other method without declaring a reference variable or instantiating an object using a new statement.)

Q: I still don't get why they're called "virtual" methods—they seem real to me!

A: The name "virtual" has to do with how .NET handles the virtual methods behind the scenes. It uses something called a virtual method table (or vtable). That's a table that .NET uses to keep track of which methods are inherited and which ones have been overridden. Don't worry—you don't need to know how it works to use virtual methods!

Q: What did you mean by only being able to move up the class diagram but not being able to move down?

A: When you've got a diagram with one class that's above another one, the class that's higher up is more *abstract* than the one that's lower down. More specific or concrete classes (like Shirt or Car) inherit from more abstract ones (like Clothing or Vehicle). When you think about it that way, it's easy to see how if all you need is any vehicle, a car or van or motorcycle will do. But if you need a car, a motorcycle won't be useful to you.

Inheritance works exactly the same way. If you have a method with Vehicle as a parameter, and if the Motorcycle class inherits from the Vehicle class, then you can pass an instance of Motorcycle to the method. But if the method takes Motorcycle as a parameter, you can't pass any Vehicle object, because it may be a Van instance. Otherwise C# wouldn't know what to do when the method tries to access the Handlebars property!

You can always pass an instance of a subclass to any method whose parameters expect a class that it inherits from.

A subclass can access its base class using the base keyword

Even when you override a method or property in your base class,
sometimes you'll still want to access it. Luckily, we can use **base**, which
lets us access any method in the base class.

Animal
NumberOfLegs
Eat()
Swallow()
Digest()

Chameleon
TongueLength
Color
CatchWithTongue()

❶ All animals eat, so the `Animal` class has an `Eat()` method that takes a
`Food` object as its parameter.

```
public class Animal {
    public virtual void Eat(Food morsel) {
        Swallow(morsel);
        Digest();
    }
}
```

❷ Chameleons eat by catching food with their tongues. So the `Chameleon` class inherits
from `Animal` but overrides `Eat()`.

```
public class Chameleon : Animal {
    public override void Eat(Food morsel) {
        CatchWithTongue(morsel);
        Swallow(morsel);
        Digest();
    }
}
```

The chameleon needs to swallow and digest the food, just like any other animal. Do we really need to duplicate this code, though?

❸ Instead of duplicating the code, we can use the **base** keyword to call the method that
was overridden. Now we have access to both the old and the new version of `Eat()`.

```
public class Chameleon : Animal {
    public override void Eat(Food morsel) {
        CatchWithTongue(morsel);
        base.Eat(morsel);
    }
}
```

This line calls the Eat() method in the base class that Chameleon inherited from.

When a base class has a constructor, your subclass needs one too

If your class has a constructor, then any class that inherits from it **must call that constructor**. The subclass's constructor can have different parameters from the base class constructor.

Add this extra line to the end of your subclass's constructor declaration to tell C# that it needs to call the base class's constructor every time the subclass is instantiated.

```
public class Subclass : BaseClass {
    public Subclass(parameter list)
        : base(the base class's parameter list) {
        // first the base class constructor is executed
        // then any statements here get executed
    }
}
```

Here's the constructor for the subclass.

The base class constructor is executed before the subclass constructor

But don't take our word for it—see for yourself!

* **Do this!**

1 **Create a base class with a constructor that pops up a messagebox**

Then add a button to a form that instantiates this **base class** and shows a messagebox:

```
public class MyBaseClass {
    public MyBaseClass(string baseClassNeedsThis) {
        MessageBox.Show("This is the base class: " + baseClassNeedsThis);
    }
}
```

This is a parameter that the base class constructor needs.

Keep an eye out for this slightly cryptic error. It means that your subclass didn't inherit the constructor properly.

2 **Try adding a subclass, but don't call the constructor**

Then add a button to a form that instantiates this **subclass** and shows a messagebox:

```
public class MySubclass : MyBaseClass{
    public MySubclass(string baseClassNeedsThis, int anotherValue) {
        MessageBox.Show("This is the subclass: " + baseClassNeedsThis
            + " and " + anotherValue);
    }
```

Select Build >> Build Solution in the IDE and you'll get an error from this code.

❸ 1 No overload for method 'MyBaseClass' takes '0' arguments

3 **Fix the error by making the constructor call the one from the base class**

Then instantiate the subclass and **see what order** the two message boxes pop up!

```
public class MySubclass : MyBaseClass{
    public MySubclass(string baseClassNeedsThis, int anotherValue)
        : base(baseClassNeedsThis)
    {
        // the rest of the subclass is the same
```

This is how we send the base class the parameter its constructor needs.

Add this line to tell C# to call the constructor in the base class. It has a parameter list that shows what gets passed to the base class constructor. Then the error will go away and you can make a button to see the two message boxes pop up!

Now you're ready to finish the job for Kathleen!

When you last left Kathleen, you'd finished adding birthday parties to her program. She needs you to charge an extra $100 for parties over 12. It seemed like you were going to have to write the same exact code twice, once for each class. Now that you know how to use inheritance, you can have them inherit from the same base class that contains all of their shared code, so you only have to write it once.

DinnerParty
NumberOfPeople
CostOfDecorations
CostOfBeveragesPerPerson
HealthyOption
CalculateCostOfDecorations()
CalculateCost()
SetHealthyOption()

BirthdayParty
NumberOfPeople
CostOfDecorations
CakeSize
CakeWriting
CalculateCostOfDecorations()
CalculateCost()

Exercise

If we play our cards right, we should be able to change the two classes without making any changes to the form!

① Let's create the new class model

We'll still have the same DinnerParty and BirthdayParty classes, but now they'll inherit from a single Party class. We need them to have exactly the same methods, properties and fields, so we don't have to make any changes to the form. But some of those methods, properties, and fields will be moved into the Party base class, and we may have to override a few of them.

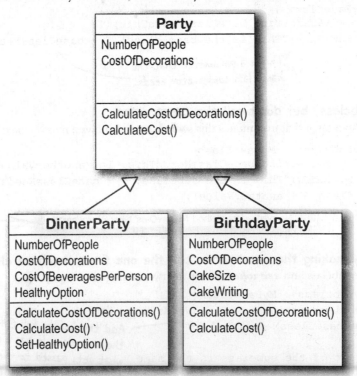

Party
NumberOfPeople
CostOfDecorations
CalculateCostOfDecorations()
CalculateCost()

DinnerParty
NumberOfPeople
CostOfDecorations
CostOfBeveragesPerPerson
HealthyOption
CalculateCostOfDecorations()
CalculateCost() `
SetHealthyOption()

BirthdayParty
NumberOfPeople
CostOfDecorations
CakeSize
CakeWriting
CalculateCostOfDecorations()
CalculateCost()

② **Build the Party base class**

Create the Party class—make sure it's public. You'll need to look really closely at the properties and methods in the class diagram, and figure out what you need to move out of DinnerParty and BirthdayParty and into Party.

★ Move the NumberOfPeople and CostOfDecorations properties into it so that they're compatible with both DinnerParty and BirthdayParty.

★ Do the same for the CalculateCostOfDecorations() and CalculateCost() methods. If those methods need any private fields, you'll need to move them too. (Remember, subclasses only inherit **public** fields—once you move a private field to Party, the DinnerParty and BirthdayParty classes won't have access to it.)

★ You'll also need a constructor. Take a close look at the BirthdayParty and DinnerParty constructors—anything they have in common should be moved to it.

★ Now **add the $100 bonus** for parties over 12 people. After all, that's why we're doing this! It's common to both birthday and dinner parties, so it belongs in Party.

③ **Make DinnerParty inherit from Party**

Now that Party does a lot of the things DinnerParty does, you can eliminate the overlap and only keep the part of DinnerParty that's unique to dinner parties.

★ Make sure the constructor is working properly. Does it do anything the Party constructor doesn't? If so, keep that and then leave everything else to the base class constructor.

★ Any logic that has to do with setting the healthy option should stay in DinnerParty.

★ You'll need to override at least one method because it does something specific to dinner parties.

④ **Make BirthdayParty inherit from Party**

Do the same thing for BirthdayParty—leave anything not specific to birthdays to the base class, and only keep the birthday-specific functionality in BirthdayParty.

★ What does the BirthdayParty constructor need to do that's not part of Party?

★ You'll need to deal with the cost of the cake inside of BirthdayParty. That touches a method and a property, so you'll need to override them.

★ Yes, you can override a property! It's just like overriding a method. When you set the value of base.NumberOfPeople, it calls the property's set accessor in the base class. You'll need to use the base keyword to both get and set the value.

Check it out—you changed the DinnerParty and BirthdayParty classes so that they inherited from the same base class, Party. Then you were able to make the change to the cost calculation to add the $100 fee, and you didn't have to change the form at all. Neat!

```
public class Party
{
    const int CostOfFoodPerPerson = 25;
    private bool fancyDecorations;
    public decimal CostOfDecorations = 0;

    public Party(int numberOfPeople, bool fancyDecorations) {
        this.fancyDecorations = fancyDecorations;
        this.NumberOfPeople = numberOfPeople;
    }

    private int numberOfPeople;
    public virtual int NumberOfPeople {
        get { return numberOfPeople; }
        set {
            numberOfPeople = value;
            CalculateCostOfDecorations(fancyDecorations);
        }
    }

    public void CalculateCostOfDecorations(bool fancy) {
        fancyDecorations = fancy;
        if (fancy)
            CostOfDecorations = (NumberOfPeople * 15.00M) + 50M;
        else
            CostOfDecorations = (NumberOfPeople * 7.50M) + 30M;
    }

    public virtual decimal CalculateCost() {
        // Each person costs $25 for food plus cost of beverages
        decimal TotalCost = CostOfDecorations + (CostOfFoodPerPerson * NumberOfPeople);
        if (NumberOfPeople > 12)
        {
            TotalCost += 100;
        }
        return TotalCost;
    }
}
```

This code was moved straight out of the DinnerParty and BirthdayParty classes and into Party.

The Party constructor does everything that was previously in both the DinnerParty and BirthdayParty constructors.

NumberOfPeople needs to be virtual because BirthdayParty needs to override it (so that a change to the number of people calculates a new cake size).

The decoration calculation is identical in both birthday and dinner parties, so it makes sense to move it to Party. That way none of the code is duplicated in multiple classes.

The cost calculation needs to be a virtual method because the birtday party overrides it (and also extends it by calling the base class method).

```
public class BirthdayParty : Party {
    public int CakeSize;

    public BirthdayParty(int numberOfPeople, bool fancyDecorations, string cakeWriting)
        : base(numberOfPeople, fancyDecorations) {
        CalculateCakeSize();
        this.CakeWriting = cakeWriting;
        CalculateCostOfDecorations(fancyDecorations);
    }

    private void CalculateCakeSize() {
        if (NumberOfPeople <= 4)
            CakeSize = 8;
        else
            CakeSize = 16;
    }

    private string cakeWriting = "";
    public string CakeWriting {
        get { return this.cakeWriting; }
        set {
            int maxLength;
            if (CakeSize == 8)
                maxLength = 16;
            else
                maxLength = 40;
            if (value.Length > maxLength) {
                MessageBox.Show("Too many letters for a " + CakeSize + " inch cake");
                if (maxLength > this.cakeWriting.Length)
                    maxLength = this.cakeWriting.Length;
                this.cakeWriting = cakeWriting.Substring(0, maxLength);
            } else
                this.cakeWriting = value;
        }
    }

    public override decimal CalculateCost() {
        decimal CakeCost;
        if (CakeSize == 8)
            CakeCost = 40M + CakeWriting.Length * .25M;
        else
            CakeCost = 75M + CakeWriting.Length * .25M;
        return base.CalculateCost() + CakeCost;
    }

    public override int NumberOfPeople {
        get { return base.NumberOfPeople; }
        set {
            base.NumberOfPeople = value;
            CalculateCakeSize();
            this.CakeWriting = cakeWriting;
        }
    }
}
```

The constructor relies on the base class to do most of the work. Then it calls CalculateCakeSize(), just like the old BirthdayParty constructor did.

The CalculateCakeSize() method is specific to birthday parties, so it stays in the BirthdayParty class.

The CakeWriting property stays intact in the BirthdayParty class too.

CalculateCost() also needs to be overridden, because it needs to first calculate the cost of the cake, and then add it to the cost that's calculated in the Party class's CalculateCost() method.

The NumberOfPeople property has to override the one in Party because the set accessor needs to recalculate the cake size. The set accessor needs to call base. NumberOfPeople so that the set accessor in Party also gets executed.

Continues on page 238.

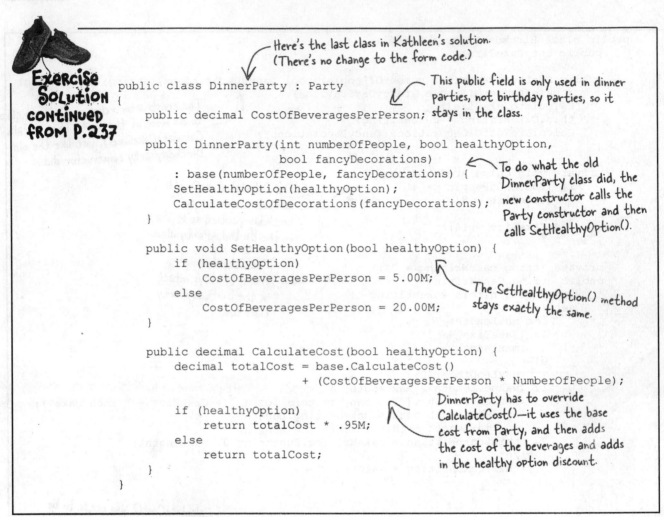

Exercise Solution continued from p.237

Here's the last class in Kathleen's solution. (There's no change to the form code.)

```
public class DinnerParty : Party
{
    public decimal CostOfBeveragesPerPerson;

    public DinnerParty(int numberOfPeople, bool healthyOption,
                    bool fancyDecorations)
        : base(numberOfPeople, fancyDecorations) {
        SetHealthyOption(healthyOption);
        CalculateCostOfDecorations(fancyDecorations);
    }

    public void SetHealthyOption(bool healthyOption) {
        if (healthyOption)
            CostOfBeveragesPerPerson = 5.00M;
        else
            CostOfBeveragesPerPerson = 20.00M;
    }

    public decimal CalculateCost(bool healthyOption) {
        decimal totalCost = base.CalculateCost()
                        + (CostOfBeveragesPerPerson * NumberOfPeople);

        if (healthyOption)
            return totalCost * .95M;
        else
            return totalCost;
    }
}
```

This public field is only used in dinner parties, not birthday parties, so it stays in the class.

To do what the old DinnerParty class did, the new constructor calls the Party constructor and then calls SetHealthyOption().

The SetHealthyOption() method stays exactly the same.

DinnerParty has to override CalculateCost()—it uses the base cost from Party, and then adds the cost of the beverages and adds in the healthy option discount.

The program's perfect. It's so much easier to run my business now—thanks so much!

Build a beehive management system

A queen bee needs your help! Her hive is out of control, and she needs a program to help manage it. She's got a beehive full of workers, and a whole bunch of jobs that need to be done around the hive. But somehow she's lost control of which bee is doing what, and whether or not she's got the beepower to do the jobs that need to be done.

It's up to you to build a beehive management system to help her keep track of her workers. Here's how it'll work:

① The queen assigns jobs to her workers

There are six possible jobs that the workers can do. Some know how to collect nectar and manufacture honey, others can maintain the hive and patrol for enemies. A few bees can do every job in the hive. So your program will need to give her a way to assign a job to any bee that's available to do it.

The bees work shifts, and most jobs require more than one shift. So the queen enters the number of shifts the job will take, and clicks the "Assign this job" button.

This dropdown list shows all six jobs that the workers can do. The queen knows what jobs need to be done, and she doesn't really care which bee does each job. So she just selects which job has to be done—the program will figure out if there's a worker available to do it and assign the job to him.

If there's a bee available to do the job, the program assigns the job to the bee and lets the queen know it's taken care of.

The queen bee says...

The job 'Honey manufacturing' will be done in 3 shifts

OK

② When the jobs are all assigned, it's time to work

Once the queen's done assinging the work, she'll tell the bees to work the next shift by clicking the "Work the next shift" button. The program then generates a shift report that tells her which bees worked that shift, what jobs they did, and how many more shifts they'll be working each job.

First you'll build the basic system

This project is divided into two parts. The first part is a bit of a review, where you'll create the basic system to manage the hive. It's got two classes, Queen and Worker. You'll build the form for the system, and hook it up to the two classes. And you'll make sure the classes are well encapsulated so they're easy to change when you move on to the second part.

Sometimes class diagrams list private fields and types.

Queen

private workers: Worker[]
private shiftNumber: int

AssignWork()
WorkTheNextShift()

CurrentJob and ShiftsLeft are read-only properties.

Worker

CurrentJob: string
ShiftsLeft: int

private jobsICanDo: string[]
private shiftsToWork: int
private shiftsWorked: int

DoThisJob()
WorkOneShift()

The program has one Queen object that manages the work being done.

★ The Queen uses an array of Worker objects to track each of the worker bees and whether or not those bees have been assigned jobs. It's stored in a private Worker[] field called `worker`.

★ The form calls the AssignWork() method, passing a string for the job that needs to be performed and an int for the number of shifts. It'll return true if it find a worker to assign the job to, or false if it couldn't find a worker to do that job.

★ The form's "Work the next shift" button calls WorkTheNextShift(), which tells the workers to work and returns a shift report to display. It tells each Worker object to work one shift, and then checks that worker's status so it can add a line to the shift report.

The queen uses an array of Worker objects to keep track of all of the workers and what jobs they're doing.

★ CurrentJob is a read-only property that tells the Queen object what job the worker's doing ("Sting patrol", "Hive maintenance", etc.) If the worker isn't doing any job, it'll return an empty string.

★ The Queen object attempts to assign a job to a worker using its DoThisJob() method. If that worker is not already doing the job, and if that's a job that he knows how to do, then he'll accept the assignment and the method returns true. Otherwise, it returns false.

★ When the WorkOneShift() method is called, the worker works a shift. He keeps track of how many shifts are left in the current job. If the job is done, then he resets his current job to an empty string so that he can take on his next assignment.

String.IsNullOrEmpty()

Since each bee stores its current job as a string, the way the worker knows whether or not he's not currently doing a job is to check if his CurrentJob property—it'll be equal to an empty string if he's waiting for his next job. C# gives you an easy way to do that: String.IsNullOrEmpty(CurrentJob) will return true if the CurrentJob string is either empty or null, false otherwise.

A queen bee needs your help! Use what you've learned about classes and objects to build a beehive management system to help her track her worker bees.

Exercise

① **Build the form**

The form is pretty simple—all of the intelligence is in the Queen and Worker classes. The form has a private Queen field, and two buttons call its AssignWork() and WorkTheNextShift() methods. You'll need to add a ComboBox control for the bee jobs (flip back to the previous page to see its list items), a NumericUpDown control, two buttons, and a multiline textbox for the shift report. You'll also need the form's constructor—it's below the screenshot.

This is a ComboBox control named workerBeeJob. Use its Items property to set the list, and set its DropDownStyle property to "DropDownList" so the user is only allowed to choose items from the list. The Shifts box is a NumericUpDown control called shifts.

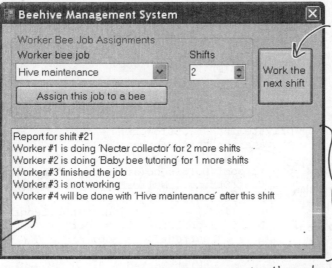

The nextShift button calls the queen's WorkTheNextShift() method, which returns a string that contains the shift report.

Look closely at this shift report, which the Queen object generates. It starts with a shift number, and then reports what each worker is doing. Use the escape sequences "\r\n" to add a line break in the middle of a string.

Name this text box "report" and set its MultiLine property to true.

```
public Form1() {
    InitializeComponent();
    Worker[] workers = new Worker[4];
    workers[0] = new Worker(new string[] { "Nectar collector", "Honey manufacturing" });
    workers[1] = new Worker(new string[] { "Egg care", "Baby bee tutoring" });
    workers[2] = new Worker(new string[] { "Hive maintenance", "Sting patrol" });
    workers[3] = new Worker(new string[] { "Nectar collector", "Honey manufacturing",
                "Egg care", "Baby bee tutoring", "Hive maintenance", "Sting patrol" });
    queen = new Queen(workers);
}
```

Each Worker object's constructor takes one parameter, an array of strings that tell it what jobs it knows how to do.

Your form will need a Queen field called queen. You'll pass that array of Worker object references to the Queen object's constructor.

② **Build the Worker and Queen classes**

You've got almost everything you need to know about the Worker and Queen classes. There are just a couple more details. Queen.AssignWork() loops through the the Queen object's `worker` array and attempts to assign the job to each Worker using its DoThisJob() method. The Worker object checks its `jobsICanDo` string array to see if it can do the job. If it can, it sets its private shiftsToWork field to the job duration, its CurrentJob to the job, and its shiftNumber to zero. When it works a shift, it decreases shiftNumber by one. The read-only ShiftsLeft property returns `shiftsToWork - shiftsWorked`—the queen uses it to see how many shifts are left on the job.

Exercise Solution

ShiftsLeft is a read-only property that calculates how many shifts are left on the current job.

CurrentJob is a read-only property that tells the queen which job needs to be done.

The queen uses the worker's DoThisJob() method to assign work to him—he checks his JobsICanDo property to see if he knows how to do the job.

```
public class Worker {
    public Worker(string[] jobsICanDo) {
        this.jobsICanDo = jobsICanDo;
    }

    public int ShiftsLeft {
        get {
            return shiftsToWork - shiftsWorked;
        }
    }

    private string currentJob = "";
    public string CurrentJob {
        get {
            return currentJob;
        }
    }

    private string[] jobsICanDo;
    private int shiftsToWork;
    private int shiftsWorked;

    public bool DoThisJob(string job, int numberOfShifts) {
        if (!String.IsNullOrEmpty(currentJob))
            return false;
        for (int i = 0; i < jobsICanDo.Length; i++)
            if (jobsICanDo[i] == job) {
                currentJob = job;
                this.shiftsToWork = numberOfShifts;
                shiftsWorked = 0;
                return true;
            }
        return false;
    }

    public bool WorkOneShift() {
        if (String.IsNullOrEmpty(currentJob))
            return false;
        shiftsWorked++;
        if (shiftsWorked > shiftsToWork) {
            shiftsWorked = 0;
            shiftsToWork = 0;
            currentJob = "";
            return true;
        }
        else
            return false;
    }
}
```

The constructor just sets the JobsICanDo property, which is a string array. It's private because we want the queen to ask the worker to do a job, rather than make her check whether he knows how to do it.

We used !—the NOT operator—to check if the string is NOT null or empty. It's just like checking to see if something's false.

The queen uses the worker's WorkOneShift() method to tell him to work the next shift. The method only returns true if this is the very last shift that he's doing the job. That way the queen can add a line to the report that the bee will be done after this shift.

Take a close look at the logic here. First it checks the currentJob field: if the worker's not working on a job, it just returns false, which stops the method. If not, then it increments ShiftsWorked, and then checks to see if this is the job's done by comparing it with ShiftsToWork. If it is, the method returns true. Otherwise it returns false.

```
public class Queen {
    public Queen(Worker[] workers) {
        this.workers = workers;
    }

    private Worker[] workers;
    private int shiftNumber = 0;

    public bool AssignWork(string job, int numberOfShifts) {
        for (int i = 0; i < workers.Length; i++)
            if (workers[i].DoThisJob(job, numberOfShifts))
                return true;
        return false;
    }

    public string WorkTheNextShift() {
        shiftNumber++;
        string report = "Report for shift #" + shiftNumber + "\r\n";
        for (int i = 0; i < workers.Length; i++)
        {
            if (workers[i].WorkOneShift())
                report += "Worker #" + (i + 1) + " finished the job\r\n";
            if (String.IsNullOrEmpty(workers[i].CurrentJob))
                report += "Worker #" + (i + 1) + " is not working\r\n";
            else
                if (workers[i].ShiftsLeft > 0)
                    report += "Worker #" + (i + 1) + " is doing '" + workers[i].CurrentJob
                        + "' for " + workers[i].ShiftsLeft + " more shifts\r\n";
                else
                    report += "Worker #" + (i + 1) + " will be done with '"
                        + workers[i].CurrentJob + "' after this shift\r\n";
        }
        return report;
    }
}
```

The queen keeps her array of workers private because once they're assigned, no other class should be able to change them... or even see them, since she's the only one who gives them orders. The constructor sets the field's value.

When she assigns work to her worker bees, she starts with the first one and tries assigning him the job. If he can't do it, she moves on to the next. When a bee who can do the job is found, the method returns (which stops the loop).

The queen's WorkTheNextShift() method tells each worker to work a shift and adds a line to the report depending on the worker's status.

We already gave you the constructor. Here's the rest of the code for the form:

The form uses its queen field to keep a reference to the Queen object, which in turn has an array of references to the worker objects.

```
Queen queen;

private void assignJob_Click(object sender, EventArgs e) {
    if (queen.AssignWork(workerBeeJob.Text, (int)shifts.Value) == false)
        MessageBox.Show("No workers are available to do the job '"
            + workerBeeJob.Text + "'", "The queen bee says...");
    else
        MessageBox.Show("The job '" + workerBeeJob.Text + "' will be done in "
            + shifts.Value + " shifts", "The queen bee says...");
}

private void nextShift_Click(object sender, EventArgs e) {
    report.Text = queen.WorkTheNextShift();
}
```

The nextShift button tells the queen to work the next shift. She generates a report, which it displays in the report text box.

The assignJob button calls the queen's AssignWork() method to assign work to a worker, and displays a messagebox depending on whether or not a worker's available to do the job.

Objectcross

Before you move on to the next part of the exercise, give your brain a break with a quick crossword.

Across

5. This method gets the value of a property.
7. This method returns true if you pass it "".
8. The constructor in a subclass class doesn't need the same _____ as the constructor in its base class.
9. A control on a form that lets you create tabbed applications.
11. This type of class can't be instantiated.

Down

1. A _____ can override methods from its base class.
2. If you want a subclass to override a method, mark the method with this keyword in the base class.
3. A method in a class that's run as soon as it's instantiated.
4. What a subclass does to replace a method in the base class.
6. This contains base classes and subclasses
7. What you're doing when add a colon to a class declaration.
10. A subclass uses this keyword to call the members of the class it inherited from.

⟶ Answers on page 250.

Use inheritance to extend the bee management system

Now that you have the basic system in place, use inheritance to let it track how much honey each bee consumes. Different bees consume different amounts of honey, and the queen consumes the most honey of all. So you'll use what you've learned about inheritance to create a Bee base class that Queen and Worker inherit from.

The Bee class has the basic honey consumption behavior. Since honey consumption requires the number of shifts left, we'll move the ShiftsLeft property into it and mark it virtual so the Worker can override it.

Bee

pblic ShiftsLeft: int

---

private
GetHoneyConsumption():
double

The worker just needs to subclass Bee override the ShiftsLeft method with the one you already wrote.

The queen needs to change her report to add honey consumption data. That means she needs to add each worker's honey consumption—and since she consumes honey herself, she'll need to inherit from Bee and override its virtual GetHoneyConsumption() method.

Queen

private workers: Worker[]
private shiftNumber: int

AssignWork()
WorkTheNextShift()

Worker

CurrentJob: string
ShiftsLeft: int

---

private jobsICanDo: string[]
private shiftsToWork: int
private shiftsWorked: int

DoThisJob()
WorkOneShift()

Add Existing Item

Whenever you have a two-part exercises, it's always a good idea to start a new project for the second part. That way you can always get back to the first solution if you need it. An easy way to do that is to right-click on the project name in the new project's Solution Explorer in the IDE, navigate to the old project's folder, and select the files you want to add. The IDE will make new copies of those files in the new project's folder, and add them to the project. There are a few things to watch out for, though. The IDE will NOT change the namespace, so you'll need to edit each class file and change its namespace line by hand. And if you add a form, make sure to add its designer (.Designer. cs) and resource (.resx) files—and make sure you change their namespaces, too.

Exercise

We're not done yet! The queen needs to keep track of how much honey the hive is spending on its workers. Here's a perfect chance to use your new inheritance skills!

① The queen needs to know how much honey the hive uses

The queen just got a call from her accountant bees, who told her that the hive isn't producing enough honey. She'll need to know how much honey she and her workers are using so she can decide whether to divert workers from egg maintenance to honey production.

★ All bees eat honey, so the hive runs through a lot of honey. That's why they need to keep making more of it.

★ Worker bees use more honey when they're working. They need the most honey when the job starts, to give them plenty of energy for the job,. They consume less and less as the job goes on. On the last shift the bee uses 10 units of honey, the second-to-last shift he uses 11 units, the shift before that he uses 12 units, etc. So if the bee's working (meaning its ShiftsLeft is greater than zero), then you can find out how many units of honey to consume by adding 9 to ShiftsLeft.

★ If a bee doesn't have a job (i.e., its ShiftsLeft is zero), he only uses 7.5 units of honey for the shift.

★ Those numbers are all for normal bees. If a bee weighs over 150 milligrams, it uses 35% more honey. This includes both workers and queens.

★ Queens require a lot of honey. A queen uses more honey when she's got more workers doing jobs, because it's a lot of work overseeing them. She needs to consume as much honey as if she'd worked as many shifts as the worker with the most shifts left on his job.

★ Then she needs even more honey: she uses 20 extra units of honey per shift if there are 2 or fewer workers working, or 30 extra units of honey if there are 3 or more worker bees doing jobs. The queen's consumption isn't subject to the 35% rule, since all queens weigh 275 milligrams.

★ The queen needs all the honey consumption numbers added to the end of each shift report.

② Create a Bee class to handle the honey calculations

Since the workers and queen all do their honey calculations in similar ways, you'll be able to avoid duplicating your code by having a Bee base class that Worker and Queen can inherit from. You know that each bee needs to know its weight (so it knows whether to multiply its honey expenditure by 35%).

★ Create a GetHoneyConsumption() method that calculates the amount of honey that a worker uses. Since the workers and queen all need to do this calculation but the queen needs to do extra calculations as well, it makes sense for the worker to inherit it and the queen to override it.

★ The GetHoneyConsumption() method needs the number of shifts left, so add a virtual read-only property called ShiftsLeft that returns zero. The worker's ShiftsLeft will override it.

★ The honey consumption calculation needs to know the bee's weight, so the Bee constructor will need to take the weight as a parameter and store it in a field. Since no other class needs to use it, you should make it private.

> Here's a good rule of thumb. You should make fields and methods private by default, and only make them public if another class needs them. That way you avoid bugs in your programs caused by one class accessing another class's properties or methods incorrectly.

Hint: You can use the slightly cryptic "no overload" error message to your advantage! Have the Worker class inherit from Bee, then build your project. When the IDE displays the error, double-click on it and the IDE will jump right to the Worker constructor automatically. How convenient!

③ Make the Worker class inherit from Bee

You'll need to set up the constructor to call the base class constructor, like you did with Kathleen. You'll need to change the Worker constructor so that it takes the bee's weight as a parameter, and pass that parameter on to the base class constructor. Then, just add the `override` keyword to the Worker's ShiftLeft method. Once you do that, each worker will be able to calculate his honey consumption for the queen... and you don't have to make any more changes to the Worker class!

④ Make the Queen class inherit from Bee

The Queen class needs a little more alteration than the Worker class, since she needs to actually do the honey calculation and add it to the shift report.

★ Override the Bee.GetHoneyConsumption() method and add the queen's extra calculation. She'll need to figure out whether she has 2 or fewer workers with jobs, so she knows whether she needs 20 or 30 units. Then she'll need to add that to the number of units she'd use if she had the same number of shifts left as the worker with the most shifts left.

★ Update the queen's WorkTheNextShift() by adding the a honey consumption line to the report. Add a loop to add up the honey consumptions for each worker and also find the worker with the largest honey consumption—do it **before** the queen tells each worker to work each shift (so she gets the consumption numbers for the current shift). She'll add those up, add her own consumption, and then add a line to the end of the shift report that says, "Total Honey Consumption: xxx units" (where xxx is the number of units of honey consumed).

★ You'll need to update the Queen constructor just like you did for Worker.

Go to the Queen class and type "public override"—when you press the space bar, the IDE automatically lists all the methods you can override. Select the method you want to override and it'll fill in the base method call automatically.

⑤ Update the form to instantiate the bees properly

Since you changed the Queen and Worker constructors, you'll also need to change the way they're called. Each constructor has a new Weight parameter, so you'll need weights to use:

★ Worker Bee #1: 175mg; Worker Bee #2: 114mg; Worker Bee #3: 149mg; Worker Bee#4: 155mg; Queen Bee: 275mg

That's the only change you'll need to make to the form!

Exercise Solution

Here's the Bee class. It does the basic honey consumption calculation that's used by both the Worker and Queen classes.

```
public class Bee {
    public Bee(double weight) {
        this.weight = weight;
    }

    public virtual int ShiftsLeft {
        get { return 0; }
    }

    private double weight;

    public virtual double GetHoneyConsumption() {
        double consumption;
        if (ShiftsLeft == 0)
            consumption = 7.5;
        else
            consumption = 9 + ShiftsLeft;
        if (weight > 150)
            consumption *= 1.35;
        return consumption;
    }
}
```

The Bee class has a constructor that sets its Weight field and a HoneyConsumption() method that calculates how much honey a worker consumes.

If a bee has 1 shift left, he consumes 10; if 2 left, he consumes 11, etc. If he has no job, then he consumes 7.5. If ShiftsLeft is zero, then the bee has no job.

If the bee weighs more than 150mg, then consumption goes up by 35%.

Inheritance made it easy for you to update your code and add the new honey consumption behavior to the Queen and Worker classes. It would have been a lot harder to make this change if you'd had a lot of duplicated code.

Only the form constructor changed—the rest of the form is exactly the same.

```
public Form1() {
    InitializeComponent();

    Worker[] workers = new Worker[4];
    workers[0] = new Worker(new string[] { "Nectar collector", "Honey manufacturing" }, 175);
    workers[1] = new Worker(new string[] { "Egg care", "Baby bee tutoring" }, 114);
    workers[2] = new Worker(new string[] { "Hive maintenance", "Sting patrol" }, 149);
    workers[3] = new Worker(new string[] { "Nectar collector", "Honey manufacturing",
            "Egg care", "Baby bee tutoring", "Hive maintenance", "Sting patrol" }, 155);
    queen = new Queen(workers);
}
```

The only change to the form is that the weights need to be added to the Worker constructors.

```
public class Worker : Bee {
    public Worker(string[] jobsICanDo, int weight)
        : base(weight) {
        this.jobsICanDo = jobsICanDo;
    }

    public override int ShiftsLeft {
    // ... the rest of the class is the same ...
```

All the Worker class needed was to inherit from Bee and have its constructor adjusted so that it takes a Weight parameter and passes it on to the base class constructor, and overrides the Bee.ShiftsLeft property by adding the override keyword to the property declaration.

The Queen class needed a few changes, starting with inheriting from Bee.

```
public class Queen : Bee {
    public Queen(Worker[] workers)
        : base(275) {
        this.workers = workers;
    }

    public string WorkTheNextShift()
    {
        double totalConsumption = 0;
        for (int i = 0; i < workers.Length; i++)
            totalConsumption += workers[i].GetHoneyConsumption();
        totalConsumption += GetHoneyConsumption();

        // ... here's where the orignal code for this method goes

        report += "Total honey consumption: " + totalConsumption + " units";
        return report;
    }

    public override double GetHoneyConsumption() {
        double consumption = 0;
        double largestWorkerConsumption = 0;
        int workersDoingJobs = 0;
        for (int i = 0; i < workers.Length; i++) {
            if (workers[i].GetHoneyConsumption() > largestWorkerConsumption)
                largestWorkerConsumption = workers[i].GetHoneyConsumption();
            if (workers[i].ShiftsLeft > 0)
                workersDoingJobs++;
        }
        consumption += largestWorkerConsumption;
        if (workersDoingJobs >= 3)
            consumption += 30;
        else
            consumption += 20;
        return consumption;
    }
}
```

The queen weighs 275mg, so her constructor calls the base Bee constructor and passes it a weight of 275.

The WorkTheNextShift() has a loop added to the top that calls each worker's GetHoneyConsumption() method, and then calls her own GetHoneyConsumption() method to come up with a total consumption.

The rest of WorkTheNextShift() is the same, except that it adds the honey line to the report.

The queen overrides the Bee's GetHoneyConsumption() method to do her honey calculation. It finds the worker with the largest consumption and adds either 20 or 30 to it based on how many workers are working.

This loop looks at the consumption of all the workers and finds the one with the largest consumption.

If there are 3 or more workers doing jobs, the queen needs 30 more units of honey; otherwise, she needs 20 more units.

Objectcross Solution

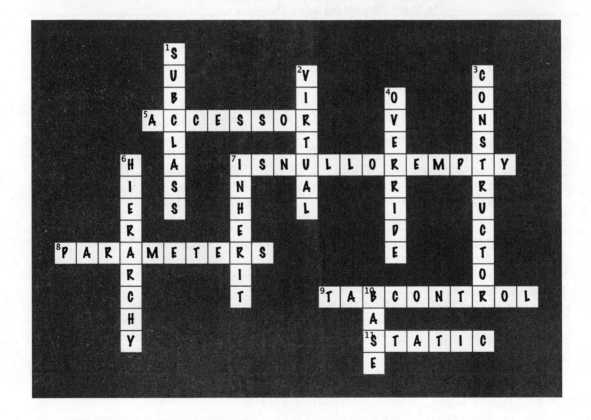

7 interfaces and abstract classes

Making classes keep their promises

> Okay, okay, I know I implemented the BookieCustomer interface, but I can't code the PayMoney() method until next weekend.

> You've got three days before I send some Thug objects by to make sure you implement the WalksWithALimp() method.

Actions speak louder than words.

Sometimes you need to group your objects together based on the **things they can do** rather than the classes they inherit from. That's where **interfaces** come in—they let you work with any class that can do the job. But with **great power comes great responsibility**, and any class that implements an interface must promise to **fulfill all of its obligations**... or the compiler will break their kneecaps, see?

Let's get back to bee-sics

The General Bee-namics corporation wants to make the Beehive Management System you created in the last chapter into a full-blown Hive Simulator. Here's an overview of the specification for the new version of the program:

General Bee-namics Hive Simulator

To better represent life in the hive, we'll need to add specialized capabilities to the worker bees.

- All bees consume honey and have a weight.

- Queens assign work, monitor shift reports, and tell workers to work the next shift.

- All worker bees work shifts.

- Sting patrol bees will need to be able to sharpen their stingers, look for enemies, and sting them.

- Nectar collector bees are responsible for finding flowers, gathering nectar and then returning to the hive.

The Bee and Worker classes don't look like they'll change much. We can extend the classes we already have to handle these new features.

Looks like we'll need to be able to store different data for the worker bees depending on the job they do.

Lots of things are still the same

The bees in the new hive simulator will still consume honey in the same way they did before. The queen still needs to be able to assign work to the workers and see the shift reports that tell who's doing what. The workers work shifts just like they did before, too, it's just that the jobs they are doing have been elaborated a little bit.

We can use inheritance to create classes for different types of bees

Here's a class hierarchy with Worker and Queen classes that inherit from Bee, and Worker has subclasses NectarCollector and StingPatrol.

Here's where information about the weight and honey consumption is stored.

Here's where all of the information about working shifts is kept.

Remember how the queen needed extra honey? Here's where we overrode her HoneyConsumption() method.

This is what the new subclasses will look like.

StingPatrol and NectarCollector inherit from the Worker class.

And these classes hold the information particular to each job.

Bee
Weight

HoneyConsumption()

Worker
Job
ShiftsToWork
ShiftsWorked
ShiftsLeft

DoThisJob()
WorkOneShift()

Queen
Worker[]
ShiftNumber

AssignWork()
WorkTheNextShift()
HoneyConsumption()

StingPatrol
StingerLength
EnemyAlert

SharpenStinger()
LookForEnemies()
Sting()

NectarCollector
Nectar

FindFlowers()
GatherNectar()
ReturnToHive()

```
class StingPatrol : Worker
{
    int StingerLength;
    bool enemyAlert;
    public bool SharpenStinger (int Length)
    {...}
    public bool LookForEnemies(){...}
    public void Sting(string Enemy){...}
}

class NectarCollector : Worker
{
    int Nectar;
    public void FindFlowers (){...}
    public void GatherNectar(){...}
    public void ReturnToHive(){...}
}
```

BRAIN POWER

What happens if you have a bee that needs to sting *and* collect nectar?

An interface tells a class that it **must** implement certain methods and properties

A class can only inherit from one other class. So creating two separate subclasses for the `StingPatrol` and `NectarCollector` bees won't help us if we have a bee that can do **both** jobs. Luckily, C# gives us **interfaces** to handle situations like that. Interfaces let you define a bunch of methods that a class **must** have.

An interface **requires** that a class has certain methods, and the way that it does that is that it **makes the compiler throw errors** if it doesn't find all the methods required by the interface in every class that implements it. Those methods can be coded directly in the class, or they can be inherited from a base class. The interface doesn't care how the methods or properties get there, as long as they're there when the code is compiled.

> You use an interface to require a class to include all of the methods and properties listed inside the interface—if it doesn't, the compiler will throw an error.

The queen's DefendTheHive() method can only tell StingPatrol objects to keep the hive safe. She'd love to train the other bees to use their stingers, but she doesn't have any way to command them to attack.

I wish you guys could help defend the hive.

By adding a class file with the IStingPatrol interface to the project and modifying the BeeCare class to use it, you give the queen a way to be sure that any BeeCare object knows how to defend the hive.

If we create an `IStingPatrol` interface, then any bee object that implements it and adds AlertLevel, StingerLength, LookForEnemies(), and SharpenStinger() can go defend the hive.

These are the same Maintenance and BeeCare objects, but now that they've implemented the `IStingPatrol` interface, they know how to sharpen their stingers and look for any enemies.

Interface names start with I

Whenever you create an interface, you should make its name start with an uppercase I. There's no rule that says you need to do it, but it makes your code a lot easier to understand. You can see for yourself just how much easier that can make your life. Just go into the IDE to any blank line inside any method and type "I". You'll see IntelliSense pop up a whole bunch of built-in .NET interfaces. Since they all start with I, it's immediately obvious that they're interfaces and not classes.

Use the `interface` keyword to define an interface

Adding an interface to your program is a lot like adding a class, except you never write any methods. You just define the methods' return type and parameters, but instead of a block of statements inside curly brackets you just end the line with a semicolon.

Interfaces do not store data, so you **can't add any fields**. But you *can* add definitions for properties. The reason is that a get or accessor is just a different kind of method, and interfaces are all about forcing classes to have certain methods with specific names, types and parameters. So if you want your interface to require a field with a certain name and type, just **use a property instead**—it'll accomplish the same thing.

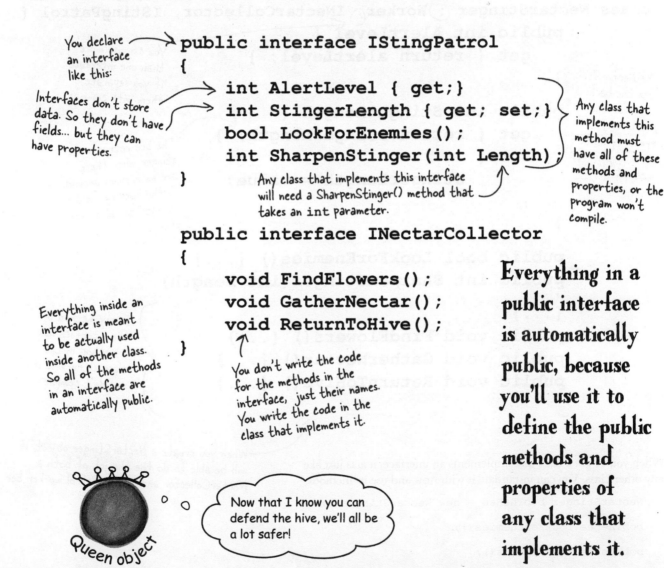

You declare an interface like this:

```
public interface IStingPatrol
{
    int AlertLevel { get;}
    int StingerLength { get; set;}
    bool LookForEnemies();
    int SharpenStinger(int Length);
}
```

Interfaces don't store data. So they don't have fields... but they can have properties.

Any class that implements this interface will need a SharpenStinger() method that takes an int parameter.

Any class that implements this method must have all of these methods and properties, or the program won't compile.

```
public interface INectarCollector
{
    void FindFlowers();
    void GatherNectar();
    void ReturnToHive();
}
```

Everything inside an interface is meant to be actually used inside another class. So all of the methods in an interface are automatically public.

You don't write the code for the methods in the interface, just their names. You write the code in the class that implements it.

Queen object

Now that I know you can defend the hive, we'll all be a lot safer!

Everything in a public interface is automatically public, because you'll use it to define the public methods and properties of any class that implements it.

Now you can create an instance of NectarStinger that does both jobs

You use the **colon operator** to declare an interface, just like you do for inheritance. It works like this: the first thing after the colon is the class it inherits from, followed by a list of interfaces -- unless it doesn't inherit from a class, in which case it's just a list of interfaces (in no particular order).

You implement an interface with a colon operator, just like you inherit.

This class inherits from Worker and implements INectarCollector and IStingPatrol.

```
class NectarStinger : Worker, INectarCollector, IStingPatrol {
    public int AlertLevel {
        get { return alertLevel; }
    }

    public int StingerLength {
        get { return stingerLength; }
        set {
            stingerLength = value;
        }
    }

    public bool LookForEnemies() {...}
    public int SharpenStinger(int Length)
    {...}
    public void FindFlowers() {...}
    public void GatherNectar() {...}
    public void ReturnToHive() {...}
}
```

The NectarStinger sets the backing field for the AlertLevel property in its LookForEnemies() method.

You can use more than one interface if you separate them with commas.

The bee retracts its stinger when there are no enemies around, so the backing field changes its value over time.

Every method in the interface has a method in the class. Otherwise it wouldn't compile.

When you create a NectarStinger object, it will be able to do the the job of both a NectarCollector and a StingPatrol worker bee.

When you've got a class that implements an interface, it acts just like any other class. You can instantiate it with new and use its methods:

```
NectarStinger bobTheBee = new NectarStinger();

bobTheBee.LookForEnemies();

bobTheBee.FindFlowers();
```

Classes that implement interfaces have to include <u>ALL</u> of the interface's methods

Implementing an interface means that you have to have a method in the class for each and every property and method that's declared in the interface—if it doesn't have every one of them, it won't compile. If a class implements more than one interface, then it needs to include all of the properties and methods in each of the interfaces it implements. But don't take our word for it...

Do this!

① **Create a new application and add a new class file called IStingPatrol.cs**
Instead of adding a class, type in the **IStingPatrol** interface on the previous page.

② **Add a Bee class to the project**
Don't add any properties or methods yet. Just have it implement IStingPatrol:

```
public class Bee : IStingPatrol {
```

③ **Try to compile the program**
Select "Rebuild" from the Build menu. Uh-oh—the compiler won't let you do it:

You'll see one of these "does not implement" errors for every member of IStingPatrol that's not implemented in the class. The compiler really wants you to implement every method in the interface.

④ **Add the methods and properties to the Bee class**
Add a LookForEnemies method and a SharpenStinger method—they don't have to do anything, they just need to compile. Then add a get accessor for an int called AlertLevel and get and set accessors for an int called StingerLength. Now the program will compile!

Get a little practice using interfaces

Interfaces are really easy to use, but the best way to understand is to start using them. So create a new Windows Forms Application project, drag a button onto the form, and get started!

Do this!

❶ Here's the TallGuy class, and the code for a button that creates it using an object initializer and calls its TalkAboutYourself() method. Nothing new here—we'll use it in a minute:

```
public class TallGuy {
    public string Name;
    public int Height;

    public void TalkAboutYourself() {
        MessageBox.Show("My name is " + Name + " and I'm "
            + Height + " inches tall.");
    }
}

private void button1_Click(object sender, EventArgs e) {
    TallGuy tallGuy = new TallGuy() { Height = 74, Name = "Jimmy" };
    tallGuy.TalkAboutYourself();
}
```

❷ Let's create an IClown interface for the class.

You already know that everything inside an interface has to be public. But don't take our word for it. Create a new project and declare an interface on your own, like this:

public interface IClown

Now try to declare a private method inside the interface:

private void Honk();

Select Build>>Build Solution in the IDE. You'll see this error:

> ⊗ 1   The modifier 'private' is not valid for this item

Now go ahead and **delete the private access modifier**—the error will go away and your program will compile just fine.

You don't need to type "public" inside the interface, because it automatically makes every property and method public.

❸ Before you go on to the next page, see if you can create the rest of the IClown interface, and modify the TallGuy class to implement this interface. Add your interface to your project just like you add a class: right-click on the project in the Solution Explorer and add a class file called IClown.cs.

Your new IClown interface should have a void method called Honk that doesn't take any parameters, and a string read-only property called FunnyThingIHave that has a get accessor but no set accessor.

❹ Here's the interface—did you get it right?

```
public interface IClown
{
    string FunnyThingIHave { get; }
    void Honk();
}
```

Here's an example of an interface that has a get accessor without a set accessor. Remember, interfaces can't contain fields, but when you implement this read-only property in a class, it'll look like a field to other objects.

Okay, now modify the TallGuy class so that it implements clown. Remember, the colon operator is always followed by the base class to inherit from (if any), and then a list of interfaces to implement, all separated by commas. Since there's no base class and only one interface to implement, the declaration looks like this:

← TallGuy will implement the IClown interface.

```
public class TallGuy : IClown  ←
```

What the IDE is telling you is that when you said TallGuy would implement IClown, you promised to add all of the properties and methods in that interface... and then you broke that promise!

Then make sure the rest of the class is the same, including the two fields and the method. Select "Build Solution" from the Build menu in the IDE to compile and build the program. You'll see two errors, including this one:

```
'TallGuy' does not implement interface
member 'IClown.Honk()'
```

❻ The errors will go away as soon as you add all of the methods and properties defined in the interface. So go ahead and implement the interface. Add a read-only string property called FunnyThingIHave with a get accessor that always returns the string "big shoes". Then add a Honk() method that pops up a message box that says, "Honk honk!".

Here's what it'll look like:

All the interface requires is that a class that implements it has a property called FunnyThingIHave with a get accessor. You can put any get accessor in there, even one that just returns the same string every time. Most get accessors won't do this, but this will work just fine if it does what you need it to do.

```
public string FunnyThingIHave {
    get { return "big shoes"; }
}

public void Honk() {
    MessageBox.Show("Honk honk!");
}
```

The interface says that you need a public void method called Honk, but it doesn't say what that method needs to do. It can do anything at all—no matter what it does, the code will compile as long as some method is there with the right signature.

❼ Now your code will compile! Update your button so that the object initializer sets the FunnyThingIHave property, and the button calls the TallGuy object's Honk() method.

You can't instantiate an interface, but you can <u>reference</u> an interface

Say you had a method that needed an object that could perform the FindFlowers() method. Any object that implemented the INectarCollector interface would do. It could be a Worker object, or a Robot object or a Dog object as long as it implements the INectarCollector interface.

That's where **interface references** come in. You can use one to refer to an object that implements the interface you need and you'll always be sure that it has the right methods for your purpose—even if you don't know much else about it.

> *If you try to the instantiate an interface, the compiler will complain.*

This won't work...

```
IStingPatrol dennis = new IStingPatrol();
```

> ⊗ 1   Cannot create an instance of the abstract class or interface

You can't use the new keyword with an interface, which makes sense—the methods and properties don't have any implementation. If you could create an object from an interface, how would it know how to behave?

...but this will.

```
NectarStinger fred = new NectarStinger();
IStingPatrol george = fred;
```

> *Remember how you could pass a BLT reference into any class that expects a Sandwich, because BLT inherits from Sandwich? Well, this is the same thing—you can use a NectarStinger in any method or statement that expects an IStingPatrol.*

> *Even though this object can do more, when you use an interface reference you only have access to the methods in the interface.*

The first line is an ordinary new statement, creating reference called Fred and pointing it to a NectarStinger object.

The second line is where things start to get interesting, because that line of code **creates a new reference variable using IStingPatrol.** That line may look a little odd when you first see it. But look at this:

```
NectarStinger ginger = fred;
```

You know what this third statement does—it creates a new NectarStinger reference called `ginger` and points it at whatever object `fred` is pointing to. The `george` statement uses IStingPatrol the same way.

So what happened?

There's only one new statement, so **only one object** was created. The second statement created a reference variable called `george` that can point to an instance of **any class that implements IStingPatrol**.

Interface references work just like object references

You already know all about how objects live on the heap. When you work with an interface reference, it's just another way to refer to the same objects you've already been dealing with. Look—it's easy!

① Create a couple of bees

This is totally familiar stuff by now.

```
StingPatrol biff = new StingPatrol();
NectarCollector bertha = new NectarCollector();
```

② Add IStingPatrol and INectarCollector references

You can use interface references just like you use any other reference type.

```
IStingPatrol defender = biff;
INectarCollector cutiePie = bertha;
```

These two statements use interfaces to create new references to existing objects. You can only point an interface reference at an instance of a class that implements it.

③ An interface reference will keep an object alive

When there aren't any references pointing to an object, it disappears. But there's no rule that says those references all have to be the same type! An interface reference is just as good as an object reference when it comes to keeping track of objects.

```
biff = null;
```

This object didn't disappear because defender is still pointing to it.

④ Assign a new instance to an interface reference

You don't actually *need* an object reference—you can create a new object and assign it straight to an interface reference variable.

```
INectarCollector gatherer = new NectarStinger();
```

You can find out if a class implements a certain interface with "is"

Sometimes you need to find out if a certain class implements an interface. Suppose we have all our worker bees in an array, called Bees. We can make the array hold the type Worker, since all worker bees will be Worker classes, or subclasses of that type.

But which of the worker bees can collect nectar? In other words, we want to know if the class implements the INectarCollector interface. We can use the **is** keyword to find out exactly that.

> All the workers are in an array of Workers. We'll use "is" to sort out which type of worker each bee is.

```
Worker[] Bees = new Worker[3];
Bees[0] = new NectarCollector();
Bees[1] = new StingPatrol();
Bees[2] = new NectarStinger();
for (int i = 0; i < Bees.Length; i++)
{
    if (Bees[i] is INectarCollector)
    {

        Bees[i].DoThisJob("Nectar Collector", 3);
    }
}
```

> We've got an array of Worker bees who are all eligible to go on a nectar collecting mission. So we'll loop though the array, and use "is" to figure out which ones have the right methods and properties to do the job.

> is works like an equals operator (==) for interfaces

> This is like saying, if this bee implements the INectarCollector interface... do this.

> Now that we know the bee is a nectar collector, we can assign it the job of collecting nectar.

BRAIN POWER

If you have some other class that doesn't inherit from Worker but **does** implement the INectarCollector interface, then it'll be able to do the job, too! But since it doesn't inherit from Worker, you can't get it into an array with other bees. Can you think of a way to get around the problem and create an array with both bees and this new class?

Interfaces can inherit from other interfaces

When we draw an interface on a class diagram, we'll show inheritance using dashed lines.

When one class inherits from another, it gets all of the methods and properties from the base class. **Interface inheritance** is even simpler. Since there's no actual method body in any interface, you don't have to worry about calling base constructors or methods. The inherited interfaces simply accumulate all of the methods and properties from the interfaces they inherit from.

```
public interface IWorker
{
    string Job { get; }
    int Left { get; }
    void DoThisJob(string Job, int Shifts)
    void WorkOneShift()
}
```

We've created a new IWorker interface that the other interfaces inherit from.

(interface) IWorker
Job ShiftsLeft
DoThisJob() WorkOneShift()

(interface) IStingPatrol
StingerLength EnemyAlert
SharpenStinger() LookForEnemies() Sting()

(interface) INectarCollector
Nectar
FindFlowers() GatherNectar() ReturnToHive()

Any class that implements an interface that inherits from IWorker <u>must implement</u> its methods and properties

When a class implements an interface, it has to include every property and method in that interface. And if that interface inherits from another one, then all of *those* properties and methods need to be implemented, too.

```
public interface IStingPatrol : IWorker
{
    int AlertLevel { get;}
    int StingerLength { get; set;}
    bool LookForEnemies();
    int SharpenStinger(int Length);
}
```

Here's the same IStingPatrol interface, but now it inherits from the IWorker interface. It looks like a tiny change, but it makes a huge difference in any class that implements IStingPatrol.

A class that implements IStingPatrol must not only implement these methods...

...but the methods of the IWorker interface this interface inherits from, too.

(interface) IWorker
Job ShiftsLeft
DoThisJob() WorkOneShift()

The RoboBee 4000 can do a worker bee's job without using valuable honey

Let's create a new bee, a RoboBee 4000, that runs on gas. We can have it inherit from the IWorker interface, though, so it can do everything a normal worker bee can.

RoboBee
ShiftsToWork
ShiftsWorked
ShiftsLeft
Job
DoThisJob()

This is our basic Robot class, so robots can run on gasoline.

```
public class Robot
{
    public void ConsumeGas() {...}
}

public class RoboBee : Robot, IWorker
{
    private int shiftsToWork;
    private int shiftsWorked;
    public int ShiftsLeft
       {get {return ShiftsToWork - ShiftsLeft;}}
    private string job;
    public string Job;{get{return job;}}
    public bool DoThisJob(string Job, int ShiftsToWork){...}
}
```

The RoboBee class inherits from Robot and implements IWorker. That means it's a robot, but can do the job of a worker bee. Perfect!

The RoboBee class implements all the methods from the IWorker interface.

If RoboBee didn't implement everything in the IWorker Interface, the code wouldn't compile.

Remember, for other classes in the application, there's no functional difference between a RoboBee and a normal worker bee. They both implement the IWorker interface, so both act like worker bees as far as the rest of the program is concerned.

But, you could distringuish between the types by using `is`:

```
if (workerBee is Robot) {
  // now we know workerBee
  // is a Robot object
}
```

We can see what class or interface workerBee implements or subclasses with "is."

Any class can implement ANY interface as long as it keeps the promise of implementing the interface's methods and properties.

<u>is</u> tells you what an object im<u>plements</u>, <u>as</u> tells the compiler how to <u>treat</u> your object

Sometimes you need to call a method that an object gets from an interface it implements. But what if you don't know if that object is the right type? You use **is** to find that out. Then, you can use **as** to treat that object—which you now know is the right type—as having the method you need to call.

```
IWorker[] Bees = new IWorker[3];
    Bees[0] = new NectarStinger();
    Bees[1] = new RoboBee();
    Bees[2] = new Worker();
```

All these bees implement IWorker, but we don't know which ones implement other interfaces, like INectarCollector.

We're looping through each bee...

```
for (int i = 0; i < Bees.Length; i++) {
    if (Bees[i] is INectarCollector) {
        INectarCollector thisCollector;
        thisCollector = workers[i] as INectarCollector;
        thisCollector.EmptyNectarBucket();
```

...and checking to see if it implements INectarCollector.

We can't call INectarCollector methods on the bees. They're of type IWorker, and don't know about INectarCollector methods.

NOW we can call INectarCollector methods.

We use "as" to say, treat this object AS an INectarCollector implementation.

Sharpen your pencil

Take a look at the array on the left. For each of these statements, write down which values of i would make it evaluate to true. Also, two of them won't compile—cross those lines out.

```
IWorker[] Bees = new IWorker[8];
Bees[0] = new NectarStinger();
Bees[1] = new RoboBee();
Bees[2] = new Worker();
Bees[3] = Bees[0] as IWorker;
Bees[4] = IStingPatrol;
Bees[5] = null;
Bees[6] = Bees[2];
Bees[7] = new INectarCollector();
```

1. (Bees[i] is INectarCollector)

....

2. (Bees[i] is IStingPatrol)

....

3. (Bees[i] is IWorker)

....

A CoffeeMaker is also an Appliance

If you're trying to figure out how to cut down your energy bill each month, you don't really care what each of your appliances does. You only really care that they consume power. So if you were writing a program to monitor your electricity consumption, you'd probably just write an Appliance class. But if you needed to be able to distinguish a coffee maker from an oven, you'd have to build a class hierarchy. So you'd add the methods and properties that are specific to a coffee maker or oven to some CoffeeMaker and Oven classes, and they'd inherit from an Appliance class that has their common methods and properties..

```
public void MonitorPower(Appliance appliance) {
    // code to add data to a household
    // power consumption database
}

    CoffeeMaker misterCoffee = new CoffeeMaker();
    MonitorPower(misterCoffee);
```

Here's a method in the program to monitor the power consumption for a house.

This code would appear later on in the program to monitor the coffee maker's power consumption.

Even though the MonitorPower() method takes a reference to an Appliance object, you can pass it the misterCoffee reference because CoffeeMaker is a subclass of Appliance.

You already saw this in the last chapter, when you saw how you could pass a BLT reference to a method that expected a Sandwich.

Sharpen your pencil
Solution

Take a look at the array on the left. For each of these statements, write down which values of i would make it evaluate to true. Also, two of them won't compile—cross them out.

```
IWorker[] Bees = new IWorker[8];
Bees[0] = new NectarStinger();
Bees[1] = new RoboBee();
Bees[2] = new Worker();
Bees[3] = Bees[0] as IWorker;
Bees[4] = IStingPatrol;
Bees[5] = null;
Bees[6] = Bees[0];
Bees[7] = new INectarCollector();
```

NectarStinger() implements the IStingPatrol interface.

All of these objects inherit from base class Worker.

1. (Bees[i] is INectarCollector)

   0, 5 and 7

2. (Bees[i] is IStingPatrol)

   0, 6

3. (Bees[i] is IWorker)

   0, 1, 2, 3, and 6

266   Chapter 7

Upcasting works with both objects and interfaces

When you substitute a subclass for a base class—like substituting a coffee maker for an appliance or a BLT for a sandwich—it's called **upcasting**. It's a really powerful tool that you get when you build class hierarchies. The only drawback to upcasting is that you can only use the properties and methods of the base class. In other words, when you treat a coffee maker like an appliance, you can't tell it to make coffee or fill it with water. But you *can* tell whether or not it's plugged in, since that's something you can do with any appliance (which is why the PluggedIn property is part of the Appliance class).

① Let's create some objects
We can create a CoffeeMaker and Oven class as usual:

```
CoffeeMaker misterCoffee = new CoffeeMaker();

Oven oldToasty = new Oven();
```

> We'll start by instantiating an Oven object and a CoffeeMaker object as usual.

② What if we want to create an array of appliances?
You can't put a CoffeeMaker in an Oven[] array, and you can't put an Oven in a CoffeeMaker[] array. But you can put both of them in an Appliance[] array:

```
Appliance[] kitchenWare = new Appliance[2];

kitchenWare[0] = misterCoffee;

kitchenWare[1] = oldToasty;
```

> You can use upcasting to create an array of appliances that can hold both coffee makers and ovens.

③ But you can't treat an appliance like an oven
When you've got an Appliance reference, you can **only** access the methods and properties that have to do with appliances. You **can't** use the coffee maker methods and properties through the Appliance reference *even if you know it's really a CoffeeMaker*. So these statements will work just fine, because they treat a CoffeeMaker object like an Appliance:

```
Appliance powerConsumer = new CoffeeMaker();

powerConsumer.ConsumePower();
```

But as soon as you try to use it like a Coffee Maker:

```
powerConsumer.MakeCoffee();
```

> This line won't compile because powerConsumer is an Appliance reference, so it can only be used to do Appliance things.

> powerConsumer is an Appliance reference pointing to a CoffeeMaker object.

your code won't compile, and the IDE will displays an error:

> ⓧ 'Appliance' does not contain a definition for 'MakeCoffee'

because once you upcast from a subclass to a base class, then you can only access the methods and properties that **match the reference** that you're using to access the object.

Downcasting lets you turn your appliance back into a coffee maker

Upcasting is a great tool, because it lets you use a coffee maker or an oven anywhere you just need an appliance. But it's got a big drawback—if you're using an Appliance reference that points to a CoffeeMaker object, you can only use the methods and properties that belong to Appliance. And that's where **downcasting** comes in: that's how you take your **previously upcast reference** and change it back. You can figure out if your Appliance is really a CoffeeMaker using the **is** keyword. And once you know that, you can convert the Appliance back to a CoffeeMaker using the **as** keyword.

① **We'll start with the coffee maker we already upcast**
Here's the code that we used:

```
Appliance powerConsumer = new CoffeeMaker();
powerConsumer.ConsumePower();
```

Here's our Appliance reference that points to a CoffeeMaker object from the last page.

② **But what if we want to turn the Appliance back into a CoffeeMaker?**
The first step in downcasting is using the `is` keyword to check if it's even an option.

```
if (powerConsumer is CoffeeMaker)
    // then we can downcast!
```

③ **Now that we know it's a CoffeeMaker, let's use it like one**
The `is` keyword is the first step. Once you know that you've got an Appliance reference that's pointing to a CoffeeMaker object, you can use `as` to downcast it. And that lets you use the CoffeeMaker class's methods and properties. And since CoffeeMaker inherits from Appliance, it still has its Appliance methods and properties.

```
if (powerConsumer is CoffeeMaker) {
    CoffeeMaker javaJoe = powerConsumer as CoffeeMaker;
    javaJoe.MakeCoffee();
}
```

The javaJoe reference points to the same CoffeeMaker object as powerConsumer. But it's a CoffeeMaker reference, so it can call the MakeCoffee() method.

When downcasting fails, `as` returns null

So what happens if you try to use as to convert an Oven object into a CoffeeMaker? It returns null—and if you try to use it, .NET will cause your program to break.

Uh-oh—these don't match!

```
if (powerConsumer is CoffeeMaker) {
    Oven foodWarmer = powerConsumer as Oven;
    foodWarmer.Preheat();
}
```

powerConsumer is NOT an Oven object. So when you try to downcast it with "as", the foodWarmer reference ends up set to null. And when you try to use a null reference, this happens...

⚠ NullReferenceException was unhandled   ✕

Upcasting and downcasting work with interfaces, too

You already know that `is` and `as` work with interfaces. Well, so do all of the upcasting and downcasting tricks. Let's add an ICooksFood interface for any class that can heat up food. And we'll add a Microwave class—both Microwave and Oven implement the ICooksFood interface. Now there are three different ways that you can access an Oven object. And the IDE's IntelliSense can help you figure out exactly what you can and can't do with each of them:

Any class that implements ICooksFood is an appliance that can heat up food.

```
Oven misterToasty = new Oven();

misterToasty.
```

As soon as you type the dot, the IntelliSense window will pop up with a list of all of the members you can use.

misterToasty is an Oven reference pointing to an Oven object, so it can access all of the methods and properties... but it's the least general type, so you can only point it at Oven objects.

```
ICooksFood cooker;

if (misterToasty is ICooksFood)

    cooker = misterToasty as ICooksFood;

    cooker.
```

cooker is an ICooksFood reference pointing to that same Oven object. It can only access ICooksFood members. But it can also point to a Microwave object.

```
Appliance powerConsumer;

if (misterToasty is Appliance)

    powerConsumer = misterToasty;

    powerConsumer.
```

powerConsumer is an Appliance reference. It only lets you get to the public fields, methods and properties in Appliance. You can also point it at a CoffeeMaker object if you want.

Three different references that point to the same object can access different methods and properties, depending on the reference's type.

there are no
Dumb Questions

Q: So back up—you told me that I can always upcast but I can't always downcast. Why?

A: Because the compiler can warn you if your upcast is wrong. The only time an upcast won't work is if you're trying to set an object equal to a class that it doesn't inherit from or an interface that it doesn't implement. And the compiler can figure out immediately that you didn't upcast properly, and will give you an error.

On the other hand, the compiler doesn't know how to check if you're downcasting *from* an object or interface reference *to* a reference that's not valid. That's because it's perfectly legal to put any class or interface name on the right-hand side of the `as` keyword. If the downcast is illegal, then the `as` statement will just return `null`. And it's a good thing that the compiler doesn't stop you from doing that, because there are plenty of times when you'd want to do that.

Q: Someone told me that an interface is like a contract, but I don't really get why. What does that mean?

A: Yes, we've heard that too—a lot of people like to say that an interface is like a contract. (That's a really common question on job interviews.) And it's true, to some extent. When you make your class implement an interface, you're telling the compiler that you promise to put certain methods into it. The compiler will hold you to that promise.

But we think that it's easier to remember how interfaces work if you think of an interface as a kind of checklist. The compiler runs through the checklist to make sure that you actually put all of the methods from the interface into your class. If you didn't, it'll bomb out and not let you compile.

Q: What if I want to put a method body into my interface? Is that okay?

A: No, the compiler won't let you do that. An interface isn't allowed to have any statements in it at all. Even though you use the colon operator to implement an interface, it's not the same thing as inheriting from a class. Implementing an interface doesn't add any behavior to your class at all, or make any changes to it. All it does is tell the compiler to make sure that your class has all of the methods that the interface says it should have.

Q: Then why would I want to use an interface? It seems like it's just adding restrictions, without actually changing my class at all.

A: Because when your class implements an interface, then an interface reference can point to any instance of that class. And that's really useful to you—it lets you create one reference type that can work a whole bunch of different kinds of objects.

Here's a quick example. A horse, an ox, a mule, and a steer can all pull a cart. But in our zoo simulator, Horse, Ox, Mule, and Steer would all be different classes. Let's say you had a cart-pulling ride in your zoo, and you wanted to create an array of any animal that could pull carts around. Uh-oh—you can't just create an array that will hold all of those. If they all inherited from the same base class, then you could create an array of those. But it turns out that they don't. So what'll you do?

That's where interfaces come in handy. You can create an `IPuller` interface that has methods for pulling carts around. Now you could declare your array like this:

```
IPuller[] pullerArray;
```

Now you can put a reference to any animal you want in that array, as long as it implements the `IPuller` interface.

Q: Is there an easier way to implement interfaces? It's a lot of typing!

A: Why yes, there is! The IDE gives you a very powerful shortcut that automatically implements an interface for you. Just start typing your class:

```
public class
   Microwave : ICooksFood
   { }
```

Click on ICooksFood—you'll see a small bar appear underneath the "I". Hover over it and you'll see an icon appear underneath it:

interface ICooksFood
ICooksFood

Click on icon and choose "Implement Interface 'ICooksFood'" from the menu. It'll automatically add any members that you haven't implemented yet. Each one has a single `throws` statement in it—they'll cause your program to halt, as a reminder in case you forget to implement one of them (You'll learn about `throws` in chapter 10.)

An interface is like a checklist that the compiler runs through to make sure your class implemented a certain set of methods.

Extend the IClown interface and use classes that implement it.

Exercise

1 Start with the `IClown` interface from the last "Do This!" on page 258

```
public interface IClown {
    string FunnyThingIHave { get; }
    void Honk();
}
```

2 Extend `IClown` by creating a new interface, `IScaryClown`, that inherits from `IClown`. It should have an additional `string` property called `ScaryThingIHave` with a get accessor but no set accessor, and a `void` method called `ScareLittleChildren()`.

3 Create these classes:

★ A funny clown class called `FunnyFunny` that uses a private string variable to store a funny thing, and use a constructor that takes a parameter called `funnyThingIHave` and uses it to set the private field. The `Honk()` method should say, "Honk honk! I have a " followed by the funny thing it has. The `FunnyThingIHave` set accessor should return the same thing.

★ A scary clown class called `ScaryScary` that uses a private variable to store an integer that was passed to it by its constructor in a parameter called `numberOfScaryThings`. The `ScaryThingIHave` get accessor should return a string consisting of the number from the constructor followed by "spiders". The `Honk()` pops up a message box that says, "Boo! Gotcha!"

4 Here's code for a button—but it's not working. Can you figure out how to fix it?

```
private void button1_Click(object sender, EventArgs e) {
    ScaryScary fingersTheClown = new ScaryScary("big shoes", 14);
    FunnyFunny someFunnyClown = fingersTheClown;
    IScaryClown someOtherScaryclown = someFunnyClown;
    someOtherScaryclown.Honk();
}
```

Fingers the Clown is scary.

You better get this one right... or else!

IClown (interface)
FunnyThingIHave
Honk()

Clown
FunnyThingIHave
Honk()

IScaryClown (interface)
ScaryThingIHave
ScareLittleChildern()

ScaryClown
ScaryThingIHave
ScareLittleChildern()

Extend the IClown interface and use classes that implement it.

```
public interface IClown {
    string FunnyThingIHave { get; }
    void Honk();
}

public interface IScaryClown : IClown {
    string ScaryThingIHave { get; }
    void ScareLittleChildren();
}

public class FunnyFunny : IClown {
    public FunnyFunny(string funnyThingIHave) {
        this.funnyThingIHave = funnyThingIHave;
    }
    private string funnyThingIHave;
    public string FunnyThingIHave {
        get { return "Honk honk! I have " + funnyThingIHave; }
    }
    public void Honk() {
        MessageBox.Show(this.FunnyThingIHave);
    }
}

public class ScaryScary : FunnyFunny, IScaryClown {
    public ScaryScary(string funnyThingIHave, int numberOfScaryThings)
        : base(funnyThingIHave) {
        this.numberOfScaryThings = numberOfScaryThings;
    }

    private int numberOfScaryThings;
    public string ScaryThingIHave {
        get { return "I have " + numberOfScaryThings + " spiders"; }
    }

    public void ScareLittleChildren() {
        MessageBox.Show("Boo! Gotcha!");
    }
}
private void button1_Click(object sender, EventArgs e) {
    ScaryScary fingersTheClown = new ScaryScary("big shoes", 14);
    FunnyFunny someFunnyClown = fingersTheClown;
    IScaryClown someOtherScaryclown = someFunnyClown as ScaryScary;
    someOtherScaryclown.Honk();
}
```

The Honk() method just uses this set accessor to display its message—no need to have the same code twice.

You could have implemented the IClown method and property again, but why not just inherit from FunnyFunny?

Since ScaryScary is a subclass of FunnyFunny and FunnyFunny implements IClown, ScaryScary implements IClown too.

You can set a FunnyFunny reference equal to a ScaryScary object because ScaryScary inherits from FunnyFunny. But you can't set any IScaryClown reference to just any clown, because you don't know if that clown is scary. That's why you need to use the as keyword.

There's more than just public and private

You already know how important the `private` keyword is, how you use it, and how it's different from `public`. C# has a name for them: they're called **access modifiers**. The name makes sense, because when you change an access modifier on a property, field, or method of a class—its **members**—or the entire class, you change the way other classes can access it. There are a few more access modifiers that you'll use, but we'll start witht he ones you know:

> We call a class's methods, fields and properties its members. Any member can be marked with the public or private access modifier.

- ⭐ **`public` means that anyone can access it**
  When you mark a class or class member `public`, you're telling C# that any member of other class can access it. It's the least restrictive access modifier. And you've already seen how it can get you in trouble—only mark class members public if you have a reason. That's how you make sure your clases are well-encapsulated.

- ⭐ **`private` means that only other members can access it**
  When you mark a class member `private`, then it can only be accessed from other members inside that class or **other instances of that class**.. And when you mark a class `private`, then it can only be used by other classes inside its namespace—unless that class **lives inside another class**, in which case it's only available to instances of its container class.

- ⭐ **`protected` means public to subclasses, private to everyone else**
  You've already seen how a subclass can't access the private fields in its base class—it has to use the `base` keyword to get to the public members of the base object. Wouldn't it be convenient if the subclass could access those private fields? That's why you have the `protected` access modifier. Any class member marked `protected` can be accessed by any other member of its class, and any member of a subclass of its class.

- ⭐ **`internal` means public only to other classes in an assembly**
  The built-in .NET Framework classes are **assemblies**—libraries of classes that are in your project's list of references. You can see a list of assemblies by right-clicking on "References" in the Solution Explorer and choosing "Add Reference..."—when you create a new Windows Forms Application, the IDE automatically includes the references you need to build a Windows application. When you build an assembly, you can use the internal keyword to keep classes private to that assembly, so you can only expose the classes you want.

- ⭐ **`sealed` says that this class can't be subclassed**
  There are some classes which you just can't inherit from. A lot of the .NET Framework classes are like this—go ahead, try to make a class that inherits from `String` (that's the class whose IsEmptyOrNull() method you used in the last chapter.) What happens? The compiler won't let you build your code—it gives you the error, "cannot derive from sealed type 'string'". You can do that with your own classes—just add `sealed` after the access modifier.

Access modifiers change scope

Let's take a closer look at the access modifers, and how they affect the **scope** of the various class members. We made two changes: the funnyThingIHave backing field is now `protected`, and we changed the ScareLittleChildren() method so that it uses the funnyThingIHave field.

Make these two changes to your own exercise solution. Then change the protected access modifier back to private and see what errors you get.

The "this" keyword also changes the scope of a variable. It says to C#, "Look at the current instance of the class to find whatever I'm connected to—even if that matches a parameter or local variable."

```csharp
public interface IClown {
    string FunnyThingIHave { get; }
    void Honk();
}

public interface IScaryClown : IClown {
    string ScaryThingIHave { get; }
    void ScareLittleChildren();
}

public class FunnyFunny : IClown {
    public FunnyFunny(string funnyThingIHave) {
        this.funnyThingIHave = funnyThingIHave;
    }
    protected string funnyThingIHave;
    public string FunnyThingIHave {
        get { return "Honk honk! I have " + funnyThingIHave; }
    }

    public void Honk() {
        MessageBox.Show(this.FunnyThingIHave);
    }
}
```

This is a really common way to use "this", since the parameter and backing field have the same name. funnyThingIHave refers to the parameter, while this.funnyThingIHave is the backing field.

By adding "this", we told C# that we're talking about the backing field, not the parameter that has the same name.

We changed this to protected. Look and see how it affects the ScaryScary.ScareLittleChildren() method.

When you use "this" with a property, it tells C# to execute the set or get accessor.

Access Modifiers
Up Close

numberOfScaryThings
is private, which is
typical of a backing
field. So only another
instance of ScaryScary
would be able to see it.

```csharp
public class ScaryScary : FunnyFunny, IScaryClown {
    public ScaryScary(string funnyThingIHave,
                      int numberOfScaryThings)
        : base(funnyThingIHave) {
        this.numberOfScaryThings = numberOfScaryThings;
    }

    private int numberOfScaryThings;
    public string ScaryThingIHave {
        get { return "I have " + numberOfScaryThings + " spiders"; }
    }

    public void ScareLittleChildren() {
        MessageBox.Show("You can't have my "
                       + base.funnyThingIHave);
    }
}
```

The "base" keyword tells C# to use the value from the base class. That's another way to change scope.

The protected keyword tells C# to make something private to everyone except instances of a subclass.

If we'd left funnyThingIHave private, this would cause the compiler to give you an error. But when we changed it to protected, that made it visible to any subclass of FunnyFunny.

```csharp
private void button1_Click(object sender, EventArgs e) {
    ScaryScary fingersTheClown = new ScaryScary("big shoes", 14);
    FunnyFunny someFunnyClown = fingersTheClown;
    IScaryClown someOtherScaryclown = someFunnyClown as ScaryScary;
    someOtherScaryclown.Honk();
}
```

Since this button click event handler is not part of FunnyFunny and ScaryScary, it can't access the protected funnyThingIHave field.

It's outside of both classes, so the statements inside it only have access to the public members of any FunnyFunny or ScaryScary objects.

there are no
Dumb Questions

Q: Why would I want to use an interface instead of just writing all of the methods I need directly into my class?

A: You might end up with a lot of different classes as you write more and more complex programs. Interfaces let you group those classes by the kind of work they do. They help you be sure that every class that's going to do a certain kind of work does it using the same methods. The class can do the work however it needs to and, because of the interface, you don't need to worry about how it does it just to get the job done.

Here's an example: you can have a truck class and a sailboat class that implement `ICarryPassenger`. Say the `ICarryPassenger` interface stipulates that any class that implements it has to have a `ConsumeEnergy()` method. Your program could use them both to carry passengers even though the sailboat class's `ConsumeEnergy()` method uses wind power and the truck class's method uses diesel fuel.

Imagine if you didn't have the `ICarryPassenger` interface. Then it would be tough to tell your program which vehicles could carry people and which couldn't. You would have to look through each class that your program might use and figure out whether or not there was a method for carrying people from one place to another. Then you'd have to call each of the vehicles your program was going to use with whatever method was defined for carrying passengers. And since there's no standard interface, they could be named all sorts of things or buried inside other methods. You can see how that'll get confusing pretty fast.

Q: Why do I need to use a property? Can't I just include a field?

A: Good question. An interface only defines the way a class should do a specific kind of job. It's not an object by itself, so you can't instantiate it and it can't store information. If you added a field that was just a variable declaration, then C# would have to store that data somewhere—and an interface can't store data by itself.

Q: What's the difference between a regular object reference and an interface reference?

A: You already know how a regular, everyday object reference works. If you create a instance of `Skateboard` called `VertBoard`, and then a new reference to it called `HalfPipeBoard`, they both point to the same thing. But if `Skateboard` implements the interface `IStreetTricks` and you create an interface reference to `Skateboard` called `StreetBoard`, it will only know the methods in the `Skateboard` class that are also in the `IStreetTricks` interface.

All three references are actually pointing to the same object. If you call the object using the `HalfPipeBoard` or `VertBoard` references, you'll be able to access any method or property in the object. If you call it using the `StreetBoard` reference, you'll only have access to the methods and properties in the interface.

Q: Then why would I ever want to use an interface reference if it limits what I can do with the object?

A: Interface references give you a way of working with a bunch of different kinds of objects that do the same thing. You can create an array using the interface reference type that will let you pass information to and from the methods in `ICarryPassenger` whether your working with a truck object, a horse object, a unicycle object, or a car object. The way each of those objects do the job is probably a little different, but with interface references, you know that they all have the same methods that take the same parameters and have the same return types. So, you can call them and pass information to them in exactly the same way.

Q: Why would I make something protected instead of private or public?

A: Because it helps you encapsulate your classes better. There are a lot of times that a subclass needs access to some internal part of its base class. For example, if you need to override a property, it's pretty common to use the backing field in the base class in the get accessor, so that it returns some sort of variation of it. But when you build classes, you should only make something public if you have a reason to do it. Using the protected access modifier lets you expose it only to the subclass that needs it, and keep it private to everyone else.

Interface references only know about the methods and properties that are defined in the interface.

Some classes should never be instantiated

Remember our zoo simulator class hierarchy? You'll definitely end up instantiating a bunch of hippos, dogs and lions. But what about the Canine and Feline classes? How about the Animal class? It turns out that there are some classes that just don't need to be instantiated... and, in fact, don't make any sense if they are. Here's an example.

Let's start with a basic class for a student shopping at the student bookstore.

```
public class Shopper {
    public void ShopTillYouDrop()
        while (TotalSpent < CreditLimit)
            BuyFavoriteStuff();
    }
    public virtual void BuyFavoriteStuff () {
        // No implementation here - we don't know
        // what our student likes to buy!
    }
}
```

Here's the ArtStudent class—it subclasses Shopper:

```
public class ArtStudent : Shopper {
    public override void BuyFavoriteStuff () {
        BuyArtSupplies();
        BuyBlackTurtlenecks();
        BuyDepressingMusic();
    }
}
```

And the EngineeringStudent class also inherits from Shopper:

```
public class EngineeringStudent : Shopper {
    public override void BuyFavoriteStuff () {
        BuyPencils();
        BuyGraphingCalculator();
        BuyPocketProtector();
    }
}
```

The ArtStudent and EngineeringStudent classes both override the BuyFavoriteStuff() method, but they buy very different things.

So what happens when you instantiate Shopper? Does it ever make sense to do it?

An abstract class is like a cross between a class and an interface

Suppose you need something like an interface, that requires classes to implement certain methods and properties. But you need to include some code in that interface, so that certain methods don't have to be implemented in each inheriting class. What you want is an **abstract class**. You get the features of an interface, but you can write code in it like a normal class.

A method that has a declaration but no statements or method body is called an <u>abstract method</u>. Inheriting classes must implement all abstract methods, just like when they inherit from an interface.

⭐ **An abstract class is <u>like</u> a normal class**
You define an abstract class just like a normal one. It has fields and methods, and you can inherit from other classes, too, exactly like with a normal class. There's almost nothing new to learn here, because you already know everything that an abstract class does!

Only abstract classes can have abstract methods. If you put an abstract method into a class, then you'll have to mark that class abstract or it won't compile. You'll learn more about how to mark a class abstract in a minute.

⭐ **An abstract class is <u>like</u> an interface**
When you create a class that implements an interface, you agree to implement all of the properties and methods defined in that interface. An abstract class works the same way—it can include declarations of properties and methods that, just like in an interface, must be implemented by inheriting classes.

The opposite of abstract is <u>concrete</u>. A concrete method is one that has a body, and all the classes you've been working with so far are concrete classes.

⭐ **But an abstract class can't be instantiated**
The biggest difference between an **abstract** class and a **concrete** class is that you can't use new to create an instance of an abstract class. If you do, C# will give you an error when you try to compile your code.

> ⊗ Cannot create an instance of the abstract class or interface 'MyClass'

This error is because you have abstract methods without any code! The compiler won't let you instantiate a class with missing code, just like it wouldn't let you instantiate an interface.

> Wait, what? A class that I can't instantiate?
> Why would I even want something like that?

Because you want to provide some code, but still require that subclasses fill in the rest of the code.

Sometimes **bad things happen** when you create objects that should never be created. The class at the top of your class diagram usually has some fields that it expects its subclasses to set. An Animal class may have a calculation that depends on a boolean called HasTail or Vertebrate, but there's no way for it to set that itself.

Here's a class that the Objectville Astrophysics Club uses to send their rockets to different planets.

Here's an example...

The astrophysicists have two missions—one to Mars, and one to Venus.

```
public class PlanetMission {
   public long RocketFuelPerMile;
   public long RocketSpeedMPH;
   public int MilesToPlanet;

   public long UnitsOfFuelNeeded() {
      return MilesToPlanet * RocketFuelPerMile;
   }

   public int TimeNeeded() {
      return MilesToPlanet / RocketSpeedMPH;
   }

   public string FuelNeeded() {
      return "You'll need "
         + MilesToPlanet * RocketFuelPerMile
         + " units of fuel to get there. It'll take "
         + TimeNeeded() + " hours.";
   }
}
```

It doesn't make sense to set these fields in the base class, because we don't know what rocket or planet we'll be using.

```
public class Venus : PlanetMission {
   public Venus() {
      MilesToPlanet = 40000000;
      RocketFuelPerMile = 100000;
      RocketSpeedMPH = 25000;
   }
}

public class Mars : PlanetMission {
   public Mars() {
      MilesToPlanet = 75000000;
      RocketFuelPerMile = 100000;
      RocketSpeedMPH = 25000;
   }
}
```

The constructors for the Mars and Venus subclasses set the three fields they inherited from Planet. But those fields won't get set if you instantiate Planet directly. So what happens when FuelNeeded() tries to use them?

```
private void button1_Click(object s, EventArgs e) {
   MarsMission mars = new Mars();
   MessageBox.Show(mars.FuelNeeded());
}
```
→ You'll need 7500000000000 units of fuel to get there. It'll take 3000 hours. [OK]

```
private void button2_Click(object s, EventArgs e) {
   VenusMission venus = new Venus();
   MessageBox.Show(venus.FuelNeeded());
}
```
→ You'll need 4000000000000 units of fuel to get there. It'll take 1600 hours. [OK]

```
private void button3_Click(object s, EventArgs e) {
   PlanetMission planet = new PlanetMission();
   MessageBox.Show(planet.FuelNeeded());
}
```
→ **Before you flip the page, try to figure out what will happen when the user clicks the third button...**

Some classes should never be instantiated

The problems all start when you create an instance of the
PlanetMission class. Its `FuelNeeded()` method expects
the fields to be set by the subclass. But when they aren't,
they get their default values—zero. And when C# tries to
divide a number by zero...

The PlanetMission class wasn't written to be instantiated. We were only supposed to inherit from it. But we did, and that's where the problems started.

```
private void button3_Click(object s, EventArgs e) {
    PlanetMission planet = new PlanetMission();
    MessageBox.Show(planet.FuelNeeded());
}
```

When the FuelNeeded() method tried to divide by RocketSpeedMPH, it was zero. And when you divide by zero, this happens.

⚠ DivideByZeroException was unhandled	✕

Attempted to divide by zero.

Troubleshooting tips:

Make sure the value of the denominator is not zero before performing a division

Get general help for this exception.

Search for more Help Online...

Actions:
View Detail...
Copy exception detail to the clipboard

Solution: use an **abstract class**

Adding the abstract keyword to the class declaration tells C# this is an abstract class, and can't be instantiated.

When you mark a class `abstract`, C# won't let you write
code to instantiate it. It's a lot like an interface—it acts like a
template for the classes that inherit from it.

```
public abstract class PlanetMission {
    public long RocketFuelPerMile;
    public long RocketSpeedMPH;
    public int MilesToPlanet;

    public long UnitsOfFuelNeeded() {
        return MilesToPlanet * RocketFuelPerMile;
    }

    // the rest of the class is defined here
}
```

Now C# will refuse to compile our program until we remove the line that creates an instance of PlanetMission.

An abstract method doesn't have a body

You know how an interface only has declarations for methods and properties, but it doesn't actually have any method bodies? That's because every method in an interface is an **abstract method**. You can have abstract methods in an abstract class, too—but you need to explicitly mark them with the **abstract** keyword, because an abstract class can also have normal methods, too.

Every method in an interface is automatically abstract, so you don't need to use the abstract keyword in an interface, just in an abstract class. Only abstract classes can have abstract methods... but they can have concrete methods too.

```
public abstract class PlanetMission {

    public abstract void SetMissionInfo(
        int MilesToPlanet, int RocketFuelPerMile,
        long RocketSpeedMPH);

    // the rest of the class...
```

This abstract method is just like an interface—it doesn't have a body, but any class that inherits from PlanetMission has to implement the SetMissionInfo() method or the program won't compile.

It really sucks to be an abstract method. You don't have a body.

If we add that method in and try to build the program, the IDE gives us an error:

> ⊗ 'VenusMission' does not implement inherited abstract member 'PlanetMission.SetMissionInfo(long, int, int)'

So let's implement it! Once we do, the error will go away.

```
public class Venus : PlanetMission {
    public Venus() {
        SetMissinInfo(40000000, 100000, 25000);
    }

    SetMissionInfo(int milesToPlanet, long rocketFuelPerMile, int rocketSpeedMPH) {
        this.MilesToPlanet = milesToPlanet;
        this.RocketFuelPerMile = rocketFuelPerMile;
        this.RocketSpeedMPH = rocketSpeedMPH;
    }
}
```

Sharpen your pencil

Here's your chance to demonstrate your artistic abilities. On the left you'll find sets of class and interface declarations. Your job is to draw the associated class diagrams on the right. We did the first one for you. Don't forget to use a dashed line for implementing an interface and a solid line for inheriting from a class.

Given:

What's the Picture?

1)
```
public interface Foo { }

public class Bar : Foo { }
```

1)

2)
```
public interface Vinn { }

public abstract class Vout : Vinn { }
```

2)

3)
```
public abstract class Muffie : Whuffie { }

public class Fluffie : Muffie { }

public interface Whuffie { }
```

3)

4)
```
public class Zoop { }

public class Boop : Zoop { }

public class Goop : Boop { }
```

4)

5)
```
public class Gamma : Delta, Epsilon { }

public interface Epsilon { }

public interface Beta { }

public class Alpha : Gamma,Beta { }

public class Delta { }
```

5)

On the left you'll find sets of class diagrams. Your job is to turn these into valid C# declarations. We did number 1 for you.

Given:

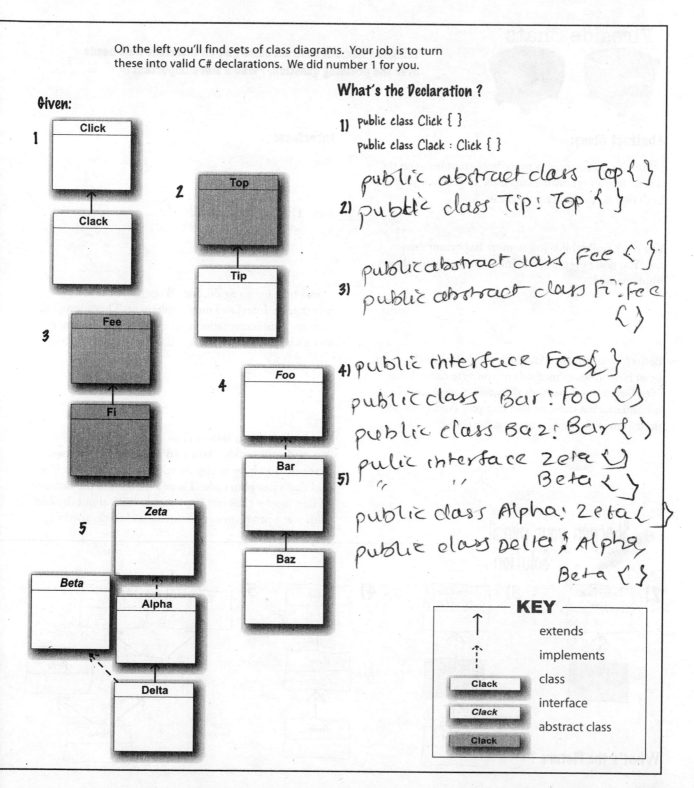

What's the Declaration ?

1) public class Click { }
   public class Clack : Click { }

2) public abstract class Top { }
   public class Tip : Top { }

3) public abstract class Fee { }
   public abstract class Fi : Fee { }

4) public interface Foo { }
   public class Bar : Foo { }
   public class Baz : Bar { }

5) public interface Zeta { }
   public interface Beta { }
   public class Alpha : Zeta { }
   public class Delta : Alpha, Beta { }

KEY

↑ extends
↑ (dashed) implements
Clack — class
Clack — interface
Clack — abstract class

Fireside Chats

Tonight's talk: **An abstract class and an interface butt heads over the pressing question, "Who's more important?"**

Abstract Class:	**Interface:**
I think it's obvious who's more important between the two of us. Programmers need me to get their jobs done. Let's face it. You don't even come close.	
	Nice. This oughta be good.
You can't really think you're more important than me. You don't even use real inheritance—you only get implemented.	
	Great, here we go again. Interfaces don't use real inheritance. Interfaces only implement. That's just plain ignorant. Implementation is as good as inheritance, in fact it's better!
Better? You're nuts. I'm much more flexible than you. I can have abstract methods or concrete ones. I can even have virtual methods if I want. Sure, I can't be instantiated but then, neither can you. And I can do pretty much anything else a regular class does.	
	Yeah? What if you want a class that inherits from you **and** your buddy? **You can't inherit from two classes.** You have to choose which class to inherit from. And that's just plan rude! There's no limit to the number of interfaces a class can implement. Talk about flexible! With me, a programmer can make a class do anything.

Sharpen your pencil Solution

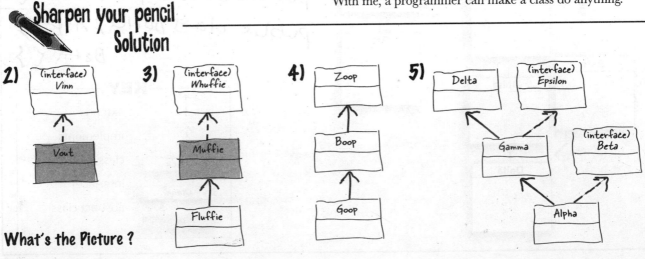

What's the Picture ?

Abstract Class:

You might be overstating your power a little bit.

That's exactly the kind of drivel I'd expect from an interface. Code is extremely important! It's what makes your programs run.

Really? I doubt that—programmers always care what's in their properties and methods.

Yeah, sure, tell a coder he can't code.

Interface:

You think that just because you can contain code, you're the greatest thing since sliced bread. But you can't change the fact that a program can only inherit from one class at a time. So, you're a little limited. Sure, I can't include any code. But really, code is overrated.

Nine times out of ten, a programmer wants to make sure an object has certain properties and methods, but doesn't really care how they're implemented.

Okay, sure. Eventually. But think about how many times you've seen a programmer write a method that takes an object that just needs to have a certain method, and it doesn't really matter right at that very moment exactly how the method's built. Just that it's there. So bang! The programmer just needs to write an interface. Problem solved!

What*ever*!

---

2) public abstract class Top { }
public class Tip : Top { }

3) public abstract class Fee { }
public abstract class Fi : Fee { }

4) public interface Foo { }
public class Bar : Foo { }
public class Baz : Bar { }

5) public interface Zeta { }
public class Alpha : Zeta { }
public interface Beta { }
public class Delta : Alpha, Beta { }

Delta inherits from Alpha and implements Beta.

What's the Declaration ?

> I'm still hung up on not being able to inherit from two classes. If I can't inherit from more than one class, so I have to use interfaces. That's a pretty big limitation of C#, right?

It's not a limitation, it's a protection.

If C# let you inherit from more than one base class, it would open up a whole can of worms. When a language lets one subclass inherit from two base classes, it's called **multiple inheritance**. And by giving you interfaces instead, C# saves you from a big fat mess that we like to call...

The Deadly Diamond of Death!

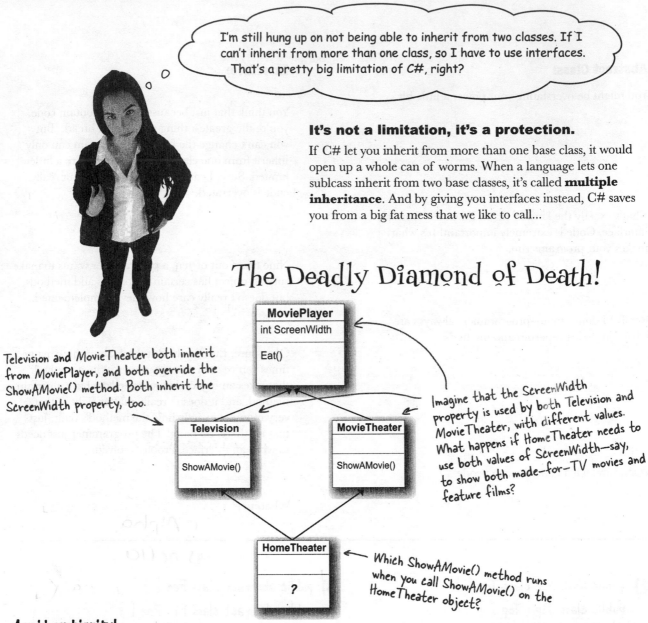

Television and MovieTheater both inherit from MoviePlayer, and both override the ShowAMovie() method. Both inherit the ScreenWidth property, too.

Imagine that the ScreenWidth property is used by both Television and MovieTheater, with different values. What happens if HomeTheater needs to use both values of ScreenWidth—say, to show both made-for-TV movies and feature films?

Which ShowAMovie() method runs when you call ShowAMovie() on the HomeTheater object?

Avoid ambiguity!

A language that allows the Deadly Diamond of Death can lead to some pretty ugly situations, because you need special rules to deal with this kind of ambiguous situation... which means extra work for you when you're building your program! C# protects you from having to deal with this by giving you interfaces. If Television and MovieTheater are interfaces instead of classes, then the same ShowAMovie() method can satisfy both of them. All the interface cares about is that there's some method called ShowAMovie().

Pool Puzzle

Your *job* is to take code snippets from the pool and place them into the blank lines in the code and output. You may use the same snippet more than once, and you won't need to use all the snippets. Your *goal* is to make a set of classes that will compile and run and produce the output listed.

```
public interface Nose {
    int Ear();
    string Face { get; }
}

public abstract class Picasso : Nose {
    public virtual int Ear()
    {
        return 7;
    }
    public Picasso(string face)
    {
        this.face = face;
    }
    public virtual string Face {
        get { return face; }
    }
    string face;
}

public class Clowns : Picasso {
    public Clowns() : base("Clowns") { }
}
```

```
public class Acts : Picasso {
    public Acts() : base("Acts") { }
    public override int Ear() {
        return 5;
    }
}
```

Here's the entry point—this is a complete C# program.

```
public class Of76 : Clowns {
    public override string Face {
        get { return "Of76"; }
    }
    public static void Main(string[] args) {
        string result = "";
        Nose[] i = new Nose[3];
        i[0] = new Acts();
        i[1] = new Clowns()
        i[2] = new Of76();
        for (int x = 0; x < 3; x++)
            result += ( i[x].Ear() + " "
                + i[x].Face) + "\n";
    }
    MessageBox.Show(result);
}
```

Output

```
5 Acts
7 Clowns
7 Of76
      OK
```

Note: each snippet from the pool can be used more once!

```
Acts();                             i
Nose();          ;                  i()
Of76();          class              i(x)        class
Clowns();        abstract           i[x]        5 class
Picasso();       interface                       7 class          Acts
                 int Ear()                        7 public class   Nose
Of76 [ ] i = new Nose[3];   this                                  Of76
Of76 [ 3 ] i;               this.         get                     Clowns
Nose [ ] i = new Nose();    face          set          i.Ear(x)   Picasso
Nose [ ] i = new Nose[3];   this.face     return       i[x].Ear()
                                                        i[x].Ear(
                                                        i[x].Face
```

→ Answers on page 306.

Okay, I think I've got a pretty good handle on objects now!

The idea that you could combine your data and your code into classes and objects was a revolutionary one when it was first introduced—but that's how you've been building all your C# programs so far, so you can think of it as just plain programming.

You're an object oriented programmer.

There's a name for what you've been doing. It's called **object oriented programming**, or OOP. Before languages like C# came along, people didn't use objects and methods when writing their code. They just used functions (which is what they called methods in a non-OOP program) that were all in one place—as if each program were just one big static class that only had static methods. It made it a lot harder to create programs that modeled the problems they were solving. Luckily, you'll never have to write programs without OOP, because it's a core part of C#.

The four princples of object oriented programming

When programmers talk about OOP, they're referring to four important principles. They should seem very familiar to you by now because you've been working with every one of them. You'll recognize the first three principles just from their names: **inheritance**, **abstraction**, and **encapsulation**. The last one's called **polymorphism**. It sounds a little odd, but it turns out that you already know all about it too.

Encapsulation means creating an object that keeps track of its state internally using private fields, and uses public properties and methods to let other classes work with only the part of the internal data that they need to see.

This just means having one class or interface that inherits from another.

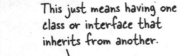 **Inheritance**

Encapsulation

The word "polymorphism" literally means "many forms". Can you think of a time when an object has taken on many forms in your code?

 Abstraction

You're using abstraction when you create a class model that starts with more general—or abstract—classes, and then has more specific classes that inherit from it.

 Polymorphism

Polymorphism means that one object can take many different forms

Any time you use a mockingbird in place of an animal or aged Vermont cheddar in a recipe that just calls for cheese, you're using **polymorphism**. That's what you're doing any time you upcast or downcast. It's taking an object and use it in a method or a statement that expects something else

Keep your eyes open for polymorphism in the next exercise!

You're about to do a really big exercise—the biggest one you've seen so far—and you'll be using a lot of polymorphism in it. So keep your eyes open for it. Here's a list of four typical ways that you'll use polymorphism. We gave you an example of each of them (you won't see these particular lines in the exercise, though). As soon as you see similar code in the code that you write for the exercise, **check it off the list**.

> You're using polymorphism when you take an instance of one class and use it in a statement or a method that expects a different type, like a parent class or an interface that the class implements.

- [ ] Taking any reference variable that uses one class and setting it equal to an instance of a different class.

  ```
  NectarStinger bertha = new NectarStinger();

  INectarCollector gatherer = bertha;
  ```

- [ ] Upcasting by using a subclass in a statement or method that expects its base class.

  ```
  spot = new Dog();

  zooKeeper.FeedAnAnimal(spot);
  ```

  If FeedAnAnimal() expects an Animal object, and Dog inherits from Animal, then you can pass Dog to FeedAnAnimal().

- [ ] Creating a reference variable whose type is an interface and pointing it to an object that implements that interface.

  ```
  IStingPatrol defender = new StingPatrol();
  ```

  This is upcasting, too!

- [ ] Downcasting using the as keyword.

  ```
  void MaintainTheHive(IWorker worker) {

      if (worker is HiveMaintainer) {

          HiveMaintainer maintainer = worker as HiveMaintainer;

          ...
  ```

  The MaintainTheHive() method takes any IWorker as a parameter. It uses as to point a HiveMaintainer reference to the worker.

LONG EXERCISE

Let's build a house! Create a model of a house using classes to represent the rooms and locations, and an interface for any place that has a door.

Location is an abstract class. That's why we shaded it darker in the class diagram.

Location
Name
Exits

Description()

1 **Start with this class model**

Every room or location in your house will be represented by its own object. The interior rooms all inherit from Room, and the outside places inherit from Outside, which subclass the same base class, Location. It has two fields: Name is the name of the location ("Kitchen"), and Exits is an array of Location objects that the current location connects to. So diningRoom.Name will be equal to "Dining Room", and diningRoom.Exits will be equal to the array { LivingRoom, Kitchen }.

→ **Create a Windows Application project and add Location, Room and Outside classes to it.**

Room
Decoration

Outside
Hot

Inside locations each have some kind of a decoration in a read-only property.

Outside locations can be hot, so the Outside class has a read-only boolean property called Hot.

2 **You'll need the blueprint for the house**

This house has three rooms, a front yard, and a garden. There are two doors: the front door connects the living room to the front yard, and the back door connects the kitchen to the back yard.

The living room connects to the dining room, which also connects to the kitchen.

Living Room

Dining Room

Front Yard

Kitchen

Back Yard

You can move between the back yard and the front yard, and both of them connect to the garden.

This symbol is an exterior door between the front yard and the living room. There's also an exterior door between the kitchen and back yard.

Garden

All rooms have doors, but only a few rooms have an exterior door that leads inside or outside the house.

3 **Use the IHasExteriorDoor interface for rooms with an exterior door**

There are two exterior doors in the house, the front door and the back door. Every location that has one (the front yard, back yard, living room, and kitchen) should implement IHasExteriorDoor. The DoorDescription read-only property contains a description of the door (the front door is "an oak door with a brass knob", the back door is "a screen door"). The DoorLocation field contains a reference to the Location where the door leads (kitchen).

IHasExteriorDoor
DoorDescription
DoorLocation

④ Here's the Location class

To get you started, here's the Location class:

```
public abstract class Location {
    public Location(string name) {
        this.name = name;
    }
    public Location[] Exits;
    private string name;
    public string Name {
        get { return name; }
    }
    public virtual string Description {
        get {
            string description = "You're standing in the " + name
                + ". You see exits to the following places: ";
            for (int i = 0; i < Exits.Length; i++) {
                description += " " + Exits[i].Name;
                if (i != Exits.Length - 1)
                    description += ",";
            }
            description += ".";
            return description;
        }
    }
}
```

The constructor sets the name field, which is the read-only Name property's backing field.

Description is a virtual method. You'll need to override it.

The public Exits field is an array of Location references that keeps track of all of the other places that this location connects to.

The Room class will override and extend Description to add the decoration, and Outside will add the temperature.

The Description property returns a string that describes the room, including the name and a list of all of the locations it connects to (which it finds in the Exits[] field). Its subclasses will need to change the description slightly, so they'll override it.

Remember, Location is an abstract class—you can inherit from it and declare reference variables of type Location, but you can't instantiate it.

⑥ Create the classes

First create the Room and Outside classes based on the class model. Then create two more classes: OutsideWithDoor, which inherits from Outside and implements IHasExteriorDoor, and RoomWithDoor, which subclasses Room and implements IHasExteriorDoor.

Here are the class declarations to give you a leg up:

Get the classes started now—we'll give you more details about them on the next page.

```
public class OutsideWithDoor : Outside, IHasExteriorDoor
{
    // The read-only DoorLocation property goes here
    // The DoorDescription property goes here
}

public class RoomWithDoor : Room, IHasExteriorDoor
{
    // The read-only DoorLocation property goes here
    // The DoorDescription property goes here
}
```

This one's going to be a pretty big exercise... but we promise it's a lot of fun! And you'll definitely know this stuff once you get through it.

We're not done yet—flip the page!

LONG EXERCISE (CONTINUED)

Now that you've got the class model, you can create the objects for all of the parts of the house, and add a form to explore it.

6 **How your house objects work**

Here's the architecture for two of your objects, `frontYard` and `diningRoom`. Since each of them has a door, they both need to be instances of a class that implements `IHasExteriorDoor`. The `DoorLocation` property keeps a reference to the location on the other side of the door.

FrontYard is an OutsideWithDoor object, which is a subclass of Outside that implements IHasExteriorDoor.

LivingRoom is an instance of RoomWithDoor, which inherits from Room and implements IHasExteriorDoor.

You started building the IHasExteriorDoor interface and add these two classes that implement it. One inherits from Room, the other is a subclass of Outside. Now it's time to finish them.

Exits is an array of Location references. LivingRoom has one exit, so its Exits array has a length of 1.

7 **Finish building the classes, and instantiate their instances**

You've got all the classes, now it's time to finish them and build your objects.

★ You'll need to make sure that the constructor for the Outside class sets the read-only Hot property and overrides the Description property to add the text "It's very hot here." if Hot is true. It's hot in the back yard but not the front yard or garden.

★ The constructor for Room needs to set the Decoration, and should override the Description property to add, "You see *(the decoration)* here." The living room has an antique carpet, the dining room has a crystal chandelier, and the kitchen has stainless steel appliances and a screen door that leads to the back yard.

★ Your form needs to create each of the objects and keep a reference to each one. So add a method to the form called `CreateObjects()` and call it from the form's constructor.

Every location will have its own field in the form class.

★ Instantiate each of the objects for the six locations in the house. Here's one of those lines:

```
RoomWithDoor livingRoom = new RoomWithDoor("Living Room",
    "an antique carpet" , "an oak door with a brass knob");
```

Exits is an array of Location references, so this line creates one and that has two references in it.

★ Your `CreateObjects()` method needs to populate the `Exits[]` field in each object:

```
frontYard.Exits = new Location[] { backYard, garden };
```

These are curly brackets. Anything else will cause an error.

8 **Build a form to explore the house**

Build a simple form to let you explore the house. It'll have a big multiline textbox called description to show the description of the current room. A ComboBox called exits lists all of the exits in the current room. It's got two buttons: goHere moves to the room selected in the ComboBox, and goThroughTheDoor is only visible when there's an exterior door.

Here's where you'll set up what populates the ComboBox.

Click the goHere button to move to another location.

This is a multiline TextBox that displays the Description() of the current location. It's name is description.

The ComboBox contains a list of all of the exits, so name it exits. Make sure its DropDownStyle is set to DropDownList.

This button is only visible when you're in a room with an exterior door. You can make it visible or invisible by setting its Visible property to true or false. It's called goThroughTheDoor.

9 **Now you just need to make the form work!**

You've got all the pieces, now you just need to put them together.

★ You'll need a field in your form called currentLocation to keep track of your current location.

★ Add a MoveToANewLocation() method that has a Location as its parameter. This method should first set currentLocation to the new location. Then it'll clear the combo box using its Items.Clear() method, and then add the name of each location in the Exits[] array using the combo box's Items.Add() method. Finally, reset the combo box so it displays the first item in the list by setting its SelectedIndex property to zero.

★ Set the textbox so that it has the description of the current location.

★ Use the **is** keyword to check if the current location has a door. If it does, make the "Go through the door" button visible using its Visible property. If not, make it invisible.

★ If the "Go here:" button is clicked, move to the location selected in the combo box.

★ If the "Go through the door" button is clicked, move to the location that the door coonects to.

Hint: When you choose an item in the combo box, its selected index in the combo box will be the same as the index of the corresponding location in the Exits[] array.

Another hint: Your form's currentLocation field is a Location reference. So even though it's pointing to an object that implements IHasExteriorDoor, you can't just type "currentLocation.DoorLocation" because DoorLocation isn't a field in Location. You'll need to downcast if you want to get the door location out of the object.

LONG EXERCISE SOLUTION

Here's the code to model the house. We used classes to represent the rooms and locations, and an interface for any place that has a door.

```
public interface IHasExteriorDoor {
    string DoorDescription { get; }
    Location DoorLocation { get; set; }
}
```

Here's the IHasExteriorDoor interface.

```
public class Room : Location {
    private string decoration;

    public Room(string name, string decoration)
        : base(name) {
        this.decoration = decoration;
    }

    public override string Description {
        get {
            return base.Description + " You see " + decoration + ".";
        }
    }
}
```

The Room class inherits from Location and adds a backing field for the read-only Decoration property. Its constructor sets the field.

```
public class RoomWithDoor : Room, IHasExteriorDoor {
    public RoomWithDoor(string name, string decoration, string doorDescription)
        : base(name, decoration)
    {
        this.doorDescription = doorDescription;
    }

    private string doorDescription;
    public string DoorDescription {
        get { return doorDescription; }
    }

    private Location doorLocation;
    public Location DoorLocation {
        get { return doorLocation; }
        set { doorLocation = value; }
    }
}
```

The RoomWithDoor class inherits from Room and implements IHasExteriorDoor. It does everything that the room does, but it adds a description of the exterior door to the constructor. It also adds DoorLocation, a reference to the location that the door leads to. DoorDescription and DoorLocation are required by IHasExteriorDoor.

```
public class Outside : Location {
    private bool hot;
    public bool Hot { get { return hot; } }

    public Outside(string name, bool hot)
        : base(name)
    {
        this.hot = hot;
    }


    public override string Description {
        get {
            string NewDescription = base.Description;
            if (hot)
                NewDescription += " It's very hot.";
            return NewDescription;
        }
    }
}

public class OutsideWithDoor : Outside, IHasExteriorDoor {
    public OutsideWithDoor(string name, bool hot, string doorDescription)
        : base(name, hot)
    {
        this.doorDescription = doorDescription;
    }

    private string doorDescription;
    public string DoorDescription {
        get { return doorDescription; }
    }

    private Location doorLocation;
    public Location DoorLocation {
        get { return doorLocation; }
        set { doorLocation = value; }
    }

    public override string Description {
        get {
            return base.Description + " You see " + doorDescription + ".";
        }
    }
}
```

Outside is a lot like Room—it inherits from Location, and adds a backing field for the Hot property, which is used in the Description() method extended from the base class.

OutsideWithDoor inherits from Outside and implements IHasExteriorDoor, and it looks a lot like RoomWithDoor.

The base class's Description property fills in whether or not the location is hot. And that relies on the original Location class's Description property to add the main description and exits.

We're not done yet—flip the page!

Long Exercise
Solution (continued)

Here's the code for the form. It's all in the Form1.cs, inside the Form1 declaration.

```
public partial class Form1 : Form
{
    Location currentLocation;

    RoomWithDoor livingRoom;
    Room diningRoom;
    RoomWithDoor kitchen;

    OutsideWithDoor frontYard;
    OutsideWithDoor backYard;
    Outside garden;

    public Form1() {
        InitializeComponent();
        CreateObjects();
        MoveToANewLocation(livingRoom);
    }

    private void CreateObjects() {
        livingRoom = new RoomWithDoor("Living Room", "an antique carpet",
                "an oak door with a brass knob");
        diningRoom = new Room("Dining Room", "a crystal chandelier");
        kitchen = new RoomWithDoor("Kitchen", "stainless steel appliances", "a screen door");

        frontYard = new OutsideWithDoor("Front Yard", false, "an oak door with a brass knob");
        backYard = new OutsideWithDoor("Back Yard", true, "a screen door");
        garden = new Outside("Garden", false);

        diningRoom.Exits = new Location[] { livingRoom, kitchen };
        livingRoom.Exits = new Location[] { diningRoom };
        kitchen.Exits = new Location[] { diningRoom };
        frontYard.Exits = new Location[] { backYard, garden };
        backYard.Exits = new Location[] { frontYard, garden };
        garden.Exits = new Location[] { backYard, frontYard };

        livingRoom.DoorLocation = frontYard;
        frontYard.DoorLocation = livingRoom;

        kitchen.DoorLocation = backYard;
        backYard.DoorLocation = kitchen;
    }
```

This is how the form keeps track of which room is being displayed.

The form uses these reference variables to keep track of each of the rooms in the house.

The form's constructor creates the objects and then uses the MoveToANewLocation method.

When the form creates the objects, first it needs to instantiate the classes and pass the right information to each one's constructor.

Here's where we pass the door description to the OutsideWithDoor constructors.

Here's where the Exits[] array for each instance is populated. We need to wait to do this until after all the instances are created, because otherwise we wouldn't have anything to put into each array!

For the IHasExteriorDoor objects, we need to set their door locations.

```
private void MoveToANewLocation(Location newLocation) {
    currentLocation = newLocation;

    exits.Items.Clear();
    for (int i = 0; i < currentLocation.Exits.Length; i++)
        exits.Items.Add(currentLocation.Exits[i].Name);
    exits.SelectedIndex = 0;

    description.Text = currentLocation.Description;

    if (currentLocation is IHasExteriorDoor)
        goThroughTheDoor.Visible = true;
    else
        goThroughTheDoor.Visible = false;
}

private void goHere_Click(object sender, EventArgs e) {
    MoveToANewLocation(currentLocation.Exits[exits.SelectedIndex]);
}

private void goThroughTheDoor_Click(object sender, EventArgs e) {
    IHasExteriorDoor hasDoor = currentLocation as IHasExteriorDoor;
    MoveToANewLocation(hasDoor.DoorLocation);
}
}
```

The MoveToANewLocation() method displays a new location in the form.

First we need to clear the combo box, then we can add each of the locations' names to it. Finally, we set its selected index (or which line is highlighted) to zero so it shows the first item in the list. Don't forget to set the ComboBox's DropDownStyle property to "DropDownList"—that way the user won't be able to type anything into the combo box.

This makes the "Go through the door" button invisible if the current location doesn't implement IHasExteriorDoor.

When the user clicks the "Go here:" button, it moves to the location selected in the combo box.

We need to use the as keyword in order to downcast currentLocation to an IHasExteriorDoor so we can get access to the DoorLocation field.

But we're not done yet!

It's fine to create a model of a house, but wouldn't it be cool to turn it into a game? Let's do it! You'll play Hide and Seek against the computer. We'll need to add an Opponent class and have him hide in a room. And we'll need to make the house a lot bigger. Oh, and he'll need someplace to hide! We'll add a new interface so that some rooms can have a hiding place. Finally, we'll update the form to let you check the hiding places, and keep track of how many moves you've made trying to find your opponent. Sound fun? Definitely!

Let's get started!

Exercise

Time for hide and seek! Build on your original house program to add more rooms, hiding places, and an opponent who hides from you.

Create a new project, and use the IDE's "Add Existing Item" feature to add the classes from the first part of the exercise.

1 Add an IHidingPlace interface

We don't need to do anything fancy here. Any Location subclass that implements IHidingPlace has a place for the opponent to hide. It just needs a string to store the name of the hiding place ("in the closet", "under the bed", etc.)

★ Give it a get accessor, but no set accessor—we'll set this in the constructor, since once a room has a hiding place we won't ever need to change it.

2 Add classes that implement IHidingPlace

You'll need two more classes: OutsideWithHidingPlace (which inherits from Outside) and RoomWithHidingPlace (which inherits from Room). Also, let's make any room with a door have a hiding place, so it'll have to inherit from RoomWithHidingPlace instead of Room. *So every room with an exterior door will also have a hiding place.*

3 Add a class for your opponent

The Opponent object will find a random hiding place in the house, and it's your job to find him.

★ He'll need a private Location field (myLocation) so he can keep track of where he is, and a private Random field (random) to use when he moves to a random hiding place.

★ The constructor takes the starting location and sets myLocation to it, and sets random to a new instance of Random. He starts in the front yard (that'll be passed in by form), and moves from hiding place to hiding place randomly. He moves 10 times when the game starts. When he encounters an exterior door, he flips a coin to figure out whether or not to go through it.

★ Add a Move() method that moves the opponent from his current location to a new location. First, if he's in a room with a door, then he flips a coin to decide whether or not to go through the door, so if random.Next(2) is equal to 1, he goes through it. Then he chooses one of the exits from his current location at random and goes through it. If it doesn't have a hiding place, then he'll do it again—he'll choose a random exit from his current location and go there, and he'll keep doing it over and over until he finds a place to hide.

★ Add a Check() method that takes a location as a parameter and returns true if he's hiding in that location, or false otherwise.

4 Add more rooms to the house

Update your CreateObjects() method to add more rooms:

★ Add **stairs** with a wooden bannister that connect the living room to the **upstairs hallway**, which has a picture of a dog and a closet to hide in.

★ The upstairs hallway connects to three rooms: a **master bedroom** with a large bed, a **second bedroom** with a small bed, and a **bathroom** with a sink and a toilet. Someone could hide under the bed in either bedroom or in the shower.

★ The front yard and back yard both connect to the **driveway**, where someone could hide in the garage. Also, someone could hide in the shed in the **garden**.

5 **Okay, time to update the form**

You'll need to add a few buttons to the form. And we'll get a little more intricate with making them visible or invisible, depending on the state of the game.

The middle button's called check. You don't need to set its Text property.

You use the top two buttons and the combo box exactly the same way as before, except that they're only visible while the game is running.

When the game first starts, the hide button is the only one displayed. When you click it, the form counts to 10 in the text box, and calls the opponent's Move() method 10 times. Then it makes this button invisible.

This is the button you'll use to check the room's hiding place. It's only visible if you're in a room that has a place to hide. When it's shown, the Text property is changed from "button3" to "Check" followed by the name of the hiding place—so for a room with a hiding place under the bed, the button will say, "Check under the bed".

6 **Make the buttons work**

There are two new buttons to add to the form.

Flip back to Chapter 2 for a refresher on DoEvents() and Sleep()—they'll come in handy.

★ The middle button checks the hiding place in the current room and is only visible when you're in a room with a place to hide using the opponent's Check() method. If you found him, then it resets the game.

★ The bottom button is how you start the game. It counts to 10 by showing "1...", waiting 200 milliseconds, then showing "2...", then "3...", etc. in the text box. After each number, it tells the opponent to move by calling his Move() method. Then it shows, "Ready or not, here I come!" for half a second, and then the game starts.

7 **Add a method to redraw the form, and another one to reset the game**

Add a RedrawForm() method that puts the right text in the description textbox, makes the buttons visible or invisible, and puts the correct label on the middle button. Then add a ResetGame() method that's run when you find the opponent. It resets the opponent object so that he starts in the front yard again—he'll hide when the user clicks the "Hide!" button. It should leave the form with nothing but the text box and "Hide!" button visible. The text box should say where you found the opponent, and how many moves it took.

8 **Keep track of how many moves the player made**

Make sure the text box displays the number of times the player checked a hiding place or moved between rooms. When you find the opponent, he should pop up a mesage box that says, "You found me in X moves!"

9 **Make it look right when you start the program**

When you first start the program, all you should see is an empty text box and the "Hide!" button. When you click the button, the fun begins!

Exercise Solution

Build on your original house program to add more rooms, hiding places, and an opponent who hides from you.

Here's the new IHidingPlace interface. It just has one string field with a get accessor that returns the name of the hiding place.

```
public interface IHidingPlace {
    string HidingPlaceName { get; }
}

public class RoomWithHidingPlace : Room, IHidingPlace {
    public RoomWithHidingPlace(string name, string decoration, string hidingPlaceName)
        : base(name, decoration)
    {
        this.hidingPlaceName = hidingPlaceName;
    }

    private string hidingPlaceName;
    public string HidingPlaceName {
        get { return hidingPlaceName; }
    }

    public override string Description {
        get {
            return base.Description + " Someone could hide " + hidingPlaceName + ".";
        }
    }
}

public class RoomWithDoor : RoomWithHidingPlace, IHasExteriorDoor {
    public RoomWithDoor(string name, string decoration,
                    string hidingPlaceName, string doorDescription)
        : base(name, decoration, hidingPlaceName)
    {
        this.doorDescription = doorDescription;
    }

    private string doorDescription;
    public string DoorDescription {
        get { return doorDescription; }
    }

    private Location doorLocation;
    public Location DoorLocation {
        get { return doorLocation; }
        set { doorLocation = value; }
    }
}
```

The RoomWithHidingPlace class inherits from Room and implements IHidingPlace by adding the HidingPlaceName property. The constructor sets its backing field.

Since we decided every room with a door also needed a hiding place, we made RoomWithDoor inherit from RoomWithHidingPlace. The only change to it is that its constructor takes a hiding place name and sends it on to the RoomWithHidingPlace constructor.

```
public class OutsideWithHidingPlace : Outside, IHidingPlace {
    public OutsideWithHidingPlace(string name, bool hot, string hidingPlaceName)
        : base(name, hot)
    { this.hidingPlaceName = hidingPlaceName; }

    private string hidingPlaceName;
    public string HidingPlaceName {
        get { return hidingPlaceName; }
    }

    public override string Description {
        get {
            return base.Description + " Someone could hide " + hidingPlaceName + ".";
        }
    }
}

public class Opponent {
    private Random random;
    private Location myLocation;
    public Opponent(Location startingLocation) {
        myLocation = startingLocation;
        random = new Random();
    }
    public void Move() {
        if (myLocation is IHasExteriorDoor) {
            IHasExteriorDoor LocationWithDoor =
                            myLocation as IHasExteriorDoor;
            if (random.Next(2) == 1)
                myLocation = LocationWithDoor.DoorLocation;
        }
        bool hidden = false;
        while (hidden) {
            int rand = random.Next(0, myLocation.Exits.Length);
            myLocation = myLocation.Exits[rand];
            if (myLocation is IHidingPlace)
                hidden = true;
        }
    }
    public bool Check(Location locationToCheck) {
        if (locationToCheck != myLocation)
            return false;
        else
            return true;
    }
}
```

The OutsideWithHidingPlace class inherits from Outside and implements IHidingPlace just like RoomWithHidingPlace does.

The Opponent class constructor takes a starting location. It creates a new instance of Random, which it uses to move randomly between rooms.

The Move() method first checks if the current room has a door using the is keyword—if so, it has a 50% chance of going through it. Then it moves to a random location, and keeps moving until it finds a hiding place.

The guts of the Move() method is this while loop. It keeps looping until the variable hidden is true—and it sets it to true when it finds a room with a hiding place.

The Check() method just checks the opponent's location against the location that was passed to it using a Location reference. If they point to the same object, then he's been found!

We're not done yet—flip the page!

Exercise Solution (continued)

Here are all the fields in the Form1 class. It uses them to keep track of the locations, the opponent and the number of moves the player has made.

```
int Moves;

Location currentLocation;

RoomWithDoor livingRoom;
RoomWithHidingPlace diningRoom;
RoomWithDoor kitchen;
Room stairs;
RoomWithHidingPlace hallway;
RoomWithHidingPlace bathroom;
RoomWithHidingPlace masterBedroom;
RoomWithHidingPlace secondBedroom;

OutsideWithDoor frontYard;
OutsideWithDoor backYard;
OutsideWithHidingPlace garden;
OutsideWithHidingPlace driveway;

Opponent opponent;
```

The Form1 constructor creates the objects, sets up the opponent, and then resets the game. We added a boolean parameter to ResetGame() so that it only displays its message when you win, not when you first start up the program.

```
public Form1() {
    InitializeComponent();
    CreateObjects();
    opponent = new Opponent(frontYard);
    ResetGame(false);
}
private void MoveToANewLocation(Location newLocation) {
    Moves++;
    currentLocation = newLocation;
    RedrawForm();
}
```

The MoveToANewLocation() method sets the new location and then redraws the form.

```
private void RedrawForm() {
    exits.Items.Clear();
    for (int i = 0; i < currentLocation.Exits.Length; i++)
        exits.Items.Add(currentLocation.Exits[i].Name);
    exits.SelectedIndex = 0;
    description.Text = currentLocation.Description + "\r\n(move #" + Moves + ")";
    if (currentLocation is IHidingPlace) {
        IHidingPlace hidingPlace = currentLocation as IHidingPlace;
        check.Text = "Check " + hidingPlace.HidingPlaceName;
        check.Visible = true;
    }
    else
        check.Visible = false;
    if (currentLocation is IHasExteriorDoor)
        goThroughTheDoor.Visible = true;
    else
        goThroughTheDoor.Visible = false;
}
```

We need the hiding place name, but we've only got the CurrentLocation object which doesn't have a HidingPlaceName property, so we can use as to downcast the reference to an IHidingPlace variable.

RedrawForm() populates the combo box list, sets the text (adding the number of moves), and then makes the buttons visible or invisible depending on whether or not there's a door or the room has a hiding place.

Wow—you could add an entire wing onto the house just by adding a couple of lines! That's why well-encapsulated classes and objects are really useful.

```
private void CreateObjects() {
    livingRoom = new RoomWithDoor("Living Room", "an antique carpet",
            "inside the closet", "an oak door with a brass handle");
    diningRoom = new RoomWithHidingPlace("Dining Room", "a crystal chandelier",
            "in the tall armoire");
    kitchen = new RoomWithDoor("Kitchen", "stainless steel appliances",
            "in the cabinet", "a screen door");
    stairs = new Room("Stairs", "a wooden bannister");
    hallway = new RoomWithHidingPlace("Upstairs Hallway", "a picture of a dog",
            "in the closet");
    bathroom = new RoomWithHidingPlace("Bathroom", "a sink and a toilet",
            "in the shower");
    masterBedroom = new RoomWithHidingPlace("Master Bedroom", "a large bed",
            "under the bed");
    secondBedroom = new RoomWithHidingPlace("Second Bedroom", "a small bed",
            "under the bed");

    frontYard = new OutsideWithDoor("Front Yard", false, "a heavy-looking oak door");
    backYard = new OutsideWithDoor("Back Yard", true, "a screen door");
    garden = new OutsideWithHidingPlace("Garden", false, "inside the shed");
    driveway = new OutsideWithHidingPlace("Driveway", true, "in the garage");

    diningRoom.Exits = new Location[] { livingRoom, kitchen };
    livingRoom.Exits = new Location[] { diningRoom, stairs };
    kitchen.Exits = new Location[] { diningRoom };
    stairs.Exits = new Location[] { livingRoom, hallway };
    hallway.Exits = new Location[] { stairs, bathroom, masterBedroom, secondBedroom };
    bathroom.Exits = new Location[] { hallway };
    masterBedroom.Exits = new Location[] { hallway };
    secondBedroom.Exits = new Location[] { hallway };
    frontYard.Exits = new Location[] { backYard, garden, driveway };
    backYard.Exits = new Location[] { frontYard, garden, driveway };
    garden.Exits = new Location[] { backYard, frontYard };
    driveway.Exits = new Location[] { backYard, frontYard };

    livingRoom.DoorLocation = frontYard;
    frontYard.DoorLocation = livingRoom;

    kitchen.DoorLocation = backYard;
    backYard.DoorLocation = kitchen;
}
```

The new CreateObjects() method creates all the objects to build the house. It's a lot like the old one, but it has a whole lot more places to go.

➝ We're still not done—flip the page!

Exercise
Solution (CONTINUED)

Here's the rest of the code for the form. The goHere and goThroughTheDoor button event handlers are identical to the ones in the first part of this exercise, so flip back a few pages to see them.

```
private void ResetGame(bool displayMessage) {
    if (displayMessage) {
        MessageBox.Show("You found me in " + Moves + " moves!");
        IHidingPlace foundLocation = currentLocation as IHidingPlace;
        description.Text = "You found your opponent in " + Moves
                + " moves! He was hiding " + foundLocation.HidingPlaceName + ".";
    }
    Moves = 0;
    hide.Visible = true;
    goHere.Visible = false;
    check.Visible = false;
    goThroughTheDoor.Visible = false;
    exits.Visible = false;
}

private void check_Click(object sender, EventArgs e) {
    Moves++;
    if (opponent.Check(currentLocation))
        ResetGame(true);
    else
        RedrawForm();
}

private void hide_Click(object sender, EventArgs e) {
    hide.Visible = false;

    for (int i = 1; i <= 10; i++) {
        opponent.Move();
        description.Text = i + "... ";
        Application.DoEvents();
        System.Threading.Thread.Sleep(200);
    }

    description.Text = "Ready or not, here I come!";
    Application.DoEvents();
    System.Threading.Thread.Sleep(500);

    goHere.Visible = true;
    exits.Visible = true;
    MoveToANewLocation(livingRoom);
}
```

The ResetGame() method resets the game. It displays the final message, then makes all the buttons except the "Hide!" one invisible.

We want to display the name of the hiding place, but CurrentLocation is a Location reference, so it doesn't give us access to the HidingPlaceName field. Luckily, we can use the as keyword to downcast it to an IHidingPlace reference that points to the same object.

When you click the check button, it checks whether or not the opponent is hiding in the current room. If he is, it resets the game. If not, it redraws the form (to update the number of moves).

The hide button is the one that starts the game. The first thing it does is make itself invisible. Then it counts to 10 and tells the opponent to move. Finally, it makes the first button and the combo box visible, and then starts off the player in the living room. The MoveToANewLocation() method calls RedrawForm().

Objectcross

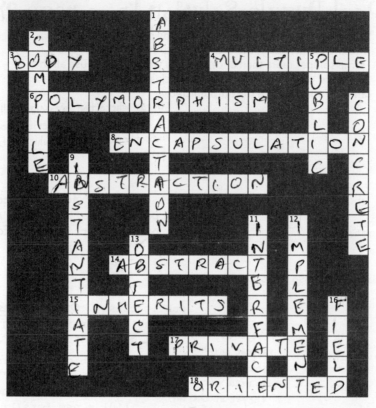

Across

3. What an abstract method doesn't have
4. C# doesn't allow _____ inheritance
6. When you use a pass subclass to a method that expects its base class, you're using this OOP principle
8. The OOP principle where you hide private data and only expose those methods and fields that other classes need access to
10. One of the four principles of OOP that you implement using the colon operator
14. Every method in an interface is automatically _____
15. Your class that implements an interface that _____ from another interface, then you need to implement all of its members too
17. An access modifier that's not valid for anything inside an interface
18. Object _____ Programming means creating programs that combine your data and code together into classes and objects

Down

1. When you move common methods from specific classes to more a general class that they all inherit from, you're using this OOP principle
2. If a class that implements an interface doesn't implement all of its methods, getters and setters, then the project won't _____.
5. Everything in an interface is automatically
7. An abstract class can include both abstract and _____ methods
9. You can't _____ an abstract class
11. A class that implements this must include all of the methods, getters and setters that it defines
12. What you do with an interface
13. The is keyword returns true if an _____ implements an interface
16. An interface can't technically include a _____, but it can define getters and setters that look just like one from the outside

Pool Puzzle Solution from page 287

Your job is to take code snippets from the pool and place them into the blank lines in the code and output. You may use the same snippet more than once, and you won't need to use all the snippets. Your goal is to make a set of classes that will compile and run and produce the output listed.

Here's where the Acts class calls the constructor in Picasso, which it inherits from. It passes "Acts" into the constructor, which gets stored in the face property.

```csharp
public    interface    Nose {
    int Ear()    ;
    string Face { get; }
}

public abstract class    Picasso : Nose    {
    public virtual int Ear()
    {
        return 7;
    }
    public Picasso(string face)
    {
        this.face    = face;
    }
    public virtual string Face {
        get { return face    ; }
    }
    string face;
}

public class    Clowns : Picasso    {
    public Clowns() : base("Clowns") { }
}
```

```csharp
public class    Acts  :  Picasso   {
    public Acts() : base("Acts") { }
    public override    int Ear()    {
        return 5;
    }
}

public class    Of76 : Clowns    {
    public override string Face {
        get { return "Of76"; }
    }
}

public static void Main(string[] args) {
    string result = "";
    Nose[] i = new Nose[3];
    i[0] = new Acts();
    i[1] = new Clowns()
    i[2] = new Of76();
    for (int x = 0; x < 3; x++) {
        result += (    i[x].Ear()    + " "
                + i[x].Face    ) + "\n";
    }
    MessageBox.Show(result);
}
```

Properties can appear anywhere in the class! It's easier to read your code if they're at the top, but it's perfectly valid to have the face property at the bottom of the Picasso class.

Face is a get accessor that returns the value of the face property. Both of them are defined in Picasso and inherited into the subclasses.

Objectcross solution

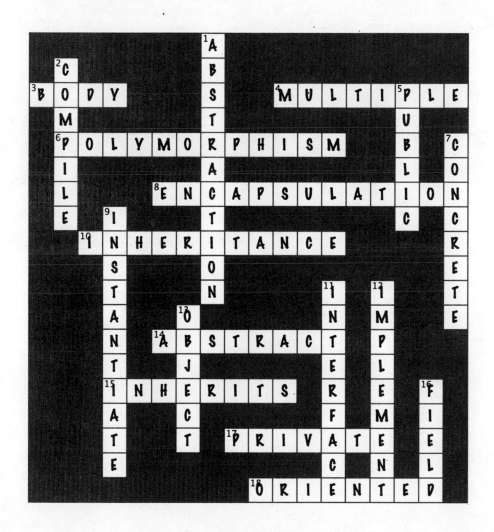

8 enums and collections

Storing lots of data

Finally, a way to organize my boyfriends!

When it rains, it pours.

In the real world, you don't get to handle your data in tiny little bits and pieces. No, your data's going to come at you in **loads, piles, and bunches**. You'll need some pretty powerful tools to organize all of it, and that's where **collections** come in. They let you **store, sort, and manage** all the data that your programs need to pore through. That way you can think about writing programs to work with your data, and let the collections worry about keeping track of it for you.

Strings don't always work for storing categories of data

Suppose you have several worker bees, all represented by
`Worker` classes. How would you write a constructor that took
a job as a parameter? If you use a string for the job name, you
might end up with code that looks like this:

*Our bee management software kept track
of each worker's job using a string like
"Sting Patrol" or "Nectar Collector".*

*Our code would allow these values to be passed
in a constructor even though the program only
supports Sting Patrol, Nectar Collector, and
other jobs that a bee does.*

```
Worker buzz = new Worker("Attorney General");
Worker clover = new Worker("Dog Walker");
Worker gladys = new Worker("Newscaster");
```

*This code compiles, no problem. But these jobs don't
make any sense for a bee. The Worker class really
shouldn't allow these types as valid data.*

You could probably add code to the `Worker` constructor to check each
string and make sure it's a valid bee job. Although, if you add new jobs
that bees can do, you've got to change this code and recompile the
Worker class. But that's a pretty short-sighted solution. What if you have
other classes that need to check for the types of worker bees they can be?
Now you've got to duplicate code, and that's a bad path to go down.

What we need is a way to say, "Hey, there are only certain values that are
allowed here." We need to **enumerate** the values that are okay to use.

Enums let you enumerate a set of valid values

An enum is a data type that only allows certain values for that piece of data. So we could define an enum called Jobs, and define the allowed jobs:

The stuff inside the brackets is called the enumerator list, and each one of them is an enumerator. The whole thing together is called an enumeration.

This is the name of the enum.

But most people just call them enums.

```
public enum Job {
    NectarCollector,
    StingPatrol,
    HiveMaintenance,
    BabyBeeTutoring,
    EggCare,
    HoneyManufacturing,
}
```

The last enumerator doesn't have to end with a comma, but using one makes it easier to rearrange them using cut and paste.

Each of these is a valid job. Any can be used as a Jobs value.

Separate each value with a comma, and end the whole thing with a curly brace.

Now, you can reference these with types like this:

This is the name of the enum.

Finally, the value you want from the enum.

```
Worker nanny = new Worker(Job.EggCare);
```

We've changed the Worker constructor to accept Worker.Jobs as its parameter type.

Any other values aren't allowed. You can't just make up a new value for the enum. If you do, the program won't compile.

```
private void button1_Click(object sender EventArgs e)
{
    Worker buzz = new Worker(Jobs.AttorneyGeneral);
}
```

Here's the error you get from the compiler.

> ⊗ 'Jobs' does not contain a definition for 'AttorneyGeneral'

Enums let you represent numbers with names

Sometimes it's easier to work with numbers if you have names for them. You can assign numbers to the values in an enum and use the names to refer to them. That way, you don't have bunch of unexplained numbers floating around in your code. Here's an enum to keep track of a the scores for tricks at a dog competition. It's **inside the DogCompetition class**, so if you want to use it outside the class you'll need to call it DogCompetition. TrickScores.

This is the DogCompetition. TrickScores enum.

```
class DogCompetition{
    public enum TrickScore {
        Sit = 7,
        Beg = 25,
        RollOver = 50,
        Fetch = 10,
        ComeHere = 5,
        Speak = 20,
    }
    ...
    // code later in the class
    int score = (int)TrickScore.Fetch * 3;
    MessageBox.Show(score.ToString());

    MessageBox.Show(TrickScore.ComeHere.ToString())
```

These don't have to be in any particular order, and you can give multiple names to the same number.

Supply a name, then "=", then the number that name stands in for.

The (int) cast tells the compiler to turn this into the number it represents. So since TrickScroe.Speak has an index of to 20, (int)TrickScore.Speak turns it into the int value 20.

*This shows "30", 10 * 3.*

ToString() returns the name... in this case, "ComeHere".

You can cast the enum as a number and do calculations with it, or you can use the ToString() method to treat the name as a string. If you don't assign any number to a name, the items in the list will be given index numbers by default. The first item will be assigned a 0 value, the second a 1, etc.

But what happens if you want to use really big numbers for one of the enumerators? The default type for the numbers in an enum is int, so you'll need to specify the type you need using the : operator, like this:

You can put an enum inside a class like this, or it can exist on its own outside of a class.

```
public enum TrickScore : long {
        Sit = 7,
        Beg = 2500000000025
}
```

This tells the compiler to treat values in the TrickScores enum as longs, not ints.

If you tried to compile this code without specifying long as the type, you'd get this message:

```
Cannot implicitly convert type 'long' to 'int'.
```

Use what you've learned about enums to build a class that holds a playing card.

Exercise

1 ## Create a new project and add a Card class
You'll need two public fields: Suit (which will either be Spades, Clubs, Diamonds, or Hearts) and Value (Ace, Two, Three ... Ten, Jack, Queen, King). And you'll need a read-only property, Name ("Ace of Spades", "Five of Diamonds").

Card
Suit
Value
Name

2 ## Use two enums to define the suits and values.
Make sure that (int) Card.Suits.Spades is equal to 0, followed by Clubs (equal to 1), Diamonds (2), and Hearts (3). Make the values equal to their face values: (int) Card.Values.Ace should equal 1, Two should be 2, Three should be 3, etc. Jack should equal 11, Queen should be 12, and King should be 13.

3 ## Add a property for the name of the card
Name should be a read-only property. The get accessor should return a string that describes the card. This code will run in a form that calls the Name property from the card class and displays it:

```
Card card = new Card(Card.Suits.Spades, Card.Values.Ace);
string cardName = card.Name;
```

The value of cardName should be "Ace of Spades".

To make this work, your Card class will need a constructor that takes two parameters.

4 ## Add a form button that pops up the name of a random card
You can get your program to create a card with a random suit and value by casting a random number between 0 and 3 as a Cards.Suits and another random number between 1 and 13 as a Cards.Values. To do this, you can take advantage of a feature of the built-in Random class that gives it three different ways to call its Next() method:

When you've got more than one way to call a method, it's called overloading. More on that later...

```
Random random = new Random();
int numberBetween0and3 = random.Next(4);
int numberBetween1and13 = random.Next(1, 14);
int anyRandomInteger = random.Next();
```

This tells Random to return a value at least 1 but under 14.

Three of Clubs

there are no
Dumb Questions

Q: Hold on a second. When I was typing in that code, I noticed that an IntelliSense window popped up that said something about "3 of 3" when I used that Random.Next() constructor. What was that about?

A: What you saw was a constructor that was **overloaded**. When a class has a method that you can call more than one way, it's called overloading. When you're using a class with an overloaded method, the IDE lets you know all of the options that you have. In this case, the Random class has three possible Next() methods. As soon as you type "random.Next(" into the code window, the IDE pops up its IntelliSense box that shows the parameters for the different overloaded methods. The up and down arrows next to the "3 of 3" let you scroll between them. That's really useful when you're dealing with a method that has dozens of overloaded definitions. So when you're doing it, make sure you choose the right overloaded Next() method! But don't worry too much now—we'll talk a lot about overloading later on in the chapter.

```
random.Next(
▲ 3 of 3 ▼  int Random.Next (int minValue, int maxValue)
minValue: The inclusive lower bound of the random number
```

Exercise Solution

A deck of cards is a great example of where limiting values is important. Nobody wants to turn over their cards and be faced with a Joker of Clubs, or a 13 of Hearts. Here's how we wrote the Card class.

```
public class Card {

    public enum Suits {
        Spades,
        Clubs,
        Diamonds,
        Hearts
    }
```

When you don't specify values, the first item in the list is equal to zero, the second is 1, the third is 2, etc.

```
    public enum Values {
        Ace = 1,
        Two = 2,
        Three = 3,
        Four = 4,
        Five = 5,
        Six = 6,
        Seven = 7,
        Eight = 8,
        Nine = 9,
        Ten = 10,
        Jack = 11,
        Queen = 12,
        King = 13
    }
```

Here's where we set the value of Card.Values.Ace to 1.

```
    public Suits Suit;
    public Values Value;
```

When you set up your Suit and Value fields, you can just use Suits instead of Card.Suits, since you're inside of the Card class.

```
    public Card(Suits suit, Values value) {
        this.Suit = suit;
        this.Value = value;
    }

    public string Name {
        get { return Value.ToString() + " of " + Suit.ToString(); }
    }
}
```

The get accessor for the Name property can take advantage of the way an enum's ToString() method returns its name converted to a string.

Here's the code for the button that pops up the name of a random card.

```
private void button1_Click(object sender, EventArgs e) {
    Random random = new Random();
    Card card = new Card((Card.Suits)random.Next(4), (Card.Values)random.Next(1, 14));
    MessageBox.Show(card.Name);
}
```

Here's where we use the overloaded Random.Next() method to generate a random number that we cast to the enum.

We <u>could</u> use an array to create a deck of cards...

What if you want to create a class to represent a deck of cards? It would need a
way to keep track of every card in the deck, and it'd need to know what order they
were in. A Card array would do the trick—the top card in the deck would be at
index 0, the next card at index 1, etc. Here's a starting point—a Deck that starts
out with a full deck of 52 cards.

```
public class Deck {
    private Card[] cards = {
        new Card(Card.Suits.Spades, Card.Values.Ace),
        new Card(Card.Suits.Spades, Card.Values.Two),
        new Card(Card.Suits.Spades, Card.Values.Three),
        // ...
        new Card(Card.Suits.Diamonds, Card.Values.Queen),
        new Card(Card.Suits.Diamonds, Card.Values.King),
    };

    public void PrintCards() {
        for (int i = 0; i < cards.Length; i++)
            Console.WriteLine(cards[i].ToString());
    }
}
```

*This array declaration
would continue all the
way through the deck.
It's just abbreviated
here to save space.*

... but what if you wanted to do more?

Think of everything you might need to do with a deck of cards, though. If
you're playing a card game, you routinely need to change the order of the
cards, and add and remove cards from the deck. You just can't do that with
an array very easily.

BRAIN POWER

How would you add a Shuffle() method to the Deck class that rearranges
the cards in random order? What about a method to deal the first card
off the top of the deck? How would you add a card to the deck?

Arrays are hard to work with

An array is fine for storing a fixed list of values or references. But once you need
to move array elements around, or add more elements than the array can hold,
things start to get a little sticky.

1 Every array has a length, and you need to know the length to work with it. You could use
null references to keep some array elements empty:

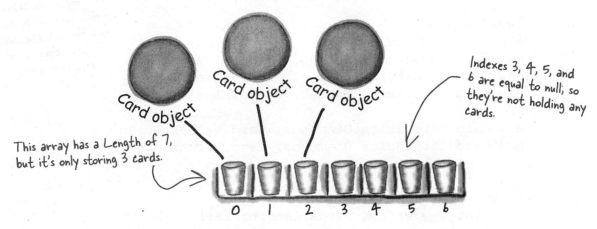

*Indexes 3, 4, 5, and
6 are equal to null; so
they're not holding any
cards.*

*This array has a Length of 7,
but it's only storing 3 cards.*

2 You'd need to keep track of how many cards are being held. So you'd need an int field,
which we could call `topCard`, which would hold the index of the last card in the array. So
our 3-card array would have a `Length` of 7, but we'd set `topCard` equal to 3.

*We'll add a topCard field to keep
track of how many cards are in the
array. Any index above topCard has a
null Card reference.*

*There's actually an Array.Resize()
method built into the .NET
Framework that does exactly that.*

3 But now things get complicated. It's easy enough to add a Peek() method that just returns a
reference to the top card—so you can peek at the top of the deck. But what if you want to add
a card? If topCard is less than the array's Length, you can just put your card in the array at that
index and add 1 to topCard. But if it the array's full, you'll need to create a new, bigger array
and copy the existing cards to it. Removing a card is easy enough—but after you subtract 1 from
toCard, you'll need to make sure to set the removed card's array index back to null. And what if
you need to remove a card **from the middle of the list**? If you remove card #4, you'll need to
move card 5 back to replace it, and then move 6 back, then 7 back...wow, what a mess!

Lists make it easy to store collections of... anything

The .NET Framework has a bunch of **collection** classes that handle all of those nasty issues that come up with you add and remove array elements. The most common sort of collection is a **List**. Once you creat a List object, it's easy to add an item, remove one from any location in the list, peek at an item, and even move an item from one place in the list to another. Here's how a list works:

① **First you create new instance of List**

Every array has a type—you don't just have an array, you have an int array, a Card array, etc. Lists are the same way. You need to specify the type of object or value that the list will hold by putting it in angle brackets <> when you use the new keyword to create it.

```
List cards = new List<Card>();
```

You specified <Card> when you created the list, so now this list only holds references to Card objects.

② **Now you can add to your List**

Once you've got a List object, you can add as many items to it as you want (as long as they match whatever type you specified when you created your new List).

```
cards.Add(new Card(Card.Suits.Diamonds, Card.Values.King);
cards.Add(new Card(Card.Suits.Clubs, Card.Values.Three);
cards.Add(new Card(Card.Suits.Hearts, Card.Values.Ace);
```

A list keeps its elements in order, just like an array. King of Diamonds is first, 3 of Clubs is second, and Ace of Hearts is third.

You can add as many cards as you want to the List – just call its Add() method. It'll make sure it's got enough "slots" for the items. If it starts to run out, it'll automatically resize itself.

Lists are more flexible than arrays

The List class is built into the .NET Framework, and it lets you do a lot of
things with objects that you can't do with a plain old array. Check out some
of the things you can do with a List.

❶ You can make one.
```
List<Egg> myCarton = new List<Egg>();
```

*A new List object is
created on the heap. But
there's nothing in it yet.*

❷ Add something to it.
```
Egg x = new Egg();
myCarton.Add(x);
```

*Now the List expands to hold
the Egg object....*

❸ Add something else to it.
```
Egg y = new Egg();

myCarton.Add(y);
```

*...and expands again to hold
the second Egg object..*

❹ Find out how many things are in it.
```
int theSize = myCarton.Count;
```

❺ Find out if it has something in particular in it.
```
bool Isin = myCarton.Contains(x);
```

*Now you can search for any
Egg inside the list. This would
definitely come back true.*

❻ Figure out where that thing is.
```
int idx = myCarton.IndexOf(y);
```

*The index for x would be 0 and the
index for y would be 1.*

❼ Find out how much the list will hold.
```
int limit = myCarton.Capacity;
```

*This will tell you the number of
objects the list can hold before it
has to resize itself.*

❽ Take something out if it.
```
myCarton.Remove(y);
```

poof!

*When we removed y, we left only x in
the List, so it shrank!*

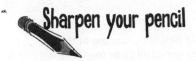

Sharpen your pencil

Fill in the rest of the table below by looking at the List code on the left and putting in what you think the code might be if it were using a regular array instead. We don't expect you to get all of them exactly right, so just make your best guess.

Assume these statements are all executed in order, one after another.

We filled in a couple for you...

List	**regular array**
`List<String> myList =` `        new List <String>();`	`String [] myList = new String[2];`
`String a = "Yay!";`	`String a = "Yay!";` ~~myList~~
`myList.Add(a);`	`String [0] = a`
`String b = "Bummer";`	`String b = "Bummer";` ~~myList~~
`myList.Add(b);`	`String [1] = b`
`object o = myList[1];`	`object o = ~~str~~ myList [1]`
`int theSize = myList.Count;`	`int theSize = myList.Length`

`bool isIn = myList.Contains(b);`
 	
Hint: You'll need than more than one line of code here.
	`for(int i=0, i< theSize; i++)`
	`{`
	`  if (myList [i] == b)`
	`      isIn = true;`
	`  else`
	`      isIn = false;`
	`}`

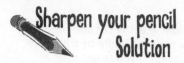

Sharpen your pencil
Solution

Your job was to fill in the rest of the table below by looking at the List code on the left and putting in what you think the code might be if it were using a regular array instead.

List

regular array

List	regular array
```List<String> myList =``` ``` new List <String>();```	```String[] myList = new String[2];```
```String a = "Yay!"``` ```myList.Add(a);```	```String a = "Yay!";``` ```myList[0] = a;```
```String b = "Bummer";``` ```myList.Add(b);```	```String b = "Bummer";``` ```myList[1] = b;```
```int theSize = myList.Count;```	```int theSize = myList.Length;```
```object o = myList[1];```	```object o = myList[1];```

```bool isIn = myList.Contains(b);```	```bool isIn = false;```
	``` for (int i = 0; i < myList.```
	``` Length; i++) {```
	``` if (b == myList[i]) {```
	``` isIn = true;```
	``` }```
	```}```

Lists are objects that use methods just like every other class you've used so far. You can see the list of methods available from within the IDE just by typing a **.** next to the List name and you pass parameters to them just the same as you would for a class you created yourself.

With arrays you're a lot more limited. You need to set the size of the array when you create it, and any logic that'll need to be performed on it will need to be written on your own.

The .NET Framework does have an Array class which makes some of these things a little easier to do... but we're concentrating on List objects because they're a lot easier to use.

Lists shrink and grow dynamically

The great thing about a `List` is that you don't need to know how long it'll be when you create it. A `List` automatically grows and shrinks to fit its contents. Here's an example of a few of the methods that make working with Lists a lot easier than arrays:

We're declaring a List of Shoe objects called ShoeCloset.

```
List<Shoe> shoeCloset = new List<Shoe>();
```

You can use a new statement inside the List.Add() method.

```
shoeCloset.Add(new Shoe()
    { Style = Style.Sneakers, Color = "Black" });
shoeCloset.Add(new Shoe()
    { Style = Style.Clogs, Color = "Brown" });
shoeCloset.Add(new Shoe()
    { Style = Style.Wingtips, Color = "Black" });
shoeCloset.Add(new Shoe()
    { Style = Style.Loafers, Color = "White" });
shoeCloset.Add(new Shoe()
    { Style = Style.Loafers, Color = "Red" });
shoeCloset.Add(new Shoe()
    { Style = Style.Sneakers, Color = "Green" });
```

foreach is special kind of loop for Lists. It will execute a statment for each object in the List. This loop creates an identifier called shoe. As the loop goes through the items, it sets shoe equal to the first item in the list, then the second, then the third, until the loop is done.

```
int numberOfShoes = shoeCloset.Count;
foreach (Shoe shoe in shoeCloset) {
    shoe.Style = Style.Flipflops;
    shoe.Color = "Orange";
}
```

This returns the total number of Shoe objects in the List.

foreach loops work on arrays, too! In fact, they work on any collection.

This foreach loop goes through each of the shoes in the closet.

The Remove() method will remove the object by it's reference; RemoveAt() does it by index number.

```
shoeCloset.RemoveAt(4);

Shoe thirdShoe = shoeCloset[3];
Shoe fifthShoe = shoeCloset[5];
shoeCloset.Clear();

shoeCloset.Add(thirdShoe);
if (shoeCloset.Contains(fifthShoe))
    Console.WriteLine("That's surprising.");
```

The Clear() method removes all of the objects in a List.

We saved references to two shoes before we cleared the list. We added one back, but the other's still missing.

This line will never run, because Contains() will return false. We only added thirdShoe into the cleared list, not fifthShoe.

Here's the Shoe class we're using...

```
public class Shoe {
    public Style Style;
    public string Color;
}


public enum Style {
    Sneakers,
    Loafers,
    Sandals,
    Flipflops,
    Wingtips,
    Clogs,
}
```

List objects can store <u>any</u> type

You've already seen that a List can store strings or Shoes. You could also make Lists of integers, or any other object you can create. That makes a List a **generic collection**. When you create a new List object, you tie it to a specific type: you can have a list of ints, or strings, or Shoe objects. That makes working with Lists easy—once you've created your list, you always know the type of data that's inside it.

> This doesn't actually mean that you add the letter T. It's notation that you'll see whenever a class or interface works with all types. The <T> part means you can put a type in there, like List<Shoe>, and limit the type.

```
List name = new List<T>();
```

> Lists can be either very flexible (allowing any type) or very restrictive. So they do what arrays do, and then quite a few things more.

The .NET Framework comes with some generic interfaces that let the collections you're building work with any and all types. List implements those interfaces and that's why you could create a List of integers and work with it using pretty much the same way that you would work with a List of Shoe objects.

➤ ***Check it out for yourself.*** Type the word, `List`, into the IDE and then right-click on it and select "Go To Definition". That will take you to the declaration for the List class. It implements a few interfaces:

> This is where RemoveAt(), IndexOf(), and Insert() come from.

```
public class List<T> : ⟨IList<T>⟩,
⟨ICollection<T>⟩ ⟨IEnumerable<T>⟩ IList,
ICollection, IEnumerable
```

> This is where Add(), Clear(), CopyTo(), and Remove() come from. It's the basis for all generic collections.

> This interface lets you use foreach among other things.

BULLET POINTS

- **List** is a class in the .NET Framework.

- A List **resizes dynamically** to whatever size is needed. It's got a certain capacity—once you add enough data to the list, it'll grow to accommodate it.

- To put something into an List, use **Add()**. To remove something from a List, use **Remove()**.

- You can remove objects using their index number using **RemoveAt()**.

- You declare the type of the List using a **type parameter**, which is a type name in angle brackets. Example: List<Frog> means the List will be able to hold only objects of type Frog.

- To find out where something is (and if it is) in a List, use **IndexOf()**.

- To get the number of elements in a List, use the **count** property.

- You can use the **Contains()** method to find out if a particular object is in a List.

- **foreach** is a special kind of loop that will iterate through all of the elements in a list and execute code on it. The syntax for a foreach loop is **foreach (string s in StringList)**. You don't have to tell the foreach loop to increment by one; it will go through the entire list all on its own.

16

Code Magnets

Can you reconstruct the code snippets to make a working Windows Form that will pop up the message box below when you click a button?

```
private void button1_Click(object sender,
EventArgs e){
```

6

```
a.RemoveAt(2);
```

1

```
List<string> a = new List<string>();
```

1a

```
public void printL (List<string> a){
```

1b

5 8

```
if (a.contains("two")) {
    a.Add(twopointtwo);
}
```

3

```
a.Add(zilch);
a.Add(first);
a.Add(second);
a.Add(third);
```

```
}
```

2a

```
string result = "";
```

4

```
if (a.Contains("three")){
    a.Add("four");
}
```

3a

4a

```
foreach (string element in a)
{
    result += "\n" + element;
}
```

5a

```
MessageBox.Show(result);
```

7

6a

```
}
```

```
if (a.IndexOf("four") != 4) {
    a.Add(fourth);
}
```

```
}
```

3b

```
printL(a);
```

2b

2

```
string zilch = "zero";
string first =  "one";
string second = "two";
string third = "three";
string fourth = "4.2";
string twopointtwo = "2.2";
```

Message box:
```
zero
one
three
four
4.2

    OK
```

Code Magnets Solution

```
private void button1_Click(object sender,
EventArgs e){

    List<string> a = new List<string>();

    string zilch = "zero";
    string first =  "one";
    string second = "two";
    string third = "three";
    string fourth = "4.2";
    string twopointtwo = "2.2";

    a.Add(zilch);
    a.Add(first);
    a.Add(second);
    a.Add(third);

    if (a.Contains("three")){
        a.Add("four");
        }

    a.RemoveAt(2);

    if (a.IndexOf("four") != 4) {
        a.Add(fourth);
            }

    if (a.contains("two")) {
        a.Add(twopointtwo);

    }

    printL(a);
}

public void printL (List<string> a){
    string result = "";

    foreach (string element in a)
    {
        result += "\n" + element;
    }

    MessageBox.Show(result);
    }
}
```

```
zero
one
three
four
4.2

    OK
```

Can you figure out why "2.2" never gets added to the list, even though it's declared here?

RemoveAt() removes the element at index #2—which is the third element in the list.

The printL() method uses a foreach loop to go through a list of strings, add each of them to one big string, and then show it in a message box.

The foreach loop goes through all of the elements in the list and prints them.

Dumb Questions
there are no

Q: So why would I ever use an enum instead of a List? Don't they solve the same problem?

A: Enums are a little different than Lists. You can think of enums as a handy way to store *lists of constants* so you can refer to them by name. They're great for keeping your code readable and making sure that you are always using the right variable names to access values that you use really frequently.

A List can store just about anything. Since it's a list of *objects*, each element in a list can have its own methods and properties. Enums, on the other hand, have to be assigned one of the **value types** in C# (like the ones on the first page of Chapter 4). So, you can't store reference variables in them.

Enums can't dynamically change their size either. They can't implement interfaces or have methods, and you'll have to cast them to another type to store a value from an enum in another variable. Add all of that up and you've got some pretty big differences between the two ways of storing data. But both are really useful in their own right.

Q: OK, it sounds like Lists are pretty powerful. So why would I ever want to use an array?

A: Arrays take up less memory and take less CPU time for your programs. If you're doing something that's really performance-intensive—like the same operation thousands and thousands of

times –then you might find that a List will cause your program to slow down significantly. Luckily, you can easily convert any list to an array using the `ToArray()` method... and you can convert an array to a list using one of the overloaded constructors for the `List` object.

Q: I don't get the name "generic". Why is it called a generic collection? Why isn't an array one?

A: A generic collection is a collection object (or a built-in object that lets you store and manage a bunch of other objects) that's been set up to store only one type.

Q: Okay, that explains the "collection" part. But what makes it "generic"?

A: Supermarkets used to carry generic items that were packaged in big white packages with black type that just said the name of what was inside ("Potato Chips", "Cola", "Soap", etc.). The generic brand was all about what's inside the bag, and not about how it's displayed.

The same thing happens with generic data types. Your List<> will work exactly the same with whatever happens to be inside it. A List of Shoe objects, Card objects, ints, longs, or even other Lists will still act at the container level. So you can always add, remove, insert, etc., no matter what's inside the list itself.

The term "generic" refers to the fact that even though a specific instance of List can only store one specific type, the List class in general works with any type.

Q: Can I have a list that doesn't have a type?

A: No. Every list—in fact, every generic collection (and you'll learn about the other generic collections in just a minute)—must have a type connected to it. C# does have non-generic lists called ArrayLists that can store any kind of object. If you want to use an ArrayList, you need to include a "`using System.Collections;`" line in your code.

Generic collections are actually a recent addition to C#—they didn't exist in the early versions of the language. But they're so useful that people rarely use non-generic collections any more... which is why we won't be talking much about them.

When you create a new List object, you always supply a type—that tells C# what type of data that it'll store. A list can store a value type (like int, bool, or string) or a class.

Okay, honestly, we're talking about a really, really tiny performance boost. Like if you have to do the same thing millions of times a second, use an array and not a list.

That's what the <T> stuff is all about. It's the way that you tie a specific instance of a List to one type. But the List class as a whole is generic enough to work with ANY type. That's why generic collections are different from anything you've seen so far.

Collection initializers work just like object initializers

C# gives you a nice bit of shorthand to cut down on typing when you need to create a list and immediately add a bunch of items to it. When you create a new List object, you can use a **collection initializer** to give it a starting list of items. It'll add them as soon as the list is created.

You saw this code a few pages ago—it creates a new List<Shoe> and fills it with new Shoe objects.

```
List<Shoe> shoeCloset = new List<Shoe>();
shoeCloset.Add(new Shoe() { Style = Style.Sneakers, Color = "Black" });
shoeCloset.Add(new Shoe() { Style = Style.Clogs, Color = "Brown" });
shoeCloset.Add(new Shoe() { Style = Style.Wingtips, Color = "Black" });
shoeCloset.Add(new Shoe() { Style = Style.Loafers, Color = "White" });
shoeCloset.Add(new Shoe() { Style = Style.Loafers, Color = "Red" });
shoeCloset.Add(new Shoe() { Style = Style.Sneakers, Color = "Green" });
```

The same code rewritten using a collection initializer

Collection Initializers are a C# 3.0 feature. If you're still using Visual Studio 2005, you should download Visual Studio 2008 Express for free from Microsoft, otherwise this code won't work.

You can create a collection initializer by taking each item that was being added using Add() and adding them to the statement that creates the list.

```
List<Shoe> shoeCloset = new List<Shoe>() {
    new Shoe() { Style = Style.Sneakers, Color = "Black" },
    new Shoe() { Style = Style.Clogs, Color = "Brown" },
    new Shoe() { Style = Style.Wingtips, Color = "Black" },
    new Shoe() { Style = Style.Loafers, Color = "White" },
    new Shoe() { Style = Style.Loafers, Color = "Red" },
    new Shoe() { Style = Style.Sneakers, Color = "Green" },
};
```

The statement to create the list is followed by curly brackets that contain separate new statement, separated by commas.

You're not limited to using new statements in the initializer—you can include variables, too.

A collection initializer makes your code more compact by letting you combine creating a list with adding an initial set of items.

Let's create a list of Ducks

Here's a duck class that keeps track of your extensive duck colleciton. (You *do* collect ducks, don't you?)

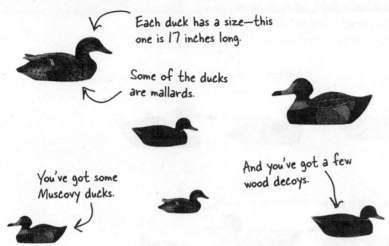

Each duck has a size—this one is 17 inches long.

Some of the ducks are mallards.

You've got some Muscovy ducks.

And you've got a few wood decoys.

Duck
Size
Kind
Quack()
Swim()
Eat()
Walk()

```
public class Duck {
    public int Size;
    public KindOfDuck Kind;
}
```

The class has two public fields. It's also got some methods, which we're not showing here.

```
public enum KindOfDuck {
    Mallard,
    Muscovy,
    Decoy
}
```

We'll use an enum called KindOfDuck to keep track of what sort of ducks are in your collection.

Here's the initializer

We've got six ducks, so we'll create a List<Duck> that has a collection initializer with six statements. Each statement in the initializer creates a new duck, using an object initializer to set each Duck object's Size and Kind field.

```
List<Duck> Ducks = new List<Duck>() {

    new Duck() { Kind = KindOfDuck.Mallard, Size = 17 },

    new Duck() { Kind = KindOfDuck.Muscovy, Size = 18 },

    new Duck() { Kind = KindOfDuck.Decoy, Size = 14 },

    new Duck() { Kind = KindOfDuck.Muscovy, Size = 11 },

    new Duck() { Kind = KindOfDuck.Mallard, Size = 14 },

    new Duck() { Kind = KindOfDuck.Decoy, Size = 13 },

}
```

Lists are easy, but <u>SORTING</u> can be tricky

It's not hard to think about ways to sort numbers or letters. But what do you sort two objects on, especially if they have multiple fields? In some cases you might want to order objects by the value in a name field, while in other cases it might make sense to order objects based on height or date of birth. There are lots of ways you can order things, and Lists support any of them.

You could sort a list of ducks by size...

Sorted smallest to biggest...

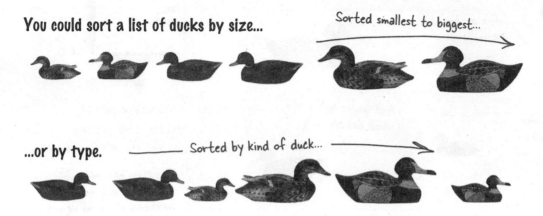

...or by type.

Sorted by kind of duck...

Lists know how to sort themselves

Every list comes with a Sort() method that rearranges all of the items in the list to put them in order. Lists already know how to sort most built-in types and classes, and it's easy to teach it how to sort your own classes.

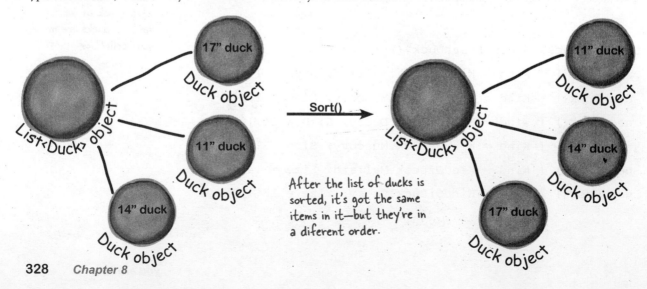

After the list of ducks is sorted, it's got the same items in it—but they're in a different order.

Two ways to sort your ducks

The List.Sort() method already knows how to sort any type or class that implements the **IComparable** interface. That interface has just one member—a method called CompareTo(). Sort() uses an object's CompareTo() method to compare it with other objects, and uses its return value (an int) to determine which comes first.

But sometimes you need to sort a list of objects that don't implement IComparable, and .NET has another interface to help with that. You can pass Sort() an instance of a class that implements IComparer. That interface also has one method. The List's Sort() method uses the comparer object's Compare() method to compare pairs of objects, in order to figure out which one comes first in the sorted list.

You can make any class work with the List's built-in Sort() method by having it implement IComparable and adding a CompareTo() method.

An object's CompareTo() method compares it with another object

One way to let our List object sort is to modify the Duck class to implement IComparable. To do that, we'd add a CompareTo() method that takes a Duck reference as a parameter. If the duck to compare should come after the current duck in the sorted list, CompareTo() returns a positive number.

Here's a Duck class that sorts itself based on duck size:

```
public class Duck : IComparable<Duck> {
    public int Size;
    public KindOfDuck Kind;


    public int CompareTo(Duck duckToCompare) {
        if (this.Size > duckToCompare.Size)
            return 1;
        else if (this.Size < duckToCompare.Size)
            return -1;
        else
            return 0;
    }
}
```

When you implement IComparable, you specify the type being compared when you have the class implement the interface.

Most CompareTo() methods look a lot like this. This method first compares the Size field against the other duck's Size field. If this duck is bigger, it returns 1. If it's smaller, it returns -1. And if they're the same size, it returns zero.

If you want to sort your list from smallest to biggest, have CompareTo() return a positive number if it's comparing to a smaller duck, and a negative number if it's comparing to a bigger one.

Use IComparer to tell your List how to sort

Lists have a special interface built into the .NET Framework that lets you build your own sorting logic. By implementing the **IComparer** interface, you are can tell your List exactly how you want it to sort your objects. You do that by implementing the Compare() method in the IComparer interface. It takes two object parameters, x and y, and returns an int. If x is less than y, it should return a negative value. If they're equal, it should return zero. And if x is greater than y, it should return a positive value.

Here's an example of how you'd declare a comparer class to compare duck objects by size:

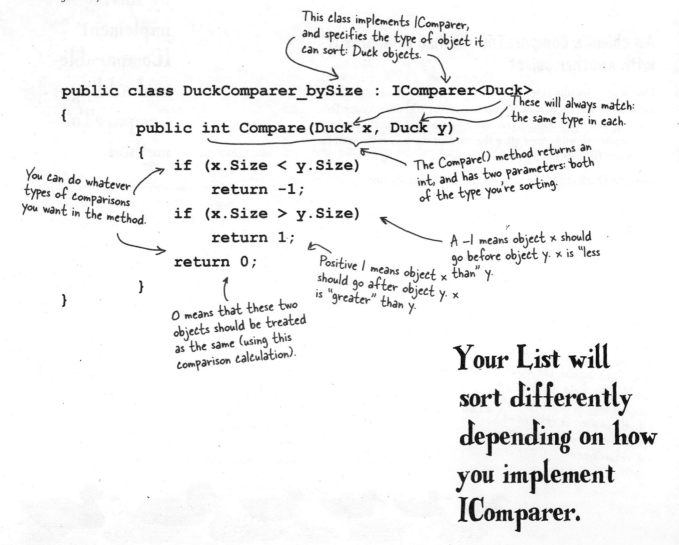

This class implements IComparer, and specifies the type of object it can sort: Duck objects.

These will always match: the same type in each.

```
public class DuckComparer_bySize : IComparer<Duck>
{
    public int Compare(Duck x, Duck y)
    {
        if (x.Size < y.Size)
            return -1;
        if (x.Size > y.Size)
            return 1;
        return 0;
    }
}
```

You can do whatever types of comparisons you want in the method.

The Compare() method returns an int, and has two parameters: both of the type you're sorting.

A –1 means object x should go before object y. x is "less than" y.

Positive 1 means object x should go after object y. x is "greater" than y.

0 means that these two objects should be treated as the same (using this comparison calculation).

Your List will sort differently depending on how you implement IComparer.

Create an instance of your comparer object

When you want to sort using IComparer, you need to create a new instance of the class that implements it. That object exists for one reason—to help List.Sort() figure out how to sort the array. But like any other (non-static) class, you need to instantiate it before you use it.

We left out the code you already saw a few pages ago to initialize the list.

```
List<Duck> ducks = new List<Duck>() { ... };

DuckComparer_bySize dc = new DuckComparer_bySize();

ducks.Sort(dc);
```

You'll pass Sort() a reference to the new DuckComparer_bySize object as its parameter.

Sorted smallest to biggest...

Multiple IComparer implementations, multiple ways to sort your objects

You can create multiple IComparer classes with different sorting logic depending on what you need to do. Then you can call the comparer you want when you need to sort in that particular way. Here's another duck comparer implementation:

This comparer sorts by duck type. Remember, when you compare the enum Kind, you're comparing their index values.

```
class DuckComparer_byKind : IComparer<Duck> {
    public int Compare(Duck x, Duck y) {
        if (x.Kind < y.Kind)
            return -1;
        if (x.Kind > y.Kind)
            return 1;
        else
            return 0;
    }
}
```

So Mallard comes before Muscovy, which comes before Decoy.

We used the value of the Type that comes from the index value in the enum Duck.Type.

Notice how "greater than" and "less than" have a different meaning here. One type is "greater than" another, just so we have an ordering we can use.

Here's an example of how enums and Lists work together. Enums stand in for numbers, and are used in sorting of lists.

```
DuckComparer_byKind dcKind = new DuckComparer_byKind();
ducks.Sort(dcKind);
```

——— Sorted by kind of duck... ———

IComparer can do complex comparisons

One advantage to creating a separate class for sorting your ducks is
that you can build more complex logic into that class—and you can
add members that help determine how the list gets sorted.

```
public class DuckComparer : IComparer<Duck> {
    public enum SortCriteria {
        SizeThenKind,
        KindThenSize,
    }

    public SortCriteria SortBy = SortCriteria.SizeThenKind;

    public int Compare(Duck x, Duck y) {
        if (SortBy == SortCriteria.SizeThenKind)
            if (x.Size > y.Size)
                return 1;
            else if (x.Size < y.Size)
                return -1;
            else
                if (x.Kind > y.Kind)
                    return 1;
                else if (x.Kind < y.Kind)
                    return -1;
                else
                    return 0;
        else
            if (x.Kind > y.Kind)
                return 1;
            else if (x.Kind < y.Kind)
                return -1;
            else
                if (x.Size > y.Size)
                    return 1;
                else if (x.Size < y.Size)
                    return -1;
                else
                    return 0;
    }
}

DuckComparer dc = new DuckComparer();

dc.SortBy = DuckComparer.SortCriteria.KindThenSize;
ducks.Sort();

dc.SortBy = DuckComparer.SortCriteria.SizeThenKind;
ducks.Sort();
```

Here's a more complex class to compare ducks. Its CompareTo() method takes the same parameters, but it looks at the public SortBy field to determine how to sort the ducks.

This enum tells the object which way to sort the ducks.

This if statement checks the SortBy field. If it's set to SizeThenKind, then it first sorts the ducks by size, and then within each size it'll sort the ducks by their kind.

Instead of just returning 0 if the two ducks are the same size, the comparer checks their kind, and only returns 0 if the two ducks are both the same size and the same kind.

If SortBy isn't set to SizeThenKind, then the comparer first sorts by the kind of duck. If the two ducks are the same kind, then it compares their size.

Here's how we'd use this comparer object. First we'd instantiate it as usual. Then we can set the object's SortBy field before calling ducks.Sort(). Now you can change the way the list sorts its ducks just by changing one field in the object.

Create five random cards and then sort them.

Exercise

Console applications that you run from the command prompt use the Console.WriteLine() method a lot, but you can use it in a Windows application too.

① Create code to make a jumbled set of cards

Add a button to a form that creates five random Card objects. After you create each object, use the built-in `Console.WriteLine()` method to write its name to the **output**. You can view everything written to the output by selecting "Output" from the View menu while the program's running.

② Create a class that implements IComparer<List> to sort the cards

Here's a good chance to use that IDE shortcut to implement an interface:

```
public class CardComparer_byValue : IComparer<Card>
```

Then click on IComparer and hover over the I. You'll see a box appear underneath it, when you click on the box, the IDE pops up a window:

If you click on "Implement interface IComparer<Card>", the IDE automatically fills in all of the methods and properties that you need to implement. In this case, it creates an empty Compare() method to compare two cards, x and y. Write the method so that it returns 1 if x is bigger than y, -1 if it's smaller, and 0 if they're the same card. In this case, make sure that any king comes after than any jack, which comes after than any four, which comes after than any ace.

③ Make sure the output looks right

Here's what your output window should look like after you click the button.

When you use the built-in Console.WriteLine() method, it adds a line to this output window.

Your IComparer object needs to sort the cards by value, so the cards with the lowest values are first in the list.

Create five random cards and then sort them.

Exercise Solution

Here's the "guts" of the card sorting, which uses the built-in List.Sort() method. Sort() takes an IComparer object, which has one method: Compare(). This implementation takes two cards and first compares their suits, then their values.

```csharp
public class CardComparer_byValue : IComparer<Card> {
    public int Compare(Card x, Card y) {
        if (x.Value < y.Value) {
            return -1;
        }
        if (x.Value > y.Value) {
            return 1;
        }
        if (x.Suit < y.Suit) {
            return -1;
        }
        if (x.Suit > y.Suit) {
            return 1;
        }
        return 0;
    }
}
```

If x has a bigger suit, return 1. If x's suit is smaller, return -1. Remember, both return statements end the method immediately.

These statements only get executed if x and y have the same suit—that means the first two return statements weren't executed.

If none of the other four return statements were hit, the cards must be the same—so return zero.

Here's a generic List of Card objects to store the cards. Once they're in the list, it's easy to sort them using an IComparer.

```csharp
private void button1_Click(object sender, EventArgs e)
{
    Console.WriteLine("Five random cards:");
    List<Card> cards = new List<Card>();
    for (int i = 0; i < 5; i++)
    {
        cards.Add(new Card((Card.Suits)random.Next(4),
                        (Card.Values)random.Next(1, 14)));
        Console.WriteLine(cards[i].Name);
    }

    Console.WriteLine("Those same cards, sorted:");
    cards.Sort(new CardComparer_byValue());
    foreach (Card card in cards)
    {
        Console.WriteLine(card.Name);
    }
}
```

Use a dictionary to store keys and values

A list is like a big long page full of names. But what if you want, for each name, an address? Or for every car in the garage list, you want details about that car? You need a **dictionary**. A dictionary lets you take a special value—the **key**—and associate that key with a bunch of data—the **value**. And one more thing: a specific key can **only appear once** in any dictionary.

> ## dic·tion·ar·y
> A book that lists the words of a language in alphabetical order and gives their meaning.

This is the key. It's how you look up a definition in (you guessed it) a dictionary.

This is the value. It's the data associated with a particular key.

Here's how you declare a Dictionary in C#:

$$\text{Dictionary <Tkey, TValue> kv = new Dictionary <TKey, TValue>();}$$

These are like List<T>. The <T> means a type goes in there. So you can declare one type for the key, and another type for the value.

The first item in the angle brackets is always the key, and the second is always the data.

And here's a Dictionary in action:

```
private void button1_Click(object sender, EventArgs e)
{
    Dictionary<string, string> wordDefinition =
        new Dictionary<string, string>();

    wordDefinition.Add ("Dictionary", "A book that lists the words of a "
                + "language in alphabetical order and gives their meaning");
    wordDefinition.Add ("Key", "A thing that provides a means of gaining access to "
                + "our understanding something.");
    wordDefinition.Add ("Value", "A magnitude, quantity, or number.");

    if (wordDefinition.ContainsKey("Key"))
        MessageBox.Show(wordDefinition["Key"]);
}
}
```

This dictionary has string values for keys, and strings as the value. It's like a real dictionary: term, and definition.

The Add() method is how you add keys and values to the dictionary.

Add() takes a key, and then the value.

ContainsKey() tells you if a key is in the dictionary. Handy, huh?

Here's how you get the value for a key. It looks kind of like an array index—get the value for the key at this index.

The Dictionary Functionality Rundown

Dictionaries are a lot like Lists. Both types are flexible in letting you work with lots of data types, and also come with lots of built-in functionality. Here are the basic `Dictionary` methods:

* **Add an item.**
  You can add an item to a dictionary by passing a key and a value to its the `Add()` method.

```
Dictionary<string, string> myDictionary = new Dictionary<string, string>();

        myDictionary.Add("some key", "some value");
```

* **Look up a value using its key.**
  The most important thing you'll do with a dictionary is look up values—which makes sense, because you stored those values in a dictionary so you could look them up using their unique keys.

```
        string lookupValue = myDictionary["some key"];
```

* **Remove an item.**
  Just like a List, you can remove and item from a dictionary using the `Remove()` method. All you need to pass to the Remove method is the Key value to have both the key and the value removed.

```
        myDictionary.Remove("some key");
```

Keys are unique in a Dictionary; any key appears exactly once. Values can appear any number of times—two keys can have the same value. That way, when you look up or remove a key, the Dictionary knows what to remove.

* **Get a list of keys.**
  You can get a list of all of the keys in a Dictionary using a `KeyCollection` and loop through it using a foreach loop. You'll usually use a Keycollection like this:

```
        foreach (string key in myDictionary.Keys) { ... };
```

Keys is a property of your dictionary object. This particular dictionary has string keys, so Keys is a collection of strings.

* **Get a list of values.**
  You can get a list of all of the values in a Dictionary using a `ValueCollection`. Most of the time, you use a ValueCollection with a foreach loop too:

```
        foreach (string value in myDictionary.Values) { ... };
```

Since this dictionary has string values, the foreach identifier will be a string.

Your key and value can be different types, too

Dictionaries are really versatile and can hold just about anything, from strings to numbers and even objects. Here's an example of a dictionary that's storing an integer as a key and a duck object as a value. The `Duck` object has a `Size` field and `Types` enum that are set inside its constructor.

Here's where the dictionary is declared. It'll store numbers and ducks. We'll add each of the ducks to the dictionary, giving it a unique ID number as the key.

```
Dictionary<int, Duck> duckDictionary = new Dictionary<int, Duck>();

duckDictionary.Add(5155, new Duck() { Kind = KindOfDuck.Mallard, Size = 15 });

duckDictionary.Add(6256, new Duck() { Kind = KindOfDuck.Mallard, Size = 14 });

duckDictionary.Add(2799, new Duck() { Kind = KindOfDuck.Mallard, Size = 13 });
```

The Count property tells how many key-value pairs are in the Dictionary.

```
int howMany = duckDictionary.Count;

Console.WriteLine("There are {0} ducks.", howMany);
```

If you need to pull the keys and values out of a dictionary, you can use a KeyValuePair<>.

This loop assigns the current key/value pair to idDuck, one at a time, through the whole loop.

```
foreach (KeyValuePair<int, Duck> idDuck in duckDictionary)

        Console.WriteLine("Key/value pair: {0}: {1}, {2}",

            idDuck.Key, idDuck.Value.Size, idDuck.Value.Kind.ToString() );
```

Every KeyValuePair has a key and a value. Since the value is a Duck, you can use its fields.

```
foreach (Duck duck in duckDictionary.Values)

    Console.WriteLine("Duck size: {0}", duck.Size);
```

This foreach loop goes through all of the values in the dictionary.

```
foreach (int key in duckDictionary.Keys)

    Console.WriteLine("ID Number: {0}", key);
```

And this foreach loop pulls each of the keys out of the dictionary.

```
Output                                          [x]
Show output from: Debug

    Key/value pair: 5155: 15, Mallard
    Key/value pair: 6256: 14, Mallard
    Key/value pair: 2799: 13, Mallard
    Duck size: 15
    Duck size: 14
    Duck size: 13
    ID Number: 5155
    ID Number: 6256
    ID Number: 2799
```

Here's the output that this code writes to the console.

Exercise ① **Build a form that lets you move cards between two decks**

You've built a card class already. Now it's time to build a class to hold any number of cards, which we'll call Deck. A real-life deck has 52 cards, but the Deck class can hold any number of cards— or no cards at all.

Then you'll build a form that shows you the contents of two Deck objects. When you first start the program, deck #1 has up to 10 random cards, and deck #2 is a complete deck of 52 cards, both sorted by suit and then value—and you can reset either deck to its initial state using two Reset buttons. The form also has buttons (labeled "<<" and ">>") to move cards between the decks.

These buttons are named moveToDeck2 (top) and moveToDeck1 (bottom). They move cards from one deck to the other.

You can use a button's Name property to give it a name to make your code easier to read. Then when you double-click on the button, its event handler is given a matching name.

Use two ListBox controls to show the two decks. When the moveToDeck1 button is clicked, it moves the selected card from deck #2 to deck #1.

These buttons are named shuffle1 and shuffle2. They call the appropriate Deck.Shuffle() method, and then redraw the deck.

Each of the reset1 and reset2 buttons first calls the RedrawDeck() method and then the ResetDeck() method.

In addition to the event handlers for the six buttons, you'll need to add two methods for the form. First add a ResetDeck() method, which resets a deck to its initial state. It takes an int as a parameter: if it's passed 1, it resets the first Deck object by reinitializing it to an empty deck and a random number of up to 10 random cards; if it's passed 2, it resets the second Deck object so that it contains a full 52-card deck. Then add this method:

The RedrawDeck() method updates the two listbox controls with whatever happens to be in the two Deck objects.

```
private void RedrawDeck(int DeckNumber) {
    if (DeckNumber == 1) {
        listBox1.Items.Clear();
        foreach (string cardName in deck1.GetCardNames())
            listBox1.Items.Add(cardName);
        label1.Text = "Deck #1 (" + deck1.Count + " cards)";
    } else {
        listBox2.Items.Clear();
        foreach (string cardName in deck2.GetCardNames())
            listBox2.Items.Add(cardName);
        label2.Text = "Deck #2 (" + deck2.Count + " cards)";
    }
}
```

Take a look at how we used the foreach loop to add each of the cards in the deck to the listbox.

❷   **Build the Deck class**

When you have the declarations for a class without the implementation, it's called a "skeleton".

Here's the skeleton for the Deck class. We've filled in several of the methods for you. You'll need to finish it by writing the Shuffle() and GetCardNames() methods, and you'll have to get the Sort() method to work. We also added two useful **overloaded constructors**: one that creates a complete deck of 52 cards, and the other that takes an array of Card obects and loads them into the deck.

The Deck stores its cards in a List—but it keeps it private to make sure it's well-encapsulated.

Deck
Count
Add()
Deal()
GetCardNames()
Shuffle()
Sort()

```
public class Deck {
    private List<Card> cards;
    private Random random = new Random();

    public Deck() {
        cards = new List<Card>();
        for (int suit = 0; suit <= 3; suit++)
            for (int value = 1; value <= 13; value++)
                cards.Add(new Card((Card.Suits)suit, (Card.Values)value));
    }

    public Deck(Card[] initialCards) {
        cards = new List<Card>(initialCards);
    }

    public int Count { get { return cards.Count; } }

    public void Add(Card cardToAdd) {
        cards.Add(cardToAdd);
    }

    public Card Deal(int index) {
        Card CardToDeal = cards[index];
        cards.RemoveAt(index);
        return CardToDeal;
    }

    public void Shuffle() {
        // this method shuffles the cards by rearranging them in a random order
    }

    public string[] GetCardNames() {
        // this method returns a string array that contains each card's name
    }

    public void Sort() {
        cards.Sort(new CardComparer_bySuit());
    }
}
```

If you don't pass parameters into the constructor, it creates a complete deck of 52 cards.

This overloaded constructor takes one parameter—an array of cards, which it loads as the initial deck.

The Deal method deals one card out of the deck—it removes the Card object from the deck and returns a reference to it. You can deal from the top by passing it 0, or deal from the middle of the deck by passing it the index of the card to deal.

Hint: The ListBox control's SelectedIndex property will be the same as the index of the card in the list. You can pass it directly to the Deal() method. If no card is selected, it'll be less than zero. In that case, the moveToDeck button should do nothing.

You'll need to write the Shuffle() method, the GetCardNames() method, and add a class that implements IComparer to make the Sort() method work. And you'll need to add the Card class you already wrote. If you use "Add Existing Item" to add it, don't forget to change its namespace.

Another hint: The form makes it really easy to test your Shuffle() method. Keep clicking the "Reset Deck #1" button until you get a three-card deck. That'll make it easy to see if your shuffling code works.

Build a class to store a deck of cards, along with a form that uses it.

Exercise Solution

Here's the constructor that creates a complete deck of 52 cards. It uses a nested for loop. The outside one loops through the four suits. That means the inside loop that goes through the 13 values runs four separate times, once per suit.

```
public class Deck {
    private List<Card> cards;
    private Random random = new Random();

    public Deck() {
        cards = new List<Card>();
        for (int suit = 0; suit <= 3; suit++)
            for (int value = 1; value <= 13; value++)
                cards.Add(new Card((Card.Suits)suit, (Card.Values)value));
    }

    public Deck(Card[] initialCards) {
        cards = new List<Card>(initialCards);
    }

    public int Count { get { return cards.Count; } }

    public void Add(Card cardToAdd) {
        cards.Add(cardToAdd);
    }

    public Card Deal(int index) {
        Card CardToDeal = cards[index];
        cards.RemoveAt(index);
        return CardToDeal;
    }

    public void Shuffle() {
        List<Card> NewCards = new List<Card>();
        while (cards.Count > 0) {
            int CardToMove = random.Next(cards.Count);
            NewCards.Add(cards[CardToMove]);
            cards.RemoveAt(CardToMove);
        }
        cards = NewCards;
    }

    public string[] GetCardNames() {
        string[] CardNames = new string[cards.Count];
        for (int i = 0; i < cards.Count; i++)
            CardNames[i] = cards[i].Name;
        return CardNames;
    }

    public void Sort() {
        cards.Sort(new CardComparer_bySuit());
    }
}
```

Here's the other constructor—this class has two overloaded constructors, each with different parameters.

The Add and Deal methods are pretty straightforward—they use the methods for the Cards list. The Deal method removes a card from the list, and the Add method adds a card to the list.

Your GetCardNames() method needs to create an array that's big enough to hold all the card names. This one uses a for loop, but it could also use foreach.

The Shuffle() method creates a new instance of List<Cards> called NewCards. Then it pulls random cards out of the Cards field and sticks them in NewCards until Cards is empty. Once it's done, it resets the Cards field to point to the new instance. The old instance won't have any more references pointing to it, so it'll get collected by the garbage collector.

```
class CardComparer_bySuit : IComparer<Card>
{
    public int Compare(Card x, Card y)
    {
        if (x.Suit > y.Suit)
            return 1;
        if (x.Suit < y.Suit)
            return -1;
        if (x.Value > y.Value)
            return 1;
        if (x.Value < y.Value)
            return -1;
        return 0;
    }
}


    Deck deck1;
    Deck deck2;
    Random random = new Random();

    public Form1() {
        InitializeComponent();
        ResetDeck(1);
        ResetDeck(2);
        RedrawDeck(1);
        RedrawDeck(2);
    }

    private void ResetDeck(int deckNumber) {
        if (deckNumber == 1) {
            int numberOfCards = random.Next(1, 11);
            deck1 = new Deck(new Card[] { });
            for (int i = 0; i < numberOfCards; i++)
                deck1.Add(new Card((Card.Suits)random.Next(4),
                                 (Card.Values)random.Next(1, 14)));
            deck1.Sort();
        } else
            deck2 = new Deck();
    }
```

Sorting by suit is a lot like sorting by value. The only difference is that in this case the suits are compared first, and then the values are compared only if the suits match.

Instead of using if/else if, we used a series of if statements. This works because each if statement only executes if the previous one didn't—otherwise the previous one would have returned.

The form's constructor needs to reset the two decks, and then it draws them.

To reset deck #1, this method first uses random.Next() to pick how many cards will go into the deck, creates a new empty deck. It uses a for loop to add that many random cards. It finishes off by sorting the deck. Resetting deck #2 is a easy—just create a new instance of Deck().

You've already got the RedrawDeck() method from the instructions.

We're not done yet—flip the page!

Exercise Solution (continued)

Naming your controls makes it a lot easier to read your code. If these were called button1_Click, button2_Click, etc., you wouldn't know which button's code you were looking at!

Here's the rest of the code for the form.

```
private void reset1_Click(object sender, EventArgs e) {
    ResetDeck(1);
    RedrawDeck(1);
}

private void reset2_Click(object sender, EventArgs e) {
    ResetDeck(2);
    RedrawDeck(2);
}

private void shuffle1_Click(object sender, EventArgs e) {
    deck1.Shuffle();
    RedrawDeck(1);
}

private void shuffle2_Click(object sender, EventArgs e) {
    deck2.Shuffle();
    RedrawDeck(2);
}

private void moveToDeck1_Click(object sender, EventArgs e) {
    if (listBox2.SelectedIndex >= 0)
        if (deck2.Count > 0) {
            deck1.Add(deck2.Deal(listBox2.SelectedIndex));
        }
    RedrawDeck(1);
    RedrawDeck(2);
}

private void moveToDeck2_Click(object sender, EventArgs e)
    if (listBox1.SelectedIndex >= 0)
        if (deck1.Count > 0)
            deck2.Add(deck1.Deal(listBox1.SelectedIndex));
    RedrawDeck(1);
    RedrawDeck(2);
    }
}
```

These buttons are pretty simple—first reset or shuffle the deck, then redraw it.

You can use the ListBox control's SelectedIndex property to figure out which card the user selected and then move it from one deck to the other. (If it's less than zero, no card was selected, so the button does nothing.) Once the card's moved, both decks need to be redrawn.

You can build your own overloaded methods

You've been using **overloaded methods** and even an overloaded constructor that were part of the built-in .NET Framework classes and objects, so you can already see how useful they are. Wouldn't it be cool if you could build overloaded methods into your own classes? Well, you can—and it's easy! All you need to do is write two or more methods that have the same name but take different parameters.

Do this!

① **Create a new project and add the Card class to it.**
You can do this easily by right-clicking on the project in the Solution Explorer and selecting "Existing Item" from the Add menu. The IDE will make a copy of the class and add it to the project. The file will **still have the namespace from the old project**, so go to the top of the Card.cs file and change the namespace line to <u>match the name of the new project you created</u>.

> *If you don't do this, you'll only be able to access the Card class by specifying its namespace (like oldnamespace.Card).*

② **Add some new overloaded methods to the card class.**
Create two static `DoesCardMatch()` methods. The first one should check a card's suit. The second should check its value. Both return true only if the card matches.

```
public static bool DoesCardMatch(Card CardToCheck, Card.Suits Suit) {
   if (CardToCheck.Suit == Suit) {
      return true;
   } else {
      return false;
   }
}
public static bool DoesCardMatch(Card CardToCheck, Card.Values Value) {
   if (CardToCheck.Value == Value) {
      return true;
   } else {
      return false;
   }
}
```

> *Overloaded methods don't have to be static, but it's good to get a little practice writing static methods.*

③ **Add a button to the form to use the new methods.**
Add this code to the button:

```
Card cardToCheck = new Card(Card.Suits.Clubs, Card.Values.Three);
bool doesItMatch = Card.DoesCardMatch(cardToCheck, Card.Suits.Hearts);
```

As soon as you type "`DoesCardMatch(`" the IDE will show you that you really did build an overloaded method:

```
Card.DoesCardMatch (
```
| ▲ 1 of 2 ▼ | bool Card.DoesCardMatch (**Card CardToCheck**, Card.Suits Suit) |

Take a minute and play around with the two methods so you can get used to overloading.

Long Exercise

Build a game of **Go Fish!** that you can play against the computer.

This exercise is a little different...

There's a good chance that you're learning C# because you want a job as a professional developer. That's why we modeled this exercise after a professional assignment. When you're working as a programmer on a team, you don't usually build a complete program from start to finish. Instead, you'll build a *piece* of a bigger program. So we're going to give you a puzzle that's got some of the pieces already filled in. The code for the form is all on the next page in step #3. You just have to type it in—which may seem like you've got a great head start, but it means that your classes **have to work with that code**. And that can be a challenge!

1 **Start with the spec**

Every professional software project starts with a specification, and this one is no exception. You'll be building a game of the classic card game **Go Fish!** Different people play the game by slightly different rules, so here's a recap of the rules you'll be using:

★ The game starts with a deck of 52 cards. Five cards are dealt to each player. The pile of cards that's left after everyone's dealt a hand is called the **stock**. Each player takes turns asking for a value ("Do you have any sevens?"). Any other player holding cards with that value must hand them over. If nobody has a card with that value, then the player must "go fish" by taking a card from the stock.

★ The goal of the game is to make books, where a book is the complete set of all four cards that have the same value. The player with the most books at the end of the game is the winner. As soon as a player collects a book, he places it face-up on the table so all the other players can see what books everyone else has.

★ When a player places a book on the table, that may cause him to run out of cards. If it does, then he has to draw five more cards from the stock. If there are fewer than five cards left in the stock, he takes all of them. The game is over as soon as the stock is out of cards. The winner is then chosen based on whoever has the most books.

★ For this computer version of Go Fish, there are two computer players and one human player. Every round starts with the human player selecting one of the cards in his hand, which is displayed at all times. He does this by choosing one of the cards and indicating that he will ask for a card. Then the two computer players will ask for their cards. The results of each round will be displayed. This will repeat until there's a winner.

★ The game will take care of all of the trading of cards and pulling out of books automatically. Once there's a winner, the game is over. The game displays the name of the winner (or winners, in case of a tie). No other action can be taken—the player will have to restart the program in order to start a new game.

> If you don't know what you're building before you start, then how would you know when you're done? That's why most professional software projects start with a specification that tells you what you're going to build.

❷ Build the form

Build the form for the Go Fish! game. It should have a ListBox control for the player's hand, two TextBox controls for the progress of the game, and a button to let the player ask for a card. To play the game, the user will select one of the cards from the hand and click the button to ask the computer players if you have that card.

This TextBox control should have its Name property set to textName. In this screenshot, it's disabled, but it should be enabled when the program starts.

Set this button's Name property to buttonStart. It's disabled in this screenshot, but it starts out enabled. It'll get disabled once the game is started.

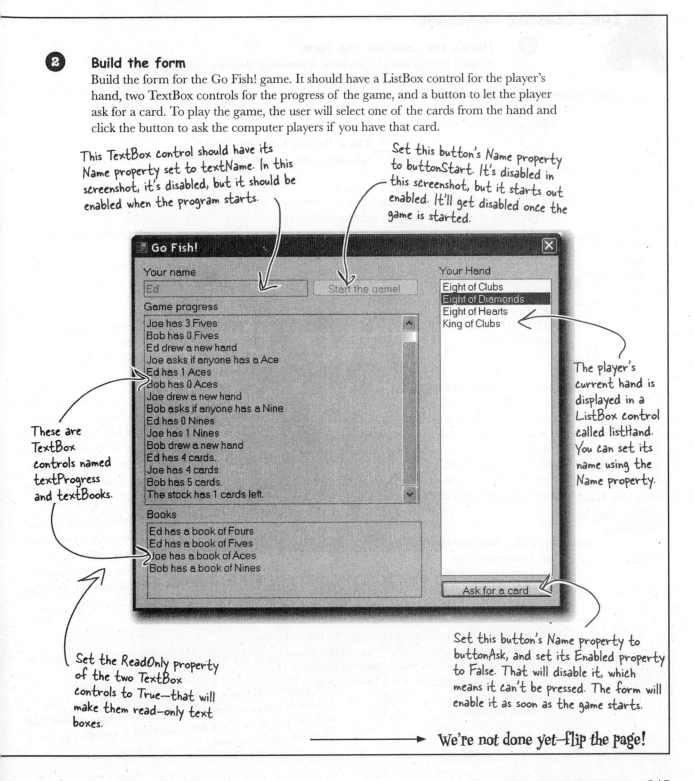

Go Fish!

Your name
`Ed`   Start the game!

Game progress
Joe has 3 Fives
Bob has 0 Fives
Ed drew a new hand
Joe asks if anyone has a Ace
Ed has 1 Aces
Bob has 0 Aces
Joe drew a new hand
Bob asks if anyone has a Nine
Ed has 0 Nines
Joe has 1 Nines
Bob drew a new hand
Ed has 4 cards.
Joe has 4 cards.
Bob has 5 cards.
The stock has 1 cards left.

Books
Ed has a book of Fours
Ed has a book of Fives
Joe has a book of Aces
Bob has a book of Nines

Your Hand
Eight of Clubs
Eight of Diamonds
Eight of Hearts
King of Clubs

Ask for a card

These are TextBox controls named textProgress and textBooks.

The player's current hand is displayed in a ListBox control called listHand. You can set its name using the Name property.

Set the ReadOnly property of the two TextBox controls to True—that will make them read-only text boxes.

Set this button's Name property to buttonAsk, and set its Enabled property to False. That will disable it, which means it can't be pressed. The form will enable it as soon as the game starts.

⟶ We're not done yet—flip the page!

Long Exercise (continued)

③ **Here's the code for the form**

Enter it exactly like you see here. The rest of the code that you write yourself will have to work with it.

```
public partial class Form1 : Form {
    public Form1() {
        InitializeComponent();
    }

    private Game game;

    private void buttonStart_Click(object sender, EventArgs e) {
        if (String.IsNullOrEmpty(textName.Text)){
            MessageBox.Show("Please enter your name", "Can't start the game yet");
            return;
        }
        game = new Game(textName.Text, new string[] { "Joe", "Bob" }, textProgress);
        buttonStart.Enabled = false;
        textName.Enabled = false;
        buttonAsk.Enabled = true;
        UpdateForm();
    }

    private void UpdateForm() {
        listHand.Items.Clear();
        foreach (String cardName in game.GetPlayerCardNames())
            listHand.Items.Add(cardName);
        textBooks.Text = game.DescribeBooks();
        textProgress.Text += game.DescribePlayerHands();
        textProgress.SelectionStart = textProgress.Text.Length;
        textProgress.ScrollToCaret();
    }

    private void buttonAsk_Click(object sender, EventArgs e) {
        textProgress.Text = "";
        if (listHand.SelectedIndex < 0) {
            MessageBox.Show("Please select a card");
            return;
        }
        if (game.PlayOneRound(listHand.SelectedIndex)) {
            textProgress.Text += "The winner is... " + game.GetWinnerName();
            textBooks.Text = game.DescribeBooks();
            buttonAsk.Enabled = false;
        } else
            UpdateForm();
    }
}
```

This is the only class that the form interacts with. It runs the whole game.

The Enabled property enables or disables a control on the form.

When you start a new game, it creates a new instance of the Game class, enables the "Ask" button, disables the "Start Game" button, and then redraws the form.

This method clears and repopulates the ListBox that holds the player's hand, and then updates the text boxes.

Using SelectionStart and ScrollToCaret() like this scrolls the text box to the end, so if there's too much text to display at once it scrolls down to the bottom.

The SelectionStart line moves the flashing textbox cursor to the end, and once it's moved, the ScrollToCaret() method scrolls the text box down to the cursor.

The player selects one of the cards and clicks the "Ask" button to see if any of the other players have a card that matches its value. The Game class plays a round using the PlayOneRound() method.

4 **You'll need this code, too**

You'll need the code you wrote before for the Card class, the Deck class and the CardComparer_byValue class. But you'll need to add a few more methods to the Deck class... and you'll need to understand them in order to use them.

```
public Card Peek(int cardNumber) {
    return cards[cardNumber];
}
```
The Peek() method lets you take a peek at one of the cards in the deck without dealing it.

```
public Card Deal() {
    return Deal(0);
}
```
Someone overloaded Deal() to make it a little easier to read. If you don't it pass any parameters, it deals a card off the top of the deck.

```
public bool ContainsValue(Card.Values value)
    foreach (Card card in cards)
        if (card.Value == value)
            return true;
    return false;
}
```
The ContainsValue() method searches through the entire deck for cards with a certain value, and returns true if it finds any. Can you guess how you'll use this in the Go Fish game?

```
public Deck PullOutValues(Card.Values value) {
    Deck deckToReturn = new Deck(new Card[] { });
    for (int i = cards.Count - 1; i >= 0; i--)
        if (cards[i].Value == value)
            deckToReturn.Add(Deal(i));
    return deckToReturn;
}
```
You'll use the PullOutValues() method when you build the code to get a book of cards from the deck. It looks for any cards that match a value, pulls them out of the deck, and returns a new deck with those cards in it.

```
public bool HasBook(Card.Values value) {
    int NumberOfCards = 0;
    foreach (Card card in cards)
        if (card.Value == value)
            NumberOfCards++;
    if (NumberOfCards == 4)
        return true;
    else
        return false;
}
```
The HasBook() method checks a deck to see if it contains a book of four cards of whatever value was passed as the parameter. It returns true if there's a book in the deck, false otherwise.

```
public void SortByValue() {
    cards.Sort(new CardComparer_byValue());
}
```
The SortByValue() method sorts the deck using the Comparer_byValue class.

→ Still not done—flip the page!

Long Exercise (continued)

5 **Now comes the HARD part: Build the Player class**
There's an instance of the Player class for each of the three players in the
game. They get created by the buttonStart button's event handler.

```
public class Player
{
    private string name;
    public string Name { get { return name; } }
    private Random random;
    private Deck cards;
    private TextBox textBoxOnForm;

    public Player(String name, Random random, TextBox textBoxOnForm) {
        // The constructor for the Player class initializes four private fields, and then
        // adds a line to the TextBox control on the form that says, "Joe has just
        // joined the game" - but use the name in the private field, and don't forget to
        // add line break ("\r\n") at the end of every line you add to the TextBox.
    }

    public List<Card.Values> PullOutBooks() {  } // see the facing page for the code

    public Card.Values GetRandomValue() {
        // This method gets a random value—but it has to be a value that's in the deck!
    }

    public Deck DoYouHaveAny(Card.Values value) {
        // This is where an opponent asks if I have any cards of a certain value
        // use Deck.PullOutValues() to pull out the values. Add a line to the TextBox
        // that says, "Joe has 3 sixes" - use the new Card.Plural() static method
    }

    public void AskForACard(List<Player> players, int myIndex, Deck stock) {
        // Here's an overloaded version of AskForACard() - choose a random value
        // from the deck using GetRandomValue() and ask for it using AskForACard()
    }

    public void AskForACard(List<Player> players, int myIndex, Deck stock, Card.Values value) {
        // Ask the other players for a value. first add a line to the TextBox: "Joe asks
        // if anyone has a Queen". Then go through the list of players that was passed in
        // as a parameter and ask each player if he has any of the value (using his
        // DoYouHaveAny() method). He'll pass you a deck of cards - add them to my deck.
        // Keep track of how many cards were added. If there weren't any, you'll need
        // to deal yourself a card from the stock (which was also passed as a parameter),
        // and you'll have to add a line to the TextBox: "Joe had to draw from the stock"
    }
    // Here's a property and a few short methods that were already written for you
    public int CardCount { get { return cards.Count; } }
    public void TakeCard(Card card) { cards.Add(card); }
    public string[] GetCardNames() { return cards.GetCardNames(); }
    public Card Peek(int cardNumber) { return cards.Peek(cardNumber); }
    public void SortHand() { cards.SortByValue(); }
}
```

Look closely at each of the comments—they tell you what the methods are supposed to do. Your job is to fill in the methods.

That Peek() method we added to the Deck class will come in handy. It lets the program look at one of the cards in the deck by giving its index number, but unlike Deal() it doesn't remove the card.

```
public List<Card.Values> PullOutBooks() {
    List<Card.Values> Books = new List<Card.Values>();
    for (int i = 1; i <= 13; i++) {
        Card.Values value = (Card.Values)i;
        int howMany = 0;
        for (int card = 0; card < cards.Count; card++)
            if (cards.Peek(card).Value == value)
                howMany++;
        if (howMany == 4) {
            Books.Add(value);
            for (int card = cards.Count - 1; card >= 0; card--)
                cards.Deal(card);
        }
    }
    return Books;
}
```

You'll have to build TWO overloaded versions of the AskForACard() method. The first one is used by the opponents when they ask for cards—it'll look through their hands and find a card to ask for. The second one is used when the player asks for the card. Both of them ask EVERY other player (both computer and human) for any cards that match the value.

6 You'll need to add this method to the Card class

It's a static method to take a value and return its plural—that way a ten will return "Tens" but a six will return "Sixes" (with "es" on the end). Since it's static, you call it with the class name—Card.Plural()—and not from an instance.

```
public partial class Card {
    public static string Plural(Card.Values value) {
        if (value == Values.Six)
            return "Sixes";
        else
            return value.ToString() + "s";
    }
}
```

Nearly there—keep flipping!

Long Exercise (continued)

7 **The rest of the job: Build the Game class**
The form keeps one instance of Game. It manages the game play. Look
closely at how it's used in the form.

```
public class Game {
    private List<Player> players;
    private Dictionary<Card.Values, Player> books;
    private Deck stock;
    private TextBox textBoxOnForm;

    public Game(string playerName, string[] opponentNames, TextBox textBoxOnForm) {
        Random random = new Random();
        this.textBoxOnForm = textBoxOnForm;
        players = new List<Player>();
        players.Add(new Player(playerName, random, textBoxOnForm));
        foreach (string player in opponentNames)
            players.Add(new Player(player, random, textBoxOnForm));
        books = new Dictionary<Card.Values, Player>();
        stock = new Deck();
        Deal();
        players[0].SortHand();
    }

    private void Deal() {
        // This is where the game starts - this method's only called at the beginning
        // of the game. Shuffle the stock, deal five cards to each player, then use a
        // foreach loop to call each player's PullOutBooks() method.
    }

    public bool PlayOneRound(int selectedPlayerCard) {
        // Play one round of the game. The parameter is the card the player selected
        // from his hand - get its value. Then go through all of the players and call
        // each one's AskForACard() methods, starting with the human player (who's at
        // at index zero in the Players list - make sure he asks for the selected
        // card's value). Then call PullOutBooks() - if it returns true, then the
        // player ran out of cards and needs to draw a new hand. After all the players
        // have gone, sort the human player's hand (so it looks nice in the form).
        // Then check the stock to see if it's out of cards. If it is, reset the
        // TextBox on the form to say, "The stock is out of cards. Game over!" and return
        // true. Otherwise, the game isn't over yet, so return false.
    }

    public bool PullOutBooks(Player player) {
        // Pull out a player's books. Return true if the player ran out of cards, otherwise
        // return false. Each book is added to the Books dictionary. A player runs out of
        // cards when he's used all of his cards to make books—and he wins the game.
    }

    public string DescribeBooks() {
        // Return a long string that describes everyone's books by looking at the Books
        // dictionary: "Joe has a book of sixes. (line break) Ed has a book of Aces."
    }
```

```
public string GetWinnerName() {
        // This method is called at the end of the game. It uses its own dictionary
        // (Dictionary<string, int> winners) to keep track of how many books each player
        // ended up with in the Books dictionary. First it uses a foreach loop
        // on Books.Keys -- foreach (Card.Values value in Books.Keys) -- to populate
        // its winners dictionary with the number of books each player ended up with.
        // Then it loops through that dictionary to find the largest number of books
        // any winner has. And finally it makes one last pass through winners to come
        // up with a list of winners in a string ("Joe and Ed"). If there's one winner,
        // it returns a string like this: "Ed with 3 books". Otherwise it returns a
        // string like this: "A tie between Joe and Bob with 2 books."
}

// Here are a couple of short methods that were already written for you:

public string[] GetPlayerCardNames() {
    return players[0].GetCardNames();
}

public string DescribePlayerHands() {
    string description = "";
    for (int i = 0; i < players.Count; i++) {
        description += players[i].Name + " has " + players[i].CardCount;
        if (players[i].CardCount == 1)
            description += " card.\r\n";
        else
            description += " cards.\r\n";
    }
    description += "The stock has " + stock.Count + " cards left.";
    return description;
}
```

Long Exercise Solution

Here are the filled-in methods in the Game class.

```
public class Game {
    private void Deal() {
        stock.Shuffle();
        for (int i = 0; i < 5; i++)
            foreach (Player player in players)
                player.TakeCard(stock.Deal());
        foreach (Player player in players)
            PullOutBooks(player);
    }

    public bool PlayOneRound(int selectedPlayerCard) {
        Card.Values cardToAskFor = players[0].Peek(selectedPlayerCard).Value;
        for (int i = 0; i < players.Count; i++) {
            if (i == 0)
                players[0].AskForACard(players, 0, stock, cardToAskFor);
            else
                players[i].AskForACard(players, i, stock);
            if (PullOutBooks(players[i])) {
                textBoxOnForm.Text += players[i].Name + " drew a new hand\r\n";
                int card = 1;
                while (card <= 5 && stock.Count > 0) {
                    players[i].TakeCard(stock.Deal());
                    card++;
                }
            }
        }
        players[0].SortHand();
        if (stock.Count == 0) {
            textBoxOnForm.Text = "The stock is out of cards. Game over!\r\n";
            return true;
        }
        return false;
    }

    public bool PullOutBooks(Player player)
    {
        List<Card.Values> BooksPulled = player.PullOutBooks();
        foreach (Card.Values value in BooksPulled)
            books.Add(value, player);
        if (player.CardCount == 0)
            return true;
        return false;
    }
}
```

The Deal() method gets called when the game first starts—it shuffles the deck and then deals five cards to each player. Then it pulls out any books that the players happened to have been dealt.

After the player or opponent asks for a card, the game pulls out any books that he made. If a player's out of books, he draws a new hand by dealing up to 5 cards from the stock.

As soon as the player clicks the "Ask for a card" button, the game calls AskForACard() with that card. Then it calls AskForACard() for each opponent.

After the round is played, the game sorts the player's hand, to make sure it's displayed in order on the form. Then it checks to see if the game's over. If it is, PlayOneRound() returns true.

PullOutBooks() looks through a player's cards to see if he's got four cards with the same value. If he does, they get added to his books dictionary. And if he's got no cards left afterwards, it returns true.

The form needs to display a list of books, so it uses DescribeTheBooks() to turn the player's books dictionary into words.

```csharp
public string DescribeBooks() {
    string whoHasWhichBooks = "";
    foreach (Card.Values value in books.Keys)
        whoHasWhichBooks += books[value].Name + " has a book of "
            + Card.Plural(value) + "\r\n";
    return whoHasWhichBooks;
}

public string GetWinnerName() {
    Dictionary<string, int> winners = new Dictionary<string, int>();
    foreach (Card.Values value in books.Keys) {
        string name = books[value].Name;
        if (winners.ContainsKey(name))
            winners[name]++;
        else
            winners.Add(name, 1);
    }
    int mostBooks = 0;
    foreach (string name in winners.Keys)
        if (winners[name] > mostBooks)
            mostBooks = winners[name];
    bool tie = false;
    string winnerList = "";
    foreach (string name in winners.Keys)
        if (winners[name] == mostBooks)
        {
            if (!String.IsNullOrEmpty(winnerList))
            {
                winnerList += " and ";
                tie = true;
            }
            winnerList += name;
        }
    winnerList += " with " + mostBooks + " books";
    if (tie)
        return "A tie between " + winnerList;
    else
        return winnerList;
}
}
```

Once the last card's been picked up, the game needs to figure out who won. That's what the GetWinnerName() does. And it'll use a dictionary called winners to do it. Each player's name is a key in the dictionary; its value is the number of books that player got during the game.

Next the game looks through the dictionary to figure the number of books that the player with the most books has. It puts that value in a variable called mostBooks.

Now that we know which player has the most books, the method can come up with a string that lists the winner (or winners).

We're not done yet—flip the page!

Long Exercise
Solution (continued)

Here are the filled-in methods in the Player class.

```
public Player(String name, Random random, TextBox textBoxOnForm) {
    this.name = name;
    this.random = random;
    this.textBoxOnForm = textBoxOnForm;
    this.cards = new Deck( new Card[] {} );
    textBoxOnForm.Text += name + " has just joined the game\r\n";
}
```

Here's the constructor for the Player class. It sets its private fields and the adds a line to the progress text box saying who joined.

```
public Card.Values GetRandomValue() {
    Card randomCard = cards.Peek(random.Next(cards.Count));
    return randomCard.Value;
}
```

The GetRandomValue() method uses Peek() to look at a random card in the player's hand.

```
public Deck DoYouHaveAny(Card.Values value) {
    Deck cardsIHave = cards.PullOutValues(value);
    textBoxOnForm.Text += Name + " has " + cardsIHave.Count + " "
        + Card.Plural(value) + "\r\n";
    return cardsIHave;
}
```

DoYouHaveAny() uses the PullOutValues() method to pull out and return all cards that match the parameter.

```
public void AskForACard(List<Player> players, int myIndex, Deck stock) {
    Card.Values randomValue = GetRandomValue();
    AskForACard(players, myIndex, stock, randomValue);
}
```

There are two overloaded AskForACard() methods. This one is used by the opponents—it gets a random card from the hand and calls the other AskorACard().

```
public void AskForACard(List<Player> players, int myIndex,
    Deck stock, Card.Values value) {
    textBoxOnForm.Text += Name + " asks if anyone has a " + value + "\r\n";
    int totalCardsGiven = 0;
    for (int i = 0; i < players.Count; i++) {
        if (i != myIndex) {
            Player player = players[i];
            Deck CardsGiven = player.DoYouHaveAny(value);
            totalCardsGiven += CardsGiven.Count;
            while (CardsGiven.Count > 0)
                cards.Add(CardsGiven.Deal());
        }
    }
    if (totalCardsGiven == 0) {
        textBoxOnForm.Text += Name + " must draw from the stock.\r\n";
        cards.Add(stock.Deal());
    }
}
```

This AskForACard() method looks through every player (except for the one asking), calls its DoYouHaveAny() method, and adds any cards handed over to the hand.

If no cards were handed over, the player has to draw from the stock using its Deal() method.

And yet <u>MORE</u> collection types...

List and Dictionary objects are two of the **built-in generic collections** that are part of the .NET framework. Lists and dictionaries are very flexible—you can access any of the data in them in any order. But sometimes you need to restrict how your program works with the data because the *thing* that you're representing inside your program works like that in the real world. For situations like that, you'll use a **Queue** or a **Stack**. Those are the other two generic collections that are similar to lists, but they're especially good at making sure that your data is processed in a certain order.

There are other types of collections, too—but these are the ones that you're most likely to come in contact with.

Use a Queue when the first object you store will be the first one you'll use, like:

★ Cars moving down a one-way street

★ People standing in line

★ Customers on hold for a customer service support line

★ Anything else that's handled on a first-come, first-served basis

A queue is first-in first-out, which means that the first object that you put into the queue is the first one you pull out of it to use.

Use a Stack when you always want to use the object you stored most recently, like:

★ Furniture loaded into the back of a moving truck

★ A stack of books where you want to read the most recently added one first

★ A pyramid of cheerleaders, where the ones on top have to dismount first... imagine the mess if the one on the bottom walked away first!

The stack is first-in last-out—the first object that goes into the stack is the last one that comes out of it.

Generic collections are an important part of the .NET framework

They're really useful—so much that the IDE automatically adds this statement to the top of every class you add to your project:

```
using System.Collections.Generic;
```

Almost every large project that you'll work on will include some sort of generic collection, because your programs need to store data. And when you're dealing with groups of similar things in the real world, they almost always naturally fall into a category that corresponds pretty well to one of these kinds collections.

You can, however, use foreach to enumerate through a stack or queue, because they implement IEnumerable!

A queue is like a list that lets you put objects on the end of the list and use the ones on the front. A stack only lets you access the last object you put into it.

A queue is <u>FIFO</u> — First In, First Out

A **queue** is a lot like a list, except that you can't just add or remove items at any index. To add an object to a queue, you **enqueue** it. That adds the object to the end of the queue. You can **dequeue** the first object from the front of the queue. When you do that, the object is removed from the queue, and the rest of the objects in the queue move up a position.

Create a new queue of strings.

```
Queue<string> myQueue = new Queue<string>();
myQueue.Enqueue("first in line");
myQueue.Enqueue("second in line");
myQueue.Enqueue("third in line");
myQueue.Enqueue("last in line");
string takeALook = myQueue.Peek();①
string getFirst = myQueue.Dequeue();②
string getNext = myQueue.Dequeue();③
int howMany = myQueue.Count;④
myQueue.Clear();
MessageBox.Show("Peek() returned: " + takeALook + "\n"
    + "The first Dequeue() returned: " + getFirst + "\n"
    + "The second Dequeue() returned: " + getNext + "\n"
    + "Count before Clear() was " + howMany + "\n"
    + "Count after Clear() is now " + myQueue.Count);⑤
```

Here's where we add four items to the queue. When we pull them out of the queue, they'll come out in the same order they went in.

Peek() lets you take a "look" at the first item in the queue without removing it.

The first Dequeue() pulls the first item out of the queue. Then the second one shifts up into the first place—the next call to Dequeue() pulls that one out next.

The Clear() method removes all objects from the queue.

The queue's Count property returns the number of items in the queue.

Objects in a queue need to wait their turn. The first one in the queue is the first one to come out of it.

```
Peek() returned: first in line①
The first Dequeue() returned: first in line②
The second Dequeue() returned: second in line
Count before Clear() was 2④                    ③
Count after Clear() is now 0⑤
```

```
OK
```

A stack is LIFO — Last In, First Out

A **stack** is really similar to a queue—with one big difference. You **push** each item onto a stack, and when you want to take an item from the stack you **pop** one of it. When you pop an item off of a stack, you end up with the most recent item that you pushed onto it. It's just like a stack of plates, magazines or anything else—you can drop something onto the top of the stack, but you need to take it off before you can get to whatever's underneath it.

Creating a stack is just like creating any other generic collection.

When you push an item onto a stack, it pushes the other items back one notch and sits on top.

```
Stack<string> myStack = new Stack<string>();
myStack.Push("first in line");
myStack.Push("second in line");
myStack.Push("third in line");
myStack.Push("last in line");
① string takeALook = myStack.Peek();
② string getFirst = myStack.Pop();
③ string getNext = myStack.Pop();
④ int howMany = myStack.Count;
myStack.Clear();
MessageBox.Show("Peek() returned: " + takeALook + "\n"
    + "The first Pop() returned: " + getFirst + "\n"
    + "The second Pop() returned: " + getNext + "\n"
    + "Count before Clear() was " + howMany + "\n"
    + "Count after Clear() is now " + myStack.Count);
⑤
```

When you pop an item off the stack, you get the most recent item that was added.

Peek() returned: last in line ①
The first Pop() returned: last in line ②
The second Pop() returned: third in line ③
Count before Clear() was 2 ④
Count after Clear() is now 0 ⑤

OK

The last object you put on a stack is the first object that you pull off of it.

> Wait a minute, something's bugging me. You haven't shown me anything I can do with a stack or a queue that I can't do with a list—they just save me a couple of lines of code. But I can't get at the items in the middle of a stack or a queue. I can do that with a list pretty easily! So why would I give that up just for a little convenience?

Don't worry—you don't give up anything when you use a queue or a stack.

It's really easy to convert a Queue object to a List object. And it's just as easy to convert a List to a Queue, a Queue to a Stack... in fact, you can create a List, Queue or Stack from any other object that implements the **IEnumerable** interface. All you have to do is use the overloaded constructor that lets you pass the collection you want to copy from as a parameter. That means you have the flexibility and convenience of representing your data with the collection that best matches the way you need to be used.

Let's set up a stack with four items—in this case, a stack of strings.

```
Stack<string> myStack = new Stack<string>();
myStack.Push("first in line");
myStack.Push("second in line");
myStack.Push("third in line");
myStack.Push("last in line");

Queue<string> myQueue = new Queue<string>(myStack);
List<string> myList = new List<string>(myQueue);
Stack<string> anotherStack = new Stack<string>(myList);
MessageBox.Show("myQueue has " + myQueue.Count + " items\n"
    + "myList has " + myList.Count + " items\n"
    + "anotherStack has " + anotherStack.Count + " items\n");
```

It's easy to convert that stack to a queue, then copy the queue to a list, and then copy the list to another stack.

All four items were copied into the new collections.

myQueue has 4 items
myList has 4 items
anotherStack has 4 items

OK

...and you can always use a foreach loop to access all of the members in a stack or a queue!

Write a program to help a cafeteria full of lumberjacks eat some flapjacks. Start with the Lumberjack class, filling in the missing code. Then design the form, and add the button event handlers to it.

Exercise

❶ Here's the Lumberjack class. Fill in the get accessor for `FlapjackCount` and the `TakeFlapjacks` and `EatFlapjacks` methods.

```
public class Lumberjack {
    private string name;
    public string Name { get { return name; } }
    private Stack<Flapjack> meal;
    public Lumberjack(string name) {
        this.name = name;
        meal = new Stack<Flapjack>();
    }
    public int FlapjackCount { get { // return the count } }
    public void TakeFlapjacks(Flapjack Food, int HowMany) {
        // Add some number of flapjacks to the Meal stack
    }
    public void EatFlapjacks() {
        // Write this output to the console
    }
}
```

```
public enum Flapjack {
    crispy,
    soggy,
    browned,
    banana
}
```

Output

```
Ed's eating flapjacks
Ed ate a crispy flapjack
Ed ate a soggy flapjack
Ed ate a browned flapjack
Ed ate a browned flapjack
Ed ate a banana flapjack
Ed ate a banana flapjack
Ed ate a banana flapjack
Ed ate a soggy flapjack
Ed ate a crispy flapjack
```

❷ Build this form. It lets you enter the names of lumberjacks into a text box so they get in the breakfast line. You can give the lumberjack at the front of the line a plate of flapjacks, and then tell him to move on to eat them using the "Next lumberjack" button. We've given you the click event handler for the "Add flapjacks" button. Use a queue called **breakfastLine** to keep track of the lumberjacks.

This listbox is called line.

This button should dequeue the next lumberjack, call his EatFlapjacks method, and then redraw the listbox.

You'll need to add a RedrawList() method to update the listbox with the contents of the queue. All three buttons will call it. Here's a hint: it uses a foreach loop.

When the user clicks "Add Lumberjack", add the name in the name text box to the BreakfastLine queue.

When you drag these RadioButton controls into the groupbox, the form automatically links them and only allows the user to check one of them at a time. Look at the addFlapjacks_Click method to figure out what they should be named.

```
private void addFlapjacks_Click(...) {
    Flapjack food;
    if (crispy.Checked == true)
        food = Flapjack.crispy;
    else if (soggy.Checked == true)
        food = Flapjack.soggy;
    else if (browned.Checked == true)
        food = Flapjack.browned;
    else
        food = Flapjack.banana;

    Lumberjack currentLumberjack = breakfastLine.Peek();
    currentLumberjack.TakeFlapjacks(food,
                      (int)howMany.Value);
    RedrawList();
}
```

Note the special "else if" syntax.

Peek() returns a reference to the first lumberjack in the queue.

The NumericUpDown control is called howMany, and the label is called nextInLine.

Exercise Solution

```
private Queue<Lumberjack> breakfastLine = new Queue<Lumberjack>();
private void addLumberjack_Click(object sender, EventArgs e) {
    breakfastLine.Enqueue(new Lumberjack(name.Text));
    name.Text = "";
    RedrawList();
}
private void RedrawList() {
    int number = 1;
    line.Items.Clear();
    foreach (Lumberjack lumberjack in breakfastLine) {
        line.Items.Add(number + ". " + lumberjack.Name);
        number++;
    }
    if (breakfastLine.Count == 0) {
        groupBox1.Enabled = false;
        nextInLine.Text = "";
    } else {
        groupBox1.Enabled = true;
        Lumberjack currentLumberjack = breakfastLine.Peek();
        nextInLine.Text = currentLumberjack.Name + " has "
            + currentLumberjack.FlapjackCount + " flapjacks";
    }
}
private void nextLumberjack_Click(object sender, EventArgs e) {
    Lumberjack nextLumberjack = breakfastLine.Dequeue();
    nextLumberjack.EatFlapjacks();
    nextInLine.Text = "";
    RedrawList();
}

public class Lumberjack {
    private string name;
    public string Name { get { return name; } }
    private Stack<Flapjack> meal;

    public Lumberjack(string name) {
        this.name = name;
        meal = new Stack<Flapjack>();
    }

    public int FlapjackCount { get { return meal.Count; } }

    public void TakeFlapjacks(Flapjack food, int howMany) {
        for (int i = 0; i < howMany; i++) {
            meal.Push(food);
        }
    }

    public void EatFlapjacks() {
        Console.WriteLine(name + "'s eating flapjacks");
        while (meal.Count > 0) {
            Console.WriteLine(name + " ate a "
                + meal.Pop().ToString() + " flapjack");
        }
    }
}
```

We called the listbox "line", the label between the two buttons "nextInLine".

The RedrawList() method uses a foreach loop to pull the lumberjacks out of their queue and add each of them to the listbox.

This if statement updates the label with information about the first lumberjack in the queue.

The TakeFlapjacks method updates the Meal stack.

The EatFlapjacks method uses a while loop to print out the lumberjack's meal.

Collectioncross

Across

3. An instance of a _____ collection only works with one specific type

6. A special kind of loop that only works on collections

9. The name of the method you use to send a string to the output

10. How you remove something from a stack

11. An object that's like an array but more flexible

13. Two methods in a class with the same name but different parameters are...

15. A method to figure out if a certain object is in a collection

19. An easy way to keep track of categories

20. All generic collections implement this interface

21. How you remove something from a queue

Down

1. The generic collection that lets you map keys to values

2. This collection is first-in, first-out

4. The built-in class that lets your program write text to the output

5. A method to find out how many things are in a collection

7. The only method in the IComparable interface

8. Most professional projects start with this

12. An object that implements this interface helps your list sort its contents

14. How you add something to a queue

16. This collection is first-in, last-out

17. How you add something to a stack

18. This method returns the next object to come off of a stack or queue

Collectioncross solution

The crossword grid contains the following answers:

- 3 Across: GENERIC
- 1 Down: DICTIONARY
- 2 Down: QUEUE
- 4 Down: CONSOLE
- 5 Down: COUNT
- 6 Across: FOREACH
- 7 Down: COMPARETO
- 8 Down: SPECIFICATION
- 9 Across: WRITELINE
- 10 Across: POP
- 11 Across: LIST
- 12 Down: ICOMP
- 13 Across: OVERLOADED
- 14 Down: EQUEUE
- 15 Across: CONTAINS
- 16 Down: STACK
- 17 Down: PUSH
- 18 Down: PEEK
- 19 Across: ENUM
- 20 Across: IENUMERABLE
- 21 Across: DEQUEUE

C# Lab

The Quest

This lab gives you a spec that describes a program for you to build, using the knowledge you've gained over the last few chapters.

This project is bigger than the ones you've seen so far. So read the whole thing before you get started, and give yourself a little time. And don't worry if you get stuck—there's nothing new in here, so you can move on in the book and come back to the lab later.

We've filled in a few design details for you, and we've made sure you've got all the pieces you need... and nothing else.

It's up to you to finish the job. You can download an executable for this lab from the website... but we won't give you the code for the answer.

The spec: build an adventure game

Your job is to build an adventure game where a mighty adventurer is on a quest to defeat level after level of deadly enemies. You'll build a **turn-based system**, which means the player makes one move and then the enemies make one move. The player can move **or** attack, and then each enemy gets a chance to move **and** attack. The game keeps going until the player either defeats all the enemies on all seven levels or dies.

The enemies get a bit of an advantage—they move every turn, and after they move they'll attack the player if he's in range.

The game window gives an overhead view of the dungeon where the player fights his enemies.

The player can pick up weapons and potions along the way.

The player and enemies move around in the dungeon.

The player moves using the four Move buttons.

Here's the player's inventory. It shows what items the player's picked up, and draws a box around the item that they're currently using. The player clicks on an item to equip it, and uses the Attack button to use the item.

The game shows you the number of hit points for the player and enemies. When the player attacks an enemy, the enemy's hit points go down. Once the hit points get down to zero, the enemy or player dies.

These four buttons are used to attack enemies and drink potions.

The player picks up weapons...

There are weapons and potions scattered around the dungeon that the player can pick up and use to defeat his enemies. All he has to do is move onto a weapon and it disappears from the floor and appears in his inventory.

A black box around a weapon means it's currently equipped. Different weapons work differently—they have different ranges, some only attack in one direction while others have a wider range, and they cause different levels of damage to the enemies they hit.

...and attacks enemies with them

Every level in the game has a weapon that the player can pick up and use to defeat his enemies. Once the weapon's picked up, it should disappear from the game floor.

The bat is to the right of the player, so he hits the Right attack button.

The attack causes the bat's hit points to drop, from 6 to 2 in this case.

Higher levels bring more enemies

There are three different kinds of enemies: a bat, a ghost, and a ghoul. The first level only has a bat. The seventh level is the last one, and it has all three enemies.

A ghoul moves quickly towards the player, and causes heavy damage when it attacks.

The bat flies around somewhat randomly. When it's near the player, it causes a small amount of damage.

The ghost moves slowly towards the player. As soon as it's close to the player, it attacks and causes a medium amount of damage.

The design: building the form

The form gives the game its unique look. Use the form's
`BackgroundImage` property to display the image of the dungeon
and the inventory, and a series of `PictureBox` controls to show
the player, weapons and enemies in the dungeon. You'll use a
`TableLayoutPanel` control to display the hit points for the player,
bat, ghost and ghoul as well as the buttons for moving and attacking.

The dungeon itself is a static image,
displayed using the BackgroundImage
property of the form.

Make sure the
BackgroundImageLayout
property is set to None.

Each of these icons is a PictureBox.

Hit points, movement buttons, and
attack buttons are all displayed in a
TableLayoutPanel.

Download the background image and the graphics for the weapons, enemies, and player from the Head First Labs website: www.headfirstlabs.com/books/hfcsharp

Everything in the dungeon is a PictureBox

Players, weapons, and enemies should all be represented by icons. Add nine PictureBox controls, and set their Visible properties to False. Then, your game can move around the controls, and toggle their Visible properties as needed.

Add nine PictureBox controls to the dungeon. Use the Size property to make each one 30x30. It doesn't matter where you place them—the form will move them around. Use the little black arrow that shows up when you click on the PictureBox to set each to one of the images from the Head First Labs web site.

After you've added the nine PictureBox controls, right-click on the player's icon and select "Bring to Front", then send the three weapon icons to back. That ensures player icons stay "above" any items that are picked up.

Controls overlap each other in the IDE, so the form needs to know which ones are in front, and which are in back. That's what the "Bring to Front" and "Send to Back" form designer commands do.

The inventory contains PictureBox controls, too

You can represent the inventory of the player as five 50x50 PictureBox controls. Set the BackColor property of each to **Transparent**. Since the picture files have a transparent background, you'll see the scroll and dungeon behind them:

You'll need five more 50x50 PictureBoxes for the inventory.

When the player equips one of the weapons, the form should set the BorderStyle of that weapon icon to FixedSingle and the rest of the icons' BorderStyle to None.

Build your stats window

The hit points are in a TableLayoutPanel, just like the attack and movement buttons. For the hit points, create two columns in the panel, and drag the column divider to the left a bit. Add four rows, each 25% height, and add in Label controls to each of the eight cells:

2 columns, 4 rows... 8 cells for your hit point statistics.

Player	playerHitPoint
Bat	batHitPoints
Ghost	ghostHitPoints
Ghoul	ghoulHitPoints

Each cell has a Label in it, and you can update those values during the game.

The architecture: using the objects

You'll need several types of objects in your game: a Player object, several sub-types of an Enemy object, and several sub-types of a Weapon object. And you'll also need one object to keep up with everything that's going on: the Game object.

This is just the general overview. We'll give you a lot more details on how the player and enemies move, how the enemy figures out if it's near the player, etc.

The form never interacts directly with the players, weapons, or enemies.

Game takes the input from the form and deals with the objects in the game.

The Game object handles turns

When one of your form's Move buttons is clicked, the form will call the Game object's Move() method. That method will let the player take a turn, and then let all the enemies move. So it's up to Game to handle the turn-based movement portion of the game.

For example, here's how the move buttons work:

There's only one weapon per level, so the game just needs a Weapon reference, not a List. The Player, however, has a List<Weapon> to hold the inventory.

The Game object keeps up with players, weapons, and a list of enemies.

We left the parameters out of this diagram. Each Move() method takes a direction, and some of them take a Random object too.

1. game.Move()

When the user clicks one of the four move buttons, the form calls Game's Move() method.

2. player.Move()

Game's Move() method first calls the Player object's Move() method to tell the player to move.

3. enemy.Move()

After the player moves, Game tells each of the enemies to Move().

4. if (NearPlayer())
       game.HitPlayer();

If any of the enemies end up near the player after they've moved, they attack the player.

The form delegates activity to the Game object

Movement, attacking, and inventory all begin in the form. So clicking a movement or attack button, or an item in inventory, triggers code in your form. But it's the Game object that controls the objects in the game. So the form has to pass on anything that happens to the Game object, and then the Game object takes it from there:

Game.Move() calls the enemies' Move() methods, which all take a random reference.

The Form object calls the game's Move(), and then calls its own UpdateCharacters() method to update the screen.

How moving works

```
1. Move(Direction.Right, random);
```

Use a Direction enum for the four button directions.

Move Button Clicked
Form object

Game object

Game handles updating locations, so when UpdateCharacters() is called, things are moved to their new locations.

```
2. UpdateCharacters();
```

When the player hits an enemy, it causes a random amount of damage (up to a maximum damage limit).

This UpdateCharacters() method is part of the form. It reads the location of the player, enemies, and any weapons currently in the dungeon and moves the PictureBoxes to match them.

How attacking works

```
1. Attack(Direction.Right, random);
```

Attack Button Clicked
Form object

Game object

Attacking is like movement... the form calls Attack() on Game, and Game handles dealing with the attack.

```
2. UpdateCharacters();
```

The UpdateCharacters() method also checks the player's inventory and makes sure the correct icons are displayed on the inventory scroll.

The inventory scroll displays all of the icons for the items that the player's picked up.

How the inventory scroll works

```
if (game.CheckPlayerInventory("Bow") {
```

Inventory Icon Clicked
Form object

Game object

```
game.Equip("Bow");
```

```
inventoryBow.BorderStyle =
        BorderStyle.FixedSingle;
```

```
inventorySword.BorderStyle =
        BorderStyle.None;
```

The BorderStyle property highlights the active item in the player's inventory.

The Quest

Building the Game class

We've gotten you started with the Game class in the code below. There's a lot for you to do—so read through this code carefully, get it into the IDE, and get ready to go to work:

```
using System.Drawing;
```
> You'll need the Rectangle class from System.Drawing, so be sure to add this to the top of your class.

```
public class Game {
  public List<Enemy> Enemies;
  public Weapon WeaponInRoom;
```
> These are okay as public properties if Enemy and Weapon are well-encapsulated... in other words, just make sure the form can't do anything inappropriate with them.

```
  private Player player;
```
> The game keeps a private Player object. The form will only interact with this through methods on Game, rather than directly.

```
  public Point PlayerLocation { get { return player.Location; } }
  public int PlayerHitPoints { get { return player.HitPoints; } }
  public List<string> PlayerWeapons { get { return player.Weapons; } }

  private int level = 0;
  public int Level { get { return level; } }
```
> The Rectangle object has a Top, Bottom, Left, and Right field, and works perfectly for the overall game area.

```
  private Rectangle boundaries;
  public Rectangle Boundaries { get { return boundaries; } }

  public Game(Rectangle boundaries) {
    this.boundaries = boundaries;
    player = new Player(this,
      new Point(boundaries.Left + 10, boundaries.Top + 70),
      boundaries);
  }
```
> Game starts out with a bounding box for the dungeon, and creates a new Player object in the dungeon.

```
  public void Move(Direction direction, Random random) {
    player.Move(direction);
    foreach (Enemy enemy in Enemies)
      enemy.Move(random);
  }
```
> Movement is simple: move the player in the direction the form gives us, and move each enemy in a random direction.

```
  public void Equip(string weaponName) {
    player.Equip(weaponName);
  }
  public bool CheckPlayerInventory(string weaponName) {
    return player.Weapons.Contains(weaponName);
  }
  public void HitPlayer(int maxDamage, Random random) {
    player.Hit(maxDamage, random);
  }
```
> These are all great examples of encapsulation... Game doesn't know how Player handles these actions, it just passes on the needed information and lets Player do the rest.

```
public void IncreasePlayerHealth(int health, Random random) {
  player.IncreaseHealth(health, random);
}

public void Attack(Direction direction, Random random) {
  player.Attack(direction, random);
  foreach (Enemy enemy in Enemies)
    enemy.Move(random);
}

private Point GetRandomLocation(Random random) {
  return new Point(boundaries.Left +
    random.Next(boundaries.Right / 10 - boundaries.Left / 10) * 10,
      boundaries.Top +
    random.Next(boundaries.Bottom / 10 - boundaries.Top / 10) * 10);
}

public void NewLevel(Random random) {
  level++;
  switch (level) {
    case 1:
      Enemies = new List<Enemy>();
      Enemies.Add(new Bat(this, GetRandomLocation(random), boundaries));
      WeaponInRoom = new Sword(this, GetRandomLocation(random));
      break;
  }
}
```

Attack() is almost exactly like Move(). The player attacks, and the enemies all get a turn to move.

GetRandomLocation() will come in handy in the NewLevel() method, which will use it to determine where to place enemies and weapons.

This is just a math trick to get a random location within the rectangle that represents the dungeon area.

We only added the case for the level 1. It's your job to add cases for the other levels.

We've only got room in the inventory for one blue potion and one red potion. So if the player already has a red potion, then the game shouldn't add a red potion to the level (and the same goes for the blue potion).

So if the blue potion is still in the player's inventory from Level 2, nothing appears on this level.

Finish the rest of the levels

It's your job to finish the NewLevel() method. Here's the breakdown for each level:

Level	Enemies	Weapons
2	Ghost	Blue potion
3	Ghoul	Bow
4	Bat, Ghost	Bow, if not picked up on 3; otherwise, blue potion
5	Bat, Ghoul	Red potion
6	Ghost, Ghoul	Mace
7	Bat, Ghost, Ghoul	Mace, if not picked up on 6; otherwise, red potion
8	N/A	N/A – end the game with Application.Exit()

This only appears if the red potion from Level 5 has already been used up.

Finding common behavior: movement

You already know that duplicate code is bad, and duplicate code usually shows up when two or more objects share the same behavior. That's the case in the dungeon game, too... both enemies and players move.

Let's create a `Mover` class, to abstract that common behavior into a single place. `Player` and `Enemy` will inherit from `Mover`. And even though weapons don't move around, they inherit from Mover too, because they need some of its properties and methods. `Mover` has a `Move()` method for moving around, and a read-only `Location` property that the form can use to position a subclass of `Mover`.

Mover is abstract, so can't be instantiated. You'll only instantiate Player and Enemy, which inherit from it.

Nearby() takes a point, and figures out if it's within a certain distance away from the object.

Move takes a direction as well as the dungeon's boundaries, and calculates where the end point of that movement would be.

Player and Enemy both inherit from Mover

The Player class overrides the Move() method.

You can call Nearby() and Move() on both Enemy and Player now.

Enemies don't have an Attack() method because their attacking is built into Move().

Add a Direction enum

The `Mover` class, as well as several other classes, need a `Direction` enum. Create this enum, and give it four enumerated values: Up, Down, Left, and Right.

The Mover class source code

Here's the code for Mover:

Since protected properties are only available to subclasses, the form object can't set the location... only read it through the public get method we define.

```csharp
public abstract class Mover {
    private const int MoveInterval = 10;
    protected Point location;
    public Point Location { get { return location; } }
    protected Game game;

    public Mover(Game game, Point location) {
        this.game = game;
        this.location = location;
    }

    public bool Nearby(Point locationToCheck, int distance) {
        if (Math.Abs(location.X - locationToCheck.X) < distance &&
            (Math.Abs(location.Y - locationToCheck.Y) < distance)) {
            return true;
        } else {
            return false;
        }
    }

    public Point Move(Direction direction, Rectangle boundaries) {
        Point newLocation = location;
        switch (direction) {
            case Direction.Up:
                if (newLocation.Y - MoveInterval >= boundaries.Top)
                    newLocation.Y -= MoveInterval;
                break;
            case Direction.Down:
                if (newLocation.Y + MoveInterval <= boundaries.Bottom)
                    newLocation.Y += MoveInterval;
                break;
            case Direction.Left:
                if (newLocation.X - MoveInterval >= boundaries.Left)
                    newLocation.X -= MoveInterval;
                break;
            case Direction.Right:
                if (newLocation.X + MoveInterval <= boundaries.Right)
                    newLocation.X += MoveInterval;
                break;
            default: break;
        }
        return newLocation;
    }
}
```

Instances of Mover take in the Game object and a current location.

The Nearby method checks a Point against this object's current location. If they're within **distance** of each other, then it returns true, otherwise it returns false.

The Move() method tries to move one step in a direction. If it can, it returns the new Point. If it hits a boundary, it returns the original Point.

If the end location is outside the boundaries, the new location stays the same as the starting point.

Finally, this new location is returned (which might still be the same as the starting location!).

The Player class keeps track of the player

Here's a start on the Player class. Start with this code in
the IDE, and then get ready to add to it.

```
public class Player : Mover {
  private Weapon equippedWeapon;
  private int hitPoints;
  public int HitPoints { get { return hitPoints; } }

  private List<Weapon> inventory = new List<Weapon>();
  public List<string> Weapons {
    get {
      List<string> names = new List<string>();
      foreach (Weapon weapon in inventory)
        names.Add(weapon.Name);
      return names;
    }
  }

  public Player(Game game, Point location, Rectangle boundaries)
          : base(game, location) {
    hitPoints = 10;
  }

  public void Hit(int maxDamage, Random random) {
    hitPoints -= random.Next(1, maxDamage);
  }

  public void IncreaseHealth(int health, Random random) {
    hitPoints += random.Next(1, health);
  }

  public void Equip(string weaponName) {
    foreach (Weapon weapon in inventory) {
      if (weapon.Name == weaponName)
        equippedWeapon = weapon;
    }
  }
}
```

All of the properties
of Player are hidden
from direct access.

A Player can hold
multiple weapons in
inventory, but can only
equip one at a time.

Player inherits
from Mover, so
this passes in
the Game and
location to that
base class.

The player's constructor sets
its hitPoints to 10 and then
calls the base class constructor.

When an enemy hits the player,
it causes a random amount of
damage. And when a potion
increases the player's health, it
increases it by a random amount.

The Equip() method tells the player
to equip one of his weapons. The Game
object calls this method when one of the
inventory icons is clicked.

A Player object can only have one Weapon
object equipped at a time.

Even though potions help the player
rather than hurt the enemy, they're
still considered weapons by the game.
That way the inventory can be a
List<Weapon>, and the game can
point to one with its WeaponInRoom
reference.

Write the Move() method for the Player

Game calls the Player's Move() method to tell a player to move in a certain direction. Move() takes in the direction to move (using the Direction enum you should have already added). Here's the start of that method: ← *This happens when one of the movement buttons on the form is clicked.*

```
public void Move(Direction direction) {
    base.location = Move(direction, game.Boundaries);
    if (!game.WeaponInRoom.PickedUp) {
        // see if the weapon is nearby, and possibly pick it up
    }
}
```

Move is in the Mover base class.

When the player picks up a weapon, it needs to disappear from the dungeon and appear in the inventory.

You've got to fill in the rest of this method. Check and see if the weapon is near the player (within a single unit of distance). If so, pick up the weapon and add it to the player's inventory.

The Weapon and form will handle making the weapon's Picturebox invisible when the player picks it up... that's not the job of the Player class.

If the weapon is the only weapon the player has, go ahead and equip it immediately. That way, the player can use it right away, on the next turn.

Add an Attack() method, too

The weapons all have an Attack() method that takes a Direction enum and a Random object. The player's Attack() will figure out which weapon is equipped and call its Attack().

Next up is the Attack() method. This is called when one of the form's attack buttons is clicked, and carries with it a direction (again, from the Direction enum). Here's the method signature:

If the weapon is a potion, then Attack() removes it from the inventory after the player drinks it.

```
public void Attack(Direction direction, Random random) {
    // Your code goes here
}
```

If the player doesn't have an equipped weapon, this method won't do anything. If the player does have an equipped weapon, this should call the weapon's Attack() method.

But potions are a special case. If a potion is used, remove it from the player's inventory, since it's not available anymore.

Potions will implement an IPotion interface (more on that in a minute), so you can use the "is" word to see if a Weapon is an implementation of IPotion.

Bats, ghosts, and ghouls inherit from the Enemy class

We'll give you another useful abstract class: Enemy. Each different sort of enemy has its own class that inherits from the Enemy class. The different kinds of enemies move in different ways, so the Enemy abstract class leaves the Move method as an abstract method—the three enemy classes will need to implement it differently, depending on how they move.

```
Enemy
(abstract)
```
```
HitPoints: int
```
```
Move(random: Random)
Hit(maxDamage: int,
      random: Random)
```

```csharp
public abstract class Enemy : Mover {
    private const int NearPlayerDistance = 25;
    private int hitPoints;
    public int HitPoints { get { return hitPoints; } }
    public bool Dead { get {
        if (hitPoints <= 0) return true;
        else return false;
    }
}

public Enemy(Game game, Point location, Rectangle boundaries, int hitPoints)
        : base(game, location) { this.hitPoints = hitPoints; }

public abstract void Move(Random random);

public void Hit(int maxDamage, Random random) {
    hitPoints -= random.Next(1, maxDamage);
}

protected bool NearPlayer() {
    return (Nearby(game.PlayerLocation,
                NearPlayerDistance));
}

protected Direction FindPlayerDirection(Point playerLocation) {
    Direction directionToMove;
    if (playerLocation.X > location.X + 10)
        directionToMove = Direction.Right;
    else if (playerLocation.X < location.X - 10)
        directionToMove = Direction.Left;
    else if (playerLocation.Y < location.Y - 10)
        directionToMove = Direction.Up;
    else
        directionToMove = Direction.Down;
    return directionToMove;
}
}
```

The form can use this read-only property to see if the enemy should be visible in the game dungeon.

Each subclass of Enemy implements this.

When the player attacks an enemy, it calls the enemy's Hit() method, which subtracts a random number from the hit points.

The NearPlayer() method uses the Mover.Nearby() static method to figure out if the enemy is near the player.

If you feed FindPlayerDirection() the player's location, it'll use the base class's location field to figure out where the player is in relation to the enemy and return a Direction enum that tells you which direction the enemy needs to move in order to move towards the player.

Write the different Enemy subclasses

The three Enemy subclasses are pretty straightforward. Each enemy has a different number of starting hit points, moves differently, and does a different amount of damage when it attacks. You'll need to have each one pass a different `startingHitPoints` parameter to the Enemy base constructor, and you'll have to write different `Move()` methods for each subclass.

Here's an example of how one of those classes might look:

```
public class Bat : Enemy {
    public Bat(Game game, Point location, Rectangle boundaries)
        : base(game, location, boundaries, 6)
    { }

    public override void Move(Random random) {
        // Your code will go here
    }
}
```

The bat starts with 6 hit points, so it passes 6 to the base class constructor.

You probably won't need any constructor for these; the base class handles everything.

Each of these subclasses the Enemy base class, which in turn subclasses Mover.

The bat flies around somewhat randomly, so it uses Random to fly in a random direction half the time.

Once an enemy has no more hit points, the form won't display it any more. But it'll still be in the game's Enemies list until the player finishes the level.

The bat starts with 6 hit points. It'll keep moving towards the player and attacking **as long as it has one or more hit points.** When it moves, there's a 50% chance that it'll move towards the player, and a 50% chance that it'll move in a random direction. After the bat moves, it checks if it's near the player—if it is, then it attacks the player with up to 2 hit points of damage.

We'll have to make sure the form sees if an enemy should be visible at every turn.

The ghost is harder to defeat than the bat, but like the bat, it will only move and attack if its hit points are greater than zero. It starts with 8 hit points. When it moves, there's a 1 in 3 chance that it'll move towards the player, and a 2 in 3 chance that it'll stand still. If it's near the player, it attacks the player with up to 3 hit points of damage.

The ghost and ghoul use Random to make them move more slowly than the player.

The ghoul is the toughest enemy. It starts with 10 hit points, and only moves and attacks if its hit points are greater than zero. When it moves, there's a 2 in 3 chance that it'll move towards the player, and a 1 in 3 chance that it'll stand still. If it's near the player, it attacks the player with up to 4 hit points of damage.

Weapon inherits from Mover, each weapon inherits from Weapon

We need a base Weapon class, just like we had a base Enemy class. And each weapon has a location, as well as a property indicating whether or not it's been picked up. Here's the base Weapon class:

> Weapon inherits from Mover because it uses its Nearby() and Move() methods in DamageEnemy().

Weapon (abstract)
PickedUp Location
PickUpWeapon() DamageEnemy()

```
public abstract class Weapon : Mover {

    protected Game game;
    private bool pickedUp;
    public bool PickedUp { get { return pickedUp; } }
    private Point location;
    public Point Location { get { return location; } }

    public Weapon(Game game, Point location) {
        this.game = game;
        this.location = location;
        pickedUp = false;
    }

    public void PickUpWeapon() { pickedUp = true; }

    public abstract string Name { get; }

    public abstract void Attack(Direction direction, Random random);

    protected bool DamageEnemy(Direction direction, int radius,
                               int damage, Random random) {
        Point target = game.PlayerLocation;
        for (int distance = 0; distance < radius; distance++) {
            foreach (Enemy enemy in game.Enemies) {
                if (Nearby(enemy.Location, target, radius)) {
                    enemy.Hit(damage, random);
                    return true;
                }
            }
            target = Move(direction, target, game.Boundaries);
        }
        return false;
    }
}
```

A pickedUp weapon shouldn't be displayed anymore... the form can use this get accessor to figure that out.

Every weapon has a location in the game dungeon.

The constructor sets the game and location fields, and sets pickedUp to false (because it hasn't been picked up yet).

Each weapon class needs to implement a Name property and an Attack() method that determines how that weapon attacks.

Each weapon's Name property returns its name ("Sword", "Mace", "Bow").

Each weapon has a different range and pattern of attack, so the weapons implement the Attack() method differently.

The DamageEnemy() method is called by Attack(). It attempts to find an enemy in a certain direction and radius. If it does, it calls the enemy's Hit() method and returns true. If no enemy's found, it returns false.

Different weapons attack in different ways

Each subclass of `Weapon` has its own name and attack logistic. Your job is to implement these classes. Here's the basic skeleton for a Weapon subclass:

```
public class Sword : Weapon {

    public Sword(Game game, Point location)
        : base(game, location) { }

    public override string Name { get { return "Sword"; } }

    public override void Attack(Direction direction, Random random) {
        // Your code goes here
    }
}
```

Each subclass represents one of the three weapons: a sword, bow, or mace.

Each subclass relies on the base class to do the initialization work.

You're basically hardcoding in the name of each weapon.

The Game object will pass on the direction to attack in.

The player can use the weapons over and over—they never get dropped or used up.

Sword

Name
Attack()

The sword is the first weapon the player picks up. It's got a wide angle of attack: if he attacks up, then it first tries to attack an enemy that's in that direction—if there's no enemy there, it looks in the direction that's clockwise from the original attack and attacks any enemy here, and if it still fails to hit then it attempts to attack an enemy counterclockwise from the original direction of attack. It's got a radius of 10, and causes 3 points of damage.

Think carefully about this... what is to the right of the direction left? What is to the left of up?

Bow

Name
Attack()

The bow has a very narrow angle of attack, but it's got a very long range—it's got an attack radius of 30, but only causes 1 point of damage. Unlike the sword, which attacks in three directions (because the player swings it in a wide arc), when the player shoots the bow in a direction, it only shoots in that one direction.

Mace

Name
Attack()

The mace is the most powerful weapon in the dungeon. It doesn't matter which direction the player attacks with it—since he swings it in a full circle, it'll attack any enemy with a radius of 20 and cause up to 6 points of damage.

The different weapons will call DamageEnemy() in various ways. The Mace attacks in all directions, so if the player's attacking to the right, it'll call DamageEnemy(Direction.Right, 20, 6, random). If that didn't hit an enemy, it'll attack Up. If there's no enemy there, it'll try Left, then Down—that makes it swing in a full circle.

Potions implement the IPotion interface

There are two potions, a blue potion and a red potion, which increase the player's health. They act just like weapons—the player picks them up in the dungeon, equips them by clicking on the inventory, and **uses them by clicking one of the attack buttons**. So it makes sense for them to inherit from the abstract Weapon class.

But potions act a little differently, too, so you'll need to add an IPotion interface so they can have extra behavior: increasing the player's health. The IPotion interface is really simple. Potions only need to add one read-only property called Used that returns false if the player hasn't used the potion, and true if he has. The form will use it to determine whether or not to display the potion in the inventory.

```
public interface IPotion {
    bool Used { get; }
}
```

IPotion makes potions usable only once. It's also possible to find out if a Weapon is a potion with "if (weapon is IPotion) because of this interface."

Weapon (abstract)
PickedUp
Location
PickUpWeapon()
DamageEnemy()

IPotion (interface)
Used

RedPotion
Name
Attack()

BluePotion
Name
Attack()

The potions inherit from the Weapon class because they're used just like weapons—the player clicks on the potion in the inventory scroll to equip it, and then clicks any of the Attack buttons to use it.

You should be able to write these classes using this class diagram and the information below.

BluePotion
Name
Attack()

The BluePotion class's Name property should return the string "Blue Potion". Its Attack() method will be called when the player uses the blue potion—it should increase the player's health by up to 5 hit points by calling the IncreasePlayerHealth() method. After the player uses the potion, the potion's Used() method should return true.

If the player picks up a blue potion on level 2, uses it, and then picks up another one on level 4, the game will end up creating two different BluePotion instances.

RedPotion
Name
Attack()

The RedPotion class is very similar to BluePotion, except that its Name property returns the string "Red Potion", and its Attack() method increases the player's health by up to 10 hit points.

The form brings it all together

There's one instance of the Game object, and it lives as a private field of your form. It's created in the form's Load event, and the various event handlers in the form use the fields and methods on the Game object to keep the game play going.

Everything begins with the form's Load event handler, which passes the Game a Rectangle that defines the boundaries of the dungeon play area. Here's some form code to get you going:

```
private Game game;
private Random random = new Random();
private void Form1_Load(object sender,
                        EventArgs e) {
    game = new Game(new Rectangle(78, 57, 420, 155));
    game.NewLevel(random);
    UpdateCharacters();
}
```

Using a Rectangle

You'll find a lot of Rectangles any time you work with forms. You can create one by passing it X, Y, Width, and Height values, or two Points (for opposite corners). Once you've got a rectangle instance, you can also access its Left, Right, Top, and Bottom, as well as its X, Y, Width, and Height values.

These are the boundaries of the dungeon in the background image you'll download and add to the form.

Remember to double-click on each PictureBox so the IDE adds a separate event handler method for each of them.

The form has a separate event handler for each of these PictureBox's Click events. When the player clicks on the sword, it first checks to make sure the sword is in the player's inventory using the Game object's CheckPlayerInventory() method. If the player's holding the sword, the form calls game.Equip() to equip it. It then sets each PictureBox's BorderStyle property to draw a box around the sword, and make sure none of the other icons have a box around them.

There's an event handler for each of the four movement buttons. They're pretty simple. First the button calls game.Move() with the appropriate Direction value, and then it calls the form's UpdateCharacters() method.

Make sure you change the buttons back when the player equips the sword, bow, or mace.

The four attack button event handlers are also really simple. Each button calls game.Attack(), and then calls the form's UpdateCharacters() method. If the player equips a potion, it's still used the same way—by calling game.Attack()—but potions have no direction. So make the Left, Right, and Down buttons invisible when the player equips a potion, and change the text on the Up button to say "Drink".

The form's UpdateCharacters() method moves the PictureBoxes into position

The last piece of the puzzle is the form's `UpdateCharacters()` method. Once all the objects have moved and acted on each other, the form updates everything... so weapons that been dropped have their PictureBoxes' Visible properties set to false, enemies and players are drawn in their new locations (and dead ones are made invisible), and inventory is updated.

Here's what you need to do:

 Update the player's position and stats

The first thing you'll do is update the player's PictureBox location and the label that shows his hit points. Then you'll need a few variables to determine whether you've shown each of the various enemies.

```
public void UpdateCharacters() {
   Player.Location = game.PlayerLocation;
   playerHitPoints.Text =
     game.PlayerHitPoints.ToString();

   bool showBat = false;
   bool showGhost = false;
   bool showGhoul = false;
   int enemiesShown = 0;
   // more code to go here...
```

> The showBat variable will be set to true if we made the bat's PictureBox visible. Same goes for showGhost and showGhoul.

 Update each enemy's location and hit points

Each enemy could be in a new location, and have a different set of hit points. You need to update each enemy after you've updated the player's location:

```
foreach (Enemy enemy in game.Enemies) {
   if (enemy is Bat) {
     bat.Location = enemy.Location;
     batHitPoints.Text = enemy.HitPoints.ToString();
     if (enemy.HitPoints > 0) {
       showBat = true;
       enemiesShown++;
     }
   }
}
// etc...
```

> This goes right after the code from above.

> This will affect the visibility of the enemy PictureBox controls in just a bit.

> You'll need two more if statements like this in your foreach loop—one for the ghost and one for the ghoul.

Once you've looped through all the enemies on the level, check the showBat variable. If the bat was killed, then showBat will still be false, so make its PictureBox invisible and clear its hit points label. Then do the same for showGhost and showGhoul.

3 **Update the weapon PictureBoxes**

Declare a `weaponControl` variable and use a big `switch` statement to set it equal to the PictureBox that corresponds to the weapon in the room.

```
sword.Visible = false;
bow.Visible = false;
redPotion.Visible = false;
bluePotion.Visible = false;
mace.Visible = false;
Control weaponControl = null;
switch (game.WeaponInRoom.Name) {
    case "Sword":
        weaponControl = sword; break;
```

Make sure your controls' names match these names. It's easy to end up with bugs that are difficult to track down if they don't match.

You'll have more cases for each weapon type.

The rest of the cases should set the variable `weaponControl` to the correct control on the form. After the `switch`, set `weaponControl.Visible` to `true` to display it.

4 **Set the Visible property on each inventory icon PictureBox**

Check use the Game object's `CheckPlayerInventory()` method to figure out whether or not to display the various inventory icons.

5 **Here's the rest of the method**

The first thing you'll do is update the player's PictureBox location and the label that shows his hit points. Then you'll need a few variables to determine whether you've shown the various enemies.

```
weaponControl.Location = game.WeaponInRoom.Location;
if (game.WeaponInRoom.PickedUp) {
  weaponControl.Visible = false;
} else {
  weaponControl.Visible = true;
}
if (game.PlayerHitPoints <= 0) {
  MessageBox.Show("You died");
  Application.Exit();
}
if (enemiesShown < 1) {
  MessageBox.Show("You have defeated the enemies on this level");
  game.NewLevel(random);
  UpdateCharacters();
}
```

Every level has one weapon. If it's been picked up, we need to make its icon invisible.

Application.Exit() immediately quits the program. It's part of System.Windows.Forms, so you'll need the appropriate using statement if you want to use it outside of a form.

If there are no more enemies on the level, then the player's defeated them all and it's time to go to the next level.

The fun's just beginning!

Seven levels, three enemies... that's a pretty decent game. But you can make it even better. Here are a few ideas to get you started...

Make the enemies smarter

Can you figure out how to change the enemies' Move() methods so that they're harder to defeat? Then see if you can change their constants to properties, and add way to change them in the game.

Add more levels

The game doesn't have to end after seven levels. See if you can add more... can you figure out how to make the game go on indefinitely? If the player does win, make a cool ending animation with dancing ghosts and bats! And the game ends pretty abruptly if the player dies. Can you think of a more user-friendly ending—maybe let the user restart the game or retry his last level.

Add different kinds of enemies

You don't need to limit the dangers to ghouls, ghosts, and bats. See if you can add more enemies to the game.

Add more weapons

The player will definitely need more help defeating any new enemies you've added. Think of new ways that the weapons can attack, or different things that potions can do. Take advantage of the fact that Weapon is a subclass of Mover—make magic weapons the player has to chase around!

Add more graphics

You can go to **www.headfirstlabs.com/books/hfcsharp/** to find more graphics files for additional enemies, weapons, and other images to help spark your imagination.

This is your chance to show off! Did you come up with a cool new version of the game? Join the Head First C# forum and claim your bragging rights: www.headfirstlabs.com/books/hfcsharp/

9 reading and writing files

Save the byte array, save the world

Okay, go ahead with our shopping list ... chicken wire ... tequila ... grape jelly ... bandages ... yes, dear, **I am** <u>writing</u> this down.

Sometimes it pays to be a little persistent.

So far, all of your programs have been pretty short-lived. They fire up, run for a while, and shut down. But that's not always enough, especially when you're dealing with important information. You need to be able to **save your work**. In this chapter, we'll look at how to **write data to a file**, and then how to **read that information back in** from a file. You'll learn about the .NET **stream classes**, and also take a look at the mysteries of **hexadecimal** and **binary**.

C# uses <u>streams</u> to read and write data

A **stream** is the .NET Framework's way of getting data in and out of your program. Any time your C# program reads or writes a file, connects to another computer over a network, or generally does anything where it **sends or receives bytes** from one place to another, you're using streams.

> Whenever you want to read data from a file or write data to a file, you'll use a <u>Stream object</u>.

Let's say you have a simple program—a form with an event handler that needs to read data from a file. You'll use a Stream object to do it.

```
input = stream.Read();
```

bytes read from the file

input contains data read from the stream

You use a Stream object...

...and the stream works with the file directly.

And if your program needs to write data out to the file, it can use another Stream object.

```
stream.Write(output);
```

output contains data to write to the stream

bytes written to the file

You use a different stream object, but the process is the same.

Different streams read and write different things

Every stream is a subclass of the abstract **Stream** class, and there are a bunch of built-in stream classes to do different things. We'll be concentrating on reading and writing regular files, but everything you learn in this chapter will just as easily apply to compressed or encrypted files, or network streams that don't use files at all.

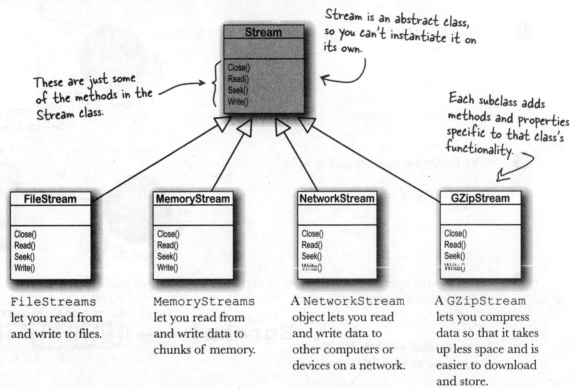

Stream is an abstract class, so you can't instantiate it on its own.

These are just some of the methods in the Stream class.

Each subclass adds methods and properties specific to that class's functionality.

FileStreams let you read from and write to files.

MemoryStreams let you read from and write data to chunks of memory.

A NetworkStream object lets you read and write data to other computers or devices on a network.

A GZipStream lets you compress data so that it takes up less space and is easier to download and store.

Things you can do with a stream:

1 Write to the stream.
You can write text or binary data to a stream and through a stream's Write() method.

2 Read from the stream.
You can use the Read() method to get data from a file, or a network, or memory, or just about anything else, using a stream.

3 Change your position within the stream.
Most streams support a Seek() method that lets you find a position within the stream so you can insert data at a specific place.

> **Streams let you read and write data. Use the right kind of stream for the data you're working with.**

A FileStream writes bytes to a file

When your program needs to write a few lines of text to a file, there are a lot of things that have to happen:

Make sure you add using System.IO; to any program that uses streams.

1 Create a new FileStream object and tell it to write to the file.

A FileStream can only be attached to one file at a time.

2 The FileStream attaches itself to a file.

3 Streams write bytes to files, so you'll need to convert the string that you want to write *to* an array of bytes.

This is called encoding, and we'll talk more about it later on...

Eureka! →

69 117 114 101 107 97 33
0 1 2 3 4 5 6

4 Call the stream's Write() method and pass it the byte array.

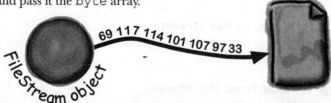

69 117 114 101 107 97 33

5 Close the file so other programs can access it.

Forgetting to close a stream is a <u>big deal</u>. Otherwise, the file will be locked, and other programs can't use that file until you close your stream.

How to write text to a file in 3 simple steps

StreamWriter creates and manages a FileStream object for you automatically.

C# comes with a convenient class called **StreamWriter** that does all of those things in one easy step. All you have to do is create a new `StreamWriter` object and give it a filename. It **automatically** creates a `FileStream` and links it to the file. Then you can use the StreamWriter's `Write()` and `WriteLine()` methods to write everything to the file you want.

1 **Use the StreamWriter's constructor to open or create a file**
You can pass a filename to the `StreamWriter()` constructor. When you do, the writer automatically opens the file. `StreamWriter` also has an overloaded constructor that also takes a `bool`: true if you want to add text to the end of an existing file (or append), or false if you want to delete the existing file and create a new file with the same name.

```
StreamWriter writer = new StreamWriter(@"C:\newfiles\toaster oven.txt", true);
```

Putting @ in front of the filename tells C# to treat this as a literal string, without escape characters, like \t for tab or \n for newline.

2 **Use the Write() and WriteLine() methods to write to the file**
These methods work just like the ones in `Console`: `Write()` writes text, and `WriteLine()` writes text and adds a line break to the end. If you include "{0}", "{1}", "{2}", etc., inside the string you're writing, the methods include parameters in the strings being written: "{0}" is replaced with the first parameter after the string being written, "{1}" is replaced with the second, etc.

```
writer.WriteLine("The {0} is set to {1} degrees.", appliance, temp.ToString());
```

3 **Call the Close() method to release the file**
If you leave the stream open and attached to a file, then it'll keep the file locked open and no other program will be able to use it. So make sure you always close your files!

```
writer.Close();
```

The Swindler launches another diabolical plan

The citizens of Objectville have long lived in fear of the Swindler.
Now he's using a StreamWriter to implement another evil plan.
Let's take a look at what's going on:

This line creates the StreamWriter object and tells it where the file will be.

The path starts with an @ sign so that the StreamWriter doesn't interpret the "\" as the start of an escape sequence.

```
StreamWriter sw = new StreamWriter(@"c:\secret_plan.txt");

sw.WriteLine("How I'll defeat Captain Amazing");

sw.WriteLine("Another genius secret plan by The Swindler");

sw.Write("I'll create an army of clones and ");

sw.WriteLine("unleash them upon the citizens of Objectville.");

string location = "the mall";

for (int number = 0; number <= 6; number++) {

    sw.WriteLine("Clone #{0} attacks {1}", number, location);

    if (location == "the mall") { location = "downtown"; }

    else { location = "the mall"; }

}

sw.Close();
```

WriteLine() adds a new line after writing. Write() sends just the text, with no extra line feeds at the end.

Can you figure out what's going on with the location variable in this code?

You can use the {} within the text to pass in variables to the string being written. {0} is replaced by the first parameter after the string, {1} by the second, and so on.

Close() frees up any connections to the file and any resources the StreamWriter is using. The text doesn't get written if you don't close the stream.

This is what the code above produces.

```
secret_plan.txt - Notepad
File  Edit  Format  View  Help
How I'll defeat Captain Amazing
Another genius secret plan by The Swindler
I'll create an army of clones and unleash them upon the citizens of Objectville.
Clone #0 attacks the mall
Clone #1 attacks downtown
Clone #2 attacks the mall
Clone #3 attacks downtown
Clone #4 attacks the mall
Clone #5 attacks downtown
Clone #6 attacks the mall
```

StreamWriter Magnets

Suppose you have the code for button1_Click() shown below. Your job is to use the magnets to build code for the Flobbo class so that, when the event handler is called, it produces the output shown at the bottom of the page. Good luck!

```
private void button1_Click(object sender, EventArgs e) {
    Flobbo f = new Flobbo("blue yellow");
    StreamWriter sw = f.Snobbo();
    f.Blobbo(f.Blobbo(f.Blobbo(sw), sw), sw);
}
```

```
sw.WriteLine(Zap);
Zap = "red orange";
return true;
```

```
}
```

```
sw.WriteLine(Zap);
sw.Close();
return false;
```

```
public bool Blobbo
    (bool Already, StreamWriter sw) {
```

```
public bool Blobbo(StreamWriter sw) {
```

```
sw.WriteLine(Zap);
Zap = "green purple";
return false;
```

```
}
```

```
return new
    StreamWriter("macaw.txt");
```

```
}
```

```
}
```

```
}
```

```
private string Zap;

public Flobbo(string Zap) {
    this.Zap = Zap;
}
```

```
public class Flobbo {
```

```
if (Already) {
```

```
} else {
```

```
public StreamWriter Snobbo() {
```

Output:

```
macaw.txt - Notepad
File  Edit  Format  View  Help
blue yellow
green purple
red orange
```

StreamWriter Magnets Solution

Your job was to construct the Flobbo class from the magnets to create the desired output.

```
private void button1_Click(object sender, EventArgs e) {
    Flobbo f = new Flobbo("blue yellow");
    StreamWriter sw = f.Snobbo();
    f.Blobbo(f.Blobbo(f.Blobbo(sw), sw), sw);
}
```

```
public class Flobbo {

    private string Zap;

    public Flobbo(string Zap) {
        this.Zap = Zap;
    }
```

```
    public StreamWriter Snobbo() {

        return new
            StreamWriter("macaw.txt");
    }
```

```
    public bool Blobbo(StreamWriter sw) {

        sw.WriteLine(Zap);
        Zap = "green purple";
        return false;
    }
```

The Blobbo() method is overloaded—it's got two declarations with different parameters.

```
    public bool Blobbo
        (bool Already, StreamWriter sw) {

        if (Already) {
```

```
            sw.WriteLine(Zap);
            sw.Close();
            return false;
```

Make sure you close files when you're done with them.

```
        } else {
```

```
            sw.WriteLine(Zap);
            Zap = "red orange";
            return true;
```

```
        }
    }
}
```

Output:

macaw.txt - Notepad

File Edit Format View Help

```
blue yellow
green purple
red orange
```

Reading and writing takes two objects

Let's read Swindler's secret plans with another stream, a `StreamReader`. `StreamReader` works just like a `StreamWriter`, except instead of writing a file you give the reader the name of the file to read in its constructor. The `ReadLine()` method returns a string that contains the next line from the file. You can write a loop that reads lines from it until its `EndOfStream` field is true—that's when it runs out of lines to read:

```
StreamReader reader =
    new StreamReader(@"d:\secret_plan.txt");
StreamWriter writer =
    new StreamWriter(@"e:\emailToCaptainAmazing.txt");
```

Pass the file you want to read from into the StreamReader's constructor.

This program uses a StreamReader to read the Swindler's plan, and a StreamWriter to write a file that will get emailed to Captain Amazing.

```
writer.WriteLine("To: CaptainAmazing@objectville.net");
writer.WriteLine("From: Commissioner@objectiville.net");
writer.WriteLine("Subject: Can you save the day... again?");
writer.WriteLine();
writer.WriteLine("We've discovered the Swindler's plan:");
while (!reader.EndOfStream) {
    string lineFromThePlan = reader.ReadLine();
    writer.WriteLine("The plan -> " + lineFromThePlan);
}
writer.WriteLine();
writer.WriteLine("Can you help us?");
writer.Close();
reader.Close();
```

An empty WriteLine() method writes a blank line.

EndOfStream is the property that tells you if there's no data left unread in the file.

This loop reads a line from the reader and writes it out to the writer.

Make sure to close every stream that you open, even if you're just reading a file.

```
emailToCaptainAmazing.txt - Notepad
File  Edit  Format  View  Help

To: CaptainAmazing@objectville.net
From: Governor@objectiville.net
Subject: Can you save the day... again?

We've discovered the Swindler's plan:
The plan -> How I'll defeat Captain Amazing
The plan -> Another genius secret plan by The Swindler
The plan -> I'll create an army of clones and unleash them upon the citizens of Objectville.
The plan -> Clone #0 attacks the mall
The plan -> Clone #1 attacks downtown
The plan -> Clone #2 attacks the mall
The plan -> Clone #3 attacks downtown
The plan -> Clone #4 attacks the mall
The plan -> Clone #5 attacks downtown
The plan -> Clone #6 attacks the mall

Can you help us?
```

Data can go through <u>more</u> <u>than</u> <u>one</u> stream

One big advantage to working with streams in .NET is that you can have your data go through more than one stream on its way to its final destination. One of the many types of streams that .NET ships with is the CryptoStream class. This lets you encrypt your data before you do anything else with it:

Stream

Close()
Read()
Seek()
Write()

CryptoStream

Close()
Read()
Seek()
Write()

Using a normal FileStream, your data gets written directly to a file as text.

FileStream object

I'll create an army of Clones and

CryptoStream inherits from the abstract Stream class, just like the other stream classes.

You write normal text to a CryptoStream.

The CryptoStream is connected to a FileStream, and gives that file stream your text, but encrypted.

Now your FileStream writes the encrypted text to the file.

I'll create an army

CryptoStream object

*3yd4ÿÖndfr56di¢L1

FileStream object

*3yd4ÿÖndfr56di¢L1

You can <u>**CHAIN**</u> streams. One stream can write to another stream, which writes to another stream... often ending with a network or file stream.

Pōol Puzzle

Your *job* is to take code snippets from the pool and place them into the blank lines in the program. You can use the same snippet more than once, and you won't need to use all the snippets. Your *goal* is to make the program produce the output shown to the right.

```
order.txt - Notepad
File  Edit  Format  View  Help
West
East
South
North
That's all folks!
```

```csharp
public class Pineapple {
  const _____ d = "delivery.txt";
  public _____ _____
       { North, South, East, West, Flamingo }
  public static void Main() {
       _____ o = new _____("order.txt");
    Pizza pz = new Pizza(new _____(d, true));
    pz._____(Fargo.Flamingo);
    for (_____ w = 3; w >= 0; w--) {
      Pizza i = new Pizza
              (new _____(d, false));
      i.Idaho((Fargo)w);
      Party p = new Party(new _____(d));
      p._____(o);
    }
    o._____("That's all folks!");
    o._____();
  }
}
```

```csharp
public class Pizza {
  private _____ _____;
  public Pizza(_____ _____) {
    _____.Writer = Writer;
  }
  public void _____(_____.Fargo f) {
    Writer._____(f.ToString());
    Writer._____();
  }
}


public class Party {
  private _____ Reader;
  public Party(_____ Reader) {
    _____.Reader = Reader;
  }
  public void HowMuch(_____ q) {
    q._____(Reader._____());
    Reader._____();
  }
}
```

Note: each snippet from the pool can be used more than once!

	int	Stream			
	long	Reader	public		
	string	Writer	private		=
	enum	StreamReader	this	for	>=
HowMany	class	StreamWriter	class	while	<=
HowMuch		Open	static	foreach	!=
HowBig		Close			==
HowSmall					++
					--

Fargo
Utah
Idaho
Dakota
Pineapple

Pool Puzzle Solution

This enum is used with its
ToString() method to print a lot
of the output.

```csharp
public class Pineapple {
    const string d = "delivery.txt";
    public enum Fargo { North, South, East, West, Flamingo }
    public static void Main() {
        StreamWriter o = new StreamWriter("order.txt");
        Pizza pz = new Pizza(new StreamWriter(d, true));
        pz.Idaho(Fargo.Flamingo);
        for (int w = 3; w >= 0; w--) {
            Pizza i = new Pizza(new StreamWriter(d, false));
            i.Idaho((Fargo)w);
            Party p = new Party(new StreamReader(d));
            p.HowMuch(o);
        }
        o.WriteLine("That's all folks!");
        o.Close();
    }
}

public class Pizza {
    private StreamWriter Writer;
    public Pizza(StreamWriter Writer) {
        this.Writer = Writer;
    }
    public void Idaho(Pineapple.Fargo f) {
        Writer.WriteLine(f.ToString());
        Writer.Close();
    }
}

public class Party {
    private StreamReader Reader;
    public Party(StreamReader Reader) {
        this.Reader = Reader;
    }
    public void HowMuch(StreamWriter q) {
        q.WriteLine(Reader.ReadLine());
        Reader.Close();
    }
}
```

Here's the entry point for
the program. It creates a
StreamWriter that it passes to
the Party class. Then it loops
through the Fargo members,
passing each of them to the
Pizza.Idaho() method to print.

The Pizza class keeps a
StreamWriter as a private
field, and its Idaho() method
writes Fargo enums to the
file using their ToString()
methods.

The Party class has a
StreamReader field, and
its HowMuch() method
reads a line from that
StreamReader and writes
it to a StreamWriter.

Use built-in objects to pop up standard dialog boxes

When you're working on a program that reads and writes files, there's a good chance that you'll need to pop up a dialog box at some point to prompt the user for a filename. That's why .NET ships with objects to pop up the standard Windows file dialog boxes.

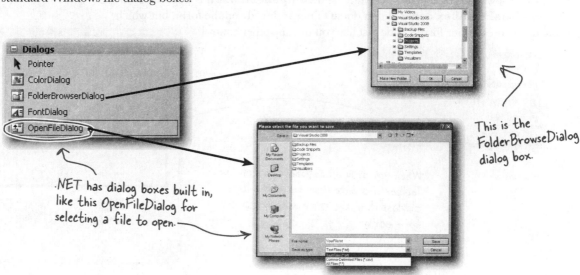

This is the FolderBrowseDialog dialog box.

.NET has dialog boxes built in, like this OpenFileDialog for selecting a file to open.

ShowDialog() pops up a dialog box

Displaying a dialog box is easy. Here's all you need to do:

We'll walk you through these steps in a minute.

1 Create an instance of the dialog box object. You can do this in code using `new`, or you can drag it onto your form out of the toolbox.

2 Set the dialog box object's properties. A few useful ones include `Title` (which sets the text in the title bar), `InitialDirectory` (which tells it which directory to open first), and `FileName` (for open and save dialog boxes).

3 Call the object's `ShowDialog()` method. That pops up the dialog box, and doesn't return until the user clicks the OK button or the Cancel button, or closes the window.

4 The `ShowDialog()` method returns a `DialogResult`, which is an enum. Some of its members are `OK` (which means the user clicked OK), `Cancel`, `Yes`, and `No` (for Yes/No dialog boxes).

Dialog boxes are just another .NET control

You can add Windows standard file dialog boxes to your program just by dragging them to your form –just drag an `OpenFileDialog` control out of the toolbox and drop it on your form. Instead of showing up as a visual control, you'll see it appear in the space below your form. That's because it's a **component**, which is a special kind of **non-visual Toolbox control** that doesn't appear directly on the form, but which you can still use in your form's code just like you use any other control.

"Non-visual" just means it doesn't appear on your form when you drag it out of the toolbox.

When you drag a component out of the Toolbox and onto your form, the IDE displays it in the space underneath the form editor.

The InitialDirectory propery changes the folder that's first displayed when the dialog opens.

The Filter Property lets you change the filters that show up on the bottom of the dialog box, such as what types of files to show.

```
openFileDialog1.InitialDirectory = @"c:\MyFolder\Default\";

openFileDialog1.Filter = "Text Files (*.txt)|*.txt|"

  + "Comma-Delimited Files (*.csv)|*.csv|All Files (*.*)|*.*";

openFileDialog1.FileName = "default_file.txt";

openFileDialog1.CheckFileExists = true;

openFileDialog1.CheckPathExists = false;

DialogResult result = openFileDialog1.ShowDialog();

if (result == DialogResult.OK){

    OpenSomeFile(openFileDialog1.FileName);

}
```

These properties tell the dialog box to display an error message if the user tries to open up a file or path that doesn't exist on the drive.

Display the dialog box using its ShowDialog() method, which returns a DialogResult. That's an enum that you can use to check whether or not the user hit the OK button. It'll be set to DialogResult.OK if the user clicked OK, and DialogResult.Cancel if he hit Cancel.

Dialog boxes are objects, too

An **OpenFileDialog** box object shows the standard Windows "Open"
window, and the **SaveFileDialog** shows its "Save" window. You can display
them by creating a new instance, setting the properties on the object, and
calling its ShowDialog() method. The ShowDialog() method returns
a DialogResult enum (because some dialog boxes have more than two
buttons or results, so a simple bool wouldn't be enough).

> When you drag a save dialog object out
> of the toolbox and onto your form, the
> IDE just adds a line like this to your
> form's InitializeComponent() method.

```
saveFileDialog1 = new SaveFileDialog();

saveFileDialog1.InitialDirectory = @"c:\MyFolder\Default\";

saveFileDialog1.Filter = "Text Files (*.txt)|*.txt|"
    + "Comma-Delimited Files (*.csv)|*.csv|All Files (*.*)|*.*";

DialogResult result = saveFileDialog1.ShowDialog();

if (result == DialogResult.OK){

    SaveTheFile(saveFileDialog1.FileName);

}
```

> The ShowDialog() and FileName
> properties work exactly the same
> as on the OpenFileDialog object.

> The SaveFileDialog
> object pops up the
> standard Windows
> "Save as..." dialog box.

> The Title property lets
> you change this text.

> The ShowDialog()
> method pops up
> the dialog box
> and opens the
> folder specified in
> the InitialFolder
> property.

> Change the "Save as
> type" list using the
> Filter property.

> When the user chooses a
> file, its full path is saved
> in the FileName property.

> The DialogResult
> returned by the
> ShowDialog() method
> lets you figure out
> which button the
> user clicked.

Use the built-in File and Directory classes to work with files and directories

Like StreamWriter, the File class creates streams for you to work with files behind the scenes. You can use its methods to do most common actions without having to create the FileStreams first. Directory objects let you work with whole directories full of files, you can use it to make changes to your file structure easily.

Things you can do with a File:

1   Find out if it exists
You can check to see if a file exists using the Exists() method. It'll return true if it does and false if it doesn't.

2   Read from and write to the file
You can use the OpenRead() method to get data from a file, or the Create() or OpenWrite() method to write to the file.

3   Append text to the file
The AppendAllText() method lets you append text to an already created file. It even creates the file if it's not there when the method runs.

4   Get information about the file
The GetLastAccessTime() and GetLastWriteTime() methods return the date and time when the file was last accessed and modified.

FileInfo works just like File

If you're going to be doing a lot of work with a file, you might want to create an instance of the FileInfo class instead of using the File class's static methods.

The FileInfo class does just about everything the File class does except you have to instantiate it to use it. You can create a new instance of FileInfo and access its Exists() method, or its OpenRead() method in just the same way.

The only difference is that the File class is faster for a small number of actions and FileInfo is better suited for big jobs.

Things you can do with a Directory:

1   Create a new directory
Create a directory using the CreateDirectory() method. All you have to do is supply the path; this method does the rest.

2   Get a list of the files in a directory
You can create an array of files in a directory using the GetFiles() method; just tell the method which directory you want to know about and it will do the rest.

3   Delete a directory
Deleting a directory is really simple too. Use the Delete() method.

there are no
Dumb Questions

Q: I still don't get that {0} and {1} thing that was part of the StreamWriter.

A: When you're printing strings to a file, you'll often find yourself in the position of having to print the contents of a bunch of variables. For example, you might have to write something like this:

```
writer.WriteLine("My name is " + name +
    "and my age is " + age);
```

It gets really tedious and somewhat error-prone to have to keep using + to combine strings. It's easier to take advantage of {0} and {1}:

```
writer.WriteLine(
    "My name is {0} and my age is {1}",
    name, age);
```

It's a lot easier to read that code, especially when many variables are included in the same line.

Q: Why did you put a @ in front of the string that contained the filename?

A: The `Write()` and `WriteLine()` methods support escape sequences like `\n` and `\r`. That makes it difficult to type filenames, which have a lot of backslash characters in them. If you put @ in front of a string, it tells C# not to interpret escape sequences. It also tells C# to include line breaks in your string, so you can hit Enter halfway through the string and it'll include that as a linebreak in the output:

```
string twoLine = @"this is a string
that spans two lines.";
```

Q: And what do \n and \t mean again?

A: Those are escape sequences. `\n` is a linefeed and `\t` is a tab. `\r` is a return character, or half of a Windows return—in Windows text files, lines have to end with `\r\n`. If you want to use an *actual* backslash in your string, and not have C# interpret it as the beginning of an escape sequence, just do a ***double*** backslash: `\\`.

Q: What was that in the beginning about converting a string to a byte array? How would that even work?

A: You've probably heard many times that files on a disk are repesented as bits and bytes. What that means is that when you write a file to a disk, the operating system treats it as one long sequence of bytes. Remember from Chapter 4 how a `byte` variable can store any number between 0 and 255? Every file on your hard drive is one long sequence of numbers between 0 and 255. It's up to the programs that read and write those files to interpret those bytes as meaningful data. When you open a file in Notepad, it converts each individal byte to a character—for example, `E` is 69 and `a` is 97. And when you type text into Notepad and save it, Notepad converts each of the characters back into a byte and saves it to disk. And if you want to write a `string` to a stream, you'll need to do the same.

Q: If I'm just using a StreamWriter to write to a file, why do I really care if it's creating a FileStream for me?

A: If you're only reading or writing lines to or from a text file in order, then all you need are `StreamReader` and `StreamWriter`. But as soon as you need to do anything more complex than that, you'll need to start working with other streams. If you ever need to write data like numbers, arrays, collections or objects to a file, a `StreamWriter` just won't do. But don't worry, we'll go into a lot more detail about how that will work in just a minute.

Q: What if I want to create my own dialog boxes? Can I do that?

A: Yes, you definitely can. You can add a new form to your project, design it to look exactly how you want. Then you can create a new instance of it with `new` (just like you created an `OpenFileDialog` object). Then you can call its `ShowDialog()` method, and it'll work just like any other dialog box. We'll talk a lot more about adding other forms to your program in Chapter 13.

Q: Why do I need to worry about closing streams after I'm done with them?

A: Have you ever had a word processor tell you it couldn't open a file because it was "busy"? When one program uses a file, Windows locks it and prevents other programs from using it. And it'll do that for your program when it opens a file. If you don't call the `Close()` method, then it's possible for your program to keep a file locked open until it ends.

Sharpen your pencil

.NET has two built-in classes with a bunch of static methods for working with files and folders. The **File** class gives methods to work with files, and the **Directory** class lets you work with directories. Write down what you think each of these lines of code does.

Code	What the code does
```if (Directory.Exists(@"c:\SYP")) { Directory.CreateDirectory(@"c:\SYP"); }```	
```if (Directory.Exists(@"c:\SYP\Bonk")) { Directory.Delete(@"c:\SYP\Bonk"); }```	
```Directory.CreateDirectory(@"c:\SYP\Bonk");```	
```Directory.SetCreationTime(@"c:\SYP\Bonk", new DateTime(1976, 09, 25));```	
```string[] files = Directory.GetFiles(@"c:\windows\", "*.log", SearchOption.AllDirectories);```	
```File.WriteAllText(@"c:\SYP\Bonk\weirdo.txt", @"This is the first line and this is the second line and this is the last line");```	
```File.Encrypt(@"c:\SYP\Bonk\weirdo.txt");``` See if you can guess what this one does—you haven't seen it yet.	
```File.Copy(@"c:\SYP\Bonk\weirdo.txt", @"c:\SYP\copy.txt");```	
```DateTime myTime = Directory.GetCreationTime(@"c:\SYP\Bonk");```	
```File.SetLastWriteTime(@"c:\SYP\copy.txt", myTime);```	
```File.Delete(@"c:\SYP\Bonk\weirdo.txt");```	

Use File Dialogs to open and save files (all with just a few lines of code)

You can build a program that opens a text file. It'll let you make
changes to the file, and saves your changes. with very little code,
all using standard .NET controls. Here's how:.

Do this

1 **Build a simple form.**

All you need is a textbox and two buttons. Drop the
OpenFileDialog and SaveFileDialog controls onto the Form
too. Double-click on the buttons to create their event handlers
and **add a private string field called name to the form**.
Don't forget to put a using statement up top for System.
IO.

2 **Hook the Open button up to the openFileDialog.**

The Open button shows an OpenFileDialog and then uses File.ReadAllText()
to read the file into the text box:

```
private void open_Click(object sender, EventArgs e) {
  if (openFileDialog1.ShowDialog() == DialogResult.OK) {
    name = openFileDialog1.FileName;
    textBox1.Clear();
    textBox1.Text = File.ReadAllText(name);
  }
}
```

Clicking Open shows the OpenFileDialog control.

3 **Now, hook up the Save button.**

The Save button uses the File.WriteAllText() method to save the file:

```
private void save_Click(object sender, EventArgs e) {
  if (saveFileDialog1.ShowDialog() == DialogResult.OK) {
    name = saveFileDialog1.FileName;
    File.WriteAllText(name, textBox1.Text);
  }
}
```

The ReadAllText() and WriteAllText() methods are part of the File class. That's coming up on the next page. We'll look at them in more detail in just a few pages.

4 **Play with the other properties of the dialog boxes.**

✦ Use the Title property of the saveFileDialog to change the text in
the title bar.

✦ Set the initialFolder property to have the dialog OpenFileDialog
start in a specified directory.

✦ Filter the OpenFileDialog so it will only show text files using the
Filter property.

If you don't add a filter, then the drop-down lists at the bottom of the open and save dialog boxes will be empty. Try using this filter: "Text Files (*.txt)|*.txt"

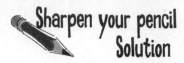

Sharpen your pencil
Solution

.NET has two built-in classes with a bunch of static methods for working with files and folders. The **File** class gives methods to work with files, and the **Directory** class lets you work with directories. Your job was to write down what each bit of code did.

Code	What the code does
```if (Directory.Exists(@"c:\SYP")) { Directory.CreateDirectory(@"c:\SYP"); }```	Check if the C:\SYP folder exists. If it doesn't, create it.
```if (Directory.Exists(@"c:\SYP\Bonk")) { Directory.Delete(@"c:\SYP\Bonk"); }```	Check if the C:\SYP\Bonk folder exists. If it does, delete it.
```Directory.CreateDirectory(@"c:\SYP\Bonk");```	Create the directory C:\SYP\Bonk.
```Directory.SetCreationTime(@"c:\SYP\Bonk", new DateTime(1976, 09, 25));```	Set the creation time for the C:\SYP\Bonk folder to September 25, 1976.
```string[] files = Directory.GetFiles(@"c:\windows\", "*.log", SearchOption.AllDirectories);```	Get a list of all files in C:\Windows that match the *.log pattern, including all matching files in any subdirectory.
```File.WriteAllText(@"c:\SYP\Bonk\weirdo.txt", @"This is the first line and this is the second line and this is the last line");```	Create a file called "weirdo.txt" (if it doesn't already exist) in the C:\SYP\Bonk folder and write three lines of text to it.
```File.Encrypt(@"c:\SYP\Bonk\weirdo.txt");``` *This is an alternative to using a CryptoStream.*	Take advantage of built-in Windows encryption to encrypt the file "weirdo.txt" using the logged in account's credentials..
```File.Copy(@"c:\SYP\Bonk\weirdo.txt", @"c:\SYP\copy.txt");```	Copy the C:\SYP\Bonk\weirdo.txt file to C:\SYP\Copy.txt.
```DateTime myTime = Directory.GetCreationTime(@"c:\SYP\Bonk");```	Declare the myTime variable and set it equal to the creation time of the C:\SYP\Bonk folder.
```File.SetLastWriteTime(@"c:\SYP\copy.txt", myTime);```	Alter the last write time of the copy.txt file in C:\SYP\ so it's equal to whatever time is stored in the myTime variable.
```File.Delete(@"c:\SYP\Bonk\weirdo.txt");```	Delete the C:\SYP\Bonk\weirdo.txt file.

IDisposable makes sure your objects are disposed properly

A lot of .NET classes implement a particularly useful interface called
IDisposable. It **only has one member**: a method called **Dispose()**.
Whenever a class implements IDisposable, it's telling you that there
are important things that it needs to do in order to shut itself down, usually
because it's **allocated resources** that it won't give back until you tell it to.
The Dispose() method is how you tell the object to release those resources.

You can use the "Go To Definition" feature in the IDE the official C#
definition of IDispoable. Go to your project and type IDisposable
anywhere inside the code. Then right-click on it and select "Go To Definition"
from the menu. It'll open a new tab with code in it. Expand all of the code
and this is what you'll see:

You'll learn more about "Go To Definition" later on.

> Declare an object in a using block and that object's Dispose() method is called **automatically**.

```
namespace System
{
```

A lot of classes allocate important resources, like memory, files, and other objects. That means they take them over, and don't give them back until you tell them it's done with those resources.

```
    // Summary:

    //     Defines a method to release allocated resources.

    public interface IDisposable
    {

        // Summary:

        //     Performs application-defined tasks

        //     associated with freeing, releasing, or

        //     resetting unmanaged resources.

        void Dispose();
    }
}
```

Any class that implements IDisposable will immediately release any resources that it took over as soon as you call its Dispose() method. It's almost always the last thing you do before you're done with the object.

Go To Definition

There's a handy feature in the IDE that lets you automatically jump to the
definition for any variable, object or method. Just right-click on it and
select "Go To Definition", and the IDE will automatically jump right to the
code that defines it.

---

al-lo-cate, verb.
to distribute resources
or duties for a particular
purpose. *The programming
team was irritated at their project
manager because he **allocated**
all of the conference rooms for a
useless management seminar.*

Avoid file system errors with <u>using</u> statements

We've been telling you all chapter that you need to **close your streams**. That's because some of the most common bugs that programmers run across when they deal with files are caused when streams aren't closed properly. Luckily, C# gives you a great tool to make sure that never happens to you: IDisposable and the Dispose() method. When you **wrap your stream code in a using statement**, it automatically closes your streams for you. All you need to do is **declare your stream reference** with a using statement, followed by a block of code (inside curly brackets) that uses that reference. When you do that, the using statement **automatically calls the stream's Dispose() method** as soon as it finishes running the block of code. Here's how it works:

These "using" statements are different from the ones at the top of your code.

A using statement is always followed by an object declaration...

...and then a block of code within curly braces.

```
using (StreamWriter sw = new StreamWriter("secret_plan.txt")) {

    sw.WriteLine("How I'll defeat Captain Amaing");

    sw.WriteLine("Another genius secret plan");

    sw.WriteLine("by The Swindler");

}
```

These statements can use the object created in the using statement above like any normal object.

When the using statement ends, the Dispose() method of the object being used is run.

In this case, the object being used is the Log Stream, so the Dispose() method of the Stream class is run... which closes the stream.

Every stream has a Dispose() method that closes the stream. So if you declare your stream in a using statement, it will always close itself!

Use multiple using statements for multiple objects

You can pile using statements on top of each other—you don't need extra sets of curly brackets or indents.

```
using (StreamReader reader = new StreamReader("secret_plan.txt");

using (StreamWriter writer = new StreamReader("email.txt");

{

    // statements that use reader and writer

}
```

You don't need to call Close() on the streams now, because the using statement will close them automatically.

Any time you use a stream, you should <u>ALWAYS</u> declare it inside a using statement. That makes sure it's always closed!

Trouble at work

Meet Brian. He likes his job as a C# developer, but he *loves* taking the occasional day off. But his boss **hates** when people take vacation days, so Brian's got to come up with a good excuse.

Sorry I've gotta leave early, boss. My cat's got a vet appointment.

That's the ninth vet appointment you've had since March, son. If I find out you're lying to me, you'd better start looking for a new job!

You can help Brian out by building a program to manage his excuses

Use what you know about reading and writing files to build an excuse manager that Brian can use to keep track of which excuses he's used recently and how well they went over with the boss.

This asterisk appears when a form has unsaved data.

Brian wants to keep all of his excuses in one place, so let's let him select a folder to store all of them.

Sometimes Brian's too lazy to think up an excuse. Let's add a button to load up a random excuse from his excuse folder.

Excuse Manager*	☒
Excuse	My dog has a headache
Results	Didn't work - boss knows I don't have a dog.
Last Used	Tuesday , March 07, 2006 ▼
File date	7/26/2007 9:48:27 AM

[Folder] [Save] [Open] [Random Excuse]

Select a folder

Save an excuse

The folder contains one text file for each excuse. When Brian clicks the Save button, the current excuse is saved out to the folder. The Open button lets him open a saved excuse.

Build the excuse manager so Brian can manage his excuses at work.

Excuse
Description: string
Results: string
LastUsed: DateTime
ExcusePath: string
OpenFile(string)
Save(string)

Exercise

1 **Build the form**

This form has a few special features:

★ When the form's first loaded, **only the Folder button should be enabled**—disable the other three buttons until the user selects a folder.

★ When the form opens or saves an excuse, it displays the file date for the excuse file using a Label control with AutoSize set to False and BorderStyle set to Fixed3D.

★ After an excuse is saved, the form pops up an "Excuse Written" messagebox.

★ The Folder button brings up a folder browser dialog box. If the user selects a folder, it enables the Save, Open, and Random Excuse buttons.

★ The form knows when there are unsaved changes. When there are no unsaved changes, the text on the form's title bar is "Excuse Manager". But when the user has changed any of the three fields, the form adds an asterisk (*) to the title bar. The asterisk goes away when the data is saved or a new excuse is opened.

★ The form will need to keep track of the current folder and whether or not the current excuse has been saved. You can figure out when the excuse hasn't been saved by **using the Changed event handlers** for the three input controls. ←— *When you drag a textbox to a form and double-click on it, you create a Changed event handler for that field.*

2 **Create an Excuse class and store an instance of it in the form**

Now add a CurrentExcuse field to the form to hold the current excuse. You'll need **three overloaded constructors**: one for when the form's first loaded, one for opening up a file, and one for a random excuse. Add methods OpenFile() to open an excuse (for the constructors to use), and Save() to save the excuse. Then add this UpdateForm() method to update the controls (it'll give you some **hints** about the class):

```
private void UpdateForm(bool Changed) {
    if (!Changed) {
        this.description.Text = currentExcuse.Description;
        this.results.Text = currentExcuse.Results;
        this.lastUsed.Value = currentExcuse.LastUsed;
        if (!string.IsNullOrEmpty(currentExcuse.ExcusePath))
            FileDate.Text = File.GetLastWriteTime(currentExcuse.ExcusePath).ToString();
        this.Text = "Excuse Manager";
    }
    else
        this.Text = "Excuse Manager*";
    this.formChanged = Changed;
}
```

This parameter indicates whether or not the form has changed. You'll need a field in your form to keep track of this status.

Remember, the ! means NOT—so this checks if the excuse path is NOT null or empty.

Double-click on the input controls so the IDE builds Changed event handlers for you. The event handlers for the three input controls will first change the Excuse instance and then call UpdateForm(true)—then it's up to you to change the fields on your form.

3 **Make the Folder button open a folder browser**

When the user clicks on the Folder button, the form should pop up a "Browse for Folder" dialog box. The form will need to store the folder in a field so that the other dialog boxes can use it. When the form **first loads**, the Save, Open, and Random Excuse buttons are **disabled**, but if the user selects a folder then the Folder button enables them.

3 **Make Save button save the current excuse to a file**

Clicking the Save button should bring up the Save As dialog box.

★ Each excuse is saved to a separate text file. The first line of the file is the excuse, the second is the result, and the third is the date last used (use the DateTimePicker's ToString() method). The Excuse class should have a Save() method to save an excuse out to a specified file.

★ When the Save As dialog box is opened, its folder should be set to the folder that the user selected using the Folder button, and the filename should be set to the excuse plus a ".txt" extension.

★ The dialog box should have two filters: Text Files (*.txt) and All Files (*.*).

★ If the user tries to save the current excuse but has left either the excuse or the result blank, the form should pop up a warning dialog box:

You can display this Exclamation icon by using the overloaded MessageBox.Show() method that allows you to specify a MessageBoxIcon parameter.

4 **Make the Open button open a saved excuse**

Clicking the Save button should bring up the Open dialog box.

★ When the Open dialog box is opened, its folder should be set to the folder that the user selected using the Folder button.

★ Add an Open() method to the Excuse class to open an excuse from a given file.

★ Use Convert.ToDateTime() to load the saved date into the DateTimePicker control.

★ If the user tries to open the current excuse but the current excuse hasn't been saved, it pops up this dialog box:

Show a Yes/No dialog box by using the overloaded MessageBox.Show() method that lets you specify the MessageBoxButtons.YesNo parameter. If the user clicks "No", then Show() returns DialogResult.No.

5 **Finally, make the Random Excuse button load a random excuse**

When the user clicks the Random Excuse button, it looks in the excuse folder, chooses one of the excuses at random, and opens it.

★ The form will need to save a Random object in a field and pass it to one of the overloaded constructors of the Excuse object.

★ If the current excuse hasn't been saved, the button should pop up the same warning dialog box as the Open button.

Build the excuse manager so Brian can manage his excuses at work.

Exercise Solution

The form uses fields to store the current Excuse object, the selected folder, remember whether or not the current excuse has changed, and keep a Random object for the Random Excuse button.

```csharp
private Excuse currentExcuse = new Excuse();
private string selectedFolder = "";
private bool formChanged = false;
Random random = new Random();

private void folder_Click(object sender, EventArgs e) {
    folderBrowserDialog1.SelectedPath = selectedFolder;
    DialogResult result = folderBrowserDialog1.ShowDialog();
    if (result == DialogResult.OK) {
        selectedFolder = folderBrowserDialog1.SelectedPath;
        save.Enabled = true;
        open.Enabled = true;
        randomExcuse.Enabled = true;
    }
}
```

If the user selected a folder, the form saves the folder name and then enables the other three buttons.

The two vertical bars mean OR—this is true if description is empty OR results is empty.

```csharp
private void save_Click(object sender, EventArgs e) {
    if (String.IsNullOrEmpty(description.Text) || String.IsNullOrEmpty(results.Text)) {
        MessageBox.Show("Please specify an excuse and a result",
            "Unable to save", MessageBoxButtons.OK, MessageBoxIcon.Exclamation);
        return;
    }
    saveFileDialog1.InitialDirectory = selectedFolder;
    saveFileDialog1.Filter = "Text files (*.txt)|*.txt|All files (*.*)|*.*";
    saveFileDialog1.FileName = description.Text + ".txt";
    DialogResult result = saveFileDialog1.ShowDialog();
    if (result == DialogResult.OK) {
        currentExcuse.Save(saveFileDialog1.FileName);
        UpdateForm(false);
        MessageBox.Show("Excuse written");
    }
}
```

Here's where the filters are set for the Save As dialog.

This will cause two rows to show up in the "Files of Type" dropdown at the bottom of the Save dialog box: one for Text Files (*.txt), and one for All Files (*.*).

```csharp
private void open_Click(object sender, EventArgs e) {
    if (CheckChanged()) {
        openFileDialog1.InitialDirectory = selectedFolder;
        openFileDialog1.Filter = "Text files (*.txt)|*.txt|All files (*.*)|*.*";
        openFileDialog1.FileName = description.Text + ".txt";
        DialogResult result = openFileDialog1.ShowDialog();
        if (result == DialogResult.OK) {
            currentExcuse = new Excuse(openFileDialog1.FileName);
            UpdateForm(false);
        }
    }
}
```

Use the DialogResult enum returned by the Open and Save dialog boxes to make sure you only open or save if the user clicked "OK", and not "Cancel".

```csharp
private void randomExcuse_Click(object sender, EventArgs e) {
    if (CheckChanged()) {
        currentExcuse = new Excuse(random, selectedFolder);
        UpdateForm(false);
    }
}
```

```
private bool CheckChanged() {
    if (formChanged) {
        DialogResult result = MessageBox.Show(
            "The current excuse has not been saved. Continue?",
            "Warning", MessageBoxButtons.YesNo, MessageBoxIcon.Warning);
        if (result == DialogResult.No)
            return false;
    }
    return true;
}
```

MessageBox.Show() also returns a DialogResult enum that we can check.

Here are the three Changed event handlers for the three input fields on the form. If any of them are triggered, that means the excuse has changed, so first we update the Excuse instance and then we call UpdateForm(), add the asterisk to the form's title bar, and set Changed to true.

```
private void description_TextChanged(object sender, EventArgs e) {
    currentExcuse.Description = description.Text;
    UpdateForm(true);
}

private void results_TextChanged(object sender, EventArgs e) {
    currentExcuse.Results = results.Text;
    UpdateForm(true);
}

private void lastUsed_ValueChanged(object sender, EventArgs e) {
    currentExcuse.LastUsed = lastUsed.Value;
    UpdateForm(true);
}
```

Passing true to UpdateForm() tells it to just mark the form as changed, but not update the input controls.

```
public class Excuse {
    public string Description;
    public string Results;
    public DateTime LastUsed;
    public string ExcusePath;
    public Excuse() {
        ExcusePath = "";
    }
    public Excuse(string excusePath) {
        OpenFile(excusePath);
    }
    public Excuse(Random random, string folder) {
        string[] fileNames = Directory.GetFiles(folder, "*.txt");
        OpenFile(fileNames[random.Next(fileNames.Length)]);
    }
    private void OpenFile(string excusePath) {
        this.ExcusePath = excusePath;
        using (StreamReader reader = new StreamReader(excusePath)) {
            Description = reader.ReadLine();
            Results = reader.ReadLine();
            LastUsed = Convert.ToDateTime(reader.ReadLine());
        }
    }
    public void Save(string fileName) {
        using (StreamWriter writer = new StreamWriter(fileName))
        {
            writer.WriteLine(Description);
            writer.WriteLine(Results);
            writer.WriteLine(LastUsed.ToString());
        }
    }
}
```

The Random Excuse button uses Directory.GetFiles() to read all of the text files in the selected folder into an array, and then chooses a random array index to open.

We made sure to use a using statement every time we opened a stream. That way our files will always be closed.

Here's where the using statement comes in. We declared the StreamWriter inside of a using statement, so its Close() method is called for us automatically!

Writing files usually involves making a lot of decisions

You'll write lots of programs that take a single input, maybe from a file, and have to decide what to do based on that input. Here's code that uses one long `if` statement—it's pretty typical. It checks the `part` variable and prints different lines to the file based on which enum it uses. There are lots of choices, so lots of `else ifs`:

```
enum BodyPart {
    Head,
    Shoulders,
    Knees,
    Toes
}
```

Here's an enum—we'll want to compare a variable against each of the four members and write a different line to the StreamWriter depending on which one it matches. We'll also write something different if none of them match.

```
private void WritePartInfo(BodyPart part, StreamWriter writer) {
    if (part == BodyPart.Head)
        writer.WriteLine("the head is hairy");
    else if (part == BodyPart.Shoulders)
        writer.WriteLine("the shoulders are broad");
    else if (part == BodyPart.Knees)
        writer.WriteLine("the knees are knobby");
    else if (part == BodyPart.Toes)
        writer.WriteLine("the toes are teeny");
    else
        writer.WriteLine("some unknown part is unknown");
    }
}
```

If we use a series of if/else statements, then we end up writing this "if (part ==[option])" over and over.

We've got a final else in case we didn't find a match.

BRAIN POWER

What sort of things can go wrong when you write code that has this many if/else statements? Think about typos and bugs caused by brackets, a single equals sign, etc.

Use a <u>switch</u> statement to choose the right option

Comparing one variable against a bunch of different values is a really common pattern that you'll see over and over again. It's especially common when you're reading and writing files. It's so common, in fact, that C# has a special kind of statement designed specifically for this situation.

A **switch statement** lets you compare one variable against many values in a way that's easy to read and is compact. Here's a switch statement that does exactly the same thing as the series of if/else statements on the opposite page:

> There's nothing about a switch statement that's specifically related to files. It's just a useful C# tool that we can use here.

A switch statement compares ONE variable against MULTIPLE possible values.

```
enum BodyPart
{
    Head,
    Shoulders,
    Knees,
    Toes,
}
```

> You'll start with the switch keyword followed by the variable that's going to be compared against a bunch of different possible values.

```
private void WritePartInfo(BodyPart part, StreamWriter writer)
{
    switch (part) {
        case BodyPart.Head:
            writer.WriteLine("the head is hairy");
            break;
        case BodyPart.Shoulders:
            writer.WriteLine("the shoulders are broad");
            break;
        case BodyPart.Knees:
            writer.WriteLine("the knees are knobby");
            break;
        case BodyPart.Toes:
            writer.WriteLine("the toes are teeny");
            break;
        default:
            writer.WriteLine("some unknown part is unknown");
            break;
    }
}
```

> The body of the switch statement is a series of cases that compare whatever follows the switch keyword against a particular value.

> Every case must end with "break;".

> Each of these cases consists of the case keyword followed by the value to compare and a colon. After that is a series of statements followed by "break;". Those statements will be executed if the case matches the comparison value.

> Switch statements can end with a default: block that gets executed if none of the other cases are matched.

Use a switch statement to let your deck of cards read from a file or write itself out to one

The switch statement lets you test one value against a bunch of cases and execute different statements depending on which one it matches.

Writing a card out to a file is straightforward—just make a loop that writes the name of each card out to a file. Here's a method you can add to the Deck object that does exactly that:

```
public void WriteCards(string Filename) {
    using (StreamWriter writer = new StreamWriter(Filename)) {
        for (int i = 0; i < Cards.Count; i++) {
            writer.WriteLine(Cards[i].Name);
        }
    }
}
```

But what about reading the file in? It's not quite so simple. That's where the switch statement can come in handy.

```
Card.Suits suit;
switch (suitString) {
    case "Spades":
        suit = Card.Suits.Spades;
        break;
    case "Clubs":
        suit = Card.Suits.Clubs;
        break;
    case "Hearts":
        suit = Card.Suits.Hearts;
        break;
    case "Diamonds":
        suit = Card.Suits.Diamonds;
        break;
    default:
        MessageBox.Show(suitString + " isn't a valid suit!");
}
```

The switch statement starts with a value to compare against. This switch statement is called from a method that has a suit stored in a string.

Each of these **case** lines compares some value against the value in the switch line. If they match, it executes all of the following statements until it hits a **break**.

The **default** line comes at the end. If none of the cases match, the statements after the default get executed instead.

Add an overloaded Deck() constructor that reads a deck of cards in from a file

You can use a switch statement to build a new constructor for the Deck class that you wrote in the last chapter. This constructor reads in a file and checks each line for a card. Any valid card gets added to the deck.

There's a method that you can find on every string that'll come in handy: Split(). It lets you split the string into an array of substrings by passing it a char[] array of separator characters that it'll use to split the string up.

> This line tells C# to split the nextCard string using a space as a separator character. That splits the string "Six of Diamonds" into the array {"Six", "of", "Diamonds"}.

```csharp
public Deck(string Filename) {
    Cards = new List<Card>();
    StreamReader reader = new StreamReader(Filename);
    while (!reader.EndOfStream) {
        bool invalidCard = false;
        string nextCard = reader.ReadLine();
        string[] cardParts = nextCard.Split(new char[] { ' ' });
        Card.Values value = Card.Values.Ace;
        switch (cardParts[0]) {
            case "Ace": value = Card.Values.Ace; break;
            case "Two": value = Card.Values.Two; break;
            case "Three": value = Card.Values.Three; break;
            case "Four": value = Card.Values.Four; break;
            case "Five": value = Card.Values.Five; break;
            case "Six": value = Card.Values.Six; break;
            case "Seven": value = Card.Values.Seven; break;
            case "Eight": value = Card.Values.Eight; break;
            case "Nine": value = Card.Values.Nine; break;
            case "Ten": value = Card.Values.Ten; break;
            case "Jack": value = Card.Values.Jack; break;
            case "Queen": value = Card.Values.Queen; break;
            case "King": value = Card.Values.King; break;
            default: invalidCard = true; break;
        }
        Card.Suits suit = Card.Suits.Clubs;
        switch (cardParts[2]) {
            case "Spades": suit = Card.Suits.Spades; break;
            case "Clubs": suit = Card.Suits.Clubs; break;
            case "Hearts": suit = Card.Suits.Hearts; break;
            case "Diamonds": suit = Card.Suits.Diamonds; break;
            default: invalidCard = true; break;
        }
        if (!invalidCard) {
            Cards.Add(new Card(suit, value));
        }
    }
}
```

> This switch statement checks the first word in the line to see if it matches a value. If it does, the right value is assigned to the value variable.

> We do the same thing for the third word in the line, except we convert this one to a suit.

All that code just to read in one simple card? That's way too much work! What if my object has a whole bunch of fields and values? Are you telling me I need to write a switch statement for each of them?

There's an easier way to store your objects in files. It's called serialization.

Instead of painstakingly writing out each field and value to a file line by line, you can save your object the easy way by serializing it out to a stream. *Serializing* an object is like **flattening it out** so you can slip it into a file. And on the other end, you can *deserialize* it, which is like taking it out of the file and **inflating** it again.

What happens to an object when it's serialized?

It seems like something mysterious has to happen to an object in order to copy it off of the heap and put it into a file, but it's actually pretty straightforward.

1 **Object on the heap**

When you create an instance of an object, it has a **state**. Everything that an object "knows" is what makes one instance of a class different from another instance of the same class.

2 **Object serialized**

When C# serializes an object, it **saves the complete state of the object**, so that an identical instance (object) can be brought back to life on the heap later.

This object has two byte fields, width and height.

The values are sucked out and pumped into the stream.

00100101
01000110

The instance variable values for width and height are saved to the file "file.dat", along with a little more info that the CLR needs to restore the object later (like the type of the object and each of its fields.)

file.dat

Width   Height

Object on the heap again

3 **And later on...**

Later—maybe days later, and in a different program—you can go back to fhe file and **deserialize** it. That pulls the original class back out of the file and restores it **exactly as it was**, with all of its fields and values intact.

But what exactly IS an object's state? What needs to be saved?

We already know that **an object stores its state in its fields**. So when an object is serialized, every one of those those fields needs to be saved to the file.

Serialization starts to get interesting when you have more complicated objects. 37 and 70 are bytes—those are value types, so they can just be written out to a file as-is. But what if an object has an instance variable that's an object *reference*? What about an object that has five instance variables that are object references? What if those object instance variables themselves have instance variables?

Think about it for a minute. What part of an object is potentially unique? Imagine what needs to be restored in order to get an object that's identical to the one that was saved. Somehow everything on the heap has to be written to the file.

BRAIN BARBELL

What has to happen for this Car object to be saved so that it gets restored back to its original state? Let's say the car has three passengers and a 3-liter engine and all-weather radial tires... aren't those things are part of the state? What should happen to them?

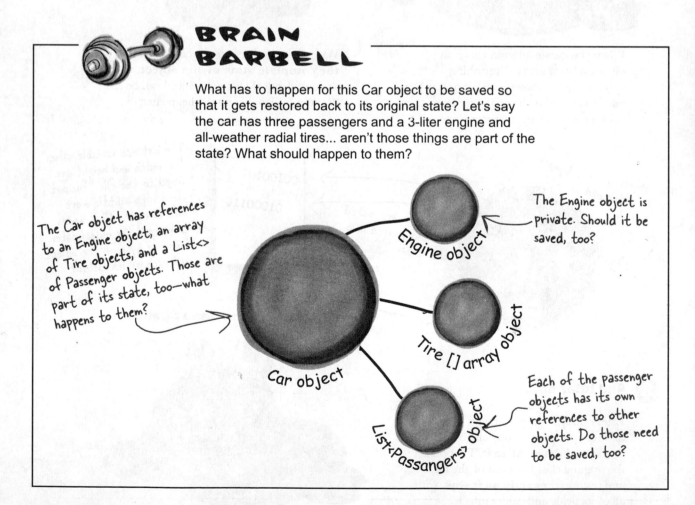

The Car object has references to an Engine object, an array of Tire objects, and a List<> of Passenger objects. Those are part of its state, too—what happens to them?

Car object

Engine object

The Engine object is private. Should it be saved, too?

Tire [] array object

List<Passangers> object

Each of the passenger objects has its own references to other objects. Do those need to be saved, too?

When an object is serialized, all of the objects it refers to get serialized too...

...and all of the objects *they* refer to, and all of the objects *those other objects* refer to, and so on and so on. But don't worry—it may sound complicated, but it all happens automatically. C# starts with the object you want to serialize and looks through its fields for other objects. Then it does the same for each of them. Every single object gets written out to the file, along with all the information C# needs to reconstitute it all when the object gets deserialized.

Some people call this whole group of connected objects a "graph."

When you ask C# to serialize the Kennel object, it looks for any field that has a reference to another object.

"Fido"

DoggyID object

Breed.Beagle
4 years old
32 pounds
14" tall

Collar object

Kennel object

Dog object

One of the fields of the Kennel object is this List<Dog> that contains two Dog objects, so C# will need to serialize them, too.

List<Dog> object

Each of the two Dog objects has references to a DoggyID object and a Collar object. They'll need to get serialized along with each Dog.

"Spike"

DoggyID object

Breed.Mutt
6 years old
18 pounds
11" tall

Collar object

Dog object

DoggyID and Collar are the end of the line—they don't have references to any other objects.

Serialization lets you read or write a whole object all at once

You're not just limited to reading and writing lines of text to your files. You can use **serialization** to let your programs copy entire objects to files and read them back in... all in just a few lines of code! There's a tiny amount of prep work you need to do—add one [Serializable] line to the top of the class to serialize—but once you do that, everything's ready to write.

It's quick to copy an object out to a file or read it in from one. You can serialize or deserialize it.

You'll need a BinaryFormatter object

If you want to serialize an object—*any* object—the first thing you do is create an instance of BinaryFormatter. It's really straightforward to do—and all it takes is one line of code (and an extra using line at the top of the class file).

```
using System.Runtime.Serialization.Formatters.Binary;
...
BinaryFormatter formatter = new BinaryFormatter();
```

Now just create a stream and read or write your objects

The File.Create() method creates a new file. You can open an existing one using File.OpenWrite().

Use the **Serialize()** method from the BinaryFormatter object to write any object out to a stream.

```
Stream output = File.Create(filenameString);
formatter.Serialize(output, objectToSerialize);
output.Close();
```

If you use a using statement, Close() will be called automatically.

The Serialize() method takes an object and writes it out to a stream. That's a whole lot easier than building a method to write it out yourself!

And once you've got an object serialized out to a file, use the BinaryFormatter object's **Deserialize()** method to read it back in. The method returns a reference, so you need to cast the output so that it matches the type of the reference variable you're copying it to.

```
Stream input = File.OpenRead(filenameString);
SomeObj obj = (SomeObj)formatter.Deserialize(input);
input.Close();
```

When you use Deserialize() to read an object back from a stream, don't forget to cast the return value to match the type of object you're reading.

If you want your class to be serializable, mark it with the [Serializable] attribute

An **attribute** is a special tag that you can add to the top of any C# class. It's how C# stores **metadata** about your code, or information about how the code should be used or treated. When you **add [Serializable] to the top of a class just above the class declaration**, you're telling C# that your class is safe for serialization. And you only use it with classes that include fields that are either value types (like an int, string, or enum) or other serializable classes. If you don't add the attribute to the class you want to serialize, or if you include a field with a type that isn't serializable, then your program will have an error when you try to run it. *See for yourself...*

Do this

① **Create a class and serialize it**

Remember the Guy Class from Chapter 3? Let's serialize Joe so we can keep a file that knows how much money he's got in his pockets even after you close your program.

```
[Serializable]
public class Guy
```

Here's code to serialize it to a file called "Guy_file.dat"—add a "Save Joe" button and a "Load Joe" button to the Form

```
using System.IO;
using System.Runtime.Serialization.Formatters.Binary;
...

private void saveJoe_Click(object sender, EventArgs e)
{
  using (Stream output = File.Create("Guy_File.dat")) {
    BinaryFormatter formatter = new BinaryFormatter();
    formatter.Serialize(output, Joe);
  }
}
private void loadJoe_Click(object sender, EventArgs e)
{
  using (Stream input = File.OpenRead("Guy_File.dat")) {
    BinaryFormatter bf = new BinaryFormatter();
    Joe = (Guy)bf.Deserialize(input);
  };
  CheckGuys();
}
```

You'll need these two using lines. The first one is for the file and stream methods, and the second is for serialization.

② **Run the program and play around with it.**

If Joe had two hundred dollars saved up from his transactions with Bob during your time running the program, it would be a pain to lose all that money just because you needed to exit. Now your program can save Joe out to a file and restore him whenever you want.

Let's serialize and deserialize a deck of cards

Take a deck of cards and write it out to a file. C# makes
serializing objects really easy. All you need to do is
create a stream and write out your objects.

Do this

❶ Create a new project and add the Deck and Card classes

Right-click on the project in the Solution Explorer and choose "Add/Existing Item", and add the
Card and Deck classes you created in Chapter 7. You'll also need to add the two card comparer
classes, since Deck uses them. The IDE will copy the files into the new project—make sure you
change the namespace line at the top of each class file to match your new project's namespace.

❷ Mark all of the classes serializable

Add the [Serializable] attribute to all of the classes you added to
the project.

> If you don't do
> this, C# won't let
> you serialize the
> classes to a file.

❸ Add a couple of useful methods to the form

The RandomDeck method creates a random deck of cards, and the
PrintCards method deals all of the cards and prints them to the console.

```
Random random = new Random();
private Deck RandomDeck(int Number) {
    Deck myDeck = new Deck(new Card[] { });
    for (int i = 0; i < Number; i++)
    {
        myDeck.Add(new Card(
            (Card.Suits)random.Next(4),
            (Card.Values)random.Next(1, 14)));
    }
    return myDeck;
}

private void DealCards(Deck DeckToDeal, string Title) {
    Console.WriteLine(Title);
    while (DeckToDeal.Count > 0)
    {
        Card nextCard = DeckToDeal.Deal();
        Console.WriteLine(nextCard.Name);
    }
    Console.WriteLine("-------------------");
}
```

> This creates an empty
> deck and then adds some
> random cards to it using
> the Card class from the
> last chapter.

> The DealCards()
> method deals each of
> the cards off of the
> deck and prints it to
> the console.

4 **Okay, prep work's done.. now serialize that deck**

Start by adding buttons to serialize a random deck to a file and read it back. Check the console output to make sure the deck you wrote out is the same as the deck you read.

```
private void button1_Click(object sender, EventArgs e) {
    Deck deckToWrite = RandomDeck(5);
    using (Stream output = File.Create("Deck1.dat")) {
        BinaryFormatter bf = new BinaryFormatter();
        bf.Serialize(output, deckToWrite);
    }
    DealCards(deckToWrite, "What I just wrote to the file");
}

private void button2_Click(object sender, EventArgs e) {
    using (Stream input = File.OpenRead("Deck1.dat")) {
        BinaryFormatter bf = new BinaryFormatter();
        Deck deckFromFile = (Deck)bf.Deserialize(input);
    }
    DealCards(deckFromFile, "What I read from the file");
}
```

The BinaryFormatter object takes any object marked with the Serializable attribute—in this case a Deck object—and writes it out to a stream using its Serialize() method.

The BinaryFormatter's Deserialize() method returns an Object, which is just the general type that every C# object inherits from—which is why we need to cast it to a Deck object.

5 **Now serialize a bunch of decks to the same file**

Once you open a stream, you can write as much as you want to it. You can serialize as many objects as you need into the same file. So now add two more buttons to write out a random number of decks to the file. Check the output to make sure everything looks good.

```
private void button3_Click(object sender, EventArgs e) {
    using (Stream output = File.Create("Deck1.dat")) {
        BinaryFormatter bf = new BinaryFormatter();
        for (int i = 1; i <= 5; i++) {
            Deck deckToWrite = RandomDeck(random.Next(1,10));
            bf.Serialize(output, deckToWrite);
            DealCards(deckToWrite, "Deck #" + i + " written");
        }
    }
}

private void button4_Click(object sender, EventArgs e) {
    using (Stream input = File.OpenRead("Deck1.dat")) {
        BinaryFormatter bf = new BinaryFormatter();
        for (int i = 1; i <= 5; i++) {
            Deck deckToRead = (Deck)bf.Deserialize(input);
            DealCards(deckToRead, "Deck #" + i + " read");
        }
    }
}
```

You can serialize one object after another to the same stream.

Notice how the line that reads a single deck from the file uses (Deck) to cast the output of Deserialize() to a Deck. That's because Deserialize() returns an object, but doesn't necessarily know what type of object.

As long as you cast the objects you read off the stream to the right type, there's no limit to the number of objects you can serialize.

6 **Take a look at the file you wrote**

Open up Deck1.dat in Notepad. It may not be quite something you'd read on the beach, but it's got all the information to restore your whole deck of cards.

> Wait a minute. I'm not sure I like all this writing objects out to some weird file that looks like garbage when I open it up. When I wrote the deck of cards as strings, I could open up the output in Notepad and see everything in it. Isn't C# supposed to make it easy for me to understand everything I'm doing?

When you serialize objects out to a file, they're written in a binary format.

But that doesn't mean it's indecipherable—just compact. That's why you can recognize the strings when you open up a file with serialized objects in it: that's the most compact way C# can write strings to a file—as strings. But writing out a number as a string would be really wasteful. Any `int` can be stored in four bytes. So it would be odd if C# stored, say, the number 49,369,144 as an 8-character string that you could read—10 characters if you include commas. That would be a waste of space!

Behind the Scenes

.NET uses **Unicode** to encode a char or string into bytes. Luckily, Windows has a useful little tool to help us figure out how unicode works. Open up the Character Map (it's in the Start menu under Accessories, or do Start / Run and type "charmap.exe").

When you look at all the letters and symbols that are used in languages all around the world, you realize just how many different *things* need to be written to a file just to store text. That's why .NET **encodes** all of its strings and characters in a format called Unicode. Encoding just means taking the logical data (like the letter H) and turning it into bytes (the number 72). It needs to do that because letters, numbers, enums and other data all end up in bytes on disk or in memory. And that's why Character Map's useful—it shows you how letters are encoded into numbers.

Select the Arial font and scroll down until you reach the Hebrew letters. Find the letter Shin and click on it.

As soon as you click on the letter, its Unicode number shows up in the status bar. The Hebrew letter Shin is number 05E9. That's a hexadecimal number—"hex" for short.

You can convert it to decimal using the Windows calculator: open it up, put it in Scientific mode, click the "Hex" radio button, enter "05E9", and then click "Dec"—it's 1,513.

Unicode is an industry standard developed by a non-profit group called the Unicode Consortium, and it works across programs and different computer platforms. Take a minute and look at their website: http://www.unicode.org/

.NET converts text to Unicode automatically

The two C# value types for storing text—string and char—keep their data in
memory as Unicode. When that data's written out as bytes to a file, each of those
Unicode numbers is written out to the file. So start a new project and drag three
buttons onto a form, and we'll use the File.WriteAllBytes() and ReadAllBytes() methods
to get a sense of exactly how Unicode data is written out to a file.

Do this!

① **Write a normal string out to a file and read it back**

Use the same WriteAllText() method that you used in the text editor to have the first button
write the string "Eureka!" out to a file called "eureka.txt". Then create a new byte array called
eurekaBytes, read the file into it, and then print out all of the bytes read:

```
File.WriteAllText("eureka.txt", "Eureka!");
byte[] eurekaBytes = File.ReadAllBytes("eureka.txt");
foreach (byte b in eurekaBytes)
    Console.Write("{0} ", b);
Console.WriteLine();
```

The ReadAllBytes() method returns a reference to a new array of bytes that contains all of the bytes that were read in from the file.

You'll see these bytes written to the output: 69 117 114 101 107 97 33. Now **open up the
file in the Simple Text Editor** that you wrote earlier in the chapter. It says "Eureka!"

② **Make the second button display the bytes as hex numbers**

It's not just Character Map that shows numbers in hex. Almost anything you read that has to do
with encoding data will show that data in hex, so it's useful to know how to work with it. Make
the code for second button's event handler in your program **identical to the first one**, except
change the Console.Write() line so it looks like this instead:

```
Console.Write("{0:x2} ", b);
```

Hex uses the numbers 0 through 9 and letters A through F to represent numbers in base 16, so 6B is equal to 107.

That tells Write() to print parameter #0 (the first one after the string to print) as a two-character
hex code. So it writes the same seven bytes in hex instead of decimal: 45 75 72 65 6b 61 21

③ **Make the third button write out Hebrew letters**

Go back to Character Map and double-click on the Shin character (or click the Select button). It'll add
it to the "Characters to copy" box. Then do the same for the rest of the letters in "Shalom": Lamed
(U+05DC), Vav (U+05D5), and Final Mem (U+05DD). Now add the code for the third button's event
handler. It'll look exactly like button 2, except for one change. Click the "Copy" button in Character
Map, and then paste the letters over "Eureka!" so it looks like this:

```
File.WriteAllText("eureka.txt", "שלום");
```

Did you notice that the IDE pasted the letters in **backwards**? That's because it knows that Hebrew is
read right-to-left, so any time it encounters Hebrew Unicode letters, it displays them right-to-left. Put
your cursor in the middle of the letters—the left and right arrow keys reversed! That makes it a lot easier
if you need to type in Hebrew. Now run the code, and look closely at the output: ff fe e9 05 dc 05
d5 05 dd 05. The first two characters are "FF FE", which is the Unicode way of saying that we're
going to have a string of two-byte characters. The rest of the bytes are the Hebrew letters—but they're
reversed, so U+05E9 appears as **e9 05**. Now open the file up in your Simple Text Editor—it looks right!

C# can use byte arrays to move data around

Since all your data ends up encoded as **bytes**, then it makes sense to think of a file as one **big byte array**. And you already know how to read and write byte arrays.

Here's the code to create a byte array, open an input stream, and read data into bytes 0 through 6 of the array.

Hello!!

```
byte[] greeting;
greeting = File.ReadAllBytes(filename);
```

7 byte variables

0	1	2	3	4	5	6
72	101	108	108	111	33	33

These numbers are the Unicode numbers for the characters in "Hello!!"

This is a static method for Arrays that reverses the order of the bytes. We're just using it to show that the changes you make to the byte array get written out to the file exactly.

```
Array.Reverse(greeting);
File.WriteAllBytes(filename, greeting);
```

When the program writes the byte array out to a file, the text is in reverse order too.

!!olleH

7 byte variables

0	1	2	3	4	5	6
33	33	111	108	108	101	72

Now the bytes are in reverse order.

Use a BinaryWriter to write binary data

You *could* encode all of your strings, chars, ints, and floats into byte arrays before
writing them out to files, but that would get pretty tedious. That's why .NET gives you
a very useful class called **BinaryWriter** that **automatically encodes your data**
and writes it to a file. All you need to do is create a FileStream and pass it into the
BinaryWriter's constructor. Then you can call its methods to write out your data. So add
another button to your program, and we'll show you how to use BinaryWriter().

Do this!

1 Start by setting up some data to write to a file.

```
int intValue = 48769414;
string stringValue = "Hello!";
byte[] byteArray = { 47, 129, 0, 116 };
float floatValue = 491.695F;
char charValue = 'E';
```

> If you use File.Create(), it'll start a new file—if there's one there already, it'll blow it away and start a brand new one. There's also the File.OpenWrite() method, which opens the existing one and starts overwriting it from the beginning.

2 To use a BinaryWriter, first you need to open a new stream with File.Create():

```
using (FileStream output = File.Create("binarydata.dat")) {
    BinaryWriter writer = new BinaryWriter(output);
```

3 Now just call its Write() method. Each time you do, it adds new bytes onto the end of the file
that contain an encoded version of whatever data you passed it as a parameter.

```
writer.Write(intValue);
writer.Write(stringValue);
writer.Write(byteArray);
writer.Write(floatValue);
writer.Write(charValue);
```

> Each Write() statement encodes one value into bytes, and then sends those bytes to the FileStream object. You can pass it any value type, and it'll encode it automatically.

> The FileStream writes the bytes to the end of the file.

Sharpen your pencil

4 Now use the same code you used before to read in the file you just wrote.

```
byte[] dataWritten = File.ReadAllBytes("binarydata.dat");
foreach (byte b in dataWritten)
    Console.Write("{0:x2} ", b);
Console.WriteLine(" - {0} bytes", dataWritten.Length);

}
```

> Here's a hint: Strings can be different lengths, so the string has to start with a number to tell .NET how long it is. Also, you can look up the string and char Unicode values using Character Map.

Write down the output in the blanks below. Can you **figure out what bytes
correspond** to each of the five Write() statements? Mark each group of bytes with
the name of the variable.

_ - __ bytes

float and int values take up four bytes when
you write them to a file. If you'd used long or
double, then they'd take up eight bytes each.

Sharpen your pencil
Solution

86 29 e8 02 06 48 65 6c 6c 6f 21 2f 81 00 74 f6 d8 f5 43 45 - 20 bytes

intValue   stringValue   byteArray   floatValue   charValue

The first byte in the string is 6—that's
the length of the string. You can use
Character Map to look up each of the
characters in "Hello!"—it starts with
U+0048 and ends with U+0021.

If you use the Windows
calculator to convert these
bytes from hex to decimal, you
can see that these are the
numbers in byteArray.

char holds a Unicode
character, and 'E' only
takes one byte—it's
encoded as U+0045.

Use BinaryReader to read the data back in

The BinaryReader class works just like BinaryWriter. You create a stream,
attach the BinaryReader object to it, and then call its methods. But the reader
doesn't know what data's in the file! And it has no way of knowing.
Your float value of 491.695F was encoded as d8 f5 43 45. But those
same bytes are a perfectly valid int—1,140,185,334. So you'll need to tell the
BinaryReader exactly what types to read from the file. Add one more button
to your form, and have it read the data you just wrote.

Don't take our word for it.
Replace the line that reads the
float with a call to ReadInt32().
(You'll need to change the type
of floatRead to int.) Then you
can see for yourself what it
reads from the file.

1 Start out by setting up the FileStream and BinaryReader objects:

```
using (FileStream input = File.OpenRead("binarydata.dat")) {
    BinaryReader reader = new BinaryReader(input);
```

2 You tell BinaryReader what type of data to read by calling its different methods.

```
int intRead = reader.ReadInt32();
string stringRead = reader.ReadString();
byte[] byteArrayRead = reader.ReadBytes(4);
float floatRead = reader.ReadSingle();
char charRead = reader.ReadChar();
}
```

Each value type has its own method in
BinaryReader() that returns the data
in the correct type. Most don't need
any parameters, but ReadBytes() takes
one parameter that tells BinaryReader
how many bytes to read.

3 You tell BinaryReader what type of data to read by calling its different methods.

```
Console.Write("int: {0}  string: {1}  bytes: ", intRead, stringRead);
foreach (byte b in byteArrayRead)
    Console.Write("{0} ", b);
Console.Write(" float: {0}  char: {1} ", floatRead, charRead);
```

Here's the output that gets printed to the console:

```
int: 48769414  string: Hello!  bytes: 47 129 0 116  float: 491.695  char: E
```

You can read and write serialized files manually, too

Serialized files don't look so pretty when you open them up in Notepad. You'll find all the files you write in your project's "bin/Debug" folder—let's take a minute and get more acquainted to the inner workings of a serialized file.

Do this!

1 **Serialize two Card objects to different files**

Use the serialization code you've already written to serialize the **Three of Clubs** to card1.dat and **Six of Hearts** to card2.dat. Check to make sure that both files were written out and are now in a folder, and that they both have the same file size. Then open one of them in Notepad:

There are some words in the file (like "Chapter9", which was the namespace we used), but it's mostly unreadable.

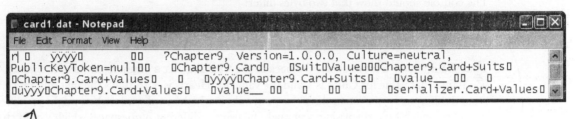

```
card1.dat - Notepad
File  Edit  Format  View  Help
r|          yyyy              ?Chapter9, Version=1.0.0.0, Culture=neutral,
PublicKeyToken=null    Chapter9.Card    SuitValueChapter9.Card+Suits
Chapter9.Card+Values        yyyyChapter9.Card+Suits     value__
üyyyyChapter9.Card+Values    value__                     serializer.Card+Values
```

2 **Write a loop to compare the two binary files**

We used the ReadByte() method to read the next byte from a stream—it returns an int that contains the value of that byte. We also used the stream's Length field to make sure we read the whole file.

```
byte[] firstFile = File.ReadAllBytes("card1.dat");
byte[] secondFile = File.ReadAllBytes("card2.dat");
for (int i = 0; i < firstFile.Length; i++)
    if (firstFile[i] != secondFile[i])
        Console.WriteLine("Byte #{0}: {1} versus {2}",
            i, firstFile[i], secondFile[i]);
```

This loop examines the first byte from each of the files and compares them, then the second byte, then the third, etc. When it finds a difference, it writes a line to the console.

The two files are read into two different byte arrays, so they can be compared byte by byte. Since the same class was serialized to two different files, they'll be almost identical... but let's see just HOW identical they are.

Watch it!

When you write to a file, you don't always start from a clean slate!

Be careful if you use File.OpenWrite(). It doesn't delete the file—it just starts overwriting the data starting at the beginning. That's why we've been using File.Create()—it creates a new file.

⟶ We're not done yet—flip the page!

Find where the files differ, and use that information to alter them

The loop you just wrote pinpoints exactly where the two serialized
Card files differ. Since the only difference between the two objects
were their Suit and Value fields, then that should be the only difference
in their files, too. So if we find the bytes that hold the suit and value,
we should be able to **change them to make a new card** with
whatever suit and value we want!

③ Take a look at the console output to see how the two files differ

The console should show that two bytes differ:

```
Byte #218: 1 versus 3
Byte #266: 3 versus 6
```

That should make a lot of sense! Go back to the `Card.Suits` enum from the last chapter, and
you'll find that value for Clubs is 1 and the value for Hearts is 3, so that's the first difference. And the
second difference—six versus three—is pretty obviously the card's value. You might see different byte
numbers, which isn't surprising: you might be using a different namespace, which would change the
length of the file.

*Remember how the namespace was included as part
of the serialized file? If your namespace is different,
then the byte numbers will be different too.*

*Hmm, if byte #218 in the serialized file
represents the suit, then we should be able to
change the suit of the card by reading that file
in, changing that one byte, and writing it out
again. (Remember, your own serialized file might
store the suit at a different location.)*

④ Write code to manually create a new file that contains King of Spades

We'll take one of the arrays that we read, alter it to contain a new card, and write it back out.

*If you found
different
byte numbers
in step #3,
substitute
them in here.*

```
firstFile[227] = (byte)Card.Suits.Spades;
firstFile[275] = (byte)Card.Values.King;
File.Delete("card3.dat");
File.WriteAllBytes("card3.dat", firstFile);
```

Now **deserialize the card from card3.dat** and see if it's the King of Spades!

*Now that you know which bytes
contain the suit and value, you
can change just those bytes
in the array before it gets
written out to card3.dat.*

Working with binary files can be tricky

What do you do if you have a file and you aren't quite sure what's inside it? You don't know what application created it, and you need to know something about it—but when you open it in Notepad, it looks like a bunch of garbage. What if you'd exhausted all your other options, and really needed to just look inside? Looking at that picture, it's pretty clear that Notepad just isn't the right tool.

Here's the serialized card, opened up in Notepad. That's not going to be useful at all.

You can make out a few things—like the enum names ("Suit" and "Value"), and the name of the namespace we used ("Chapter9"). But that's not all that helpful.

There's another option—it's a format called a "hex dump", and it's a pretty standard way to look at binary data. It's definitely more informative than looking at the file in Notepad. Hexadecimal—or "hex"—is a convenient way to display bytes in a file. Every byte takes 2 characters to display in hex, so you can see a lot of data in a really small space, and a format that makes it easy to spot patterns. Also, it's useful to display binary data in rows that are 8, 16, or 32 bytes long because most binary data tends to break down in chunks of 4, 8, 16, or 32...like all the types in C#. For example, an `int` takes up 4 bytes, and is 4 bytes long when serialized on disk. Here's what that same file looks like as a hex dump, using one of any number of free hex dump programs available for Windows:

You can immediately see the numeric value of each byte in the file.

The number at the beginning of each line is the offset (or distance into the file) of the first byte in the line.

You still get to see the original text, but the garbage characters are stripped out.

Use file streams to build a hex dumper

A **hex dump** is a *hexadecimal* view of the contents of a file, and it's
a really common way for programmers to take a deep look at a file's
internal structure. Most operating systems ship with a built-in hex
dump utility. Unfortunately, Windows doesn't. So let's build one!

How to make a hex dump

Start with some familiar text:

    We the people of the United States, in order to form a more perfect union...

Here's what a hex dump of that text would look like:

Again, you can immediately see the numeric value of each byte in the file.

```
0000: 57 65 20 74 68 65 (20) 70 -- 65 6f 70 6c 65 20 6f 66    We the people of
0010: 20 74 68 65 20 55 6e 69 -- 74 65 64 20 53 74 61 74     the United Stat
0020: 65 73 2c 20 69 6e 20 6f -- 72 64 65 72 20 74 6f 20    es, in order to
0030: 66 6f 72 6d 20 61 20 6d -- 6f 72 65 20 70 65 72 66    form a more perf
0040: 65 63 74 20 75 6e 69 6f -- 6e 2e 2e 2e                 ect union...
```

And we'll need to replace the garbage characters with periods.

We'll add the number at the beginning of each line by using the offset of the first byte in the line.

Each of those numbers—57, 65, 6F—is the value of one byte in the file. The reason some of the "numbers"
have letter values is that they're *hexadecimal* (or hex). That's just another way of writing a number. Instead of
using ten digits from 0 to 9, it uses sixteen digits from 0 to 9 plus the letters A through F.

Each line in our hex dump represents sixteen characters in the input that was used to generate it. In our
dump, the first four characters are the offset in the file—the first line starts at character 0, the next at
character 16 (or hex 10), then character 32 (hex 20), etc. (Other hex dumps look slightly different, but this
one will do for us.)

Working with hex

You can put hex numbers directly into your program—just add the
characters 0x in front of the number:

```
int j = 0x20;
MessageBox.Show("The value is " + j);
```

When you use the + operator to concatenate a number into a
string, it gets converted to decimal. You can use the static String.
Format() method to convert your number to a hex-formatted
string instead:

String.Format() uses parameters just lke Console.WriteLine(), so you don't need to learn anything new to use it.

```
string h = String.Format("{0:x2}", j);
```

StreamReader and StreamWriter will do just fine

Our hex dumper will write its dump out to a file, and since it's just writing text a StreamWriter will do just fine. But we can also take advantage of the **ReadBlock()** method in StreamReader. It reads a block of characers into a `char` array—you specify the number of characters you want to read, and it'll either read that many characters or, if there are fewer than that many left in the file, it'll read the rest of the file. Since we're displaying 16 characters per line we'll read blocks of 16 characters.

So add one more button to your program—add this hex dumper to it. Change the first two lines so that they point to real files on your hard drive. Start with a serialized Card file. Then see if you can modify it to use the Open and Save As dialog boxes.

```
using (StreamReader reader = new StreamReader(@"c:\files\inputFile.txt"))
using (StreamWriter writer = new StreamWriter(@"c:\files\outputFile.txt", false))
{
  int position = 0;

  while (!reader.EndOfStream) {
    char[] buffer = new char[16];
    int charactersRead = reader.ReadBlock(buffer, 0, 16);
    writer.Write("{0}: ", String.Format("{0:x4}", position));
    position += charactersRead;

    for (int i = 0; i < 16; i++) {
      if (i < charactersRead) {
        string hex = String.Format("{0:x2}", (byte)buffer[i]);
        writer.Write(hex + " ");
      }
      else
        writer.Write("   ");

      if (i == 7) { writer.Write("-- "); }
      if (buffer[i] < 32 || buffer[i] > 250) { buffer[i] = '.'; }
    }
    string bufferContents = new string(buffer);
    writer.WriteLine("   " + bufferContents.Substring(0, charactersRead));
  }
}
```

A StreamReader's EndofStream field returns false if there are characters still left to read in the file.

This ReadBlock() call reads up to 16 characters into a char array.

The static String.Format method converts numbers to strings. "{0:x4}" tells Format() to print the second parameter—in this case, position—as a 4-character hex number.

This loop goes through the characters and prints each of them to a line in the output.

Some characters with an value under 32 don't print, so we'll replace all of them with a period.

You can convert a char[] array to a string by passing it to the overloaded constructor for string.

Every string has a substring method that returns a piece of the string. In this case, it returns the first charactersRead characters starting at the beginning (position 0). (Look back at the top of the loop to see where charactersRead is set—the ReadBlock() method returns the number of characters that it read into the array.

there are no
Dumb Questions

Q: Why didn't I have to use the `Close()` method to close the file after I used `File.ReadAllText()` and `File.WriteAllText()`?

A: The `File` class has several very useful static methods that automatically open up a file, read or write data, and then **close it automatically**. In addition to the `ReadAllText()` and `WriteAllText()` methods, there are `ReadAllBytes()` and `WriteAllBytes()` that work with byte arrays, and `ReadAllLines()` and `WriteAllLines()`, which read and write string arrays, where each string in the array is a separate line in the file. All of these methods automatically open and close the streams, so you can do your whole file operation in a single statement.

Q: If the `FileStream` has methods for reading and writing, why do I ever need to use `StreamReader` and `StreamWriter`?

A: The `FileStream` class is really useful for reading and writing bytes to binary files. Its methods for reading and writing operate with bytes and byte arrays. But a lot of programs work exclusively with text files—like the first version of the Excuse Generator, which only wrote strings out to files. That's where the `StreamReader` and `StreamWriter` come in really handy. They have methods that are built specifically for reading and writing lines of text. Without them, if you wanted to read a line of text in from a file, you'd have to first read a byte array and then write a loop to search through that array for a linebreak—so it's easy to see how they make your life easier.

Q: When should I use `File`, and when should I use `FileInfo`?

A: The main difference between the `File` and `FileInfo` classes is that the methods in `File` are static, so you don't need to create an instance of them. On the other hand, `FileInfo` requires that you instantiate it with a filename. In some cases, that would be more cumbersome, like if you only need to perform a single file operation (like just deleting or moving one file). On the other hand, if you need to do many file operations to the same file, then it's more efficient to use `FileInfo`, because you only need to pass it the filename once. You should decide which one to use based on the particular situation you encounter. In other words, if you're doing one file operation, use File. If you're doing a lot of file operations in a row, use FileInfo.

Q: Back up a minute. Why was "Eureka!" written out with one byte per character, but when I wrote out the Hebrew letters they took up two bytes? And what was that "FF FE" thing at the beginning of the bytes?

A: What you're seeing is the difference between two **closely related** Unicode encodings. Plain English letters, numbers, normal punctuation marks, and some standard characters (like curly brackets, ampersands, and other things you see on your keyboard) all have very low Unicode numbers—between 0 and 127. (If you've used ASCII before, they're the same as the ASCII characters.) If a file only contains those Unicode characters with low numbers, it just prints out their bytes.

Things get a little more complicated when you add higher-numbered Unicode characters into the mix. One byte can only hold a number between 0 and 255. But two bytes in a row can store numbers between 0 and 65,536—which, in hex, is FFFF. The file needs to be able to tell whatever program opens it up that it's going to contain these higher-numbered characters. So it puts a special reserved byte sequence at the beginning of the file: "FF FE". That's called the "byte order mark". As soon as a program sees that, it knows that all of the characters are encoded with two bytes each. (So an E is encoded as 00 45—with leading zeroes.)

Q: Why is it called a byte order mark?

A: Remember how your bytes were reversed? Shin's Unicode value of U+05E9 was written to the file as E9 05. That's called "little endian". Go back to the code that wrote out those bytes and add a third parameter to WriteAllText(): Encoding.BigEndianUnicode. That tells it to write the data out in "big endian", which doesn't flip the bytes around. You'll see the bytes come out as "05 E9" this time. You'll also see a different byte order mark: "FE FF". And your Simple Text Editor is smart enough to read both of them!

> If you're writing a string that only has Unicode characters with low numbers, it writes one byte per character. But if it's got high-numbered characters, they'll be written using two bytes each.

ExeRcise

Change Brian's Excuse Generator so it uses binary files with serialized Excuse objects instead of text files.

① **Make the Excuse class serializable**

Mark the Excuse class with the [Serializable] attribute to make it serializable. Also, you'll need to add the using line:

```
using System.Runtime.Serialization.Formatters.Binary;
```

② **Change the Excuse.Save() method to serialize the excuse**

When the Save() method writes a file out to the folder, instead of using StreamWriter to write the file out, have it open a file and serialize itself out. You'll need to figure out how the current class can deserialize itself.

Hint: What keyword can you use inside of a class that returns a reference to itself?

③ **Change the Excuse.OpenFile() method to deserialize an excuse**

You'll need to create a temporary Excuse object to deserialize from the file, and then copy its fields into the current class.

④ **Now just change the form so it uses a new file extension**

There's just one very small change you need to make to the form. Since we're no longer working with text files, we shouldn't use the `.txt` extension any more. Change the dialog boxes, default filenames and directory search code so that they work with `*.excuse` files instead.

---

o O

Wow, that was really easy! All the code for saving and opening excuses was inside the Excuse class. I just had to change the class—I barely had to touch the form at all. It's like the form doesn't even care how the class saves its data. It just passes in the filename and knows everything will get saved properly.

That's right! Your code was very easy to change because the class was well encapsulated.

When you've got a class that hides its internal operations from the rest of the program and only exposes the behavior that needs to be exposed, it's called a **well encapsulated class**. In the Excuse Manager program, the form doesn't have any information about how excuses are saved to files. It just passes a filename into the excuse class, and the class takes care of the rest. That makes it very easy to make big changes to how your class works with files. The better you encapsulate your classes, the easier they are to alter later on.

Remember how encapsulation was one of the four core OOP principles? Here's an example of how using those principles makes your programs better.

Exercise Solution

Change Brian's Excuse Generator so it uses binary files with serialized
Excuse objects instead of text files.

You only need to change these four lines in the form:
two lines in the save button's Click event, and two in
the open button's—they just change the dialogs to use
the .excuse extension.

```
private void save_Click(object sender, EventArgs e) {
    // existing code
    saveFileDialog1.Filter = "Excuse files (*.excuse)|*.excuse|All files (*.*)|*.*";
    saveFileDialog1.FileName = description.Text + ".excuse";
    // existing code
}
private void save_Click(object sender, EventArgs e) {
    // existing code
    openFileDialog1.Filter =
        "Excuse files (*.excuse)|*.excuse|All files (*.*)|*.*";
    openFileDialog1.FileName = description.Text + ".excuse";
    // existing code
}
```

Standard save and
open dialog boxes do
the trick here.

The only change to the form
is to have it change the file
extension it passes to the
Excuse class.

```
[Serializable]
public class Excuse {
    public string Description;
    public string Results;
    public DateTime LastUsed;
    public string ExcusePath;

    public Excuse() {
        ExcusePath = "";
    }
    public Excuse(string excusePath) {
        OpenFile(ExcusePath);
    }
    public Excuse(Random random, string folder) {
        string[] fileNames = Directory.GetFiles(folder, "*.excuse");
        OpenFile(fileNames[random.Next(fileNames.Length)]);
    }
    private void OpenFile(string excusePath) {
        this.ExcusePath = excusePath;
        BinaryFormatter formatter = new BinaryFormatter();
        Excuse tempExcuse;
        using (Stream input = File.OpenRead(excusePath)) {
            tempExcuse = (Excuse)formatter.Deserialize(input);
        }
        Description = tempExcuse.Description;
        Results = tempExcuse.Results;
        LastUsed = tempExcuse.LastUsed;
    }

    public void Save(string fileName) {
        BinaryFormatter formatter = new BinaryFormatter();
        using (Stream output = File.OpenWrite(fileName)) {
            formatter.Serialize(output, this);
        }
    }
}
```

The constructor for loading
random excuses needs to look
for the ".excuse" extension
instead of "*.txt" files.

We pass in "this"
because we want this
class to be serialized.

Filecross

Across

6. The method in the File class that checks whether or not a specific file is on the drive

9. This statement indicates the end of a case inside a switch statement

10. The abstract class that FileStream inherits from

11. A non-visual control that lets you pop up the standard Windows "Save As" dialog box

15. How you write numbers in base-16

16. If you don't call this method, your stream could be locked open so other methods or programs can't open it

17. The StreamReader method that reads data into a char[] array

18. An encoding system that assigns a uniue number to each character

19. Use this statement to indicate which statements should be executed when the value being tested in a switch statement does not match any of the cases

Down

1. This class has a method that writes any value type to a file

2. The static method in the Array class that turns an array backwards

3. The event handler that gets run whenever someone modifies the data in an input control

4. This class has many static methods that let you manipulate folders

5. Using this OOP principle makes it a lot easier to maintain your code

7. If you don't use this attribute to indicate that a class can be written to a stream, BinaryFormatter will generate an error

8. This BinaryFormatter method reads an object from a stream

12. \n and \r are examples of this kind of sequence

13. This class lets you perform all the operations in the File class for a specific file

14. This method sends text to a stream followed by a line break

Filecross solution

The crossword grid solution:

Across:
- 6. EXIST
- 9. BREAK
- 10. STREAM
- 11. SAVEFILE
- 12. DIALOG
- 15. HEXADECIMAL
- 16. CLOSE
- 17. READBLOCK
- 18. UNICODE
- 19. DEFAULT

Down:
- 1. BINARY
- 2. REVERSE
- 3. CHANGE
- 4. DIRECTORY
- 5. ENCAPSULATION
- 7. SERIALIZABLE
- 8. DESERIALIZE
- 11. SWRITER
- 12. DESCAPP
- 14. WRITELINE
- 17. FILEINF

10 exception handling

Putting out fires gets old

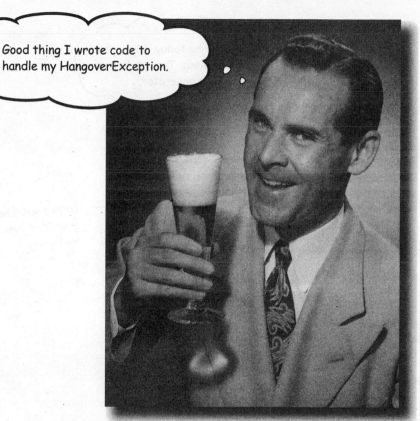

Good thing I wrote code to handle my HangoverException.

Programmers aren't meant to be firefighters.

You've worked your tail off, waded through technical manuals and a few engaging Head First books, and you've reached the pinnacle of your profession: **master programmer**. But you're still getting pages from work because **your program crashes**, or **doesn't behave like it's supposed to**. Nothing pulls you out of the programming groove like having to fix a strange bug…but with **exception handling**, you can write code to **deal with problems** that come up. Better yet, you can even react to those problems, and **keep things running**.

Brian needs his excuses to be mobile

Brian recently got reassigned to the international division. Now he flies all over the world. But he still needs to keep track of his excuses, so he installed the program you built on his laptop, and takes it with him everywhere.

Work's boring today. I want to go scuba diving. Time to fire up the Excuse generator.

Brian's got the excuse generator running on his laptop.

Same ol' Brian... always looking for an excuse to get out of work.

But the program isn't working!

Brian clicks the "Random Excuse" button, and gets a pretty nasty looking error. Something about not finding his excuses. What gives?

Excuse Manager

Unhandled exception has occurred in your application. If you click Continue, the application will ignore this error and attempt to continue. If you click Quit, the application will close immediately.

Index was outside the bounds of the array.

▼ Details   Continue   Quit

An unhandled exception... must have been a problem we didn't account for.

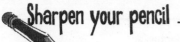

Sharpen your pencil

Here's another example of some broken code. There are five different exceptions that this code throws, and the error messages are shown on the right. It's your job to match the line of code that has a problem with the exception that line generates. Read the exception messages for a good hint.

```csharp
public static void BeeProcessor() {
    object myBee = new HoneyBee(36.5, "Zippo");
    float howMuchHoney = (float)myBee;

    HoneyBee anotherBee = new HoneyBee(12.5, "Buzzy");
    double beeName = double.Parse(anotherBee.MyName);

    double totalHoney = 36.5 + 12.5;
    string beesWeCanFeed = "";
    for (int i = 1; i < (int) totalHoney; i++) {
        beesWeCanFeed += i.ToString();
    }
    float f =
        float.Parse(beesWeCanFeed);

    int drones = 4;
    int queens = 0;
    int dronesPerQueen = drones / queens;

    anotherBee = null;
    if (dronesPerQueen < 10) {
        anotherBee.DoMyJob();
    }
}
```

Calling double.Parse("32") will parse a string and return a double value, like 32.

When you have a reference that doesn't point to any object, it gets a special value called null. Setting a reference to null, tells C# it doesn't point to anything.

(1) OverflowException was unhandled
Value was either too large or too small for a Single.

(2) NullReferenceException was unhandled
Object reference not set to an instance of an object.

(3) InvalidCastException was unhandled
Specified cast is not valid.

(4) DivideByZeroException was unhandled
Attempted to divide by zero.
Troubleshooting tips:
Make sure the value of the denominator is not zero before performing a division operation.
Get general help for this exception.
Search for more Help Online...

(5) FormatException was unhandled
Input string was not in a correct format.
Troubleshooting tips:
Make sure your method arguments are in the right format.
When converting a string to DateTime, parse the string to take the date before putting each variable into the DateTime object.
Get general help for this exception.
Search for more Help Online...

Sharpen your pencil
Solution

Your job was to match the line of code that has a problem with the exception that line generates.

C# has no idea how to cast a HoneyBee object to a float, and trying to do it will cause an InvalidCastException.

```
object myBee = new HoneyBee(36.5, "Zippo");
float howMuchHoney = (float)myBee;
```

⚠ **InvalidCastException was unhandled**   ✕

Specified cast is not valid.

The Parse() method wants you to give it a string in a certain format. "Buzzy" isn't a string it knows how to convert to a number. That's why it throws a FormatException.

```
HoneyBee anotherBee = new HoneyBee(12.5, "Buzzy");
double beeName = double.Parse(anotherBee.MyName);
```

⚠ **FormatException was unhandled**   ✕

Input string was not in a correct format.

Troubleshooting tips:

Make sure your method arguments are in the right format.

When converting a string to DateTime, parse the string to take the date before putting each variable into the DateTime object.

Get general help for this exception.

Search for more Help Online...

```
double totalHoney = 36.5 + 12.5;
string beesWeCanFeed = "";
for (int i = 1; i < (int) totalHoney; i++) {
    beesWeCanFeed += i.ToString();
}
float f = float.Parse(beesWeCanFeed);
```

The for loop will create a string called beesWeCanFeed that contains a number with over 60 digits in it. There's no way a float can hold a number that big, and trying to cram it into a float will throw an OverflowException.

⚠ **OverflowException was unhandled**

Value was either too large or too small for a Single.

You'd never actually get all these exceptions in a row. The program would throw the first exception and then stop. You'd only get to the second exception if you fixed the first.

```
int drones = 4;
int queens = 0;
int dronesPerQueen = drones / queens;
```

It's really easy to throw a DivideByZeroException. Just divide any number by zero.

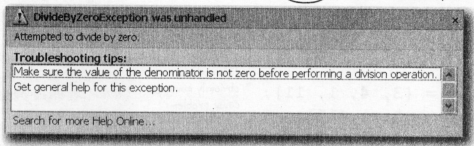

Dividing any number by zero always throws this kind of exception. Even if you don't know the value of queens, you can prevent it just by checking the value to make sure it's not zero **before** you divide it into drones.

```
anotherBee = null;
if (dronesPerQueen < 10) {
    anotherBee.DoMyJob();
}
```

Setting the anotherBee reference variable equal to null tells C# that it doesn't point to anything. So instead of pointing to an object, it points to nothing. Throwing a NullReferenceException is C#'s way of telling you that there's no object whose DoMyJob() method can be called.

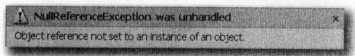

That DivideByZero error didn't have to happen. You can see just by looking at the code that there's something wrong. The same goes for the other exceptions. These problems were preventable—and the more you know about exceptions, the better you'll be at keeping your code from crashing.

When your program throws an exception, .NET generates an <u>Exception</u> object.

You've been looking at .NET's way of telling you something went wrong in your program: an **exception**. In C#, when an exception occurs, an object is created to represent the problem. It's called, no surprise here, Exception.

For example, suppose you have an array with four items. Then, you try and access the sixteenth item (index 15, since we're zero-based here):

```
int anArray = {3, 4, 1, 11};
int aValue = anArray[15];
```

> This code is obviously going to cause problems.

ex-cep-tion, noun.
a person or thing that is excluded from a general statement or does not follow a rule. *While Jim usually hates peanut butter, he made an* **exception** *for Ken's peanut butter fudge.*

As soon as your program runs into an unhandled exception, it generates an object with all the data it has about it.

Exception object

You can see this detail by clicking on the View Detail link in the unhandled exception window.

The exception object has a message that tells you what's wrong and a list of all of the calls that were made to the system's memory leading up to the event that caused the exception.

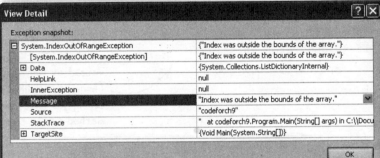

.NET goes to the trouble of creating an object because it wants to give you all the information about what caused the exception. You may have code to fix, or you may just need to make some changes to how you handle a particular situation in your program.

In this case, an **IndexOutOfRangeException** indicates you have a bug: you're trying to access an index in the array that's out of range. You've also got information about exactly where in the code the problem occurred, making it easy to track down the problem (even if you've got thousands of lines of code).

Dumb Questions
there are no

Q: Why are there so many kinds of exceptions?

A: There are all sorts of ways that you can write code that C# simply doesn't know how to deal with. It would be difficult to troubleshoot your problems if your program simply gave a generic error message ("A problem occurred at line 37"). It's a lot easier to track down and fix problems in your code when you know specifically what kind of error occurred.

Q: So what *is* an exception, really?

A: It's an object that .NET creates when there's a problem (more about that in a minute).

Q: Wait, what? It's an *object*?

A: Yes, an exception is an **object**. The properties in the object tell you information about the exception. For example, it's got a Message property that has a useful string like "Specified cast was invalid" and "Value was either too large or too small for a Single", which is what it used to generate the exception window. The reason that .NET generates it is to give you as much information as it can about exactly what was going on when it executed the statement that threw the exception.

Q: Okay, I still don't get it. Sorry. Why are there so many different kinds of exceptions, again?

A: Because there are so many ways that your code can act in unexpected ways. There are a lot of situations that will cause your code to simply crash. It would be really hard to troubleshoot the problems if you didn't know why the crash happened. By throwing different kinds of exceptions under different circumstances, .NET is giving you a lot of really valuable information to help you track down and correct the problem.

Q: So exceptions are there to help me, not just cause a pain in my butt?

A: Yes! Exceptions are all about helping you expect the unexpected. A lot of people get frustrated when they see code throw an exception. But if you think about an exception as .NET's way of helping you track down and debug your program, it really helps out when you're trying to track down what's causing the code to bomb out.

Q: So when my code throws an exception, it's not necessarily because I did something wrong?

A: Exactly. Sometimes your data's different than you expected it to be—like you've got a method that's dealing with an array that's a lot longer or shorter than you anticipated when you first wrote it. And don't forget that human beings are using your program, and they almost always act in an unpredictable way. Exceptions are .NET's way to help you handle those unexpected situations so that your code still runs smoothly and doesn't simply crash or give a cryptic, useless error message.

Q: Once I knew what I was looking for, it was pretty clear that the code on the previous page was going to crash. Are all exceptions easy to spot?

A: No. Unfortunately, there are times when your code will have problems, and it'll be really hard to figure out what's causing them just by looking at it. That's why the IDE gives you a really useful tool called the **debugger**. It lets you pause your program and execute it statement by statement, inspecting the value of each individual variable and field as you go. That makes it a lot easier for you to figure out where your code is acting in a way that's different from how you expect it to act. That's when you have the best chance of finding and fixing the exceptions—or, even better, preventing them in the first place.

> **Exceptions are all about helping you find and fix situations where your code behaves in ways you didn't expect.**

Brian's code did something unexpected

When Brian wrote his excuse manager, he never expected
the user to try to pull a random excuse out of an empty
directory.

 The problem happened when Brian pointed his Excuse Manager program at an
empty folder on his laptop and clicked the Random button. Let's take a look at
it and see if we can figure out what went wrong. Here's the unhandled exception
window that popped up when he ran the program outside the IDE:

2 Okay, that's a good starting point. It's telling us that the index was outside the
bounds of the array, right? So let's look for an array in the code for the Random
Excuse button's event handler:

```
private void RandomExcuseButton_Click(object sender, EventArgs e) {
    if (CheckChanged() == true) {
        CurrentExcuse = new Excuse(random, Folder);
        UpdateForm(false);
    }
}
```

3 Hmm, no arrays in there. But it creates a new `Excuse` object using one of the
overloaded constructors. Maybe there's an array in the constructor code:

```
public Excuse(Random random, string Folder) {
    string[] fileNames = Directory.GetFiles(Folder, "*.excuse");
    OpenFile(fileNames[random.Next(fileNames.Length)]);
}
```

Bingo! There's the array.
We must be trying to use
an index that's past the
end of the array.

4 It turns out that `Directory.GetFiles()` returns an empty array when you
point it at a directory with no files in it. Hey, we can test for that! All we need
to do is add a check to **make sure the directory's not empty** before we
open a file, and the nasty unhandled exception window will be replaced with an
informative messagebox.

```
private void RandomExcuseButton_Click(object sender, EventArgs e) {
    string[] fileNames = Directory.GetFiles(Folder, "*.excuse");
    if (fileNames.Length == 0) {
        MessageBox.Show("Please specify a folder with excuse files in it",
                        "No excuse files found");
    } else {
        if (CheckChanged() == true) {
            CurrentExcuse = new Excuse(random, Folder);
            UpdateForm(false);
        }
    }
}
```

*By checking for excuse
files in the folder **before**
we create the Excuse
object, we can prevent
the exception from being
thrown—and pop up a
helpful message box, too.*

*Oh, I get it. Exceptions aren't always bad.
Sometimes they identify bugs, but a lot of the time
they're just telling me that something happened
that was different from what I expected.*

**That's right. Exceptions are a really useful tool
that you can use to find places where your code
acts in ways you don't expect.**

A lot of programmers get frustrated the first time they see an
exception. But exceptions are really useful, and you can use them to
your advantage. When you see an exception, it's giving you a lot of
clues to help you figure out when your code is reacting to a situation
that you didn't anticipate. And that's good for you: it lets you know
about a new scenario that your program has to handle, and it gives
you an opportunity to **do something about it**.

All exception objects inherit from `Exception`

.NET has lots of different exceptions it may need to report. Since many of these have a lot of similar features, inheritance comes into play. .NET defines a base class, called Exception, that all specific exceptions types inherit from.

The Exception class has a couple of useful members. The `Message` properties stores an easy-to-read message about what went wrong. And `StackTrace` tells you what was going on in memory when the exception occurred, and what led up to the exception. (There are others, too, but we'll use those first.)

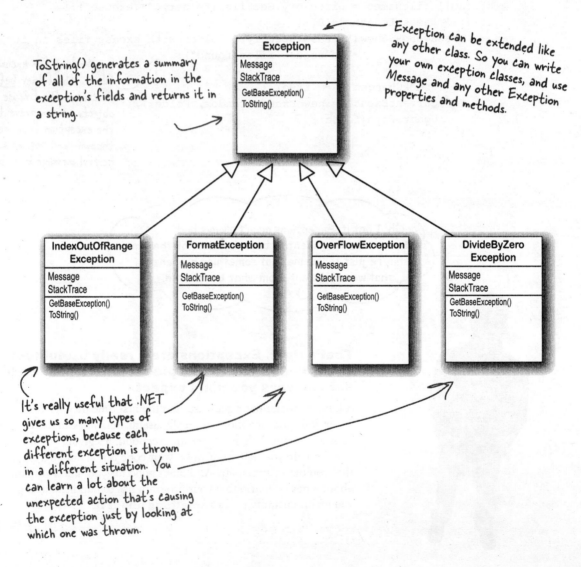

ToString() generates a summary of all of the information in the exception's fields and returns it in a string.

Exception can be extended like any other class. So you can write your own exception classes, and use Message and any other Exception properties and methods.

It's really useful that .NET gives us so many types of exceptions, because each different exception is thrown in a different situation. You can learn a lot about the unexpected action that's causing the exception just by looking at which one was thrown.

The debugger helps you track down and prevent exceptions in your code

Before you can add exception handling to your program, you need to know which statements in your program are throwing the exception. That's where the **debugger** that's built into the IDE can be really helpful. When you run the debugger, the IDE pops up a toolbar with some really useful buttons. Take a minute and hover your mouse cursor over each of them to see its name and shortcut key. (Those shortcut keys come in really handy.)

The Debug toolbar only shows up when you're debugging your program in the IDE. So you'll have to run a program in order to hover over the toolbar icons.

Stop: end the program and exit the debugger.

Show next statement: scroll to the next statement that's going to be executed.

Step over: execute the next statement. If it's a method, execute it as a single statement.

Continue: run until the next breakpoint is hit or the program ends.

Step out: run the rest of the statements in the current method, and break when it's done.

Break all: break the program immediately and jump to the statement being executed.

Restart: stop execution and start the program again.

Step into: execute the next statement. If it's a method, execute the first statement in the method.

Debugging means running your code line by line to see what happens

Whenever you run your program inside the IDE, you can always pause it at any time by hitting the **Break All** button in the toolbar (or choosing the command from the Debug menu). This causes your program to **stop in its tracks** and show you the line of code that it's about to run. It turns that line of code yellow to show you that it's the one that'll run next. If you press **Continue**, then your program will keep running as if you'd never stopped it. But you can also step through your code, which means executing the current line and going to the next one. If the next line is a method, then you can **step into** the method, which causes the debugger to jump to the first line of the method and highlight it. Or you can **step over** the method, which executes the whole thing. If you're inside a method, you can **step out** of it, which causes the debugger to execute the rest of the statements in the method and break at the first line after it returns from the method.

You can also inspect and change variables and fields in your code using the **Watch window**. Just right-click on a variable in the code and select "Add Watch", and it'll appear in the Watch window—or you can type it directly into the Watch window. Then its value will be displayed. If it's an object, you can drill down into its fields.

Watch			
Name	Value	Type	
🔵 fileNames.Length	0	int	

When you break inside the debugger, the IDE stops your program and displays the next line of code that it's about to run highlighted in yellow. Then you can move forward line by line until you find your problem.

Use the IDE's debugger to ferret out exactly what went wrong in the excuse manager

Let's use the debugger to take a closer look at the problem that we ran into in the excuse manager. It's a good place to get some practice with the debugger, because you know exactly what you're looking for. (That's a luxury that you don't have most of the time!)

Debug this

1 **Use a breakpoint to break—or pause—your program**

You've got a starting point—the exception happens when the Random Excuse button is clicked after an empty folder is selected. So open up the code for the button, click anywhere in the first line of the method, and select "Toggle Breakpoint" from the Debug menu (or press F9):

> *The debugger shows your breakpoints as red lines with a big red dot in the left-hand margin.*

```
private void RandomExcuseButton_Click(object sender, EventArgs e)
{
    string[] fileNames = Directory.GetFiles(Folder, "*.excuse");
    if (fileNames.Length == 0) {
        MessageBox.Sho  ● fileNames.Length 0  fy a folder with excuse files in it", "No excuse files found");
    } else {
        if (CheckChanged() == true) {
            CurrentExcuse = new Excuse(random, Folder);
            UpdateForm(false);
        }
    }
}
```

> *Hover over any field or variable and the IDE will show you its value.*

> *The yellow line with a yellow arrow in the left-hand margin is the next line the debugger will execute when it runs.*

The IDE turned the line red and put a circle in the left-hand margin. That's the debugger's way of telling you that it set a **breakpoint** on the line. Now, when you debug the program in the IDE, execution will stop on that line. Give it a try—run the program in the IDE (using the same "Start Debugging" command you've been using all along). When you reproduce the problem, the line should turn yellow, with an arrow pointing to the code. Now your program's temporarily paused. The "Start Debugging" menu item's turned into "Continue Debugging," too. Click it—the program will pick up exactly where it left off, starting with the line you put the breakpoint on.

> *Now you know why the IDE command for running a program is "Start Debugging"—because you're using the debugger built into the IDE.*

> *Start Debugging – when you have no breakpoints set – is the same as running your program.*

2 **Step through the application**

Use the **Step Into** command (using either the toolbar or the F11 key) to move through the application line by line. When it gets to the line that creates the new Excuse object, it'll jump straight into the constructor that you fixed. Step past the first line so it sets the fileNames variable. Then hover over the variable to see its value.

③ **Use the Watch window to reproduce the problem**

One really powerful feature of the debugger is the **Watch** window, which lets you check the value of variables and fields in your objects. Hover your mouse cursor over the "Length" part of `fileNames.Length`. Then select all of `fileNames.Length`, right-click, and select "Add Watch" from the menu. It'll get added to the Watch window (which is in the same pane as Output—you can bring it up by selecting "Watch" under Windows in the Debug menu). Then add each piece of the statement: first `random.Next(fileNames.Length)`. It should look something like this, depending on how many files are in the folder you pointed to—in this case, we had five, so `fileNames` has five elements:

We'll use the Watch window to reproduce the problem that caused the exception. We'll start by adding the fileNames array.

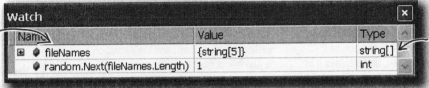

You need to break (pause) the program before you can add a watch.

④ **Set fileNames equal to an empty string array**

Double-click in the empty space in the Watch window underneath the two watch variables. You'll get a cursor. Type this in: **`fileNames = new string[0]`**. Watch the top row in the window—as soon as you hit enter, the value of `fileNames` will change to {`string[0]`}. A re-evaluate icon ⓦ should show up next to the `random.Next` line—click on it and its value gets set to 0. So what happened?

The Watch window has another very useful feature—it lets you **change the value** of variables and fields that it's displaying. And it even lets you **execute methods and create new objects**—and when you do, it displays its re-evaluate icon (ⓦ) that you can click to tell it to execute that line again, because sometimes running the same method twice will generate different results (like with Random).

We know the problem happened with an empty fileNames array, so we'll use the Watch window to change its value to an empty string array.

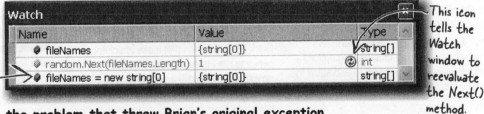

This icon tells the Watch window to reevaluate the Next() method.

⑤ **Reproduce the problem that threw Brian's original exception**

Here's where debugging gets really interesting. Add one more line to the debugger—the statement that actually threw the exception: `fileNames[random.Next(fileNames.Length)]`. As soon as you type it in, the Watch window evaluates it... and that throws the exception. It tells you that it found the exception by displaying an exclamation point, and displays the text of the exception in the Value column.

This exclamation point is the Watch window's way of telling you it found an exception.

Watch			☒
Name	Value	Type	
● fileNames	{string[0]}	string[]	
◈ random.Next(fileNames.Length)	1	ⓦ int	
◈ fileNames = new string[0]	{string[0]}	ⓦ string[]	
❶ fileNames[random.Next(fileName	Out of bounds array index	ⓦ string	

When you get an exception, you can go back and reproduce it in the debugger. That's another way that more descriptive exception messages can help you fix your code.

Q: How come Brian's unhandled exception window looked different than the one in the IDE?

A: Because when you run a program inside the IDE, you're running it in the debugger, which **breaks the program** (as if you'd pressed the Break All button or inserted a breakpoint) as soon as it intercepts an exception, and displays it in a useful window. That lets you inspect the Exception object and your program's fields and variables so you can track down the problem.

When Brian ran his program, he wasn't running it from inside the IDE. He'd published his program and installed it, just like you did back in Chapter 1 with the Contact List program. You can run your program outside the IDE any time without publishing it—just build your program, which causes Visual Studio to create an executable file. Just look inside your project's folder for the `bin/` folder—one of its subdirectories should have the `exe` file for your application. If you run that, any exceptions that it throws will be unhandled and show the same window that Brian saw.

Q: So that's it? When an exception happens outside the IDE, my program just stops and there's nothing I can do about it?

A: Well, your program does stop when there's an *unhandled* exception. But that doesn't mean that all of your exceptions have to be unhandled! We'll talk a lot more about how you can handle exceptions in your code. There's no reason your users ever have to see an unhandled exception.

Q: How do I know where to put a breakpoint?

A: That's a really good question, and there's no one right answer. When your code throws an exception, it's always a good idea to start with the statement that threw it. But usually, the problem actually happened earlier in the program, and the exception is just fallout from it. For example, the statement that throws a divide by zero error could be dividing values that were generated 10 statements earlier but just haven't been used yet. So there's no one good answer to where you should put a breakpoint, because every situation is different. But as long as you've got a good idea how your code works, you should be able to figure out a good starting point.

Q: Can I run any method in the Watch window?

A: Yes. Any statement that's valid in your program will work inside the Watch window, even things that make absolutely no sense to run inside a Watch window. Here's an example. Bring up a program, start it running, break it, and then add this to the Watch window: `System.Threading.Thread.Sleep(2000)`. (Remember, that method causes your program to delay for two seconds.)There's no reason you'd ever do that in real life, but it's interesting to see what happens: you'll get an hourglass for two seconds while the method evaluates. Then, since `Sleep()` has no return value, the Watch window will display the value, "`Expression has been evaluated and has no value`" to let you know that it didn't return anything. But it did evaluate it. Not only that, but it displays IntelliSense pop-ups to

help you type code into the window. That's useful because it'll tell you what methods are available to an object when your program is running.

Q: Wait, so isn't it possible for me to run something in the Watch window that'll change the way my program runs?

A: Yes! Not permanently, but it can definitely affect your program's output. But even better, just *hovering* over fields inside the debugger can cause your program to change its behavior, because hovering over a property *executes its get accessor*. If you have a property that's got a get accessor that executes a method, then hovering over that property will cause that method to execute. And if that method sets a value in your program, then that value will stay set if you run the program again. And that can cause some pretty unpredictable results inside the debugger. Programmers have a name for results that seem to be unpredictable and random: they're called **heisenbugs** (which is a joke that makes sense to physicists and cats in boxes).

> **When you run your program inside the IDE, an unhandled exception will cause it to break as if it had run into a breakpoint.**

Uh-oh—the code's still got problems...

Brian was happily using his Excuse Manager, when he remembered that he had a folder full of excuses that he made when he first built the program—but he forgot that he made that folder *before* he added serialization to the program. Let's see what happens....

No, not again!

1 You can re-create Brian's problem—just create your own text-based Excuse file using Notepad. The first line should be the description, the second should be the results, and the third should be the last used date ("10/4/2007 12:08:13 PM").

2 Pop open the Excuse Manager and open up the excuse. It throws an exception! But this time, click on the Details button so we can take a closer look at what it says. Pay attention to the **call stack**—that's what it's called when a method is called by another method, which is called by another method, etc.

The program threw a `SerializationException`. Can we figure out what line threw it from the exception details?

Excuse Manager

Unhandled excepti
Continue, the applic
you click Quit, the a

Index was outside t

▼ Details

It looks like there was a problem with the BinaryFormatter—which makes sense, because it was trying to deserialize a text file.

You can learn a lot from the call stack, which tells you which methods were running. You can see that the Excuse class's `OpenFile()` method was being called from its constructor (".ctor"), which was called from the "Random Excuse" button's click event handler.

************** Exception Text **************

System.Runtime.Serialization.**SerializationException**: End of Stream encountered before parsing was completed.

at System.Runtime.Serialization.Formatters.Binary.__BinaryParser.Run()

at System.Runtime.Serialization.Formatters.Binary.ObjectReader.Deserialize(HeaderHandler handler, __BinaryParser serParser, Boolean fCheck, Boolean isCrossAppDomain, IMethodCallMessage methodCallMessage)

at System.Runtime.Serialization.Formatters.Binary.BinaryFormatter.Deserialize(Stream serializationStream, HeaderHandler handler, Boolean fCheck, Boolean isCrossAppDomain, IMethodCallMessage methodCallMessage)

at System.Runtime.Serialization.Formatters.Binary.**BinaryFormatter.Deserialize**(Stream serializationStream)

at Chapter10.**Excuse.OpenFile(String ExcusePath)** in C:\Documents and Settings\Administrator\My Documents\Visual Studio 2005\Projects\Chapter10\Chapter10\Excuse.cs:line 40

at Chapter10.**Excuse..ctor(Random random, String Folder)** in C:\Documents and Settings\Administrator\My Documents\Visual Studio 2005\Projects\Chapter10\Chapter10\Excuse.cs:line 30

at Chapter10.**Form1.RandomExcuseButton_Click(Object sender, EventArgs e)** in C:\Documents and Settings\Administrator\My Documents\Visual Studio 2005\Projects\Chapter10\Chapter10\Form1.cs:line 146

3 So the Details button in the unhandled exception window tells you a lot about what caused this problem. *Can you think of anything you can do about it?*

> Wait a second. Of course the program's gonna crash—I gave it a bad file. Users screw up all the time. You can't expect me to do anything about that, right?

Actually, there is something you can do about it.

Yes, it's true that users screw up all the time. That's a fact of life. But that doesn't mean you can't do anything about it. There's a name for programs that deal with bad data, malformed input, and other unexpected situations gracefully: they're called **robust**. And C# gives you some really powerful exception handling tools to help you make your programs more robust. Because while you *can't* control what your users do, you *can* make sure that your program doesn't crash when they do it.

ro-bust, adj.
sturdy in construction; able to withstand or overcome adverse conditions. *After the Tacoma Narrows Bridge disaster, the civil engineering team looked for a more **robust** design for the bridge that would replace it.*

Watch it!

BinaryFormatter will throw an exception if there's anything at all wrong with a serialized file.

It's easy to get the Excuse Manager to throw a SerializationException—just feed it any file that's not a serialized Excuse object. When you try to deserialize an object from a file, BinaryFormatter expects the file to contain a serialized object that matches the class that it's trying to read. If the file contains anything else, anything at all, then the Deserialize() method will throw a SerializationException.

Handle exceptions with try and catch

In C#, you can basically say, "**Try** this code, and if an exception occurs, **catch** it with this *other* bit of code." The part of code you're trying is the **try block**, and the part where you deal with exceptions is called the **catch block**. In the catch block, you can do thinks like print a friendly error message, instead of letting your program come to a screeching halt:

```csharp
private void RandomExcuseButton_Click(object sender,
EventArgs e) {

    // ... code you added a few pages ago goes here ...

    try {

        if (CheckChanged() == true) {

            CurrentExcuse = new Excuse(random, Folder);

            UpdateForm(false);

        }

    }

    catch {

        MessageBox.Show(

            "Your excuse file was invalid.",

            "Unable to open a random excuse");

    }

}
```

This is the try block. You start exception handling with try.

The catch keyword means that the block immediately following it contains an exception handler.

Put the code that might throw an exception inside the try block. If no exception happens, it'll get run exactly as usual, and the statements in the catch block will be ignored. But if a statement in the try block throws an exception, the rest of the try block won't get executed.

When an exception is thrown, the program immediately jumps to the catch statement and starts executing the catch block.

This is the simplest kind of exception handling: stop the program, write out the exception message, and keep running.

BRAIN POWER

If throwing an exception makes your code automatically jump to the catch block, what happens to the objects and data you were working with before the exception happened?

What happens when a method you want to call is risky?

Users are unpredictable. They feed all sorts of weird data into your program, and click on things in ways you never expected. And that's just fine, because you can handle unexpected input with good exception handling.

(1) **Let's say your user is using your code, and gives it some input that it didn't expect.**

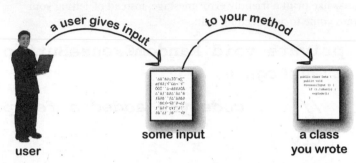

a user gives input   to your method

some input

a class you wrote

user

(2) **That method does something risky, something that might not work at runtime.**

a class you wrote

```
public void
    Process(Input i) {
    if (i.IsBad()) {
        explode();
    }
}
```

"Runtime" just means "while your program is running". Some people refer to exceptions as "runtime errors".

(3) **You need to *know* that the method you're calling is risky.**

I wonder what happens if I click here...

My Process() method will blow up if it gets bad input data!

a class you wrote

user

(4) **You then write code that can handle the failure if it *does* happen. You need to be prepared, just in case.**

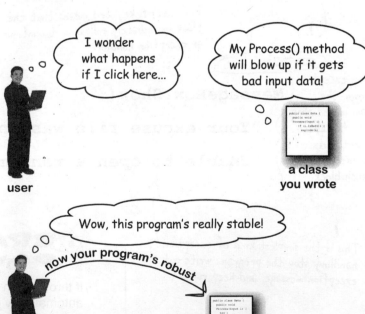

Wow, this program's really stable!

now your program's robust

your class, now with exception handling

user

there are no Dumb Questions

Q: So when do I use try and catch?

A: Any time you're writing risky code, or code that could throw an exception. The trick is figuring out which code is risky, and which code is safer.

You've already seen that code that uses input provided by a user can be risky. Users give you incorrect files, words instead of numbers, names instead of dates, and they pretty much click everywhere you could possibly imagine. And a good program will take all that input and work in a calm, predictable way. It might not give the users a result they can use, but it will let them know that it found the problem and hopefully suggest a solution.

Q: How can a program suggest a solution to a problem it doesn't even know about in advance?

A: That's what the catch block is for. A catch block is only executed when code in the try block throws an exception. It's your chance to make sure the user knows that something went wrong, and to let the user know that it's a situation that might be corrected.

If the excuse manager simply crashes when there's bad input, that's not particularly useful. But if it tries to read the input and displays garbage in the form, that's also not

useful—fact, some people might say that it's worse. But if you have the program display an error message telling the user that it couldn't read the file, then the user has an idea of what went wrong, and information that he can use to fix the problem.

Q: Is the debugger only used to troubleshoot exceptions?

A: No. The debugger's actually a really useful tool that you can use to examine any code you've written. Sometimes it's useful to step through your code and check the value of certain fields and variables—like when you've got a really complex method, and you want to make sure it's working properly.

But as you may have guessed from the name "debugger," its most common use is to track down and remove bugs. Sometimes those bugs are exceptions that get thrown. But a lot of the time, you'll be using the debugger to try to find other kinds of problems, like code that gives a result that you don't expect.

Q: I'm not sure I totally got the Watch window. What's it for, again?

A: When you're debugging a program, you usually want to pay attention to how a few variables and fields change. That's where the Watch window comes in. If you

add watches for a few variables, the Watch window updates their values every time you step into, out of or over code. That lets you monitor exactly what happens to them after every statement, which can be really useful when you're trying to track down a problem.

The Watch window also lets you type in any statement you want, and it'll evaluate it. If the statement updates any of the fields and variables in your program, then it does that, too. That lets you change values while your program is running, which can be another really useful tool for reproducing exceptions and other bugs.

Any changes you make in the Watch window just affect the data in memory, and only last as long as the program is running. Restart your program, and values that you changed will be undone.

The catch block is only executed when code in the try block throws an exception. It gives you a chance to make sure your user has the information to fix the problem.

Use the debugger to follow the try/catch flow

An important part of exception handling is that when a statement in your try block throws an exception, the rest of the code in the block gets **short-circuited**. The program's execution immediately jumps to the first line in the catch block. *But don't take our word for it...*

Debug this

1 Make sure that you've incorporated all of the code from this chapter into the Random Excuse button in your Excuse Manager. Place a breakpoint on the first line in the Random Excuse button's Click event handler. Then run your program in the IDE. Click the Folder button and specify a folder with a single excuse file in it—and make sure it's a **not a valid excuse file** (any other sort of file will cause it to throw an exception). Press the Random Excuse button. The debugger should break the program at the breakpoint you placed. Press the "Step Over" button (or F10) six times to get to the statement that calls the Excuse constructor. Here's what your debugger screen should look like:

Place a breakpoint on the first line of the Random Excuse button event handler.

Step over the statements until your yellow "next statement" bar shows that the next statement to get executed will create the new Excuse object.

```
private void RandomExcuseButton_Click(object sender, EventArgs e) {
    string[] fileNames = Directory.GetFiles(Folder, "*.excuse");
    if (fileNames.Length == 0) {
        MessageBox.Show("Please specify a folder with excuse files in it",
                        "No excuse files found");
    } else {
        try {
            if (CheckChanged()) {
                CurrentExcuse = new Excuse(random, Folder);
                UpdateForm(false);
            }
        }
        catch {
            MessageBox.Show(
                "Your excuse file was invalid.",
                "Unable to open a random excuse");
        }
    }
}
```

Make sure you use the Step Over (F10) command in the debugger so it doesn't step into the CheckChanged() method.

2 Use Step Into (F11) to step into the new statement. The debugger will jump to the Excuse constructor, and position its yellow "next statement" bar over the declaration line in the code. Keep hitting Step Into (F11) to step into the OpenFile() method. Watch what happens when you hit the `Deserialize()` line.

As soon as you step into the new statement that creates the Excuse object, the debugger jumps to the constructor code.

```
public Excuse(Random random, string folder)
{
    string[] fileNames = Directory.GetFiles(folder, "*.excuse");
    OpenFile(fileNames[random.Next(fileNames.Length)]);
}
```

3 As soon as the debugger executes the Deserialize() statement, the exception is thrown and the program jumps straight to the first statement in the catch block. It **short-circuited** right past the call to UpdateForm() and **jumped straight to the catch block**.

The debugger will highlight the catch statement with its yellow "next statement" block, but it shows the rest of the block in grey to show you that it's about to execute the whole thing.

```
private void RandomExcuseButton_Click(object sender, EventArgs e) {
    string[] fileNames = Directory.GetFiles(Folder, "*.excuse");
    if (fileNames.Length == 0) {
        MessageBox.Show("Please specify a folder with excuse files in it",
                        "No excuse files found");
    } else {
        try {
            if (CheckChanged()) {
                CurrentExcuse = new Excuse(random, Folder);
                UpdateForm(false);
            }
        }
        catch {
            MessageBox.Show(
                "Your excuse file was invalid.",
                "Unable to open a random excuse");
        }
    }
}
```

4 Start the program again by pressing the Continue button (or F5). It'll begin running the program again, starting with whatever's highlighted by the yellow "next statement" block—in this case, the catch block.

Unable to open a random excuse ⊠

Your excuse file was invalid.

OK

Here's a career tip: a lot of C# programming job interviews include a question about how you deal with exceptions in a constructor.

Watch it!

Be careful with exceptions in a constructor!

You've noticed by now that a constructor doesn't have a return value, not even void*. That's because a constructor doesn't actually return anything. Its only purpose is to initialize an object—which is a problem for exception handling inside the constructor. When an exception is thrown inside the constructor, then the statement that tried to instantiate the class **won't end up with an instance of the object**. That's why you had to move the try/catch block to the button's event handler. That way, if there's an exception in the constructor, the code won't expect CurrentExcuse to contain a valid Excuse object.*

If you have code that <u>ALWAYS</u> should run, use a finally block

When your program throws an exception, a couple of things can happen. If the exception ***isn't*** handled, your program will stop processing and crash. If the exception ***is*** handled, your code jumps to the `catch` block. But what about the rest of the code in your try block? What if you were closing a stream, or cleaning up important resources? That code needs to run, even if an exception occurs, or you're going to make a mess of your program's state. That's where the **finally** block comes in really handy. It comes after the `try` and `catch` blocks. The **finally block always runs**, whether or not an exception was thrown. Here's how you'd use it to finish the event handling in the Random Excuse button:

```
private void RandomExcuseButton_Click(object sender, EventArgs e) {
    string[] fileNames = Directory.GetFiles(Folder, "*.excuse");
    if (fileNames.Length == 0) {
        MessageBox.Show("Please specify a folder with excuse files in it",
                    "No excuse files found");
    } else {
        try {
            if (CheckChanged() == true) {
                CurrentExcuse = new Excuse(random, Folder);
            }
        }
        catch (Exception) {
            CurrentExcuse = new Excuse();
            CurrentExcuse.Description = "";
            CurrentExcuse.Results = "";
            CurrentExcuse.LastUsed = DateTime.Now;
            MessageBox.Show(
                "Your excuse file was invalid.",
                "Unable to open a random excuse");
        }
        finally {
            UpdateForm(false);
        }
    }
}
```

> If the Excuse constructor throws an exception, we have <u>no way of knowing what's in CurrentExcuse</u>. But you <u>do</u> know that no instance of Excuse was created. So the catch block creates a new Excuse object and clears out all its fields.

> The `finally` block makes sure that `UpdateForm()` gets run whether or not an exception was thrown. So if the Excuse constructor successfully read an excuse, it'll call `UpdateForm()`, but it'll also call it if the constructor threw an exception and cleared out the excuse.

Did you notice how catch was followed by (Exception)? When you have a `catch` statement, you can follow it with a specific kind of exception telling it what to catch. If you specify **(Exception)** or leave it out, it catches all exceptions. But if you only wanted to catch a `SerializationException`, you could specify that inside the parentheses instead. Or you could use an <u>**IOException,**</u> which will catch **any file input or output problem**.

① Update the **Random Excuse** button's event handler with the code on the facing page. Then place a breakpoint on the first line in the method and debug the program.

② Run the program normally, and make sure that the Random Excuse button works when you set the program's folder to one with a bunch of normal excuse files in it. The debugger should break at the breakpoint you set:

> When the "next statement" bar and the breakpoint are on the same line, the IDE shows you the yellow arrow placed over the big red dot in the margin.

```
private void RandomExcuseButton_Click(object sender, EventArgs e) {
    string[] fileNames = Directory.GetFiles(Folder, "*.excuse");
    if (fileNames.Length == 0) {
        MessageBox.Show("Please specify a folder with excuse files in it",
                        "No excuse files found");
    } else {
        try
        {
            if (CheckChanged()) {
                CurrentExcuse = new Excuse(random, Folder);
            }
        }
        catch (Exception) {
            CurrentExcuse = new Excuse();
            CurrentExcuse.Description = "";
            CurrentExcuse.Results = "";
            CurrentExcuse.LastUsed = DateTime.Now;
            MessageBox.Show(
                "Your excuse file was invalid.",
                "Unable to open a random excuse");
        }
        finally {
            UpdateForm(false);
        }
    }
}
```

③ Step through the rest of the Random Excuse button's event handler and make sure it runs the way you expect it to. It should finish the `try` block, skip over the `catch` block (because no exceptions were thrown), and then execute the `finally` block.

④ Now set the program's folder so that it's pointed to the folder with one malformed excuse file in it and click the Random excuse button. It should start executing the `try` block, and then jump to the `catch` block when it throws the exception. After it finishes all of the statements in the `catch` block, it'll execute the `finally` block.

there are no Dumb Questions

Q: Back up a second. So every time my program runs into an exception, it's going to stop whatever it's doing unless I specifically write code to catch it. How is that a good thing?

A: One of the best things about exceptions is that they make it really obvious when you run into problems. Imagine how easy it could be in a complex application for you to lose track of all of the objects your program was working with. Exceptions call attention to your problems and help you root out their causes so that you always know that your program is doing what it's supposed to do.

Any time an exception occurs in your program, something you expected to happen didn't. Maybe an object reference wasn't pointing where you thought it was, or it was possible for a user to supply a value you hadn't considered, or a file you thought you'd be working with suddenly isn't available. If something like that happened and you didn't know it, it's likely that the output of your program would be wrong, and the behavior from that point on would be pretty different than you expected when you wrote the program.

Now imagine that you had no idea the error had occurred and your users started calling you up with incorrect data and telling you that your program was unstable. That's why it's a *good* thing that exceptions disrupt everything your program is doing. They force you to deal with the problem while it's easy to find and fix.

Q: Okay, so now what's a handled exception and what's an unhandled exception?

A: Whenever your program throws an exception, the runtime environment will search through your code looking for a catch block to that matches it. If you've written one, the catch block will execute and do whatever you specified for that particular exception. Since you wrote a catch block to deal with that error up front, that exception is considered handled. If the runtime can't find a catch block to match the exception, it stops everything your program is doing and raises an error. Then, you'd call the exception unhandled.

Q: What was that bit about specifying a particular kind of exception to catch? Why would I ever want to do that?

A: You *usually* don't want to catch every kind of exception. In fact, you should do your best to avoid catching `Exception`, and instead catch specific exceptions. For example, let's say you wanted your Excuse class to prevent a `FileNotFoundException` from getting back to the form—say, if you wanted to make it so that if you tried to open a file that wasn't found, it would automatically create a excuse file with that filename and give it some default values. Then you could add a `try` block followed by `catch` (`FileNotFoundException`). Then if a file isn't found, the class can handle it—but an `IOException` or `SerializationException` would not get caught, and the exception handler you added to the form would catch it. But if you do that, you have to make sure that there's *some* method in the call stack that does have a catch-all exception handler, otherwise the exception would be unhandled. And that would cause the users to see the ugly "unhandled exception" crash.

Q: What happens when you have a catch that doesn't specify a particular exception?

A: A catch block like that will catch any kind of exception the try block can throw.

Q: If a catch block with no specified exception will catch anything, why would I ever want to specify?

A: Good question. Because certain exceptions might require different actions to keep your program moving. An exception that happens when you divide by zero might have a catch block where you go back and set some number values to save some of the data you've been working with. A null reference exception might require that you create new instances of an object if you're going to recover.

Q: Does all error handling happen in a try/catch/finally sequence?

A: No. You can mix it up a bit. You could have **multiple catch blocks** if you wanted to deal with lots of different kinds of errors. You could also have no catch block at all. It's legal to have a try/finally block. That wouldn't handle any exceptions, but it would make sure that the code in the finally block ran even if you got stopped half way through the try block. But we'll talk a lot more about that in a minute...

An unhandled exception means your program will run unpredictably. That's why the program stops whenever it runs into one.

Pool Puzzle

Your *job* is to take code snippets from the pool and place them into the blank lines in the program. You can use the same snippet more than once, and you won't need to use all the snippets. Your *goal* is to make the program produce the output.

Output: ⟶ **G'day Mate!**

```
using System.IO;
public static void Main() {
    Kangaroo Joey = new Kangaroo();
    int Koala = Joey.Wombat(
        Joey.Wombat(Joey.Wombat(1)));
    try {
        Console.WriteLine((15 / Koala)
                + " eggs per pound");
    }
    catch (_____) {
        Console.WriteLine("G'Day Mate!");
    }
}
```

```
public class Kangaroo {
    _____ fs;
    int Croc;
    int Dingo = 0;
    public int Wombat(int Wallaby) {
        _____ __;
        try {
            if (_____ > 0) {
                __ = _____.OpenWrite("wobbiegong");
                Croc = 0;
            } else if (_____ < 0) {
                Croc = 3;
            } else {
                ___ = _____.OpenRead("wobbiegong");
                Croc = 1;
            }
        }
        catch (IOException) {
            Croc = -3;
        }
        catch {
            Croc = 4;
        }
        finally {
            if (_____ > 2) {
                Croc ___ Dingo;
            }
        }
        _____ _____;
    }
}
```

Note: each snippet from the pool can be used more than once!

Exception	ef		++	Dingo
IOException	i	FileInfo	-=	Wallaby
NullPointerException	fs	File	+=	Koala
DivideByZeroException	int	Directory	==	Croc
InvalidCastException	j	Stream	!=	Platypus
OutOfMemoryException		FileStream		

Pool Puzzle Solution

Joey.Wombat() is called three times, and the third time it returns zero. That causes the WriteLine() to throw a **DivideByZeroException**.

```
public static void Main() {
    Kangaroo Joey = new Kangaroo();
    int Koala = Joey.Wombat(Joey.Wombat(Joey.Wombat(1)));
    try {
        Console.WriteLine((15 / Koala) + " eggs per pound");
    }
    catch (DivideByZeroException) {
        Console.WriteLine("G'Day Mate!");
    }
}
```

This **catch** block only catches exceptions where the code divides by zero.

The clue that this is a FileStream is that it has an OpenRead() method and throws an IOException.

```
public class Kangaroo {
    FileStream fs;
    int Croc;
    int Dingo = 0;
    public int Wombat(int Wallaby) {
        Dingo ++;
        try {
            if (Wallaby > 0) {
                fs = File.OpenWrite("wobbiegong");
                Croc = 0;
            } else if (Wallaby < 0) {
                Croc = 3;
            } else {
                fs = File.OpenRead("wobbiegong");
                Croc = 1;
            }
        }
        catch (IOException) {
            Croc = -3;
        }
        catch {
            Croc = 4;
        }
        finally {
            if (Dingo > 2) {
                Croc -= Dingo;
            }
        }
        return Croc;
    }
}
```

This code opens a file called "wobbiegong" and keeps it open the first time it's called. Later on, it opens the file again. But it never closed the file, which causes it to throw an IOException.

You already know that you always have to close files when you're done with them. If you don't, the file will be locked open, and if you try to open it again it'll throw an IOException.

Use the Exception object to get information about the problem

We've been saying all along that .NET generates an Exception object when an exception is thrown. When you write your catch block, you have access to that object. Here's how it works:

1 An object is humming along, doing its thing, when it encounters some something unexpected and throws an exception.

Uh-oh—what the heck happened?

An object

2 Luckily, its try/catch block caught the exception. Inside the catch block, it gave the Exception a name: **ex**.

```
try {
    DoSomethingRisky();
}
catch (Exception ex) {
    string message = ex.Message;
    MessageBox.Show(message, "An error occurred");
}
```

When you specify a specific type of exception in the catch block, if you provide a variable name then your code can use it to access the Exception object.

3 The exception object stays around until the catch block is done. Then the **ex** reference disappears, and it's garbage collected.

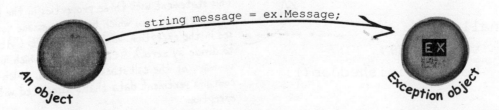

string message = ex.Message;

An object

EX

Exception object

Use more than one catch block to handle multiple types of exceptions

You know that you can catch a specific type of exception . . . but what if you write code where more than one problem can occur? In these cases, you may want to write code that handles each different type of exception. That's where using more than one catch block comes in. Here's an example from code from the beehive nectar processing plant. You can see how it catches several kinds of exceptions. In some cases it uses properties in the Exception object. It's pretty common to use the **Message** property, which usually contains a description of the exception that was thrown.

> You can also call the exception's ToString() method to get a lot of the pertinent data into your MessageBox.

```
public void ProcessNectar(NectarVat vat, Bee worker, HiveLog log) {
    try {
        NectarUnit[] units = worker.EmptyVat(vat);
        for (int count = 0; count < worker.UnitsExpected, count++) {
            stream hiveLogFile = log.OpenLogFile();
            worker.AddLogEntry(hiveLogFile);
        }
    }
    catch (IndexOutOfRangeException) {
        vat.Emptied = true;
    }
    catch (IOException ex) {
        worker.AlertQueen("Log file is corrupted: " + ex.Message);
    }
    catch (Exception ex) {
        worker.AlertQueen("An unspecified error happened: "
            + "Message: " + ex.Message + "\r\n"
            + "Stack trace: " + ex.StackTrace + "\r\n"
            + "Data: " + ex.Data + "\r\n");
    }
    finally {
        vat.Seal();
        worker.FinishedJob();
    }
}
```

> If you won't use the Exception object, there's no need to declare it.

> When you have several catch blocks, they're examined in order. In this code, first it checks to see if there was an index out of range. If not, then it'll check for a file I/O exception. The last catch block is a general catch-all exception that will get executed for any exception that wasn't already caught.

> This catch block assigns the exception to the variable ex, which it can use to get information from the Exception object.

> It's fine for two blocks to use the same name ("ex") for the Exception.

> This statement uses three properties in the Exception object: Message, which has the message you'd normally see in the exception window in the IDE ("Attempted to divide by zero"); StackTrace, which gives you a summary of the call stack; and Data, which sometimes contains pertinent data that's associated with the exception.

One class __throws__ an exception, another class __catches__ the exception

When you're building a class, you don't always know how it's going to be used. Sometimes other people will end up using your objects in a way that causes problems –and sometimes you do it yourself! That's where exceptions come in.

The whole point behind throwing an exception is to see what might go wrong, so you can put in place some sort of contingency plan. You don't usually see a method that throws an exception and then catches it. An exception is usually thrown in one method and then caught in a totally different one—usually in a different object.

Of course, one method in a single class can throw and catch its own exceptions.

Instead of this...

Without good exception handling, one exception can halt the entire program. Here's how it would work in a program that manages bee profiles for a queen bee.

This BeeProfile object's constructor expects the filename for a profile data file that it'll open using File.Open(). If there's a problem opening the file, the program bombs out.

```
stream = File.Open(profile);
```

The BeeProfile object tried to read a file but it wasn't there so File.Open() threw an exception. The hive didn't catch it, so it went unhandled.

> ⚠️ FileNotFoundException was unhandled
>
> Unable to find the specified file.

Notice how the BeeProfile object intercepts the exception, logs it using its WriteLogEntry() method, and then throws it again so it's passed along to the hive.

```
try {
    stream = File.Open(profile);
} catch (FileNotFoundException ex) {
    WriteLogEntry("unable to open " +
        profile + ": " + ex.Message());
    throw ex;
}
```

...we can do this.

The BeeProfile object can intercept the exception and add a log entry. Then it can turn around and throw the exception back to the hive, which catches it and recovers gracefully.

```
try {
    prof = new BeeProfile("prof.dat");
} catch (FileNotFoundException) {
    Hive.RecreateBeeProfile("prof.dat");
}
```

Now when the hive tries to create a new BeeProfile object by passing it an invalid filename, it can trust BeeProfile to log the error and then alert it to the problem by throwing an exception. The Hive can catch the exception and take some corrective action—in this case, recreating the bee profile.

Bees need an OutOfHoney exception

Your classes can throw their own exceptions. For example, if you get a null parameter in a method that was expecting a value, it's pretty common to throw the same exception a .NET method would:

```
throw new ArgumentNullException();
```

But sometimes you want your program to throw an exception because of a special condition that could happen when it runs. The bees we created in the hive, for example, consume honey at a different rate depending on their weight. If there's no honey left to consume, it makes sense to have the hive throw an exception. You can create a custom exception to deal with that specific error condition just by creating your own class that inherits from `Exception` and then throwing the exception whenever you encounter a specific error.

Exception
Message StackTrace
GetBaseException() ToString()

your Exception
Message StackTrace
GetBaseException() ToString()

```
public class OutOfHoneyException : System.Exception {
    public OutOfHoneyException(string message) : base(message) { }
}
public class HoneyDeliverySystem {
    ...
    public void FeedHoneyToEggs() {
        if (honeyLevel == 0) {
            throw new OutOfHoneyException("The hive is out of honey.");
        } else {
            foreach (Egg egg in Eggs) {
                ...
}
public partial class Form1 : Form {
...

    private void consumeHoney_Click(object sender, EventArgs e) {
        HoneyDeliverySystem delivery = new HoneyDeliverySystem();
        try {
            FeedHoneyToEggs()
        }
        catch (OutOfHoneyException ex){
            MessageBox.Show(ex.Message, "Warning: Resetting Hive");
            Hive.Reset();
        }
    }
}
```

You need to create a class for your exception and make sure that it inherits from System. Exception. Notice how we're overloading the constructor so we can pass an exception message.

This throws a new instance of the exception object.

If there's honey in the hive, the exception will never get thrown and this code will run.

You can catch a custom exception by name just like any other exception, and do whatever you need to do to handle it.

In this case, if the hive is out of honey none of the bees can work, so the simulator can't continue. The only way to keep the program working once the hive runs out of honey is to reset it, and we can do that by putting the code to reset it in the catch block.

Warning: Resetting hive
The hive is out of honey.
OK

Exception Magnets

Arrange the magnets so the application writes the output to the console.

```
public static void Main() {
    Console.Write("when it ");
    ExTestDrive.Zero("yes");
    Console.Write(" it ");
    ExTestDrive.Zero("no");
    Console.WriteLine(".");
}

class MyException : Exception { }
```

output:

when it thaws it throws.

Every value type—including constants like "yes" or 37 or true—has built-in methods. So "yes".Equals(t) returns true if the variable t contains the string "yes".

```
}
}
}
```

```
if ("yes".Equals(t)) {
```

```
Console.Write("a");
```

```
Console.Write("o");
```

```
Console.Write("t");
```

```
Console.Write("w");
```

```
Console.Write("s");
```

```
try {
```

```
} catch (MyException) {
```

```
throw new MyException();
```

```
} finally {
```

```
doRisky(test);
```

```
Console.Write("r");
    }
}
```

```
public class ExTestDrive {
    public static void Zero(string test) {
```

```
static void doRisky(String t) {
    Console.Write("h");
```

```
public static void Main() {
    Console.Write("when it ");
    ExTestDrive.Zero("yes");
    Console.Write(" it ");
    ExTestDrive.Zero("no");
    Console.WriteLine(".");
}
```

Exception Magnets Solution

Arrange the magnets so the application writes the output to the console.

output:

→ **when it thaws it throws.**

```
class MyException : Exception { }
```

This line defines a custom exception called **MyException**, which gets caught in a catch block in the code.

```
public class ExTestDrive {
    public static void Zero(string test) {
        try {
            Console.Write("t");
            doRisky(test);
            Console.Write("o");
        } catch (MyException) {
            Console.Write("a");
        } finally {
            Console.Write("w");
        }
        Console.Write("s");
    }

    static void doRisky(String t) {
        Console.Write("h");
        if ("yes".Equals(t)) {
            throw new MyException();
        }
        Console.Write("r");
    }
}
```

The Zero() method either prints "thaws" or "throws", depending on whether it was passed "yes" or something else as its test parameter.

The **finally** block makes sure that the method always prints "w". And the "s" is printed outside the exception handler, so it always prints, too.

This line only gets executed if doRisky() doesn't throw the exception.

The doRisky() method only throws an exception if it's passed the string "yes".

BULLET POINTS

- Any statement can throw an exception if something fails at runtime.

- Use a `try`/`catch` block to handle exceptions. Unhandled exceptions will cause your program to stop execution and pop up an error window.

- Any exception in the block of code after the `try` statement will cause the program's execution to immediately jump to the first statement in the block of code after `catch`.

- The `Exception` object gives you information about the exception that was caught. If you specify an `Exception` variable in your `catch` statement, that variable will contain information about any exception thrown in the `try` block:

```
try {
   // statements that might
   // throw exceptions
} catch (IOException ex) {
   // if an exception is thrown,
   // ex has information about it
}
```

- There are many different kinds of exception that you can catch. Each has its own object that inherits from `Exception`. Try to avoid just catching `Exception`—catch specific exceptions.

- Each `try` can have more than one `catch`:

```
try { ... }
catch (NullReferenceException ex) {
   // these statements will run if a
   // NullReferenceException is thrown
}
catch (OverflowException ex) { ... }
catch (Exception ex) {
   // Any exception that hasn't been
   // caught will jump to this block
}
```

- Your code can throw an exception using `throw`:

```
throw;

throw new Exception("Exception message");
```

- You can create a custom exception by inheriting from the `Exception` base class.

```
class CustomException : Exception;
```

- Most of the time, you only need to throw exceptions that are built into .NET, like ArgumentException. The reason you use different kinds of exceptions is so that you can **give more information to your users**. Popping up a window with the text "An unknown error has occurred" is not nearly as useful as an error message that says "The excuse folder is empty. Please select a different folder if you want to read excuses."

An easy way to avoid a lot of problems: using gives you try and finally for free

Remember, when you declare a reference in a "using" statement, its Dispose() method is automatically called at the end of the block.

You already know that `using` is an easy way to make sure that your files always get closed. But what you didn't know that it's really **just a C# shortcut** for `try` and `finally`!

```
using (YourClass c
        = new YourClass() ) {

   // code

}
```

is the same as this

```
YourClass c = new
YourClass();

try {

   // code

} finally {

   c.Dispose();

}
```

When you use a using statement, you're taking advantage of finally to make sure its Dispose() method is always called.

Exception avoidance: implement IDisposable to do your own clean up

Streams are great, because they already have code written to close themselves when the object is disposed of. But what if you have your own custom object, and it always needs to do something when it's disposed of? Wouldn't it be great if you could write your own code that got run if your object was used in a `using` statement?

> IDisposable is a really effective way to avoid common exceptions and problems. Make sure you use using statements any time you're working with any class that implements it.

C# lets you do just that with the `IDisposable` interface. Implement `IDisposable`, and write your clean up code in the `Dispose()` method, like this:

> You can only use a class in a "using" statement if it implements IDisposable; otherwise, your program won't compile.

> Your object must implement IDisposable if you want to use your object within a using statement.

```
class Nectar : IDisposable {
    private double amount;
    private BeeHive hive;
    private Stream hiveLog;
    public Nectar(double amount, BeeHive hive, Stream hiveLog) {
        this.amount = amount;
        this.hive = hive;
        this.hiveLog = hiveLog;
    }
    public void Dispose() {
        Hive.Add(amount);
        Hive.WriteHiveLogEntry(hiveLog,
            amount + "mg of nectar was added");
    }
}
```

> The IDisposable interface only has one member: the Dispose() method. Whatever you put in this method will get executed at the end of the using statement.

> This particular code always logs the amount of nectar added. It's important, and must happen, so we put it in the Dispose() method.

We can use multiple using statements now. First, let's use a built-in object that implements `IDisposable`, `Stream`. Then, we'll work with our updated `Nectar` object, which also implements `IDisposable`:

> You'll often see one using statement inside of another.

```
using (Stream Log = new File.Write("log.txt"))
using (Nectar nect = new Nectar(16.3, hive, Log)) {
    Bee.FlyTo(flower);
    Bee.Harvest(nect);
    Bee.FlyTo(hive);
}
```

> The Nectar object uses the Log stream, which will close automatically at the end of the outer using statement.

> Then the Bee object uses the nect object, which will log automatically at the end of the inner using statement.

there are no
Dumb Questions

Q: Can I only use objects that implement **IDisposable** with a using statement?

A: Yes. IDisposable is tailor-made to work with using statements, and adding a using statement is just like creating a new instance of a class, except that it always calls its Dispose() method.

Q: Can you put any statement inside a using block?

A: Definitely. The whole idea with using is that it helps you make sure that every object you create with it is disposed. But what you do with those objects is entirely up to you. In fact, you can create an object with a using statement and never even use it inside the block. But that would be pretty useless, so we don't recommend doing that.

Q: Can you call **Dispose()** outside of a **using** statement?

A: Yes. You don't ever actually **need** to use a using statement. You can call Dispose() yourself when you're done with the object. Or you can do whatever cleanup is necessary—like calling a stream's Close() method manually. But if you use a using statement, it'll make your code easier to understand and prevent problems that happen if you don't dispose your objects.

Q: You mentioned a "try/finally" block. Does that mean it's okay to have a try and finally without a catch?

A: Yes! You can definitely have a try block without a catch, and just a finally. It looks like this:

```
try {
    DoSomethingRisky();
    SomethingElseRisky();
}
finally {
    AlwaysExecuteThis();
}
```

If SomethingRisky() throws an exception, then the finally block will immediately run.

Q: Does Dispose() only work with files and streams?

A: No, there are a lot of classes that implement IDisposable, and when you're using one you should always use a using statement. (You'll see some of them in the next few chapters.) And if you write a class that has to be disposed in a certain way, then you can implement IDisposable, too.

If try/catch is so great, why doesn't the IDE just put it around everything? Then we wouldn't have to write all these try/catch blocks on our own, right?

You want to know what <u>type</u> of exception is thrown, so you can handle <u>that</u> exception.

There's more to exception handling than just printing out a generic error message. For instance, in the excuse finder, if we know we've got a FileNotFoundException, we might print an error that suggested where the right files should be located. If we have an exception related to databases, we might send an email to the database administrator. All that depends on you catching *specific* exception types.

This is why there are so many classes that inherit from Exception, and why you may even want to write your own classes to inherit from Exception.

The worst catch block <u>EVER</u>: comments

A catch block will let your program keep running if you want. An exception gets thrown, you catch the exception, and instead of shutting down and giving an error message, you keep going. But sometimes, that's not such a good thing.

Take a look at the DivisorCalculator, which seems to be acting funny all the time. What's going on?

```
public class Calculator {

...

    public void Divide(float dividend, float divisor) {

        try {

            this.quotient = dividend / divisor;

        } catch {

            // Note from Jim: we need to figure out a way to prevent

            // people from entering in zero in a division problem.

        }
    }
}
```

Here's the problem. If divisor is zero, this will create a DivdeByZeroException.

But there's a catch block. So why are we still getting errors?

The programmer thought that he could <u>bury</u> his exceptions by using an empty catch block, but he just caused a headache for whoever had to track down problems with it later.

You should <u>handle</u> your exceptions, not <u>bury</u> them

Just because you can keep your program running doesn't mean you've *handled* your exceptions. In the code above, the calculator won't crash... at least, not in the Divide() method. But what if some other code calls that method, and tries to print the results? If the divisor was zero, then the method probably returned an incorrect (and unexpected) value.

Instead of just adding a comment, and burying the exception, you need to **handle the exception**. And if you're not able to handle the problem, ***don't leave empty or commented catch blocks!*** That just makes it harder for someone else to track down what's going on. It's better to let the program continue to throw exceptions, because then it's easy to figure out what's going wrong.

Temporary solutions are okay (temporarily)

Sometimes you find a problem, and know it's a problem, but aren't sure what to do about it. In these cases, you might want to log the problem, and note what's going on. That's not as good as handling the exception, but it's better than doing nothing.

Here's a temporary solution to the calculator:

```
public class Calculator {

...

    public void Divide(float dividend, float divisor) {

        try {

            this.quotient = dividend / divisor;

        } catch (Exception ex) {

            StreamWriter sw = new StreamWriter(@"C:\Logs\errors.txt");

            sw.WriteLine(ex.getMessage());

            sw.Close();

        }

    }

}
```

This still needs to be fixed, but short-term, this makes it clear where the problem occurred.

> I get it. It's sort of like using exception handling to place a marker in the problem area.

Handling exceptions doesn't always mean the same thing as FIXING exceptions.

It's never good to have your program bomb out. But it's way worse to have no idea why it's crashing or what it's doing to users' data. That's why you need to be sure that you're always dealing with the errors you can predict and logging the ones you can't.

A few simple ideas for exception handling

Design your code to handle failures GRACEFULLY.

Give your users USEFUL error messages.

Throw built-in .NET exceptions where you can. Only throw custom exceptions if you need to give custom information.

Think about code in your try block that COULD get short-circuited.

 ... and most of all ...

Avoid unnecessary file system errors... ALWAYS USE A USING BLOCK ANY TIME YOU USE A STREAM! ALWAYS ALWAYS ALWAYS!

Use what you know about `try/catch/finally` to improve the exception handling in Brian's excuse manager.

1 Add exception handling to the Open button's Click event handler. Just make a simple try/catch block that pops up a message box. Here's what it should pop up if you try to open up a file that's not a real excuse file:

You'll get this exception message with a really small file, but a bigger one will give you a different error ("The input stream is not a valid binary format..."). Your message box should work either way.

3 You're not done yet. Open up the excuse manager, select a folder, enter data into the "Description" and "Last Results" boxes, **but don't enter a Last Used date**. Now select a folder and try saving the excuse. Did you get this `ArgumentOutOfRange` exception?

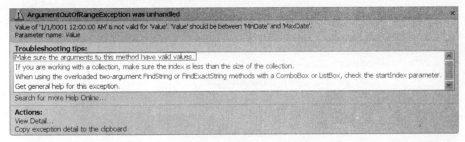

Use the debugger to track down the exception. This particular exception is totally avoidable—you can fix the program and make sure that the exception never happens? *(Hint: This has nothing to do with adding a try/catch block. You'll need to **figure out why** the "Last Used" date is causing a problem. Look carefully at the exception message for clues.)*

4 One last thing. Before the program threw the `ArgumentOutOfRange` exception, it saved out a file. Load that file in—you should get the same exception. And you'll get a different exception if you try to open a file that's not a valid excuse file. Add an exception handling block **nested inside the one you added in step 2** to make sure it doesn't fail when you try to load an invalid excuse file (which can happen in several situations). Here's what to do:

1. Declare a boolean variable called `clearForm` above the try/catch block. You'll set this to true if there's an exception, and check it later to see if the form should be cleared.

2. Add another try/catch block inside the one you just added to the Open button.

3. Add a `finally` block to the outer `try/catch` to reset the form to its original empty state. Reset `LastUsed.Value` to `DateTime.Now` (which returns the current date) if the `clearForm` variable is set to `true`.

Use what you know about `try`/`catch`/`finally` to improve the exception handling to Brian's excuse manager.

```
private void open_Click(object sender, EventArgs e) {
    if (CheckChanged()) {
        openFileDialog1.InitialDirectory = selectedFolder;
        openFileDialog1.Filter =
          "Excuse files (*.excuse)|*.excuse|All files (*.*)|*.*";
        openFileDialog1.FileName = description.Text + ".excuse";
        DialogResult result = openFileDialog1.ShowDialog();
        if (result == DialogResult.OK) {
            bool clearForm = false;
            try {
                currentExcuse = new Excuse(openFileDialog1.FileName);
                try {
                    UpdateForm(false);
                }
                catch {
                    MessageBox.Show("The excuse file '"
                        + openFileDialog1.FileName + "' is invalid",
                        "Unable to open the excuse");
                    clearForm = true;
                }
            }
            catch (Exception ex) {
                MessageBox.Show("An error occurred while opening the excuse '"
                    + openFileDialog1.FileName + "'\n" + ex.Message,
                    "Unable to open the excuse", MessageBoxButtons.OK,
                    MessageBoxIcon.Error);
                clearForm = true;
            }
            finally {
                if (clearForm) {
                    description.Text = "";
                    results.Text = "";
                    lastUsed.Value = DateTime.Now;
                }
```

Here's the try/catch block to create a pop up error, in case problems occur when the form calls the Excuse constructor to load an excuse.

Here's a nested try/catch. It handles exceptions that happen if the file gets loaded but has invalid data in it. That's not the same as problems arising from the Excuse constructor.

Here's the messagebox from the outer try/catch block. It prints the exception message.

Both catch blocks set clearForm to true so that this finally block knows that the form should be reset. It's okay to have code that interacts with your finally block, since you know finally blocks will always run.

Exceptioncross

Across

5. The base class that DivideByZeroException and FormatException inherit from

8. An _____Exception happens when you try to cast a value to a variable that can't hold it

10. If the next statement is a method, "Step _____" tells the debugger to execute all the statements in the method and break immediately afterwards

12. If you _____ your exceptions, it can make them hard to track down

13. This method is always called at the end of a using block

14. The field in the Exception object that contains a string with a description

15. One try block can have multiple _____ blocks

17. The _____ block contains any statements that absolutely must be run after an exception is handled

18. An _____Exception means you tried to cram a number that was too big into a variable that couldn't hold it

Down

1. The window in the IDE that you can use to check your variables' values

2. You'll get an exception if you try to divide by this

3. Toggle this if you want the debugger to stop execution when it hits a specific line of code

4. "Step _____" tells the debugger to execute the rest of the statements in the current method and then break

6. What a reference contains if it doesn't point to anything

7. You can only declare a variable with a using statement if it implements this interface

9. When a statement has a problem, it _____ an exception

11. A program that handles errors well

16. If the next statement is a method, "Step _____" tells the debugger to execute the first statement in that method

Exceptioncross Solution

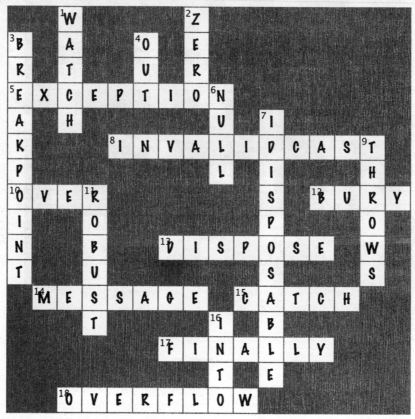

The completed crossword grid reads:

- 1 Down: WATCH
- 2 Down: ZERO
- 3 Down: BREAKPOINT
- 4 Down: OUT... (OULL)
- 5 Across: EXCEPTION
- 6 Down: NULL
- 7 Down: ISPOSS... (LISPOSS)
- 8 Across: INVALIDCAST
- 9 Down: THROWS
- 10 Across: OVE... (OVER)
- 11 Down: ROBUST
- 12 Across: BURY
- 13 Across: DISPOSE
- 14 Across: MESSAGE
- 15 Across: CATCH
- 16 Down: ITE... (BITE)
- 17 Across: FINALLY
- 18 Across: OVERFLOW

Brian <u>finally</u> gets his vacation...

Now that Brian's got a handle on his exceptions, his job's going smoothly and he can take that well-deserved (and boss-approved!) vacation day.

...and things are looking up back home!

Your exception handling skills did more than just prevent problems. They ensured that Brian's boss has no idea anything went wrong in the first place!

> Good ol' Brian. Never misses a day of work unless he's got a **real** problem.

Good exception handling is <u>invisible</u> to your users. The program never crashes, and if there are problems, they are handled gracefully, without confusing error messages.

11 events and delegates

What your code does when you're not looking

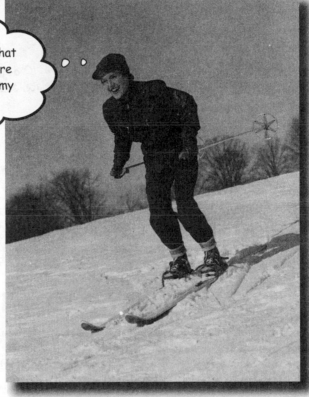

I'd better subscribe to that TreePopsUpOutOfNowhere event, or I'll have to call my OnBrokenLeg() method.

Your objects are starting to think for themselves.

You can't always control what your objects are doing. Sometimes things... happen. And when they do, you want your objects to be smart enough to **respond to anything** that pops up. And that's what events are all about. One object *publishes* an event, other objects *subscibe*, and everyone works together to keep things moving. Which is great, until you've got too many objects responding to the same event. And that's when **callbacks** will come in handy.

Ever wish your objects could think for themselves?

Suppose you're writing a baseball simulator. You're going to model a game, sell the software to the Yankees (they've got deep pockets, right?), and make a million bucks. You create your `Ball`, `Pitcher`, `Umpire`, and `Fan` objects, and a whole lot more. You even write code so that the `Pitcher` object can catch a ball.

Now you just need to connect everything together. You add an `OnBallInPlay()` method to `Ball`, and now you want your `Pitcher` object to respond with its event handler method. Once the methods are written, you just need to tie the separate methods together:

That's a standard way of naming methods—we'll talk more about it later.

When the ball gets hit, BallHasBeenHit() gets called.

The ball was hit with a 70 degree trajectory from homeplate, and it's going to travel 82 feet.

`Ball.OnBallInPlay(70, 82)`

We want the Pitcher to catch this ball.

The pitcher can handle the angle the ball was hit, and the distance (90 is greater than 82).

`Pitcher.CatchBall(70, 90)`

Ball object

Pitcher object

But how does an object <u>KNOW</u> to respond?

Here's the problem. You really want your `Ball` object to only worry about getting hit, and your `Pitcher` to object only worry about catching balls that come its way. In other words, you really don't want the `Ball` telling the `Pitcher`, "I'm coming to you."

Ball object

The Ball doesn't know which fielder will pick it up... maybe the Pitcher, or maybe the Catcher, or maybe ThirdBaseman who decided to ScootIn().

This doesn't mean that objects can't interact. It just means that a Ball shouldn't determine who fields it. That's not the Ball's job.

You want an object to worry about itself, not other objects. You're <u>separating</u> the <u>concerns</u> of each object.

When an <u>EVENT</u> occurs... objects listen

What you need to do when the ball is hit is use an **event**. An event is simply *something that's happened* in your program. Then, other objects can respond to that event—like our `Pitcher` object.

Even better, more than one object can listen for events. So the Pitcher could listen for a ball-being-hit event, as well as a `Catcher`, `ThirdBaseman`, an `Umpire`, even a `Fan`. And each object can respond to the event differently.

So what we want is a `Ball` object that can **raise an event**. Then, we want to have other objects to **subscribe to that particular type of event**... that just means listen to it, and get notified when that event occurs.

> **event, noun.**
> a **thing** that happens, especially something of importance. *The solar eclipse was an amazing **event** to behold.*

Any object can <u>subscribe</u> to this event... and the Ball object doesn't need to know what objects are subscribed.

When a Ball gets hit, it <u>raises</u> a BallInPlay event.

BallInPlay event raised

If we subscribe to the BallInPlay event, we'll always get notified when the ball's in play.

Ball object

Pitcher object

Umpire object

Fan object

Events look like lightning bolts in the IDE too. You'll see a an icon like this next to events in IntelliSense and in the properties window.

The Pitcher and other players want to try and field the ball.

The umpire checks every ball to see if it's fair or foul, and monitor what happens.

The Fan object subscribes in case a ball goes into the seats.

Want to DO SOMETHING with an event?
You need an <u>event</u> handler

Once your object "hears" about an event, you can set up some code to run. That code is called an **event handler**. An event handler gets information about the event, and runs every time that event occurs.

Remember, all this happens *without your intervention* at runtime. So you write code to raise an event, and then you write code to handle those events, and fire up your application. Then, whenever an event is raised, your handlers kick into action... *without you doing anything*. And, best of all, your objects have <u>separate</u> <u>concerns</u>. They're worrying about themselves, not other objects.

We've been doing this all along. Every time you click a button, an event is raised, and your code responds to that event.

One object <u>raises</u> its event, others listen for it...

Let's take a look at how events, event handlers, and subscription
works in C#:

① **First, other objects subscribe to the event**

Before the `Ball` can raise its `BallInPlay` event, other objects need to
subscribe to it. That's their way of saying, anytime a `BallInPlay` event
occurs, we want to know about it.

Every object adds its own
event handler to listen for
the event—just like you add
button1_Click() to your
programs to listen for Click
events.

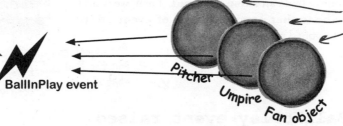

These objects are saying
they want to know anytime a
BallInPlay event is raised.

② **Something triggers an event**

The ball gets hit. It's time for the `Ball` object to raise a new event.

The Ball object starts everything
rolling. It's job is to raise an event
when it gets hit, and goes into play.

Sometimes we'll talk
about raising an event,
or firing it, or invoking
it—they're all the same
thing. People just use
different names for it.

③ **The ball raises an event**

A new event gets created (we'll talk about exactly how that works in just a minute).
That event also has some arguments, like the velocity of the ball, as well as
its trajectory. Those arguments are attached to the event as an instance of an
EventArgs object, and then the event is sent off, available to anyone listening for it.

BallInPlay is an event that gets
fired off by by Ball.

BallInPlay references a new
object, BallEventArgs, which is
just a class that defines fields
for Velocity and Trajectory.

Then, the other objects <u>handle</u> the event

Once an event is raised, all the objects subscribed to that event get notification, and can do something:

④ Subscribrs get notification

Since the `Pitcher`, `Umpire`, and `Fan` object subscribed to the `Ball` object's `BallInPlay` event, they all get notified—all of their event handler methods get called one after another.

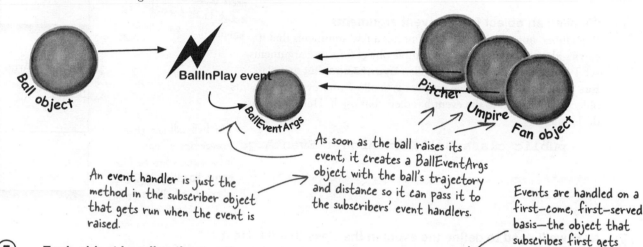

An event handler is just the method in the subscriber object that gets run when the event is raised.

As soon as the ball raises its event, it creates a BallEventArgs object with the ball's trajectory and distance so it can pass it to the subscribers' event handlers.

Events are handled on a first-come, first-served basis—the object that subscribes first gets notified first.

⑤ Each object handles the event

Now, `Pitcher`, `Umpire`, and `Fan` can all handle the `BallInPlay` event in their own way. But they don't all run at the same time—their event handlers get called one after another, with a reference to a `BallEventArgs` object as its parameter.

Here's what each object gets to work with... notice that the Ball that raised the event is nowhere to be found.

The Pitcher object checks BallEventArgs, and if the ball is close, it fields the ball.

The Fan objects checks BallEventArgs to see if the ball is close enough to catch.

The Umpire watches. It might even subscribe to other events, like BallFielded or BallThrown, to further react what happens.

Connecting the dots

Now that you've got a handle on what's going on,
let's take a closer look at how the pieces fit together.
Luckily, there are only a few moving parts.

It's a good idea (although not required) for your event argument objects to inherit from EventArgs. That's an empty class—it has no public members.

It means that you can upcast your EventArgs object in case you need to send it to an event that doesn't handle it in particular.

EventArgs

BallEventArgs
Trajectory
Distance

① **We need an object for the event arguments**
Remember, our `BallInPlay` event has a few arguments that it
carries along. So we need a very simple object for those arguments.
.NET has a standard class for it called **EventArgs**, but that class
has no members. Its sole purpose is to allow your event arguments
object to be passed to the event handlers that use it. Here's the class
declaration:

> **public class BallEventArgs : EventArgs**

The ball will use these properties to pass information hit to the event handlers about where the ball's been hit.

② **Next we'll need to define the event in the class that'll raise it**
The ball class will have a line with the **event keyword**—this is how it informs
other objects about the event, so they can subscribe to it. This line can be
anywhere in the class—it's usually near the property declarations. But as long as
it's in the Ball class, other objects can subscribe to a ball's event. It looks like this:

> **public event EventHandler BallInPlay;**

Events are usually public. This event is defined in the Ball class, but we'll want Pitcher, Umpire, etc., to be able to reference it. You could make it private if you only wanted other instances of the same class to subscribe to it.

After the event keyword comes EventHandler. That's not a reserved C# keyword—it's defined as part of .NET. The reason you need it is to tell the objects subscribing to the event what their event handler methods should look like.

When you use EventHandler, you're telling other methods that their event handlers need to take two parameters, an object named sender and an EventArgs reference named e.

(3) **The subscribing classes need event handler methods**

Every object that has to subscribe to the Ball's BallInPlay event needs to have an event handler. You already know how event handlers work—every time you added a method to handle a Button's Click event or a NumericUpDown's ValueChanged event, the IDE added an **event handler method** to your class. The Ball's BallInPlay event is no different, and an event handler for it should look pretty familiar:

```
void ball_BallInPlay(object sender, EventArgs e)
```

There's no C# rule that says your event handlers need to be named a certain way, but there's a pretty standard naming convention: the name of the object reference, followed by an underscore, followed by the name of the event.

The BallInPlay event declaration listed its event type as EventHandler, which means that it needs to take two parameters—an object called sender and an EventArgs called e—and have no return value.

The class that has this particular event handler method has a Ball reference variable called `ball`, so its BallInPlay event handler starts with "`ball_`", followed by the name of the event being handled, "`BallInPlay`".

(4) **Each individual object subscribes to the event**

Once we've got the event handler set up, the various Pitcher, Umpire, ThirdBaseman, and Fan objects need to hook up their own event handlers. Each one of them will have its own specific `ball_BallInPlay` method that responds differently to the event. So if there's a Ball object reference variable or field called `ball`, then the += operator will hook up the event handler:

```
ball.BallInPlay += new EventHandler(ball_BallInPlay);
```

This tells C# to hook the event handler up to the BallInPlay event of whatever object the ball reference is pointing to.

The += operator tells C# subscribe an event handler to an event.

This part specifies which event handler method to subscribe to the event.

The event handler method's signature (its parameters and return value) has to match the one defined by EventHandler or the program won't compile.

Turn the page, there's a little more...

⑤ A Ball object raises its event to notify subscribers that it's in play

Now that the events are all set up, the Ball can **raise its event** in response to something else that happens in the simulator. Raising an event is easy—it just calls the BallInPlay event.

```
if (BallInPlay != null)

    BallInPlay(this, e);
```

e is a new BallEventArgs object.

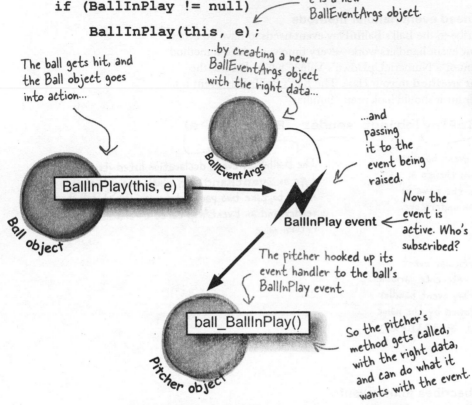

The ball gets hit, and the Ball object goes into action...

...by creating a new BallEventArgs object with the right data...

...and passing it to the event being raised.

BallInPlay(this, e)

Ball object

BallEventArgs

BallInPlay event

Now the event is active. Who's subscribed?

The pitcher hooked up its event handler to the ball's BallInPlay event.

ball_BallInPlay()

pitcher object

So the pitcher's method gets called, with the right data, and can do what it wants with the event.

Watch it!

If you raise an event with no handlers, it'll throw an exception.

If no other objects have added their event handlers to an event, it'll be null. So always check to make sure your event handler isn't equal to null before you raise it. If you don't, it'll throw a NullReferenceException.

Use a standard name when you add a method to raise an event

Take a minute and go the code for any form and type the keyword override any place you'd declare a method. As soon as you press space, an IntelliSense window pops up:

```
override
    OnCursorChanged(EventArgs e)
    OnDeactivate(EventArgs e)
    OnDockChanged(EventArgs e)
    OnDoubleClick(EventArgs e)
    OnDragDrop(DragEventArgs drgevent)
```

Notice how each of these methods takes an EventArgs as a parameter? They all pass that parameter on to the event when they raise it.

There are a huge number of events that a Form object can raise, and every one of them has its own method that raises it. The form's OnDoubleClick() raises the DoubleClick event, and that's the whole reason it's there. So the Ball event will follow the same convention: we'll make sure it **has a method called OnBallInPlay** that takes a BallEventArgs object as a parameter. The baseball simulator will call that method any time it needs the ball to raise its BallInPlay event—so when the simulator detects that the bat hit the ball, it'll create a new instance of BallEventArgs with the ball's trajectory and distance and pass it to OnBallInPlay().

there are no Dumb Questions

Q: Why do I need to include the word EventHandler when I declare an event? I thought the event handler was what the other objects used to subscribe to the events.

A: That's true—when you need to subscribe to an event, you write a method called an event handler. But did you notice how we used `EventHandler` in the the event declaration (step #2) *and* the in line to subscribe the event handler to it (step #4)? What `EventHandler` does is it defines the **signature** of the event—it tells the objects subscribing to the event exactly how they need to define their event handler methods. Specifically, it says that if you want to subscribe a method to this event, it needs to take two parameters (an `object` and an `EventArgs` reference) and have a `void` return value.

Q: What happens if I try to use a method that doesn't match the ones that are defined by EventHandler?

A: Then your program won't compile. The compiler will make sure that you don't ever accidentally subscribe an incompatible event handler method to an event. That's why the standard event handler, `EventHandler`, is so useful—as soon as you see it, you know exactly what your event handler method needs to look like.

Q: Wait, "standard" event handler? There are other kinds of event handlers?

A: Yes! Your events don't *have to* send an object and an EventArgs. In fact, they can send anything at all—or nothing at all! Look at the last line in the IntelliSense window on the bottom on the facing page. Notice how the OnDragDrop method takes a DragEventArgs reference instead of an EventArgs reference? DragEventArgs inherits from EventArgs, just like BallEventArgs does. The form's DragDrop event doesn't use EventHandler. It uses something else, DragEventHandler, and if you want to handle it your event handler method needs to take an object and a DragEventArgs reference.

The parameters of the event are defined by something called a *delegate*—EventHandler and DragEventArgs are two examples of delegates. But we'll talk more about that in a minute.

Q: So I can probably have my event handlers return something other than void, too, right?

A: Well, you can, but it's often a bad idea. If you don't return void from your handler, you can't *chain* event handlers. That means you can't connect more than one handler to each event. Since chaining is a handy feature, you'd do best to always return void from your event handlers.

Q: Chaining? What's that?

A: It's how more than one object can subscribe to the same event—they chain their event handlers onto the event, one after

another. We'll talk a lot more about that in a minute, too.

Q: Is that why I used += when when I added my event handler? Like I'm somehow adding a new handler to existing handlers?

A: Exactly! Anytime you add an event handler, you want to use +=. That way, your handler doesn't replace existing handlers. It just becomes one in what may be a very long chain of other event handlers, all of which are listening to the same event.

Q: Why does the ball use "this" when it raises the BallInPlay() event?

A: Because that's the first parameter of the standard event handler. Have you noticed how every Click event handler method has a parameter "object sender"? That parameter is a **reference to the object that's raising the event**. So if you're handling a button click, `sender` points to the button that was clicked. And if you're handling a BallInPlay event, `sender` will point to the Ball object that's in play—and the ball sets that parameter to `this` when it raises the event.

A **SINGLE** event is always raised by a **SINGLE** object.

But a **SINGLE** event can be responded to by **MULTIPLE** objects.

The IDE creates event handlers for you automatically

Most programmers follow the same convention for naming their event handlers. If there's a `Ball` object that has a `BallInPlay` event, and the name of the reference holding the object is called `ball`, then the event handler would typically be named `ball_BallInPlay()`. That's not a hard-and-fast rule, but if you write your code like that, it'll be a lot easier for other programmers to read.

Luckily, the IDE makes it really easy to name your event handlers properly. It has a feature that **automatically adds event handler methods for you** when you're working with a class that raises an event. It shouldn't be too surprising that the IDE can do this for you—after all, this is exactly what it does when you double-click on a button in your form.

Do this

1 **Start a new Windows application and add the Ball and BallEventArgs**
Here's the Ball class:

```
public class Ball {
    public event EventHandler BallInPlay;
    public void OnBallInPlay(BallEventArgs e) {
        if (BallInPlay != null)
            BallInPlay(this, e);
    }
}
```

And here's the BallEventArgs class:

```
public class BallEventArgs : EventArgs {
    public int Trajectory { get; private set; }
    public int Distance { get; private set; }
    public BallEventArgs(int Trajectory, int Distance) {
        this.Trajectory = Trajectory;
        this.Distance = Distance;
    }
}
```

2 **Start adding the Pitcher's constructor**
Add a new Pitcher class to your project. Then give it a constructor that takes a `Ball` reference called `ball` as a parameter. There will be one line of code in the constructor to add its event handler to `ball.BallInPlay`. Start typing the statement, but **don't type += yet**.

```
public Pitcher(Ball ball) {
    ball.BallInPlay
}
```

③ Type += and the IDE will finish the statement for you

As soon as you type += in the statement, the IDE displays a very useful little box:

```
public Pitcher(Ball ball) {
    ball.BallInPlay +=
}                         new EventHandler(ball_BallInPlay);   (Press TAB to Insert)
```

As soon as you press the tab key, the IDE will finish the statement for you. It'll look like this:

```
public Pitcher(Ball ball) {
    ball.BallInPlay += new EventHandler(ball_BallInPlay);
}
```

When you double-click on a button in the form designer, the IDE does the exact same trick—adding an event handler automatically—except that it adds the code to the form's InitializeComponent() method in the Form1. Designer.cs file instead of just adding it to the end of the class file.

④ The IDE will add your event handler, too

You're not done—you still need to add a method to chain onto the event. Luckily, the IDE takes care of that for you, too.

```
new EventHandler(ball_BallInPlay);
                 Press TAB to generate handler 'ball_BallInPlay' in this class
```

Hit the tab key again to make the IDE add this event handler method to your Pitcher class. The IDE will always follow the objectName_HandlerName() convention:

```
void ball_BallInPlay(object sender, EventArgs e) {
    throw new NotImplementedException();
}
```

The IDE always fills in this NotImplementedException() as a placeholder so if you run the code it'll throw an exception that tells you that you still need to implement something it filled in automatically.

⑤ Finish the pitcher's event handler

Now that you've got the event handler's skeleton added to your class, fill in the rest of its code. The pitcher should catch any low balls, otherwise he covers first base. *Since BallEventArgs is a subclass of EventArgs, we'll downcast it using the as keyword so we can use its properties.*

```
void ball_BallInPlay(BallEventArgs e) {
    if (e is BallEventArgs) {
        BallEventArgs ballEventArgs = e as BallEventArgs;
        if ((ballEventArgs.Distance < 95) && (ballEventArgs.Trajectory < 60))
            CatchBall();
        else
            CoverFirstBase();
    }
}
```

You'll add these methods in a minute.

It's time to put what you've learned so far into practice. Your job is to complete the Ball and Pitcher classes, add a Fan class, and make sure they all work together with a very basic version of your baseball simulator.

1 **Complete the Pitcher class.**

Below is what we've got for `Pitcher`. Add the `CatchBall()` and `CoverFirstBase()` methods. Both should print out that the catcher has either caught the ball, or run to first base.

```
public class Pitcher {
    public Pitcher(Ball ball) {
        ball.BallInPlay += new EventHandler(ball_BallInPlay);
    }

    void ball_BallInPlay(object sender, EventArgs e) {
        if (e is BallEventArgs){
            BallEventArgs ballEventArgs = e as BallEventArgs;
            if ((ballEventArgs.Distance < 95) && (ballEventArgs.Trajectory < 60))
                CatchBall();
            else
                CoverFirstBase();
        }
    }
}
```

> You'll need to implement these two methods to write a line of output to the console.

Pitcher object

2 **Write a Fan class.**

Create another class called Fan. Fan should also subscribe to the BallInPlay event in its constructor. The fan's event handler should see if the distance is greater than 400 feet and the trajectory is greater than 30 (a home run), and grab for a glove to try and catch the ball if it is. If not, the fan should scream and yell. Write out what's going on with the fan to the console.

> Look at the output window on the facing page to see exactly what it should print.

Fan object

4 **Build a very simple simulator.**

Create a new application. The application should have two NumericUpDown controls: one for the ball's distance, and one for its trajectory. Add a button, labeled "Play ball!" When "Play ball!" is clicked, a ball is hit with the values in the two NumericUpDowns. Your form should look something like this:

The value for trajectory can range from 0 to 100, so set its Minimum property to 0, Maximum to 100 and Value to 20.

Don't forget to cast the Value properties to ints before you use them.

The Distance can range from 0 to 500, with a default value of 100.

5 **Create the following output.**

See if you can make your simulator generate this output with three successive balls put into play. Write down the values you used to get the result below:

Ball 1:

Trajectory: ....

Distance: ....

Ball 2:

Trajectory: ....

Distance: ....

Ball 3:

Trajectory: ....

Distance: ....

Exercise Solution

It's time to put what you've learned so far into practice. Your job is to complete the Ball and Pitcher classes, add a Fan class, and make sure they all work together with a very basic version of your baseball simulator.

```
public class Ball
{
    public event EventHandler BallInPlay;
    public void OnBallInPlay(BallEventArgs e)
    {
        if (BallInPlay != null)
            BallInPlay(this, e);
    }
}
```

The OnBallInlay() method just raises the BallInPlay event—but it has to check make sure it's not null, otherwise it'll throw an exception.

Read-only automatic properties work really well in event arguments because the event handlers only read the data passed to them.

```
public class BallEventArgs {

    public int Trajectory { get; private set; }
    public int Distance { get; private set; }
    public BallEventArgs(int Trajectory, int Distance)
    {
        this.Trajectory = Trajectory;
        this.Distance = Distance;
    }
}
```

The Fan object's constructor chains its event handler onto the BallInPlay event.

```
public class Fan {
    public Fan(Ball ball)
    {
        ball.BallInPlay += new EventHandler(ball_BallInPlay);
    }

    void ball_BallInPlay(object sender, EventArgs e)
    {
        if (e is BallEventArgs) {
            BallEventArgs ballEventArgs = e as BallEventArgs;
            if (ballEventArgs.Distance > 400 && ballEventArgs.Trajectory > 30)
                Console.WriteLine("Fan: Home run! I'm going for the ball!");
            else
                Console.WriteLine("Fan: Woo-hoo! Yeah!");
        }
    }
}
```

The fan's BallInPlay event handler looks for any ball that's high and long.

```
public class Pitcher {
    public Pitcher(Ball ball) {
        ball.BallInPlay += new EventHandler(ball_BallInPlay);
    }

    void ball_BallInPlay(object sender, EventArgs e) {
        if (e is BallEventArgs) {
            BallEventArgs ballEventArgs = e as BallEventArgs;
            if ((ballEventArgs.Distance < 95) && (ballEventArgs.Trajectory < 60))
                CatchBall();
            else
                CoverFirstBase();
        }
    }

    private void CatchBall() {
        Console.WriteLine("Pitcher: I caught the ball");
    }

    private void CoverFirstBase() {
        Console.WriteLine("Pitcher: I covered first base");
    }
}
```

You already have the pitcher's BallInPlay event handler. It looks for any low balls.

```
public partial class Form1 : Form {
    Ball ball = new Ball();
    Pitcher pitcher;
    Fan fan;

    public Form1() {
        InitializeComponent();
        pitcher = new Pitcher(ball);
        fan = new Fan(ball);
    }

    private void playBall_Click(object sender, EventArgs e) {
        BallEventArgs ballEventArgs = new BallEventArgs(
            (int)trajectory.Value, (int)distance.Value);
        ball.OnBallInPlay(ballEventArgs);
    }
}
```

The form needs one ball, one fan, and one pitcher. It hooks the fan and pitcher up to the ball in its constructor.

When the button's clicked, the form tells the pitcher to pitch the ball to the batter, which tells the ball to fire off its BallInPlay event, which calls the event handlers in the pitcher and fan objects.

Here are the values we used to get the output. Yours might be a little different.

Ball 1:

Trajectory: 75

Distance: 105

Ball 2:

Trajectory: 48

Distance: 80

Ball 3:

Trajectory: 40

Distance: 435

The forms you've been building all use events

Every time you've created a button, double-clicked on it in the designer, and written code for a method like `button1_Click()`, you've been working with events.

Do this

① Create a new Windows Application project. Bring up the form, and go to the Properties window. There are icons at the top of the window—click on the one that's got a lightning bolt icon on it. That will bring up **the events page in the Properties window**:

You can see all of the pre-made events for a control by click on it and then click on this events button in the properties window.

Scroll down to Click and double-click on the word "Click". When you do, the IDE will add a new click event handler to your form that gets fired every time you click on it. And it'll add a line to Form1.Designer.cs to hook the event handler up to the event.

You can create an event that will fire every time someone clicks on the form by selecting Form1_Click next to Click in the events window.

② Double-click on the "Click" row in the events page. The IDE will automatically add an event handler method to your form called Form1_Click. Add this line of code to it:

```
private void Form1_Click(object sender, EventArgs e) {
    MessageBox.Show("You just on clicked the form");
}
```

③ Visual Studio did more than just write a little method declaration for you, though. It also hooked the event handler up to the Form objects Click event. Open up Form1.Designer.cs and use the Quick Find feature in the IDE to search for the text Form1_Click in the current project. You'll find this line of code:

```
this.Click += new System.EventHandler(this.Form1_Click);
```

Now run the program and make sure your code works!

Watch it!

Event handlers always need to be "hooked up".

If you drag a button onto your form and add a method called `button1_Click()`, *that has the right parameters, but **isn't registered to listen to your button**, the method won't ever get called. Double-click on the button in the designer—the IDE will see the default event handler name is taken, so it'll add an event handler for the button called* `button1_Click_1()`.

One event, multiple handlers

Here's a really useful thing that you can do with events: you can **chain** them
so that one event or delegate calls many methods, one after another. Let's
add a few buttons to your application to see how it works.

4   Add these two methods to your form:

```
private void SaySomething(object sender, EventArgs e) {
    MessageBox.Show("Something");
}
private void SaySomethingElse(object sender, EventArgs e) {
    MessageBox.Show("Something else");
}
```

5   Now add two buttons to your form. Double-click on each button to add its event handler.
Here's the code for both event handlers:

```
private void button1_Click(object sender, EventArgs e) {
    this.Click +=new EventHandler(SaySomething);
}
private void button2_Click(object sender, EventArgs e) {
    this.Click +=new EventHandler(SaySomethingElse);
}
```

6   Now run your program and do this:

★   **Click the form**—you'll see a message box pop up that says, "You just clicked on the form".

★   Now **click button1** and then **click on the form again**. You'll see two message boxes
pop up: "You just clicked on the form" and then "Something".

★   **Click button2 twice** and then **click on the form again**. You'll see four message boxes:
"You just clicked on the form", "Something", "Something else", and "Something else".

So what happened?

Every time you clicked one of the buttons, you chained another method—either Something() or
SomethingElse()—onto the form's Click event. You can keep clicking the buttons, and they'll keep
chaining the same methods onto the event. The event doesn't care how many methods are
chained on, or even if the same method is in the chain more than once. It'll just call them all every
time the event fires, one after another, in the order they were added.

Connecting event <u>senders</u> with event <u>receivers</u>

One of the trickiest things about events is that the **sender** of the event has to know what kind of event to send—including the arguments to pass to the event. And the **receiver** of the event has to know about the return type and the arguments its handler methods must use.

But—and here's the tricky part—you can't tie the sender and receiver *together*. You want the sender to send the event and *not worry about who receives it*. And the receiver cares about the event, *not the object that raised the event*. So both sender and receiver focus on the event, not each other.

Ball needs to know about BallInPlay, because it needs to raise that event.

Pitcher needs to know about BallInPlay, so it can respond to that event, and build an appropriate event handler.

BallInPlay event

Ball object

Pitcher object

Ball does <u>NOT</u> want to worry about Pitcher. It doesn't care what type of object works with it: Fan, Pitcher, Umpire, etc.

"My people will get in touch with your people."

You know what this code does:

```
Ball currentBall;
```

It creates a **reference variable** that can point to any Ball object. It's not tied to a single Ball. Instead, it can point to any ball object—or it can be null, and not point to anything at all.

An event needs a similar kind of reference—except instead of pointing to an object, it needs one that **points to a method**. Every event needs to keep track of a list of methods that are subscribed to it. You've already seen that they can be in other classes, and they can even be private. So how does it keep track of all of the event handler methods that it needs to call?

A delegate STANDS IN for an actual method

One of the most useful aspects of events is that when an event fires, it **has no idea** whose event handler methods it's calling. Anyone who happens to subscribe to an event gets his event handler called. So how does the event manage that?

It uses a C# type called a **delegate**. A delegate lets you create a reference variable, but instead of referring to an instance of a class, it **refers to a method inside a class.**

You've actually already been using delegates thoughout this chapter! When you created the BallInPlay event, you used EventHandler. Well, an EventHandler is just a delegate. If you right-click on EventHandler in the IDE and select "Go to definition", this is what you'll see (try it yourself):

> When you create a delegate, all you need to do is specify the signature of methods that it can point to.
>
> So this delegate can be used to reference any method that takes an object and an EventArgs and has no return value.

```
public delegate void EventHandler(object sender, EventArgs e);
```

This specifies the return value of the delegate's signature—which means an EventHandler can only point to methods with void return values.

The name of this delegate is EventHandler.

Do this

A delegate adds a new type to your project

When you add a delegate to your project, you're adding a **delegate type**. And when you use it to create a field or variable, you're creating an **instance** of that delegate type. **So create a new project**. Then add a new class file to the project called ReturnsAString.cs. But instead of putting a class inside it, add a single line:

```
public delegate string ReturnsAString();
```

ReturnsAString is a delegate type that you've added to your project. Now you can use it to declare variables and fields.

Go to the form code and add this field to the form:

```
ReturnsAString someMethod;
```

someMethod is an instance of the delegate type ReturnsAString.

Now build your program—it compiles! (It gets a warning because you never used that field—that's okay.) As soon as you added your new delegate to the program, it created a new type called ReturnsAString. If you use that type to declare a variable, you can set that variable equal to any method that takes no parameters and returns a string. Try it out—add this method to your code:

```
private string HiThere() {
    return "Hi there!";
}
```

This method's signature matches ReturnsAString.

Add a button that has these three lines. Click it and see what happens:

```
someMethod = new ReturnsAString(HiThere);
string message = someMethod();
MessageBox.Show(message);
```

You can set someMethod just like any other variable. But when you call it like a method, it calls whatever method it happens to point to.

del-e-gate, noun.
a person sent or authorized to represent others. *The president sent a **delegate** to the summit.*

Delegates in action

There's nothing mysterious about delegates—in fact, they
don't take much code at all to use. Let's use them to help a
restaurant owner sort out his top chef's secret ingredients.

Do this

1 **Create a new Windows project and add a delegate**
Delegates usually appear outside of any other classes, so add a new class file to your project and
call it AddSecretIngredient.cs. It will have exactly one line of code in it:

```
public delegate string GetSecretIngredient(int amount);
```

This delegate can be used to create a variable that can point to any method that takes one int
parameter and returns a string.

2 **Add a class for the first chef, Suzanne**
Suzanne.cs will hold a class that keeps track of the first chef's secret ingredient. It has a private
method called SuzannesSecretIngredient() with a signature that matches GetSecretIngredient.
But it also has a read-only property—and check out that property's type. It returns a
GetSecretIngredient. So other objects can use that property to get a reference to her
SuzannesIngredientList() method.

```
public class Suzanne {
    public GetSecretIngredient MySecretIngredientMethod {
        get {
            return new GetSecretIngredient(SuzannesSecretIngredient);
        }
    }
    private string SuzannesSecretIngredient(int amount) {
        return amount.ToString() + " ounces of cloves";
    }
}
```

*Suzanne's secret
ingredient method
takes an int
called amount and
returns a string
that describes her
secret ingredient.*

3 **Then add a class for the second chef, Amy**
Amy's method works a lot like Suzanne's:

*Amy's GetSecretIngredient property
returns a new instance of the
GetSecretIngredient delegate that's
pointing to her secret ingredient method.*

```
public class Amy {
    public GetSecretIngredient AmysSecretIngredientMethod {
        get {
            return new GetSecretIngredient(AmysSecretIngredient);
        }
    }
    private string AmysSecretIngredient(int amount) {
        if (amount < 10)
            return amount.ToString()
                    + " cans of sardines -- you need more!";
        else
            return amount.ToString() + " cans of sardines";
    }
}
```

*Amy's secret
ingredient method
also takes an int
called amount and
returns a string,
but it returns a
different string
from Suzanne's.*

4 **Create a new Windows project and add a delegate**
Build this form. ───────────────────────────►

Here's the code for the form:

```
GetSecretIngredient ingredientMethod = null;
Suzanne suzanne = new Suzanne();
Amy amy = new Amy();

private void useIngredient_Click(object sender, EventArgs e) {
    if (ingredientMethod != null)
        Console.WriteLine("I'll add " + ingredientMethod((int)amount.Value));
    else
        Console.WriteLine("I don't have a secret ingredient!");
}

private void getSuzanne_Click(object sender, EventArgs e) {
    ingredientMethod = new GetSecretIngredient(suzanne.MySecretIngredientMethod);
}

private void getAmy_Click(object sender, EventArgs e) {
    ingredientMethod = new GetSecretIngredient(amy.AmysSecretIngredientMethod);
}
```

5 **Use the debugger to explore how delegates work**
You've got a great tool—the IDE's debugger—that really help you get a handle on how delegates work. Do the following steps:

★ Start by running your program. First click the "Get the ingredient" button—it should write a line to the console that says, "I don't have a secret ingredient."

★ Click the "Use Suzanne's delegate" button—that takes the form's ingredientMethod field (which is a GetSecretIngredient delegate) and set it equal to whatever Suzanne's GetSecretIngredient property returns. That property returns a new instance of the GetSecretIngredient type that's pointing to the SuzannesSecretIngredient() method.

★ Click the "Get the ingredient" button again. Now that the form's ingredientMethod field is pointing to SuzannesSecretIngredient(), it calls that, passing it the value in the numericUpDown control and writing its output to the console.

★ Click the "Use Amy's delegate" button. It uses the Amy.GetSecretIngredient property to set the form's ingredientMethod field to point to the AmysSecretIngredient() method.

★ Click the "Get the ingredient" method one more time. Now it calls Amy's method.

★ Now **use the debugger** to see exactly what's going on. Place a breakpoint on the first line of each of the three methods in the form. Then **restart the program** (which resets the ingredientMethod so that it's equal to null), and start over with the above five steps. Use the Step Into (F11) feature of the debugger to step through every line of code. Watch what happens when you click "Get the ingredient". It steps right into the Suzanne and Amy classes, depending on which method the ingredientMethod field is pointing to.

Pool Puzzle

Your *job* is to take snippets from the pool and place them into the blank lines in the code. You can use the same snippet more than once, and you won't need to use all the snippets. Your *goal* is to complete the code for a form that writes this output to the console when its **button1** button is clicked.

Output
```
Fingers is coming to get you!
```

Note: each thing from the pool can be used more than once

```
public Form1() {
    InitializeComponent();
    this._____ += new EventHandler(_____);
    this._____ += new EventHandler(_____);
}

void Towtruck(object sender, EventArgs e) {
    Console.Write("is coming ");
}

void Motorcycle(object sender, EventArgs e) {
    button1._____ += new EventHandler(_____);
}

void Bicycle(object sender, EventArgs e) {
    Console.WriteLine("to get you!");
}

void _____(object sender, EventArgs e) {
    button1._____ += new EventHandler(Dumptruck);
    button1._____ += new EventHandler(_____);
}

void _____(object sender, EventArgs e) {
    Console.Write("Fingers ");
}
```

```
      +
      ++
      ==
      -=
      !=

Van              Load          event           Airplane
Car              Save          delegate        Bicycle
Minivan          Open          int             Dumptruck
Motorcycle       Close         private         Towtruck
Tricycle         Click         public          Flatbed
                 Scroll
```

Any object can subscribe to a public event...

Suppose we add a new class to our simulator, a Bat class, and that class adds a HitTheBall event into the mix. Here's how it works: if the simulator detects that the player hit the ball, it calls the Bat object's OnHitTheBall() method, which raises a HitTheBall event.

So now we can add a bat_HitTheBall method to the Ball class that subscribes to the Bat object's HitTheBall event. Then when the ball gets hit, its own event handler calls its OnBallInPlay() method to raise its own event, BallInPlay, and the chain reaction begins. Fielders field, fans scream, umpires yell... we've got a ball game.

Now its event handler can take information about how hard the swing was, figure out the distance and trajectory, and raise a BallInPlay event.

The simulator detects that the bat collided with the ball, so it calls the bat object's OnHitTheBall() method.

Ball subscribed to the HitTheBall event.

...but that's not always a good thing!

There's only ever going to be one ball in play at any time. But if the Bat object uses an event to announce to the ball that it's been hit, then any Ball object can subscribe to it. And that means we've set ourself up for a nasty little bug—what happens if a programmer accidentally adds three more Ball objects? Then the batter will swing, hit, and **four different balls will fly** out into the field!

Uh-oh! These balls were supposed to be held in reserve in case the first one was hit out of the park.

But a careless programmer subscribed them all to the bat's HitTheBall event... so when the bat hit the ball that the pitcher threw, all four of them flew out into the field!

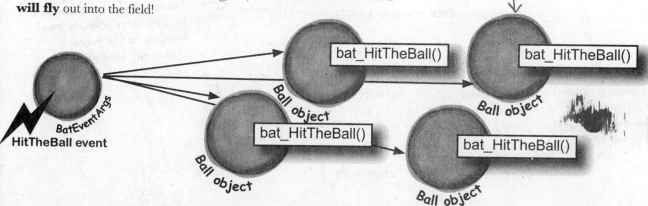

The Case of the Golden Crustacean

Five Minute Mystery

Henry "Flatfoot" Hodgkins is a TreasureHunter. He's hot on the trail of one of the most prized possessions in the rare and unusual aquatic-themed jewelry markets: a jade-encrusted translucent gold crab. But so are lots of other TreasureHunters. They all got a reference to the same crab in their constructor, but Henry wants to claim the prize *first*.

In a stolen set of class diagrams, Henry discovers that the GoldenCrab class raises a RunForCover event every time anyone gets close to it. Even better, the event includes NewLocationArgs, which detail where the crab is moving to. But none of the other treasure hunters know about the event, so Henry figures he can cash in.

Henry adds code to his constructor to register his ListenForClues() method as an event handler for the RunForCover event, on the crab reference he's got. Then, he sends a lowly underling after the crab, knowing it will run away, hide, and raise the RunForCover event—giving Henry's ListenForClues() method all the information he needs.

Everything goes according to plan, until Henry gets the new location and rushes to grab the crab. He's stunned to see three other TreasureHunters already there, fighting over the crab.

How did the other treasure hunters beat Henry to the crab?

→ Answers on page 511.

Pool Puzzle Solution

```
public Form1() {
    InitializeComponent();
    this.Load += new EventHandler(Minivan);
    this.Load += new EventHandler(Motorcycle);
}
void Towtruck(object sender, EventArgs e) {
    Console.Write("is coming ");
}
void Motorcycle(object sender, EventArgs e) {
    button1.Click += new EventHandler(Bicycle);
}
void Bicycle(object sender, EventArgs e) {
    Console.WriteLine("to get you!");
}
void Minivan(object sender, EventArgs e) {
    button1.Click += new EventHandler(Dumptruck);
    button1.Click += new EventHandler(Towtruck);
}
void Dumptruck(object sender, EventArgs e) {
    Console.Write("Fingers ");
}
```

The constructor chains two event handlers onto the load events. They get fired off as soon as the form is loaded.

When the button is clicked, it calls the three event handlers that are chained to it.

The two Load event handlers hook up three separate event handlers to the button's Click event handler.

Use a callback instead of an event to hook up exactly <u>one</u> <u>object</u> to a delegate

Our system of events only works if we've got one `Ball` and one `Bat`. If you've got several `Ball` objects, and they all subscribe to the public event `HitTheBall`, then they'll all go flying when the event is raised. But that doesn't make any sense... it's really only one `Ball` object that got hit. We need to let the one ball that's being pitched hook itself up to the bat, but we need to do it in a way that doesn't allow any other balls to hook themselves up. And that's what a **callback** is—it's a way of using a delegate so the object that's calling it is guaranteed to only call the one method that it needs to call, and no other method can chain itself onto the delegate.

Here's how the callback will work:

1 **The Bat will keep its delegate field private**
The easiest way to keep the wrong Ball objects from chaining themselves onto the Bat's delegate is for the bat to make it private. That way, it has control over which Ball object's method gets called.

2 **The Ball's constructor takes a delegate that points to a method in the ball**
When the ball is in play, it creates the new instance of the bat, and it passes the Bat object a pointer to its OnBallInPlay() method. This is called a **callback method** because the Bat is using it to call back to the object that instantiated it.

The Ball object passes a delegate reference to its own OnBallInPlay() method to the Bat's constructor. The bat saves that delegate in its private hitTheBallCallback field.

3 **When the bat hits the ball, it calls the callback method**
But since the bat kept its delegate private, it can be 100% sure that no other ball has been hit. That solves the problem!

The other balls can't chain themselves onto the delegate because it's a private field in the Bat object.

Now the Bat object can call its hitBallCallback delegate, which calls the Ball object's OnBallInPlay() method.

Callbacks use delegates, but <u>NOT</u> events

A callback is a **different way of using a delegate**. It's not a new
keyword or operator. It just describes a **pattern**—a way that you use
delegates with your classes so that one object can tell another object,
"Notify me when this happens—and don't tell anyone else!"

Do this

① Add another delegate to your Baseball project

Since the Bat will have a private delegate field that points to the Ball object's OnBallInPlay()
method, we'll need a delegate that matches its signature:

```
public delegate void BatCallback(BallEventArgs e);
```

The Bat object's callback will point to a
Ball object's OnBallInPlay() method, so
the callback's delegate needs to match the
signature of OnBallInPlay()—so it needs to
take a BallEventArgs parameter and have
a void return value.

② Add the Bat class to the project

The Bat class is simple. It's got a HitTheBall() method that the simulator will call every time
a ball is hit. That HitTheBall() method uses the hitBallCallback() delegate to call the ball's
OnBallInPlay() method (or whatever method is passed into its constructor).

```
public class Bat {
    private BatCallback hitBallCallback;
    public Bat(BatCallback callbackDelegate) {
        this.hitBallCallback = new BatCallback(callbackDelegate);
    }
    public void HitTheBall(BallEventArgs e) {
        if (hitBallCallback != null)
            hitBallCallback(e);
    }
}
```

Make sure you
check every
delegate to
make sure
it's not null,
otherwise it
could throw a
null reference
exception.

We used = instead of += because
there's no need to chain. This delegate
only gets set once. But if you really
feel like using += instead, it'll work
just fine.

③ We'll need to hook the bat up to a ball

So how does the Bat's constructor get a reference to a particular ball's OnBallInPlay() method?
Easy—just call that Ball object's GetNewBat() method, which you'll have to add to Ball:

```
public Bat GetNewBat()
{
    return new Bat(new BatCallback(OnBallInPlay));
}
```

We set the callback in the Bat object's constructor.
But in some cases, it makes more sense to set up the
callback method using a public method or property's
set accessor.

The Ball's GetNewBat() method
creates a new Bat object, and it uses
the BatCallBack delegate to pass a
reference to its own OnBallInPlay()
method to the new bat. That's the
callback method the bat will use when
it hits the ball.

④ **Now we can encapsulate the Ball class a little better**

It's unusual for one of the On... methods that raise an event to be public. You can check this for yourself—go to the form and try to call the playBall button's OnClick() event. You won't be able to, because it's protected (so a subclass can override it). So let's follow that pattern with our ball too, by making its OnBallInPlay() method protected:

```
protected void OnBallInPlay(BallEventArgs e)
{
    if (BallInPlay != null)
        BallInPlay(this, e);
}
```

This is a really standard pattern that you'll see over and over again when you work with .NET classes. When a .NET class has an event that gets fired, you'll almost always find a protected method that starts with "On".

⑤ **All that's left to do is hook up the form**

The form can't call the Ball object's OnBallInPlay() method anymore—which is exactly what we wanted. That's why we set up the Ball.GetNewBat() method. Now the form needs to ask the Ball for a new bat in order to hit the ball. And when it does, the Ball object will make sure that its OnBallInPlay() method is hooked up to the bat's callback.

```
private void playBall_Click(object sender, EventArgs e)
{
    Bat bat = ball.GetNewBat();
    BallEventArgs ballEventArgs = new BallEventArgs(
        (int)trajectory.Value, (int)distance.Value);
    bat.HitTheBall(ballEventArgs);
}
```

If the form (or the simulator) wants to hit a Ball object, it needs to get a new Bat object from that ball. The ball will make sure that the callback is hooked up to the bat. Now when the form calls the bat's HitTheBall() method, it calls the ball's OnBallInPlay() method, which fires its BallInPlay event.

Now **run the program**—it should work exactly like it did before. But it's now **protected** from any problems that would be caused by more than one ball listening for the same event.

But don't take our word for it—pop it open in the debugger!

BULLET POINTS

- When you add a delegate to your project, you're **creating a new type** that stores references to methods.

- Events use delegates to notify objects that actions have occurred.

- Objects subscribe to an object's event if they need to react to something that happened in that object.

- An EventHandler is a kind of delegate that's really common when you work with events.

- You chain several event handlers onto one event. That's why you use += to assign an handler to an event.

- Always check that an event or delegate is not null before you use it to avoid a NullReferenceException.

- All of the controls in the toolbox use events to make things happen in your programs.

- When one object passes a reference to a method to another object so it—and only it—can return information, it's called a callback.

- Events let any method subscribe to your object's events anonymously, while callbacks let your objects exercise more control over which delegates they accept.

- Both callbacks and events use delegates to reference and call methods in other objects.

- The debugger is a really useful tool to help you understand how events, delegates, and callbacks work. Take advantage of it!

there are no
Dumb Questions

Q: **How are callbacks different from events?**

A: Events are part of C#. They're a way for one object to announce to other objects that something specific has happened. When one object publishes an event, any number of other objects can subscribe to it without the publishing object knowing or caring. When an object fires off an event, if anyone happens to have subscribed to it then it calls each of their event handlers.

Callbacks are not published. Instead, a callback establishes a relationship between two clases where one object automatically reacts to another. A callback is generally kept private, and the class that stores the callback maintains control over who has access to it. A callback is often set up in an object's

Q: **So a callback isn't an actual type in C#?**

A: No, it isn't. A callback is a *pattern*—it's just a novel way of using the existing types, keywords and tools that C# comes with. Go back and take another look at the callback code you just wrote for the Bat and Ball. Did you see any new keywords that we haven't used before? Nope!

It turns out that there are a lot of patterns that you can use. In fact, there's a whole area of programming called *design patterns*. There are a lot problems that you'll run into which have been solved before, and the ones that pop up over and over again have their own design patterns that you can benefit from.

Q: **So callbacks are just private events?**

A: Not quite. It seems easy to think about it that way, but private events are a different beast altogether. Remember what the `private` access modifier really means? When you mark a class member private, only instances of that same class can access it. So if you mark an event `private`, then other instances if the same class can subscribe to it. That's different from a callback, because it still involves one or more objects anonymously subscribing to an event.

Q: **But it looks just like an event, except with the event keyword, right?**

A: The reason a callback looks so much like an event is that they both use **delegates**. And it makes sense that they both use delegates, because that's C#'s tool for letting one object pass another object a reference to one of its methods.

But the big difference between normal events and callbacks is that an event is a way for a class to publish to the world that some specific thing has happened. A callback, on the other hand, is never published. It's private, and the method that's doing the calling keeps tight control over who it's calling.

↑

Check out "Head First Design Patterns" at the Head First Labs website. It's a great way to learn about different patterns that you can apply to your own programs.

www.headfirstlabs.com/books/hfdp/

←

The first one you'll learn about is called the "Publisher-Subscriber" pattern, and it'll look really familiar to you. One object publishes information, and other objects subscribe to it. Hmmm...

The Case of the Golden Crustacean

How did the other treasure hunters beat Henry to the crab?

The crux of the mystery lies in how the treasure hunter seeks his quarry. But first we'll need to see exactly what Henry found in the stolen diagrams.

In a stolen set of class diagrams, Henry discovers that the GoldenCrab class raises a RunForCover event every time anyone gets close to it. Even better, the event includes NewLocationArgs, which detail where the crab is moving to. But none of the other treasure hunters know about the event, so Henry figures he can cash in.

```
public class GoldenCrab {
    public delegate void Escape(NewLocationArgs e);
    public event Escape RunForCover;
    public void SomeonesNearby() {
        NewLocationArgs e = new NewLocationArgs("Under the rock");
        RunForCover(e);
    }
}
public class NewLocationArgs {
    public NewLocationArgs(HidingPlace newLocation) {
        this.newLocation = newLocation;
    }
    private HidingPlace newLocation;
    public HidingPlace NewLocation { get { return newLocation; } }
}
```

> Any time someone comes close to the golden crab, its SomeonesNearby() method fires off a RunForCover event, and it finds a place to hide.

So how did Henry take advantage of his newfound insider information?

Henry adds code to his constructor to register his ListenForClues() method as an event handler for the RunForCover event, on the crab reference he's got. Then, he sends a lowly underling after the crab, knowing it will run away, hide, and raise the RunForCover event—giving Henry's ListenForClues() method all the information he needs.

```
public class TreasureHunter {
    public TreasureHunter(GoldenCrab treasure) {
        treasure.RunForCover += new GoldenCrab.Escape(treasure_RunForCover);
    }
    void treasure_RunForCover(NewLocationArgs e) {
        MoveHere(e.NewLocation);
    }
    void MoveHere(HidingPlace Location) {
        // ... code to move to a new location ...
    }
}
```

> Henry thought he was being clever by altering his class's constructor to add an event handler that calls his MoveHere() method every time the crab raises its RunForCover event. But he forgot that the other treasure hunters inherit from the same class, and his clever code adds their event handlers to the chain, too!

And that explains why Henry's plan backfired. When he added the event handler to the TreasureHunter constructor, he was inadvertently ***doing the same thing for all of the treasure hunters!*** And that meant that every treasure hunter's event handler got chained onto the same RunForCover event. So when the Golden Crustacean ran for cover, everyone was notified about the event.. And all of that that would have been fine if Henry were the first one to get the message. But Henry had no way of knowing when the other treasure hunters would have been called—if they subscribed before he did, they'd get the event first.

Sharpen your pencil

Fill in the blanks to make this game of Whack-a-mole work. You need to supply the code that does the callbacks. Once you've got it filled in, go ahead and type it into the IDE. Or you can try to get it working in the IDE, and then fill in the blanks afterwards. It's fun!

```csharp
public partial class Form1 : Form {
    Mole mole;
    Random random = new Random();
    public Form1() {
        InitializeComponent();

        mole = new Mole(random, new Mole._____(_____));
        timer1.Interval = random.Next(500, 1000);
        timer1.Start();
    }
    private void timer1_Tick(object sender, EventArgs e) {
        timer1.Stop();
        ToggleMole();
    }
    private void ToggleMole() {
        if (mole.Hidden == true)
            mole.Show();
        else
            mole.HideAgain();
        timer1.Interval = random.Next(500, 1000);
        timer1.Start();
    }
    private void MoleCallBack(int MoleNumber, bool Show) {
        if (MoleNumber < 0) {
            timer1.Stop();
            return;
        }
        Button button;
        switch (MoleNumber) {
            case 0: button = button1; break;
            case 1: button = button2; break;
            case 2: button = button3; break;
            case 3: button = button4; break;
            default: button = button5; break;
        }
        if (Show == true)  {
            button.Text = "HIT ME!";
            button.BackColor = Color.Red;
        } else {
            button.Text = "";
            button.BackColor = SystemColors.Control;
        }
        timer1.Interval = random.Next(500, 1000);
        timer1.Start();
    }
    private void button1_Click(object sender, EventArgs e) {
        mole.Smacked(0);
    } .
}
```

The form passes a delegate pointing to a callback method into the mole's constructor. Fill it in.

When you double-click on the timer in the form (after you drag it out of the toolbox), the IDE will create this event handler for it. Timers fire the Tick event over and over again. You'll learn all about them in the next chapter.

This method's called to pop up or hide the mole when the timer's elapsed.

This switch makes sure that the right button changes its color and text.

Form1.cs [Design]   ▼ ×

Whack-a-mole   ☒

⏲ timer1

This is a Timer control. Drag it out of the toolbox, then double-click on it.

When you type in the code, add five button event handlers. Have button2_click() call mole.Smacked(1), and then make button3 call mole.Smacked(2), and make button4 call mole.Smacked(3) and button5 call mole.Smacked(4).

Just add these event handlers the usual way by double-clicking in the form designer.

```
public class Mole {

    public _____ void PopUp(int hole, bool show);

    private _____ popUpCallback;
    private bool hidden;
    public bool Hidden { get { return hidden; } }
    private int timesHit = 0;
    private int timesShown = 0;
    private int hole = 0;
    Random random;

    public Mole(Random random, PopUp popUpCallback) {
        if (popUpCallback == null)
            throw new ArgumentException("popUpCallback can't be null");
        this.random = random;

        this._____ = _____;
        hidden = true;
    }

    public void Show() {
        timesShown++;
        hidden = false;
        hole = random.Next(5);

        _____(hole, true);
    }

    public void HideAgain() {
        hidden = true;

        _____(hole, false);
        CheckForGameOver();
    }

    public void Smacked(int holeSmacked) {
        if (holeSmacked == hole) {
            timesHit++;
            hidden = true;
            CheckForGameOver();

            _____(hole, false);
        }
    }

    private void CheckForGameOver() {
        if (timesShown >= 10) {
            popUpCallback(-1, false);
            MessageBox.Show("You scored " + timesHit, "Game over");
            Application.Exit();
        }
    }
}
```

Fill in the delegate and field to hold the delegate—they're both at the top of the Mole class.

Here's where we make sure the callback is not null—if it is, the Mole object throws an ArgumentException.

When the form creates a new Mole object, it passes it a reference to its callback method. Take a look in the form to see how the constructor is called, and then fill in this blank.

After the mole shows itself, it needs to call the method on the form that displays the mole by turning the button red and showing the text "HIT ME!"

The HideAgain() and Smacked() methods also use the callback delegate to call the method on the form.

The way the game works is that it uses the timer to wait a random period of time between half a second and 1.5 seconds. Once that time is elapsed, it tells the mole to show itself. The form gives the Mole object a callback that it uses to tell the form to show or hide the mole in one of the five holes. The form uses its timer to wait between .5 and 1.5 seconds again, and then tells the mole to hide itself.

The game's over after the mole shows itself 10 times. Your score is the number of times you hit it.

Sharpen your pencil
Solution

Fill in the blanks to make this game of Whack-a-mole work. You need to supply the code that does the callbacks. Once you've got it filled in, go ahead and type it into the IDE. It's fun!

```
public partial class Form1 : Form {
    private void Form1_Load(object sender, EventArgs e)   {

        mole = new Mole(random, new Mole.   PopUp  (   MoleCallBack   ));;
        timer1.Interval = random.Next(500, 1000);
        timer1.Start();
    }
.}
```

This is where the form passes a reference to its MoleCallBack() method into the Mole object. That lets the mole call its method.

```
public class Mole {

    public   delegate   void PopUp(int hole, bool show);

    private   PopUp   popUpCallback;

    ...

    public Mole(Random random, PopUp popUpCallback) {
        this.random = random;

        this.   popUpCallback   =   popUpCallback   ;
        hidden = true;
    }
```

Here's where the mole defines its delegate and uses it to set up a private field to hold a reference to the method on the form that changes the colors of the buttons.

```
    public void Show() {
        timesShown++;
        hidden = false;
        hole = random.Next(5);

        popUpCallback   (hole, true);
    }
```

When the form creates a new instance of the Mole object, it passes a reference to its MoleCallBack() method to the constructor as a parameter. This line in the constructor copies that reference to its popUpCallback field. Its methods can use that field to call the MoleCallBack() method in the form.

```
    public void HideAgain() {
        hidden = true;

        popUpCallback   (hole, false);
        CheckForGameOver();
    }

    public void Smacked(int holeSmacked) {
        if (holeSmacked == hole) {
            timesHit++;
            hidden = true;
            CheckForGameOver();

            popUpCallback   (hole, false);
        }
    }
```

When the mole shows itself, hides again, or gets smacked, the Mole object uses its popUpCallback delegate field to call the method on the form that changes the color and text of one of the buttons.

12 review and preview

Knowledge, power, and building cool stuff

> I just know I read about how upcasting and downcasting make event handling easier somewhere...

Learning's no good until you BUILD something.

Until you've actually written working code, it's hard to be sure if you really *get* some of the tougher concepts in C#. In this chapter, we're going to learn about some new odds and ends: **timers** and dealing with collections using **LINQ** (to name a couple). We're also going to build phase I of a **really complex application**, and make sure you've got a good handle on what you've already learned from earlier chapters. So buckle up...it's time to build some **cool software**.

You've come a long way, ~~baby~~

[note from human resources: "baby" is no longer politically correct. Please use age-challenged or infant to avoid offending readers.]

We've come a long way since we first used the IDE to help us rescue the Objectville Paper Company. Here's just a few of the things you've done over the last several hundreds pages:

You've built forms, used the .NET framework, and even talked with databases.

.NET Framework solutions

Form Objects

Data access

Objects, classes, instances... all these strange terms are now part of your everyday programming toolbox.

You've used inheritance, as well as interfaces and subclasses, to build object trees.

Party
NumberOfPeople
CostOfDecorations

CalculateCostOfDecorations()
CalculateCost()

Navigator
SetDestination()
ModifyRouteToAvoid()
ModifyRouteToInclude()
GetRoute()
GetTimeToDestination()
TotalDistance()

navigator1
3.5 miles
Navigator object

navigator2
3.8 miles
Navigator object

navigator3
4.2 miles
Navigator object

DinnerParty
NumberOfPeople
CostOfDecorations
CostOfBeveragesPerPerson
HealthyOption
CalculateCostOfDecorations()
CalculateCost()
SetHealthyOption()

BirthdayParty
NumberOfPeople
CostOfDecorations
CakeSize
CakeWriting
CalculateCostOfDecorations()
CalculateCost()

Even complex types like arrays are no big deal to work with.

7 int variables

| 0 | 1 | 2 | 3 | 4 | 5 | 6 |
| int | int | int | int | int | int | int |

HEIGHTS()

You've used events to notify objects about certain things that happen, while keeping your objects' concerns separate.

Ball object

BallInPlay event

BallEventArgs

Pitcher

Umpire

Fan object

Debugging and exceptions are part of your problem-eliminating techniques.

```
private void RandomExcuseButton_Click(object sender, EventArgs e)
{
    if (CheckChanged() == true) {
        CurrentExcuse = new Excuse(random, Folder);
        UpdateForm(false);
    }
}
```

We've also become beekeepers

Back in Chapter 6, we built some bee classes. Remember these?

We had different bees doing different jobs...

...and even shifts that the bees worked on.

But we can do a lot better now...

You've learned a lot since Chapter 6, though. So let's start from scratch, and build an **animated beehive simulator** over the next few chapters. We'll end up with a user interface that shows us the hive and the field the bees are keeping, and even a stats window letting users know what their bees are doing.

The stats window lets us monitor the simulation in detail.

The Hive window shows us what's happening.

We can even watch the bees work a field of flowers.

The beehive simulator architecture

Here's the architecture for the bee simulator. Even though the simulator will be controlling a lot of different bees, the overall object model is pretty simple.

The World object keeps track of everything in the simulator: the state of the hive, every bee, and every flower.

This is the object for the main window that shows the bee stats and messages.

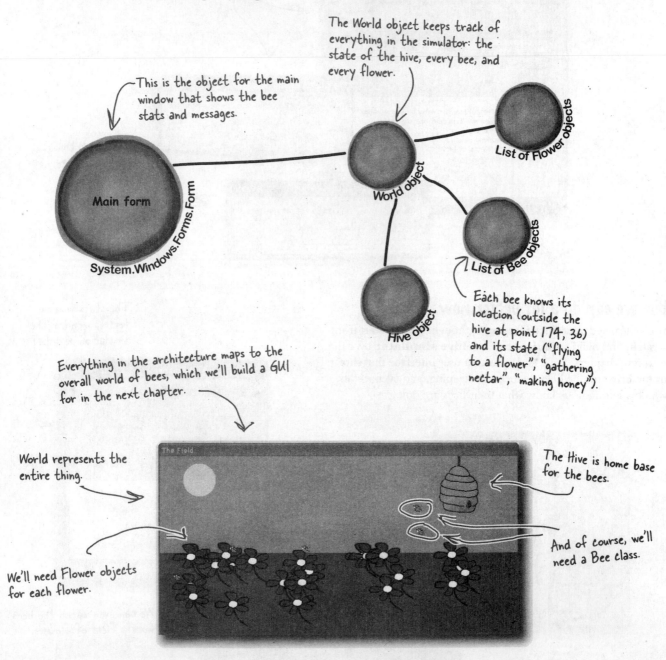

Main form

System.Windows.Forms.Form

World object

List of Flower objects

List of Bee objects

Hive object

Each bee knows its location (outside the hive at point 174, 36) and its state ("flying to a flower", "gathering nectar", "making honey").

Everything in the architecture maps to the overall world of bees, which we'll build a GUI for in the next chapter.

World represents the entire thing.

The Field

We'll need Flower objects for each flower.

The Hive is home base for the bees.

And of course, we'll need a Bee class.

Building the beehive simulator

Of course, we've never built anything this complex before, so it's going to take us a couple of chapters to put all the pieces together. Along the way, you'll add timers, LINQ, and a lot of graphical skill to your toolkit.

Here's what you're going to do in this chapter (more to come in the next):

1 **Build a Flower class that ages, produces nectar, and eventually wilts and dies.**

2 **Build a Bee class that has several different states (gathering nectar from a flower, returning to the Hive), and knows what to do based on its state.**

3 **Build a Hive class that has an entrance, exit, nursery for new bees, and honey factory for turning collected nectar into honey.**

4 **Build a World class that manages the hive, flowers, and bees for any given moment.**

5 **Build a main form that collects statistics from the other classes, and keeps the world going.**

Exercise

Let's jump right into some code. First up, we need a Flower class. The Flower class has a location, defined by a Point, an age, and a lifespan. As time goes on, the flower gets older. Then, when its age reaches its lifespan, the flower dies. It's your job to put all this into action.

A class "skeleton" is just its field, property and method declarations, with no implementation.

1 **Write the skeleton code for Flower**

Below is the class diagram for `Flower`. Write the basic class skeleton. `Location`, `Age`, `Alive`, `Nectar`, and `NectarHarvested` are **automatic properties**. `NectarHarvested` is writable, the other four are **read-only**. For now, leave the methods blank; we'll come back to those in a minute.

All of these should be read-only properties. →

This is used only in the class, so it just needs to be a private field →

Flower

Location: Point
Age: int
Alive: bool
Nectar: double
NectarHarvested: double
lifespan: int

HarvestNectar(): double
Go()

The type after the colon is the type of the variable...

...or the return type of the method.

2 **Add several constants to the class**

We need lots of constants for flowers. Add six to your `Flower` class:

* `LifeSpanMin`, the shortest flower lifespan
* `LifeSpanMax`, the longest flower lifespan
* `InitialNectar`, how much nectar a flower starts with
* `MaxNectar`, how much nectar a flower can hold
* `NectarAddedPerTurn`, how much nectar gets added each time the flower grows older
* `NectarGatheredPerTurn`, how much nectar gets collected during a cycle

FYI, you don't usually show constants in a class diagram.

You should be able to figure out the types for each constant based on their values. Flowers live between 15,000 and 30,000 cycles, and have 1.5 units of nectar when they start out. They can store up to 5 units of nectar. In each cycle of life, a flower adds 0.01 units of nectar, and in a single cycle, 0.3 units can be collected.

You'll need to add `using System.Drawing;` **to the top of any class file that uses a** `Point`.

③ Build the constructor

The constructor for `Flower` should take in a `Point`, indicating the flower's location, and an instance of the `Random` class. You should be able to use those arguments to set the location of the flower, and then set its age to 0, set the flower to alive, and set its nectar to the initial amount of nectar for a flower. Since no nectar has been harvested yet, set that variable correctly, as well. Finally, figure out the flower's lifespan. Here's a line of code to help you:

```
lifeSpan = random.Next(LifeSpanMin, LifeSpanMax + 1);
```

This will only work if you've got your variables and constants named right, as well as the argument to the Flower constructor.

④ Write code for the HarvestNectar() method

Every time this method is called, it should check to see if the nectar gathered every cycle is larger than the amount of nectar left. If so, return 0. Otherwise, you should remove the amount collected in a cycle from the nectar the flower has left, and return how much nectar was collected. Oh, and don't forget to add that amount to the `NectarHarvested` variable, which keeps up with the total nectar collected from this particular flower.

*Hint: We used NectarGatheredPerTurn, nectar, and NectarHarvested in this method, but nothing else.

⑤ Write code for the Go() method

This is the method that makes the flower go. Assume every time this method is called, one cycle passes, so update the flower's age appropriately. You'll also need to see if the age is greater than the flower's lifespan. If so, the flower dies.

Assuming the flower stays alive, you'll need to add the amount of nectar each flower gets in a cycle. Be sure and check against the maximum nectar your flower can store, and don't overrun that.

The final product will be animated, with little pictures of bees flying around. The Go() method will be called once every frame, and there will be several frames run per second.

Answers on the next page... try and finish your code and compile it before peeking.

Your job was to build the Flower class for our beehive simulator.

Exercise Solution

Flower
Location: Point
Age: int
Alive: bool
Nectar: double
NectarHarvested: double
lifespan: int
HarvestNectar(): double
Go()

```csharp
public class Flower {
    private const int LifeSpanMin = 15000;
    private const int LifeSpanMax = 30000;
    private const double InitialNectar = 1.5;
    private const double MaxNectar = 5.0;
    private const double NectarAddedPerTurn = 0.01;
    private const double NectarGatheredPerTurn = 0.3;

    public Point Location { get; private set; }

    public int Age { get; private set; }

    public bool Alive { get; private set; }

    public double Nectar { get; private set; }

    public double NectarHarvested { get; set; }

    private int lifeSpan;

    public Flower(Point location, Random random) {
        Location = location;
        Age = 0;
        Alive = true;
        Nectar = InitialNectar;
        NectarHarvested = 0;
        lifeSpan = random.Next(LifeSpanMin, LifeSpanMax + 1);
    }

    public double HarvestNectar() {
        if (NectarGatheredPerTurn > Nectar)
            return 0;
        else {
            Nectar -= NectarGatheredPerTurn;
            NectarHarvested += NectarGatheredPerTurn;
            return NectarGatheredPerTurn;
        }
    }

    public void Go() {
        Age++;
        if (Age > lifeSpan)
            Alive = false;
        else {
            Nectar += NectarAddedPerTurn;
            if (Nectar > MaxNectar)
                Nectar = MaxNectar;
        }
    }
}
```

Location, Age, Alive, Alive, and Nectar are all read-only automatic properties.

NectarHarvested will need to be accessible to other classes.

Flowers have random lifespans so that the field of flowers doesn't all change exactly at once.

A bee calls HarvestNectar() to get nectar out of a flower. A bee can only harvest a little bit of nectar at a time, so he'll have to sit near the flower for several turns until the nectar's all gone.

As part of the simulator's animation, the Go() method will be called each frame. This makes the flower age just a tiny little bit per frame—as the simulator runs, those tiny bits will add up over time.

Make sure the flower stops adding nectar after it's dead.

Point lives in the System.Drawing namespace, so make sure you added using System.Drawing; **to the top of the class file.**

Life and death of a flower

Our flower goes through a basic turn, living, adding nectar, having nectar harvested, and eventually dying:

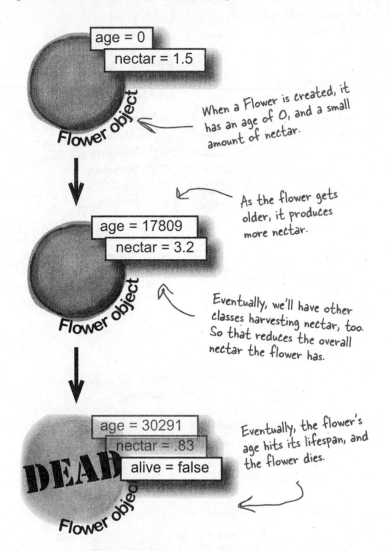

age = 0
nectar = 1.5

Flower object

When a Flower is created, it has an age of 0, and a small amount of nectar.

age = 17809
nectar = 3.2

Flower object

As the flower gets older, it produces more nectar.

Eventually, we'll have other classes harvesting nectar, too. So that reduces the overall nectar the flower has.

age = 30291
nectar = .83
alive = false

DEAD

Flower object

Eventually, the flower's age hits its lifespan, and the flower dies.

BRAIN POWER

If Go() increases the age of the Flower by 1, and the lifespan range is between 15,000 and 30,000, that means Go() will get called at least 15,000 times for each flower before it dies. How would you handle calling the method that many times? What if there are 10 flowers? 100? 1000?

Now we need a Bee class

With flowers ready to be harvested, we need a Bee class. Below is
the basic code for Bee. The Bee knows its age, whether or not its
in the hive, and how much nectar it can collect. We've also added a
method to move the bee towards a specific destination point.

```
public class Bee {
    private const double HoneyConsumed = 0.5;
    private const int MoveRate = 3;
    private const double MinimumFlowerNectar = 1.5;
    private const int CareerSpan = 1000;

    public int Age { get; private set; }
    public bool InsideHive { get; private set; }
    public double NectarCollected { get; private set; }

    private Point location;
    public Point Location { get { return location; } }

    private int ID;
    private Flower destinationFlower;

    public Bee(int id, Point location) {
        this.ID = ID;
        Age = 0;
        this.location = location;
        InsideHive = true;
        destinationFlower = null;
        NectarCollected = 0;
    }

    public void Go(Random random) {
        Age++;
    }
}
```

*Like the Flower class, there
are several bee-specific
constants we need to define.*

*MinimumFlowerNectar is
how the bee figures out
which flowers are eligible
for harvesting.*

*We used a backing field for location.
If we'd used an automatic property,
MoveTowardsLocation() wouldn't
be able to set its members directly
("Location.X -= MoveRate").*

*Each bee will be assigned its own
unique ID number.*

*A bee needs an ID and
an initial location.*

*Bees start out inside the
hive, they don't have a
flower to go to, and they
don't have any nectar.*

*We'll have to add a lot
more code to Go() before
we're done, but this will
get us started.*

Here we used Math.Abs() to calculate the absolute value of the difference between the destination {and the current location.

```
private bool MoveTowardsLocation(Point destination) {
    if (destination != null) {
        if (Math.Abs(destination.X - location.X) <= MoveRate &&
            Math.Abs(destination.Y - location.Y) <= MoveRate)
            return true;
        if (destination.X > location.X)
            location.X += MoveRate;
        else if (destination.X < location.X)
            location.X -= MoveRate;
        if (destination.Y > location.Y)
            location.Y += MoveRate;
        else if (destination.Y < location.Y)
            location.Y -= MoveRate;
    }
    return false;
}
```

If the bee has no destination, its field will be set to null. So we only move towards it if its destination is NOT null.

This method starts by figuring out if we're already within our MoveRate of being at the destination.

If we're not close enough, then we move towards the destination by our move rate.

We return false, since we're not yet at the destination point. We need to keep moving.

The MoveTowardsLocation() destination moves the bee's current location by changing the X and Y values of its location field. It returns true if the bee's reached its destination.

Exercise

Bees have lots of things they can do. Below is a list. Create a new enum that Bee uses called BeeState. You should also create a read-only automatic property called CurrentState for each Bee to track that bee's state. Set a bee's initial state to idle, and in the Go() method, add a switch statement that has an option for each item in the enum.

The enum item	What the item means
Idle	The bee isn't doing anything
FlyingToFlower	The bee's flying to a flower
GatheringNectar	The bee's gathering nectar from a flower
ReturningToHive	The bee's heading back to the hive
MakingHoney	The bee's making honey
Retired	The bee's hung up his wings

Bees have lots of things they can do. Below is a list. Create a new enum that Bee uses called BeeState. You should also create a private currentState field for each Bee to track that bee's state. Set a bee's initial state to idle, and in the Go() method, add a switch statement that has an option for each item in the enum.

```
public enum BeeState {
    Idle,
    FlyingToFlower,
    GatheringNectar,
    ReturningToHive,
    MakingHoney,
    Retired
}
```

> Here's the enum with all the different bee states.

```
public class Bee {
    // constant declarations
    // variable declarations
```

> We also need a variable to track the state of each bee.

```
    public BeeState CurrentState { get; private set; }

    public Bee(int ID, Point InitialLocation) {
        this.ID = ID;
        Age = 0;
        location = InitialLocation;
        InsideHive = true;
        CurrentState = BeeState.Idle;
        destinationFlower = null;
        NectarCollected = 0;
    }
}
```

> The bee starts out idle.

Did you remember to add using System.Drawing; to the top of the class file (because it uses Point)?

We've filled out a few of the states. It's okay if you didn't come up with this code, but go ahead and add it in now.

```
public void Go(Random random) {
    Age++;
    switch (CurrentState) {
      case BeeState.Idle:
        if (Age > CareerSpan) {
          CurrentState = BeeState.Retired;
        } else {
          // What do we do if we're idle?
        }
        break;
      case BeeState.FlyingToFlower:
        // move towards the flower we're heading to
        break;
      case BeeState.GatheringNectar:
        double nectar = destinationFlower.HarvestNectar();
        if (nectar > 0)
          NectarCollected += nectar;
        else
          CurrentState = BeeState.ReturningToHive;
        break;
      case BeeState.ReturningToHive:
        if (!InsideHive) {
          // move towards the hive
        } else {
          // what do we do if we're inside the hive?
        } break;
      case BeeState.MakingHoney:
        if (NectarCollected < 0.5) {
          NectarCollected = 0;
          CurrentState = BeeState.Idle;
        } else {
          // once we have a Hive, we'll turn the nectar into honey
        }
        break;
      case BeeState.Retired:
        // Do nothing! We're retired!
        break;
    }
  }
}
```

Here's the switch() statement to handle each bee's state.

If the age reaches the bee's lifespan, the bee retires. But he'll finish the current job before he does.

We'll fill this code in a bit later.

Here, we harvest nectar from the flower we're working....

...and if there's nectar left, add it to what we've already collected...

...but if there's no nectar left, head for the hive.

You should have each of these states covered.

Returning to the hive is different based on whether we're already in the hive or not.

The bee adds half a unit of nectar to the honey factory at a time. If there's not enough nectar to add, the factory can't use it so the bee just discards it.

P. A. H. B. (Programmers Against Homeless Bees)

We've got bees, and flowers full of nectar. We need to write code so the bees can collect nectar, but before that happens, where do the bees get created in the first place? And where do they take all that nectar? That's where a `Hive` class comes in.

The hive isn't just a place for bees to come back to, though. It has several locations within it, all with different points in the world. There's the entrance and the exit, as well as a nursery for birthing more bees and a honey factory for turning nectar into honey.

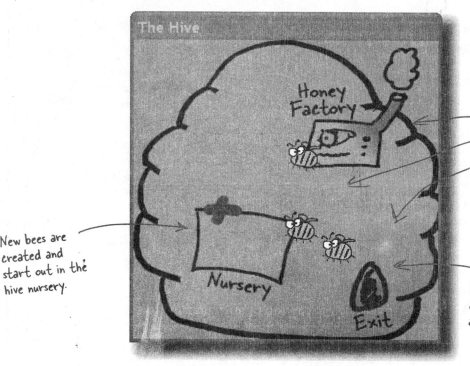

New bees are created and start out in the hive nursery.

Each location is distinct, and bees can travel from one to the other just like they can go from the hive to a flower.

Bees come in the entrance, and leave from the exit. It's all very orderly.

The hive runs on honey

The other big part that the hive plays is keeping up with how much honey it has stored up. It takes honey for the hive to keep running, and if new bees need to be created, that takes honey, too. On top of that, the honey factory has to take nectar that bees collect and turn that into honey. For every unit of nectar that comes in, .25 units of honey can be created.

Think about this for a second... as time passes, the hive uses honey to run, and to create more bees. Meanwhile, other bees are bringing in nectar, which gets turned into honey, which keeps things going longer.

It's up to you (with some help) to model all of this in the simulator code.

It's up to you to write the code for Hive.

Exercise

Hive
Honey: double
locations: Dictionary<string, Point>
beeCount: int
InitializeLocations()
AddHoney(Nectar: double): bool
ConsumeHoney(amount: double): bool
AddBee(random: Random)
Go(random: Random)
getLocation(location: string): Point

① Write the skeleton code for Hive

Like we did with the `Flower` class, you should start with a basic skeleton for `Hive`. The class diagram is shown to the right. Make the `Honey` a read-only automatic property, `locations` should be private, and `beeCount` is only used internally, so can be a private field.

② Define the constants for the Hive

You need a constant for the initial number of bees (6), the amount of honey the hive starts with (3.2), the maximum amount of honey the hive can store (15), and ratio of units of nectar produced from units of honey (.25), the maximum number of bees (8), and the minimum honey required for the hive to birth new bees (4). ◄———

You'll have to figure out good names for each, as well as the types. For types, don't just think about initial values, but also the values these constants will be used with. Doubles pair best with other doubles, ints with other ints.

③ Write the code to work with Locations

First, write the `GetLocation()` method. It should take in a string, look up that string in the Locations dictionary, and return the associated point. If it's not there, throw an ArgumentException.

Then, write the `InitializeLocations()` method. This method should set up the following locations in the hive:

- Entrance, at (600, 100)
- Nursery, at (95, 174)
- HoneyFactory, at (157, 98)
- Exit, at (194, 213)

Each of these maps to a location within the 2D space that our hive takes up. Later on, we'll have to make sure the simulator makes the hive cover all these points.

In this simulation, we're just assuming one hive, with fixed points. If you wanted multiple hives, you might make the points relative to the hive, instead of the overall world.

④ Build the Hive constructor

When a hive is constructed, it should set its honey to the initial amount of honey all hives have. It should setup the locations in the hive, and also create a new instance of `Random`. Then, `AddBee()` should be called—passing in the `Random` instance you just created—once for each bee that starts out in the hive.

AddBee() needs a Random object because it adds a random value to the Nursery location—that way the bees don't start on top of each other.

Exercise Solution

Your job was to start building the Hive class.

Make sure you add "using System. Drawing;" because this code uses Point. ↓

You might have different names for your constants. That's okay, as long as you're consistent in the rest of your code.

```csharp
public class Hive {
    private const int InitialBees = 6;
    private const double InitialHoney = 3.2;
    private const double MaximumHoney = 15.0;
    private const double NectarHoneyRatio = .25;
    private const double MinimumHoneyForCreatingBees = 4.0;
    private const int MaximumBees = 8;

    private Dictionary<string, Point> locations;
    private int beeCount = 0;

    public double Honey { get; private set; }

    private void InitializeLocations() {
        locations = new Dictionary<string, Point>();
        locations.Add("Entrance", new Point(600, 100));
        locations.Add("Nursery", new Point(95, 174));
        locations.Add("HoneyFactory", new Point(157, 98));
        locations.Add("Exit", new Point(194, 213));
    }

    public Point GetLocation(string location) {
        if (locations.Keys.Contains(location))
            return locations[location];
        else
            throw new ArgumentException("Unknown location: " + location);
    }

    public Hive() {
        Honey = InitialHoney;
        InitializeLocations();
        Random random = new Random();
        for (int i = 0; i < InitialBees; i++)
            AddBee(random);
    }

    public bool AddHoney(double Nectar) { return true; }
    public bool ConsumeHoney(double Amount) { return true; }
    private void AddBee(Random random) { }
    public void Go(Random random) { }
}
```

We made MaximumHoney a double, since it can range from InitialHoney (3.2) to this value. Since InitialHoney will need to be a double, it's best to make this a double, too.

Remember dictionaries? Ours stores a location, keyed with a string value.

Don't forget to create a new instance of Dictionary, or this won't work.

The rest of this method is pretty straightforward.

This method protects other classes from working with our locations dictionary and changing something they shouldn't. It's an example of encapsulation.

You should have called AddBee() once for each bee that a hive starts with.

We don't have code for these yet, but you should have built empty methods as placeholders.

> Isn't this sort of a weird way to build code? Our bees don't know about flowers yet, and our hive is full of empty method declarations. Nothing actually works yet, right?

Real code is built bit by bit

It would be nice if you could write all the code for a single class at one time, compile it, test it, and put it away, and **then** start on your next class. Unfortunately, that's almost never possible.

More often than not, you'll write code just the way we are in this chapter: piece by piece. We were able to build pretty much the entire Flower class, but when it came to Bee, we've still got some work to do (mostly telling it what to do for each state).

And now, with Hive, we've got lots of empty methods to fill in. Plus, we haven't hooked any Bees up to the Hive. And there's still that nagging problem about how to call the Go() method in all these objects thousands of times...

> But we didn't **really** start out by putting the classes together! We figured out the architecture first, and **then** started building.

First you design, <u>then</u> you build

We started out the project knowing exactly what we wanted to build: a beehive simulator. And we know a lot about how the bees, flowers, hive, and world all worked together. That's why we started out with the **architecture**, which told us how the classes would work with each other. Then we could move onto each class, designing them individually.

Projects always go a lot more smoothly if you have a good idea of what you're building **before** you start building it. That seems pretty straightforward and common-sense. But it makes all the difference in the final product.

Filling out the Hive class

Let's get back to the `Hive` class, and fill in a few of those missing methods:

```
public class Hive {
  // constant declarations
  // variable declarations

  // InitializeLocations()
  // GetLocation()
  // Hive constructor

  public bool AddHoney(double nectar) {
    double honeyToAdd = nectar * NectarHoneyRatio;
    if (honeyToAdd + Honey > MaximumHoney)
      return false;
    Honey += honeyToAdd;
    return true;
  }
  public bool ConsumeHoney(double amount) {
    if (amount > Honey)
      return false;
    else {
      Honey -= amount;
      return true;
    }
  }
  private void AddBee(Random random) {
    beeCount++;
    int r1 = random.Next(100) - 50;
    int r2 = random.Next(100) - 50;
    Point startPoint = new Point(locations["Nursery"].X + r1,
                                 locations["Nursery"].Y + r2);
    Bee newBee = new Bee(beeCount, startPoint);
    // Once we have a system, we need to add this bee to the system
  }
  public void Go(Random random) { }
}
```

First, we figure out how much honey this nectar can be converted to...

...and then see if there's room in the hive for that much more honey.

If there's room, we add the honey to the hive.

This method takes an amount of honey, and tries to consume it from the hive's stores.

If there's not enough honey in the hive to meet the demand, we return false.

If there's enough, remove it from the hive's stores and return true.

This is private... only Hive instances can create bees.

This creates a point within 50 units in both the X and Y direction from the nursery location.

Add a new bee, at the designated location.

We'll finish AddBee() and fill in the Go() method soon...

The hive's Go() method

We've already written a Go() method for Flower, and a Go() method for Bee (even though we've got some additional code to add in). Here's the Go() method for Hive:

```
public void Go(Random random) {

   if (Honey > MinimumHoneyForCreatingBees)

      AddBee(random);

}
```

The only constraint (at least for now) is the hive must have enough honey to create more bees.

The same instance of Random that got passed to Go() gets sent to the AddBee() method.

Unfortunately, this isn't very realistic. Lots of times in a busy hive, the queen doesn't have time to create more bees. We don't have a QueenBee class, but let's assume that when there's enough honey to create bees, a new bee actually gets created 10% of the time. We can model that like this:

```
public void Go(Random random) {

   if (Honey > MinimumHoneyForCreatingBees

      && random.Next(10) == 1) {

      AddBee(random);

   }

}
```

This is an easy way to simulate a 1 in 10 chance of a bee getting created. It comes up with a random number between 0 and 9. If the number is 1, then create the bee.

One reason to leave it out is so that you can save the Random seed—that way you can re-run a specific simulation... if you feel like doing that later!

---

there are no Dumb Questions

Q: So the hive can create an infinite number of bees?

A: Right now it can—or, at least, it's got a very large limit—but you're right, that's not very realistic. Later on, we'll come back to this, and add a constraint that only lets so many bees exist in our simulator world at one time.

Q: Couldn't we assign that instance of Random to a property of the class, instead of passing it on to AddBee()?

A: You sure could. Then AddBee could use that property, rather than a parameter passed in. There's not really a right answer to this one; it's up to you.

Q: I still don't understand how all of these Go() methods are getting called.

A: That's okay, we're just about to get to that. First, though, we need one more object: the World class, which will keep track of everything that's going on in the hive, track all the bees, and even keep up with flowers.

We're ready for the World

With a `Hive`, `Bee`, and `Flower` class in place, we can
finally build the `World` class. `World` handles coordination
between all the individual pieces of our simulaor: keeping
up with all the bees, telling the hive if there is room for
more bees, locating flowers, etc.:

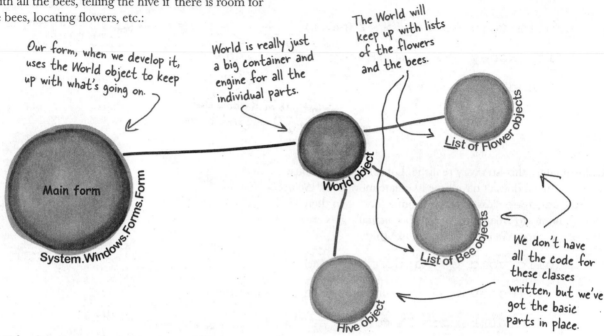

Our form, when we develop it,
uses the World object to keep
up with what's going on.

World is really just
a big container and
engine for all the
individual parts.

The World will
keep up with lists
of the flowers
and the bees.

Main form

System.Windows.Forms.Form

World object

List of Flower objects

List of Bee objects

Hive object

We don't have
all the code for
these classes
written, but we've
got the basic
parts in place.

The World object keeps everything `Go()`ing

One of the biggest tasks of the `World` object is, for each turn in
the simulator, to call `Go()` on every `Flower`, `Bee`, and `Hive`
instance. In other words, `World` makes sure that life continues
in the simulator world.

Go() in World calls Go() on all
the other objects in the world.

Main form

System.Windows.Forms.Form

Go()

World object

We still have to deal with
calling World's Go() method,
but we'll come back to that.

```
foreach (Flower flower in Flowers)
    flower.Go(random);
```

```
foreach (Bee bee in Bees)
    bee.Go(random);
```

```
hive.Go(random);
```

List of Flower objects

List of Bee objects

Hive object

We're building a <u>turn-based</u> system

Our Go() methods in each object are supposed to run each **turn**, or **cycle**, of our simulator. A turn in this case just means an arbitrary amount of time... for instance, a turn could be every 10 seconds, or every 60 seconds, or every 10 minutes.

The main thing is that a turn affects every object in the world. The hive ages by one "turn", checking to see if it needs to add more bees. Then each bee takes a turn, moving a very small distance towards its destination or doing one small action, and getting older. Then each flower takes a turn, manufacturing a little nectar and getting older too. And that's what World does: it makes sure that every time its Go() method is called, every object in the world gets a turn to act.

Each "turn" will be drawn as a single frame of animation, so the world only needs to change a tiny little bit each turn.

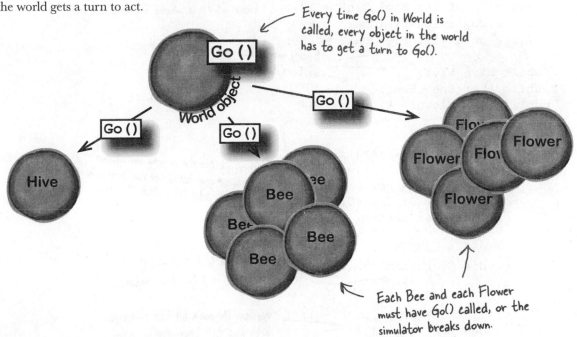

Every time Go() in World is called, every object in the world has to get a turn to Go().

Each Bee and each Flower must have Go() called, or the simulator breaks down.

Sharpen your pencil

One of the big object-oriented principles we've been using in the simulator is encapsulation (flip back to Chapter 5 for a refresher). See if you can look over the code we've developed so far and come up with two examples of encapsulation for each class you've built.

Hive	Bee	Flower
1.	1.	1. ....
....	....	....
2.	2.	2. ....
....	....	....

Here's the code for World

The World class is actually one of the simpler classes in our simulator. Here's the code:

```csharp
using System.Drawing;
public class World {
    private const double NectarHarvestedPerNewFlower = 50.0;
    private const int FieldMinX = 15;
    private const int FieldMinY = 177;
    private const int FieldMaxX = 690;
    private const int FieldMaxY = 290;

    public Hive Hive;
    public List<Bee> Bees;
    public List<Flower> Flowers;

    public World() {
        Bees = new List<Bee>();
        Flowers = new List<Flower>();
        Random random = new Random();
        for (int i = 0; i < 10; i++)
            AddFlower(random);
    }

    public void Go(Random random) {
        Hive.Go(random);

        for (int i = Bees.Count - 1; i >= 0; i--) {
            Bee bee = Bees[i];
            bee.Go(random);
            if (bee.CurrentState == BeeState.Retired)
                Bees.Remove(bee);
        }

        double totalNectarHarvested = 0;
        for (int i = Flowers.Count - 1; i >= 0; i--) {
            Flower flower = Flowers[i];
            flower.Go();
            totalNectarHarvested += flower.NectarHarvested;
            if (!flower.Alive)
                Flowers.Remove(flower);
        }
```

These define the bounds of the field, which is where flowers can live.

Every world has one hive, a list of bees, and a list of flowers.

When we create a new world, we initialize our lists, create a new hive, and then add 10 initial flowers.

This is easy... we just tell the Hive to Go(), passing in a Random instance.

We run through all the current bees and tell them Go().

If a bee's retired, we need to take it out of the world.

We run through each flower and tell it to Go().

We need to keep up with how much nectar's been collected this turn, too. So we get that by summing up the nectar collected from each flower.

Just like bees, we remove any flowers that die during this turn.

Sharpen your pencil
Solution

One of the big object-oriented principles we've been using in the simulator is encapsulation (flip back to Chapter 5 for a refresher). See if you can look over the code we've developed so far and come up with two examples of encapsulation for each class you've built.

Here are the ones we came up with. Did you come up with any others?

Hive

1. The hive's Locations dictionary is private

2. It gives the bees a method to add honey

Bee

1. The bee's location is read-only

2. So is its age. So other classes can't write to them

Flower

1. The flower provides a method to gather nectar

2. And it keeps its alive boolean private

```
if (totalNectarHarvested > NectarHarvestedPerNewFlower) {
    foreach (Flower flower in Flowers)
        flower.NectarHarvested = 0;
    AddFlower(random);
    }
}
```

Bees pollinate flowers as they harvest nectar. Once they've harvested enough nectar from the flowers, they've pollinated enough for the world to add a new flower.

If there's enough nectar in the field, true, the world adds a new flower.

```
private void AddFlower(Random random)
{
    Point location = new Point(random.Next(FieldMinX, FieldMaxX),
                               random.Next(FieldMinY, FieldMaxY));
    Flower newFlower = new Flower(location, random);
    Flowers.Add(newFlower);
}
}
```

This handles coming up with a random location in the field...

...and then adding a new flower in that location.

---

there are no
Dumb Questions

Q: Why don't you use foreach loops to remove dead flowers and retired bees?

A: Because you **can't remove items** from a collection from inside a foreach loop that's iterating on it. If you do, .NET will throw an exception.

Q: Okay, then why does each of those for loops start at the end of the list and count down to 0?

A: Because each loop needs to preserve the numbering of the list. Let's say you started at the beginning of a list of five bees, and your loop discovered that one of the flowers in the middle was dead. If it removes

the flower at index #3, now the list only has 4 flowers in it, and there's a new flower at index #3—and that flower will end up getting skipped, because the next time through the loop it'll look at index #4.

If the loop starts at the end, then the flower that moves into the empty slot will already have been looked at by the loop, so there's no chance of missing a flower.

Exercise

With all four of our core classes in place, we've got some work to do to tie them all together. Follow the steps below, and you should have working Bee, Hive, Flower, and World classes. But beware: you'll have to make changes to almost every class, in several places, before you're done.

① **Update Bee to take in a Hive and World reference.**
Now that we've got a class for `Hive` and a class for `World`, `Bee` objects need to know about both. Update your code to take in references to a bee's hive and world in the constructor and save those references for later use.

② **Update Hive to take in a World reference.**
Just as a `Bee` needs to know about its `Hive`, a `Hive` needs to know about its `World`. Update `Hive` to take in a `World` reference in its constructor, and save that reference. You should also update the code in `Hive` that creates new bees to pass into the Bee a reference to itself (the `Hive`), and the `World`.

③ **Update World to pass itself into a new Hive.**
Update your `World` class so that when it creates a new `Hive`, it passes in a reference to itself.

STOP! At this point, you should be able to compile all of your code. If you can't, check through it and correct any mistakes before continuing on.

④ **Place an upper limit on the bees that Hive can create.**
The Hive class has a MaximumBees constant that determines how many bees the Hive can support (inside and outside the hive, combined). Now that the Hive has access to the World, you should be able to enforce that constraint.

Hint: Look at code near where you create or add bees. There are two places where code related to this occurs in Hive, so be careful.

⑤ **When the Hive creates bees, let the World know.**
The World class keeps up with all the bees that exist. When the Hive creates a new Bee, make sure that Bee gets added to the overall list that the World is keeping up with.

there are no
Dumb Questions

Q: Why did you throw an exception in the Hive class's GetLocation() method?

A: Because we needed a way to deal with bad data passed into the parameter. The hive has a few locations, but the parameter to GetLocations() can pass any string. What happens if there's a bug in the program that causes an invalid string (like an empty string, or the name of a location that's not in the locations dictionary) to be sent as the parameter? What should the method return?

When you've got an invalid parameter and it's not clear what to do with it, it's always a good idea to throw a new ArgumentException. Here's how the GetLocation() method does it:

```
throw new ArgumentException(
       "Unknown location: " + location);
```

This statement causes the Hive class to throw an ArgumentException with the message "Unknown location:" that contains the location that it couldn't find.

The reason this is useful is that it immediately alerts you if a bad location parameter is passed to the method. And by including the parameter in the exception message, you're giving yourself a some valuable information that will help you debug the problem.

Q: What's the point of storing all the locations in a `Point` object if we're not drawing anything?

A: Every bee has a location, whether or not you draw it on the screen in that location. The job of the `Bee` object is to keep track of where it is in the world. Each time its `Go()` method is called, it needs to move a very small distance towards its destination.

Now, even though we may not be drawing a picture of the bee yet, the bee still needs to keep track of where it is inside the hive or in the field, because it needs to know if it's arrived at its destination.

Q: Then why use `Point` to store the location, and not something else? Aren't `Point`s specifically for drawing?

A: Yes, a `Point` is what all of the visual controls use for their Location properties. However, just becase .NET uses them that way, that doesn't mean it's not also useful for us to keep track of locations. Yes, we could have created our own `BeeLocation` class with integer fields called X and Y. No reason reinvent the wheel when C# and .NET give us `Point` for free!

It's almost always easier to repurpose or extend an existing class that does MOSTLY what you want it to do, rather than creating an all new class from scratch.

Exercise
Solution

With all four of our core classes in place, we've got some work to do to tie them all together. Follow the steps below, and you should have working Bee, Hive, Flower, and World classes. Here's how we made the changes to put this into place.

1 **Update Bee to take in a Hive and World reference.**
Now that we've got a class for `Hive` and a class for `World`, `Bee` objects need to know about both. Update your code to take in references to a bee's hive and world in the constructor and save those references for later use.

```
public class Bee {
  // existing constant declarations
  // existing variable declarations
  private World world;
  private Hive hive;

  public Bee(int ID, Point InitialLocation, World world, Hive hive) {
    // existing code
    this.world = world;
    this.hive = hive;
  }
}
```

This is pretty straightforward... take these in, assign them to local variables.

2 **Update Hive to take in a World reference.**
Just as a `Bee` needs to know about its `Hive`, a `Hive` needs to know about its `World`. Update `Hive` to take in a `World` reference in its constructor, and save that reference. You should also update the code in `Hive` that creates new bees to pass into the Bee a reference to itself (the `Hive`), and the `World`.

```
public class Hive {
  private World world;

  public Hive(World world) {
    this.world = world;
    // existing code
  }
  public void AddBee(Random random) {
    // other bee creation code
    Bee newBee = new Bee(beeCount, startPoint, world, this);
  }
}
```

More basic code... get the reference, assign it locally. You want to assign the world FIRST because the rest of the constructor needs to use it.

New bees need a reference to the world, and to the hive, now.

If you're having trouble getting this running, you can download the code for this exercise (and all the others, too) from http://www. headfirstlabs.com/books/hfcsharp/

③ Update World to pass itself into a new Hive.
Update your `World` class so that when it creates a new `Hive`, it passes in a reference to itself.

```
public World() {
  Bees = new List<Bee>();
  Flowers = new List<Flower>();
  Hive = new Hive(this);
  Random random = new Random();
    for (int i = 0; i < 10; i++)
      AddFlower(random);
}
```

this passes in the reference to the Hive.

④ Place an upper limit on the bees that Hive can create.
The Hive class has a MaximumBees constant that determines how many bees the Hive can support (inside and outside the hive, combined). Now that the Hive has access to the World, you should be able to enforce that constraint.

```
public void Go(Random random) {
  if (world.Bees.Count < MaximumBees
      && Honey > MinimumHoneyForCreatingBees
      && random.Next(10) == 1) {
    AddBee(random);
  }
}
```

We can use the World object to see how many total bees there are, and compare that to the maximum bees for this hive.

We put that comparison first. If there's no room for bees, no sense in seeing if there's enough honey to create bees.

⑤ When the Hive creates bees, let the World know.
The World class keeps up with all the bees that exist. When the Hive creates a new Bee, make sure that Bee gets added to the overall list that the World is keeping up with.

```
private void AddBee(Random random) {
  beeCount++;
  // Calculate the starting point
  Point startPoint = // start the near the nursery
  Bee newBee = new Bee(beeCount, startPoint, world, this);
  world.Bees.Add(newBee);
}
```

We add the new bee to the world's overall bee list.

This demonstrates one of the reasons we need a world reference in the Hive class.

Giving the bees behavior

The one big piece of code that's missing in our current classes is the Bee's Go() method. We were able to code a few of the states earlier, but there are plenty left (Idle is incomplete, FlyingToFlower, and part of MakingHoney).

Let's finish up those remaining states now:

```
public void Go(Random random) {
    Age++;
    switch (CurrentState) {
        case BeeState.Idle:
            if (Age > CareerSpan)
                CurrentState = BeeState.Retired;
            else if (world.Flowers.Count > 0
                    && hive.ConsumeHoney(HoneyConsumed)) {
                Flower flower =
                    world.Flowers[random.Next(world.Flowers.Count)];
                if (flower.Nectar >= MinimumFlowerNectar && flower.Alive) {
                    destinationFlower = flower;
                    CurrentState = BeeState.FlyingToFlower;
                }
            }
            break;
        case BeeState.FlyingToFlower:
            if (!world.Flowers.Contains(destinationFlower))
                CurrentState = BeeState.ReturningToHive;
            else if (InsideHive) {
                if (MoveTowardsLocation(hive.GetLocation("Exit"))) {
                    InsideHive = false;
                    location = hive.GetLocation("Entrance");
                }
            }
            else
                if (MoveTowardsLocation(destinationFlower.Location))
                    CurrentState = BeeState.GatheringNectar;
            break;
        case BeeState.GatheringNectar:
            double nectar = destinationFlower.HarvestNectar();
            if (nectar > 0)
                NectarCollected += nectar;
            else
                CurrentState = BeeState.ReturningToHive;
            break;
```

If we're idle, we want to go find another flower to harvest from.

See if there are flowers left, and then consume enough honey to keep on going. Otherwise, we're stuck.

We need another living flower with nectar.

Assuming that all works out, go to the new flower.

Make sure the flower hasn't died as we're heading toward it.

That's why we passed a reference to the hive to the Bee constructor.

If we can get to the exit, then we're out of the hive. Update our location. Since we're now on the field form, we should fly out near the entrance.

If we're out of the hive, and the flower is alive, get to it and start gathering nectar.

This is the exit. When the hive stores its "Exit" location, it corresponds to the point on the Hive form that shows the picture of the exit.

This is the entrance. When the bees fly back to the hive, they fly towards the entrance of the hive on the field form.

That's why the location dictionary stores two separate "Exit" and "Entrance" locations.

```
case BeeState.ReturningToHive:
    if (!InsideHive) {
        if (MoveTowardsLocation(hive.GetLocation("Entrance"))) {
            InsideHive = true;
            location = hive.GetLocation("Exit");
        }
    }
    else
        if (MoveTowardsLocation(hive.GetLocation("HoneyFactory")))
            CurrentState = BeeState.MakingHoney;
    break;
case BeeState.MakingHoney:
    if (NectarCollected < 0.5) {
        NectarCollected = 0;
        CurrentState = BeeState.Idle;
    }
    else
        if (hive.AddHoney(0.5))
            NectarCollected -= 0.5;
        else
            NectarCollected = 0;
    break;
case BeeState.Retired:
    // Do nothing! We're retired!
    break;
}
}
```

If we've made it to the hive, update our location and the insideHive status.

If we're already in the hive, head to the honey factory.

Try and give this nectar to the hive.

If the hive could use the nectar to make honey...

...remove it from the bee.

If the hive's full, AddHoney() will return false, so the bee just dumps the rest of the nectar so he can fly out on another mission.

Once the bee's retired, he just has to wait around until the Hive removes him from the list. Then he's off to Miami!

⚛ BRAIN POWER

Suppose you wanted to change the simulator so it took two turns to reach a flower, and two turns to go from a flower back to the hive. Without writing any code, which *methods* of which classes would you have to change to put this new behavior into place?

The main form tells the world to Go()

Okay, so you know that the world advances by one frame every turn its Go() method is called. But what calls that Go() method? Why, the main form, of course! Time to lay it out.

Go ahead and add a new form to your project. Make it look like the form below. We're using some new controls, but we'll explain them all over the next several pages.

The ToolStrip control puts a toolstrip at the top of your form. You can add the two buttons using the dropdown that appears on the form. Set each button's DisplayStyle to Text.

Each of these labels lives in one cell of a TableLayoutPanel control. You lay it out just like a table in Microsoft Word. Click on the little black arrow to add, remove, and resize columns and rows.

Add a StatusStrip to put a status bar on the bottom. Use the dropdown to add a StatusLabel to it.

Add a Timer control to the form. It doesn't show up at all—it's a non-visual component that the form designer displays as an icon in the space below the form.

The ToolStrip control adds a toolbar to the top of your form, and StatusStrip adds a status bar to the bottom. But they also appear as icons in the area below the form, so you can edit their properties.

We're finally getting to the code that moves the World object along.

```
foreach (Flower flower in Flowers)
    flower.Go(random);
```

```
foreach (Bee bee in Bees)
    bee.Go(random);
```

```
hive.Go(random);
```

Go()

Main form

System.Windows.Forms.Form

World object

List of Flower objects

List of Bee objects

Hive object

We can use World to get statistics

Now we want to update all these controls. But we don't need click handlers for each one; instead, let's use a single method that will update the different statistics in the simulator window:

This indicates how long passes for a turn... we'll have to send this parameter in from somwhere else, in just a few pages.

```
private void UpdateStats(TimeSpan frameDuration) {
    Bees.Text = world.Bees.Count.ToString();
    Flowers.Text = world.Flowers.Count.ToString();
    HoneyInHive.Text = String.Format("{0:f3}", world.Hive.Honey);
    double nectar = 0;
    foreach (Flower flower in world.Flowers)
        nectar += flower.Nectar;
    NectarInFlowers.Text = String.Format("{0:f3}", nectar);
    FramesRun.Text = framesRun.ToString();
    double milliSeconds = frameDuration.TotalMilliseconds;
    if (milliSeconds != 0.0)
        FrameRate.Text = string.Format("{0:f0} ({1:f1}ms)",
                         1000 / milliSeconds, milliSeconds);
    else
        FrameRate.Text = "N/A";
}
```

Most of this just involves getting data from the world and updating labels.

Be sure you match your label names on the form with your code.

Print the first parameter as a number with no decimals, then a space, then print the second parameter with one decimal followed by the letters "ms" (in parentheses)

The frame rate is the number of frames run per second. We're using a TimeSpan object to store how long it took to run the frame. We divide 1000 by the number of milliseconds it took to run the frame—that gives us the total number of milliseconds it took to run the last frame.

Add this method into Form1.

> Whoa! Where did that World object come from... we haven't created that yet, have we? And what's all that time and frame stuff?

We'll talk more about this when we create that TimeSpan object.

Let's create a World

You're right, we need to create the World object. Add this line to your form's constructor:

```
public Form1() {
    InitializeComponent();
    world = new World();
}
```

This code uses the same String.Format() method you used in the hex dump. But instead of printing in hex using "x2", you use "f3" to display a number with three decimal places.

Go ahead and add a private World field to your form called world.

That just leaves all the time-related code. We've always said we needed a way to run Go() in World over and over... sounds like we need some sort of timer.

Timers fire events over and over again

Take a minute and create a new project so you can see how timers work. Then we'll get back to the simulator and put your new knowledge to work.

Remember how you used a loop to animate the greyhounds? Well, there's a better way to do it. A **Timer** is an especially useful component that triggers an event over and over again, up to a thousand times a second.

Do this

1 **Create a new project with a timer and three buttons**
You don't have to close your current project—just pop open a new Visual Studio and start up a new project. Drag a timer and three buttons onto the form. Click on the timer icon at the bottom of the designer and set its Interval property to 1000. That number is measured in milliseconds—it tells the timer to fire its tick event once a second.

2 **Open the IDE's Properties window and click on the Events button.**
(Remember, the Events button looks like a lightning bolt, and it lets you manage the events for any of your form's controls.) The timer control has exactly one event, Tick. **Click on the Timer** icon in the designer, then **double-click on its row** in the Events page,, and the IDE will create a new event handler method for you and hook it up to the property automatically.

The Events button in the Properties window lets you work with all the events for each of your controls.

The Timer control has one event called Tick. If you double-click here, the IDE creates an event handler method for you automatically.

The bottom of the window has a description of the event.

3 **Add code to the Tick event and to your buttons.**
Here's some code that will help you get a sense of how the timer works:

This statement writes the current date and time to the output. Check the output window to make sure the tick event is fired once a second (every 1000 milliseconds).

```
private void timer1_Tick(object sender, EventArgs e) {
    Console.WriteLine(DateTime.Now.ToString());
}
private void toggleEnabled_Click(object sender, EventArgs e) {
    if (timer1.Enabled)
        timer1.Enabled = false;
    else
        timer1.Enabled = true;
}
private void startTimer_Click(object sender, EventArgs e){
    timer1.Start();
    Console.WriteLine("Enabled = " + timer1.Enabled);
}
private void stopTimer_Click(object sender, EventArgs e) {
    timer1.Stop();
    Console.WriteLine("Enabled = " + timer1.Enabled);
}
```

These buttons let you play with the Enabled property and the Start() and Stop() methods. The first one switches Enabled between true and false, and the other two call the Start() and Stop() methods.

The timer's Enabled property starts and stops the timer.

The timer's Start() method starts the timer and sets Enabled to true. The Stop() method stops the timer and sets Enabled to false.

The timer's using a delegate behind the scenes

The timer's Tick event is an average, everyday event handler, just like the ones to handle button clicks.

How do C# and .NET tell the timer what to do every tick? How does the `timer1_Tick()` method get run every time your timer ticks? Well, we're back to **events** and **delegates**, just like we talked about in the last chapter. Use the IDE's "Go To Definition" feature to remind yourself how the Event Handler delegate works:

Right-click on your timer1 variable and select "Go To Definition"
The "Go To Definition" feature will cause the IDE to automatically jump to the location in the code where the `timer1` variable is defined. The IDE will jump you to the code it created to add `timer1` as a property in the Form1 object in Form1.Designer.cs. Scroll up in the file until you find this line:

```
this.timer1.Tick += new System.EventHandler(this.timer1_Tick);
```

This is the Tick event of your timer control. You've set this to occur every 1000 milliseconds.

Here's one of the System's delegates: the basic event handler. It's a delegate... a pointer to one or more methods.

Here's the method you just wrote, timer1_Tick(). You're telling the delegate to point to that method.

Now right-click on EventHandler and select "Go To Definition"
The IDE will automatically jump to the code that defines `EventHandler`. Take a look at the name of new tab that it opened to show you the code: "EventHandler [from metadata]". This means that the code to define EventHandler isn't in your code. It's built into the .NET framework, and the IDE generated a "fake" line of code to show you how it's represented:

```
public delegate void EventHandler(object sender, EventArgs e);
```

Each event is of type EventHandler. So our Tick event now points to the timer1_Tick() method.

Here's why every event in C# generally takes an Object and EventArgs parameter—that's the form of the delegate that C# defines for event handling.

BRAIN POWER

What code would you write to run the World's Go() method every 500 milliseconds in our beehive simulator?

Add a Timer to the simulator

Let's add a timer to the simulator. You've already got a timer control, probably called `timer1`. Instead of using the IDE to generate a `timer1_Tick()` method, though, we can wire the timer to an event handler method called RunFrame() manually:

TimeSpan has properties like Days, Hours, Seconds, and Milliseconds that let you measure the span in different units.

DateTime & TimeSpan

.NET uses the DateTime class to store information about a time, and its Now property returns the current date and time. If you want to find the difference between two times, use a TimeSpan object: just subtract one DateTime object from another, and that'll return a TimeSpan obect that holds the difference between them.

```
public partial class Form1 : Form {
   World world;
   private Random random = new Random();
   private DateTime start = DateTime.Now;
   private DateTime end;
   private int framesRun = 0;

   public Form1() {
      InitializeComponent();
      world = new World();

      timer1.Interval = 50;
      timer1.Tick += new EventHandler(RunFrame);
      timer1.Enabled = false;
      UpdateStats(new TimeSpan());
   }

   private void UpdateStats(TimeSpan frameDuration) {
      // Code from earlier to update the statistics
   }


   public void RunFrame(object sender, EventArgs e) {
      framesRun++;
      world.Go(random);
      end = DateTime.Now;
      TimeSpan frameDuration = end - start;
      start = end;
      UpdateStats(frameDuration);
   }
}
```

You should have a World property from earlier.

These will be used to figure out how long the simulator's been running at any given point.

We want to keep up with how many frames—or turns—have passed.

Run every 50 milliseconds.

We set the handler to our own method, RunFrame().

Timer starts off.

We also start out by updating stats, with a new TimeSpan (0 time elapsed).

A second is 1000 milliseconds, so our timer will tick 200 times a second.

Increase the frame count, and tell the world to Go().

Next, we figure out the time elapsed since the last frame was run.

Finally, update the stats again, with the new time duration.

Exercise

If you haven't dragged a ToolStrip and StatusStrip out of the toolbox and onto your form, do it now.

Your job is to write the event handlers for the **startSimulation** and **reset** buttons in the ToolStrip. Here's what each button should do:

1. Initially, the first button should read "Start Simulation." Pressing it causes the simulation to start, and the label to change to "Pause Simulation." If the simulation is paused, the button should read, "Resume simulation."

2. The second button should say "Reset." When it's pressed, the world should be recreated. If the timer is paused, the text of the first button should change from "Resume simulation" to "Start Simulation."

There's no single answer to this question—we just want you to think about what's left to do.

Sharpen your pencil

What do you think is left to be done in this phase of the simulator? Try running the program. Write down everything you think we still need to take care of before moving on to the graphical stuff.

....

....

....

....

....

....

....

there are no Dumb Questions

Q: We've been using the term "turn," but now you're talking about frames. What's the difference?

A: Semantics, really. We're still dealing in turns: little chunks of time where every object in the world gets to act. But since we'll soon be putting some heavy-duty graphics in place, we've started using "frame", as in a graphical game's frame-rate.

EXERCISE
SOLUTION

Your job was to write the event handlers for the Start Simulation and Reset buttons.

Form1.cs [Design]* ▾ ✕

Beehive Simulator ▬ ⊡ ✕

Start Simulation Reset

# Bees	Bees
# Flowers	Flowers
Total honey in the hive	HoneyInHive
Total nectar in the field	NectarInFlowers
Frames run	FramesRun
Frame rate	FrameRate

Simulation paused

🖳 toolStrip1   ▭ statusStrip1   ⏱ timer1

```
public partial class Form1 : Form {
  // variable declarations

  public Form1() {
    InitializeComponent();
    world = new World();
  }
  private void Form1_Load(object sender, tArgs e) {
    // code to start simulator
  }
  private void UpdateStats(TimeSpan frameDuration) {
    // Code from earlier to update the statistics
  }
  public void RunFrame(object sender, EventArgs e) {
    // event handler for timer
  }


  private void startSimulation_Click(object sender, EventArgs e) {
    if (timer1.Enabled) {
      toolStrip1.Items[0].Text = "Resume simulation";
      timer1.Stop();
    } else {
      toolStrip1.Items[0].Text = "Pause simulation";
      timer1.Start();
    }
  }


  private void reset_Click(object sender, EventArgs e) {
    framesRun = 0;
    if (!timer1.Enabled)
      toolStrip1.Items[0].Text = "Start simulation";
  }
}
```

Be sure your form's control names match up with what you use in your code.

Toggle the timer, and update the message.

Resetting the simulator is just a matter of recreating the World instance and resetting framesRun.

The only time we need to change the first button's label is if it says, "Resume simulation." If it says, "Pause simuation," it doesn't need to change.

Test drive

You've done a ton of work. Compile your code, fix any typos, and run the simulator. How's it look?

Your start/pause and reset buttons should all work.

Looks pretty good! All these numbers should update as the world moves along.

Hmmm... our status strip seems to be the only thing not working.

Exercise

Here's your chance to put together everything you've learned. We need to allow bees to tell our simulator what they're doing. When they do, we want our simulator to update the status message in the simulator.

This time, it's up to you to not only write most of the code, but figure out what code you need to write. How can you have a method in your simulator that gets called everytime a bee changes its state?

To give you a little help, we've written the method to add to the form. The Bee class should call this method any time its state changes:

```
private void SendMessage(int ID, string Message) {
    statusStrip1.Items[0].Text = "Bee #" + ID + ": " + Message;
}
```

* Okay, one more hint. You'll need to make changes to all but one of your classes to make this work.

Exercise Solution

Your job was to come up with a way for Bees to let the simulator know about what they're doing.

Here's what we added to the Bee class.

We used a callback to hook each individual bee object up to the form's SendMessage() method.

```
public class Bee {
    // all our existing code
    public delegate void BeeMessage(int ID, string Message);
    public BeeMessage MessageSender;

    public void Go(Random random) {
        Age++;
        BeeState oldState = CurrentState;
        switch (currentState) {
         // the rest of the switch statement is the same
        }
        if (oldState != CurrentState
            && MessageSender != null)
                MessageSender(ID, CurrentState.ToString());
    }
}
```

BeeMessage is our delegate. It's also a match with the SendMessage() method we wrote in the form.

If the status of the Bee changed, we call back the method our BeeMessage delegate points to, and let that method know about the status change.

Here are the changes we made to the Hive.

```
public class Hive {
    // all our existing code
    public Bee.BeeMessage MessageSender;

    public Hive(World world, Bee.BeeMessage MessageSender) {
        this.MessageSender = MessageSender;
        // existing constructor code
    }

    public void AddBee(Random random) {
        // existing AddBee() code
        Bee newBee = new Bee(beeCount, startPoint, world, this);
        newBee.MessageSender += this.MessageSender;
        world.Bees.Add(newBee);
    }
}
```

Hive needs a delegate too, so it can pass on the methods for each bee to call when they're created in AddBee().

AddBee() now has to make sure that each new bee gets the method to point at.

Hive required some changes, as well.

```
public class World {
    // all our existing code

    public World(Bee.BeeMessage messageSender) {
        Bees = new List<Bee>();
        Flowers = new List<Flower>();
        Hive = new Hive(this, messageSender);
        Random random = new Random();
        for (int i = 0; i < 10; i++)
            AddFlower(random);
    }
}
```

World doesn't need to have a delegate of its own. It just passes on the method to call to the Hive instance.

Last but not least, here's the updated form. Anything not shown stayed the same.

```
public partial class Form1 : Form {
    // variable declarations

    public Form1() {
        InitializeComponent();
        world = new World(new Bee.BeeMessage(SendMessage));
        // the rest of the Form1 constructor
    }

    private void reset_Click(object sender, EventArgs e) {
        framesRun = 0;
        world = new World(new Bee.BeeMessage(SendMessage));
        if (!timer1.Enabled)
            toolStrip1.Items[0].Text = "Start simulation";
    }

    private void SendMessage(int ID, string Message) {
        statusStrip1.Items[0].Text = "Bee #" + ID + ": " + Message;
    }
}
```

We create a new delegate from the Bee class (make sure you declared BeeMessage public), and point it at our SendMessage() method.

Same thing here... create the world with the method for bees to call back.

This is the method we gave you... be sure to add it in, too.

Let's work with <u>groups</u> of bees

Your bees should be buzzing around the hive and the field, and your simulation should be running! How cool is that? But since we don't have the visual part of the simulator working yet—that's what we're doing in the next chapter—all the information we have so far is the messages that the bees are sending back to the main form with their callback. So let's add more information about what the bees are doing.

You already have the form updating these stats and displaying the messages that the bees send as they do their jobs.

Go ahead and add a ListBox to your form. We'll use it to display some extra stats about the bees in the world.

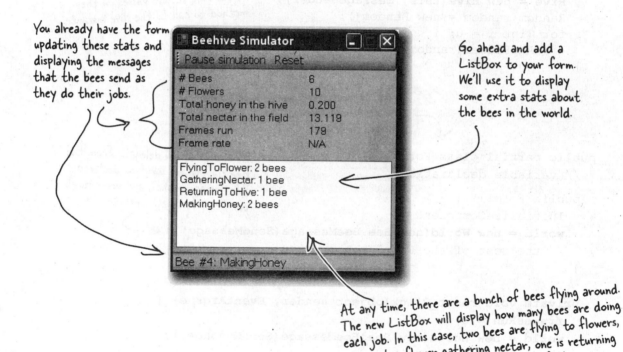

At any time, there are a bunch of bees flying around. The new ListBox will display how many bees are doing each job. In this case, two bees are flying to flowers, one is at a flower gathering nectar, one is returning to the hive, and two are in the honey factory turning nectar into honey.

You know enough to gather the information you'd need to populate that ListBox—take a minute and think through how that would work. But it's a little more complex than it seems at first. What would you need to do to figure out how many bees are in each of the various `Bee.State` states?

A collection collects... <u>DATA</u>

Our bees are stored in a List, which is one of C#'s collection types. And collection types really just store data... a lot like a database does. So each bee is like a row of data, complete with a state, and ID, and so on. Here's how our bees look as a collection of objects:

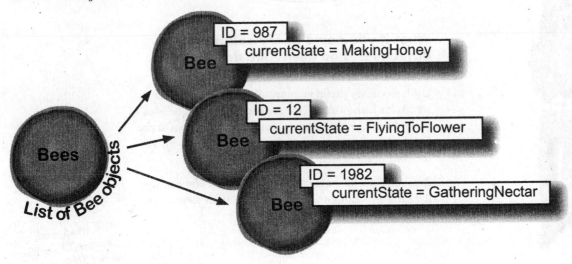

There's a lot of data in the Bee objects' fields. You can *almost* think of a collection of objects the same way you think of rows in a database. Each object holds data in its fields, the same way each row in a database holds data in its columns.

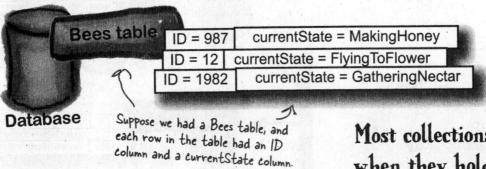

Suppose we had a Bees table, and each row in the table had an *ID* column and a *currentState* column.

Most collections—especially when they hold objects—can be thought of as data stores, just like a database.

Who cares if you can **think** about a collection as a database if you can't **use** a collection like a database? What a total waste of time...

What if you could query collections, databases, and even XML documents with the same basic syntax?

C# has a really useful feature called **LINQ** (which stands for **Langauge INtegrated Query**). The idea behind LINQ is that it gives you a way to take an array, list, stack, queue, or other collection and work with all the data inside it all at once in a single operation.

But what's really great about LINQ is that you can use the same syntax that works with collections as you can for working with databases.

We'll spend most of Chapter 15 working with LINQ.

This LINQ query works essentially the same with data in a collection or a database.

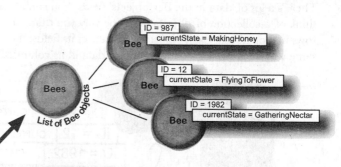

```
var beeGroups =
   from bee in world.Bees
   group bee by bee.CurrentState
   into beeGroup
   orderby beeGroup.Key
   select beeGroup;
```

LINQ

List of Bee objects

Bees	ID = 987, currentState = MakingHoney
	ID = 12, currentState = FlyingToFlower
	ID = 1982, currentState = GatheringNectar

Bees table — Database

ID = 987	currentState = MakingHoney
ID = 12	currentState = FlyingToFlower
ID = 1982	currentState = GatheringNectar

If we had our bee data in a database—or even an XML file—LINQ could work with them in exactly the same way.

XML
```
<bee id="987" currentState="MakingHoney" />
<bee id="12" currentState="FlyingToFlower" />
<bee id="1982" currentState="GatheringNectar" />
```

LINQ makes working with data in collections and databases easy

We're going to spend an entire chapter on LINQ before long, but we can use LINQ and some Ready Bake Code to add some extra features to our simulator. Ready Bake Code is code you should type in, and it's okay if you don't understand it all. You'll learn how it all works in Chapter 15.

Ready Bake Code

```
private void SendMessage(int ID, string Message) {
    statusStrip1.Items[0].Text = "Bee #" + ID + ": " + Message;
    var beeGroups =
        from bee in world.Bees
        group bee by bee.CurrentState into beeGroup
        orderby beeGroup.Key
        select beeGroup;
    listBox1.Items.Clear();
    foreach (var group in beeGroups) {
        string s;
        if (group.Count() == 1)
            s = "";
        else
            s = "s";
        listBox1.Items.Add(group.Key.ToString() + ": "
                + group.Count() + " bee" + s);
        if (group.Key == BeeState.Idle
          && group.Count() == world.Bees.Count()
          && framesRun > 0) {
            listBox1.Items.Add("Simulation ended: all bees are idle");
            toolStrip1.Items[0].Text = "Simulation ended";
            statusStrip1.Items[0].Text = "Simulation ended";
            timer1.Enabled = false;
        }
    }
}
```

This is a LINQ query. It takes all the bees in the Bees collection, and groups them by their CurrentState property.

The group's Key is the bee's CurrentState, so that's the order the states will be displayed on the form.

Make sure this matches the list box control's name on your form.

beeGroups is from the LINQ query. We can count the members, and iterate over them.

This bit of code makes sure it says, "1 bee" and "3 bees", keeping the plural right.

Finally, add the group status (its key) and count to the list box.

Here's another nice feature: Since we know how many bees are idle...

...we can see if ALL bees are idle. If so, the hive's out of honey, so let's stop the simulation.

Relax

> **We'll learn a lot more about LINQ in upcoming chapters.**
>
> You don't need to memorize LINQ syntax or try to drill all of this into your head right now. You'll get a lot more practice working with LINQ in Chapter 15.

Test drive (Part 2)

Go ahead and compile your code and run your project. If
you get any errors, double-check your syntax, especially
with the new LINQ code. Then, fire up your simulator!

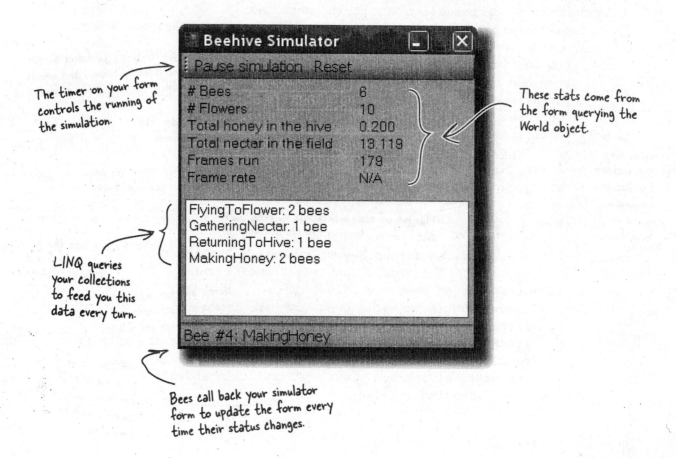

The timer on your form controls the running of the simulation.

These stats come from the form querying the World object.

LINQ queries your collections to feed you this data every turn.

Bees call back your simulator form to update the form every time their status changes.

One final challenge: Open and Save

We're almost ready to take on graphics, and add some visual eye candy to our simulator. First, though, let's do one more thing to this version: allow loading, saving, and printing of bee statistics.

❶ Add the Open, Save, and Print icons

The ToolStrip control has a really useful feature—it can automatically insert picture buttons for standard icons: new, open, save, print, cut, copy, paste, and help. Just right-click on the ToolStrip icon at the bottom of the Form Designer window and select "Insert Standard Items". Then click on the first item—that's the "new" icon—and delete it. Keep the next three items, because they're the ones we need (open, save and print). After that comes a separator; you can either delete it or move it between the Reset button and the save buton. Then delete the rest of the buttons.

> You'll add the Print button now—we'll make it print a status page for the hive in the next chapter.

❷ Add the button event handlers

The new standard buttons are named openToolStripButton, saveToolStripButton and printToolStripButton. Just double-click on them to add their event handlers.

Exercise

Add code to make the save and open buttons work.

1. Make the save button serialize the world to a file. Stop the timer (you can restart it after saving). Set **MessageSender** to **null** for the hive and all the bees, so .NET doesn't try and serialize the code your delegates point to: the form itself. Display a Save dialog box, and then serialize the World object, and the number of frames that have been run. Don't forget to reattach the SendMessage() when you're done saving.

2. Make the open button deserialize the world from a file. Take care of the timer just like in the save button, pop up an Open dialog box, and deserialize the world and the number of frames run from the selected file. Then you can hook up the MessageSender delegates again and restart the timer (if necessary).

3. Don't forget about exception handling! Make sure the world is intact if there's a problem reading or writing the file. Consider popping up a human-readable error message indicating what went wrong.

Your job was to make the Save and Open buttons work.

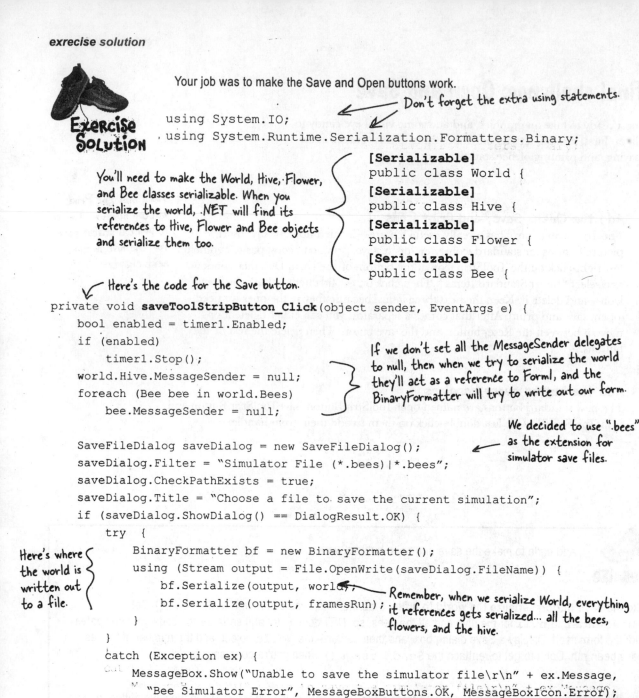

Exercise Solution

Don't forget the extra using statements.

```
using System.IO;
using System.Runtime.Serialization.Formatters.Binary;
```

You'll need to make the World, Hive, Flower, and Bee classes serializable. When you serialize the world, .NET will find its references to Hive, Flower and Bee objects and serialize them too.

```
[Serializable]
public class World {
[Serializable]
public class Hive {
[Serializable]
public class Flower {
[Serializable]
public class Bee {
```

Here's the code for the Save button.

```
private void saveToolStripButton_Click(object sender, EventArgs e) {
    bool enabled = timer1.Enabled;
    if (enabled)
        timer1.Stop();
    world.Hive.MessageSender = null;
    foreach (Bee bee in world.Bees)
        bee.MessageSender = null;
```

If we don't set all the MessageSender delegates to null, then when we try to serialize the world they'll act as a reference to Form1, and the BinaryFormatter will try to write out our form.

We decided to use ".bees" as the extension for simulator save files.

```
    SaveFileDialog saveDialog = new SaveFileDialog();
    saveDialog.Filter = "Simulator File (*.bees)|*.bees";
    saveDialog.CheckPathExists = true;
    saveDialog.Title = "Choose a file to save the current simulation";
    if (saveDialog.ShowDialog() == DialogResult.OK) {
        try {
            BinaryFormatter bf = new BinaryFormatter();
            using (Stream output = File.OpenWrite(saveDialog.FileName)) {
                bf.Serialize(output, world);
                bf.Serialize(output, framesRun);
            }
        }
        catch (Exception ex) {
            MessageBox.Show("Unable to save the simulator file\r\n" + ex.Message,
                "Bee Simulator Error", MessageBoxButtons.OK, MessageBoxIcon.Error);
        }
    }
    world.Hive.MessageSender = new Bee.BeeMessage(SendMessage);
    foreach (Bee bee in world.Bees)
        bee.MessageSender = new Bee.BeeMessage(SendMessage);
    if (enabled)
        timer1.Start();
}
```

Here's where the world is written out to a file.

Remember, when we serialize World, everything it references gets serialized... all the bees, flowers, and the hive.

After we save the file, we need to hook up the MessageSender delegates again, and then restart the timer (if we stopped it).

Here's the code for the
Open button.

```csharp
private void openToolStripButton_Click(object sender, EventArgs e) {
    World currentWorld = world;
    int currentFramesRun = framesRun;

    bool enabled = timer1.Enabled;
    if (enabled)
        timer1.Stop();


    OpenFileDialog openDialog = new OpenFileDialog();
    openDialog.Filter = "Simulator File (*.bees)|*.bees";
    openDialog.CheckPathExists = true;
    openDialog.CheckFileExists = true;
    openDialog.Title = "Choose a file with a simulation to load";
    if (openDialog.ShowDialog() == DialogResult.OK) {
        try {
            BinaryFormatter bf = new BinaryFormatter();
            using (Stream output = File.OpenRead(openDialog.FileName)) {
                world = (World)bf.Deserialize(output);
                framesRun = (int)bf.Deserialize(output);
            }
        }
        catch (Exception ex) {
    MessageBox.Show("Unable to read the simulator file\r\n" + ex.Message,
    "Bee Simulator Error", MessageBoxButtons.OK, MessageBoxIcon.Error);
            world = currentWorld;
            framesRun = currentFramesRun;
        }
    }

    world.Hive.MessageSender = new Bee.BeeMessage(SendMessage);
    foreach (Bee bee in world.Bees)
        bee.MessageSender = new Bee.BeeMessage(SendMessage);
    if (enabled)
        timer1.Start();
}
```

Before opening the file and reading from it, save a reference to the current world and framesRun. If there's a problem, you can revert to these and keep running.

Set up the Open File dialog box and pop it up.

using ensures the stream gets closed.

Here's where we serialize the world and the number of frames run to the file.

If the file operations throw an exception, we restore the current world and framesRun.

Once everything is loaded, we hook back up the delegates and restart the timer.

You'll need to get your simulator up and running before you move on to the next chapter. You can download a working version from the Head First Labs website: www.headfirstlabs.com/books/hfcsharp/

13 controls and graphics

Make it pretty

Sometimes you have to take graphics into your own hands.

We've spent a lot of time on relying on controls to handle everything visual in our applications. But sometimes that's not enough—like when you want to **animate a picture**. And once you get into animation, you'll end up **creating your own controls** for your .NET programs, maybe adding a little **double buffering**, and even **drawing directly onto your forms**. It all begins with the **Graphics** object, **Bitmap**s, and a determination to not accept the graphics status quo.

You've been using controls all along to interact with your programs

TextBoxes, PictureBoxes, Labels... you've got a pretty good handle by now on how you can use the controls in the IDE's toolbox. But what do you *really* know about them? There's a lot more to a control than just dragging an icon onto your form.

⭐ **You can create your own controls**
The controls in the toolbox are really useful for building forms and applications, but there's nothing magical about them. They're just classes, like the classes that you've been writing on your own. In fact, C# makes it really easy for you to create controls yourself, just by inheriting from the right base class.

⭐ **Your custom controls show up in the IDE's toolbox**
There's also nothing mysterious about the toolbox in the IDE. It just looks in your project's classes and the built-in .NET classes for any controls. If it finds a control—a class that implements the right interface—then it displays an icon for the class. If you add your own custom controls, they'll show up in the toolbox, too.

> You can create a class that inherits from any of the existing control classes—even if it doesn't have any other code in it—and it'll automatically show up in the toolbox.

⭐ **You can write code to add controls to your form, and even remove controls, while your program's running**
Just because you lay out a form in the IDE's form designer, that doesn't mean that it has to stay like that. You've already moved plenty of PictureBox controls around (like when you built the greyhound race). But you can also add or remove controls, too. In fact, when you build a form in the IDE, all it's doing is writing the code that adds the controls to the form... which means you can write similar code, and run that code whenever you want.

Form controls are just <u>objects</u>

You already know how important **controls** are to your forms. You've been using buttons, text boxes, picture boxes, check boxes, group boxes, labels, and other forms since chapter 1. Well, it turns out that those controls are just objects, just like everything else you've been working with.

A control is just an object, like any other object—it just happens to know how to draw itself. The Form object form keeps track of its controls using a special collection called **Controls**, which you can use to add or remove controls in your own code.

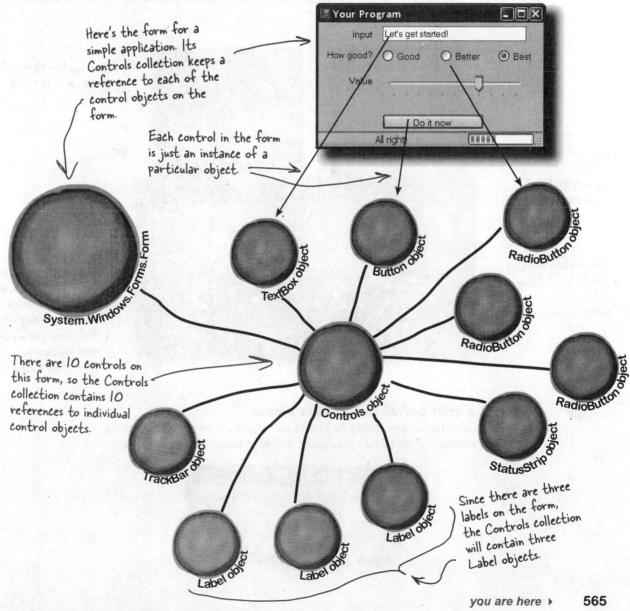

Here's the form for a simple application. Its Controls collection keeps a reference to each of the control objects on the form.

Each control in the form is just an instance of a particular object.

There are 10 controls on this form, so the Controls collection contains 10 references to individual control objects.

Since there are three labels on the form, the Controls collection will contain three Label objects.

System.Windows.Forms.Form

TextBox object

Button object

RadioButton object

RadioButton object

RadioButton object

Controls object

StatusStrip object

Label object

Label object

Label object

TrackBar object

Your Program — Input: Let's get started! — How good? ○ Good ○ Better ◉ Best — Value — Do it now — All right

Use controls to animate the beehive simulator

You've built a great simulator, but it's not much to look at. It's time to create a
really stunning visualization that shows those bees in action. You're about to
build a renderer that animates the beehive…and controls are the key.

1 **The user interface shows you everything that's going on**

Your simulator will have three different windows. You've already built the main "heads-up display"
stats window that shows stats about the current simulation and updates from the bees. Now you'll
add a window that shows you what's going in inside the hive, and a window that shows the field of
flowers where the bees gather nectar.

The form you built
in the last chapter
becomes the heads-
up display for the
simulator.

This window shows what's
going on in the hive.

These two windows are
<u>child</u> windows—when
you minimize the main
window, the other two
disappear along with it.
And when you move the
main window around, the
other two follow it.

This window displays
the field of flowers
and the bees
gathering nectar.

2 **We'll add a Print button to the stats window**

The stats window has an open and save button already. Once we add the graphics,
we can add a button to the toolbar to print an info page about what's going on.

3 **The hive window shows you what's going on inside the hive**
As the bees fly around the world, you'll need to animate each one. Sometimes they're inside the hive, and when they are, they show up in this window.

The hive has three important locations in it. The bees are born in the nursery, they have to fly to the exit to leave the hive to gather nectar from the flowers, and when they come back they need to go to the honey factory to make honey.

The hive exit is on the hive form, and the entrance is on the field form. (That's why we put both of them in the Hive's locations dictionary.)

Here's the entrance to the hive. When bees fly into it, they disappear from the field form and reappear near the Exit in the hive form.

4 **The field window is where the bees collect the nectar**
Bees have one big job: collect nectar from the flowers, and bring it back to the hive to make honey. Then they eat honey to give them energy to fly out and get more nectar.

Add a renderer to your architecture

We need another class that reads the information in the world and uses it to draw the hive, bees and flowers on the two new forms. We'll add a class called **Renderer** to do exactly that. And since your other classes are well-encapsulated, that won't require a lot of changes to your existing code.

You've already built these objects.

The World object keeps track of everything in the simulator: the state of the hive, every bee and every flower.

This is the object for the main window that you've already built.

List of Flower objects

World object

Main form

System.Windows.Forms.Form

List of Bee objects

Each bee knows its location—and we can use that location to draw the bee on the form.

Hive object

Renderer object

The Hive and Field objects are forms, tied to your main form.

Hive form

The renderer reads the information from the World object and uses that information to update the <u>two</u> forms. It keeps a reference to the World object, as well as the Hive form object and the Field form object.

Field form

ren-der, verb.
to represent or depict artistically.
*Sally's art teacher asked the class to look at all of the shadows and lines in the model and **render** them on the page.*

Because Bee, Hive, Flower, and World are <u>well-encapsulated</u>, a class that renders those objects can be added <u>without</u> lots of changes to existing code.

The renderer draws everything in the World on the two forms

The World object keeps track of everything in the simulation: the hive, the bees, and the flowers. But it doesn't actually draw anything or produce any output. That's the job of the Renderer object. It reads all of the information in the World, Hive, Bee, and Flower objects and draws them on the forms.

checks fields for state

draws the bees in the hive

World object

Renderer object

returns the state of the objects

draws the bees and flowers in the field

The World is encapsulated, so Renderer only needs to use the properties on World and its related objects to get the information it needs, and render the information on the display windows.

The simulator renders the world after each frame

After the main form calls the world's Go() method, it should call the renderer's Render() method to redraw the display windows. For example, each flower will be displayed using a PictureBox control. But let's go further with bees and create an animated control. You'll create this new control, called BeeControl, and define its behavior yourself.

Main form

System.Windows.Forms.Form

renderer.Render()

Renderer object

moves each bee's BeeControl

Hive form

moves each BeeControl and flower PictureBox

Field form

The renderer keeps track of which visual control is used to represent a particular bee or flower using Dictionary objects, where the Bee or Flower object is the key.

Controls are well-suited for visual display elements

When a new bee is added to the hive, we'll want our simulator to add a new
`BeeControl` to the Hive form and change its location as it moves around the
world. When that bee flies out of the hive, our simulator will need to remove the
control from the Hive form and add it to the Field form. And when it flies back to
the hive with its load of nectar, its control needs to be removed from the Field form
and added back to the Hive form. And all the while, we'll want the animated bee
picture to flap its wings... and controls will make it easy to do all of that.

1 The world adds a new bee, and the renderer creates a new `BeeControl`
and adds it to the Hive form's `Controls` collection.

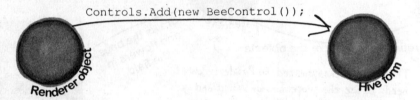

`Controls.Add(new BeeControl());`

2 When the bee flies out of the hive and enters the field, the renderer
removes the `BeeControl` from the hive's `Controls` collection and adds
it to the field form's `Controls` collection.

`Controls.Remove(theBee);`

`Controls.Add(theBee);`

3 A bee will retire if it's idle and it's gotten too old. If the renderer checks
the world's Bees list and finds that the bee is no longer there, it removes the
control from the Hive form.

`Controls.Remove(theBee);`

Sharpen your pencil

Can you figure out what each of these code snippets does? Assume each snippet is inside a form, and write down your best guess.

```
this.Controls.Add(new Button());
```

....
....
....

```
Form2 childWindow = new Form2();
childWindow.BackgroundImage =
        Properties.Resources.Mosaic;
childWindow.BackgroundImageLayout =
        ImageLayout.Tile;
childWindow.Show();
```

....
....
....
....
....
....

If you've got a ListBox on your form, you can use its AddRange() method to add list items.

```
Label myLabel = new Label();
myLabel.Text = "What animal do you like?";
myLabel.Location = new Point(10, 10);
ListBox myList = new ListBox();
myList.Items.AddRange( new object[]
        { "Cat", "Dog", "Fish", "None" } );
myList.Location = new Point(10, 40);
Controls.Add(myLabel);
Controls.Add(myList);
```

....
....
....
....
....
....
....

You don't need to write down each line, as much as summarize what's going on in the code block.

```
Label controlToRemove = null;
foreach (Control control in Controls) {
    if (control is Label
            && control.Text == "Bobby")
        controlToRemove = control as Label;
}
Controls.Remove(controlToRemove);
controlToRemove.Dispose();
```

....
....
....
....
....

Bonus question: Why do you think we didn't put the Controls.Remove() statement inside the foreach loop?

....
....
....

Try it out if you want, and write why you think you got the result that .NET gave you.

buzz buzz buzz

Sharpen your pencil
Solution

Can you figure out what each of these code snippets does? Assume each snippet is inside a form, and write down what you think it does.

```
this.Controls.Add(new Button());
```

Create a new button and add it to the form. It'll have default values (e.g., the Text property will be empty).

```
Form2 childWindow = new Form2();
childWindow.BackgroundImage =
        Properties.Resources.Mosaic;
childWindow.BackgroundImageLayout =
        ImageLayout.Tile;
childWindow.Show();
```

There's a second Form in the application called Form2, so this creates it, sets its background image to a resource image called "Mosaic", makes the background image so it's tiled instead of stretched, and then displays the window to the user.

```
Label myLabel = new Label();
myLabel.Text = "What animal do you like?";
myLabel.Location = new Point(10, 10);
ListBox myList = new ListBox();
myList.Items.AddRange( new object[]
        { "Cat", "Dog", "Fish", "None" } );
myList.Location = new Point(10, 40);
Controls.Add(myLabel);
Controls.Add(myList);
```

This code creates a new label, sets its text, and moves it to a new position. Then it creates a new listbox, adds four items to the list, and moves it just underneath the label. It adds the label and listbox to the form, so they both get displayed immediately.

```
Label controlToRemove = null;
foreach (Control control in Controls) {
    if (control is Label
        && control.Text == "Bobby")
        controlToRemove = control as Label;
}
Controls.Remove(controlToRemove);
controlToRemove.Dispose();
```

This loop searches through all the controls on the form until it finds a label with the text "Bobby". Once it finds the label, it removes it from the form.

If you try, .NET will throw an exception. It needs the collection intact, otherwise it'll lose its place and give you unpredictable results. That's why you'd use a for loop for this instead.

Bonus question: Why do you think we didn't put the Controls.Remove() statement inside the foreach loop?

You can't modify the Controls collection (or any other collection) in the middle of a foreach loop that's iterating through it.

Build your first animated control

You're going to **build your own control** that draws an animated bee picture. If you've never done animation, it's not as hard as it sounds: you draw a sequence of pictures one after another, and produce the illusion of movement. Lucky for us, the way C# and .NET handle resources makes it really easy for us to do animation.

Once you download the four bee animation pictures (Bee animation 1.png through Bee animation 4.png) from Head First Labs, you'll add them to your project's resources. When you flash these four bees quickly one after another, it'll look like their wings are flapping.

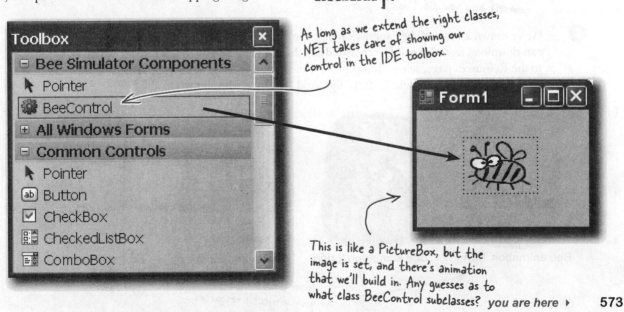

We want a control in the toolbox

If you build `BeeControl` right, it'll appear as a control that you can drag out of your toolbox and onto your form. It'll look just like a `PictureBox` showing a picture of a bee, except that it'll have animated flapping wings.

Download the images for this chapter from the Head First Labs website: www.headfirstlabs.com/books/ hfcsharp/

As long as we extend the right classes, .NET takes care of showing our control in the IDE toolbox.

Toolbox

- □ **Bee Simulator Components**
  - ▶ Pointer
  - ⚙ BeeControl
- ⊞ **All Windows Forms**
- □ **Common Controls**
  - ▶ Pointer
  - ab Button
  - ☑ CheckBox
  - CheckedListBox
  - ComboBox

Form1

This is like a PictureBox, but the image is set, and there's animation that we'll build in. Any guesses as to what class BeeControl subclasses? *you are here ▸* **573**

BeeControl is UNDERLINE a PictureBox... so let's start by UNDERLINE from PictureBox

Since every control in the Toolbox is just an object, it's easy to make a new control. All you need to do is add a new class to your project that inherits from an existing control, and add any new behavior you want your control to perform.

We want a control—let's call it a **BeeControl**—that shows an animated picture of a bee flapping its wings, but we'll start with a control that shows a *non*-animated picture, and then just add animation. So we'll start with a PictureBox, and then we'll add code to draw an animated bee on it.

Animate this!

① **Create a new project** and add the four animation cells to the project's resources, just like you added the Objectville Paper Company logo to your project way back in Chapter 1. But instead of adding them to the *form* resources, add them to the *project's* resources.

In Chapter 1, we added the logo graphic to the <u>form</u>'s Resources file. This time we're adding the resources to the <u>project</u>'s global collection of resources, which makes them available to every class in the project (through the Properties.Resources collection).

Take a minute and flip back to Chapter 1 to remind yourself how you did this.

These appear under your project, not a particular form.

② We've drawn a four-cell bee animation that you can import into your resources that you can download from **http://www.headfirstlabs.com/books/hfcsharp/**. Then, go to the Resources page, select "Images" from the first dropdown at the top of the screen, and select "Add Existing File..." from the "Add Resource" dropdown.

Bee animation 1.png   Bee animation 2.png   Bee animation 3.png   Bee animation 4.png

Import each of these images into your project's resources.

❸ When you add images or other resources to the project's Resources file, you can access them using the `Properties.Resources` class. Just go to any line in your code and type `Properties.Resources.` — as soon as you do, the IntelliSense pops up a dropdown list that shows all of the pictures you've imported.

Note that "." at the end… that's what tells the IDE to pop up the properties and methods of the class you typed in.

```
Resources.resx                       ▾ ✕
📄 Images  ▾  📄 Add Resource ▾
```

Bee_animation_1   Bee_animation_2

Bee_animation_3   Bee_animation_4

```
pictureBox1.Image =
  Properties.Resources.Bee_animation_1;
```

This sets the image used for a particular PictureBox's image (and for our starting image).

These images are stored as public properties of the Properties.Resources class.

You'll need to add a "using System.Windows. Forms" line for the PictureBox and Timer.

❹ **Now add your BeeControl!** Just add this BeeControl class to your project:

```csharp
public class BeeControl : PictureBox {
  private Timer animationTimer = new Timer();
  public BeeControl() {
    animationTimer.Tick += new EventHandler(animationTimer_Tick);
    animationTimer.Interval = 150;
    animationTimer.Start();
    BackColor = System.Drawing.Color.Transparent;
    BackgroundImageLayout = ImageLayout.Stretch;
  }

  private int cell = 0;
  void animationTimer_Tick(object sender, EventArgs e) {
    cell++;
    switch (cell) {
      case 1: BackgroundImage = Properties.Resources.Bee_animation_1; break;
      case 2: BackgroundImage = Properties.Resources.Bee_animation_2; break;
      case 3: BackgroundImage = Properties.Resources.Bee_animation_3; break;
      case 4: BackgroundImage = Properties.Resources.Bee_animation_4; break;
      case 5: BackgroundImage = Properties.Resources.Bee_animation_3; break;
      default: BackgroundImage = Properties.Resources.Bee_animation_2;
        cell = 0; break;
    }
  }
}
```

Here's where you initialize the timer by instantiating it, setting its Interval property, and then adding its tick event handler.

Once we get back to frame #1, we'll reset cell back to 0.

Each time the timer's tick event fires, it increments cell, and then does a switch based on it to assign the right picture to the Image property (inherited from PictureBox).

When you change the code for a control, you need to rebuild your program to make your changes show up in the designer.

Then **rebuild your program**. Go back to the form designer and look in the toolbox, the BeeControl is there. Drag it onto your form—you get an **animated** bee!

Create a button to add the BeeControl to your form

It's easy to add a control to a form—just add it to the Controls collection. And it's just as easy to remove from the form by removing it from Controls. But controls implement IDisposable, so make sure you **always dispose your control** after you remove it.

Now do this

1 **Remove the BeeControl from your form, and then add a button**
Go to the form designer and **delete the BeeControl from the form**. Then add a button. We'll make the button add and remove a BeeControl.

> You can use an object initializer to set the BeeControl properties after it's instantiated.

2 **Add a button to and and remove the bee control**
Here's the event handler for it:

> When you add a control to the Controls collection, it appears on the form immediately.

```
BeeControl control = null;
private void button1_Click(object sender, EventArgs e) {
    if (control == null) {
        control = new BeeControl() { Location = new Point(100, 100) };
        Controls.Add(control);
    } else {
        Controls.Remove(control);
        control.Dispose();
        control = null;
    }
}
```

> All you need to do to remove the control is remove it from the Controls collection. But make sure you dispose it—otherwise it'll keep taking up resources!

Now when you run your program, if you click the button once it'll add a new BeeControl to the form. Click it again and it'll delete it. It uses the private control field to hold the reference to the control. (It sets the reference to null when there's no control on the form.)

Behind the Scenes

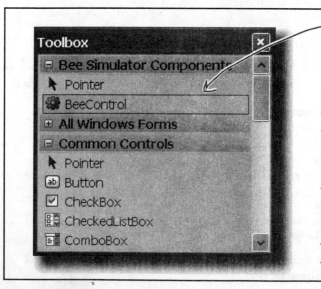

> You can add your own control to the toolbox just by creating a class that inherits from Control.

Every visual control in your toolbox inherits from System. Windows.Forms.Control. That class implements the has some members which should be pretty familiar by now: Visible, Width, Height, Text, Location, BackColor, BackgroundImage... all of those familiar properties you see in the form's Properties window.

Your controls need to dispose <u>their</u> controls, too!

There's a problem with the BeeControl. Controls need to be disposed after they're done. But the BeeControl creates a new instance of Timer, which is a control that shows up in the toolbox... and it never gets disposed! That's a problem. Luckily, it's easy to fix—just override the Dispose() method.

The control class implements IDisposable, so you need to make sure every control you use gets disposed.

③ Override the Dispose() method and dispose of the timer

Since BeeControl inherits from a control, then that control must have a Dispose() method. So we can just override and extend that method to dispose our timer. Just go into the control and type `override`:

```
public class BeeControl : PictureBox {
    override
```

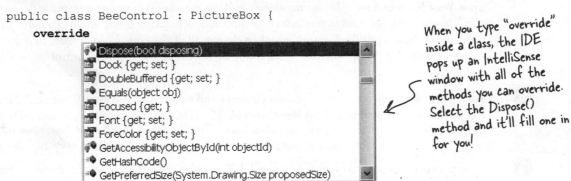

When you type "override" inside a class, the IDE pops up an IntelliSense window with all of the methods you can override. Select the Dispose() method and it'll fill one in for you!

As soon as you click on Dispose(), the IDE will fill in the method with a call to base.Dispose():

```
protected override void Dispose(bool disposing) {
    base.Dispose(disposing);
}
```

③ Add the code to dispose the timer

Since BeeControl inherits from a control, then that control must have a Dispose() method. So we can just override and extend that method to dispose our timer. Just add a line to the Dispose() method that the IDE filled in for you:

```
protected override void Dispose(bool disposing) {
    animationTimer.Dispose();
    base.Dispose(disposing);
}
```

Now the BeeControl will dispose of its timer as part of its own Dispose() method. It cleans up after itself!

Now your BeeControl will dispose of the timer that it created in its constructor. The IDE filled in a call to the PictureBox base class's Dispose() method—leave it in so the PictureBox can dispose itself, too.

Any control that you write from scratch is responsible for disposing any other controls (or disposable objects) that it creates.

A UserControl is an easy way to build a control

There's an easier way to build your own Toolbox controls. Instead of creating a class that inherits from an existing control, all you need to do is **use the IDE to add a UserControl to your project**. You work with a UserControl just like a form. You can drag other controls out of the toolbox and onto it—it uses the normal form designer in the IDE. And you can use its events just like you do with a form. So let's rebuild the BeeControl using a UserControl.

Do this

1 Right-click on BeeControl.cs in the IDE and rename it to OldBeeControl.cs. The IDE will **pop up a Yes/No window**: *"You are renaming a file. Would you also like to perform a rename in this project of all references to the code element 'BeeControl'?"*—this window is asking if you want to rename the BeeControl class to OldBeeControl, and then change all of the code in the project to reflect this change. **Click the "Yes" button** to rename your BeeControl to OldBeeControl.

2 Right-click on the project in the Solution Explorer and select "Add >> User Control..." Have the IDE **add a user control called BeeControl**. The IDE will open up the new control in the form designer. *Use the animationTimer_Tick() method (you'll need to rename it) and the cell field from the old bee control—but don't copy anything else.*

3 Drag a Timer control onto your user control. It'll show up at the bottom of the designer, just like with a form. Use the Properties window to set its `Interval` to 150 and its `Enabled` to true. Then double-click on it—the IDE will add its Tick event handler. Just use the same Tick event handler that you used earlier to animate the first bee control.

4 Now update the BeeControl's constructor:

```
public BeeControl() {
    InitializeComponent();
    BackColor = System.Drawing.Color.Transparent;
    BackgroundImageLayout = ImageLayout.Stretch;
}
```

You can also do this from the Properties page in the IDE, instead of using code.

5 Go back to the button event handler on the form. When you renamed the first BeeControl to OldBeeControl, it changed the form code as well. So change the two lines back to BeeControl so it uses your new UserControl instead of the PictureBox:

```
BeeControl control = null;
private void button1_Click(...) {
    if (control == null) {
        control = new BeeControl() { ...
```

Now **run your program**—it should work exactly the same as before. The button now adds and removes your UserControl-based BeeControl.

A UserControl is an easy way to add a control to the toolbox. Edit a UserControl just like a form—you can drag other controls out of the toolbox onto it, and you can use its events exactly like a form's events.

But I've been using controls all this time, and I've never disposed a single one of them! Why should I start now?

You didn't dispose your controls because your forms did it for you.

But don't take our word for it. Use the IDE's search function to search your project for the word "Dispose", and you'll find that the IDE added a method in Form1.Designer.cs to override the Dispose() method that calls its own `base.Dispose()`. When the form is disposed, **it automatically disposes everything in its Controls collection** so you don't have to worry about it. But once you start removing controls from that collection or creating new instances of controls (like the Timer in the BeeControl) outside of the Controls collection, then you need to do the disposal yourself.

---

there are no
Dumb Questions

Q: Why does the form code for the PictureBox-based BeeControl work exactly the same with the UserControl-based BeeControl?

A: Because the code doesn't care how the BeeControl object is implemented. It just cares that it can add the object to the form's Controls method.

Q: I double-clicked on my OldBeeControl class in the Solution Explorer, and it had a message about adding components to my class. What's that about?

A: When you create a control by adding a class to your project that inherits from PictureBox or another control, the IDE does some clever things. One of the things it does is let you work with **components**, those non-visual controls like Timer and

OpenFileDialog that show up in the space beneath your form when you work with them.

Give it a try—create an empty class that inherits from PictureBox. Then rebuild your project and double-click on it in the IDE. You'll get this message:

To add components to your class, drag them from the Toolbox and use the Properties window to set their properties.

Drag an OpenFileDialog out of the Toolbox and onto your new class. It'll appear as an icon. You can click on it and set its properties. Set a few of them. Now go back to the code for your class. Check out the constructor—the IDE added code to instantiate the OpenFileDialog object and set its properties.

Q: When I changed the properties in the OpenFileDialog, I noticed an error message in the IDE: "You must rebuild your project for the changes to show up in any open designers." Why did I get this error?

A: Because the desginer runs your control, and until you rebuild your code it's not running the latest version of the control.

Remember how the wings of the bee were flapping when you first created your BeeControl, even when you dragged it out of the toolbox and into the designer? You weren't running your program yet, but the code that you wrote was being executed. The timer was firing its Tick event, and your event handler was changing the picture. The only way the IDE can make that happen is if the code were actually compiled and running in memory somewhere. So it's reminding you to update your code so it can display your controls properly.

The renderer uses your BeeControl to draw animated bees on your forms

With a BeeControl class and two forms, you just need a way to position bees, move them from one form to the other, and keep up with the bees. You'll also need to position flowers on the FieldForm, although since flowers don't move, that's pretty simple. All of this is code that we can put into a new class, Renderer. Here's what that class does:

1 **The stats form will be the parent of the hive and field forms**
The first step in adding graphics to the Beehive Simulator will be adding two forms to the project. You'll add one called HiveForm (to show the inside of the hive) and one called FieldForm (which will show the field of flowers). Then you'll add lines to the main form's constructor to show its two child forms to tell Windows that the stats form is their **owner**:

```
public Form1() {
    // other code in the Form1 constructor
    hiveForm.Show(this);
    fieldForm.Show(this);
```

> You'll want the hive and field forms "linked" to the stats form—that does useful things like minimizing the hive and field forms when you minimize the stats form. You can do this by telling Windows that the stats form is their owner.

> Every form object has a Show() method. If you want to set another form as its owner, just pass a reference to that form to Show().

2 **The renderer keeps a reference to the world and each child form**
At the very top of the Renderer class you'll need a few important fields. The class has to know the location of each bee and flower, so it needs a reference to the World. And it'll need to add, move, and remove controls in the two forms, so it needs a reference to each of those forms:

```
public class Renderer {
    private World world;
    private HiveForm hiveForm;
    private FieldForm fieldForm;
```

> Start your Renderer class with these lines. We'll add to this class throughout the chapter.

3 **The renderer uses dictionaries to keep track of the controls**
World keeps track of its Bee objects using a List<Bee> and a List<Flower> to store its flowers. The renderer needs to be able to look at each of those Bee and Flower objects and figure out what BeeControl and PictureBox they correspond to—or, if it can't find a corresponding control, it needs to create one. So here's a perfect opportunity to use dictionaries. So we'll need two more private fields in Renderer:

```
private Dictionary<Flower, PictureBox> flowerLookup =
        new Dictionary<Flower, PictureBox>();
private Dictionary<Bee, BeeControl> beeLookup =
        new Dictionary<Bee, BeeControl>();
```

> These dictionaries become one-to-one mappings between a bee or flower and the control for that bee or flower.

> These two dictionary collections let the renderer store exactly one control for each bee or flower in the world.

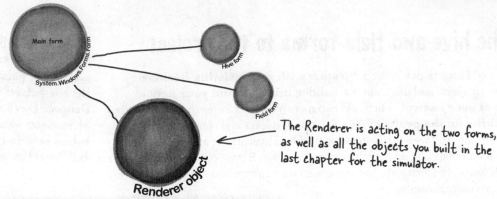

The Renderer is acting on the two forms, as well as all the objects you built in the last chapter for the simulator.

④ The bees and flowers already know their locations

There's a reason we stored each bee and flower location using a Point. Once we have a Bee object, we can easily look up its BeeControl and set its location.

```
beeControl = beeLookup[bee];
beeControl.Location = bee.Location;
```

For each bee or flower, we can look up the matching control. Then, set that control's location to match the location of the bee or flower object.

⑤ If a bee doesn't have a control, the renderer adds it to the hive form

It's easy enough for the renderer to figure out if a particular bee or flower has a control. If the dictionary's ContainsKey() method returns false for a particular Bee object, that means there's no control on the form for that bee. So Renderer needs to create a BeeControl, add it to the dictionary, and then add the control to the form. (It also calls the control's BringToFront() method, to make sure the control doesn't get hidden behind the flower PictureBoxes):

```
if (!beeLookup.ContainsKey(bee)) {
    if (!beeLookup.ContainsKey(bee)) {
        beeControl = new BeeControl() { Width = 40, Height = 40 };
        beeLookup.Add(bee, beeControl);
        hiveForm.Controls.Add(beeControl);
        beeControl.BringToFront();
} else
    beeControl = beeLookup[bee];
```

ContainsKey() tells us if the bee exists in the dictionary. If not, then we need to add that bee, along with a corresponding control.

BringToFront() ensures the bee appears "on top of" any flowers on the FieldForm, and on top of the background of the HiveForm.

Remember how a dictionary can use anything as a key? Well, this one uses a Bee object as a key. The renderer needs to know which BeeControl on the form belongs to a particular bee. So it looks up that bee's object in the dictionary, which spits out the correct control. Now the renderer can move it around.

Add the hive and field forms to the project

Now you need forms to put bees on. So **start with your existing Beehive Simulator project**, and use "Add >> Existing Item…" to **add your new BeeControl user control**. Then add two more Windows forms to the project by **right-clicking on the project** in the Solution Explorer and choosing "Windows Form…" from the Add menu. If you name the files HiveForm.cs and FieldForm.cs, the IDE will automatically set their Name properties to `HiveForm` and `FieldForm`. You already know that forms are just objects, so `HiveForm` and `FieldForm` are really just two more classes.

This is a PictureBox control with its BackgroundImage set to the outside hive picture. When you load the hive pictures into the Resource Designer, they'll show up in the list of resources when you click the "…" button next to BackgroundImage in the Properties window.

Make sure you resize both forms so they look like these screenshots.

You'll need the inside and outside hive images—"Hive (inside).png" and "Hive (outside).png"—loaded into your resources. Then add these two forms. Set each form's <u>FormBorderStyle</u> property to FixedSingle (so the user can't resize it), the <u>ControlBox</u> property to false (to take away its minimize and maximize controls), and <u>StartPosition to Manual</u> (so its Location property is settable).

Set the form's BackgroundImage property to the inside hive picture.

Figure out where <u>your</u> locations are

Remember, go to the Properties window, click on the lightning-bolt icon to bring up the Events window, scroll down to the MouseClick row and double-click on it. The IDE will add the event handler for you.

You need to figure out where the hive is on your FieldForm. Using the Properties window, create a handler for the MouseClick event, and add this code:

```
private void Form1_MouseClick(object sender, MouseEventArgs e) {
    MessageBox.Show(e.Location.ToString());
}
```

Now you can run the form, and click on the location of the hive. That will give you a set of coordinates for your hive on the field.

Add the same handler to HiveForm, and run it. Then, by clicking, get the coordinates of the exit, the nursery, and the honey factory. Using all these locations, you can update the `ResetLocations()` method you wrote in the `Hive` class in the last chapter:

```
private void ResetLocations()
{
    locations = new Dictionary<string, Point>();
    locations.Add("Entrance", new Point(600, 100));
    locations.Add("Nursery", new Point(95, 174));
    locations.Add("HoneyFactory", new Point(157, 98));
    locations.Add("Exit", new Point(194, 213));
}
```

These are the coordinates that worked for us, but if you're forms a little bigger or smaller, your coordinates will be different.

{X=236,Y=166}

OK

Remove the mouse click handler when you're done… you just needed it to get the locations on your forms.

Build the Renderer

Here's the complete `Renderer` class. The main form calls this class's `Render()` method right after it calls `World.Go()` to draw the bees and flowers on the forms. You'll need to make sure that the flower graphic (`Flower.png`) is loaded into the project, just like the animated bee images.

Renderer

Render()
Reset()

All fields in the renderer are private because no other class needs to update to any of its properties. It's fully encapsulated. The world just calls Render() to draw the world to the forms, and Reset() to clear the controls on the forms if it needs to reset.

The renderer keeps references to the world and the two forms it draws the bees on.

The world uses Bee and Flower objects to keep track of every bee and flower in the world. The forms use a PictureBox to display each flower and a BeeControl to display each bee. The renderer uses these dictionaries to connect each bee and flower to its own BeeControl or PictureBox.

When a flower dies or a bee retires, it uses the deadFlowers and retiredBees lists to clean out the dictionaries.

```
public class Renderer {
    private World world;
    private HiveForm hiveForm;
    private FieldForm fieldForm;

    private Dictionary<Flower, PictureBox> flowerLookup =
        new Dictionary<Flower, PictureBox>();
    private List<Flower> deadFlowers = new List<Flower>();

    private Dictionary<Bee, BeeControl> beeLookup =
        new Dictionary<Bee, BeeControl>();
    private List<Bee> retiredBees = new List<Bee>();

    public Renderer(World world, HiveForm hiveForm, FieldForm fieldForm) {
        this.world = world;
        this.hiveForm = hiveForm;
        this.fieldForm = fieldForm;
    }

    public void Render() {
        DrawBees();
        DrawFlowers();
        RemoveRetiredBeesAndDeadFlowers();
    }

    public void Reset() {
        foreach (PictureBox flower in flowerLookup.Values) {
            fieldForm.Controls.Remove(flower);
            flower.Dispose();
        }
        foreach (BeeControl bee in beeLookup.Values) {
            hiveForm.Controls.Remove(bee);
            fieldForm.Controls.Remove(bee);
            bee.Dispose();
        }
        flowerLookup.Clear();
        beeLookup.Clear();
    }
```

The timer on the main form that runs the animation calls the Render() method, which updates the bees and the flowers, and then cleans out its dictionaries.

If the simulator is reset, it calls the RemoveAllControls() method to completely clear out the controls on the two forms. It finds all of the controls in each of its two dictionaries and removes them from the forms, calling Dispose() on each of them. Then it clears the two dictionaries.

It takes two foreach loops to draw the flowers. The first looks for new flowers and adds their PictureBoxes. The second looks for dead flowers and removes their PictureBoxes.

The first foreach loop uses the flowerLookup dictionary to check each flower to see if it's got a control on the form. If it doesn't, it creates a new PictureBox using an object initializer, adds it to the form, and then adds it to the flowerLookup dictionary.

```
private void DrawFlowers() {
    foreach (Flower flower in world.Flowers)
        if (!flowerLookup.ContainsKey(flower)) {
            PictureBox flowerControl = new PictureBox() {
                Width = 45,
                Height = 55,
                Image = Properties.Resources.Flower,
                SizeMode = PictureBoxSizeMode.StretchImage,
                Location = flower.Location
            };
            flowerLookup.Add(flower, flowerControl);
            fieldForm.Controls.Add(flowerControl);
        }

    foreach (Flower flower in flowerLookup.Keys) {
        if (!world.Flowers.Contains(flower)) {
            PictureBox flowerControlToRemove = flowerLookup[flower];
            fieldForm.Controls.Remove(flowerControlToRemove);
            flowerControlToRemove.Dispose();
            deadFlowers.Add(flower);
        }
    }
}

private void DrawBees() {
    BeeControl beeControl;
    foreach (Bee bee in world.Bees) {
        beeControl = GetBeeControl(bee);
        if (bee.InsideHive) {
            if (fieldForm.Controls.Contains(beeControl))
                MoveBeeFromFieldToHive(beeControl);
        } else if (hiveForm.Controls.Contains(beeControl))
            MoveBeeFromHiveToField(beeControl, bee);
        beeControl.Location = bee.Location;
    }

    foreach (Bee bee in beeLookup.Keys) {
        if (!world.Bees.Contains(bee)) {
            beeControl = beeLookup[bee];
            if (fieldForm.Controls.Contains(beeControl))
                fieldForm.Controls.Remove(beeControl);
            if (hiveForm.Controls.Contains(beeControl))
                hiveForm.Controls.Remove(beeControl);
            beeControl.Dispose();
            retiredBees.Add(bee);
        }
    }
}
```

DrawFlowers() uses the Location property in the Flower object to set the PictureBox's location on the form.

The second foreach loop looks for any PictureBox in the flowerLookup dictionary that's no longer on the form and removes it.

After it removes the PictureBox, it calls its Dispose() method. Then it adds the Flower object to deadFlowers so it'll get cleared later.

DrawBees() also uses two foreach loops, and it does the same basic things as DrawFlowers(). But it's a little more complex, so we split some of its behavior out into separate methods to make it easier to understand.

DrawBees() checks if a bee is in the hive but its control is on the FieldForm, or vice versa. It uses two extra methds to move the BeeControls between the forms.

Once the BeeControl is removed, we need to call its Dispose() method—the user control will dispose of its timer for us.

The second foreach loop works just like in DrawFlowers(), except it needs to remove the BeeControl from the right form.

You'll need to make sure you've got using System.Drawing
and using System.Windows.Forms at the top of the
Renderer class file.

GetBeeControl() looks up a bee in the
beeLookup dictionary and returns it. If
it's not there, it creates a new 40 x 40
BeeControl and adds it to the hive form
(since that's where bees are born).

```
private BeeControl GetBeeControl(Bee bee) {
    BeeControl beeControl;
    if (!beeLookup.ContainsKey(bee)) {
        beeControl = new BeeControl() { Width = 40, Height = 40 };
        beeLookup.Add(bee, beeControl);
        hiveForm.Controls.Add(beeControl);
        beeControl.BringToFront();
    }
    else
        beeControl = beeLookup[bee];
    return beeControl;
}
```

Don't forget that
the ! means NOT.

MoveBeeFromHiveToField() takes a specific
BeeControl out of the hive form's Controls
collection and adds it to the field form's
Controls collection.

```
private void MoveBeeFromHiveToField(BeeControl beeControl, Bee bee) {
    hiveForm.Controls.Remove(beeControl);
    beeControl.Size = new Size(20, 20);
    fieldForm.Controls.Add(beeControl);
    beeControl.BringToFront();
}
```

The bees on the field form are smaller than
the ones on the hive form, so the method
needs to change BeeControl's Size property.

```
private void MoveBeeFromFieldToHive(BeeControl beeControl) {
    fieldForm.Controls.Remove(beeControl);
    beeControl.Size = new Size(40, 40);
    hiveForm.Controls.Add(beeControl);
    beeControl.BringToFront();
}
```

MoveBeeFromFieldToHive() moves a
BeeControl back to the hive form.
It has to make it bigger again.

```
private void RemoveRetiredBeesAndDeadFlowers() {
    foreach (Bee bee in retiredBees)
        beeLookup.Remove(bee);
    retiredBees.Clear();
    foreach (Flower flower in deadFlowers)
        flowerLookup.Remove(flower);
    deadFlowers.Clear();
}
```

Whenever DrawBees() and DrawFlowers()
found that a flower or bee was no longer
in the world, it added them to the
deadFlowers and retiredBees lists to be
removed at the end of the frame.

After all the controls are moved around,
the renderer calls this method to clear
any dead flowers and retired bees out of
the two dictionaries.

Now connect the main form to your two new forms, HiveForm and FieldForm

It's great to have a Renderer, but so far, there aren't any forms to render onto. We can fix that by going back to the main Form class (probably called Form1), and making some code changes:

When the main form loads, it creates an instance of each of the other two forms. They're just objects in the heap for now—they won't be displayed until their Show() methods are called.

```csharp
public partial class Form1 : Form {
    HiveForm hiveForm = new HiveForm();
    FieldForm fieldForm = new FieldForm();
    Renderer renderer;

    // the rest of the fields

    public Form1() {
        InitializeComponent();

        MoveChildForms();
        hiveForm.Show(this);
        fieldForm.Show(this);
        ResetSimulator();

        // The rest of the code stays the same
    }
```

Move the code to instantiate the World into the ResetSimulator() method.

The form passes a reference to itself into Form.Show() so it becomes the parent form.

The main form's constructor moves the two child forms in place, then displays them. Then it calls ResetSimulator(), which instantiates Renderer.

Everything else that used to be in the constructor will be moved to the ResetSimulator() method.

```csharp
    private void MoveChildForms() {
        hiveForm.Location = new Point(Location.X + Width + 10, Location.Y);
        fieldForm.Location = new Point(Location.X,
            Location.Y + Math.Max(Height, hiveForm.Height) + 10);
    }

    public void RunFrame(object sender, EventArgs e) {
        framesRun++;
        world.Go(random);
        renderer.Render();
        // previous code
    }

    private void Form1_Move(object sender, EventArgs e) {
        MoveChildForms();
    }
```

This code moves the two forms so that the hive form is next to the main stats form and the field form is below both of them.

Adding this one line to RunFrame makes the simulator update the graphics after each time the world's Go() method is called.

The Move event is fired every time the main form is moved. Calling MoveChildForms() makes sure the child forms always move along with the main form.

Use the Events button in the Properties window to add the Move event handler.

Make sure you've set the field and hive forms' StartPosition property to Manual, or else MoveChildForms() won't work.

Here's where we create new instances of
the World and Renderer classes, which
resets the simulator.

```
private void ResetSimulator() {
    framesRun = 0;
    world = new World(new Bee.BeeMessage(SendMessage));
    renderer = new Renderer(world, hiveForm, fieldForm);
}

private void reset_Click(object sender, EventArgs e) {
    renderer.Reset();
    ResetSimulator();
    if (!timer1.Enabled)
        toolStrip1.Items[0].Text = "Start simulation";
}

private void openToolStripButton_Click(object sender, EventArgs e) {
    // The rest of the code in this button stays exactly the same.

    renderer.Reset();
    renderer = new Renderer(world, hiveForm, fieldForm);
}
}
```

The Reset button needs to
call Reset() to clear out all
the BeeControls and flower
PictureBoxes, and then reset
the simulator.

Finally, you'll need to add code to
the Open button on the ToolStrip
to use the Reset() method to
remove the bees and flowers from
the two forms' Controls collections.
and then create a new renderer
using the newly loaded world.

there are no
Dumb Questions

Q: I saw that you showed the form using a `Show()` method, but I don't quite get what was going on with passing `this` as a parameter.

A: This all comes down to the idea that a form is just another class. When you display a form you're just instantiating that class and calling its `Show()` method. There's an overloaded version of `Show()` that takes one parameter, a parent window. When one form is a parent of another, it causes Windows to set up a special relationship between them—for example, when you minimize the parent window, it automatically minimizes all of that form's child windows, too.

Q: Can you alter the preexisting controls and muck around with their code?

A: No, you can't actually access the code inside the controls that ship with Visual Studio. However, every single one of those controls is a class that you can inherit, just like you inherited from `PictureBox` to create your `BeeControl`. If you want to add or change behavior in any of those controls, you add your own methods and properties that manipulate the ones in the base class.

Test drive... ahem... buzz

Compile all your code, chase down any errors you're
getting, and run your simulator.

Your bees should be happily
flapping their wings now.

Try changing the
constants on your
simulator, and seeing how
the Renderer handles
more bees or flowers.

Looks great, but something's not quite right...

Look closely at the bees buzzing around the hive and the flowers, and you'll notice some problems with the way they're being rendered. Remember how you set each BeeControl's BackColor property to Color.Transparent? Unfortunately, that wasn't enough to keep the simulator from having some problems which are actually pretty typical of graphics programs.

① **There are some <u>serious</u> performance issues**
Did you notice how the whole simulator slows down when all the bees are inside the hive? If not, try adding more bees by increasing the constants in the World class. Keep your eye on the frame rate—add more bees, and it starts to drop significantly.

② **The flowers' backgrounds aren't really transparent**
And there's another, completely *separate* problem. When we saved the graphics files for the flowers, we gave them transparent backgrounds. But while that made sure that each flower's background matched the background of the form, it doesn't look so nice when flowers overlap each other.

> When you set a PictureBox's background color to Transparent, it draws any transparent pixels in the image so they match the background of the _form_... which isn't always the right thing to do.

> When one PictureBox overlaps another, C# draws the transparent pixels so they match the form, not the other control that it overlaps, causing weird rectangular "cut-outs" any time two flowers overlap.

③ **The bees' backgrounds aren't transparent, either**
It turns out that Color.Transparent really does have some limitations. When the bees are hovering over the flowers, the same "cut-out" glitch happens. Transparency works a little better with the hive form, where the form's background image does show through the transparent areas of of the bee graphics. But when the bees overlap, the same problems occur. And if you watch closely as the bees move around the hive, you'll see some glitches where the bee image are sometimes distorted when they move.

Let's take a closer look at those performance issues

Each bee picture you downloaded is big. Really big. Pop one of them open in Windows Picture Viewer and see for yourself. That means the PictureBox needs to shrink it down every time it changes the image, and scaling an image up or down takes time. The reason the bees move a lot slower when there's a lot of them flying around inside the hive is because the inside hive picture is HUGE. And when you made the background for the BeeControl transparent, it needs to do double work: first it has to shrink the bee picture down, and then it needs to shrink a portion of the form's background down so that it can draw it in the transparent area behind the bee.

Bee animation 1.png

The bee picture is really big, and the PictureBox needs time to shrink it down every time it displays a new animation frame.

Hive (Inside).png

Honey Factory

Nursery

Exit

The graphics files for the bees are really BIG. When the PictureBox needs to scale the picture down to size every time it displays a new animation frame. That takes a lot of time...

The inside hive picture is huge. Every time a bee flies in front of it, its PictureBox needs to scale it down to the size of the control. It needs to do that to show part of the picture any place the bee picture's transparent background lets it show through.

...so all we need to do to speed up the simulator's performance is to shrink down all the pictures *before* we try to display them.

All we need to do to speed up the graphics performance is add a method to the renderer that scales any image to a different size. Then we can **resize each picture once when it's loaded**, and only use the scaled down version in the bee control and for the hive form's background.

1. Add the ResizeImage method to the renderer

All of the pictures in your project (like `Properties.Resources.Flower`) are stored as `Bitmap` objects. Here's a static method that resizes bitmaps—add it to the Renderer class:

```
public static Bitmap ResizeImage(Bitmap picture, int width, int height) {
    Bitmap resizedPicture = new Bitmap(width, height);
    using (Graphics graphics = Graphics.FromImage(resizedPicture)) {
        graphics.DrawImage(picture, 0, 0, width, height);
    }
    return resizedPicture;
}
```

> We'll take a closer look at what this Graphics object is and how this method works in the next few pages

2. Add this ResizeCells method to your BeeControl

Your BeeControl can store its own Bitmap objects—an array of four of them. Here's a control that'll populate that array, resizing each one so that it's exactly the right size for the control:

```
private Bitmap[] cells = new Bitmap[4];
private void ResizeCells() {
    cells[0] = Renderer.ResizeImage(Properties.Resources.Bee_animation_1, Width, Height);
    cells[1] = Renderer.ResizeImage(Properties.Resources.Bee_animation_2, Width, Height);
    cells[2] = Renderer.ResizeImage(Properties.Resources.Bee_animation_3, Width, Height);
    cells[3] = Renderer.ResizeImage(Properties.Resources.Bee_animation_4, Width, Height);
}
```

3. Change the switch statement so that it uses the cells array, not the resources

The BeeControl's Tick event handler has a switch statement that sets its BackgroundImage:

```
BackgroundImage = Properties.Resources.Bee_animation_1;
```

Replace `Properties.Resources.Bee_animation_1` with `cells[0]`. Now replace the rest of the **case** lines, so that case 2 one uses `cells[1]`, case 3 uses `cells[2]`, case 4 uses `cells[3]`, case 5 uses `cells[2]`, and the default case uses `cells[1]`. That way only the resized image is displayed.

4. Add calls to ResizeCells() to the BeeControl

You'll need to add two calls to the new ResizeCells() method. First, **add it** to the bottom of the constructor—and **change the BackgroundImageLayout property to None**. Then go back to the IDE designer by double-clicking on the BeeControl in the Properites window. Go over to the Events page in the Properties window (by clicking on the lightning bolt icon), scroll down to Resize, and double-click on it to **add a Resize event handler**. Make the new Resize event handler call ResizeCells() too—that way it'll resize its animation pictures every time the form is resized.

5. Set the form's background image manually

Go to the Properties window and set the hive form's background image to (none). Then go to its constructor and set the image to one that's sized properly.

```
public partial class HiveForm : Form {
    public HiveForm() {
        InitializeComponent();
        BackgroundImage = Renderer.ResizeImage(
            Properties.Resources.Hive__inside_,
            ClientRectangle.Width, ClientRectangle.Height);
    }
}
```

> Your form has a ClientRectangle property that contains a Rectangle which has the dimensions of its display area.

Now run the simulator—it's much faster!

You resized your Bitmaps using a <u>Graphics</u> object

Let's take a closer look at that `ResizeImage()` method you added to the renderer. The first thing it does is create a new `Bitmap` object that's the size that the picture will be resized to. Then it uses `Graphics.FromImage()` to **create a new Graphics object**. It uses that Graphics object's `DrawImage()` method to draw the picture onto the `Bitmap`. Notice how you passed the `width` and `height` parameters to `DrawImage()`—that's how you tell it to scale the image down to the new size. Finally you returned the new `Bitmap` you created, so it can be used as the form's background image or one of the four animation cells.

> Forms and controls have a CreateGraphics() method that returns a new Graphics object. You'll see a lot more about that shortly.

> You pass a picture into the method, along with a new width and height that it'll be resized to.

```
public static Bitmap ResizeImage(Bitmap picture, int width, int height) {

    Bitmap resizedPicture = new Bitmap(width, height);

    using (Graphics graphics = Graphics.FromImage(resizedPicture)) {

        graphics.DrawImage(picture, 0, 0, width, height);

    }

    return resizedPicture;

}
```

> The FromImage() method returns a new Graphics object that lets you draw graphics onto that image. Take a minute and use the IDE's IntelliSense to look at the methods in the Graphics class. When you call DrawImage(), it copies the image into the resizedPicture bitmap at the location (0, 0) and scaled to the width and height parameters.

Let's see image resizing in action

Drag a button onto the Field form and add this code. It creates a new PictureBox control that's 100 x100 pixels, setting its border to a black line so you can see how big it is. Then it uses `ResizeImage()` to make a bee picture that's squished down to 80 x 40 pixels and assigns that new picture to its `Image` property. Once the PictureBox is added to the form, the bee is displayed.

> Just do this temporarily. Delete the button and code when you're done.

```
private void button1_Click(object sender, EventArgs e)
{
    PictureBox beePicture = new PictureBox();
    beePicture.Location = new Point(10, 10);
    beePicture.Size = new Size(100, 100);
    beePicture.BorderStyle = BorderStyle.FixedSingle;
    beePicture.Image = ResizeImage(
        Properties.Resources.Bee_animation_1, 80, 40);
    Controls.Add(beePicture);
}
```

> You can see the image resizing in action—the squished bee image is much smaller than the PictureBox. ResizeImage() squished it down.

The ResizeImage() method creates a Graphics object to draw on an invisible Bitmap object. It returns that Bitmap so it can be displayed on a form or in PictureBox.

Your image resources are stored in Bitmap objects

When you import graphics files into your project's resources, what happens to them? You already know that you can access them using `Properties.Resources`. But what, exactly, is your program doing with them once they're imported?

.NET turns your image into a new **Bitmap** object:

The Bitmap class has several overloaded constructors. This one loads a graphics file from disk. You can also pass it integers for width and height—that'll create a new Bitmap with no picture.

Bee animation 1.png

`Bitmap bee = new Bitmap("Bee animation 1.png")`

Bitmap object

Then each Bitmap is drawn to the screen

Once your images are in `Bitmap` objects, your form draws them to the screen, with a call like this:

This call gets a Graphics object to draw on the form. We use a using statment to make sure the Graphics object is disposed.

```
using (Graphics g = CreateGraphics()) {
    g.DrawImage(myBitmap, 30, 30, 150, 150);
}
```

DrawImage() takes a Bitmap, the image to draw...

...a starting X, Y coordinate...

...and a size, 150x150 pixels.

The bigger they are...

Did you notice those last two parameters to `DrawImage()`? What if the image in the `Bitmap` is 175 by 175? The graphics library must then resize the image to fit 150 by 150. What if the `Bitmap` contains an image that's 1,500 by 2,025? Then the scaling becomes even trickier...

Resizing images takes a lot of processing power! If you do it once, it's no big deal. But if you do it <u>EVERY FRAME</u>, your program will slow down. We gave you REALLY BIG images for the bees and the hive. When the renderer moves the bees around (especially in front of the inside hive picture), it has to resize them over and over again. And that was causing the performance problems!

This image, which is 300x300 pixels...

← 150 →

150

...gets shrunk to this size, which is (for example) 150x150 pixels. And that slows your simulator down!

Use System.Drawing to **TAKE CONTROL** of graphics yourself

The Graphics object is part of the System.Drawing namespace. The .NET Framework comes with some pretty powerful graphics tools that go a lot further than the simple PictureBox control that's in the toolbox. You can draw shapes, use fonts, and do all sorts of complex graphics... and it all starts with a Graphics object. Any time you want to add or modify any object's graphics or images, you'll create a Graphics object that's **linked to the object you want to draw on**, and then use the Graphics object's methods to draw on your target.

> **System.Drawing**
>
> The graphics methods in the System.Drawing namespace are sometimes referred to as GDI+, which stands for Graphics Device Interface. When you draw graphics with GDI+, you start with a Graphics object that's hooked up to a Bitmap, form, control, or another object that you want to draw on using the Graphics object's methods.

1 **Start with the object you want to draw on**
For instance, think about a form. When you call the form's `CreateGraphics()` method, it returns an instance of `Graphics` that's set up to draw on itself.

`this.CreateGraphics()`

System.Windows.Forms.Form

Graphics object

Calls on this instance of Graphics affect the form that created the Graphics object.

The form can call its own CreateGraphics() method, or another object can call it. Either way, the method returns a reference to a Graphics object whose methods will draw on it.

You don't draw on the graphics object itself. You only use it to draw on other objects.

2 **Use the Graphics object's methods to draw on your object**
Every `Graphics` object has methods that let you draw on the object that created it. When you call methods in the `Graphics` object to draw lines, circles, rectangles, text, and images, they appear on the form.

Even though you're calling methods in this Graphics object, the actual graphics appear on the object that created it.

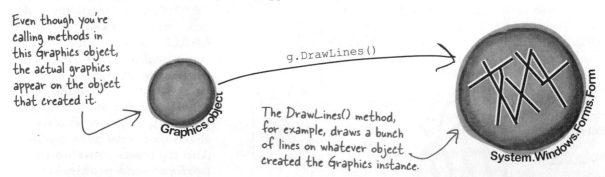

`g.DrawLines()`

Graphics object

System.Windows.Forms.Form

The DrawLines() method, for example, draws a bunch of lines on whatever object created the Graphics instance.

A 30-second tour of GDI+ graphics

There are all sorts of shapes and pictures that you can draw once you've created a `Graphics` object. All you need to do is call its methods, and it'll draw directly onto the object that created it.

1 The first step is always to grab yourself a Graphics object. Use a form's `CreateGraphics()` method, or have a `Graphics` object passed in. Remember, Graphics implements the `IDisposable()` interface, so if you create a new one use a `using` statement:

```
using (Graphics g = this.CreateGraphics()) {
```

Remember, this draws on the object that created this instance.

2 If you want to draw a line, call `DrawLine()` with starting point and ending point, each represented by X and Y coordinates:

The start coordinate...

```
g.DrawLine(Pens.Blue, 30, 10, 100, 45);
```

...and the end coordinate.

or you can do it using a couple of `Points`:

```
g.DrawLine(Pens.Blue, new Point(30, 45), new Point(100, 10));
```

3 Here's code that draws a filled slate gray rectangle, and then gives it a sky blue border. It uses a `Rectangle` to define the dimensions—in this case, the upper left hand corner is at (150, 15), and it's 140 pixels wide and 90 pixels high.

```
g.FillRectangle(Brushes.SlateGray, new Rectangle(150, 15, 140, 90));
g.DrawRectangle(Pens.SkyBlue, new Rectangle(150, 15, 140, 90));
```

There are a whole lot of colors you can use—just type "Color", "Pens" or "Brushes" followed by a dot and the IntelliSense window will display them.

4 You can draw an ellipse or a circle using the `DrawCircle()` or `FillCircle()` methods, which also use a `Rectangle` to specify how big the shape should be. This code draws two ellipses that are slightly offset to give a shadow effect:

```
g.FillEllipse(Brushes.DarkGray, new Rectangle(45, 65, 200, 100));
g.FillEllipse(Brushes.Silver, new Rectangle(40, 60, 200, 100));
```

5 Use the `DrawString()` method to draw text in any font and color. To do that, you'll need to create a `Font` object. It implements `IDisposable`, so use a `using` statement:

```
using (Font arial24Bold = new Font("Arial", 24, FontStyle.Bold)) {
    g.DrawString("Hi there!", arial24Bold, Brushes.Red, 50, 75);
}
```

If the above statements are executed in order, this is what will end up on the form. Each of the statements above matches up with the numbers here. The upper left-hand corner is coordinate (0, 0).

There's no step 1 on this picture, since that was creating the actual Graphics object.

Use graphics to draw a picture on a form

Let's create a new Windows application that draws a
picture on a form **when you click on it**.

Draw this

① Start by adding a Click event to the form
Go to the **Events page in the Properties window** (by clicking on the lightning-bolt icon),
scroll down to the Click event and double-click on it.

Start the event handler with a `using` line to create
the Graphics object. When you work with GDI+, you
use a lot of objects that implement `IDisposable`. If
you don't dispose of them, they'll slowly suck up your
computer's resources until you quit the program. So
you'll end up using a lot of `using` statements:

```
using (Graphics g = CreateGraphics()) {
```

Here's the first line in your Form1_Click()
event handler method. We'll give you all
the lines for the event handler—put them
together to draw the picture.

② Pay attention to the order you draw things on our form
We want a sky blue background for this picture, so you'll draw a big blue rectangle first—then
anything else you draw afterwards will be drawn **on top of it**. You'll take advantage of one of
the form's properties called `ClientRectangle`. It's a `Rectangle` that defines the boundaries
of the form's drawing area. `Rectangle`s are really useful—you can create a new rectangle
by specifying a `Point` for its upper left-hand corner, its width and its height. Once you do that,
it'll automatically calculate its `Top`, `Left`, `Right` and `Bottom` properties for you. And it's got
useful methods like `Contains()`, which will return true if a given point is inside it.

```
g.FillRectangle(Brushes.SkyBlue, ClientRectangle);
```

This will come in really
handy later on in the
book! What do you
think you'll be doing
with Contains()?

③ Draw the bee and the flower
You already know how the `DrawImage()` method works.

```
g.DrawImage(Properties.Resources.Bee_animation_1, 50, 20, 75, 75);
g.DrawImage(Properties.Resources.Flower, 10, 130, 100, 150);
```

Pens are for drawing lines, and they have a
width. If you want to draw a filled shape or
some text, you'll need a Brush.

④ Add a pen that you can draw with
Every time you draw a line, you use a Pen object to determine its color and thickness. There's a
built-in `Pens` class that gives you plenty of pens (`Pens.Red` is a thin red pen, for example). But
you can create your own pen using the `Pen` class constructor, which takes a `Brush` object and a
thickness (it's a float, so make sure it ends with F). Brushes are how you draw filled graphics (like
filled rectangles and ellipses), and there's a `Brushes` class that gives you brushes in various colors.

```
using (Pen thickBlackPen = new Pen(Brushes.Black, 3.0F)) {
```

This goes inside the inner using statement that created the Pen.

⑤ Add an arrow that points to the flower

There are some Graphics methods that take an array of Points, and connect them using a series of lines or curves. We'll use the DrawLines() method to draw the arrow head, and the DrawCurve() method to draw its shaft. There are other methods that take point arrays, too (like DrawPolygon(), which draws a closed shape, and FillPolygon(), which fills it in.)

```
g.DrawLines(thickBlackPen, new Point[] {
    new Point(130, 110), new Point(120, 160), new Point(155, 163)});
g.DrawCurve(thickBlackPen, new Point[] {
    new Point(120, 160), new Point(175, 120), new Point(215, 70) });
}
```

Here's where the using block ends—we don't need the thickBlackPen any more, so it'll get disposed.

When you pass an array of points to DrawCurve(), it draws a smooth curve that connects them all in order.

⑥ Add a font to draw the text

Whenever you work with drawing text, the first thing you need to do is create a Font object. Again, use a using statement because Font implements IDisposable. Creating a font is straightforward. There are several overloaded constructors—the simplest one takes a font name, font size, and FontStyle enum.

```
using (Font font = new Font("Arial", 16, FontStyle.Italic)) {
```

⑦ Add some text that says "Nectar here"

Now that you've got a font, you can figure out where to put the string by measuring how big it will be when it's drawn. The MeasureString() method returns a SizeF that defines its size. (SizeF is just the float version of Size—and both of them just define a width and height.) Since we know where the arrow ends, we'll use the string measurements to position its center just above the arrow.

```
SizeF size = g.MeasureString("Nectar here", font);
g.DrawString("Nectar here", font, Brushes.Red, new Point(
    215 - (int)size.Width / 2, 70 - (int)size.Height));
}
}
```

Make sure you close out both using blocks.

You can create a Rectangle by giving it a point and a Size (or width and height). Once you've got it, you can find its boundaries and check its Contains() method to see if it contains a Point.

what's it look like?

Sharpen your pencil

1. Most of your work with Graphics will involve thinking about your forms as a grid of X, Y coordinates. Here's the code to build the grid shown below; your job is to fill in the missing parts.

```
using (Graphics g = this.CreateGraphics())
using (Font f = new Font("Arial", 6, FontStyle.Regular)) {
  for (int x = 0; x < this.Width; x += 20) {

    ........................................................................

  } ........................................................................
  for (int y = 0; y < this.Height; y += 20) {

    ........................................................................

  } ........................................................................
}
```

2. Can you figure out what happens when you run the code below? Draw the output onto the form, using the grid you just rendered for locating specific points.

```
using (Pen pen =
        new Pen(Brushes.Black, 3.0F)) {
  g.DrawCurve(pen, new Point[] {
    new Point(80, 60),
    new Point(200,40),
    new Point(180, 60),
    new Point(300,40),
  });
  g.DrawCurve(pen, new Point[] {
    new Point(300,180), new Point(180, 200),
    new Point(200,180), new Point(80, 200),
  });
  g.DrawLine(pen, 300, 40, 300, 180);
  g.DrawLine(pen, 80, 60, 80, 200);
  g.DrawEllipse(pen, 40, 40, 20, 20);
  g.DrawRectangle(pen, 40, 60, 20, 300);
  g.DrawLine(pen, 60, 60, 80, 60);
  g.DrawLine(pen, 60, 200, 80, 200);
}
```

FillPolygon(), DrawLines(), and a few other graphics methods have a constructor that takes an array of Points that define the vertices of a series of connected lines.

3. Here's some more graphics code, dealing with irregular shapes. Figure out what's drawn using the grid we've given you below.

```
g.FillPolygon(Brushes.Black, new Point[] {
      new Point(60,40), new Point(140,80), new Point(200,40),
      new Point(300,80), new Point(380,60), new Point(340,140),
      new Point(320,180), new Point(380,240), new Point(320,300),
      new Point(340,340), new Point(240,320), new Point(180,340),
      new Point(20,320), new Point(60, 280), new Point(100, 240),
      new Point(40, 220), new Point(80,160),
   });

using (Font big = new Font("Times New Roman", 24, FontStyle.Italic)) {
      g.DrawString("Pow!", big, Brushes.White, new Point(80, 80));
      g.DrawString("Pow!", big, Brushes.White, new Point(120, 120));
      g.DrawString("Pow!", big, Brushes.White, new Point(160, 160));
      g.DrawString("Pow!", big, Brushes.White, new Point(200, 200));
      g.DrawString("Pow!", big, Brushes.White, new Point(240, 240));
}
```

looks good, except...

Sharpen your pencil
Solution

Your job was to fill in the missing code to draw a grid, and plot two chunks of code on the grids.

```
using (Graphics g = this.CreateGraphics())
using (Font f = new Font("Arial", 6, FontStyle.Regular)) {
    for (int x = 0; x < this.Width; x += 20) {
        g.DrawLine(Pens.Black, x, 0, x, this.Height);
        g.DrawString(x.ToString(), f, Brushes.Black, x, 0);
    }
    for (int y = 0; y < this.Height; y += 20) {
        g.DrawLine(Pens.Black, 0, y, this.Width, y);
        g.DrawString(y.ToString(), f, Brushes.Black, 0, y);
    }
}
```

First we draw the vertical lines and the numbers along the y axis. There's a vertical line every 20 pixels along the X axis.

We used using statements to make sure the Graphics and Font object get disposed after the form's drawn.

Next we draw the horizontal lines and X axis numbers. To draw a horizontal line, you choose a Y value and draw a line from (0, y) on the left of the form to (0, this.Width) on the right-hand side of the form.

Graphics can fix our transparency problem...

The renderer drew the bees so that they looked weird when they overlapped.

You've probably figured out by now that DrawImage() is the key to fixing the problem in the renderer where the images were drawing those boxes around the bees and flowers that caused the overlap issues. So let's tackle them! Go back to your Windows application with the picture.

Do this

1 Add a DrawBee() method that draws a bee on any Graphics object. It uses the overloaded DrawImage() constructor that takes a Rectangle to determine where to draw the image, and how big to draw it.

```
public void DrawBee(Graphics g, Rectangle rect) {
    g.DrawImage(Properties.Resources.Bee_animation_1, rect);
}
```

Much better—click on the form and the bees overlap just fine.

2 Here's the new **Click event handler for the form**. Take a close look at how it works—it draws the hive so that its upper left-hand corner is way off the form, at location (-Width, -Height), and it draws it at twice the width and height of the form—so you can resize the form and it'll still draw okay. Then it draws four bees using the DrawBee() method.

```
private void Form1_Click(object sender, EventArgs e) {
    using (Graphics g = CreateGraphics()) {
        g.DrawImage(Properties.Resources.Hive__inside_,
            -Width, -Height, Width * 2, Height * 2);
        Size size = new Size(Width / 5, Height / 5);
        DrawBee(g, new Rectangle(
            new Point(Width / 2 - 50, Height / 2 - 40), size));
        DrawBee(g, new Rectangle(
            new Point(Width / 2 - 20, Height / 2 - 60), size));
        DrawBee(g, new Rectangle(
            new Point(Width / 2 - 80, Height / 2 - 30), size));
        DrawBee(g, new Rectangle(
            new Point(Width / 2 - 90, Height / 2 - 80), size));
    }
}
```

First we'll draw the hive backround, with its corner far off the page so we only see a small piece of it. Then we'll draw four bees so that they overlap—if they don't, make your form bigger and then click on it again so they do.

...but there's a catch

But look what happens if you drag it off the side of the screen and back! Oh no!

3 Run your program and click on the form, and watch it draw the bees! But something's wrong. When you drag the form off the side of the screen and back again, **the picture disappears!** Now go back and check the "Nectar here" program you wrote a few pages ago—**it's got the same problem!**

What do you think happened?

Use the Paint event to make your graphics stick

Forms and controls have a Paint event that gives you a Graphics object. Anything you draw on it is repainted automatically.

What good are graphics if they disappear from your form as soon as part of your form gets covered up? They're no good at all. Luckily, there's an easy way to make sure your graphics stay on your form: just **write a Paint event handler**. Your form fires a Paint event every time it needs to redraw itself—like when it's dragged off the screen. One of the properties of its `PaintEventArgs` parameter is a Graphics object called `Graphics`, and anything that you draw with it will "stick".

1 **Add a Paint event handler**

Double-click on "Paint" in the Events page in the Properties window to add a Paint event handler. The Paint event is fired any time the image on your form gets "dirty". So drawing your graphics inside of it will make your image will stick around.

Double-click on Paint to add a Paint event handler. Its PaintEventArgs has a property called Graphics—and anything you draw with it will stick to your form. ⟶

2 **Use the Graphics object from the Paint event's EventArgs**

Instead of starting with a using statement, make your event handler start like this:

```
private void UserControl1_Paint(object sender, PaintEventArgs e) {
    Graphics g = e.Graphics;
```

You **don't** have to use a **using** statement—since you didn't create it, **you don't have to dispose it**.

3 **Copy the code that draws the overlapping bees and hive**

Add the new DrawBees() method from the previous page into your new user control. Then copy the code from the Click event into your new Paint event—**except for the first line with the using statement**, since you already have a Graphics object called g. (Since you don't have the using statement any more, make sure you take out its closing curly bracket.) Now run your program. **The graphics stick!**

Do the same with your "Nectar here" drawing to make it stick, too.

Forms and controls redraw themselves all the time

It may not look like it, but your forms have to redraw themselves all the time. Any time you have controls on a form, they're displaying graphics—labels display text, buttons display a picture of a button, checkboxes draw a little box with an X in it. You work with them as controls that you drag around, but each control actually draws its own image. Any time you drag a form off the screen or under another form and then drag it back or uncover it, the part of the form that was covered up is now <u>invalid</u>, which means that it no longer shows the image that it's supposed to. That's when .NET sends a message to the form telling it to redraw itself. The form fires off a Paint event any time it's "dirty" and needs to be redrawn. If you ever want your form or user control to redraw itself, you can tell .NET to make it "dirty" by calling its <u>Invalidate()</u> method.

Exercise

See if you can combine your knowledge of forms and user controls—and get a little more practice using `Bitmap` objects and and the `DrawImage()` method—by building a user control that uses TrackBars to zoom an image in and out.

 Add two TrackBar controls to a new user control

Create a new Windows Application project. **Add a User Control**—call it Zoomer—and set its `Size` property to (300, 300). Drag two TrackBar controls out of the toolbox and onto it. Drag `trackBar1` to the bottom of the control. Then drag `trackBar2` to the right-hand side of the control and set its `Orientation` property to `Horizontal`. Both should have the `Minimum` property set to 1, `Maximum` set to 175, `Value` set to 175, and `TickStyle` set to `None`. Set each TrackBar's background color to white. Finally, double-click on each trackbar to add a `Scroll` event handler. Make both event handlers call the control's `Invalidate()` method.

You user control has a Paint event, and it works just like the one you just used in the form. Just use its **PaintEventArgs** parameter e. It has a property called **Graphics**, and anything that you draw with that Graphics object will be painted onto any instance of the user control you drag out of the Toolbox.

Give the two trackbars white backgrounds because you'll be drawing a white rectangle behind everything, and you want them to blend in.

 Load a picture into a Bitmap object and draw it on the control

Add a private `Bitmap` field called `photo` to your Zoomer user control. When you create the instance of `Bitmap`, use its constructor to load your favorite image file—we used a picture of a fluffy dog. Then add a `Paint` event to the control. The event handler should create a graphics object to draw on the control, draw a white filled rectangle over the entire control, and then use `DrawImage()` to draw the contents of your `photo` field onto your control so its upper left-hand corner is at (10, 10), its width is `trackBar1.Value`, and its height is `trackBar2.Value`. Then drag your control onto the form—make sure to resize the form so the trackbars are at the edges.

When you move the trackbars, the picture will shrink and grow!

Whenever the user scrolls one of the TrackBars, they call the user control's Invalidate() method. That will cause the user control to fire its Paint event and resize the photo. Remember, since you didn't create the Graphics object—it was passed to you in **PaintEventArgs**—you don't need to dispose it. So you don't have to use a **using** statement with it. Just draw the image inside the Paint event handler.

Exercise Solution

Get a little more practice using `Bitmap` objects and and the `DrawImage()` method by building a form that uses them to load a picture from a file and zoom it in and out.

This particular Bitmap constructor loads its picture from a file. It's got other overloaded constructors, including one that lets you specify a width and height—that one creates an empty bitmap.

```
public partial class Zoomer : UserControl {

    Bitmap photo = new Bitmap(@"c:\Graphics\fluffy_dog.jpg");

    public Zoomer() {
        InitializeComponent();
    }

    private void Zoomer_Paint(object sender, PaintEventArgs e) {
        Graphics g = e.Graphics;
        g.FillRectangle(Brushes.White, 0, 0, Width, Height);
        g.DrawImage(photo, 10, 10, trackBar1.Value, trackBar2.Value);
    }
}
```

First we draw a big white rectangle so it fills up the whole control, then we draw the photo on top of it. The last two parameters determine the size of the image being drawn—trackBar1 sets the width, trackBar2 sets the height.

```
    private void trackBar1_Scroll(object sender, EventArgs e) {
        Invalidate();
    }
    private void trackBar2_Scroll(object sender, EventArgs e) {
        Invalidate();
    }
}
```

Every time the user slides one of the trackbar controls, it fires off a Scroll event. By making the event handlers call the control's Invalidate() method, we cause the form to repaint itself... and when it does, it draws a new copy of the image with a different size.

Zoom!

Each drag here is causing another image resize from DrawImage().

```
g.DrawImage(myBitmap, 30, 30, 150, 150);
```

← ??? →

↑
???
↓

A closer look at how forms and controls repaint themselves

Behind the Scenes

Remember earlier, we said that when you start working with Graphics objects, you're really taking control of graphics. It's like you tell .NET, "Hey, I know what I'm doing, I can handle the extra responsibility." In the case of drawing and redrawing, you may not want to redraw when a form is minimized and maximized... or you may want to redraw **more often**. Once you know what's going on behind the scenes with your form or control, you can take control of redrawing yourself:

1 **Every form has a Paint event that draws the graphics on the form**

Go to the event list for any form and find the event called **Paint**. Whenever the form has to repaint itself, this event is fired. Every form and control uses a `Paint` event internally to decide when to redraw itself. But what fires that event? It's called by a method called **OnPaint** that the form or user control inherits from the Control class. (That method follows the pattern you saw in Chapter 11, where methods that fire an event are named "On" followed by the event name.) Go to any form and override OnPaint:

Do this just like you did earlier with Dispose()

Override OnPaint on any form and add this line.

```
protected override void OnPaint(PaintEventArgs e) {
    Console.WriteLine("OnPaint {0} {1}", DateTime.Now, e.ClipRectangle);
    base.OnPaint(e);
}
```

Drag your form around—drag it halfway off the screen, minimize it, hide it behind other windows. Watch closely at the output that it writes. You'll see that your OnPaint method fires off a Paint event any time part of it is "dirty"—or **invalid**—and needs to be redrawn. And if you look closely at the ClipRectangle, you'll see that it's a rectangle that describes the part of the form that needs to be repainted. That gets passed to the Paint event's `PaintEventArgs` so it can improve performance by only redrawing the portion that's invalid.

2 **Invalidate() controls when to redraw, and WHAT to redraw**

.NET fires the Paint event when something on a form is interfered with, covered up, or moved offscreen, and then shown again. It calls `Invalidate()`, and passes the method a `Rectangle`. The `Rectangle` tells the `Invalidate()` method what part of the form needs to be redrawn... what part of the form is "dirty." Then .NET calls OnPaint to tell your form to fire a `Paint` event and repaint the dirty area.

Invalidate() essentially says, some part of the form might be "invalid," so redraw that part to make sure it's got the right things showing.

3 **The Update() method gives your Invalidate request top priority**

You may not realize it, but your form is getting messages all the time. The same system that tells it that it's been covered up and calls OnPaint has all sorts of other messages it needs to send. See for yourself: type `override` and scroll through all the methods that start with "On"—every one of them is a message your form responds to. The `Update()` method moves the Invalidate message to the top of the message list.

So when you call it yourself, you're telling .NET that your whole form or control is invalid, and the whole thing needs to be redrawn. You can pass it your own clip rectangle if you want—that'll get passed along to the Paint event's PaintEventArgs.

4 **The form's Refresh() method is Invalidate() plus Update()**

Forms and controls give you a shortcut. They have a Refresh() method that first calls Invalidate() to invalidate the whole client area, and then calls Update() to make sure that message moves to the top of the list.

Q: It still seems like just resizing the graphics in a program like Paint or PhotoShop would be better. Why can't I do that?

A: You can, if you're in control of the images you work with in your applications, and if they'll always stay the same size. But that's not often the case. Lots of times, you'll get images from another source, whether it's online or a co-worker in the design group. Or, you may be pulling an image from a read-only source, and you have to size it programmatically.

Q: But if I can resize it outside of .NET, that's better, right?

A: If you're sure you'll never need a larger size, it could be. But if your program might need to display the image in multiple sizes during the program, you'll have to resize at some point anyway. Plus, if your image ever needs to be displayed larger than the resize, you'll end up in real trouble. It's much easier to size down than it is to size up.

More often than not, it's better to be able to resize an image programmatically, than to be limited by an external program or constraints like read-only files.

Q: I get that CreateGraphics() gets the Graphics object for drawing on a form, but what was that FromImage() call in the ResizeImage() method about?

A: `FromImage()` retrieves the `Graphics` object for a `Bitmap` object. And just as `CreateGraphics()` called on a form returns the `Graphics` object for drawing on that form, `FromImage()` retrieves a `Graphics` object for drawing on the `Bitmap` the method was called on.

Q: So a Graphics object isn't just for drawing on a form?

A: Actually, a Graphics object is for drawing on, well, anything that gives you a Graphics object. The Bitmap gives you a Graphics object that you can use to draw onto an invisible image that you can use later. And you'll find Graphics objects on a lot more than forms. Drag a button onto a form, then go into your code and type its name followed by a period. Check out the IntelliSense window that popped up—it's got CreateGraphics() method that returns a Graphics object. Anything you draw on it will show up on the button! Same goes for Label, PictureBox, StatusStrip... almost every toolbox control has a Graphics object.

Q: Wait, I thought `using` was just something I used with streams. Why am I using `using` with graphics?

A: The `using` keyword comes in handy with streams, but it's something that you use with *any* class that implements the `IDisposable` interface. When a class implements `IDisposable`, any time you instantiate it you should call its `Dispose()` method. With streams, the `Dispose()` method makes sure that any file that was opened gets closed.

`Graphics`, `Pen`, and `Brush` objects are also disposable. When you create any of them, they take up some small amount of memory and other resources, and they don't always give them back immediately. If you're just drawing something once, you won't notice a difference. But most of the time, your graphics code will be called over and over and over again—like in a `Paint` event handler, which could get called many times a second for a particularly busy form. That's why you should always

`Dispose()` of your graphics-related objects. And the easiest way to make sure that you do is to use a `using` line, and let .NET worry about disposal. Any object you create with `using` will automatically have its `Dispose()` method called at the end of the block following the `using` statement. That will guarantee that your program won't slowly take up more and more memory if it runs for a long time.

Q: If I'm creating a new control, should I use a UserControl or should I create a class that inherits from one of the toolbox controls?

A: That depends on what you want your new control to do. If you're building a control that's really similar to one that's already in the toolbox, then you'll probably find it easiest to inherit from that control. But most of the time, when programmers create new controls in C#, they use user controls. One useful advantage of a user control is that you can **drag toolbox controls onto it**. It works a lot like a `GroupBox` or other container control—you can drag a button or checkbox onto your user control, and work with them just like you'd work with controls on a form. The IDE's form designer becomes a powerful tool to help you design user controls. You'll see more about that in just a minute.

> *A user control can host other controls. The IDE's form designer lets you drag controls out of the toolbox and onto your new user control.*

I noticed a whole lot of flickering in my Zoomer control. With all this talk of taking control of graphics, I'll bet there's something we can do about that! But why does it happen?

Even without resizing, it takes time to draw an image to a form.

Suppose you've got every image in the simulator resized. It still takes time to draw all those bees and flowers and the hive. And right now, we're drawing right to the Graphics object on the form. So if your eye catches the tail end of a render, you're going to perceive it as a little flicker.

The problem is that a lot of drawing is happening, so there's a good chance that some flickering will occur, even with our resizing. And that's why you run into problems with most amateur computer games... the human eye catches the end of a rendering cycle, and perceives it as a little bit of flickering on the screen.

How could you get rid of this flicker? If drawing lots of images to the form causes flickering, and you have to draw lots of images, how do you think you might be able to avoid all the flickering?

Double buffering makes animation look a lot smoother

Go back to your image zoomer and fiddle with the trackbars. Notice how there's a whole lot of flickering when you move the bars? That's because the Paint event handler first has to draw the white rectangle and then draw the image every time the trackbar moves a tiny little bit. When your eyes see alternating white rectangles and images many times a second, they interpret that as flicker. It's irritating... and it's avoidable using a technique called **double buffering**. That means drawing each frame or cell of animation to an invisible bitmap (a "buffer"), and only displaying the new frame once it's been drawn entirely. Here's how it would work with a Bitmap:

1 Here's a typical program that draws some graphics on a form using its Graphics object.

```
using (graphics g =
    Form.CreateGraphics()) {
        DrawOneFrame(g); }
```

Renderer object

System.Windows.Forms.Form

The users saw a lot of flickering because each frame was drawn in pieces.

2 To do double buffering, we can add a Bitmap object to the program to act as a buffer. Every time our form or control needs to be repainted, instead of drawing the graphics directly on the form, we draw on the buffer instead.

```
using (graphics g =
    Graphics.FromImage(bitmap)) {
        DrawOneFrame(g); }
```

Renderer object

Graphics object

By drawing each frame to an invisible bitmap, the users won't see the flicker any more. They'll only see the finished frame when we copy it from the bitmap back to the form.

3 Now that the frame is completely drawn out to the invisible Bitmap object, we can use DrawImageUnscaled() to copy the object back to the form's Graphics. It all gets copied at once, and that eliminates the flicker.

```
using (graphics g =
    Form.CreateGraphics()) {
        g.DrawImageUnscaled(bitmap, 0, 0); }
```

Renderer object

Graphics object

System.Windows.Forms.Form

Double buffering is <u>built into</u> forms and controls

You can do double buffering yourself using a `Bitmap`, but C# and .NET make it even easier with built-in support for double buffering. **All you need to do is set its DoubleBuffered property to true.** Try it out on your Zoomer user control—go to its Properties window, set DoubleBuffered to true, and your control will stop flickering! Now **go back to your BeeControl** and do the same. That won't fix all of the graphics problems—we'll do that in a minute—but it *will* make a difference.

Now you're ready to fix the graphics problems in the simulator!

Overhaul the Beehive Simulator

In the next exercise, you'll take your Beehive Simulator and completely overhaul it. You'll probably want to create a whole new project and use "Add >> Existing Item..." to add the current files to it so you have a backup of your current simulator. (Don't forget to change their namespace to match your new project.)

Here's what you're going to do:

1 You'll start by removing the BeeControl user control
There won't be any controls on the hive and field at all. No BeeControls, no PictureBoxes, nothing. The bees, flowers, and hive pictures will all be drawn using GDI+ graphics. So right-click on BeeControl.cs (and OldBeeControl.cs) in the Solution Explorer and click Delete—they'll be removed from the project and permanently deleted.

2 You'll need a timer to handle the bee wing flapping
The bees flap their wings much more slowly than the simulator's frame rate, so you'll need a second, slower timer. This shouldn't be too surprising, since the BeeControl had its own timer to do the same thing.

3 The big step: overhaul the renderer
You'll need to throw out the current renderer entirely, because it does everything with controls. You won't need those lookup dictionaries, because there won't be any PictureBoxes or BeeControls to look up. Instead, it'll have two important methods: DrawHive(g) will draw a Hive form on a graphics object, and DrawField(g) will draw a Field form.

4 Last of all, you'll hook up the new renderer
The Hive and Field forms will need Paint event handlers. Each of them will call the Renderer object's DrawField(g) or DrawHive(g) methods. The two timers—one for telling the simulator to draw the next frame, and the other to flap the bees' wings—will call the two forms' Invalidate() methods to repaint themselves. When they do, their Paint event handlers will render the frame.

When you use the Paint event for all your graphics, you can turn on double buffered painting simply by changing one property.

Let's get started! ⟶

Exercise

It's time to get rid of the graphics glitches in the beehive simulator. Use graphics and double buffering to make the simulator look polished.

1 **Change the main form's RunFrame() method**

You'll need to remove the call to Renderer.Render() and add two Invalidate() statements.

```
public void RunFrame(object sender, EventArgs e) {
    framesRun++;
    world.Go(random);
    end = DateTime.Now;
    TimeSpan frameDuration = end - start;
    start = end;
    UpdateStats(frameDuration);
    hiveForm.Invalidate();
    fieldForm.Invalidate();
}
```

You'll need to remove the call to renderer.Render(), since that method will go away.

As long as you keep the world up to date and both forms have a reference to the renderer object, all you need to do to animate them is call their Invalidate() methods. Their Paint event handlers will take care of the rest.

2 **Add a second timer to the main form to make the bees' wings flap**

Drag a new timer onto the main form, set its Interval to 150ms and Enabled to true. Then double-click on it and add this event handler:

```
private void timer2_Tick(object sender, EventArgs e) {
    renderer.AnimateBees();
}
```

Then add this AnimateBees() method to the renderer to make the bees' wings flap:

```
private int Cell = 0;
private int Frame = 0;
private void AnimateBees() {
    Frame++;
    if (Frame >= 6)
    Frame = 0;
    switch (Frame) {
        case 0: Cell = 0; break;
        case 1: Cell = 1; break;
        case 2: Cell = 2; break;
        case 3: Cell = 3; break;
        case 4: Cell = 2; break;
        case 5: Cell = 1; break;
        default: Cell = 0; break;
    }
    hiveForm.Invalidate();
    fieldForm.Invalidate();
}
```

The whole idea here is to set a field called Cell that you can use when you're drawing the bees in the renderer. Make sure you're always drawing BeeAnimationLarge[Cell] in the hive form and BeeAnimationSmall[Cell] in the field form. The timer will constantly call the AnimateBees() method, which will cause the Cell field to keep changing, which will cause your bees to flap their wings.

③ **Set up the hive and field forms for double-buffered animation**

Remove the code from the hive form's constructor that sets the background image. Then remove all controls from both forms and **set their DoubleBuffered properties to true**. Finally, add a Paint event handler to each of them. Here's the handler for the hive form—the field form's Paint event handler is identical, except that it calls renderer.PaintField() instead of renderer.PaintHive():

```
private void HiveForm_Paint(object sender, PaintEventArgs e) {
    renderer.PaintHive(e.Graphics);
}
```

Make sure you turn on double buffering, or your forms will flicker!

④ **The hive form and field form both need a public renderer property**

Add a public field to the hive form and the field form:

```
public Renderer renderer;
```

There are two places where you create a new Renderer(): in the open button (underneath a call to renderer.Reset() and in the ResetSimulator() method. Remove all calls to renderer.Reset(), and replace each of the new renderer statements with a call to this new CreateRenderer() method that you'll add:

```
private void CreateRenderer() {
    renderer = new Renderer(world, hiveForm, fieldForm);
    hiveForm.renderer = renderer;
    fieldForm.renderer = renderer;
}
```

You won't need a Reset() method in the renderer any more. All it did was remove the controls from the forms, and there won't be any controls to remove.

⑤ **Overhaul the renderer by removing control-based code and adding graphics**

Here's what you need to do to fix the renderer:

★ Remove the two dictionaries, since there aren't any more controls. And while you're at it, you don't need the BeeControl any more, or the Render(), DrawBees(), or DrawFlowers() methods..

★ Add some Bitmap fields called HiveInside, HiveOutside, and Flower to store the images. Then create two Bitmap[] arrays called BeeAnimationLarge and BeeAnimationSmall. Each of them will hold four bee pictures—the large ones are 40x40 and the small are 20x20. Create a method called InitializeImages() to resize the resources and store them in these fields, and call it from the Renderer class constructor.

★ Add the PaintHive() method that takes a Graphics object as a parameter and paints the hive form onto it. First draw a sky blue rectangle, then use DrawImageUnscaled() to draw the inside hive picture, then use DrawImageUnscaled() to draw each of the bees that are inside the hive.

★ Finally, add the PaintField() method. It should draw a sky blue rectangle on the top half of the form, and a green rectangle on the bottom half. You'll find two form properties helpful for this: ClientSize and ClientRectangle tell you how big the drawing area is, so you can find half of its height using ClientSize.Height / 2. Then use FillEllipse() to draw a yellow sun in the sky, DrawLine() to draw a thick line for a branch the hive can hang from, and DrawImageUnscaled() to draw the outside hive picture. Then draw each flower onto the form. Finally, draw each bee (using the small bee pictures)—draw them last so they're in front of the flowers.

★ When you're drawing the bees, remember that AnimateBees() sets the Cell field.

Exercise Solution

It's time to get rid of the graphics glitches in the beehive simulator. Use graphics and double buffering to make the simulator look polished.

Here's the complete Renderer class, including the AnimateBees() method that we gave you. Make sure you make all the modifications to the three forms—especially the Paint event handlers in the hive and field forms. Those event handlers call the renderer's PaintHive() and PaintField() methods, which do all of the animation.

```csharp
using System.Drawing;

public class Renderer {
    private World world;
    private HiveForm hiveForm;
    private FieldForm fieldForm;

    public Renderer(World TheWorld, HiveForm hiveForm, FieldForm fieldForm) {
        this.world = TheWorld;
        this.hiveForm = hiveForm;
        this.fieldForm = fieldForm;
        InitializeImages();
    }

    public static Bitmap ResizeImage(Image ImageToResize, int Width, int Height) {
        Bitmap bitmap = new Bitmap(Width, Height);
        using (Graphics graphics = Graphics.FromImage(bitmap)) {
            graphics.DrawImage(ImageToResize, 0, 0, Width, Height);
        }
        return bitmap;
    }

    Bitmap HiveInside;
    Bitmap HiveOutside;
    Bitmap Flower;
    Bitmap[] BeeAnimationSmall;
    Bitmap[] BeeAnimationLarge;
    private void InitializeImages() {
        HiveOutside = ResizeImage(Properties.Resources.Hive__outside_, 85, 100);
        Flower = ResizeImage(Properties.Resources.Flower, 75, 75);
        HiveInside = ResizeImage(Properties.Resources.Hive__inside_,
            hiveForm.ClientRectangle.Width, hiveForm.ClientRectangle.Height);
        BeeAnimationLarge = new Bitmap[4];
        BeeAnimationLarge[0] = ResizeImage(Properties.Resources.Bee_animation_1, 40, 40);
        BeeAnimationLarge[1] = ResizeImage(Properties.Resources.Bee_animation_2, 40, 40);
        BeeAnimationLarge[2] = ResizeImage(Properties.Resources.Bee_animation_3, 40, 40);
        BeeAnimationLarge[3] = ResizeImage(Properties.Resources.Bee_animation_4, 40, 40);
        BeeAnimationSmall = new Bitmap[4];
        BeeAnimationSmall[0] = ResizeImage(Properties.Resources.Bee_animation_1, 20, 20);
        BeeAnimationSmall[1] = ResizeImage(Properties.Resources.Bee_animation_2, 20, 20);
        BeeAnimationSmall[2] = ResizeImage(Properties.Resources.Bee_animation_3, 20, 20);
        BeeAnimationSmall[3] = ResizeImage(Properties.Resources.Bee_animation_4, 20, 20);
    }
}
```

The InitializeImages() method resizes all of the image resources and stores them in Bitmap fields inside the Renderer object. That way the PaintHive() and PaintForm() methods can draw the images unscaled using the forms' Graphics objects' DrawImageUnscaled() methods.

```
public void PaintHive(Graphics g) {
    g.FillRectangle(Brushes.SkyBlue, hiveForm.ClientRectangle);
    g.DrawImageUnscaled(HiveInside, 0, 0);
    foreach (Bee bee in world.Bees) {
        if (bee.InsideHive)
            g.DrawImageUnscaled(BeeAnimationLarge[Cell],
                                bee.Location.X, bee.Location.Y);
    }
}
```

A form's ClientSize property is a Rectangle that tells you how big its drawing area is.

```
public void PaintField(Graphics g) {
    using (Pen brownPen = new Pen(Color.Brown, 6.0F)) {
        g.FillRectangle(Brushes.SkyBlue, 0, 0,
                fieldForm.ClientSize.Width, fieldForm.ClientSize.Height / 2);
        g.FillEllipse(Brushes.Yellow, new RectangleF(50, 15, 70, 70));
        g.FillRectangle(Brushes.Green, 0, fieldForm.ClientSize.Height / 2,
                fieldForm.ClientSize.Width, fieldForm.ClientSize.Height / 2);
        g.DrawLine(brownPen, new Point(643, 0), new Point(643, 30));
        g.DrawImageUnscaled(HiveOutside, 600, 20);
        foreach (Flower flower in world.Flowers) {
            g.DrawImageUnscaled(Flower, flower.Location.X, flower.Location.Y);
        }
        foreach (Bee bee in world.Bees) {
            if (!bee.InsideHive)
                g.DrawImageUnscaled(BeeAnimationSmall[Cell],
                                    bee.Location.X, bee.Location.Y);
        }
    }
}

private int Cell = 0;
private int Frame = 0;
public void AnimateBees()
{
    Frame++;
    if (Frame >= 6)
        Frame = 0;
    switch (Frame) {
        case 0: Cell = 0; break;
        case 1: Cell = 1; break;
        case 2: Cell = 2; break;
        case 3: Cell = 3; break;
        case 4: Cell = 2; break;
        case 5: Cell = 1; break;
        default: Cell = 0; break;
    }
    hiveForm.Invalidate();
    fieldForm.Invalidate();
}
```

The PaintField() method looks at the bees and flowers in the world and draws a field using their locations. First it draws the sky and the ground, then it draws the sun, and then the beehive. After that, it draws the flowers and the bees. It's important that everything is drawn in the right order—if it were to draw the flowers before the bees, then the bees would look like they were flying behind the flowers.

Here's the same AnimateBees() method from the exercise. It cycles through the animations using the Frame field—first it shows cell 0, then cell 1, then 2, then 3, and then back to 2, then 1 again. That way the bee flapping animation is smooth.

Use a Graphics object and an event handler for printing

The Graphics methods you've been using to draw on your forms are **the same ones you use to print**. .NET's printing objects in System.Drawing.Printing make it really easy to add printing and print preview to your applications. All you need to do is **create a PrintDocument object**. It's got an event called PrintPage, which you can use exactly like you use a timer's Tick event. Then call the PrintDocument object's Print() method and it prints the document. And remember, the IDE makes it especially easy to add the event handler. Here's how:

Print this

1 **Start a new Windows application** and add a button to the form. Go to the form code and add a **using System.Drawing.Printing;** line to the top. Double-click on the button and add the event handler. Watch what happens as soon as you type **+=**:

```
private void button1_Click(object sender, EventArgs e) {
    PrintDocument document = new PrintDocument();
    document.PrintPage +=
```
new PrintPageEventHandler(document_PrintPage);   (Press TAB to insert)

2 Press Tab and the IDE automatically fills in the rest of the line. This is just like how you added event handlers in Chapter 11:

```
private void button1_Click(object sender, EventArgs e) {
    PrintDocument document = new PrintDocument();
    document.PrintPage += new PrintPageEventHandler(document_PrintPage);
```
Press TAB to generate handler 'document_PrintPage' in this class

3 As soon as you press Tab, the IDE generates an event handler method and adds it to the form.

```
void document_PrintPage(object sender, PrintPageEventArgs e) {
    throw new NotImplementedException();
}
```
Now you can put ANY graphics code here—just replace the throw line and use e.Graphics for all of the drawing. We'll show you how in a minute...

The PrintPageEventArgs parameter e has a Graphics property. Just replace the throw statement with code that calls the e.Graphics object's drawing methods.

4 Now finish off the button1_Click event handler by calling **document.Print()**. When that method is called, the PrintDocument object creates a Graphics object and then fires off a PrintPage event with the Graphics object as a parameter. Anything that the event handler draws onto the Graphics object will get sent to the printer.

```
private void button1_Click(object sender, EventArgs e) {
    PrintDocument document = new PrintDocument();
    document.PrintPage += new PrintPageEventHandler(document_PrintPage);
    document.Print();
}
```

PrintDocument works with the print dialog and print preview window objects

Adding a print preview window or a print dialog box is a lot like adding an open or save dialog box. All you need to do is create a `PrintDialog` or `PrintPreviewDialog` object, set its `Document` property to your `Document` object, and then call the dialog's `Show()` method. The dialog will take care of sending the document to the printer—no need to call its `Print()` method. So let's add this to the button you created in step 1:

Once you've got a PrintDocument and an event handler to print the page, you can pop up a print preview window just by creating a new PrintPreviewDialog object.

```
private void button1_Click(object sender, EventArgs e) {
    PrintDocument document = new PrintDocument();
    document.PrintPage += new PrintPageEventHandler(document_PrintPage);
    PrintPreviewDialog preview = new PrintPreviewDialog();
    preview.Document = document;
    preview.ShowDialog(this);
}

void document_PrintPage(object sender,
                        PrintPageEventArgs e) {
    DrawBee(e.Graphics, new Rectangle(0, 0, 300, 300));
}
```

Use e.HasMorePages to print multi-page documents

If you need to print more than one page, all you need to do is have your `PrintPage` event handler set `e.HasMorePages` to true. That tells the `Document` that you've got another page to print. It'll call the event handler over and over again, once per page, as long as the event handler keeps setting `e.HasMorePages` to true. So modify your Document's event handler to print two pages:

```
bool firstPage = true;
void document_PrintPage(object sender, PrintPageEventArgs e) {
    DrawBee(e.Graphics, new Rectangle(0, 0, 300, 300));
    using (Font font = new Font("Arial", 36, FontStyle.Bold)) {
        if (firstPage) {
            e.Graphics.DrawString("First page", Font, Brushes.Black, 0, 0);
            e.HasMorePages = true;
            firstPage = false;
        } else {
            e.Graphics.DrawString("Second page", Font, Brushes.Black, 0, 0);
            firstPage = true;
        }
    }
}
```

If you set e.HasMorePages to true, the Document object will call the event handler again to print the next page.

Now run your program again, and make sure it's displaying two pages in the print preview.

Write the code for the Print button in the simulator so that it pops up a print preview window showing the bee stats and pictures of the hive and the field.

Exercise

① Make the button pop up a print preview window

Add an event handler for the button's click event that pauses the simulator, pops up the print preview dialog, and then resumes the simulator when it's done. (If the simulator is paused when the button is clicked, make sure it stays paused after the preview is shown.)

② Create the document's PrintPage event handler

It should create a page that looks exactly like the one on the facing page. We'll start you off:

```
private void document_PrintPage(object sender, PrintPageEventArgs e) {
    Graphics g = e.Graphics;
    Size stringSize;
    using (Font arial24bold = new Font("Arial", 24, FontStyle.Bold)) {
        stringSize = Size.Ceiling(
            g.MeasureString("Bee Simulator", arial24bold));
        g.FillEllipse(Brushes.Gray,
            new Rectangle(e.MarginBounds.X + 2, e.MarginBounds.Y + 2,
            stringSize.Width + 30, stringSize.Height + 30));
        g.FillEllipse(Brushes.Black,
            new Rectangle(e.MarginBounds.X, e.MarginBounds.Y,
            stringSize.Width + 30, stringSize.Height + 30));
        g.DrawString("Bee Simulator", arial24bold,
            Brushes.Gray, e.MarginBounds.X + 17, e.MarginBounds.Y + 17);
        g.DrawString("Bee Simulator", arial24bold,
            Brushes.White, e.MarginBounds.X + 15, e.MarginBounds.Y + 15);
    }
    int tableX = e.MarginBounds.X + (int)stringSize.Width + 50;
    int tableWidth = e.MarginBounds.X + e.MarginBounds.Width - tableX - 20;
    int firstColumnX = tableX + 2;
    int secondColumnX = tableX + (tableWidth / 2) + 5;
    int tableY = e.MarginBounds.Y;
    // Your job: fill in the rest of the method to make it print this
```

We created the oval with text in it using the MeasureString() method, which returns a Size that contains the size of a string. We drew the oval and text twice to give it a shadow effect.

You'll need these to build the table.

③ This PrintTableRow() method will come in handy

You'll find this method useful when you create the table of bee stats at the top of the page.

```
private int PrintTableRow(Graphics printGraphics, int tableX,
                int tableWidth, int firstColumnX, int secondColumnX,
                int tableY, string firstColumn, string secondColumn) {
    Font arial12 = new Font("Arial", 12);
    Size stringSize = Size.Ceiling(printGraphics.MeasureString(firstColumn, arial12))
    tableY += 2;
    printGraphics.DrawString(firstColumn, arial12, Brushes.Black,
                firstColumnX, tableY);
    printGraphics.DrawString(secondColumn, arial12, Brushes.Black,
                secondColumnX, tableY);
    tableY += (int)stringSize.Height + 2;
    printGraphics.DrawLine(Pens.Black, tableX, tableY, tableX + tableWidth, tableY);
    arial12.Dispose();
    return tableY;
}
```

Each time you call PrintTableRow(), it adds the height of the row it printed to tableY and returns the new value.

Take a close look at the notes we wrote on the printout. This is a little complex—take your time!

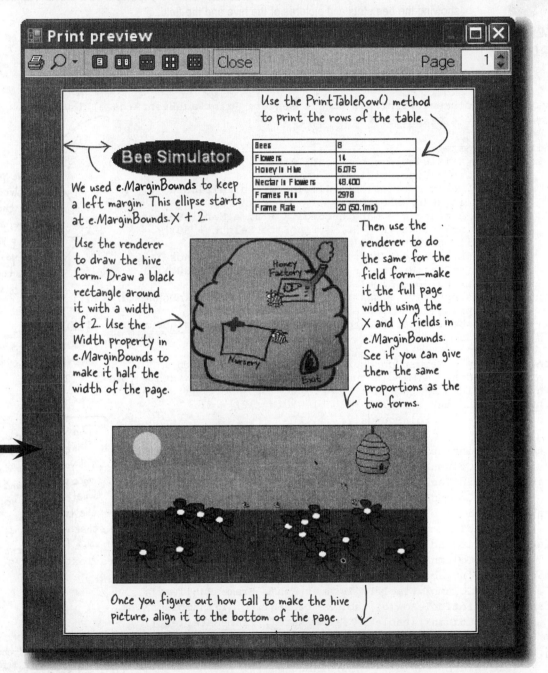

Print preview

Close   Page 1

Use the PrintTableRow() method to print the rows of the table.

Bee Simulator

Bees	8
Flowers	14
Honey In Hive	6.075
Nectar In Flowers	48.400
Frames Run	2978
Frame Rate	20 (50.1ms)

We used e.MarginBounds to keep a left margin. This ellipse starts at e.MarginBounds.X + 2.

Use the renderer to draw the hive form. Draw a black rectangle around it with a width of 2. Use the Width property in e.MarginBounds to make it half the width of the page.

Honey Factory

Nursery

Exit

Then use the renderer to do the same for the field form—make it the full page width using the X and Y fields in e.MarginBounds. See if you can give them the same proportions as the two forms.

Once you figure out how tall to make the hive picture, align it to the bottom of the page.

Here's a hint: To find the height of each form, find the ratio of its height divided by its width and multiply that by the final width. You can locate the top of the field form by subtracting its height from the bottom margin of the page: (e.MarginBounds.Y + e.MarginBounds.Height – fieldHeight).

Write the code for the Print button in the simulator so that it pops up a print preview window showing the bee stats and pictures of the hive and the field.

Exercise Solution

Here's the event handler for the Document's PrintPage event. It goes in the form.

```
using System.Drawing.Printing;

private void document_PrintPage(object sender, PrintPageEventArgs e) {
    Graphics g = e.Graphics;

    Size stringSize;
    using (Font arial24bold = new Font("Arial", 24, FontStyle.Bold)) {
        stringSize = Size.Ceiling(
                g.MeasureString("Bee Simulator", arial24bold));
        g.FillEllipse(Brushes.Gray,
            new Rectangle(e.MarginBounds.X + 2, e.MarginBounds.Y + 2,
            stringSize.Width + 30, stringSize.Height + 30));
        g.FillEllipse(Brushes.Black,
            new Rectangle(e.MarginBounds.X, e.MarginBounds.Y,
            stringSize.Width + 30, stringSize.Height + 30));
        g.DrawString("Bee Simulator", arial24bold,
            Brushes.Gray, e.MarginBounds.X + 17, e.MarginBounds.Y + 17);
        g.DrawString("Bee Simulator", arial24bold,
            Brushes.White, e.MarginBounds.X + 15, e.MarginBounds.Y + 15);
    }

    int tableX = e.MarginBounds.X + (int)stringSize.Width + 50;
    int tableWidth = e.MarginBounds.X + e.MarginBounds.Width - tableX - 20;
    int firstColumnX = tableX + 2;
    int secondColumnX = tableX + (tableWidth / 2) + 5;
    int tableY = e.MarginBounds.Y;

    tableY = PrintTableRow(g, tableX, tableWidth, firstColumnX,
        secondColumnX, tableY, "Bees", Bees.Text);
    tableY = PrintTableRow(g, tableX, tableWidth, firstColumnX,
        secondColumnX, tableY, "Flowers", Flowers.Text);
    tableY = PrintTableRow(g, tableX, tableWidth, firstColumnX,
        secondColumnX, tableY, "Honey in Hive", HoneyInHive.Text);
    tableY = PrintTableRow(g, tableX, tableWidth, firstColumnX,
        secondColumnX, tableY, "Nectar in Flowers", NectarInFlowers.Text);
    tableY = PrintTableRow(g, tableX, tableWidth, firstColumnX,
        secondColumnX, tableY, "Frames Run", FramesRun.Text);
    tableY = PrintTableRow(g, tableX, tableWidth, firstColumnX,
        secondColumnX, tableY, "Frame Rate", FrameRate.Text);

    g.DrawRectangle(Pens.Black, tableX, e.MarginBounds.Y,
        tableWidth, tableY - e.MarginBounds.Y);
    g.DrawLine(Pens.Black, secondColumnX, e.MarginBounds.Y,
        secondColumnX, tableY);
```

We gave you this part already. It draws the oval header, and sets up variables that you'll use to draw the table of bee stats.

Did you figure out how the PrintTableRow() method works? All you need to do is call it once per row, and it prints whatever text you want in the two columns. The trick is that it returns the new tableY value for the next row.

Don't forget to draw the rectangle around the table and the line between the columns.

Since the pen and the two bitmaps need to be disposed, we put them all in one big using block.

```
using (Pen blackPen = new Pen(Brushes.Black, 2))
using (Bitmap hiveBitmap = new Bitmap(hiveForm.ClientSize.Width,
                             hiveForm.ClientSize.Height))
using (Bitmap fieldBitmap = new Bitmap(fieldForm.ClientSize.Width,
                             fieldForm.ClientSize.Height))
```

You'll need a black pen that's 2 pixels wide to draw the lines around the screenshots.

The bitmaps need to be the same size as the form's drawing area, so ClientSize. comes in handy.

```
using (Graphics hiveGraphics = Graphics.FromImage(hiveBitmap))
{
    renderer.PaintHive(hiveGraphics);
}
```

The PaintHive() method needs a Graphics object to draw on, so this code creates an empty Bitmap object and passes it to PaintHive().

```
int hiveWidth = e.MarginBounds.Width / 2;
float ratio = (float)hiveBitmap.Height / (float)hiveBitmap.Width;
int hiveHeight = (int)(hiveWidth * ratio);
int hiveX = e.MarginBounds.X + (e.MarginBounds.Width - hiveWidth) / 2;
int hiveY = e.MarginBounds.Height / 3;
g.DrawImage(hiveBitmap, hiveX, hiveY, hiveWidth, hiveHeight);
g.DrawRectangle(blackPen, hiveX, hiveY, hiveWidth, hiveHeight);

using (Graphics fieldGraphics = Graphics.FromImage(fieldBitmap))
{
    renderer.PaintField(fieldGraphics);
}
int fieldWidth = e.MarginBounds.Width;
ratio = (float)fieldBitmap.Height / (float)fieldBitmap.Width;
int fieldHeight = (int)(fieldWidth * ratio);
int fieldX = e.MarginBounds.X;
int fieldY = e.MarginBounds.Y + e.MarginBounds.Height - fieldHeight;
g.DrawImage(fieldBitmap, fieldX, fieldY, fieldWidth, fieldHeight);
g.DrawRectangle(blackPen, fieldX, fieldY, fieldWidth, fieldHeight);
    }
}
```

e.MarginBounds.Width has the width of the printable area of the page. That's how wide the field screenshot should be drawn.

Here's where the height of the screenshot is calculated using the form's height–width ratio.

```
private void printToolStripButton_Click(object sender, EventArgs e) {
    bool stoppedTimer = false;
    if (timer1.Enabled) {
        timer1.Stop();
        stoppedTimer = true;
    }
    PrintPreviewDialog preview = new PrintPreviewDialog();
    PrintDocument document = new PrintDocument();
    preview.Document = document;
    document.PrintPage += new PrintPageEventHandler(document_PrintPage);
    preview.ShowDialog(this);
    if (stoppedTimer)
        timer1.Start();
}
```

Here's the code for the Print button. It pauses the simulator (if it's running), creates a PrintDocument, hooks it up to the PrintPage event handler, shows the dialog, and then restarts the simulator.

There's so much more to be done...

You've built a pretty neat little simulator, but why stop now?
There's a whole lot more that you can do on your own. Here are
some ideas—see if you can implement some of them.

Add a control panel
Convert the constants in the World and Hive classes to properties. Then
add a new form with a control panel that has sliders to control them.

Add enemies
Add enemies that attack the hive. The more flowers there are, the more
enemies are attracted to the hive. Then add Sting Patrol bees to defend
against the enemies and Hive Maintenance bees to defend and repair the
hive. Those bees take extra honey.

*A good
simulation will
have lots of
tradeoffs, and
will give the
user ways to
decide which
tradeoffs
to make to
influence the
progress of
the hive.*

Add hive upgrades
If the hive gets enough honey, it gets bigger. A bigger hive can hold more
bees, but takes more honey and attracts more enemies. If enemies cause
too much damage, the hive gets smaller again.

Add a queen bee who lays eggs
The eggs need Baby Bee Care worker bees to take care of them. More
honey in the hive causes the queen to lay more eggs, which need more
workers to care for them, who consume more honey.

Add animation
Animate the background of the Hive form so the sun slowly travels
across the sky. Make it get dark at night, and draw stars and a moon.
Add some perspective—make the bees get smaller the further they get
from the hive in the field of flowers.

Use your imagination!
Try to think of other ways you can make the simulation more interesting
or more interactive.

Did you come up with a cool modification to the simulator? Show off your skills—upload your project's source code to the Head First C# forums at www.headfirstlabs.com/books/hfcsharp/.

CAPTAIN AMAZING

THE DEATH
OF THE OBJECT

Head First Labs

$2.98 Chapter 14

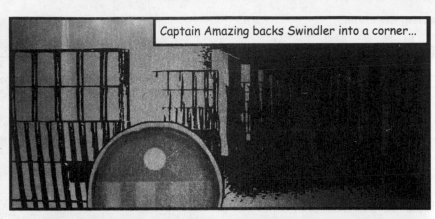
Captain Amazing backs Swindler into a corner...

...but ends up trapped himself.

CLANG

SELF DESTRUCT

A FEW MINUTES FROM NOW, YOU **AND** MY ARMY WILL BE GARBAGE (COLLECTED, THAT IS)

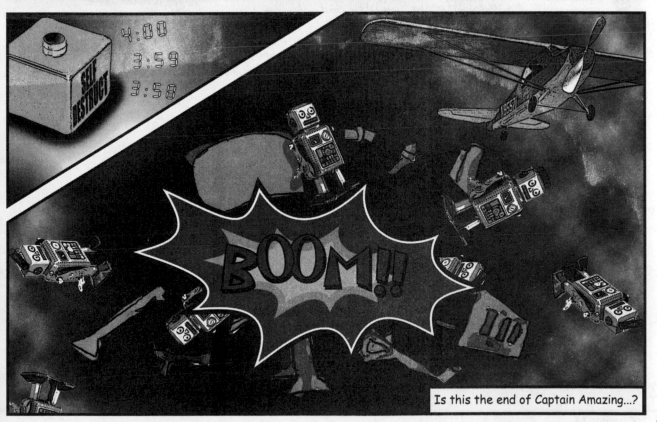
4:00
3:59
3:58

BOOM!!

Is this the end of Captain Amazing...?

Sharpen your pencil

Below is the code detailing the fight between Captain Amazing and Swindler (not to mention his clone army). Your job is to draw out what's going on in memory when the FinalBattle class is instantiated.

You can assume that Clones was set using an object initializer.

```
public class FinalBattle {
  public CloneFactory Factory = new CloneFactory();
  public List<Clone> Clones = new List<Clone>();
  public SwindlersEscapePlane escapePlane;

  public FinalBattle() {
    public Villain swindler = new Villain(this);
    using (Superhero captainAmazing = new Superhero()) {
      Factory.PeopleInFactory.Add(captainAmazing);
      Factory.PeopleInFactory.Add(swindler);    ❶
      captainAmazing.Think("I'll take down each of the clones' references,
                            one by one");
      captainAmazing.IdentifyTheClones(Clones);
      captainAmazing.RemoveTheClones(Clones);
      swindler.Think("A few minutes from now, you AND my army will be garbage");
      swindler.Think("(collected, that is!)");
      escapePlane = new SwindlersEscapePlane(swindler);    ❷
      swindler.TrapCaptainAmazing(Factory);
      MessageBox.Show("The Swindler escaped");
    }
  }                                                        ❸
}
```

We've gotten you started here, with what's going on in the factory object.

Draw what's going on right here, when the SwindlersEscapePlane object is instantiated.

Draw a picture of what the heap will look like exactly one second after the FinalBattle constructor runs.

```
[Serializable]
public class Superhero : IDisposable {
    private List<Clone> clonesToRemove = new List<Clone>();
    public void IdentifyTheClones(List<Clone> clones) {
        foreach (Clone clone in clones)
            clonesToRemove.Add(clone);
    }
    public void RemoveTheClones(List<Clone> clones) {
        foreach (Clone clone in clonesToRemove)
            clones.Remove(clone);
    }
    ...
    }
}
```

There's more code here (including the Dispose() method) that we aren't showing you, but you don't need it to answer this.

```
public class Villain {
  private FinalBattle finalBattle;
  public Villain(FinalBattle finalBattle) {
    this.finalBattle = finalBattle;
  }
  public void TrapCaptainAmazing(CloneFactory factory) {
    factory.SelfDestruct.Tick += new EventHandler(SelfDestruct_Tick);
    factory.SelfDestruct.Interval = 600;
    factory.SelfDestruct.Start();
  }
  private void SelfDestruct_Tick(object sender, EventArgs e) {
    finalBattle.factory = null;
  }
}
```

```
public class SwindlersEscapePlane {
    public Villain PilotsSeat;
    public SwindlersEscapePlane(Villain escapee) {
        PilotsSeat = escapee;
    }
}

public class CloneFactory {
    public Timer SelfDestruct = new Timer();
    public List<object> PeopleInFactory = new List<object>();
    ...
}
```

There's a clone class and that we're not showing you in this code too. You don't need it to answer the questions.

Make sure you add labels to your objects to show the reference variables that are pointing to them.

We started the first one for you. Make sure you draw in lines showing the architecture—we drew a line from the clone factory to the Superhero object, because the factory has references to it (via its PeopleInFactory field).

①

FACTORY
CloneFactory

SWINDLER
Villain object

We've left space, as there is more to be drawn at this stage.

You can leave out the Clone and List objects, and focus on first-order objects in these drawings.

②

③

Your job is to draw what's going on in these two bits of memory, too.

Based on your diagrams, where in the code did Captain Amazing die?

....
....
....
....

Be sure and annotate that on your diagram, too.

Sharpen your pencil
Solution

Draw what's happening in memory with the FinalBattle program.

1

Here's the object you should have added to this diagram.

The captainAmazing reference points to a Superhero object, and the swindler reference points to a Villain object, and the clone factory's PeopleInFactory list contains references to both of them.

2

As long as there's a reference to swindler from the escapePlane, he won't get garbage collected.

The escapePlane reference now points to a new instance of the SwindlersEscapePlane object, and its PilotSeat field points to the Villain object

When the selfDestruct fires, the factory reference variable is set to null, and eligible for garbage collection. So it's gone in this drawing.

3

As soon as the factory reference was gone, it took the CloneFactory object with it—and that caused the List object referenced by its PeopleInFactory field to disappear... and that was the only thing keeping the SuperHero object alive. Now he'll be destroyed the next time the garbage collector runs.

Based on your diagrams, where in the code did Captain Amazing die?

```
void SelfDestruct_Tick(object sender, EventArgs e) {
    finalBattle.factory = null;
}
```

One second after the FinalBattle constructor ran, the hero was gone.

Once finalBattleFactory was set to null, it was ready for garbage collection. And it took the last reference to the Captain with it!

Once the Superhero instance had no clone factory referencing it, it was marked for garbage collection too.

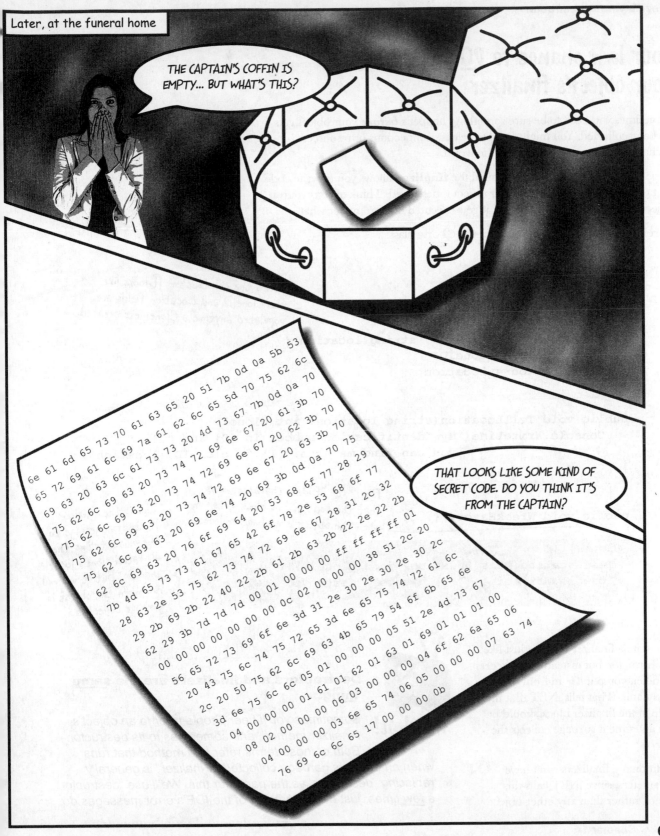

Your last chance to DO something... your object's finalizer

Sometimes you need to be sure something happens **before** your object gets garbage collected. You might want to release connections or resources... or perhaps send a coded message to the world.

A special method in your object called the **finalizer** allows you to write code that will always execute when your object is destroyed. Think of it as your object's personal `finally` block: it gets executed last, no matter what.

Here's an example of a destructor in the `Clone` class:

```
[Serializable]
public class Clone {
  string Location;
  int CloneID;

  public Clone (int cloneID, string location){
    this.CloneID = cloneID;
    this.Location = location;
  }

  public void TellLocation(string location, int cloneID){
    Console.WriteLine("My Identification number is {0} and " +
                "you can find me here: {1}.", cloneID, location);
  }

  public void WreakHavoc(){...}

  ~Clone() {
    TellLocation(this.Location, this.CloneID);
    Console.WriteLine ("{0} has been destroyed", CloneID);
  }
}
```

Here's the constructor. It looks like the CloneID and Location fields are populated anytime a Clone gets created.

This ~ (or "tilde") character says that the code in this block gets run when the object is garbage collected.

This is the finalizer. It sends a message to the villain telling the ill-fated clone's location and ID. But it will only run when the object is garbage collected.

You write a finalizer method just like a constructor, but instead of an access modifier, you put a ~ in front of the class name. That tells .NET that the code in the finalizer block should be run any time it garbage collects the object.

Additionally, finalizers can't have parameters, since .NET calls this object, rather than any other object.

Watch it!

Destructors and finalizers are the same thing.

Sometimes you'll hear people refer to an object's Finalizer method, and sometimes to its destructor. Both of those terms refer to a method that runs when an object is garbage collected. "Finalizer" is generally replacing "destructor" as the name for this. We'll use "destructor" a few times, just because some of the IDE's error messages do.

When **<u>EXACTLY</u>** does a finalizer run?

The finalizer you build for your object runs when that object gets garbage collected. And garbage collection happens after **all** references to your object go away. But garbage collection doesn't always happen *right after* the references are gone.

Suppose you have an object with a reference to it. .NET sends the garbage collector to work, and it checks out your object. But since there are references to your object, the garbage collector ignores it and moves along. Your object keeps living on in memory.

Then, something happens. That last object holding a reference to *your* object decides to move on. Now, your object is sitting in memory, with no references. It can't be accessed. It's basically a **dead object**.

But here's the thing. ***Garbage collection is something that .NET controls,*** not your objects. So if the garbage collector isn't sent out again for, say, a few seconds, or maybe even a few minutes, your object still lives on in memory. It's unusable, but it hasn't been garbage collected. **And any finalizer your object has does not (yet) get run.**

Finally, .NET sends the garbage collector out again. This time, your object is dead, and the collector tosses it away. Here, finally, your destructor runs... possibly several minutes after the last reference to the object was removed or changed.

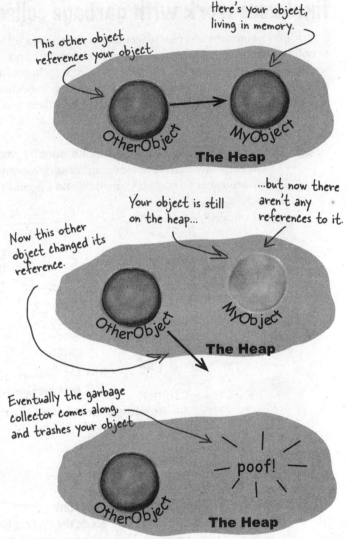

This other object references your object.

Here's your object, living in memory.

The Heap

Now this other object changed its reference.

Your object is still on the heap...

...but now there aren't any references to it.

The Heap

Eventually the garbage collector comes along, and trashes your object.

— poof! —

The Heap

You can <u>SUGGEST</u> to .NET that it's time to collect the garbage

.NET does let you *suggest* that garbage collection would be a good idea. **Most times, you'll never use this method, because garbage collection is tuned to respond to a lot of conditions in the CLR and calling it *isn't really a good idea*.** But just to see how a finalizer works, you could call for garbage collection on your own. If that's what you want to do, just call `GC.collect()`.

Be careful, though. That method doesn't **force** .NET to garbage collect things immediately. It just says, "Do garbage collection as soon as possible."

```
public void RemoveTheClones(
            List<Clone> clones) {
   foreach (Clone clone in clonesToRemove)
   clones.Remove(clone);
   GC.Collect();
}
```

Dispose() works with using, finalizers work with garbage collection

`Dispose()` runs whenever an object that is created in a `using` statement is set to null or loses all of its references. If you don't use a `using` statement, then just setting the reference to null won't cause `Dispose()` to get called—you'll need to call it directly. An object's finalizer runs at garbage collection for that particular object. Let's create a couple of objects, and see how these two methods differ:

Do this!

① Create a Clone class and make sure it implements IDisposable.
The class should have one `int` automatic property called ID. It has a constructor, a `Dispose()` method and a finalizer:

```
public class Clone : IDisposable {
    public int ID { get; private set; }

    public Clone(int ID) {
        this.ID = ID;
    }

    public void Dispose() {
        MessageBox.Show("I've been disposed!",
                "Clone #" + ID + " says...");
    }

    ~Clone() {
        MessageBox.Show("Aaargh! You got me!",
                "Clone #" + ID + " says...");
    }
}
```

> Since the class implements IDisposable, it has to have a Dispose() method.

> Here's the finalizer. It will run when the object gets garbage collected.

② Create a Form with three buttons.
Create one instance of `Clone` inside the `Click` handler for the first button with a `using` statement. Here's the first part of the code for the button:

> Here's the form you should create.

The method creates a new Clone and then immediately kills it by taking away its reference.

```
private void clone1_Click(object sender, EventArgs e)
    using (Clone clone1 = new Clone(1)) {
        // Do nothing!
    }
}
```

> Since we declared clone1 with a using statement, its Dispose() method gets run.

> As soon as the using block is done and the Clone object's Dispose() method is called, there's no more reference to it and it gets marked for garbage collection.

③ Implement the other two buttons.

Create another instance of `Clone` in the second button's `Click` handler, and set it to `null` manually:

```
private void clone2_Click(object sender, EventArgs e) {
    Clone clone2 = new Clone(2);
    clone2 = null;
}
```

Since this doesn't use a using statement, Dispose() won't ever get run, but the finalizer will.

For the third button, add a call to `GC.Collect()` to suggest garbage collection occur.

```
private void gc_Click(object sender, EventArgs e) {
    GC.Collect();
}
```

This suggests that garbage collection run.

Remember, normally it's not a great idea to do this. But it's fine here, because it's a good way to learn about garbage collection.

④ Run the program and play with Dispose() and finalizers.

Click on the first button and check out the message box: `Dispose()` runs first.

In most cases, you **won't** see the garbage collection message box. Because your object is set to null, but garbage collection hasn't run yet.

Now click on the second button... Nothing happens. right? That's because we didn't use a `using` statement, so no `Dispose()` method. And until the garbage collector runs, you won't see the message boxes from the finalizer.

Now click the third button, to suggest garbage collection. You should see the finalizer from both `Clone1` and `Clone2` fire up and display message boxes.

Even though the Clone1 object has been set to null and its Dispose method has run, it's still on the heap waiting for garbage collection.

Now Clone2 is on the heap, too, but without any references to it.

When GC.Collect() is run, both objects run their finalizers and disappear.

Play around with the program. Click the Clone #1 button, then the Clone #2 button, then the GC button. Do it a few times. Sometimes clone #1 is collected first, and sometimes clone #2 is. And once in a while, the garbage collector runs even though you didn't ask it to using GC.Collect().

Finalizers <u>can't</u> depend on stability

When you write a finalizer, you can't depend on it running at any one time. Even if you call GC.Collect()—which you should avoid, unless you have a really good reason to do it—you're only *suggesting* that the garbage collector is run. It's not a guarantee that it'll happen right now. And when it does, you have no way of knowing what order the objects will be collected.

So what does that mean, in practical terms? Well, think about what happens if you've got two objects that have references to each other. If object #1 is collected first, then object #2's reference to it is pointing to an object that's no longer there. But if object #2 is collected first, then object #1's reference is invalid. So what that means is that *you can't depend on references in your object's finalizer*. Which means that it's a really bad idea to try to do something inside a finalizer that depends on references being valid.

Serialization is a really good example of something that you **shouldn't do inside a finalizer**. If your object's got a bunch of references to other objects, serialization depends on *all* of those objects still being in memory... and all of the objects they reference, and the ones those objects reference, and so on. So if you try to serialize when garbage collection is happening, you could end up **missing** vital parts of your program because some objects could've been collected *before* the finalizer ran.

Luckily, C# gives us a really good solution to this: IDisposable. Anything that could modify your core data or that depends on other objects being in memory needs to happen as part of a Dispose() method, not a finalizer.

Some people like to think of a finalizers as a kind of failsafe for the Dispose() method. And that makes sense—you saw with your Clone object that just because you implement IDisposable, that doesn't mean the object's Dispose() method will get called. But you need to be careful—if your Dispose() method depends on other objects that are on the heap, then calling Dispose() from your finalizer can cause trouble. The best way around this is to make sure you **always use a using statement** any time you're creating an IDispoable object.

Let's say you've got two objects that have references to each other...

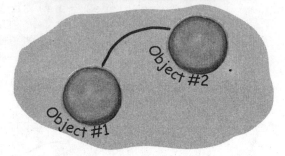

...if they're both marked for garbage collection at the same time, then object #1 could disappear first...

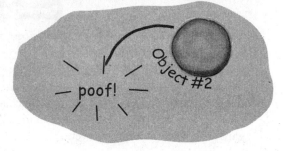

...on the other hand, object #2 could disappear before object #1. You've got no way of knowing the order...

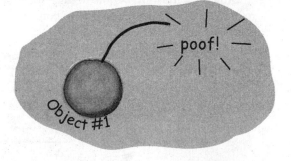

...and that's why one object's finalizer can't rely on any other object still being on the heap.

Make an object serialize itself in its Dispose()

Once you understand the difference between Dispose() and a finalizer, it's pretty easy to write objects that serialize themselves out automatically when they're disposed of.

Do this!

1 **Make the Clone class (from page 630) Serializable.**

Just add the Serializeable attribute on top of the class so that we can save the file out.

```
[Serializable]
public class Clone : IDisposable
```

2 **Modify Clone's Dispose() method to Serialize itself out to a file.**

Let's use a BinaryFormatter to write Clone out to a file in Dispose():

```
using System.IO;
using System.Runtime.Serialization.Formatters.Binary;

// existing code

public void Dispose() {
    string filename = "C:\\Temp\\Clone.dat";
    string dirname = "C:\\Temp\\";
    if (File.Exists(filename) == false) {
        Directory.CreateDirectory(dirname);
    }
    BinaryFormatter bf = new BinaryFormatter();
    using (Stream output = File.OpenWrite(filename)) {
        bf.Serialize(output, this);
    }
    MessageBox.Show("This is " + this.ID +
                    " must.. serialize..object.");
}
```

> You'll need a few more using statements to access the I/O classes we'll use.

> This is straight serialization, although we do hardcode in the file, since Dispose() can't take any parameters.

> You could set a class like this up to take in a filename to write itself to in its constructor.

3 **Run the application.**

You'll see the same behavior you saw on the last few pages... but before the Clone1 object is garbage collected, it's serialized to a file. Look inside the file and you'll see the binary representation of the object.

BRAIN POWER

What do you think the rest of the SuperHero object's code looked like? We showed you part of it on page 624. Could you write the rest now?

Fireside Chats

Tonight's talk: **The Dispose() method and a finalizer spar over who's more valuable.**

Dispose:

To be honest, I'm a little surprised I was invited here. I thought the programming world had come to a consensus. I mean, I'm way more valuable than you are. Really, you're pretty feeble. You can't even serialize yourself out, alter core data, anything. Pretty unstable, aren't you?

Finalizer:

Excuse me? That's rich. I'm feeble... OK. Well, I didn't want to get into this, but since we're already stooping this low... at least I don't need an interface to get started. Without IDisposable, you're just another useless method.

There's an interface specifically **because** I'm so important. In fact, I'm the only method in it!

Right, right... keep telling yourself that. And what happens when someone forgets to use a using statement when they instantiate their object? Then you're nowhere to be found.

OK, you're right, programmers need to know they're going to need me and either call me directly or use a using statement to call me. But they always know when I'm gonna run, and they can use me to do whatever they need to do to clean up after their object. I'm powerful, reliable, and easy to use. I'm a triple threat. And you? Nobody knows exactly when you'll run or what the state of the application will be when you finally do decide to show up.

> Handles are what your programs use when they go around .NET and the CLR and interact directly with Windows. Since .NET doesn't know about them, it can't clean them up for you.

OK, but if you need to do something at the very last moment when an object is garbage collected, there's no way to do it without me. I can free up network resources and windows handles and streams and anything else that might cause a problem for the rest of the program if you don't clean it up. I can make sure that your objects deal with being trashed more gracefully, and that's nothing to sneeze at.

So there's basically nothing you can do that I can't do. But you think you're a big shot because you run when garbage collection happens.

I'll take that over your flash and attitude any day, pal.

Dumb Questions

there are no

Q: Can a finalizer use all of an object's fields and methods?

A: Sure. While you can't pass parameters to a finalizer method, you can use any of the fields in an object, either directly or using `this`—but be careful, because if those fields reference other objects, then the other objects may have already been collected. But you can definitely call other methods in the object being finalized (as long as those methods don't depend on other objects).

Q: What happens to exceptions that get thrown in a finalizer?

A: Good question. It's totally legal to put a `try/catch` block inside a finalizer method. Give it a try yourself. Create a divide by zero exception inside a try block in the `Clone` program we just wrote. Catch it and throw up a message box that says "I just caught an exception." right before the "...I've been destroyed." box we'd already written. Now run the program and click on the first button and then the GC button. You'll see both the exception box and the destroyed box pop up. (Of course, it generally a **really bad idea** to pop up message boxes in finalizers for objects that are more than just toys... and those message boxes may never actually pop up.)

Q: How often does the garbage collector run automatically?

A: There's no good answer to that one. It doesn't run on an easily predictable cycle, and you don't have any firm control over it. You can be sure it will be run when your program exits. But if you want to be sure it'll run, you have to use GC.Collect() to set it off... and even then, timing is an issue.

Q: How soon after I call GC.Collect() will .NET start garbage collection?

A: When you run `GC.Collect()`, you're telling .NET to garbage collect soon as possible. That's **usually** as soon as .NET finishes whatever its doing. That means it'll happen pretty soon, but you can't actually control when.

Q: If I absolutely need something to run, I put it in a finalizer, right?

A: It's possible that your finalizer won't run. It's possible to suppress finalizers when garbage collection happens. Or the process could end entirely. But as a general rule, your finalizer should run.

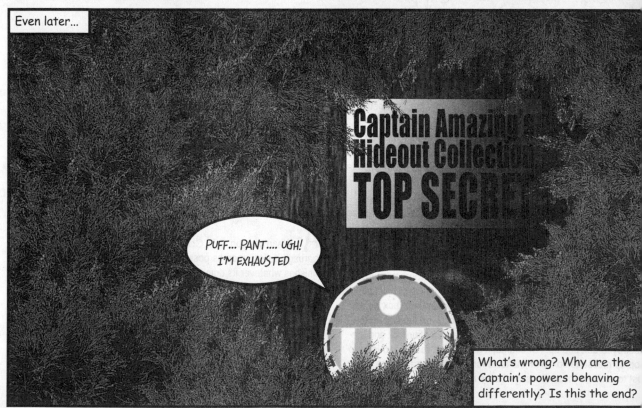

A struct *looks* like an object...

One of the types in .NET we haven't talked about much is the `struct`.
`struct` is short for **structure**, and `struct`s look a lot like objects.
They have fields and properties, just like objects. And you can even pass
them into a method that takes an `object` type parameter:

```
public struct AlmostSuperhero : IDisposable {
    public int SuperStrength;
    public int SuperSpeed { get; private set; }

    public void RemoveVillain(Villain villain)
    {
        Console.WriteLine("OK, " + villain.Name +
            " surrender and stop all the madness!");
        if (villain.Surrendered)
            villain.GoToJail();
        else
            villain.Kill();
    }

    public void Dispose() { ... }
}
```

Structs can implement interfaces but can't subclass other classes.

A struct can have properties and fields...

...and define methods.

..but *isn't* on the heap

But `struct`s **aren't** objects on the heap. They can have methods and
fields, but they can't have finalizers. They also can't inherit from other
classes or `struct`s, or have classes or `struct`s inherit from them.

structs can't inherit from other objects.

You can mimic a standalone object with a struct, but structs don't stand in very well for complex inheritance hierarchies.

The power of objects lies in their ability to mimic real-world behavior, through inheritance and polymorphism.

Structs are best used for storing data, but are not as useful as objects when it comes to representing actual behavior.

Values get copied, references get assigned

You already have a sense of how some types are different than others. On one hand you've got **value types** like int, bool, and string. On the other hand, you've got **objects** like List, Stream, and Exception. And they don't quite work exactly the same way, do they?

Here's a quick refresher on value types vs. objects.

When you use the equals sign to set one value type variable to another, it **makes a copy of the value**, and afterwards the two variables aren't connected to each other. On the other hand, when you use the equals sign with references, what you're doing is **pointing both references at the same object**.

★ Variable declaration and assignment works the same with value types or object types:

```
int howMany = 37;
string name = "Fingers";
List<float> temperatures = new List<float>();
Exception ex = new Exception("Does not compute");
```

int and string are value types, List and Exception are object types.

These are all initialized in the same basic way.

★ Differences creep in when you start to assign values, though. Value types all are handled with copying. Here's an example:

This line copies the value that's stored in the fifteenMore variable into the howMany variable and adds 15 to it.

Changing the fifteenMore variable has no effect on howMany, and vice versa.

```
int fifteenMore = howMany;
fifteenMore += 15;
Console.WriteLine("howMany has {0}, fifteenMore has {1}",
                  howMany, fifteenMore);
```

The output here shows that fifteenMore and howMany are **not** connected:

```
howMany has 25, fifteenMore has 40
```

★ With object assignments, though, you're assigning references, not actual values:

This line sets the differentList reference to point to the same object as the temperatures reference.

```
temperatures.Add(56.5F);
temperatures.Add(27.4F);
List<float> differentList = temperatures;
differentList.Add(62.9F);
```

Both references point at the same actual object.

TEMPERATURES
DIFFERENTLIST

List<float>

So changing the List means both references see the update... since they both point to a single List object.

```
Console.WriteLine("temperatures has {0}, differentlist has {1}",
                  temperatures.Count(), differentList.Count());
```

The output here demonstrates that differentList and temperatures are actually pointing to the **same** object:

```
temperatures has 3, differentList has 3
```

When you called differentList.Add(), it added a new temperature to the object that both differentList and temperatures point to.

Structs are <u>value</u> types; objects are <u>reference</u> types

When you create a `struct`, you're creating a **value type**. What that means is when you use equals to set one `struct` variable equal to another, you're creating a fresh *copy* of the struct in the new variable. So even though a `struct` *looks* like an object, it doesn't act like one.

Do this

1 **Create a struct called Dog**

Here's simple struct to keep track of a dog. It looks just like an object, but it's not.

```
public struct Dog {
    public string Name;
    public string Breed;

    public Dog(string name, string breed) {
        this.Name = name;
        this.Breed = breed;
    }

    public void Speak() {
        Console.WriteLine("My name is {0} and I'm a {1}.", Name, Breed);
    }
}
```

Yes, this is not good encapsulation. Bear with us—we're making a point.

2 **Create a class called Canine**

Make an exact copy of the Dog struct, except replace `struct` with `class` and then replace Dog with Canine. Now you'll have a Canine class that you can play with, which is almost exactly equivalent to the Dog struct.

3 **Add a button that makes some copies of Dogs and Canines**

Here's the code:

```
Canine spot = new Canine("Spot", "pug");
Canine bob = spot;
bob.Name = "Spike";
bob.Breed = "beagle";
spot.Speak();

Dog jake = new Dog("Jake", "poodle");
Dog betty = jake;
betty.Name = "Betty";
betty.Breed = "pit bull";
jake.Speak();
```

4 **Before you press that button...**

Write down the what you think will be written to the console when you run this code:

....

....

Sharpen your pencil

Sharpen your pencil
Solution

What did you think would get written to the console?

My name is Spike and I'm a beagle.
My name is Jake and I'm a poodle.

Here's what happened...

The bob and spot references both point to the same object, so both changed the same fields and accessed the same Speak() method. But structs don't work that way. When you created betty, you made a fresh copy of the data in jake. The two structs are completely independent of each other.

A new Canine object was created and the spot reference points to it.

```
Canine spot = new Canine("Spot", "pug"); (1)
```

```
Canine bob = spot; (2)
```

The new reference variable bob was created, but no new object was added to the heap—the bob variable points to the same object as spot.

```
bob.Name = "Spike";
```

```
bob.Breed = "beagle";
```

```
spot.Speak(); (3)
```

Since spot and bob both point to the same object, spot.Speak() and bob.Speak() both call the same method, and both of them produce the same output with "Spike" and "beagle".

① SPOT — Spot pug — Canine object

② SPOT BOB — Spot pug — Canine object

③ SPOT BOB — Spike beagle — Canine object

```
Dog jake = new Dog("Jake", "poodle"); (4)
```

```
Dog betty = jake; (5)
```

```
betty.Name = "Betty";
```

```
betty.Breed = "pit bull";
```

```
jake.Speak(); (6)
```

When you create a new struct, it looks really similar to creating an object—you've got a variable that you can use to access its fields and methods.

④ Jake poodle — jake

Here's the big difference. When you added the betty variable, you created a whole *new* struct, even though you didn't use the new keyword.

⑤ Jake poodle — betty | Jake poodle — jake

When you set one struct equal to another, you're creating a fresh <u>COPY</u> of the data inside the struct. That's because struct is a VALUE TYPE.

Since you created a fresh copy of the data, jake was unaffected when you changed betty's fields.

⑥ Betty pit bull — betty | Jake poodle — jake

The stack vs. the heap: more on memory

It's easy to understand how a `struct` differs from an object—you can make a fresh copy of a struct just using equals, which you can't do with an object. But what's really going on behind the scenes? The reason `structs` act like other value types is that **value types don't live on the heap**. The .NET CLR divides your data into two places in memory. You already know that objects live on the **heap**. It also keeps another part of memory called the **stack** to store all of the local variables you declare in your methods, and the parameters that you pass into those methods. You can think of the stack as a bunch of slots that you can stick values in. When a method gets called, the CLR adds more slots to the top of the stack. When it returns, its slots are removed.

Behind the Scenes

Remember, when your program's running, the CLR is actively managing memory, dealing with the heap and collecting garbage.

Even though you can set an object variable equal to a struct, structs and objects are different.

The Code

Here's code that you might see in a program.

Here's what the stack looks like after these two lines of code run.

The Stack

This is where structs and local variables hang out.

```
Canine spot = new Canine("Spot", "pug");

Dog jake = new Dog("Jake", "poodle");
```

```
Canine spot = new Canine("Spot", "pug");

Dog jake = new Dog("Jake", "poodle");

Dog betty = jake;
```

When you create a new struct—or any other value type variable—a new "slot" gets added onto the stack. That slot is a copy of the value in your type.

```
Canine spot = new Canine("Spot", "pug");

Dog jake = new Dog("Jake", "poodle");

Dog betty = jake;

SpeakThreeTimes(jake);

public SpeakThreeTimes(Dog dog) {
    int i;
    for (i = 0; i < 5; i++)
        dog.Speak();
}
```

When you call a method, the CLR puts its local variables on the top of the stack. It takes them off when it's done.

> Wait a minute. Didn't you just say that you can set an object variable equal to a struct? If an object's on the heap, and a struct is on the stack, what happens?

When you set an object equal to a value type, it gets <u>boxed</u>.

There are some times that you need to be able to write a method that can take either a value type *or* a reference type—perhaps a method that can work with either a `Dog` `struct` or a `Canine` object. If you find yourself in that situation, you can use the `object` keyword:

```
public WalkDogOrCanine(object anything) { ... }
```

If you send this method a struct, the struct gets **boxed** into a special object "wrapper" that allows it to live on the heap. While the wrapper's on the heap, you can't do much with the struct. You have to "unwrap" the struct to work with it. Luckily, all of this happens *automatically* when you set an object equal to a value type, or pass a value type into a method that expects an object.

You can also use the "is" keyword to see if an object is a struct, or any other value type, that's been boxed and put on the heap.

1 Here's what the stack and heap look like after you create an object variable and set it equal to a Dog struct.

```
Dog sid = new Dog("Sid", "husky");
Object obj = sid;
```

After a struct is boxed, there are two copies of the data: on the stack, and the copy boxed on the heap.

Dog sid (boxed)

2 If you want to unbox the object, all you need to do is cast it to the right type, and it gets unboxed automatically. This is where the is keyword comes in handy.

```
if (obj is Dog)
    Dog happy = (Dog) obj;
```

These are structs, so unless they're boxed, they don't live on the heap.

After this line runs, you've got a third copy of the data in a new struct called happy, which gets its own slot on the stack.

Dog sid (boxed)

Pool Puzzle

Your **job** is to take snippets from the pool and place them into the blank lines in the code. You **may** use the same snippet more than once, and you won't need to use all the snippets. Your **goal** is to make the code write this output to the console when a **new instance of the Faucet class is created**:

```
public class Faucet {
    public Faucet() {
        Table wine = new Table();
        Hinge book = new Hinge();
        wine.SetA(book);
        book.SetB(wine);
        wine.Lamp(10);
        book.Garden.Lamp("back in");
        book.Bulb *= 2;
        wine.Lamp("minutes");
        wine.Lamp(book);
    }
}
```

Output when you create a new Faucet object:

back in 20 minutes ←

Here's the goal... to get this output.

```
public _____ Table {
    public string Stairs;
    public Hinge Floor;
    public void Set(Hinge b) {
        Floor = b;
    }
    public void Lamp(object oil) {
        if (oil ____ int)
            _____.Bulb = (int)oil;
        else if (oil ____ string)
            Stairs = (string)oil;
        else if (oil ____ Hinge) {
            _____ vine = oil ____ _____;
            Console.WriteLine(vine.Table()
          + " " + _____.Bulb + " " + Stairs);
        }
    }
}
public _____ Hinge {
    public int Bulb;
    public Table Garden;
    public void Set(Table a) {
        Garden = a;
    }
    public string Table() {
        return _____.Stairs;
    }
}
```

Bonus points: Circle the lines where boxing happens.

Note: each thing from the pool can be used more than once.

public
private
class
new
abstract
interface

Brush
Lamp
Bulb
Table
Stairs

if
or
is
on
as
oop

Garden
Floor
Window
Door
Hinge

+
-
++
--
=
==

struct
string
int
float
single
double

Answers on page 652.

there are no
Dumb Questions

Q: Okay, back up a minute. Why do I care about the stack?

A: Because understanding the difference between the stack and the heap helps you keep your reference types and value types straight. It's easy to forget that structs and objects work very differently—when you use the equals sign with both of them, they look really similar. Having some idea of how .NET and the CLR handle things under the hood helps you understand *why* reference and value types are different.

Q: And boxing? Why is that important to me?

A: Because you need to know when things end up on the stack, and you need to know when data's being copied back and forth. Boxing takes extra memory and more time. When you're only doing it a few times (or a few hundred times) in your program, then you won't notice the difference. But let's say you're writing a program that does the same thing over and over again, millions of times a second. That's not too far-fetched, since that's exactly what your beehive simulator did. If you find that your program's taking up more and more memory, or going slower and slower, then it's possible that you can make it more efficient by avoiding boxing in the part of the program that repeats.

Q: I get how you get a fresh copy of a struct when you set one struct variable equal to another one. But why is that useful to me?

A: One place that's really helpful is with **encapsulation**. Take a look at this familiar field from a class that knows its location:

```
private Point location;
public Point Location {
  get { return location; }
}
```

If `Point` were a class, then this would be terrible encapsulation. It wouldn't matter that `location` is private, because you made a public read-only property that returns a reference to it, so any other object would be able to access it.

Lucky for us, `Point` is actually a struct. And that means that the public `Location` property returns a fresh copy of the point. The object that uses it can do whatever it wants to that copy—none of those changes will make it to the private `location` field.

Q: If Point is a struct, does that mean there are *other* structs that I've been working with all along?

A: Yes! One struct that's really useful and very common when you're working with graphics and forms is **Rectangle**. It's got some very useful methods that come in really handy when you need to figure out boundaries and check whether points are inside or outside of the rectangle. All you need to do is set its location and size, and it'll automatically compute its top, bottom, left, right, width, and height.

Another useful struct that you'll run into is **Size**. You've already seen it in action—you used it when you were determining the size of a string using the `MeasureString()` method. It's a struct, too.

Q: How do I know whether to use a struct or a class?

A: Most of the time, programmers use classes. Structs have a lot of limitations that can really make it hard to work with them for large jobs. They don't support inheritance, abstraction, or polymorphism, and you already know how important those things are for building programs easily.

Where structs come in really handy is if you have a small, limited type of data that you need to work with repeatedly. Rectangles and points are good examples—there's not much you'll do with them, but you'll use them over and over again. Structs tend to be relatively small and limited in scope. If you find that you have a small chunk of a few different kinds of data that you want to store in a field in a class or pass to a method as a parameter, that's probably a good candidate for a struct.

A struct can be very valuable when you want to add good encapsulation to your class, because a read-only property that returns a struct always makes a fresh copy of it.

← Pop quiz, hotshot!
Answer's on page 646.

Sharpen your pencil

This method is supposed to kill a Clone object, but it doesn't work. Why not?

```
private void SetCloneToNull(Clone clone) {
    clone = null;
}
```

....

....

Captain Amazing... not so much

With all this talk of boxing, you should have a pretty good idea of what was going on with the less-powerful, more-tired Captain Amazing. In fact, it wasn't Captain Amazing at all, but a boxed struct:

struct

VS.

SuperHero

That's one big advantage of structs (and other value types)—you can easily make copies of them.

1 **Structs can't inherit from classes or implement interfaces**
No wonder the Captain's superpowers seemed a little weak! He didn't get any inherited behavior.

2 **Structs can only live on the heap when they're boxed**
The struct couldn't get onto the heap without being boxed up.

1 **You can't create a fresh copy of an object**
When you set one object variable equal to another, you're copying a ***reference*** to the ***same*** variable.

2 **You can use the "as" keyword with an object**
Objects allow for polymorphism by allowing an object to function as any of the objects it inherits from.

Back at the Lab

I THINK I'VE FOUND A WAY TO GIVE HIS POWERS TO A NORMAL CITIZEN!

ESSENCE OF AMAZING

Extension methods add new behavior to <u>EXISTING</u> classes

Sometimes you need to extend a class that you can't inherit from, like a `sealed` class (a lot of the .NET classes are sealed, so you can't inherit from them). And C# gives you a powerful tool for that: **extension methods**. When you add a class with extension methods to your project, it **adds new methods to classes** that already exist. All you have to do is create a static class, and add a static method that accepts an instance of the class as its first parameter using the `this` keyword.

So let's say you've got an OrdinaryHuman class:

```
public sealed class OrdinaryHuman {
    private int age;
    int weight;

    public OrdinaryHuman(int weight){
        this.weight = weight;
    }

    public void GoToWork() { // code to go to work }
    public void PayBills() { // code to pay bills  }
}
```

The OrdinaryHuman class is sealed, so it can't be subclassed. But what if we want to add a method to it?

You use an extension method by specifying the first parameter using the "this" keyword.

Since we want to extend the OrdinaryHuman class, we make the first parameter `this OrdinaryHuman`.

The SuperSolierSerum method adds an extension method to OrdinaryHuman:

```
public static class SuperSoldierSerum {
    public static string BreakWalls(this OrdinaryHuman h, double wallDensity) {
        return ("I broke through a wall of " + wallDensity + " density.");
    }
}
```

Extension methods are always static methods, and they have to live in static classes.

As soon as the SuperSoldierSerum class is added to the project, OrdinaryHuman gets a BreakWalls method. So now a form can use it:

```
private void button1_Click(object sender, EventArgs e) {
    OrdinaryHuman steve = new OrdinaryHuman(185);
    Console.WriteLine(steve.BreakWalls(89.2));
}
```

When the form creates an instance of the OrdinaryHuman class, it can access the BreakWalls() method directly—as long as it has access to the SuperSoldierSerum class.

Sharpen your pencil — Solution

This method is supposed to kill a Clone object, but it doesn't work. Why not?

```
private void SetCloneToNull(Clone clone) {
    clone = null;
}
```

So the clone parameter is just on the stack, so setting it to null doesn't do anything to the heap.

All this method does is set its own parameter to null, but that parameter's just a reference to a Clone. It's like sticking a label on an object and peeling it off again.

Q: Tell me again why I wouldn't add the new methods I need directly to my class code, instead of using extensions?

A: You could do that, and you probably should if you're just talking about adding a method to one class. Extension methods should be used pretty sparingly, and only in cases where you absolutely can't change the class you're working with for some reason (like it's part of the .NET Framework or another third party). Where extension methods really become powerful is when you need to extend the behavior of something you *wouldn't normally have access to*, like a type or an object that comes for free with the .NET framework or another library.

Q: Why use extension methods at all? Why not just extend the class with inheritance?

A: Sure. But then you'd need to use your custom objects, and any existing code that used the original, non-extended objects would have to change. With extension methods, you can change the behavior of whole groups of objects, and even add functionality to some of the most basic classes in the .NET Framework.

Extending a class gives you new behavior, but requires that you use the new subclass if you want to use that new behavior.

Q: Does my extension method affect all instances of a class, or just a certain instance of the class?

A: It will affect all instances of a class that you extend. In fact, once you've created an extension method, the new method will show up in your IDE alongside of the extended class's normal methods.

Oh, I get it! So you'd use extension methods to add new behavior to one of the built-in .NET Framework classes, right?

That's another thing you just can't do with inheritance—there's no way to inherit from an interface.

Exactly! There are some classes that you can't inherit from.

Pop open any project, add a class, and try typing this:

```
public class x : string { }
```

Try to compile your code—the IDE will give you an error. The reason is that some .NET classes are **sealed**, which means that you can't inherit from them. (You can do this with your own classes, too! Just add the sealed keyword to your class after the `public` access modifier, and no other class will be allowed to inherit from it.) Extension methods give you a way to extend it, even if you can't inherit from it.

But that's not all you can do with extension methods. In addition to extending classes, you can also extend **interfaces**. All you have to do is use an interface name in place of the class, after the `this` keyword in the extension method's first parameter. When you do, the extension method is added to **every class that implements that interface**. Remember that LINQ code you added to your simulator in chapter 12? LINQ was built entirely with extension methods, extending the `IEnumerable` class. (You'll learn a lot more about LINQ in Chapter 15.)

Extending a fundamental type: string

You don't often get to change the behavior of a language's
most fundamental types, like strings. But with extension
methods, you can do just that!

Do this!

① **Put all of your extension methods in a separate namespace.**
It's a good idea to keep all of your extensions in a different namespace than the rest of
your code. That way, you won't have trouble finding them for use in other programs. Set
up a static class for your method to live in, too.

Using a separate namespace is a good organizational tool.

```
namespace Emergency {
    public static class HumanExtensions {
```

The class your extension method is defined in must be static.

② **Create the static extension method, and defines its first parameter as**
`this` and then the type you're extending.
The two main things you need to know when you declare an extension method is that the
method needs to be static and have the class it's extending as its first parameter.

"this string" says we're extending the string class.

```
public static bool IsDistressCall (this string s){
```

The extension method must be static, too.

③ **Put the code to evaluate the string in the method.**

```
public static class HumanExtensions {
    public static bool IsDistressCall(this string s){
        if (s.Contains("Help!"))
            return true;
        else
            return false;
    }
}
```

This checks the string for a certain value... something definitely not in the default string class.

④ **Create a form and add a string.**
Add `using Emergency;` to your code. Now, when you use a string, you get the extension methods
for free. You can see this for yourself by typing the name of a string variable and a period:

```
string message1;
message1 = "An army of clones is wreaking havoc at the factory. Help!";
message1.
```

As soon as you type the dot, The IDE pops up a helper window with all of string's methods... including your extension method.

- GetTypeCode
- IndexOf
- IndexOfAny
- Insert
- IsDistressCall
- IsNormalized
- LastIndexOf
- LastIndexOfAny
- Length
- Normalize

Comment out the using line and the extension method will disappear from the IntelliSense window.

**This toy example just shows you the
syntax of extension methods. To get
a real sense of how useful they are,
just wait until the next chapter. It's
all about LINQ, which is implemented
entirely with extension methods.**

Extension Magnets

Arrange the magnets to produce this output:

`a buck begets more bucks`

```
namespace Upside {

    public static class Margin {

        public static void SendIt
```

```
namespace Sideways {
    using Upside;

        public static class Ticker {
```

```
        }
```

```
        public static string ToPrice
```

```
}
```

```
}
```
```
}
```
```
}
```

```
}
```
```
}
```
```
}
```

```
s.SendIt()
```
```
i = 3;
```
```
b = false;
```
```
i.ToPrice()
```
```
bool b = true;
```
```
if (b == true)
```
```
else
```
```
(this bool b) {
```
```
Console.Write(s);
```
```
    return "be";
```
```
        return " more bucks";
```
```
int i = 1;
```
```
public static string Green
```
```
(this string s) {
```
```
(this int n) {
```
```
if (n == 1)
```
```
b.Green();
```
```
b.Green();
```
```
public static void Main {
```
```
    return "a buck ";
```
```
.SendIt();
```
```
else
```
```
    return "gets";
```
```
string s = i.ToPrice()
```

Extension Magnets

Your job was to arrange the magnets to produce this output:

`a buck begets more bucks`

The Upside namespace has the extensions. The Sideways namespace has the entry point.

The Margin class extends string by adding a method called SendIt() that just writes the string to the console, and it extends int by adding a method called ToPrice() that returns "a buck" if the int's equal to 1, or "more bucks" if it's not.

The entry point method uses the extensions that you added in the Margin class.

```
namespace Upside {
    public static class Margin {
        public static void SendIt (this string s) {
            Console.Write(s);
        }
        public static string ToPrice (this int n) {
            if (n == 1)
                return "a buck ";
            else
                return " more bucks";
        }
        public static string Green (this bool b) {
            if (b == true)
                return "be";
            else
                return "gets";
        }
    }
}
```

The Green method extends a bool—it returns the string "be" if the bool is true, and "gets" if it's false.

Here's where the Margin class extends bool by adding a Green() method to it. If the bool is true, Green returns "be", otherwise it returns "gets".

```
namespace Sideways {
    using Upside;
    public static class Ticker {
        public static void Main {
            int i = 1;
            string s = i.ToPrice()
            s.SendIt()
            bool b = true;
            b.Green();
            b = false;
            b.Green();
            i = 3;
            i.ToPrice() .SendIt();
        }
    }
}
```

*The*UNIVERSE 🌐

CAPTAIN AMAZING REBORN

Death was not the end!

By Bucky Barnes
UNIVERSE STAFF WRITER

OBJECTVILLE

Captain Amazing deserializes himself, makes stunning comeback

In a stunning turn of events, Captain Amazing has returned to Objectville. Last month, Captain Amazing's coffin was found empty, and only a strange note left where his body should have been. Analysis of the note revealed Captain Amazing's object DNA—all his last fields and values, captured faithfully in binary format.

Today, that data has sprung to life. The Captain is back, deserialized from his own brilliant note. When asked how he conceived of such a plan, the Captain merely shrugged and mumbled, "Chapter 9." Sources close to the Captain refused to comment on the meaning of his cryptic reply, but did admit that prior to his failed assault on Swindler, the Captain has spent a lot of time reading books, studying Dispose methods and persistence. We expect Captain Amazing…

…see AMAZING on A-5

Captain Amazing is back!

Pool Puzzle Solution

The Lamp() method sets the various strings and ints. If you call it with an int, then it sets the Bulb field in whatever object Hinge points to.

```csharp
public struct Table {
    public string Stairs;
    public Hinge Floor;
    public void Set(Hinge b) {
        Floor = b;
    }
    public void Lamp(object oil) {
        if (oil is int)
            Floor.Bulb = (int)oil;
        else if (oil is string)
            Stairs = (string)oil;
        else if (oil is Hinge) {
            Hinge vine = oil as Hinge;
            Console.WriteLine(vine.Table()
                + " " + Floor.Bulb + " " + Stairs);
        }
    }
}
```

If you pass a string to Lamp, it sets the Stairs field to whatever is in that string.

Remember, the as keyword only works with classes, not structs.

Output when you create a new Faucet object:
`back in 20 minutes`

```csharp
public class Faucet {
    public Faucet() {
        Table wine = new Table();
        Hinge book = new Hinge();
        wine.Set(book);
        book.Set(wine);
        wine.Lamp(10);
        book.Garden.Lamp("back in");
        book.Bulb *= 2;
        wine.Lamp("minutes");
        wine.Lamp(book);
    }
}
```

Here's why Table has to be a struct. If it were a class, then wine would point to the same object as book.Garden, which would cause this to overwrite the "back in" string.

Bonus question: Circle the lines where boxing happens.

Since the Lamp() method takes an object parameter, boxing automatically happens when it's passed an int or a string.

```csharp
public class Hinge {
    public int Bulb;
    public Table Garden;
    public void Set(Table a) {
        Garden = a;
    }
    public string Table() {
        return Garden.Stairs;
    }
}
```

Both Hinge and Table have a Set() method. Hinge's Set() sets its Table field called Garden, and Table's Set() method sets its Hinge field called Floor.

15 LINQ

Get control of your data

So if you take the first word from this article, and the second word in that list, and add it to the fifth word over here... you get secret messages from the government!

It's a data-driven world... you better know how to live in it.

Gone are the days when you could program for days, even weeks, without dealing with **loads of data**. But today, *everything is about data*. In fact, you'll often have to work with data from **more than one place**... and in more than one format. Databases, XML, collections from other programs... it's all part of the job of a good C# programmer. And that's where **LINQ** comes in. LINQ not only lets you **query data** in a simple, intuitive way, but it lets you **group data**, and **merge data from different data sources**.

An easy project...

Objectville Paper Company wants to do a cross-promotion with
Starbuzz Coffee. Starbuzz has a frequent customer program where
they know who buys which drink and how often they buy it. Objectville
Paper wants to figure out **which of their customers are also
Starbuzz regulars** and send them a free mug and a coupon for
their favorite coffee drink... and it's up to you to combine the data and
generate the list of customers to send mugs and coupons to.

> All of Objectville Paper's
> customers who are Starbuzz
> regulars get a free mug. Just tell us
> who the mugs need to go to and what
> their favorite drinks are, okay?

...but the data's all over the place

Starbuzz keeps all their data in classes, grouped together in a big `List`. But the Objectville data is in a database (from way back in Chapter 1). We want to find any Starbuzz customers who spent more than $90, match them to the Objectville Paper contact list, and make a final list of people: **we want each person's name, the company they work for, and their favorite Starbuzz drink**.

The Starbuzz data's in a List<>

The Starbuzz people provided a program that connects to their website and pulls all the data into a List of StarbuzzData class.

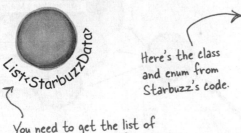

List<StarbuzzData>

You need to get the list of Starbuzz data, and find the customers that match Objectville customers.

```
public class StarbuzzData
{
    public string Name { get; set; }
    public Drink FavoriteDrink { get; set; }
    public int MoneySpent { get; set; }
    public int Visits { get; set; }
}


public enum Drink {
    BoringCoffee,
    ChocoRockoLatte,
    TripleEspresso,
    ZestyLemonChai,
    DoubleCappuccino,
    HalfCafAmericano,
    ChocoMacchiato,
    BananaSplitInACup,
}
```

Here's the class and enum from Starbuzz's code.

You've already got the customer data

You built the Objectville Paper Company contact list back in Chapter 1—it's got part of the data you need.

ContactDB database

All of the Objectville customer data is in a database.

BRAIN POWER

How would you combine the data from Starbuzz and Objectville paper to get a complete contact list?

you are here ▶   655

LINQ can pull data from multiple sources

You used LINQ in the Hive Simulator to track what groups of Bees were doing. You took advantage of the power of LINQ there to write simple queries to pull data out of a collection. LINQ can work with the Starbuzz data just like it worked with the bees, helping you use queries to pull out customer data. As long as a collection implements the `IEnumerable` interface, you can use LINQ queries with it.

But LINQ also lets you work with more than just collections. You can use the same queries to pull data from a database, or even an XML document. So once we get collections under control, we can use LINQ on the Objectville database.

In the simulator, the bees were in a collection.

Here was the query we used in the bee simulator to group and order bees by their state.

```
var beeGroups =
    from bee in world.Bees
    group bee by bee.CurrentState
    into beeGroup
    orderby beeGroup.Key
    select beeGroup;
```

LINQ

We need a similar query to pull data from the Starbuzz customer data, which is also in a collection.

The nice thing about LINQ is that the same query works on a database or XML document, of bees or customers or anything else.

LINQ works with pretty much every kind of data source you could use in .NET. Your code needs a `using System.Linq;` at the top of your file, but that's it. Even better, the IDE automatically puts a reference to LINQ in the header of any code files that are created in Visual Studio 2008. So if you're using Visual Studio 2008 or later, just start coding, and LINQ is available to you.

.NET collections are already set up for LINQ

All of the collection types in .NET implement the IEnumerable interface. Type System.Collections.Generic.IEnumerable into your IDE window, right-click on the line, and select Go To Definition. You'll see that the IEnumerable interface defines a GetEnumerator() method:

All collections and arrays implement IEnumerable. Many of them do it by implementing IEnumerable<T>, which inherits from IEnumerable.

```
namespace System.Collections.Generic {
    public interface IEnumerable<T>: IEnumerable {
    //   Summary:
    //       Returns an enumerator that iterates through the collection.
    //
    //   Returns:
    //       A System.Collections.Generic.IEnumerator<T> that can be
    //           used to iterate through the collection.
    IEnumerator<T> GetEnumerator();
    }
}
```

This T means that IEnumerable will work with any object or type.

This is the only method in the interface. Each collection implements this method. You could create your own kind of collection that implemented IEnumerable too... And if you did, you could use LINQ with your collection.

This method requires collections to define a way to move through the collection, one element at a time. That's all LINQ requires as a prerequisite. If you can move through a list of data, item-by-item, LINQ can query the collection.

Behind the Scenes

LINQ uses **extension methods** to let you query, sort, and update data. Check it out for yourself. Create an int array called linqtest, put some numbers in the array, and then type this line of code (don't worry, you'll learn what it does in a minute):

```
var result = from i in linqtest where i < 3 select i;
```

Now comment out the using System.Linq; line up in the header of the file you've created. When you try to rebuild the solution, you'll see that this line doesn't compile anymore. The methods you're calling when you use LINQ are just extension methods that are being used to extend the array.

Now you can see why extension methods were so important in Chapter 14... they let .NET (and you) add all kinds of cool behavior to existing types.

LINQ makes queries easy

Here's a simple example of LINQ syntax. It selects all the numbers in an int array that are under 37 and puts those numbers in ascending order. It does that using four **clauses** that tell it what collection to query, what criteria to use to determine which members of the collection to select, how to sort the results, and how the results should be returned.

```
int[] values = new int[] {0, 12, 44, 36, 92, 54, 13, 8};

var result = from v in values

             where v < 37

             orderby v

             select v;

foreach(int i in result)

    Console.WriteLine(i);
```

This assigns the letter "v" to stand in for each of the values array in the query. So v is 0, then 12, then 44, then 36... etc.

This LINQ query has four clauses: the from clause, a where clause, an orderby clause, and the select clause.

This says, select each v in the array that is less than 37.

Then, put those values in order (lowest to highest).

If you've used SQL before, it may seem weird to put the select at the end, but that's how things work in LINQ.

Now you can iterate through the results array and print out each item in the LINQ result.

Output:
```
0, 8, 12, 13, 36
```

var

var is a keyword that tells the compiler to figure out the type of a variable <u>at compilation time</u>. .NET detects the type from the type of the local variable that you're using LINQ to query. When you build your solution, the compiler will replace var with the right type for the data you're working with.

In the example above, when this line is compiled:
```
var result = from v in values
```
The compiler <u>replaces</u> "var" with this:
```
IEnumerable<int>
```

Watch it!

LINQ is a new feature that's part of C# 3.0 and Visual Studio 2008.

If you're using an earlier version of C#, take a few minutes to download and install Visual C# 2008 Express Edition. It's free from Microsoft, and it can be installed alongside previous versions.

LINQ is simple, but your queries don't have to be

Jimmy just sold his start-up company to a big investor, and wants to take some
of his profits and buy the most expensive issues of Captain Amazing that he can
find. But all he's got is data. How can LINQ help him scour his two collections
and figure out which comics are the most expensive?

1 Jimmy downloaded a list of Captain Amazing issues from a Captain Amazing fan page. He put
them in a List<> of Comic objects that have two fields, Name and Issue.

```
public class Comic {
    public string Name { get; set; }
    public int Issue { get; set; }
}
```

Jimmy used object initializers and a collection initializer to build his catalog:

```
private static List<Comic> BuildCatalog() {
    List<Comic> comics = new List<Comic>();
    comics.Add(new Comic("Johnny America vs. the Pinko", 6));
    comics.Add(new Comic("Rock and Roll (limited edition)", 19));
    comics.Add(new Comic("Woman's Work", 36));
    comics.Add(new Comic("Hippie Madness (misprinted)", 57));
    comics.Add(new Comic("Revenge of the New Wave Freak (damaged)", 68));
    comics.Add(new Comic("Black Monday", 74));
    comics.Add(new Comic("Tribal Tattoo Madness", 83));
    comics.Add(new Comic("The Death of an Object", 97));
    return comics;
}
```

Issue #74 of Captain Amazing
is called "Black Monday"

2 Luckily, there's a thriving marketplace for Captain Amazing comics on Greg's List. He knows that
issue #57, "Hippie Madness," was misprinted and the almost all of the run was destroyed by the
publisher, and he found a rare copy recently sold on Greg's List for $13,525. After a few hours of
searching, Jimmy was able to build a Dictionary<> that mapped issue numbers to values.

```
private static Dictionary<int, int> GetPrices() {
    Dictionary<int, int> values = new Dictionary<int, int>();
    values.Add(6, 3600);
    values.Add(19, 500);
    values.Add(36, 650);
    values.Add(57, 13525);
    values.Add(68, 250);
    values.Add(74, 75);
    values.Add(83, 25);
    values.Add(97, 35);
    return values;
}
```

Issue #57 is worth $13,525.

BRAIN POWER

Look closely at the LINQ query on page 658.
What do you think Jim has to put in his query
to find the most expensive issues?

Anatomy of a query

It's easy to mine Jimmy's data with one LINQ query. The `where` clause tells LINQ which items from the collection should be included in the results. But that clause doesn't just have to be a simple comparison. It can include any valid C# statement—like using the `values` dictionary to tell it to return only comics worth more than $500. And the `orderby` clause works the same way—we can tell LINQ to order the comics by their value.

```
List<Comic> comics = BuildCatalog();

Dictionary<int, int> values = GetPrices();
```

> The LINQ query pulls Comic objects out of the comics list, using the data in the values dictionary to decide which comics to select.

```
var mostExpensive =
```

> The first clause in the query is the from clause. This one tells LINQ to query the comics collection, and that the name comic will be used in the query to specify how to treat each individual piece of data in the collection.

```
    from comic in comics
    where values[comic.Issue] > 500
    orderby values[comic.Issue] descending
    select comic;
```

> You can choose any name you want when you use a from clause. We chose "comic".

> The where and orderby clauses can include ANY C# statement, so we can use the values dictionary to select only those comics worth more than $500 and we can sort the results so the most expensive ones come first.

> The name comic was defined in the from clause specifically so it could be used in the where and orderby clauses.

```
foreach (Comic comic in mostExpensive)

    Console.WriteLine("{0} is worth {1:c}",

                comic.Name, values[comic.Issue]);
```

> When you add "{1:c}" to the WriteLine output, that tells it to print the second parameter in the local currency format.

> The query returned its results into a collection called mostExpensive. The select clause determines what goes into the results—since it selected comic, the query returned Comic objects.

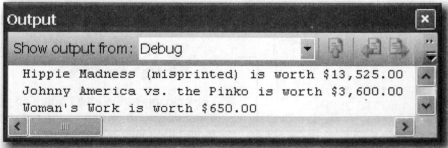

```
Output                                              [×]
Show output from: Debug          ▼  [ ] [ ] [ ]
    Hippie Madness (misprinted) is worth $13,525.00  ▲
    Johnny America vs. the Pinko is worth $3,600.00
    Woman's Work is worth $650.00                    ▼
    ◄      IIII                              ►
```

Don't worry if you've never used SQL—you don't need to know anything about it to work with LINQ. But if you're curious, check out "Head First SQL."

> I don't buy this. I know SQL already—isn't writing a LINQ query just like writing SQL?

LINQ may *look* like SQL, but it doesn't *work* like SQL.

If you've done a lot of work with SQL, it may be tempting to dismiss all this LINQ stuff as intuitive and obvious—and you wouldn't be alone, because a lot of developers make that mistake. It's true that LINQ uses the `select`, `from`, `where`, `ascending`, and `join` keywords, which are borrowed from SQL. But LINQ is very different from SQL, and if you try to think about LINQ the way you think about SQL you'll end up with code that **doesn't do what you expect**.

One big difference between the two is that SQL operates on *tables*, which are very different from *collections*. When you execute a SQL `select` against a table, you can be sure that the table is not going to be updated. SQL has all sorts of built-in data security that you can trust. And SQL queries are set operations, which means they don't examine the rows in the table in any predictable order. A collection, on the other hand, can store *anything*—values, structs, objects, anything—and collections have a specific order. (A table's rows aren't in any particular order until you make a SQL query that orders them; items inside a List, on the other hand, are in order.) And LINQ lets you perform any operation that's supported by whatever happens to be in the collection—it can even call methods on the objects in the collection. And LINQ loops through the collection, which means that it does its operations in a specific order. That may not seem all that important, but if you're used to dealing with SQL, it means your LINQ queries will surprise you if you expect them to act like SQL.

There are a lot of other differences between LINQ and SQL too, but you don't need to understand them in order to work with LINQ successfully. Just approach it with an open mind, and don't expect it to work the way SQL works.

LINQ is <u>versatile</u>

You can do a lot more than just pull a few items out of a collection. You can modify the items before you return them. And once you've generated a set of result collections, LINQ gives you a bunch of methods that work with them. Top to bottom, LINQ gives you the tools you need to manage your data.

⭐ **Modify every item returned from the query**

This code will add a string onto the end of each string in an array. It doesn't change the array itself—it **creates a new collection** of modified strings.

```
string[] sandwiches = { "ham and cheese", "salami with mayo",
                        "turkey and swiss", "chicken cutlet" };
var sandwichesOnRye =
    from sandwich in sandwiches
    select sandwich + " on rye";

foreach (var sandwich in sandwichesOnRye)
    Console.WriteLine(sandwich);
```

This adds the string " on rye" to every item in the results from the query.

Notice that all the items returned have " on rye" added to the end.

Output:

ham and cheese on rye
salami with mayo on rye
turkey and swiss on rye
chicken cutlet on rye

This change is made to the items in the results of your query... but not to the items in the original collection or database.

⭐ **Perform calculations on collections**

Remember, we said LINQ adds new methods to your collections (and database access objects)... and some of those are pretty handy on their own, without actual requiring a query:

```
List<int> listOfNumbers = new List<int>();
int length = random.Next(50, 150);
for (int i = 0; i < length; i++)
    listOfNumbers.Add(random.Next(100));

Console.WriteLine("There are {0} numbers",
                    listOfNumbers.Count());
Console.WriteLine("The smallest is {0}",
                    listOfNumbers.Min());
Console.WriteLine("The biggest is {0}",
                    listOfNumbers.Max());
Console.WriteLine("The sum is {0}",
                    listOfNumbers.Sum());
Console.WriteLine("The average is {0:F2}",
                    listOfNumbers.Average());
```

As long as you're using C# 3.0 (which is part of Visual Studio 2008), any collection you create has LINQ capabilities.

None of these methods are part of the .NET collections classes... they're all defined by LINQ.

These are all extension methods defined in the Enumerable class in the System.Linq namespace.

★ **Store all or part of your results in a new collection**
Sometimes you'll want to keep your results from a LINQ query around. You can use the `ToList()` command to do just that:

```
var under50sorted =
    from number in listOfNumbers
    where number < 50
    orderby number descending
    select number;

List<int> newList = under50sorted.ToList();
```

This time, we're sorting a list of numbers descending, from highest to lowest.

You can even take just a subset of the results, using the `Take()` method:

```
var firstFive = under50sorted.Take(6);

List<int> shortList = firstFive.ToList();
foreach (int n in shortList)
    Console.WriteLine(n);
```

ToList() converts a LINQ var into a list object, so you can keep results of a query around. There's also ToArray() and ToDictionary() methods, which do just what you'd expect.

Take() pulls out the supplied number of items, from the first of the results from a LINQ query. You can put these into another var, and then convert that into a list.

> **Watch it!**
>
> **LINQ queries aren't run until you access their results!**
>
> *It's called "lazy evaluation"—the LINQ query doesn't actually do any looping until a statement is executed that uses the results of the query. That's why ToList() is important: it tells LINQ to evaluate the query immediately.*

★ **Check out Microsoft's official "101 LINQ Samples" page**
There's way more that LINQ can do. Luckily, Microsoft gave you a great little reference to help you along.

`http://msdn2.microsoft.com/en-us/vcsharp/aa336746.aspx`

---

there are no Dumb Questions

Q: That's a lot of new keywords—from, where, orderby, select... it's like a whole different language. Why does it look so different from the rest of C#?

A: Because it serves a different purpose. Most of the C# syntax was built to do one small operation or calculation at a time. You can start a loop, or set a variable, or do a mathematical operation, or call a method... those are all single operations.

LINQ queries look different because a single LINQ query usually does a whole bunch of things at once. Let's take a closer look at a straightforward query:

```
var under10 =
    from number in numberArray
    where number < 10
    select number;
```

It looks really simple—not a lot of stuff there, right? But this is actually a pretty complex piece of code. Think about what's got to happen for the program to actually select all the numbers from `numberArray` that are less than 10. First, you need to loop through the entire array. Then, each number is compared to 10. Then those results need to be gathered together so your code can use them.

And that's why LINQ looks a little odd: because C# has to cram a whole lot of behavior into a very small space.

LINQ lets you write queries that do very complex things using very little code.

BULLET POINTS

- **from** is how you specify the collection that you're querying. It's always followed by the name of a variable, followed by **in** and the name of the collection (`from value in values`).

- **where** generally follows the `from` clause. That's where you use normal C# conditions to tell LINQ which items to pull out of the collection (`where value < 10`).

- **orderby** lets you order the results. It's followed by the criteria that you're using to sort them, and optionally **descending** to tell it to reverse the sort (`orderby value descending`).

- **select** is how you specify what goes into the results (`select value`).

- **Take** lets you pull the first items out of the results of a LINQ query (`results.Take(10)`). LINQ gives you other methods for each collection: `Min()`, `Max()`, `Sum()`, and `Average()`.

- You can `select` anything—you're not limited to selecting the name that you created in the `from` clause. Here's an example: if your LINQ query pulls a set of prices out of an array of `int` values and names them `value` in the `from` clause, you can return a collection of price strings like this: `select String.Format("{0:c}", value.`

This is just like the {0:x} you used in Chapter 9 when you built the hex dumper. There's also {0:d} and {0:D} for short and long dates, and {0:P} or {0:Pn} to print a percent (with n decimal places).

there are no Dumb Questions

Q: How does the `from` clause work?

A: It's a lot like the first line of a `foreach` loop. One thing that makes thinking about LINQ queries a little tricky is that you're not just doing one operation. Most C# statements just do one single thing.

A LINQ query does the same thing over and over again for each item in a collection. The `from` clause does two things: it tells LINQ which collection to use for the query, and it assigns a name to use for each member of the collection that's being queried.

The way the `from` clause creates a new name for each item in the collection is really similar to how a `foreach` loop does it. Here's the first line of a `foreach` loop:

```
foreach (int i in values)
```

That foreach loop temporarily creates a variable called `i`, which it assigns sequentially to each item in the `values` collection. Now look at a `from` clause in a LINQ query on the same collection:

```
from i in values
```

That clause does pretty much the same thing. It creates a temporary variable called `i` and assigns it sequentially to each item in the `values` collection. The `foreach` loop runs the same block of code for each item in the collection, while the LINQ query applies the same criteria in the `where` clause to each item in the collection to determine whether or not to include it in the results.

Q: How does LINQ decide what goes into the results?

A: That's what the `select` clause is for. Every LINQ query returns a collection, and every item in a collection is of the same type. It tells LINQ exactly what that collection should contain. When you're querying an array or list of a single type—like an array of `int`s or a `List<string>`—it's obvious what goes into the `select` clause. But what if you're selecting from a list of `Comic` objects? You could do what Jimmy did and select the whole class. But you could also change the last line of the query to `select comic.Name` to tell it to return a collection of `string`s. Or you could do `select comic.Issue` and have it return a collection of `int`s.

LINQ Magnets

Rearrange the magnets so they produce
the output at the bottom of the page.

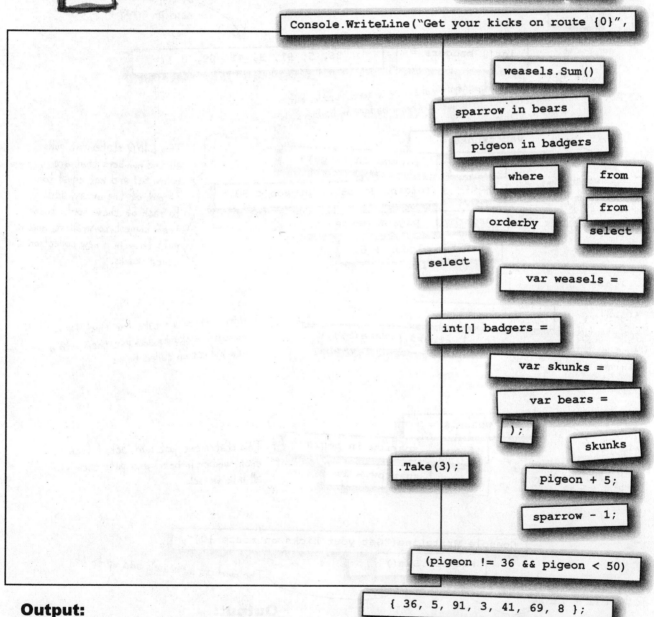

```
pigeon descending

Console.WriteLine("Get your kicks on route {0}",

weasels.Sum()

sparrow in bears

pigeon in badgers

where            from

                 from
orderby          select

select

var weasels =

int[] badgers =

var skunks =

var bears =

);

skunks

.Take(3);       pigeon + 5;

sparrow - 1;

(pigeon != 36 && pigeon < 50)

{ 36, 5, 91, 3, 41, 69, 8 };
```

Output:
Get your kicks on route 66

LINQ Magnets Solution

Rearrange the magnets so they produce the output at the bottom of the page.

LINQ starts with some sort of collection or array—in this case, an array of integers.

```
int[] badgers =          { 36, 5, 91, 3, 41, 69, 8 };
```

"from pigeon in badgers" makes for a good puzzle, but an unreadable LINQ query. "from badger in badgers" is more readable.

```
var skunks =
      from        pigeon in badgers
      where       (pigeon != 36 && pigeon < 50)
      orderby     pigeon descending
      select      pigeon + 5;
```

After this statement, skunks contains four numbers: 46, 13, 10 and 8.

This LINQ statement pulls all the numbers that are below 50 and not equal to 36 out of the array, adds 5 to each of them, sorts them from biggest to smallest, and puts them in a new collection called skunks.

```
var bears =
      skunks     .Take(3);
```

After this statement, bears contains three numbers: 46, 13 and 10.

Here's where we take the first three numbers in skunks and put them into a new collection called bears.

```
var weasels =
      from      sparrow in bears
      select    sparrow - 1;
```

After this statement, weasels contains four numbers: 45, 12, and 9.

This statement just subtracts 1 from each number in bears and puts them all into weasels.

```
Console.WriteLine("Get your kicks on route {0}",
      weasels.Sum() );
```

The numbers in weasels add up to 66.

45 + 12 + 9 = 66

Output:
Get your kicks on route 66

LINQ can combine your results into groups

You already know that you can use LINQ to build your results into groups, because that's what we did with the beehive simulator. Let's take a closer look at that query and see how it works.

①

The query starts out just like the other queries you've seen—by pulling individual bee objects out of the `world.Bees` collection, a `List<Bee>` object.

```
var beeGroups =

    from bee in world.Bees

    group bee by bee.CurrentState

    into beeGroup

    orderby beeGroup.Key

    select beeGroup;
```

②

The next line in the query has a new keyword: **group**. This tells the query to return **groups** of bees. What that means is that rather than returning one single collection, the query will return a **collection of collections**. `group bee by bee.CurrentState` tells LINQ to return one group for each unique `CurrentState` property that it finds in the bees that it selects. Finally, we need to give LINQ a name for the group. That's what the next line is for: `into beeGroup` says that the name "beeGroup" refers to the new groups.

③

Now that we've got groups, we can manipulate them. Since we're returning a collection of groups, we can use the `orderby` keyword to put the groups in order of the CurrentState enum values (Idle, FlyingToFlower, etc.): `orderby beeGroup.Key` tells the query to put the collection of groups in order, sorting them by the group key. Since we grouped the bees by their `CurrentState`, that's what being used as a key.

④

Now we just have to use the `select` keyword to indicate what's being returned by the query. Since we're returning groups, we select the group name: `select beeGroup;`

Since the bees were grouped by their state, we call that state the "key". A group's key is the criteria it was grouped by.

Note that this query returns groups of bees, not individual bees.

Combine Jimmy's values into groups

Jimmy buys a lot of cheap comic books, some midrange comic books, and a few expensive ones, and he wants to know what his options are before he decides what comics to buy. He's got those prices he got from Greg's List and put into a `Dictionary<int, int>` using his `GetPrices()` method—let's use LINQ to group them into three groups: one for cheap comics that cost under $100, one for midrange comics that cost between $100 and $1000, and expensive ones that cost over $1000. We'll create a `PriceRange` enum that we'll use as the key for the groups, and a method called EvaluatePrice() that'll evaluate a price and return a `PriceRange`.

❶ Every group needs a key—we'll use an enum for that

The group's key is the thing that all of its members have in common. The key can be anything: a string, a number, even an object reference. We'll be looking at the prices that Jimmy got from Greg's list. Each group that the query returns will be a collection of issue numbers, and the group's key will be a `PriceRange` enum. And the `EvaluatePrice()` method takes a price as a parameter and returns a `PriceRange`:

```
public enum PriceRange { cheap, midrange, expensive }

public PriceRange EvaluatePrice(int price) {
    if (price < 100) return PriceRange.cheap;
    else if (price < 1000) return PriceRange.midrange;
    else return PriceRange.expensive;
}
```

❷ Now we can group the comics by their price categories

The LINQ query returns a **collection of collections**. Each of the collections inside the results has a Key property, which matches the `PriceRange` that was returned by `EvaluatePrice()`. Look closely at the `group by` clause—we're pulling pairs out of the Dictionary, and using the name `pair` for each of them: `pair.Key` is the issue number, and `pair.Value` is the price from Greg's list. Adding `group pair.Key` tells LINQ to create groups of issue numbers, and then bundles all of those groups up based on the price category that's returned by `EvaluatePrice()`:

```
Dictionary<int, int> values = GetPrices();

var priceGroups =
    from pair in values
    group pair.Key by EvaluatePrice(pair.Value)
        into priceGroup
        orderby priceGroup.Key descending
        select priceGroup;

foreach (var group in priceGroups) {
    Console.Write("I found {0} {1} comics: issues ", group.Count(), group.Key);
    foreach (var price in group)
        Console.Write(price.ToString() + " ");
    Console.WriteLine();
}
```

The query figures out which group a particular price belongs to by sending its price to EvaluatePrice(). That returns a PriceRange enum, which it uses as the group's key.

Each of the groups is a collection, so we added an inner foreach loop to pull each of the prices out of the group.

```
Output                                              [×]
Show output from: Debug          [▼] [🔲] [🔲] [🔲]
  I found 2 expensive comics: issues 6 57
  I found 3 midrange comics: issues 19 36 68
  I found 3 cheap comics: issues 74 83 97
```

Pool Puzzle

Your **job** is to take snippets from the pool and place them into the blank lines in the program. You can use the same snippet more than once, and you won't need to use all the snippets. Your **goal** is to make the code produce this **output**:

↓

Horses enjoy eating carrots, but they love eating apples.

```
public class Line {
    public string[] Words;
    public int Value;
    public Line(string[] Words, int Value) {
        this.Words = Words; this.Value = Value;
    }  }
```

Hint: LINQ sorts strings in alphabetical order.

```
Line[] lines = {
  new Line( { "eating", "carrots,",
          "but", "enjoy", "Horses" } , 1),
  new Line( { "zebras?", "hay",
          "Cows", "bridge.", "bolted" } , 2),
  new Line( { "fork", "dogs!",
          "Engine", "and" }, 3 ) ,
  new Line( { "love", "they",
          "apples.", "eating" }, 2 ) ,
  new Line( { "whistled.", "Bump" }, 1 ) };
```

Note: each snippet from the pool can be used more once!

```
var _____ =
    from _____ in _____
        _____ line by line._____
    into wordGroups
    orderby _____._____
    select _____;

____ _____ = words._____(2);
foreach (var group in twoGroups)
{
    int i = 0;
    foreach (_____ inner in _____) {
        i++;
        if (i == _____.Key) {
            var poem =
                _____ word in _____._____
                    _____ word descending
                    _____ word + ____;
            foreach (var word in _____)
                Console.Write(word);
        }
    }
}
```

		from	Line[]			
	+	to	lines	talk		int
	-	select	new	word		string
	+=	inside	line	Take	Value	var
in	-=	outside	group	poem	Key	[]
by	""	orderby	groups	write	Words	[1]
Key	" "	into	wordGroups	length	words	[2]
Value		output	twoGroups		this	
					inner	

Pool Puzzle Solution

```
public class Line {
    public string[] Words;
    public int Value;
    public Line(string[] Words, int Value) {
        this.Words = Words; this.Value = Value;
    }
}

Line[] lines = {
    new Line( new { "eating", "carrots,", "but", "enjoy", "Horses" } , 1),
    new Line( new { "zebras?", "hay", "Cows", "bridge.", "bolted" } , 2),
    new Line( new { "fork", "dogs!", "Engine", "and" }, 3 ) ,
    new Line( new { "love", "they", "apples.", "eating" }, 2 ) ,
    new Line( new { "whistled.", "Bump" }, 1 )
};

var words =
    from line in lines
    group line by line.Value
    into wordGroups
    orderby wordGroups.Key
    select wordGroups;

var twoGroups = words.Take(2);

foreach (var group in twoGroups)
{
    int i = 0;
    foreach (var inner in group) {
        i++;
        if (i == group.Key) {
            var poem =
                from word in inner.Words
                orderby word descending
                select word + " ";
            foreach (var word in poem)
                Console.Write(word);
        }
    }
}
```

This first LINQ query divides the Line objects in the lines[] array into two groups, grouped by their Value, in ascending order of the Value key.

The first two groups are the lines with Values 1 and 2.

This loop does a LINQ query on the first Line object in the first group and the second Line object in the second group.

Did you figure out that the two phrases "Horses enjoy eating carrots, but" and "they love eating apples" are in descending alphabetical order?

Output: **Horses enjoy eating carrots, but they love eating apples.**

Use join to combine two collections into one query

Jimmy's got a whole collection of comics he's purchased, and he wants to compare them with the prices he found on Greg's List to see if the prices he's been getting are better or worse. He's been tracking his purchases using a `Purchase` class with two fields, `Issue` and `Price`. And he's got a `List<Purchase>` called `purchases` that's got all the comics he's bought. But now he needs to match up the purchases he's made with the prices he found on Greg's List. How's he going to do it?

LINQ to the rescue! Its `join` keyword lets you **combine data from two collections** into a single query. It does it by comparing items in the first collection their matching items in the second collection. (LINQ is smart enough to do this efficiently—it doesn't actually compare every pair of items unless it has to.) The end result is a final result that combines every pair that matches.

Jimmy's got his data in a collection of Purchase objects called **purchases**.

1 Start off your query with the usual `from` clause. But instead of following it up with the criteria it'll use to determine what goes into the results, you add:

> `join` *name* `in` *collection*

The `join` clause tells LINQ to loop through both collections to match up pairs of one member from each collection. It assigns *name* to the member it'll pull out of the joined collection in each iteration. You'll use that name in the where clause.

```
public class Purchase {
    public int Issue
                { get; set; };
    public int Price;
                { get; set; };
}
```

List<Comic> *from comic in comics*

Jimmy's joining his comics to **purchases**, *a list of comics he's bought.*

join purchase in purchases

List<Purchases>

You've already seen anonymous types. When you use an object initializer, you create an anonymous by typing a series of names and values inside curly brackets.

3 You'll continue the LINQ query with `where` and `orderby` clauses as usual. You could finish it with a normal `select` clause, but you usually want to return results that pulls some data from one collection and other data from the other. That's where you use **select new** to create a custom set of results using an **anonymous type**.

`on` `comic.Issue`
`equals` `purchase.Issue`

The select new is followed by curly brackets that contain the data to return in the results.

2 Next you'll add the **on** clause, which tells LINQ how to match the two collections together. You'll follow it with the name of the member of the first collection you're matching, followed by **equals** and the name of the member of the second collection to match it to.

`select new` `{ comic.Name,`
`comic.Issue, purchase.Price }`

results

LINQ Collection

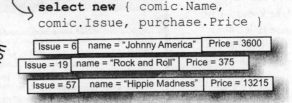

Issue = 6	name = "Johnny America"	Price = 3600
Issue = 19	name = "Rock and Roll"	Price = 375
Issue = 57	name = "Hippie Madness"	Price = 13215

Jimmy saved a bunch of dough

It looks like Jimmy drives a hard bargain. He created a list of
Purchase classes that contained his purchases, and compared them
with the prices he found on Greg's List.

1 **First Jimmy created his collection to join.**

Jimmy already had his first collection—he just used his `BuildCatalog()` method from before. So
all he had to do was write a `FindPurchases()` method to build his list of `Purchase` classes.

```
public sList<Purchase> FindPurchases() {
    List<Purchase> purchases = new List<Purchase>() {
        new Purchase() { Issue = 68, Price = 225 },
        new Purchase() { Issue = 19, Price = 375 },
        new Purchase() { Issue = 6, Price = 3600 },
        new Purchase() { Issue = 57, Price = 13215 },
        new Purchase() { Issue = 36, Price = 660 },
    };
    return purchases;
}
```

Jimmy paid $13,215 for issue #57.

2 **Now he could do the join!**

You've seen all the parts of this query already... now here they are, put together in one piece.

```
List<Comic> comics = BuildCatalog();
Dictionary<int, int> values = GetPrices();
List<Purchase> purchases = FindPurchases();

var results =
    from comic in comics
    join purchase in purchases
    on comic.Issue equals purchase.Issue
    orderby comic.Issue ascending
    select new { comic.Name, comic.Issue, purchase.Price };
int gregsListValue = 0;
int totalSpent = 0;
foreach (var result in results) {
    gregsListValue += values[result.Issue];
    totalSpent += result.Price;
    Console.WriteLine("Issue #{0} ({1}) bought for {2:c}",
            result.Issue, result.Name, result.Price);
}
Console.WriteLine("I spent {0:c} on comics worth {1:c}",
        totalSpent, gregsListValue);
```

When Jimmy used a join clause, LINQ compared every item in the comics collection with each item in purchases to see which ones have comic.Issue equal to purchase.Issue.

The select new clause creates a result set with Name and Issue from the comic member, and Price from the purchase member.

Jimmy's real happy that he knows LINQ, because it let him see just how hard a bargain he can drive!

```
Output                                                          ×
Show output from: Debug          ▼  🗗 🗗 🗗 🗗 🖼 🔁
    Issue #6 (Johnny America vs. the Pinko) bought for $3,600.00
    Issue #19 (Rock and Roll (limited edition)) bought for $375.00
    Issue #36 (Woman's Work) bought for $660.00
    Issue #57 (Hippie Madness (misprinted)) bought for $13,215.00
    Issue #68 (Revenge of the New Wave Freak (damaged)) bought for $225.00
I spent $18,075.00 on comics worth $18,525.00
```

Okay, so now I know Jimmy played with his comic books using LINQ queries to query his collections... but what about the Starbuzz promotion problem? I still don't see how LINQ works with databases.

Even though LINQ to SQL is very different under the hood, when you write your code it looks really similar to other LINQ queries.

LINQ uses the <u>same</u> syntax with databases as it does with collections.

You've already seen in Chapter 1 how easy .NET makes it to work with a database. The IDE gives you a really convenient way to connect with databases, add tables, and even link data in those tables to your forms.

Now, you can take that same database you already connected to and query it with LINQ. Not only that, LINQ lets you combine your data from your database with data from your objects seamlessly.

In fact, you can use the same exact query syntax... all you need is to get access to your database so you can run a LINQ query against it.

ContactDB database

List<StarbuzzData>

The Objectville Contact Database has the addresses.

The StarBuzz frequent customer data's here.

LINQ

results

LINQ Collection

We can use LINQ to compare and combine data from more than one source and create a collection of results.

Connect LINQ to a SQL database

LINQ operates on collections that implement the IEnumerable interface, right? So it should make sense that you access your SQL database using an object that implements IEnumerable. And C# makes it easy to add that object to your project.

— Do this

① **Add the Objectville Contact Database to a new project**
Back in Chapter 1, you created a database of contacts for the Objectville Paper Company and saved it in a file called ContactDB.mdf. Start a new Windows Application project, right-click on your project in the Solution Explorer, select "Add Existing Item" and add the database. Make sure you select "Data Files" from the "Objects of Type" filter list.

② **The IDE will pop up the Data Source Configuration Wizard**
Choose the People table by selecting its checkbox. Click Finish—the wizard will create a dataset called ContactDBDataSet and add it to your project automatically.

This is the same wizard that you used in Chapter 1 when you first created the database. It adds classes to your project that let you access the database directly.

Take a minute and flip back to Chapter 1 to see how you built it.

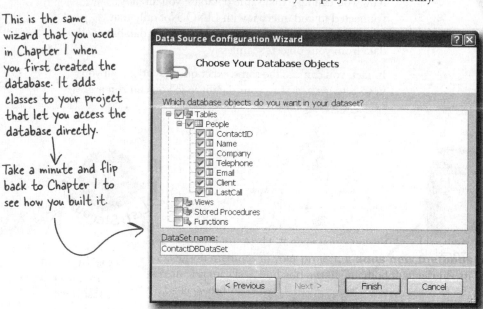

③ **Add the LINQ to SQL Classes to your project**
Right-click on the project in the Solution Explorer and choose "Add New Item". It'll display the familiar list of icons—choose the **LINQ to SQL Classes** and call it ContactDB.dbml.

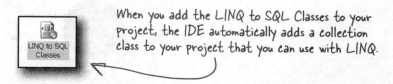

When you add the LINQ to SQL Classes to your project, the IDE automatically adds a collection class to your project that you can use with LINQ.

④ The IDE has a designer to build your SQL collection

As soon as you add the LINQ to SQL Classes to your project, the IDE pops up an empty window called the Object Relational Designer. Here's what it looks like:

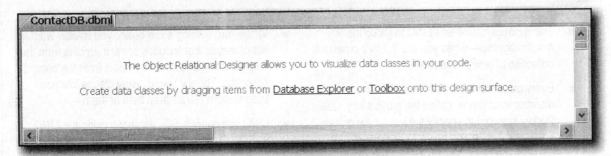

⑤ Drag the People table to the Object Relational Designer

Click on the <u>Database Explorer</u> link in the Object Relational Designer window—the IDE will pop up a Database Explorer window. Expand the Tables node, click on the People table icon, drag it into the Object Relational Designer window, and save the project.

The DataContext is a little too smart for its own good. It knows that it's got a People table, so it assumes that the table contains a bunch of rows, one for each "People"... so it has a member called Peoples to contain each individual People.

As soon as you save the project, the IDE automatically adds a class called a DataContext to your project—one of its properties is the collection you can query with LINQ, which is connected to the database.

⑥ You're all set to write LINQ queries that pull data out of the database

Add a button to the form—here's the code for it. Notice how we used the **select new** keyword to create custom results that only contain the Name and Company.

```
ContactDBDataContext context = new ContactDBDataContext();

var peopleData =
    from person in context.Peoples
    select new { person.Name, person.Company };

foreach (var person in peopleData)
    Console.WriteLine("{0} works at {1}", person.Name, person.Company);
```

Get some practice using **select new**. It'll pull just the values from the Name and Company columns from the database.

BULLET POINTS

- The **group** clause tells LINQ to group the results together—when you use it, LINQ creates a collection of group collections.

- Every group contains members that have one member in common, called the group's **key**. Use the **by** keyword to specify the key for the group. Each group collection has a **Key** member that contains the group's key.

- Use a **join** clause to tell LINQ to combine two collections into a single query. When you do, LINQ compares every member of the first collection with every member of the second collection, including the matching pairs in the results.

- Join queries use an **on ... equals** clause to tell LINQ how to match the pairs of items.

- When you're doing a join query, you usually want a set of results that includes some members from the first collection and other members from the second collection. The **select new** clause lets you build custom results from both of them.

- LINQ can query a SQL database using the **LINQ to SQL Classes**. Since LINQ only works with collections that implement IEnumerable, they provide a collection that lets you access the tables and queries as if they were a collection.

- The IDE's Object Relational Designer lets you choose the tables that you want to access via LINQ. When you specify the tables you want to access, it adds a DataContext class to your project. When it's instantiated, add its members to your LINQ queries to access the SQL tables.

there are no
Dumb Questions

Q: Can you rewind a minute and explain what var is again?

A: Yes, definitely. The var keyword solves a tricky problem that LINQ brings with it. Normally, when you call a method or execute a statement, it's absolutely clear exactly what types you're working with. If you've got a method that returns a string, for instance, then you can only store its results in a string variable or field.

But LINQ isn't quite so simple. When you build a LINQ statement, it usually returns a type that *isn't defined anywhere in your program*. Yes, you know that it's going to be a collection of some sort. But what kind of collection will it be? You don't know—because the objects that are contained in the collection depend entirely on what you put in your LINQ query.

Take this query, for example:
```
var mostExpensive =
    from comic in comics
    where values[comic.Issue] > 500
    select comic;
```

What if you changed the last line to this:
```
    select comic.Issue;
```

That's a perfectly valid LINQ query. Instead of returning a collection of Comic objects, it'll return a collection of values. And that presents a problem for C#—those are two different types, and we'd have to add extra statements to define those types. So instead, C# gives us the var keyword, which tells the compiler, "Okay, we know that this is a valid type, but we can't exactly tell you what it is right now. So why don't you just figure that out yourself and not bother us with it? Thanks so much."

there are no
Dumb Questions

Q: I don't quite get how join works.

A: Join works with any two collections. Let's say you've got a collection of football players called `players`—its items are objects that have a `Name` property, a `Position` property and a `Number` property. So we could pull out the players whose jerseys have a number bigger than 10 with this query:

```
var results =
  from player in players
  where player.Number > 10
  select player;
```

Let's say we wanted to figure out each player's shirt size, and we've got a `jerseys` collection whose items have a `Number` property and a `Size` property. A join would work really well for that:

```
var results =
  from player in players
  where player.Number > 10
  join shirt in jerseys
  on player.Number
  equals shirt.Number
  select shirt;
```

Q: Hold on, that query will just give me a bunch of shirts. What if I want to connect each player to his shirt size, and I don't care about his number at all?

A: That's what `select new` is for. It lets you construct an **anonymous type** that only has the data you want in it. And it lets you pick and choose from the various collections that you're joining together, too.

So you can select the player's name and the shirt's size, and nothing else:

```
var results =
  from player in players
  where player.Number > 10
  join shirt in jerseys
  on player.Number
  equals shirt.Number
  select new {
      player.Name,
      shirt.Size
};
```

The IDE is smart enough to figure out exactly what results you'll be creating with your query. If you create a loop to enumerate through the results, as soon as you type the variable name the IDE will pop up an IntelliSense list.

```
foreach (var r in results)
   r.
```

Notice how the list has Name and Size in it. If you added more items to the `select new` clause, they'd show up in the list too. That's because the query would create a different anonymous type with different members.

Q: But does that only work with joins?

A: No, you can use `select new` with any LINQ query where you want to build a results collection that only includes certain items in it.

Q: Do I always have to add those LINQ to SQL Classes if I want to use LINQ to query a SQL database? What are they?

A: Yes, you do have to create them. LINQ object that implements the `IEnumerable` interface. A SQL database doesn't normally implement that interface... or any interface, really, because it's not an object. So if you want LINQ to work with SQL—or any other source of data that you can query—then you need an object that interacts with it and implements the `IEnumerable` interface.

That's why the IDE provides the LINQ to SQL classes for you. When you add it to your project, it automatically does everything you need in order to connect LINQ to a SQL database: it lets you drag database objects into its Object Relational Designer, and when you do it automatically reads your database's tables and creates classes (like the People class) that LINQ can use to access them.

You can use "select new" to construct custom LINQ query results that include only the items that you want in your result collection.

Use a join query to connect Starbuzz and Objectville

Now you have all the tools that you need to combine the data from Starbuzz and Objectville Paper Company into one final result set.

— Do this

❶ Add the SQL data to your project

If you haven't already done it, create a new Windows application project and add the ContactDB SQL database to it. Then add the LINQ to SQL classes to the project, and write a simple test query just to make sure it's all working.

❷ Build the Starbuzz objects

Here's the list that contains the Starbuzz customer data. Add them to your project:

```
public class StarbuzzData { {
    public string Name { get; set; }
    public Drink FavoriteDrink { get; set; }
    public int MoneySpent { get; set; }
    public int Visits { get; set; }
}
public enum Drink {
    BoringCoffee, ChocoRockoLatte, TripleEspresso,
    ZestyLemonChai, DoubleCappuccino, HalfCafAmericano,
    ChocoMacchiato, BananaSplitInACup,
}
```

> *The Starbuzz data comes as a collection of StarbuzzData objects. It's got a lot of data—you won't need it all for the promotion, so you'll have to select only the data you need in the LINQ query.*

> *Starbuzz has plenty of great drinks, and each customer has his or her favorite.*

You'll also need a method to generate some sample data:

```
public List<StarbuzzData> GetStarbuzzData() {
    List<StarbuzzData> list = new List<StarbuzzData>() {
        new StarbuzzData() {
            Name = "Janet Venutian", FavoriteDrink = Drink.ChocoMacchiato,
            MoneySpent = 255, Visits = 50 },
        new StarbuzzData() {
            Name = "Liz Nelson", FavoriteDrink = Drink.DoubleCappuccino,
            MoneySpent = 150, Visits = 35 },
        new StarbuzzData() {
            Name = "Matt Franks", FavoriteDrink = Drink.ZestyLemonChai,
            MoneySpent = 75, Visits = 15 },
        new StarbuzzData() {
            Name = "Joe Ng", FavoriteDrink = Drink.BananaSplitInACup,
            MoneySpent = 60, Visits = 10 },
        new StarbuzzData() {
            Name = "Sarah Kalter", FavoriteDrink = Drink.BoringCoffee,
            MoneySpent = 110, Visits = 15 }
    };
    return list;
}
```

> *GetStarbuzzData() uses a collection initializer and object initializers to set up the Starbuzz objects.*

> *We built this method so that it has some names that also appear in the Objectville contact list. If you used different names, make sure you've got matching data here.*

3 **Now join the SQL database to the Starbuzz collection**

Add a button to the project that will execute the query and display the results in the console. Here's the code for the query:

```
List<StarbuzzData> starbuzzList = GetStarbuzzData();
ContactDBDataContext context = new ContactDBDataContext();

var results =
        from starbuzzCustomer in starbuzzList
        where starbuzzCustomer.MoneySpent > 90
        join person in dataContext.Peoples
        on starbuzzCustomer.Name equals person.Name
        select new { person.Name, person.Company,
                    starbuzzCustomer.FavoriteDrink };
```

We'll need to do a join to combine the Starbuzz data with the customer data in the People table.

Here's where the select new clause pulls the name and company from the database and the favorite drink from the Starbuzz data into one single result collection.

The Peoples member in the DataContext is a collection that gives you access to the People table in the database.

and it's easy enough to write to the console:

```
foreach (var row in results){
    Console.WriteLine("{0} at {1} likes {2}",
                row.Name, row.Company, row.FavoriteDrink);
}
```

Check your results—make sure it works the way you expect it to.

> Nice work... with this new promotion, I'll bet we'll get tons of repeat business. I'll definitely be calling you again.

Edit queries with LINQPad

There's a great learning tool for exploring and using LINQ. It's called LINQPad, and it's available for free from Joe Albahari (one of the tech reviewers who helped make sure "Head First C#" was reasonably error-free). You can download it here:

http://www.albahari.com/linqpad.html

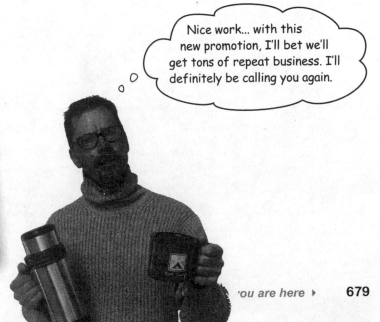

C# Lab

Invaders

This lab gives you a spec that describes a program for you to build, using the knowledge you've gained over the last few chapters.

This project is bigger than the ones you've seen so far. So read the whole thing before you get started, and give yourself a little time. And don't worry if you get stuck—there's nothing new in here, so you can move on in the book and come back to the lab later.

We've filled in a few design details for you, and we've made sure you've got all the pieces you need... and nothing else.

It's up to you to finish the job. You can download an executable for this lab from the website... but we won't give you the code for the answer.

The grandfather of video games

In this lab you'll pay homage to one of the most popular, revered and replicated icons in video game history, a game that needs no further introduction. **It's time to build Invaders.**

As the player destroys the invaders, the score goes up. It's displayed in the upper left-hand corner.

The invaders attack in waves of 30. The first wave moves slowly and fires a few shots at a time. The next wave moves faster, and fires more shots more frequently. If all 30 invaders in a wave are destroyed, the next wave attacks.

The player starts out with three ships. The first ship is in play, and the other two are kept in reserve. His spare ships are shown in the upper right-hand corner.

The player moves the ship left and right, and fires shots at the invaders. If a shot hits an invader, the invader is destroyed and the player's score goes up.

The invaders return fire. If one of the shots hits the ship, the player loses a life. Once all lives are gone, or if the invaders reach the bottom of the screen, the game ends and a big "GAME OVER" is displayed in the middle of the screen.

The multicolored stars in the background twinkle on and off, but don't affect gameplay at all.

Your mission: defend the planet against wave after wave of invaders

The invaders attack in waves, where each wave is a tight formation of 30 individual invaders. As the player destroys invaders, the score goes up. The bottom invaders are shaped like stars and worth 10 points. The spaceships are worth 20, the saucers are worth 30, the bugs are worth 40, and the satellites are worth 50. The player starts with three lives. If he loses all three lives or the invaders reach the bottom of the screen, the game's over.

There are five different types of invaders, but they all behave the same way. They start at the top of the screen and move left until they reach the edge. Then they drop down and start moving right. When they reach the right-hand boundary, they drop down and move left again. If the invaders reach the bottom of the screen, the game's over.

 10

 20

 30

 40

 50

The first wave of invaders can fire two shots at once—the invaders will hold their fire if there are more than two shots on the screen. The next wave fires three, the next fires four, etc.

The spacebar shoots. But there can only be two shots on the screen at once. As soon as a shot hits something or disappears, another shot can be fired.

If a shot hits an invader, both disappear. Otherwise, the shot disappears when it gets to the top of the screen.

The game should keep track of all keypresses. So pressing right and spacebar would cause the ship to move to the right and fire (if two shots aren't already on the screen).

Fire!

`SPACE`

`← LEFT`

The left arrow moves the ship towards the left-hand edge of the screen.

`RIGHT →`

The right arrow key moves the ship to the right.

The architecture of Invaders

Invaders needs to keep track of a wave of 30 invaders (including their locations, type, and score value), the player's ship, shots that the player and invaders fire at each other, and stars in the background. As you did in the Quest lab, you'll need a Game object to keep up with all this, and coordinate between the form and the game objects.

Here's an overview of what you'll need to create:

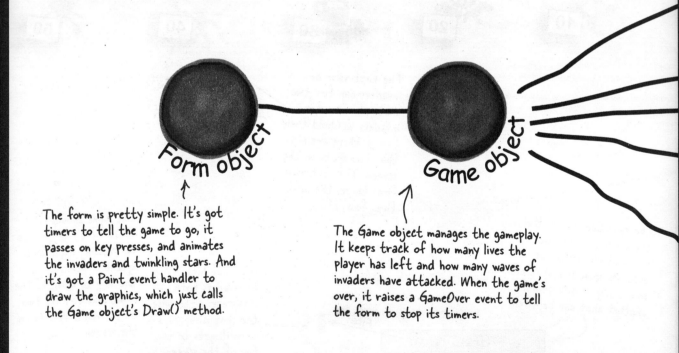

The form is pretty simple. It's got timers to tell the game to go, it passes on key presses, and animates the invaders and twinkling stars. And it's got a Paint event handler to draw the graphics, which just calls the Game object's Draw() method.

The Game object manages the gameplay. It keeps track of how many lives the player has left and how many waves of invaders have attacked. When the game's over, it raises a GameOver event to tell the form to stop its timers.

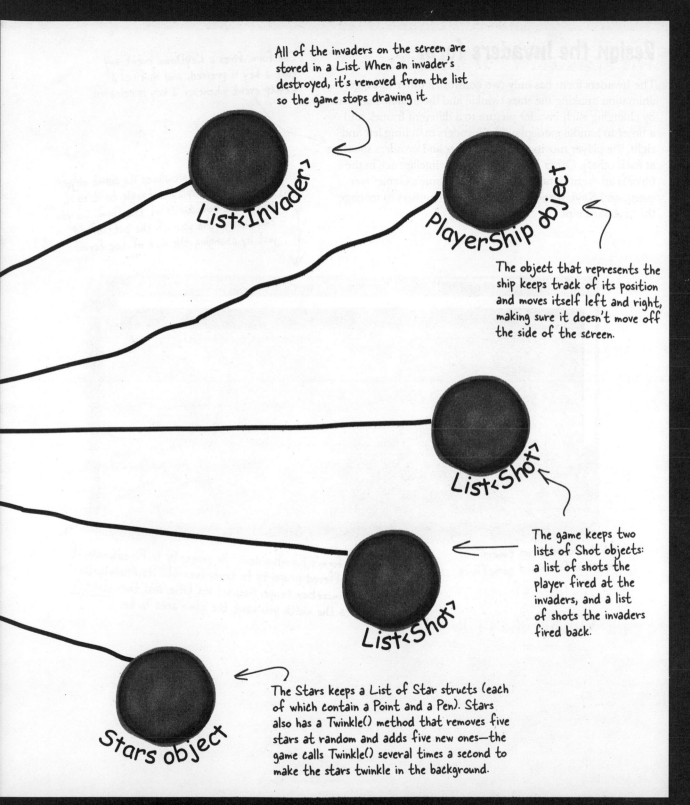

All of the invaders on the screen are stored in a List. When an invader's destroyed, it's removed from the list so the game stops drawing it.

List<Invader>

PlayerShip object

The object that represents the ship keeps track of its position and moves itself left and right, making sure it doesn't move off the side of the screen.

List<Shot>

The game keeps two lists of Shot objects: a list of shots the player fired at the invaders, and a list of shots the invaders fired back.

List<Shot>

The Stars keeps a List of Star structs (each of which contain a Point and a Pen). Stars also has a Twinkle() method that removes five stars at random and adds five new ones—the game calls Twinkle() several times a second to make the stars twinkle in the background.

Stars object

Design the Invaders form

The Invaders form has only two controls: a timer to trigger animation (making the stars twinkle and the invaders animate by changing each invader picture to a different frame), and a timer to handle gameplay (the invaders marching left and right, the player moving, and the player and invaders shooting at each other). Other than that, the only intelligence in the form is an event handler to handle the game's GameOver event, and KeyUp and KeyDown event handlers to manage the keyboard input.

The form fires a KeyDown event any time a key is pressed, and it fires a KeyUp event whenever a key is released.

When the form initializes its Game object, it passes its DisplayRectangle to it so it knows the boundaries of the form. So you can change the size of the battlefield just by changing the size of the form.

You should add two timers: animationTimer and gameTimer.

Set the form's FormBorderStyle property to FixedSingle, its DoubleBuffered property to true, turn off its MinimizeBox and MaximizeBox properties, set its title, and then <u>stretch</u> it out to the width you want the game area to be.

The animation timer handles the eye candy

The stars in the game's background and the invader animation don't affect gameplay, and they continue when the game is paused or stopped. So we need a separate timer for those.

Add code for the animation timer's tick event

Your code should have a counter that cycles from 0 to 3 and then back down to 0. That counter is used to update each of the four-cell invader animations (creating a smooth animation). Your handler should also call the Game object's Twinkle() method, which will cause the stars to twinkle. Finally, it needs to call the form's Refresh() method to repaint the screen.

Try a timer interval of 33ms, which will give you about 30 frames per second. Make sure you set the game timer to a shorter interval, though. The ship should move and gameplay should occur more quickly than the stars twinkle.

Animation occurs even when gameplay doesn't. That means that the stars twinkle and the invaders animate even if the game is over, paused, or hasn't been started.

Adjust the timer for smooth animation

With a 33ms interval for animation, set the game timer to 10ms. That way, the main gameplay will occur more quickly than the animation (which is really just background eye candy). At the same time, the Go() method in Game (fired by the game timer, which we'll talk about in a little bit) can take a lot of CPU cycles. If the CPU is busy handling gameplay, the animation timer will just wait until the CPU gets to it, and then fire (and animate the stars and invaders).

Alternately, you can just set both timers to an interval of 5ms, and the game will run and animate about as fast as your system can handle (although on fast machines, animation could get annoyingly quick).

If the animation timer is set to 33ms, but the Game object's Go() method takes longer than that to run, then animation will occur once Go() completes.

An invader starts with cell 0, goes to cell 1, then 2, then 3...

We tried things out on a slow machine, and found that setting the animation interval to 100ms and the gameplay timer interval to 50ms gave us a frame rate of about 10 frames per second, which was definitely playable. Try starting there and reducing each interval until you're happy.

...and then reverses, going back to 2, then 1, then 0.

Respond to keyboard input

Before we can code the game timer, we need to write event handlers for the KeyDown and KeyUp events. KeyDown is triggered when a key is pressed, and KeyUp when a key is released. For most keys, we can simply take action, by firing a shot or quitting the game.

So if the player's holding down the left arrow and space bar at the same time, the list will contain Keys.Left and Keys.Space.

For some keys, like the right or left arrow, we want to store those in a list that our game timer can then use to move the player's ship. So we'll also need a list of pressed keys in the form object:

We need a list of keys so we can track which keys have been pressed. Our game timer will need that list for movement in just a bit.

```
List<Keys> keysPressed = new List<Keys>();

private void Form1_KeyDown(object sender, KeyEventArgs e) {
    if (e.KeyCode == Keys.Q)
        Application.Exit();

    if (gameOver)
        if (e.KeyCode == Keys.S) {
            // code to reset the game and restart the timers
            return;
        }

    if (e.KeyCode == Keys.Space)
        game.FireShot();
    if (keysPressed.Contains(e.KeyCode))
        keysPressed.Remove(e.KeyCode);
    keysPressed.Add(e.KeyCode);
}

private void Form1_KeyUp(object sender, KeyEventArgs e) {
    if (keysPressed.Contains(e.KeyCode))
        keysPressed.Remove(e.KeyCode);
}
```

The 'Q' key quits the game.

If the game has ended, reset the game and start over.

But we only want this to work if the game's over. Pressing S shouldn't restart a game that's already in progress.

The Keys enum defines all the keys you might want to check key codes against.

You'll need to fill in this code.

The spacebar fires a shot.

By removing the key and then re-adding it, it makes the key the last (most current) item in the list.

The key that's pressed gets added to our key list, which we'll use in a second.

We want the most current key pressed to be at the very top of the list, so that if the player mashes a few keys at the same time, the game responds to the one that hit most recently. Then, when he lets up one key, the game responds to the next one in the list.

When a key is released, we remove it from our list of pressed keys.

The game timer handles movement and gameplay

The main job of the form's game timer is to call Go() in the
Game class. But it also has to respond to any keys pressed, so it
has to check the keysPressed list to find any keys caught by the
KeyDown and KeyUp events:

gameTimer

*Make sure your naming matches up with
what you call your handler methods.*

```
private void gameTimer_Tick(object sender, EventArgs e) {
    if (keysPressed.Count() >= 1) {
        switch (keysPressed[0]) {
            case Keys.Left:
                game.MovePlayer(Direction.Left);
                break;
            case Keys.Right:
                game.MovePlayer(Direction.Right);
                break;
        }
    }
    game.Go();
}
```

*keysPressed is your List<Keys>
object managed by the KeyDown
and KeyUp event handlers. The
key at index zero will always be
the most recent key pressed.*

*The KeyUp and KeyDown
events use the Keys enum
to specify a key. We'll use
Keys.Left and Keys.Right
to move the ship.*

*We only need to deal with
movement. Other keys, like
spacebar, and 'Q' for quit, are
handled in the KeyDown()
method you just wrote.*

*Finally, we call Go() on the Game
object to let game play continue.*

*Shots move up and down, the player moves left
and right, and the invaders move left, right,
and down. You'll need this enum to keep all
those directions straight.*

```
public enum Direction {
    Left,
    Right,
    Up,
    Down,
}
```

One more form detail: the GameOver event

Add a private bool field called gameOver to the form that's true only
when the game is over. Then add an event handler for the Game object's
GameOver event that stops the game timer (but not the animation timer, so
the stars still twinkle and the invaders still animate), sets gameOver to true,
and calls the form's Refresh() method.

*Here's an example of adding
another event to a form
without using the IDE. This is
all manual coding.*

When you write the form's Paint event handler, have it check gameOver.
If it's true, have it write GAME OVER in big yellow letters in the middle of
the screen. Then have it write "Press S to start a new game or Q to quit" in
the lower right-hand corner.

*The game over event and its
delegate live in the Game class,
which you'll see in just a minute.*

The form's game timer tells the game to Go()

In addition to handling movement left and right, the main job of the game timer is to call the Game object's Go() method. That's where all of the gameplay is managed. The Game object keeps track of the state of the game, and its Go() method advances the game by one frame. That involves:

1 **Checking to see if the player died**, using its Alive property. When the player dies, the game shows a little animation of the ship collapsing (using DrawImage() to squish the ship down to nothing). The animation is done by the PlayerShip class, so Go() just needs to check to see if it's dead. If it is, it returns—that way, it keeps the invaders from moving or shooting while the player gets a small break (and watches his ship get crushed).

2 **Moving each of the shots.** Shots fired by the invaders move down, and shots fired by the player move up. Game keeps two List<Shot> objects, one for the invaders' shots and one for the player's. Any shot that's moved off the screen needs to be removed from the list.

3 **Moving each of the invaders.** Game calls each Invader object's Move() method, and tells the invaders which way to move. Game also keeps up with where the invaders are in case they need to move down a row or switch directions. Then, Game checks to see if it's time for the invaders to return fire, and if so, it adds new Shot objects to the List<>.

4 **Checking for hits**. If a player's shot hit any invaders, Game removes the invaders from the appropriate List<>. Then Game checks to see if any of the invader shots have collided with the player's ship, and if so, it kills the player by setting its Alive property to false. If the player's out of lives, then Game raises the GameOver event to tell the form that the game's over. The form's GameOver event handler stops its game timer, so Go() isn't called again.

Here's where that GameOver event from the last page comes into play.

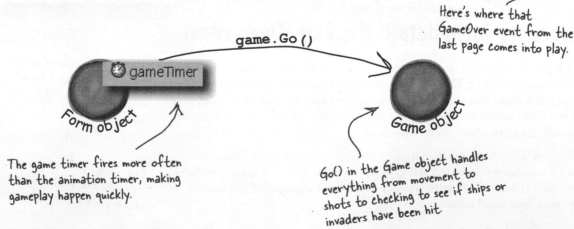

game.Go()

gameTimer

Form object

Game object

The game timer fires more often than the animation timer, making gameplay happen quickly.

Go() in the Game object handles everything from movement to shots to checking to see if ships or invaders have been hit.

Taking control of graphics

In earlier labs, the form used controls for the graphics. But now that you know how to use `Graphics` and double-buffering, the `Game` object should handle a lot of the drawing.

So the form should have a `Paint` event handler (which you'll put your double-buffering inside). But you'll delegate the rest of the drawing to the `Game` object every time that event fires.

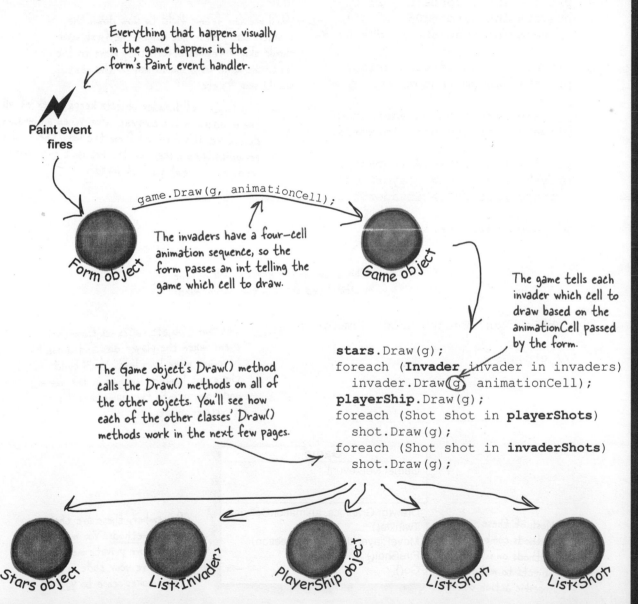

Everything that happens visually in the game happens in the form's Paint event handler.

Paint event fires

Form object

game.Draw(g, animationCell);

The invaders have a four-cell animation sequence, so the form passes an int telling the game which cell to draw.

Game object

The game tells each invader which cell to draw based on the animationCell passed by the form.

```
stars.Draw(g);
foreach (Invader invader in invaders)
    invader.Draw(g, animationCell);
playerShip.Draw(g);
foreach (Shot shot in playerShots)
    shot.Draw(g);
foreach (Shot shot in invaderShots)
    shot.Draw(g);
```

The Game object's Draw() method calls the Draw() methods on all of the other objects. You'll see how each of the other classes' Draw() methods work in the next few pages.

Stars object

List<Invader>

PlayerShip object

List<Shot>

List<Shot>

Building the Game class

The Game class is the controller for the Invaders game. Here's a start on what this class should look like, although there's lots of work still for you to do.

```
public class Game {
    private int score = 0;
    private int livesLeft = 2;
    private int wave = 0;
    private int framesSkipped = 0;

    private Rectangle boundaries;
    private Random random;

    private Direction invaderDirection;
    private List<Invader> invaders;

    private PlayerShip playerShip;
    private List<Shot> playerShots;
    private List<Shot> invaderShots;

    private Stars stars;


    public event EventHandler GameOver;

    // etc...
}
```

The score, livesLeft, and wave fields keep track of some basic information about the state of the game.

You'll use the frame field to slow down the invaders early on in the game—the first wave should skip 6 frames before they move to the left, the next wave should skip 5, the next should skip 4, etc.

This List<> of Invader objects keeps track of all of the invaders in the current wave. When an invader is destroyed, it's removed from the list. The game checks periodically to make sure the list isn't empty—if it is, it sends in the next wave of invaders.

This Stars object keeps track of the multicolored stars in the background.

The Game object raises its GameOver event when the player dies and doesn't have any more lives left. You'll build the event handler method in the form, and hook it into the Game object's GameOver event.

Game
GameOver: event
Draw(g: Graphics, animationCell: int) Twinkle() MovePlayer(direction: Direction) FireShot() Go()

Most of these methods combine methods on other objects to make a specific action occur.

Remember, these are the <u>public methods</u>. You may need a lot more private methods to structure your code in a way that makes sense to <u>you</u>.

The Game class methods

The Game class has five public methods that get triggered
by different events happening in the form.

1 **The Draw() method draws the game on a graphics object**

The Draw() method takes two parameters: a Graphics object and an integer that contains
the animation cell (a number from 0 to 3). First, it should draw a black rectangle that fills up
the whole form (using the display rectangle stored in boundaries, received from the form).
Then the method should draw the stars, the invaders, then the player's ship, and then the
shots. Finally, it should draw the score in the upper left-hand corner, the player's ships in the
upper right-hand corner, and a big "GAME OVER" in yellow letters if gameOver is true.

2 **The Twinkle() method twinkles the stars**

The form's animation timer event handler needs to be able to twinkle the stars, so the Game
object needs a one-line method to call stars.Twinkle().

↖ *— We'll write code for the Stars
object in a few more pages.*

3 **The MovePlayer() method moves the player**

The form's keyboard timer event handler needs to move the player's ship, so the Game object
also needs a two-line method that takes a Direction enum as a parameter, checks whether
or not the player's dead, and calls playerShip.Move() to affect that movement.

4 **The FireShot() method makes the player fire a shot at the invaders**

The FireShot() method checks to see if there are fewer than two player shots on screen. If
there are, the method should add a new shot to the playerShots list at the right location.

5 **The Go() method makes the game go**

The form's animation timer calls the Game object's Go() method anywhere between 10
and 30 times a second (depending on the computer's CPU speed). The Go() method does
everything the game needs to do to advance itself by a frame:

★ The game checks if the player's dead using its **Alive** property. If he's still alive, the
game isn't over yet—if it were, the form would have stopped the animation timer with
its Stop() method. So the Go() method won't do anything else until the ship's alive
again—it'll just return.

★ Every shot needs to be updated. The game needs to loop through both List<Shot>
objects, calling each shot's Move() method. If any shot's Move() returns false, that
means the shot went off the edge of the screen—so it gets deleted from the list.

★ The game then moves each invader, and allows them to return fire.

★ Finally, it checks for collisions: first for any shot that overlaps an invader (and removing
both from their List<>s), and then to see if the player's been shot. We'll add a
Rectangle property called Area to the Invader and PlayerShip classes—so we
can use the Contains() method to see if the ships' area overlaps with a shot.

Filling out the Game class

The problem with class diagrams is that they usually leave out any non-public properties and methods. So even after you've got the methods from page 693 done, you've still got a lot of work to do. Here are some things to think about:

The constructor sets everything up

The Game object needs to create all of the other objects—the Invader objects, the PlayerShip object, the List objects to hold the shots, and the Stars object. The form passes in an initialized Random object and its own DisplayRectangle struct (so the Game can **figure out the boundaries of the battlefield**, which it uses to determine when shots are out of range and when the invaders reached the edge and need to drop and reverse direction). Then, your code should create everything else in the game world.

We'll talk about most of these individual objects over the next several pages of this lab.

Build a NextWave() method

A simple method to create the next wave of invaders will come in handy. It should assign a new List of Invader objects to the invaders field, add the 30 invaders in 6 columns so that they're in their starting positions, increase the wave field by 1, and set the invaderDirection field to start them moving towards the right-hand side of the screen. You'll also change the framesSkipped field.

Here's an example of a private method that will really help out your Game class organization.

A few other ideas for private methods

Here are a few of the private method ideas you might play with, and see if these would also help the design of your Game class:

- ✓ A method to see if the player's been hit (CheckForPlayerCollisions())
- ✓ A method to see if any invaders have been hit (CheckForInvaderCollisions())
- ✓ A method to move all the invaders (MoveInvaders())
- ✓ A method allowing invaders to return fire (ReturnFire())

BRAIN POWER

It's possible to show protected and private properties and methods on a class diagram, but you'll rarely see that put into practice. Why do you think that is?

LINQ makes collision detection much easier

You've got collections of invaders and shots, and you need to search through those collections to find certain invaders and shots. Anytime you hear collections and searching in the same sentence, you should think LINQ. Here's what you need to do:

This seems really complex when you first read it, but each LINQ query is just a couple of lines of code. Here's a hint: don't overcomplicate it!

① Figure out if the invaders' formation has reached the edge of the battlefield

The invaders need to change direction if any one invader is within 100 pixels of the edge of the battlefield. When the invaders are marching to the right, once they reach the right-hand side of the form the game needs to tell them to drop down and start marching to the left. And when the invaders are marching to the left, the game needs to check if they've reached the left edge. To make this happen, add a private `MoveInvaders()` method that gets called by `Go()`. The first thing it should do is check and update the private `framesSkipped` field, and `return` if this frame should be skipped (depending on the level). Then it should check which direction the invaders are moving. If the invaders are moving to the right, `MoveInvaders()` should use LINQ to search the `invaderCollection` list for any invader whose location's X value is within 100 pixels of the right-hand boundary. If it finds any, then it should tell the invaders to march downwards and then set `invaderDirection` equal to `Direction.Left`; if not, it can tell each invader to march to the right. On the other hand, if the invaders are moving to the left, then it should do the opposite, using another LINQ query to see if the invaders are within 100 pixels of the left-hand boundary, marching them down and changing direction if they are.

② Determine which invaders can return fire

Add a private method called `ReturnFire()` that gets called by `Go()`. First, it should `return` if the invaders' shot list already has `wave + 1` shots. It should also `return` if `random.Next(10) < 10 - wave`. (That makes the invaders fire at random, and not all the time.) If it gets past both tests, it can use LINQ to group the invaders by their `Location.X` and sort them `descending`. Once it's got those groups, it can choose a group at random, and use its `First()` method to find the invader at the bottom of the column. All right, now you've got the shooter—you can add a shot to the invader's shot list just below the middle of the invader (use the invader's `Area` to set the shot's location).

When any invader reaches the edge, the formation turns around.

Only the invaders at the bottom of the formation fire shots at the player.

If any invader reaches the bottom of the screen, the game's over.

③ Check for invader and player collisions

You'll want to create a method to check for collisions. There are three collisions to check for, and the `Rectangle` struct's `Contains()` method will come in really handy—just pass it any `Point`, and it'll return `true` if that point is inside the rectangle.

★ Use LINQ to find any dead invaders by looping through the shots in the player's shot list and selecting any invader where `invader.Area` contains the shot's location. Remove the invader and the shot.

★ Add a query to figure out if any invaders reached the bottom of the screen—if so, end the game.

★ You don't need LINQ to look for shots that collided with the player, just a loop and the player's `Area` property. (Remember, **you can't modify a collection inside a foreach loop**. If you do, you'll get an InvalidOperationException with a message that the collection was modified.)

Crafting the Invader class

The Invader class keeps track of a single invader. So when the Game
object creates a new wave of invaders, it adds 30 instances of Invader to
a List<Invader> object. Every time its Go() method is called, it calls
each invader's Move() method to tell it to move. And every time its Draw()
method is called, it calls each invader object's Draw() method. So you'll
need to build out the Move() and Draw() methods. And you'll want to add
a private method called InvaderImage() too—it'll come in really handy
when you're drawing the invader. Make sure you call it inside the Draw()
method to keep the image field up to date:

```
public class Invader {
   private const int HorizontalInterval = 10;
   private const int VerticalInterval = 40;
   public enum Type {
      Bug,
      Saucer,
      Satellite,
      Spaceship,
      Star,
   }

   private Bitmap image;

   public Point Location { get; private set; }

   public Type InvaderType { get; private set; }

   public Rectangle Area { get {
      return new Rectangle(location, image.Size); }
   }

   public int Score { get; private set; }

   public Invader(Type invaderType, Point location, int score) {
      this.InvaderType = invaderType;
      this.Location = location;
      this.Score = score;
      image = InvaderImage(0);
   }

   // Additional methods will go here
}
```

The HorizontalInterval constant determines how many pixels an invader moves every time it marches left or right. VerticalInterval is the number of pixels it drops down when the formation reaches the edge of the battlefield.

The invader uses the Type enum to figure out what kind of enemy ship it is.

Check out what we did with the Area property. Since we know the invader's location and we know its size (from its image field), we can add a get accessor that calculates a Rectangle for the area it covers... which means you can use the Rectangle's Contains() method inside a LINQ query to detect any shots that collided with an invader.

Invader

Location: Point
InvaderType: Type
Area: Rectangle
Score: int

Draw(g: Graphics, animationCell: int)
Move(direction: Direction)

Build the Invaders' methods

The three core methods for `Invader` are `Move()`, `Draw()`, and `InvaderImage()`. Let's look at each in turn:

There are five types of invaders, and each of them has four different animation cell pictures.

Move the invader ships

First, you need a method to move the invader ships. The `Game` object should send in a direction, using the `Direction` enum, and then the ship should move. Remember, the `Game` object handles figuring out if an invader needs to move down or change direction, so your `Invader` class doesn't have to worry about that.

```
public void Move(Direction direction) {
    // This method needs to move the ship in the
    //    specified direction
}
```

Draw the ship - and the right animation cell

Each `Invader` knows how to draw itself. Given a `Graphics` object to draw to, and the animation cell to use, the invader can display itself onto the game board using the `Graphics` object the `Game` gives it.

```
public void Draw(Graphics g, int animationCell) {
    // This method needs to draw the image of
    //    the ship, using the correct animation cell
}
```

Get the right Invader image

You're going to need to grab the right image based on the animation cell a lot, so you may want to pull that code into its own method. Build an `InvaderImage()` method that returns a specific `Bitmap` given an animation cell.

```
private Bitmap InvaderImage(int animationCell) {
    // This is mostly a convenience method, and
    //    returns the right bitmap for the specified cell
}
```

Each invader knows its type. So if you give its InvaderImage() method a number for its animation cell, it can return a Bitmap that's got the right graphic in it.

The player's ship can move and die

The PlayerShip class keeps track of the player's ship. It's similar to the Invaders class, but even simpler.

The Location and Area properties are exactly like the ones in the Invader class.

When the ship's hit with a shot, the game sets the ship's Alive property to false. The game then keeps the invaders from moving until the ship resets its Alive property back to true.

PlayerShip

Location: Point
Area: Rectangle
Alive: bool

Draw(g: Graphics)
Move(direction: Direction)

The Draw() method just draws the player's ship in the right location—unless the player died, in which case it draws an animation of the ship getting crushed by the shot.

The Move() method takes one parameter, a Direction enum, and moves the player in that direction.

PlayerShip needs to take in a Rectangle with the game's boundaries in its constructor, and make sure the ship doesn't get moved out of the game's boundaries in Move().

Animate the player ship when it's hit

The Draw() method should take a Graphics object as a parameter. Then it checks its Alive property. If it's alive, it draws itself using its Location property. If it's dead, then instead of drawing the regular bitmap on the graphics, the PlayerShip object uses its private deadShipHeight field to animate the player ship slowly getting crushed by the shot. After three seconds of being dead, it should flip its Alive property back to true.

Waiting three seconds is easy—just use the Alive property's set accessor to set a private DateTime field to DateTime.Now. The first thing the ship's Go() method does is use a TimeSpan to check if three seconds have elapsed. If three seconds haven't elapsed, continue doing the crushing ship animation. As soon as three seconds have elapsed, set Alive back to true so the game knows it should continue gameplay. (You used a similar trick in the beehive simulator.)

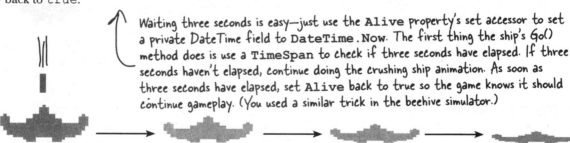

```
public void Draw(Graphics g) {
    if (!Alive) {

        Reset the deadShipHeight field and draw the ship.

    } else {

        Check the deadShipHeight field. If it's greater than zero, decrease it by 1
        and use DrawImage() to draw the ship a little flatter.

    }

}
```

"Shots fired!"

Game has two lists of `Shot` objects: one for the player's shots, moving up the screen, and one for enemy shots, moving down the screen. `Shot` only needs a few things to work: a `Point` location, a method to draw the shot, and a method to move. Here's the class diagram:

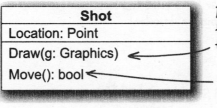

Shot
Location: Point
Draw(g: Graphics)
Move(): bool

Draw() handles drawing the little rectangle for this shot. Game will call this every time the screen needs to be updated.

Move() moves the shot up or down, and keeps up with whether the shot is within the game's boundaries.

Here's a start on the `Shot` class:

```
public class Shot {
   private const int moveInterval = 20;
   private const int width = 5;
   private const int height = 15;

   public Point Location { get; private set; }

   private Direction direction;
   private Rectangle boundaries;

   public Shot(Point location, Direction direction,
              Rectangle boundaries) {
     this.Location = location;
     this.direction = direction;
     this.boundaries = boundaries;
   }

   // Your code goes here
}
```

You can adjust these to make the game easier or harder... smaller shots are easier to dodge, faster shots are harder to avoid.

The shot updates its own location in the Move() method, so location can be a read-only automatic property.

Direction is the enum with Up and Down defined.

The game passes the form's display rectangle into the constructor's boundaries parameter so the shot can tell when it's off of the screen.

Your job is to make sure `Draw()` takes in a `Graphics` object and draws the shot as a yellow rectangle. Then, `Move()` should move the shot up or down, and return true if the shot is still within the game boundaries.

Twinkle, twinkle... it's up to you

The last class you'll need is the Stars class. There are 300 stars, and this class keeps up with all of them, causing 5 to display and 5 to disappear every time `Twinkle()` is called.

First, though, you'll need a `struct` for each star:

```
private struct Star {
  public Point point;
  public Pen pen;

  public Star(Point point, Pen pen) {
    this.point = point;
    this.pen = pen;
  }
}
```

Each star has a point (its location) and a pen (for its color).

All Star does is hold this data... no behavior.

> Here's another hint: start out the project with just a form, a Game class and Stars class. See if you can get it to draw a black sky with twinkling stars. That'll give you a solid foundation to add the other classes and methods.

The Stars class should keep a `List<Star>` for storing 300 of these `Star` structs. You'll need to build a constructor for `Stars` that populates that list. The constructor will get a `Rectangle` with the display boundaries, and a `Random` instance for use in creating the random Points to place each star in a random location.

Here's the class diagram for `Stars`, with the other methods you'll need:

You can define the Star struct inside Stars.cs, as only Stars needs to use that struct.

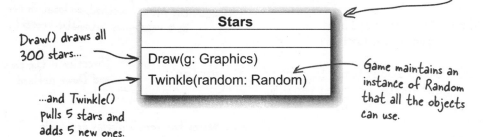

Stars
Draw(g: Graphics)
Twinkle(random: Random)

Draw() draws all 300 stars...

...and Twinkle() pulls 5 stars and adds 5 new ones.

Game maintains an instance of Random that all the objects can use.

`Draw()` should draw all the stars in the list, and `Twinkle()` should remove five random stars and add five new stars in their place.

You might also want to create a `RandomPen()` method so you can get a random color for the stars every time you create a new star easily. It should return one of the five colors stars come in, by generating a number between 0 and 4, and selecting the matching `Pen` object.

And yet there's more to do...

Think the game's looking pretty good? You can take it to the
next level with a few more additions:

Add animated explosions

Make each invader explode after it's hit, then briefly display a number to
tell the player how many points the invader was worth.

Add a mothership

Once in a while, a mothership worth 250 points can travel across the top
of the battlefield. If the player hits it, they get a bonus.

Add shields

Add floating shields the player can hide behind. You can add simple
shields the enemies and player can't shoot through. Then, if you really
want your game to shine, add breakable shields that the player and
invaders can blast holes through after a certain number of hits.

Try making the shields last for fewer hits at higher levels of the game.

Add divebombers

Create a special type of enemy that divebombs the player. A divebombing
enemy should break formation, take off towards the enemy, fly down
around the bottom of the screen, and then resume its position.

Add more weapons

Start an arms race! Smart bombs, lasers, guided missiles... there are all
sorts of weapons that both the player and the invaders can use to attack
each other. See if you can add three new weapons to the game.

Add more graphics

You can go to **www.headfirstlabs.com/books/hfcsharp/** to find more
graphics files for simple shields, a mothership, and more. We provided
blocky, pixelated graphics to give it that stylized '80s look. Can you come
up with your own graphics to give the game a new style?

A good class design should let you change out graphics with minimal code changes.

**This is your chance to show off! Did you come up with a cool new
version of the game? Join the Head First C# forum and claim your
bragging rights: www.headfirstlabs.com/books/hfcsharp/**

The top 5 things we wanted to include in this book

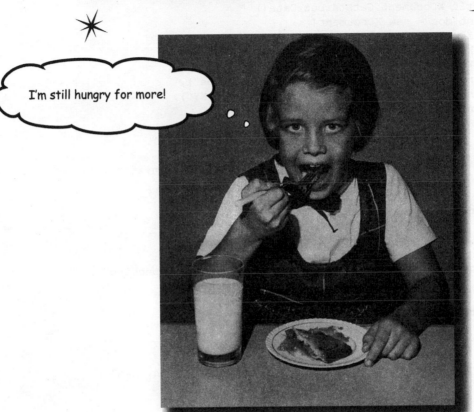

I'm still hungry for more!

The fun's just beginning!

We've shown you a lot of great tools to build some really **powerful software** with C#. But there's no way that we could include **every single tool, technology, or technique** in this book—there just aren't enough pages. We had to make some *really tough choices* about what to include and what to leave out. Here are some of the topics that didn't make the cut. But even though we couldn't get to them, we still think that they're **important and useful**, and we wanted to give you a small head start with them.

#1 LINQ to XML

XML—or **E**xtensible **M**arkup **L**anguage—is a format for files and data streams that represents complex data as text. The .NET framework gives you some really powerful tools for creating, loading and saving XML files. And once you've got your hands on XML data, you can use LINQ to query it. Add add "`using System.Xml.Linq;`" to the top of a file and enter this method—it generates an XML document to store Starbuzz customer loyalty data.

```
private static XDocument GetStarbuzzData() {
    XDocument doc = new XDocument(
        new XDeclaration("1.0", "utf-8", "yes"),
        new XComment("Starbuzz Customer Loyalty Data"),
        new XElement("starbuzzData",
            new XAttribute("storeName", "Park Slope"),
            new XAttribute("location", "Brooklyn, NY"),
            new XElement("person",
                new XElement("personalInfo",
                    new XElement("name", "Janet Venutian"),
                    new XElement("zip", 11215)),
                new XElement("favoriteDrink", "Choco Macchiato"),
                new XElement("moneySpent", 255),
                new XElement("visits", 50)),
            new XElement("person",
                new XElement("personalInfo",
                    new XElement("name", "Liz Nelson"),
                    new XElement("zip", 11238)),
                new XElement("favoriteDrink", "Double Cappuccino"),
                new XElement("moneySpent", 150),
                new XElement("visits", 35)),
            new XElement("person",
                new XElement("personalInfo",
                    new XElement("name", "Matt Franks"),
                    new XElement("zip", 11217)),
                new XElement("favoriteDrink", "Zesty Lemon Chai"),
                new XElement("moneySpent", 75),
                new XElement("visits", 15)),
            new XElement("person",
                new XElement("personalInfo",
                    new XElement("name", "Joe Ng"),
                    new XElement("zip", 11217)),
                new XElement("favoriteDrink", "Banana Split in a Cup"),
                new XElement("moneySpent", 60),
                new XElement("visits", 10)),
            new XElement("person",
                new XElement("personalInfo",
                    new XElement("name", "Sarah Kalter"),
                    new XElement("zip", 11215)),
                new XElement("favoriteDrink", "Boring Coffee"),
                new XElement("moneySpent", 110),
                new XElement("visits", 15))));
    return doc;
}
```

Save and load XML files

You can write an XDocument object to the console or save it to a file, and you can load an XML file into it:

```
XDocument doc = GetStarbuzzData();
Console.WriteLine(doc.ToString());
doc.Save("starbuzzData.xml");
XDocument anotherDoc = XDocument.Load("starbuzzData.xml");
```

The XDocument object's Load() and Save() methods read and write XML files. And its ToString() method renders everything inside it as one big XML document.

Query your data

Here's a simple LINQ query that queries the Starbuzz data using its XDocument:

```
var data = from item in doc.Descendants("person")
    select new { drink = item.Element("favoriteDrink").Value,
        moneySpent = item.Element("moneySpent").Value,
        zipCode = item.Element("personalInfo").Element("zip").Value };
foreach (var p in data)
    Console.WriteLine(p.ToString());
```

The Descendants() method returns a reference to an object that you can plug right into LINQ.

You already know that LINQ lets you call methods and use them as part of the query, and that works really well with the Element() method.

And you can do more complex queries too:

```
var zipcodeGroups = from item in doc.Descendants("person")
    group item.Element("favoriteDrink").Value
    by item.Element("personalInfo").Element("zip").Value
        into zipcodeGroup
        select zipcodeGroup;
foreach (var group in zipcodeGroups)
    Console.WriteLine("{0} favorite drinks in {1}",
                    group.Distinct().Count(), group.Key);
```

Element() returns an XElement object, and you can use its properties to check specific values in your XML document.

Read data from an RSS feed

You can do some pretty powerful things with LINQ to XML. Here's a simple query to **read articles from our blog**:

```
XDocument ourBlog = XDocument.Load("http://www.stellman-greene.com/feed");
Console.WriteLine(ourBlog.Element("rss").Element("channel").Element("title").Value);
var posts = from post in ourBlog.Descendants("item")
    select new { Title = post.Element("title").Value,
        Date = post.Element("pubDate").Value};
foreach (var post in posts)
    Console.WriteLine(post.ToString());
```

The XDocument.Load() method has several overloaded constructors. This one pulls XML data from a URL.

Stick a button on a form, make sure you've got "using System.Xml.Linq;" at the top, type this query into its event handler, and check out what it prints to the console.

We used the URL of our blog, Building Better Software. http://www.stellman-greene.com/

#2 Refactoring

Refactoring means changing the way your code is structured without changing its behavior. Whenever you write a complex method, you should take a few minutes to step back and figure out how you can change it so that you make it easier to understand. Luckily, the IDE has some very useful refactoring tools built in. There are all sorts of refactorings you can do—here are some we use often.

Extract a method

When we were writing the control-based renderer for Chapter 13, we originally included this foreach loop:

```
foreach (Bee bee in world.Bees) {
    beeControl = GetBeeControl(bee);
    if (bee.InsideHive) {
        if (fieldForm.Controls.Contains(beeControl)) {
            fieldForm.Controls.Remove(beeControl);
            beeControl.Size = new Size(40, 40);
            hiveForm.Controls.Add(beeControl);
            beeControl.BringToFront();
        } else if (hiveForm.Controls.Contains(beeControl)) {
            hiveForm.Controls.Remove(beeControl);
            beeControl.Size = new Size(20, 20);
            fieldForm.Controls.Add(beeControl);
            beeControl.BringToFront();
        }
        beeControl.Location = bee.Location;
    }
}
```

These four lines move a BeeControl from the Field form to the Hive form.

And these four lines move a BeeControl from the Hive form to the Field form.

One of our tech reviewers, Joe Albahari, pointed out that this was a little hard to read. He suggested that we **extract those two four-line blocks into methods**. So we selected the first block, right-clicked on it, and selected "Refactor >> Extract Method..."—this window popped up:

We typed in a name for the new method. We decided to call it MoveBeeFromFieldToHive() because that pretty much describes what the code does.

The IDE examined the code that we selected and figured out that it uses a BeeControl variable called beeControl, so it added it as a parameter to the method.

Then we did the same thing for the other four-line block, extracting it into a method that we named MoveBeeFromHiveToField(). Here's how that foreach loop ended up—it's a lot easier to read:

```
foreach (Bee bee in world.Bees) {
    beeControl = GetBeeControl(bee);
    if (bee.InsideHive) {
        if (fieldForm.Controls.Contains(beeControl))
            MoveBeeFromFieldToHive(beeControl);
    } else if (hiveForm.Controls.Contains(beeControl))
        MoveBeeFromHiveToField(beeControl, bee);
    beeControl.Location = bee.Location;
}
```

Rename a variable

Back in Chapter 3, we explained how choosing intuitive names for your classes, methods, fields, and variables makes your code a lot easier to understand. The IDE can really help you out when it comes to naming things in your code. Just right-click on any class, variable, field, property, namespace, constant—pretty much anything that you can name—and choose "Refactor >> Rename". We did it with "beeControl" in the code from the simulator. Here's what popped up:

This window lets you choose a new name for the item. If we renamed this, say, "Bobbo", then the IDE would go through the code and change every single occurrence of it to "Bobbo".

The IDE does a really thorough job of renaming. If you rename a class, it'll change every statement that instantiates it or uses it. You can click on any occurrence of the name, anywhere in the code, and the IDE will make the change everywhere in your program.

Consolidate a conditional expression

Here's a neat way to use the "Extract Method" feature. Open up any program, add a button, and add this code to its event handler:

```
private void button1_Click(object sender, EventArgs e) {
    int value = 5;
    string text = "Hi there";
    if (value == 36 || text.Contains("there"))
        MessageBox.Show("Pow!");
}
```

Select everything inside the if statement: `value == 36 || text.Contains("there")`. Then right-click on it and select "Refactor >> Extract Method...". Here's what pops up:

Every conditional expression evaluates to a bool, so the IDE will create a method that returns a bool and replace the conditional test with a call to that method.

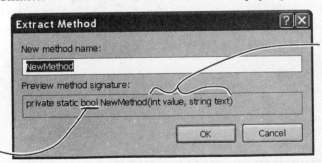

The expression uses two variables called value and text, so the IDE added parameters to the method using those names.

Not only will this make the code easier to read, but now you've got a new method that you can reuse elsewhere!

#3 Some of our favorite Toolbox components

This was a book about learning C#, not learning the ins and outs of the components that ship with .NET. Still, we've got our favorites, and we thought we'd share a few of them with you.

BackgroundWorker is one of those non-visual components (like Timer) that you can drag onto your form that does something really neat—it lets you easily build multithreaded applications.

Just drag one on your form and double-click on it (or, if you want, instantiate it—but don't forget to dispose it!). Then add an event handler to do the work that you want to run in the background.

🖻 backgroundWorker1

When you call its RunWorkerAsync() method, it fires off the DoWork() method—but the catch is that it runs it in **another thread**. That means it does its work in parallel with the other stuff your program's doing.

Your process can report its progress back to you by calling the BackgroundWorker's ReportProgress() method—that causes it to raise its ProgressChanged event.

We set up this "Happiness" counter in the "Feelings" category, and fed it data using PerformanceCounter.

FileSystemWatcher pretty much does what it sounds like it does—it watches your filesystem to see if something's changed.

You set its Filter property to the type of file it should look for (like *.txt), set the Path property to the directory it needs to watch, and you can tell it to look in subdirectories with its IncludeSubdirectories property.

fileSystemWatcher1

Once you've set it up, it watches the directory for any new or changed files. As soon as a file's added, changed, or deleted, it raises its Changed event. It's also got Created, Deleted, and Renamed events to do more specific tracking.

When the FileSystemWatcher raises an event, it passes information about the file that was changed (or added, or deleted, etc.) using a FileSystemEventArgs object.

When you're writing a program that runs continuously, it's really useful to monitor it. And Windows ships with a nifty tool called Performance Monitor (perfmon.exe) that lets you monitor processes.

The PerformanceCounter component lets you make information about your program available to the Windows performance monitoring system. Use Increment() and Decrement() or set its RawValue property. As soon as you do, you can see the data in the Performance Monitor.

performanceCounter1

Windows keeps its performance counters in categories, so you'll need to create a category—there are methods in System.Diagnostics that let you do that. Then just hook up your PerformanceCounter to the category you created, and start sending diagnostic info to your heart's delight!

#4 Console Applications

Most C# books start with console applications. We thought that was boring. It's a lot more satisfying to build programs that look like, well…that look like anything at all. And that's what a console program isn't. But sometimes you do need to write a command-line application. Luckily, it's pretty straightforward. Here's how:

 Create a Console Application project

Any project can be a console application. Go to a project, select "Properties" from the Project menu, and change the "Output type" to "Console Application". But it's easier to create one from scratch.

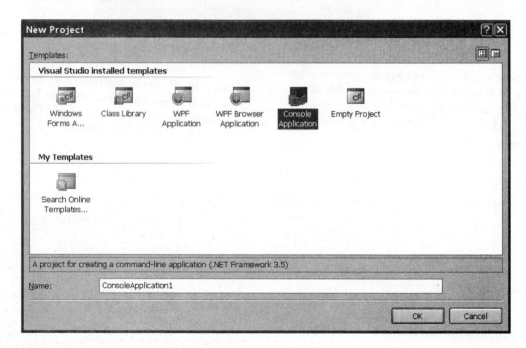

The IDE only adds one file—Program.cs

And it's got an empty entry point... and that's it.

```
class Program
{
    static void Main(string[] args)
    {

    }
}
```

Here's a little project for you: Take the hex dumper you built in Chapter 9 and turn it into a console applicaiton. Have it read a filename that you pass it on the command-line and print it out as a hex dump. Have it take data from standard input (using the Console. ReadLine() and dump that data out as a hex dump. Then look up the Unix command "od" and see if you can reproduce it in C#.

3 ## Use the args parameter for command-line arguments

Your entry point takes one parameter, a string array called `args` that contains the command-line arguments. You already know how to use the Console.WriteLine() method—there are some other useful console methods, including ReadLine() and ReadKey().

```
class Program {
    static void Main(string[] args) {
        Console.WriteLine("I got {0} arguments", args.Length);
        for (int i = 1; i <= args.Length; i++)
            Console.WriteLine("Argument #{0} is {1}", i, args[i - 1]);
        Console.Write("Enter some text: ");
        string input = Console.ReadLine();
        Console.WriteLine("You entered: {0}", input);
        Console.WriteLine("Press any key to end...");
        Console.ReadKey();
    }
}
```

4 ## Debug your program in a console window

When you debug your program, the IDE pops up a console window. The ReadLine() and ReadKey() methods get their input from that window—just type into it. And instead of writing to the Output window, a console application writes to this console window instead. You can set the command-line arguments in the "Debug" page of the Project Properties window.

#5 Windows Presentation Framework

Windows Presentation Framework, or WPF, is Microsoft's next-generation platform for building visual applications. It's pretty amazing—it has XML-based layout, scalable controls, a totally new system for controls, 2-D and 3-D graphics and animation, text flow and document formatting, and there's even a cross-platform web browser plugin that uses it.

Unfortunately, while WPF is a really cool and highly capable technology, it's not a particularly good tool for teaching C#. And that was our goal—getting C# concepts into your brain as quickly and easily as possible.

Take a second and create a new WPF application Just create a new project using the IDE, but don't create a new Windows Forms Application project. Instead, **select WPF Application**. You'll immediately notice a difference in the IDE:

The biggest difference you'll notice is that the form designer looks nothing like the one you're used to. We'll take a closer look at it in a minute.

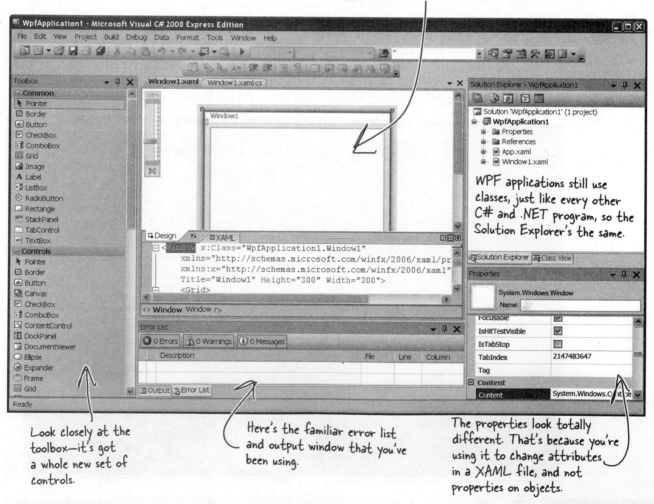

WPF applications still use classes, just like every other C# and .NET program, so the Solution Explorer's the same.

Look closely at the toolbox—it's got a whole new set of controls.

Here's the familiar error list and output window that you've been using.

The properties look totally different. That's because you're using it to change attributes in a XAML file, and not properties on objects.

Drag a button out of the toolbox and onto the form. If this were a Windows Forms application, the IDE would add code to Form1.Designer.cs to add a control to the Form1 object. But WPF is different—it uses an XML-based language called XAML to define how the user interface is laid out.

Drag this slider up and down to zoom in and out. When you zoom in really close, your user interface still looks good—it doesn't get pixelated.

XAML stands for "Extensible Application Markup Language," and it's the XML-based language that WPF applications use to determine where all of the controls go and other UI elements go.

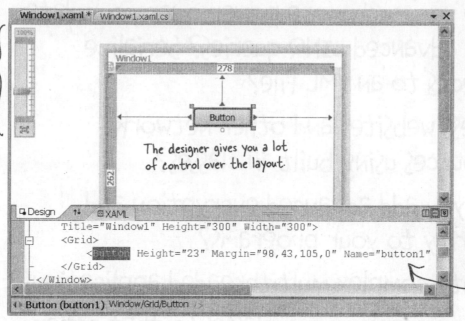

The designer gives you a lot of control over the layout.

The IDE has a really powerful XML editor that's optimized for working with XAML.

Go to the XML editor and add a second button by typing the **bold** line below into the XAML editor. You'll notice how the IDE's IntelliSense does a good job of helping you enter all the XML tags.

```
<Grid>
    <Button Height="23" Margin="98,43,105,0" Name="button1"
                VerticalAlignment="Top" Click="button1_Click">Button</Button>
    <Button Height="23" Margin="5,5,100,20" Name="button2"
                VerticalAlignment="Top" Click="button2_Click">Another button</Button>
</Grid>
```

When you get to the "**Click="button2_Click"**" part of the line, don't type in the name of the event handler. Instead, use the IntelliSense window that pops up to tell the IDE to add a new event handler. As soon as you finish the line, you'll see a new button appear in the designer. Switch over to the Window1.xaml.cs tab, and you'll find a a new button2_Click method there.

That's all the WPF and XAML that we can include here. But now that you've got the tools to start learning about WPF, we definitely recommend that you take a look at *Programming WPF* by Chris Sells and Ian Griffiths. It's available from the O'Reilly website: **http://www.oreilly.com/**.

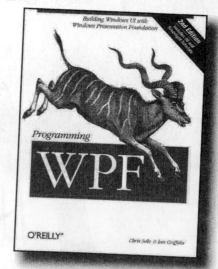

Did you know that C# and the .NET Framework can...

* ★ Give you much more power over your data with advanced LINQ queries? Serialize objects to an XML file?

* ★ Access websites and other network resources using built-in classes?

* ★ Let you add advanced encryption and security to your programs?

* ★ Create complex multithreaded applications?

* ★ Let you deploy your classes so that other people can use them?

* ★ Use regular expressions to do advanced text searching?

I had no idea! Where can I learn more?

There's a great book that explains it all!

It's called *C# 3.0 in a Nutshell* by Joseph Albahari and Ben Albahari, and it's a thorough guide to everything that C# has to offer. You'll learn about advanced C# language features, you'll see all of the essential .NET Framework classes and tools, and you'll **learn more** about what's really going on under the hood of C#.

Check it out at **http://www.oreilly.com/**.

3rd Edition
Covers LINQ and
.NET 3.5 CLR and Core Classes

C# 3.0
IN A NUTSHELL
A Desktop Quick Reference

O'REILLY®

*Joseph Albahari
& Ben Albahari*

Joseph Albahari
helped us out a
whole lot by giving
this book a really
thorough tech review.
Thanks so much for
all your help, Joe!

Index

Symbols

!= operator 68

&& operator 68, 77

*= operator 64, 136

* operator 64

+= operator 64

+ operator 64

    casting 129

-= operator 136

- operator 64

// (slashes) 66

/ operator 64

< operator 68

== operator 67, 68

= operator 64, 67

> operator 68

@ in front of filenames 389, 401

\n 15, 66, 401

\t 401

|| operator 68

A

abstract classes 278–285

    Fireside Chat 284–285

    usefulness 279–280

abstraction as principle of OOP 288

abstract keyword 281

abstract methods 278, 281

access modifiers 273–274

    internal 273

    private 273

protected 273

protected versus private or public 276

public 273

scope 274

sealed 273

Adventure Game program (see labs, #2 The Quest)

Albahari, Joe 706

allocate, defined 405

allocated resources 405

Anatomy of a program 52–53

    .NET Framework 52

    classes 52, 53

    methods 52, 53

    namespaces 52

    parameters 53

    statements 53

    using lines 52

Anatomy of a query 660

AND operator 68

animal inheritance program 216–222

animation 566–567

    building control 573

    double buffering 608–613

AppendAllText( ) method 400

Appliance project 266–270

    Appliance class 266

    downcasting 268

        interfaces 269

    upcasting 267

        interfaces 269

application design (see design)

applications

    compiling 47

    console 710–711

    debugging 47

applications (*continued*)
 deploying 37, 38
 running 36
 running in IDE 36

architecture 531

args parameter 711

arrays 148–149, 262
 deck of cards 315–316
 finding length 149
 versus Lists 318–320, 325

assemblies 273

attributes 421

B

BackColor property 51

BackgroundWorker 708

backing field 193, 198

Baseball Simulator project 484–501
 callbacks 507–509
 Fan class 494–497
 Pitcher class 494–497
 subscription and public events 505

base classes 214, 217
 colon (:) 222
 constructors 233
 extending 221
 subclasses accessing with base keyword 232
 upcasting 267
 using subclasses instead 227

base keyword 232, 275

Beehive Simulator project 239–249, 252–265
 adding new form 544
 AnimateBees( ) method 613
 animating with controls 566–567
  building control 573–575
  images 574–575
  timer 575
 Bee class 524–525
  Go( ) method 533–535, 542–543
 BeeControl 574–579

 animating bees on form 580–581
 creating button to add to form 576
 creating from UserControl 578
 disposing 577
 implementation 579
 ResizeCells method 591
BeeState enum 525–527
Bitmap class 593
building form 241
building Worker and Queen classes 241
class hierarchy with Worker and Queen classes 253
collection of bees 555
Color.Transparent 589
creating Bee class 246
DateTime class 548
Dictionary objects 569
double buffering 609–613
drawing picture on form 596–597
encapsulation 537
extending through inheritance 245–249
fixing transparency problems 601
Flower class 520–522
for loops 537
forms
 adding hive and field 582
 clearing out all controls 583
 FieldForm 586–587
 FormBorderStyle property 582
 HiveForm 586–587
 Location property 582
 Reset button 587
Graphics object 592
Hive class 529–530
 adding methods 532–533
 exceptions 539
 updates 540–541
honey production 246
interfaces 254–263
 inheritance 263
 references 260–261
making Queen class inherit from Bee class 247
making Worker class inherit from Bee class 247
NectarHarvested variable 523
number of bees 533
object model 518

OutOfHoneyException 468

overview of what's to be added 519

Paint event handler 602

performance issues 589–591

Point object 539

printing 616–619

    code for the Print button 619

    event handler for the Document's PrintPage
      event 618

    PrintTableRow( ) method 618

read-only automatic properties 523

RemoveAllControls( ) method 583

removing dead flowers and retired bees 537

Renderer 568–569

Renderer class 583–585

    DrawBees( ) 584

    DrawFlowers( ) 584

    GetBeeControl( ) 585

    MoveBeeFromFieldToHive( ) 585

    MoveBeeFromHiveToField( ) 585

    RemoveRetiredBeesAndDeadFlowers( ) 585

    ResizeImage method 591

resizing images 592–593

Show( ) method 587

timers 546

    adding to program 548

    disposing 577

    events and delegates 547

    Render( ) method 583

ToolStrip control, adding Open, Save, and Print 559

updating form to instantiate bees 247

using World to get statistics 545

World class 534–535

    code 536

behavior 12

Behind the Scenes

    how forms and controls repaint themselves 605

    LINQ using extension methods 657

    The stack vs. the heap: more on memory 641

    Unicode 424

    visual components 576

binary and decimal, converting between 125

binary files 424

    comparing 429

    hex dump 431

    working with 431

    writing 427

BinaryFormatter 420

    Deserialize( ) method 420, 423

    Serializable attribute 423

    SerializationException 454

BinaryReader 428

BinaryWriter 427

Birthday Party project 206–214

    BirthdayParty.CalculateCost( ) 213

    BirthdayParty class 207

    CakeWriting method 212

    CalculateCost( ) method 212

    inheriting from Party class 234–238

Bitmap class 593

blank space 66

boilerplate code 44

bool type 63, 64, 124, 126

bound 32

boxed objects and structs 642, 644

boxed struct 645

breakpoints 450

    knowing where to put 452

BringToFront( ) method 581

Brush object 606

Build menu 47

Build Solution 47

built-in features 55

Bullet Points

    delegates 509

    event handlers 509

    exception handling 471

    LINQ query statements 664

    Lists 322

Bullet Points (*continued*)
reference variables 154
statements 73
try/catch blocks 471
types 154
buttons 44
adding code to interact with objects 113
adding to form 51, 112
BackColor property 51
Name property 51
Size property 51
Text property 51
byte arrays 401
moving text around in 426
byte order mark 434
byte type 124, 126

C

C#
what you can do with 714
what you get with Visual Studio and 2
why you should learn 2
C# 3.0
automatic properties 195
object initializers 115
Calculator program 474–475
temporary solution 475
callbacks 507
versus events 510
call stack 453
camelCase 201
Candy Control System 102–108
capitalization 201
Captain Amazing 622–626, 635, 636, 645, 651
casting 128–130
+ operator 129
automatic 130
wrapping numbers 129

catch blocks 455, 457
followed by (Exception) 460
following in debugger 458–459
multiple 466
with no specified exceptions 462
chaining 491, 499
Character Map 424, 425
char type 125, 126
checkbox 75
class diagrams 90, 104, 106
moving up, not down 231
private fields and types 240
classes 52, 53, 73
abstract (see abstract classes)
adding 56
collection 317
concrete 278
copying 90
creating example 111
curly braces 66
declaration 54
defining 66
designing intuitive classes 116
finding out if class implements specific interface 262
instances (see instances)
internal 273
looking for common 219
members 273
message about adding components to my class 579
MessageBox 56
multiple in same namespace 61
naming 102–103
natural structure 104
never instantiated 277
organizing 106
partial (see partial classes)
private 273
protected 273
public 273
sealed 273
serializable 421

similarities between 116
static 97
subscribing 489
using to build objects 92
versus structs 644
why some should never be instantiated 280
you can't inherit from 647

class hierarchy 215, 220
Hive Simulator 253

Clone class
implementing IDisposable 630, 631

CLR (Common Language Runtime) 47, 153

code
avoiding duplication 217
blocks 73
boilerplate 44
copying 90
looking at auto-generated 15
renaming things in code 707
repeating 213
similar 214
unwanted code from IDE 11
using IDE to help write code 48–49

collection initializers 326–327

collections 317, 555
Dictionary (see dictionaries)
generic 325
LINQ 556–558
List (see lists)
performing calculations on 662
Queue (see queues)
Stack (see stack)
using join to combine two collections into one query 671, 672
versus tables 661

colon (:) 222

colon operator 256

Color.Transparent 589

colors 76

columns 20

command-line arguments 711

comments 66

CompareTo( ) method 329

compiler 47

compiler errors
interfaces 254
troubleshooting 49

compiling application 36, 47

compound operators 136

concatenation 130

concrete classes 278

conditional expressions, consolidating 707

conditional operators 68–70

conditional tests 68–70, 73

configuration files 37

Console.WriteLine( ) method 194

console applications 710–711

console window, debugging in 711

constructors 197, 198, 199
base class 233
building new with switch statement 415
exceptions in 459
overloaded 313
subclasses 233

ContactDB.mdf 18, 29, 31

ContactDBDataSet 31, 32

ContactDBDataSet.Designer.cs 31

ContainsKey( ) method 581

controls
adding code 564
altering reexisting 587
animating Behive simulator 566–567
as objects 565
bound to database 32
clearing out all on forms 583
custom 564
animation 573
disposable objects 577
database-driven 32–33
disposing 577, 579

controls (*continued*)
  how forms and controls repaint themselves 605
  redrawing themselves 602
  removing 564
  visual display elements 570

Controls collection 565

count ++ 64

count -- 64

count = 64

Create( ) method 400

CreateDirectory( ) method 400

CryptoStream 394

curly braces 66, 73

curly brackets 58, 111
  single-line blocks 212

D

data
  pulling data from multiple sources 656
  storing categories of 310

database-driven controls 32–33

database diagram 26
  saving 27

Database Explorer 18, 675

databases 3
  adding table 20
  adding to project 18
  connecting forms to 17, 30
    (see also data source)
  connecting LINQ to SQL database 674–675
  entering data 28–29
  LINQ 673
  LINQ querying SQL database 677
  multiple tables 26
  SQL 18, 19
  SQL Server Express 7

data source
  adding new 30
  configuring 31
  database-driven controls 32

Data Source Configuration Wizard 18

data storage 7

data types 20
  generic 325

DateTime class 548

debugger
  Break All button 449
  Bullet Points 471
  catch blocks
    followed by (Exception) 460
    following flow 458–459
    multiple 466
    with no specified exceptions 462
  Continue button 449
  exploring delegates 503
  finally block 460
  knowing where to put breakpoints 452
  Restart button 449
  Show next statement button 449
  Step into button 449
  Step Into command 450
  Step out button 449
  Step over button 449
  try blocks 458–459
  unhandled exception window 452
  uses for 457
  Watch window 449, 457
    running methods in 452
    (see also exception handling)

debugging 16, 47, 449
  console window 711
  Excuse Management program 450–451

Debug menu 47

decimal and binary, converting between 125

decimal type 125, 126

declaration 54

delay 76, 79

delegates
 Bullet Points 509
 defined 501
 exploring in debugger 503
 hooking up to one event 507–509
 in action 502–503
 multiple events 499

Delete( ) method 400

deploying application 37, 38

deployment package 7

design 531
 intuitive applications 34–35
 intuitive classes 116
 making code intuitive with class and method names
  102–103
 professional looking applications 35
 user's needs 5

destructor 628

dialog boxes 398–400
 as objects 399
 customized 401
 popping up 397

DialogResult 397–399
 excuse management program 410

dictionaries 335–337
 Add( ) method 335
 adding or removing items 336
 ContainsKey( ) 335
 getting list of keys 336
 getting list of values 336
 keys 335
 keys and values 337
 looking up values using keys 336
 renderer 580

Dictionary objects 569

Dinner Party Planning project 174–185
 CalculateCostOfDecorations( ) method 184
 cost estimate 175

DinnerParty class
 class diagram 176
 exercise solution 178–179
 fixing calculator 203–204
 inheriting from Party class 234–238
 numericUpDown control 183
 recalculating new individual costs 183

directories
 creating new 400
 deleting 400
 getting list of files 400

Dispose( ) method 406, 577
 finalizers 632, 634
 making object serialize in 633
 using statement 630–632

DivideByZero error 443

DivideByZeroException 443, 448

dividing any number by zero 443

DogCompetition class 312

double buffering 608–613

double type 125, 126

downcasting 268, 269
 failure 270

E

encapsulation 183–204, 435, 644
 as principle of OOP 288
 automatic properties 195
 better 276
 defined 185
 example 192
 ideas for 191
 properties 193
 Renderer 568

entry point 55, 58, 231
 changing 56

enumeration 310–311

enums 311–315
 big numbers 312
 representing numbers with names 312
 versus Lists 325

equal signs 67

error handling 462

Error List 49, 58

errors

    avoiding file system errors with using statements 406

    compiler errors and interfaces 254

    DivideByZero 443

    invalid arguments 131

    You must rebuild your project for the changes to show up in any open designers. 579

escape sequence 66

EventHandler 488, 491

    using methods that do match others defined by EventHandler 491

event handlers 177, 188, 485

    adding 491

    automatic 492–493

    Bullet Points 509

    excuse management program 408

    hooking up 498

    how they work 486–487

    printing 614

    returning something other than void 491

    types of 491

event keyword 488

events

    callbacks 507–509

    connecting senders with receivers 500

    defined 485

    delegates 499

    forms 498

    how they work 486–487

    naming methods when raising events 490

    raising 490

    raising events with no handlers 490

    reference variables 500

    subscription and public events 505

    versus callbacks 510

    (see also event handlers)

exception, defined 444

exception handling 439–482

    Bullet Points 471

    catch block 455, 457

    catching specific exception types 473

    DivideByZeroException 443, 448

    dividing any number by zero 443

    exceptions in constructors 459

    exceptions versus unhandled exceptions 462

    Excuse Management program 477–478

    FileNotFoundException 462

    finalizers 635

    FormatException 448

    handling, not burying 474

    handling versus fixing 475

    IDisposable interface 472

    IndexOutOfRangeException 448

    IOException 460

    NullReferenceException 443

    OverFlowException 448

    program stopping with exceptions 462

    SerializationException 453, 460

    simple ideas for 476

    specifying particular kinds of exceptions 462

    spotting exceptions 445

    throwing and catching exceptions 467

    try block 455, 457

    unexpected input 456

    unhandled exceptions 452

    using exceptions to find bugs 447

    using statement 471

    why there are so many exceptions 445

    (see also debugger)

Exception objects 444, 445

    inheriting from Exception class 448

    Message property 466

    using to get information about the problem 465

Excuse Management project 407–411

    binary files with serialized objects 436

    building the form 408

    code problems 453

    debugging 450–451

        Random Excuse button 461

DialogResult 410
event handlers 408
exception handling 477–478
Folder button 408
Random Excuse button 411
Save As dialog 410
solution 410–411
unexpected user behavior 446–447
using debugger to follow try/catch flow 458–459
executable file 47
executing application 36
Exists( ) method 400
Expand Tables 28
extension methods 646, 647
LINQ 657
strings 648

F

Farmer class 192–198
constructors 197
fully encapsulating 195
testing 194–195
features 3
built-in 55
fields 98
backing field 193
initializing public fields 196
interfaces 255
lining up 34
masking 198
method's parameter has same name as a field 198
private 185–188
constructors 197
declaring 201
public 191
versus methods 98
versus properties 276
with no access 188
File.Create( ) 429
File.OpenWrite( ) 429

File.ReadAllBytes( ) 425, 426, 434
File.ReadAllLines( ) 434
File.ReadAllText( ) 434
File.WriteAllBytes( ) 425, 426, 434
File.WriteAllLines( ) 434
File.WriteAllText( ) 434
File class
Close( ) method 434
ReadAllText( ) method 403
static methods 434
versus FileInfo class 434
WriteAllText( ) method 403
FileDialogs 403
FileInfo class 400
versus File class 434
filenames, @ in front of 389
FileNotFoundException 462
files
appending text to 400
finding out if exists 400
get information about 400
reading from or writing to 400
(see also streams)
where Visual Studio stores them 16
writing 412
FileStreams 387, 388
BinaryWriter 427
StreamWriter 389
versus StreamReader and StreamWriter 434
FileSystemWatcher 709
Filter property 398
finalizers 628
Dispose( ) method 632, 634
exceptions 635
fields and methods 635
garbage collection 629–631
references 632
stability 632
when they run 629
finally block 460

Fireside Chats
    abstract classes 284–285
    Dispose( ) method and finalizers 634

Five Minute Mystery
    The Case of the Golden Crustacean 506
        mystery solved 511

flickering images 607

float type 124, 126
    assigning 129

foreach loop (lists) 321, 358

for loops 65, 69

Form1.cs 8

Form1.Designer.cs 8, 45, 50
    changing control properties 12

Form1.resx 14

Form1 form, programs without 231

FormatException 448

FormBorderStyle property 582

Form Designer 3

forms
    adding buttons 112
    adding method 113
    adding variables 112
    as objects 152–153
    connecting to databases 17, 30
        (see also data source)
    CreateGraphics( ) method 594
    database-driven controls 32
    events 498
    how forms and controls repaint themselves 605
    OnPaint method 605
    Paint event 605
    PaintEventArgs 605
    redrawing themselves 602
    Refresh( ) method 605
    (see also Beehive Simulator project, forms)

frames versus turns 549

from clause 664, 667

FromImage( ) 606

G

garbage collection 140, 153, 635
    finalizers 629–631

GDI+ 594–595

generic collections 325, 355

generic data types 325

get accessor 193, 199
    interfaces with get accessor without set accssor 259

GetFiles( ) method 400

GetLastAccessTime( ) method 400

GetLastWriteTime( ) method 400

Go To Definition 405

GPS navigation system 87

graphical user interface (see GUI)

graphics
    drawing picture on form 596–597
    how forms and controls repaint themselves 605
    Rectangle 597
    using keyword 606

Graphics object 592, 594, 606
    CreateGraphics( ) method 595
    DrawBee( ) method 601
    DrawCircle( ) method 595
    DrawString( ) method 595
    FillCircle( ) method 595
    Invalidate( ) controls 605
    Paint event handler 602
    printing 614
    Update( ) method 605

green arrow button 16

GroupBox control 207, 606

group keyword 667, 668

GUI (Graphical User Interface) 94
    labs, #1 A Day at the Races 170

guys (Two Guys project) 110–115, 117–118
    building form
        adding a method 113
        adding buttons 112

adding code to interact with objects 113
adding variables 112, 113
creating Guy class and two instances 110
sample code 111
GZipStreams 387

H

heap 100, 101
garbage collection 140
structs 637
versus stack 641
Hebrew letters 425
hex dump 431
StreamReader and StreamWriter 433
using file streams to build hex dumper 432
hexadecimal 431
working with 432
hierarchy 215
defined 221

I

IClown interface 258
access modifiers 274–275
extending 271–272
IComparable interface 329
IComparer interface 330
complex comparisons 332
creating instance 331
multiple classes 331
SortBy field 332
IDE
auto-generated code 73
behind the scenes 14
buttons 44
changing names of files 11
changing things in 50
compiler errors, troubleshooting 49
creating new projects 8
Error List 49
green arrow 16

helping users code 48–49
importing images 14
making changes in 45
New Project window 8
Properties window 44
renaming things in code 707
Reset Window Layout command 11
running program in 36
SQL statements 19
stored procedures 19
unwanted code 11
using tabs to switch between open files 48
visual tools 73
what it does in typical application 44–45
what the IDE automates 2
where data is stored 29
Windows Forms Application project 44
XAML 713
IDE toolbar
green arrow button 16
Save icon 15
Stop Debugging button 16
IDisposable interface 405, 473, 630
avoiding exceptions 472
IDs
auto-generated 21
unique 20
if/else statements 67
if statements 131
images
drawing picture on form 596–597
fixing transparency problems 601
flickering 607
performance issues 590
Rectangle 597
resizing 592–593, 606
TrackBars to zoom an image in and out 603–604
images, importing 14
index (arrays) 148–149
IndexOutOfRangeException 448
infinite loops 71

inherit, defined 215

inheritance 213–250
    as principle of OOP 288
    avoiding duplication of code 217
    classes you can't inherit from 647
    class hierarchy, Hive Simulator 253
    class that contains entry point 231
    looking for common classes 219
    multiple 286
    passing instance of subclass 231
    subclasses 225–226
    (see also interfaces)

InitialDirectory propery 398

initialization 115

InitializeComponent( ) method 198

installation, testing 39

instances 93
    creating 94
        example 111
        heap 101
        static keyword 99
    defined 93
    fields 98
    keeping track of things 98
    non-static methods 97

instantiation, interfaces 260

int 63

integers, using in code 137

IntelliSense window 577, 595
    CreateGraphics( ) method 606

interface keyword 255

interfaces 254–276
    colon operator 256
    compiler errors 254
    containing statements 270
    downcasting 269
    easy way to implement 270
    example code 258
    fields 255

finding out if class implements specific interface 262
    get accessor without a set accssor 259
    implementing 257–258
    inheriting from other interfaces 263
    is keyword 262, 265
    like contracts 270
    naming 254
    new keyword 260
    object references versus interface references 276
    properties 255
    public 255
    public void method 259
    references 260–261
        why use 276
    upcasting 269
    void method 258
    why use 270, 276

internal access modifier 273

int type 124, 126, 127
    assigning value 137
    declaring 137

invalid arguments error 131

IOException 460

is keyword 262, 265

J

join clause 671, 672, 677, 678

L

labels 75
    lining up 34

labels for objects (see reference variables)

labs
    #1 A Day at the Races
        application architecture 168
        Bet class 167
        Bet object 169
        Betting Parlor groupbox 171
        dogs array 168

finished executable 172
Greyhound class 166
Greyhound object initializer 166
GUI 170
Guy class 167
Guy object 169
guys array 168
PictureBox control 166, 168, 170
RadioButton controls 168
this keyword 167
#2 The Quest 363–384
    Bat subclass 377
    BluePotion class 380
    Bow subclass 379
    Enemy class 376
    Enemy subclasses 377
    form, bringing it all together 381–383
    form, building 366–367
    form, UpdateCharacters( ) method 382
    Game class 370–371
    Ghost subclass 377
    Ghoul subclass 377
    IPotion interface 380
    Mace subclass 379
    Mover class 372–373
    Mover class source code 373
    Player class 374
    Player class Attack( ) method 375
    Player class Move( ) method 375
    RedPotion class 380
    Sword subclass 379
    using objects 368–369
    Weapon class 378
#3 Invaders 681–702
    additions 701
    animation timer 687
    architecture 684–685
    designing the form 686–690
    Form object 684
    Game class 692
    Game class, filling out 694
    Game class methods 693
    Game object 684–685
    Game object's Draw( ) method 691
    gameOver event 689
    game timer 689, 690

    graphics 691
    Invader class 696
    Invader class methods 697
    KeyDown and KeyUp events 688
    LINQ 695
    movements 683
    Paint event handler 691
    PlayerShip class 698
    PlayerShip object 685
    Shot objects 699
    Stars class 700
    Stars object 685
    types of invaders 683
line break 15, 66
LINQ (Langauge INtegrated Query) 556–558
    101 LINQ Samples 663
    combining results into groups 667, 668
    connecting to SQL database 674–675
    databases 673
    extension methods 657
    from clause 664, 667
    Invaders lab 695
    modifying items 662
    .NET collections 657
    orderby clause 664, 667
    performing calculations on collections 662
    pulling data from multiple sources 656
    queries 658, 663
    querying SQL database 677
    query statements 664
    scouring comic collections 659
    select clause 664
    Take statement 664
    to XML 704–705
        reading RSS feed 705
    using join to combine two collections into one query
        671, 672
    versus SQL 661
    where clause 664
LINQPad 679
lists 317–334
    Bullet Points 322
    CompareTo( ) method 329

lists (*continued*)
    converting from stacks or queues 358
    creating new 325
    dynamically shrinking and growing 321
    foreach loop 321
    IComparable interface 329
    IComparer interface 330
        complex comparisons 332
        creating instance 331
        multiple classes 331
    Sort( ) method 328
    sorting 328–329
    storing types 322
    things you can do with 318
    versus arrays 318–320, 325
    versus enums 325
literals 125
Location property 582
logical operators 68
long type 124, 126
loops 65, 69
    infinite 71
    nested 77
lowercasing 201

M

Main( ) method 54, 55
masking fields 198
Math class 66
Maximize and Minimize buttons 35
MaximizeBox property 35
members (class) 273
memory 100
MemoryStreams 387
message about adding components to my class 579
MessageBox 56
methods 15, 52, 53
    abstract 278, 281
    adding for form 113

calling specific 221
curly braces 66
declaration 54
defining 66
entry point 54, 55
extension (see extension methods)
extracting 706
implementing interfaces 257–258
Main( ) 54, 55
naming 102–103
objects 92
overloaded (see overloaded methods)
overriding 218, 226
parameter has same name as a field 198
private 187–188
public 191
    accessing private fields 188
    capitalization 201
return values 88
set and get accessors 199
Show( ) 56
static (see static methods)
variables matching types of parameters 131
versus fields 98
with no return value 197
MinimizeBox property 35
multiple inheritance 286

N

Name property 51
namespaces 46, 52, 55
    multiple classes in same 61
    reserved 73
Navigation project 86–98
nested loops 77
.NET collections, LINQ 657
.NET Database Objects 6
.NET Framework 46
    colors 76
    Random class 150–151

tools 52
what you can do with 714
.NET Visual Objects 6, 17
NetworkStreams 387
new keyword 91
   interfaces 260
No Dumb Questions
   @ in front of filenames 401
   \n 15, 401
   \t 401
   Beehive Simulator project
      BeeControl 579
      for loops 537
      Go( ) methods 533
      Hive class exceptions 539
      NectarHarvested variable 523
      number of bees 533
      Point object 539
      read-only automatic properties 523
      removing dead flowers and retired bees 537
      Show( ) method 587
   BirthdayParty class 207
   boxed objects and structs 644
   byte order mark 434
   capitalization 201
   catch block 457
      with no specified exceptions 462
   chaining 491
   changing names of files generated by IDE 11
   changing types 154
   class diagrams, moving up, not down 231
   classes 73
      versus structs 644
   Close( ) method 434
   closing streams 401
   columns 20
   constructors 198, 199
   controls, altering reexisting 587
   converting strings to byte array 401
   creating new Lists 325
   curly brackets 58
   customized dialog boxes 401
   data types 20

debugger 457
   Watch window 457
easy way to implement interfaces 270
encapsulation 188, 276
entry point 58, 231
error handling 462
Error List 58
errors, You must rebuild your project for the changes
      to show up in any open designers. 579
EventHandler 491
event handlers 188
   adding 491
   returning something other than void 491
   types of 491
events versus callbacks 510
Exception object 445
exceptions versus unhandled exceptions 462
extension methods 647
fields with no access 188
File class versus FileInfo class 434
FileStreams versus StreamReader
      and StreamWriter 434
finalizers
   exceptions 635
   using fields and methods 635
forms as objects 153
frames versus turns 549
from clause 664
FromImage( ) 606
garbage collection 153, 635
generic collections 325
generic data types 325
get accessor 199
graphics, using keyword 606
Graphics object 606
guys (Two Guys project) 114
IDE
   auto-generated code 73
   where data is stored 29
IDE toolbar
   green arrow 16
   Reset Window Layout command 11
   Stop Debugging button 16

No Dumb Questions (*continued*)
    IDisposable interface 473
    instances, non-static methods 97
    interface references, why use 276
    interfaces
        containing statements 270
        like contracts 270
        why use 276
    join clause 677
    knowing where to put breakpoints 452
    line break 15
    LINQ 663
    LINQ querying SQL database 677
    Lists versus arrays 325
    Lists versus enums 325
    message about adding components to my class 579
    method 15
    namespaces, reserved 73
    new projects, Visual Studio 2008 11
    null keyword 153
    object references versus interface references 276
    OpenFileDialog, changing properties 579
    overloaded constructors 313
    partial classes 73
    patterns, callbacks 510
    Point 644
    private data 188
    program stopping with exceptions 462
    programs without Form1 form 231
    properties
        statements 199
        versus fields 276
    protected versus private or public 276
    record data 29
    reference variables, how they work 154
    resizing images 606
    select clause 664
    select new clause 677
    set accessor 199
    setting structs equal to another 644
    specifying particular kinds of exceptions 462
    spotting exceptions 445
    stack 644

    static and non-static methods 97
    static methods, when to use 97
    StreamReader 401
    StreamWriter 401
    subclasses
        and base classes 222
        passing instance of 231
    this variable 154
    try/finally block 473
    try block 457
    unhandled exceptions 452
    unhandled exception window 452
    Unicode 434
    unique IDs 20
    unwanted code from IDE 11
    upcasting, but not downcasting 270
    UserControl 606
    using methods that do match others defined
        by EventHandler 491
    using statement 473
    using this keyword to raise event 491
    virtual methods 231
    Visual Studio Express 11
    Watch window, running methods in 452
    why there are so many exceptions 445
    why use interfaces 270
null keyword 153
NullReferenceException 443
NumericUpDown control 89

O

object initializers 115, 196, 197
object oriented programming (OOP) 288
object references, versus interface references 276
Object Relational Designer window 675
objects 91
    accessing fields inside object 185
    accidently misusing 184
    assigning value 137
    as variables 137

boxed 642
building from classes 92
declaring 137
encapsulation (see encapsulation)
event arguments 488
finalizers (see finalizers)
garbage collection 140
instances (see instances)
knowing when to respond 484
null keyword 153
reading entire with serialization 420
references 261
reference variables (see reference variables)
setting equal to value type 642
states 418
talking to other objects 152
versus structs 639

object type 125

Objectville Paper Co. logo 13

OOP (object oriented programming) 288

OpenFileDialog 579
changing properties 579
initialFolder property 403

OpenFileDialog control 398, 403

OpenRead( ) method 400

OpenWrite( ) method 400

operators 64
compound 136

orderby clause 664, 667

OR operator 68, 410

Oven class 266

OverFlowException 448

overloaded constructors 313
excuse management program 408

overloaded methods 343

override keyword 226

overriding methods 218

P

PaintEventArgs 605

Paint event handler 602

parameters 53, 88, 89
capitalization 201
same name as a field 198

partial classes 45, 50, 53, 59–61, 73, 78

PascalCase 201

patterns
callbacks 508, 510

Pen object 606

PerformanceCounter 709

performance issues
Beehive Simulator project 589–591
images 590

PictureBox control 12
adding to form 50
double-clicking 15
labs, #1 A Day at the Races 166, 168, 170
transparent background 589
Zoom mode 13

PictureBox control 217

Point 581, 644

polymorphism 289
as principle of OOP 288

popping up dialog boxes 397

primary key 20–24, 27

Primary Key button 20

PrintDocument object 614–615

printing
Beehive Simulator project 616–619
Graphics object and event handler 614

PrintPage event handler 615

private access modifier 258, 273

private fields 185–188
    constructors 197
    declaring 201

private methods 187–188

Problem Up Close, recalculating new
    individual costs 183

Program.cs 8, 54

programs (see applications)

properties 98
    automatic 195
    encapsulation 193
    initializing public properties 196
    interfaces 255
    public, capitalization 201
    read-only 195, 196
    statements 199
    versus fields 276

Properties window 35, 44

protected access modifier 273

protected keyword 275

public access modifier 273

public fields 191
    initializing 196

public methods 191
    accessing private fields 188
    capitalization 201

public properties
    capitalization 201
    initializing 196

public void method 259

publish/ folder 38

Publish Contacts 37

Publish Wizard 37

Q

queries 19
    anatomy of 660
    editing with LINQPad 679

LINQ 658, 663
    using join to combine two collections into one
        query 671

queues 355
    converting to lists 358
    enqueuing and dequeuing 356
    foreach loop 358

R

Racetrack Simulator (see labs, #1 A Day at the Races)

Random class 150–151

randomizing results 150–151

read-only properties 195, 196

record data 29

refactoring 706–707

references
    interfaces 260–261
    objects 261
    versus values 638

reference variables 138–140, 500
    garbage collection 140
    how they work 154
    multiple 139
    multiple references and their side effects 142
    multiple references and unintentional changes 147
    objects talking to other objects 152

Refresh( ) method 605

RemoveAllControls( ) method 583

render, defined 568

Renderer class 568–569, 583–585
    animating bees on form 580–581
    dictionaries 580
    ResizeImage method 591

reserved words 154

Reset Window Layout command 11

Resource Designer 582

resource files 14

result += 64

result = 64

return statements 88

return type 88

return values 53, 88

risky code 456–473

RoboBee class 264

robust, defined 454

RSS feed, LINQ to XML 705

S

SaveFileDialog control 399, 403
    Title property 403

Save icon 15

sbyte type 124

scope 274

sealed access modifier 273

select new clause 671, 672, 675–679

select statement 664

semicolons 66

serialization 416–425
    making classes serializable 421
    making object serialize in Dispose( ) method 633
    object states 418
    reading and writing serialized files 429
    reading entire object 420
    serializing and deserializing deck of cards 422–423
    serializing objects out to file 424
    what happens to objects 417, 419

SerializationException 453, 460
    BinaryFormatter 454

Server Explorer 18

Service-Based Database 18

set accessor 193, 199
    interfaces with get accessor without set accssor 259

Setup executable 37

short type 124, 126, 127

Show( ) method 56

ShowDialog( ) method 397, 399

similar behaviors 214

similar code 214

Size property 51

slashes (//) 66

Sloppy Joe's Random Menu Item project 150–151

solution (.sln) file 46

Solution Explorer 18, 46, 48

Sort( ) method 328

SortBy field 332

source code files 46

Spy project 186–188

SQL (Structured Query Language) 19
    connecting LINQ to SQL database 674–675
    LINQ querying SQL database 677
    versus LINQ 661

SQL databases 18, 19

SQL Server Express
    database 7
    file 29

stack 355, 644
    converting to lists 358
    foreach loop 358
    popping items off 357
    versus heap 641

Starbuzz Coffee project 654–656
    join clause 678–679

Start Debugging 47

statements 19, 53, 73

static keyword 97
    creating instances 99

static methods 97
    when to use 97

static void Main( ) 55

Step out button 449

Step over button 449

Stop Debugging button 16

stored procedures 19

Stream object 386

StreamReader 393, 401
   hex dump 433
   versus FileStreams 434

streams 386
   chaining 394
   closing 401
   different types 387
   Dispose( ) method 406
   forgetting to close 388
   serializing objects 423
   things you can do with 387
   using file streams to build hex dumper 432
   using statements 406
   writing text to files 389

StreamWriter 389–393, 401
   [0] and [1] 401
   hex dump 433
   versus FileStreams 434
   Write( ) and WriteLine( ) methods 389

String.IsNullOrEmpty( ) 240

string literals 389, 401

strings 63
   converting to byte array 401
   extension methods 648
   formatting 179
   storing categories of data 310

string type 124, 126
   concatenation 130
   converting 130

structs 637
   boxed 642, 645
   Point 644
   setting one equal to another 640, 644
   versus classes 644
   versus objects 639

Structured Query Language (see SQL)

subclasses 214, 221
   accessing base class with base keyword 232
   constructors 233
   inheriting from base class 222
   modifying 225–226
   overriding methods 226
   passing instance of 231
   upcasting 267
   using instead of base classes 227

subscription
   how it works 486–487
   public events 505
   subscribing classes 489

switch statements 413–415
   building new constructors with 415

syntax 66

System.Drawing 594

System.Windows.Forms 46, 89, 111

System.Windows.Forms.Control 576

System namespace, Math class 66

T

TabControl 207

Table grid 28

tables
   adding columns 20
   adding to database 20
   finish building 25
   multiple 26
   saving 25
   versus collections 661

Take statement 664

testing installation 39

Textbox control 89

Text property 51
   changing 34

The Problem Up Close, recalculating new
     individual costs 183

this keyword 201, 274
    labs, #1 A Day at the Races 167
    using to raise event 491

this variable 154

Timer 579

timer 575, 583
    disposing 577

timers 546, 548
    events and delegates 547

Title property 399

Toolbox components 708–709
    BackgroundWorker 708
    FileSystemWatcher 709
    PerformanceCounter 709

Toolbox controls, easier way to build 578

ToString( ) method 130, 179

TrackBars to zoom an image in and out 603–604

try/finally block 473

try blocks 455, 457
    following in debugger 458–459

turns versus frames 549

types
    object 125
    (see also value types)

U

uint type 124

ulong type 124

unexpected input 456

unhandled exceptions 452
    versus exceptions 462

Unicode 424, 434
    converting text to 425

unique IDs 20

unwanted code from IDE 11

upcasting 267, 269
    but not downcasting 270

Up Close, access modifiers 274–275

uppercasing 201

user's needs 5

UserControl 578, 606

user interface 3
    developing 12

ushort type 124

using keyword, graphics 606

using lines 52

using statements 406, 473
    Dispose( ) 630
    exception handling 471

V

values versus references 638

value types 124, 154
    bool (see bool type)
    byte (see byte type)
    casting 128–130
    changing 154
    char (see char type)
    decimal (see decimal type)
    double (see double type)
    float (see float type)
    int (see int type)
    long (see long type)
    sbyte 124
    short (see short type)
    string (see string type)
    uint 124
    ulong 124
    ushort 124
    variables matching types of parameters 131

variables 62, 73, 126
    adding to form 112
    assigning 128
    assigning values 63
    declaring 66
    matching types of parameters 131

variables (*continued*)
  naming 136
  reference (see reference variables)
  value types (see types)
var keyword 658
vertical bars 410
virtual keyword 226
virtual machines 47, 153
virtual methods 231
visual components 576
visual display elements 570
Visual Studio, what you get with C# and 2
Visual Studio 2008, new projects 11
Visual Studio 2008 Express 11
  downloading xxxvi
  setting up xxxvi
Visual Studio Integrated Development Environment (see IDE)
void method
  interfaces 258
  public 259
void return type 88, 103, 113

W

Watch it!
  = operator versus == operator 67
  automatic properties 195
  destructors and finalizers 628
  event handlers, hooking up 498
  exceptions in constructors 459
  LINQ 658
  LINQ queries 663
  method's parameter has same name as a field 198
  object initializers 115

raising events with no handlers 490
SerializationException 454
Server Explorer versus Database Explorer 18
things looking different in your IDE 8
writing to files 429
where clause 664
while loops 65, 69, 73
white space 66
Windows calculator 125
Windows Forms Application project 44, 66
Windows installer 7
Windows Presentation Framework (WPF) 712–713
Write( ) method 401
WriteLine( ) method 401

X

XAML (Extensible Application Markup Language) 713
XML, LINQ to XML 704–705
  reading RSS feed 705

Y

yesNo = 64

Z

zooming, TrackBars to zoom an image in and out 603–604
Zoo Simulator project 216–222
  class hierarchy 220
  extending base class 221
  inheriting from base class 221
  overriding methods 218

SHROFF PUBLISHERS & DISTRIBUTORS PVT. LTD. SPD

Shroff / O'Reilly

TITLES AT REDUCED PRICES

ISBN	Title	Author	Price
8173663661	.NET Framework Essentials, *324 Pages*	Thai	25.00
818404027X	**Access 2003 for Starters: The Missing Manual, *408 Pages***	**Chase**	**75.00**
8173664277	Access Cookbook for 97, 2000 & 2002 **(Book / CD-ROM)**, *724 Pages*	Getz	100.00
8173662231	ActionScriprt: The Definitive Guide, *726 Pages*	Moock	150.00
8173662886	Building Oracle XML Applications **(Book / CD-ROM)**, *824 Pages*	Muench	100.00
8173665621	Building Secure Servers with Linux, *454 Pages*	Bauer	100.00
8173664250	Building Wireless Community Networks, *144 Pages*	Flickenger	50.00
8173662584	Cascading Style Sheets: The Definitive Guide, *476 Pages*	Meyer	75.00
8173669066	**Cascading Style Sheets: The Definitive Guide (Covers CSS2 & CSS 2.1), 2/ed, *538 Pages***	**Meyer**	**100.00**
8173667241	**Cisco Cookbook, *918 Pages***	**Dooley**	**150.00**
8173662878	Developing ASP Components 2/ed, *864 Pages*	Powers	100.00
8173663882	**Designing Large Scale LANs, *408 Pages***	**Dooley**	**75.00**
817366272X	DHCP for Windows 2000, *288 Pages*	Alcott	75.00
8173663580	**Essential SNMP, *338 Pages***	**Mauro**	**75.00**
8173662754	**Excel 2000 In a Nutshell: A Power User's Quick Reference, *560 Pgs***	**Simon**	**50.00**
8173669406	**Excel Annoyances: How to Fix the Most Annoying Things about Your Favorite Spreadsheet , *266 Pages***	**Frye**	**75.00**
8173668612	**Excel Hacks: 100 Industrial Strength Tips & Tools, *316 Pages***	**David**	**75.00**
8173663599	Exim: The Mail Transport Agent, *638 Pages*	Hazel	75.00
8173669325	**Google: The Missing Manual, *312 Pages***	**Milstein**	**75.00**
817366448X	**IPv6 Essentials, *362 Pages***	**Hagen**	**75.00**
8173660573	Java Threads, 2/ed, *336 Pages*	Oaks	100.00
8173664145	Java Cookbook, *890 Pages*	Darwin	150.00
8173664625	**Java Enterprise in a Nutshell: A Desktop Quick Reference, 2/ed, *1,004 Pages***	**Farley**	**100.00**
8173660557	Java Foundation Classes in a Nutshell, *752 Pages*	Flanagan	75.00
8173662711	Java Internationalization, *456 Pages*	Deitsch	75.00
8173663807	Java Programming with Oracle SQLJ, *404 Pages*	Price	75.00
8173661103	JavaScript Application Cookbook, *512 Pages*	Bradenbaugh	75.00
8173661111	JavaScript Pocket Reference, *96 Pages*	Flanagan	25.00
8173662509	Jini in a Nutshell, *420 Pages*	Oaks	75.00
8173665168	**Learning C#, *374 Pages***	**Liberty**	**75.00**
8173662320	Learning Java **(Book / CD-ROM)**, *732 Pages*	Niemeyer	75.00
8173660603	Learning Perl/Tk, *380 Pages*	Walsh	75.00
8173661677	Learning Web Design: A Beginner's Guide to HTML, Graphics & Web Environment (2 Color Book), *432 Pages*	Niederst	100.00
8173663173	Learning WML & WMLScript, *204 Pages*	Frost	50.00
8173663149	Learning XML, *376 Pages*	Ray	75.00
8173662193	MCSD in a Nutshell: The Visual Basic Exams, *636 Pages*	Foxall	75.00
8173662398	MCSE in a Nutshell: The Windows 2000 Exams, *504 Pages*	Moncur	75.00
8173662517	MP3: The Definitive Guide, *408 Pages*	Hacker	75.00
8173665648	MySQL Cookbook (Covers MySQL 4.0), *1,028 Pages*	DuBois	150.00
8173665613	**Object-Oriented Programming with Visual Basic .NET, *306 Pgs***	**Hamilton**	**50.00**
8173663246	**Oracle Net8 Configuration & Troubleshooting, *412 Pages***	**Toledo**	**75.00**
8173660697	Oracle PL/SQL Language Pocket Reference, *80 Pages*	Feuerstein	25.00
8173667195	**Perl 6 Essentials, *208 Pages***	**Randal**	**75.00**

ISBN	Title	Author	Price
8173661243	Perl/Tk Pocket Reference, *104 Pages*	Lidie	25.00
817366269X	PHP Pocket Reference, *124 Pages*	Lerdorf	25.00
8173661251	PNG: The Definitive Guide, *344 Pages*	Roelofs	50.00
817366126X	Practical Internet Groupware, *520 Pages*	Udell	75.00
8173660751	Practical UNIX & Internet Security, 2/ed, *1,008 Pages*	Garfinkel	150.00
8173660190	QuarkXPress in a Nutshell, *552 Pages*	O'Quinn	50.00
8173662487	sed & awk Pocket Reference, *60 Pages*	Robbins	25.00
8173661294	sendmail Desktop Reference, *74 Pages*	Costales	25.00
8173664161	**Server Load Balancing,*198 Pages***	**Bourke**	**50.00**
8173663866	Solaris 8 Administrator's Guide, *308 Pages*	Watters	100.00
8173662924	**SSH: The Secure Shell: The Definitive Guide, *564 Pages***	**Barrett**	**75.00**
8173662606	Tcl/Tk Pocket Reference, *100 Pages*	Raines	25.00
8173664374	VB .NET Core Classes in a Nutshell: A Desktop Quick Reference (Book / CD-ROM), *584 Pages*	Kurniawan	75.00
817366501X	**Visual Studio Hacks: Tips & Tools for Turbocharging the IDE, *304 Pages***	**Avery**	**75.00**
8173665931	**WebLogic Server 6.1 Workbook for Enterprise JavaBeans, 3/ed, *264 Pages***	**Nyberg**	**50.00**
8173663475	Web Database Applications with PHP & MySQL, *600 Pages*	Williams	75.00
8173661359	Webmaster in a Nutshell, 2/ed, *540 Pages*	Spainhour	75.00
8173662630	Windows 2000 Active Directory, *624 Pages*	Lowe-Norris	75.00
8173662789	**Windows 2000 Administration in a Nutshell: A Desktop Quick Reference, *1,000 Pages***	**Tulloch**	**50.00**
8173663327	Windows 2000 Performance Guide, *650 Pages*	Friedman	75.00
8173660743	**Windows 2000 Quick Fixes, *304 Pages***	**Boyce**	**50.00**
8173666903	**Windows Server 2003 in a Nutshell: A Desktop Quick Reference, *672 Pages***	**Tulloch**	**75.00**
8173663564	**Windows XP in a Nutshell: A Desktop Quick Reference, *640 Pages***	**Karp**	**75.00**
8173665915	**Windows XP Unwired: A Guide for Home, Office, and the Road, *316 Pages***	**Lee**	**75.00**
8173662770	**Word 2000 in a Nutshell: A Power User's Quick Reference, *516 Pages***	**Glenn**	**50.00**
8173666113	**Word Annoyances, *218 Pages***	**Hart**	**75.00**
8173668094	**Xlib Programming Manual (Version 11): Volume One, *824 Pages***	**Nye**	**100.00**
8173668108	**Xlib Reference Manual (Version 11), 3/ed: Volume Two, *948 Pages***	**Nye**	**100.00**
8173668086	**X Protocol Reference Manual (Version X11): Volume Zero, *468 Pgs***	**Nye**	**75.00**
8173662096	XSLT, *486 Pages*	Tidwell	100.00

PUBLISHED TITLES

ISBN	Title	Author	Price
8173666539	.NET and XML, *484 Pages*	Bornstein	425.00
8173669201	.NET Compact Framework Pocket Guide, *122 Pages*	Lee	125.00
8173666547	.NET Framework Essentials, 3/ed, *392 Pages*	Thai	325.00
8173665729	.NET Gotchas: 75 Ways to Improve Your C# and VB.NET Programs, *402 Pgs*	Subramaniam	300.00
8173665753	802.11 Security, *200 Pages*	Potter	175.00
8184041632	**802.11 Wireless Networks: The Definitive Guide, 2/ed, *668 Pages***	**Gast**	**550.00**
9788184043099	**A+, Network+, Security+ Exams in a Nutshell (Cover Essentials 220-602,220-603,220-604 N10-00, *826 Pages***	**Bhardwaj**	**600.00**
8173661995	**Access 2003 Personal Trainer (Book / CD-ROM), (2 Color book), *372 Pages***	**CustomGuide**	**400.00**
9788184042573	**Access 2007: The Missing Manual, *776 Pages***	**MacDonald**	**525.00**
9788184042924	**Access 2007 For Starters: The Missing Manual, *426 Pages***	**MacDonald**	**375.00**
9788184043334	**Access Data Analysis Cookbook, *384 Pages***	**Bluttman**	**375.00**
8173664285	Access Database Design & Programming, 3/ed, *454 Pages*	Roman	325.00
8173666377	Access Hacks: Tips & Tools for Wrangling·Your Data, *362 Pgs*	Bluttman	325.00
8173667233	ActionScript Cookbook, *904 Pages*	Lott	675.00
9788184042832	**ActionScript 3.0 Cookbook, *600 Pages***	**Lott**	**475.00**
9788184043747	**ActionScript 3.0 Design Patterns, *548 Pages***	**Sanders**	**450.00**
8173666555	ActionScript for Flash MX Pocket Reference, *152 Pages*	Moock	125.00
8173665761	ActionScript for Flash MX: The Definitive Guide, 2/ed, *904 Pages*	Colin Moock	750.00
8173667357	Active Directory Cookbook for Windows Server 2003 and Windows 2000, *632 Pages*	Allen	525.00

ISBN	Title	Author	Price
8173666563	Active Directory for Windows Server 2003, 2/ed, *692 Pages*	Allen	575.00
9788184043501	**Adding Ajax, *418 Pages***	**Power**	**400.00**
817366725X	ADO .NET Cookbook, *636 Pages*	Hamilton	500.00
8173665222	ADO .NET for Visual Basic .NET 2003 in a Nutshell: A Desktop Quick Reference (**Book / CD-ROM**), *626 Pages*	Hamilton	500.00
9788184043563	**Adobe Integrated Runtime(AIR) for JavaScript Developers Pocket Reference, *192 Pages***	**Dura**	**150.00**
8173668302	Advanced Perl Programming, 2/ed, *308 Pages*	Cozens	325.00
8173668205	AI for Game Developers, *400 Pages*	Bourg	375.00
8184041578	**Ajax Design Patterns, *668 Pages***	**Mahemoff**	**500.00**
8184041063	**Ajax Hacks: Tips & Tools for Creating Responsive Web Sites, *304 Pages***	**Perry**	**350.00**
9788184043082	**Ajax on Java, *176 Pages***	**Olson**	**250.00**
9788184042610	**Ajax on Rails, *364 Pages***	**Raymond**	**350.00**
8173667292	Amazon Hacks: 100 Industrial Strength Tips & Tricks, *312 Pages*	Bausch	250.00
8173667799	**Analyzing Business Data with Excel, *276 Pages***	**Knight**	**275.00**
8184040806	**ANT: The Definitive Guide, 2/ed (Cover ANT 1.6), *346 Pages***	**Holzner**	**325.00**
8173667446	Apache Cookbook (Covers Apache 2.0 & 1.3), *264 Pages*	Coar	250.00
8173662525	Apache Pocket Reference, *112 Pages*	Ford	75.00
8173662274	Apache Security, *428 Pages*	Ristic	400.00
8173665133	Apache: The Definitive Guide (Covers Apache 2.0 & 1.3) 3/ed, *594 Pages*	Laurie	500.00
8184040393	Applied Software Project Management, *304 Pages*	Stellman	350.00
9788184043549	**Apollo for Adobe Flex Developers Pocket Guide, *154 Pages***	**Dixon**	**125.00**
8173667837	The Art of Project Management, *512 Pages*	Berkun	350.00
8184041411	**The Art of SQL, *382 Pages***	**Faroult**	**350.00**
8184041020	**ASP .NET 2.0 Cookbook (Cover ASP .NET 2.0), *1,028 Pages***	**Kittel**	**675.00**
8173664587	**ASP .NET 2.0: Developer's Notebook, *358 Pages***	**Lee**	**325.00**
8173667306	ASP .NET in a Nutshell: A Desktop Quick Reference, 2/ed, *1,008 Pages*	Duthie	600.00
8173669384	AspectJ Cookbook, *364 Pages*	Miles	350.00
8184040016	Asterisk: The Future of Telephony, *414 Pages*	Meggelen	375.00
9788184042702	**Astronomy Hacks, *420 Pages***	**Thompson**	**450.00**
8173662347	AutoCAD 2000 In a Nutshell: A Command Reference Guide, *592 Pages*	Kent	325.00
9788184042900	**BacKup & Recovery, *774 Pages***	**Preston**	**600.00**
9788184043471	**Bash Cookbook, *636 Pages***	**Albing**	**500.00**
8173663955	Beginning Perl for Bioinformatics, *390 Pages*	Tisdall	300.00
8173668981	Better, Faster, Lighter Java, *270 Pages*	Tate	250.00
9788184043556	**Beautiful Code: Leading Programmers Explain How They Think, *634 Pages***	**Wilson**	**500.00**
8184040032	Beyond Java, *206 Pages*	Tate	200.00
9788173666582	BGP, *292 Pages*	van Beijnum	275.00
8184040547	**Blackberry Hacks: Tips & Tools for Your Mobile Office, *350 Pages***	**Mabe**	**350.00**
8173665125	BLAST, *372 Pages*	Korf	325.00
817366899X	BSD Hacks:100 Industrial-Strength Tips & Tools, *458 Pages*	Lavigne	375.00
8173666598	**Building Embedded Linux Systems, *422 Pages***	**Yaghmour**	**350.00**
9780596101367	**Building Extreme PCs, *192 Pages***	**Hardwidge**	**1,200.00**
8173661014	Building Internet Firewalls 2/ed, *904 Pages*	Chapman	650.00
8173662282	Building Java Enterprise Applications: Vol. 1 - Architecture, *324 Pages*	McLaughlin	225.00
8173661391	Building Linux Clusters (**Book / CD-ROM**), *360 Pages*	Spector	350.00
8184041543	**Building Scalable Web Sites, *362 Pages***	**Henderson**	**325.00**
8173664749	**Building the Perfect PC, *360 Pages***	**Thompson**	**350.00**
8173664439	C# & VB .NET Conversion Pocket Reference, *156 Pages*	Mojica	75.00
8184040938	**C# Cookbook, 2/ed (Updated for C# 2.0 and .NET 2.0), *1,196 Pgs***	**Hilyard**	**600.00**
8173664293	C# Essentials, 2/ed, *224 Pages*	Albahari	175.00
8173663726	C# in a Nutshell: A Desktop Quick Reference, *864 Pages*	Drayton	600.00
9788184043846	**C# in a Nutshell 3/ed, *874 Pages***	**Albahari**	**600.00**
8173665192	C# Language Pocket Reference, *132 Pages*	Drayton	100.00

ISBN	Title	Author	Price
8184040490	**C in a Nutshell**, *618 Pages*	**Prinz**	**350.00**
8173666601	C Pocket Reference, *142 Pages*	Prinz	100.00
8184040369	**C++ Cookbook**, *604 Pages*	**Stephens**	**400.00**
8173666628	C++ in a Nutshell, (Cover ISO/IEC 14882 STD) *816 Pages*	Lischner	500.00
8173667101	C++ Pocket Reference, *148 Pages*	Loudon	100.00
8173662266	CDO & MAPI Programming with Visual Basic, *388 Pages*	Grundgeiger	175.00
8173664269	CGI Programming on the World Wide Web, *454 Pages*	Gundavaram	300.00
817366045X	CGI Programming with Perl 2/ed, *476 Pages*	Gundavaram	350.00
9788184042849	**Cisco IOS Cookbook, 2/ed, 1,250 Pages**	**Dooley**	**850.00**
8173669848	Cisco IOS in a Nutshell, 2/ed: A Desktop Quick Reference for IOS on IP Network, *808 Pages*	Boney	500.00
8173668469	Classic Shell Scripting, *568 Pages*	Robbins	425.00
8173663645	COM+ Programming with Visual Basic, *372 Pages*	Mojica	225.00
8173663653	COM & .NET Component Services, *390 Pages*	Lowy	250.00
8184040199	**Computer Privacy Annoyances, 218 Pages**	**Tynan**	**225.00**
8184041586	**Computer Security Basics, 2/ed, 324 Pages**	**Lehtinen**	**325.00**
8173660638	Creating Effective JavaHelp, *196 Pages*	Lewis	125.00
8184040180	**Creating WebSites: The Missing Manual, 559 Pages**	**MacDonald**	**400.00**
8173669163	CSS Cookbook (Cover CSS 2.1), *280 Pages*	Schmitt	275.00
9788184042733	**CSS Cookbook, 2/ed, 552 Pages**	**Schmitt**	**475.00**
8184042000	**CSS: The Missing Manual, 494 Pages**	**McFarland**	**450.00**
9788184042788	**CSS: The Definitive Guide, 3/ed, 550 Pages**	**Meyer**	**500.00**
9788184042658	**CSS Pocket Reference, 2/ed, 142 Pages**	**Meyer**	**125.00**
8173667802	Database In Depth: The Relational Model for Practitioners, *250 Pages*	C.J.Date	250.00
8173662363	Database Nation: The Death of Privacy in the 21st Century, *336 Pages*	Garfinkel	235.00
9788173662898	Database Programming with JDBC & Java 2/ed, *348 Pages*	Reese	150.00
8173665664	Designing Embedded Hardware, *324 Pages*	Catsoulis	250.00
9788184042597	**Designing Embedded Hardware, 2/ed, 406 Pages**	**Catsoulis**	**275.00**
8173662428	Developing Bio-informatics Computer Skills, *504 Pages*	Gibas	225.00
8173669473	Developing Feeds with RSS and Atom, *280 Pages*	Hammersley	300.00
8184040113	Digital Identity, *266 Pages*	Windley	275.00
8173665672	DNS & BIND Cookbook, *248 Pages*	Liu	250.00
8184041969	**DNS & BIND (Covers BIND 9.3), 5/ed, 654 Pages**	**Albitz**	**550.00**
8173663785	DNS on Windows 2000, 2/ed, *376 Pages*	Larson	275.00
8173660506	DNS on Windows NT, *352 Pages*	Albitz	195.00
8184041039	**Dreamweaver 8: The Missing Manual, 964 Pages**	**David**	**600.00**
8184041209	**Dreamweaver 8 Design and Construction, 330 Pages**	**Campbell**	**375.00**
8173662991	Dreamweaver MX: The Missing Manual, *750 Pages*	McFarland	600.00
8173665281	Dynamic HTML: The Definitive Reference, 2/ed, *1,428 Pages*	Goodman	650.00
9788184042771	**Dynamic HTML: The Definitive Reference, 3/ed, 1,336 Pages**	**Goodman**	**800.00**
8173669015	Eclipse (Coverage of 3.0), *344 Pages*	Holzner	325.00
8173669309	Eclipse Cookbook (Cover 3.0), *372 Pages*	Holzner	350.00
8173669945	Eclipse IDE Pocket Guide, *140 Pages*	Burnette	125.00
8173663017	Effective awk Programming, 3/ed, *454 Pages*	Robbins	325.00
8173667268	Enterprise JavaBeans (Covers EJB 2.1 & EJB 2.0 Includes workbook for JBoss 4.0), 4/ed, *798 Pages*	Monson - Haefel	500.00
8184041195	**Enterprise JavaBeans 3.0, 5/ed, 774 Pages**	**Monson-Haefel**	**500.00**
9788173668166	Enterprise Service Architecture - O'Reilly SAP Series, *236 Pages*	Woods	225.00
8173666784	Enterprise Service Bus, *284 Pages*	Chappell	300.00
8184041446	**Enterprise SOA, 466 Pages**	**Woods**	**375.00**
8173669317	Essential ActionScript 2.0, *528 Pages*	Moock	400.00
8184040105	Essential Business Process Modeling, *362 Pages*	Havey	350.00
9788184042757	**Essential CVS, 2/ed, 442 Pages**	**Vesperman**	**425.00**
818404092X	**Essential Microsoft Operation Manager, 400 Pages**	**Fox**	**350.00**

ISBN	Title	Author	Price
8184040245	Essentail PHP Security, *310 Pages*	Shiflett	125.00
8173669430	Essentail SharePoint, *338 Pages*	Webb	325.00
9788184042825	**Essentail SNMP, 2/ed, *480 Pages***	**Mauro**	**400.00**
817366529X	Essential System Administration, 3/ed, *1,178 Pages*	Frisch	525.00
8173666644	Essential System Administration Pocket Reference, *152 Pages*	Frisch	125.00
8173660255	Essential Windows NT System Administration, *488 Pages*	Frisch	225.00
8173662495	Ethernet: The Definitive Guide, *528 Pages*	Spurgeon	300.00
9788173669613	Excel 2003 Personal Trainer (**Book / CD-ROM**), (2 Color book) *490 Pages*	CustomGuide	550.00
8173668299	Excel 2003 Programming: A Developer's Notebook, *330 Pages*	Webb	325.00
8184040288	**Excel 2003 for Starters: The Missing Manual, *408 Pages***	**MacDonald**	**275.00**
9788184042559	**Excel 2007: The Missing Manual, *870 Pages***	**MacDonald**	**550.00**
9788184042955	**Excel 2007 For Starters: The Missing Manual, *364 Pages***	**MacDonald**	**350.00**
9788184043518	**Excel Hacks, 2/Ed Tips & Tools for Streamlining Your Spreadsheets, *428 Pages***	**David**	**400.00**
8173668035	Excel: The Missing Manual, *802 Pages*	MacDonald	550.00
8184040849	**Excel Scientific and Engineering Cookbook, *442 Pages***	**Bourg**	**400.00**
8173665257	Exploring the JDS Linux Desktop (**Book / CD-ROM**), *418 Pages*	Adelstein	400.00
8184042175	**Fedora Linux, *672 Pages***	**Tyler**	**500.00**
8184041365	**Flash 8 Cookbook, *548 Pages***	**Lott**	**400.00**
8184041047	**Flash 8 Project for Learning Animation and Interactivity (Book / CD-ROM), *372 Pages***	**Shupe**	**400.00**
9788184043488	**Flash CS3 the Missing Manual, *544 Pages***	**Veer**	**500.00**
8173667470	Flash Hacks: 100 Industrial Strength Tips & Tools, *504 Pages*	Bhangal	400.00
8173668590	Flash Out of the Box: A User-Centric Beginner's Guide to Flash (**Book / CD-ROM**), *264 Pages*	Hoekman	300.00
8173667314	Flash Remoting MX: The Definitive Guide, *652 Pages*	Muck	550.00
0596002874	Free As In Freedom: Richard Stallman's Crusade for Free Software, *243 Pages*	Williams	750.00
8184040504	**FrontPage 2003: The Missing Manual, *446 Pages***	**Mantaro**	**400.00**
817366868X	GDB Pocket Reference, *78 Pages*	Robbins	75.00
9788184042856	**Google: The Missing Manual, 2/ed, *478 Pages***	**Milstein**	**425.00**
8184040857	**Google Advertising Tools, *366 Pages***	**Davis**	**375.00**
817366949X	Google Hacks: Tips & Tools for Smarter Searching 2/ed, *496 Pages*	Calishain	350.00
8184040873	**Google Maps Hacks: Tips & Tools for Geographic Searching & Remixing, *366 Pages***	**Gibson**	**350.00**
8173667136	Google Pocket Guide, *144 Pages*	Calishain	125.00
0596006624	Hackers & Painters: Big Ideas from the Computer Age, *272 Pages*	Graham	700.00
8173668256	Hardcore Java, *354 Pages*	Simmons	300.00
8173663424	Hardening Cisco Routers, *196 Pages*	Akin	150.00
8173668213	Hardware Hacking Projects for Geeks, *358 Pages*	Fullam	350.00
9788173664663	Head First Design Patterns, *688 Pages*	Sierra	500.00
9788173665264	Head First EJB: Passing the Sun Certified Business Component Developer Exam, *744 Pages*	Sierra	450.00
9788184040821	**Head First HTML with CSS & XHTML, *694 Pages***	**Freeman**	**500.00**
9788173666025	Head First Java (Covers Java 5.0) 2/ed, *730 Pages*	Sierra	450.00
9788184042214	**Head First Object - Oriented Analysis & Design, *648 Pgs***	**McLaughlin**	**425.00**
9788184040418	**Head First PMP, *712 Pages***	**Greene**	**550.00**
9788173664038	Head First Servlets & JSP: Passing the Sun Certified Web Component Developer Exam, *666 Pages*	Sierra	600.00
8184041055	**Head Rush Ajax, *464 Pages***	**McLaughlin**	**375.00**
9788173669347	Hibernate: A Developer's Notebook, *190 Pages*	Elliott	200.00
8173669260	High Performance Linux Cluster with OSCAR, Rocks, OpenMosix, and MPI, *380 Pages*	Sloan	350.00
9788184043808	**High Performance Web Sites Essential Knowledge for Frontend Engineers, *184 Pages***	**Souders**	**200.00**

ISBN	Title	Author	Price
8173669023	High Performance MySQL: Optimization, Backups, Replication & Load Balancing, *304 Pages*	Zawodny	300.00
8173663165	Home Hacking Projects for Geeks, *346 Pages*	Faulkner	325.00
8173669449	Home Networking Annoyances: How to Fix the Most Annoying Things About Your Home Network, *234 Pages*	Ivens	250.00
8184040202	Home Networking: The Missing Manual, *263 Pages*	Lowe	275.00
8184042140	**HTML & XHTML the Definitive Guide, 6/ed, *692 Pages***	**Musciano**	**500.00**
8173664323	HTML Pocket Reference, 2/ed, *100 Pages*	Niederst	70.00
9788184042696	**HTML & XHTML Pocket Reference, 3/ed, *118 Pages***	**Robbins**	**125.00**
8173665109	Information Architecture for the World Wide Web, 2/ed, *492 Pages*	Rosenfeld	400.00
9788184042917	Information Architecture for The World Wide Web, 3/ed, 540 Pages	Morville	500.00
8184040385	Integrating Excel and Access, *232 Pages*	Schmalz	250.00
9788184043600	**Intel Threading Building Blocks Out fitting C++ for Multi-Core Processor Parallelism, *348 Pages***	**Reinders**	**350.00**
8184040997	**Intermediate Perl, *290 Pages***	**Schwartz**	**300.00**
8173669414	Internet Annoyances: How to Fix the Most Annoying Things about Going Online, *266 Pages*	Gralla	250.00
8173661057	Internet Core Protocols: The Definitive Guide (**Book / CD-ROM**), *476 Pages*	Hall	375.00
8184040156	Internet Forensics, *250 Pages*	Jones	275.00
8173660158	Internet in a Nutshell, *456 Pages*	Quercia	215.00
8184041810	**The Internet: The Missing Manual, *466 Pages***	**Biersdorfer**	**350.00**
8173663378	IP Routing, *244 Pages*	Malhotra	200.00
9788184042818	**IPv6 Essentials, 2/ed, *450 Pages***	**Hagen**	**450.00**
8173663025	IPv6 Network Administration, *316 Pages*	Murphy	325.00
8173667489	IRC Hack: 100 Industrial-Strength Tips & Tools, *442 Pages*	Mutton	400.00
8173667373	J2EE Design Patterns, *390 Pages*	Crawford	325.00
8173663432	J2ME in a Nutshell: A Desktop Quick Reference, *474 Pages*	Topley	400.00
8173669295	Jakarta Commons Cookbook, *412 Pages*	O'Brien	375.00
8173669481	Jakarta Struts Cookbook, *536 Pages*	Siggelkow	400.00
8173667144	Jakarta Struts Pocket Reference, *142 Pages*	Cavaness	125.00
8173664471	Java & SOAP, *286 Pages*	Englander	275.00
8173664498	Java & XML Data Binding, *224 Pages*	McLaughlin	225.00
817366367X	Java & XML, 2/ed, *534 Pages*	McLaughlin	450.00
9788184043068	Java & XML, 3/ed, 496 Pages	McLaughlin	450.00
8173663793	Java & XSLT, *534 Pages*	Burke	350.00
8173668477	Java 1.5 Tiger: A Developer's Notebook, *210 Pages*	McLaughlin	175.00
8173669368	Java Cookbook (Coverage of 1.5), 2/ed, *872 Pages*	Darwin	600.00
8173666679	Java Data Objects, *568 Pages*	Jordan	350.00
8173666660	Java Database Best Practices, *304 Pages*	Eckstein	275.00
817366577X	Java Enterprise Best Practices, *296 Pages*	Eckstein	275.00
9788184042870	**Java Enterprise in a Nutshell, 3/ed, *906 Pages***	**Farley**	**600.00**
8173662843	Java Examples in a Nutshell 2/ed, *592 Pages*	Flanagan	225.00
8173668639	Java Examples in a Nutshell: A Tutorial Companion to Java in a Nutshell, 3/ed, *728 Pages*	Flanagan	400.00
8173666687	Java Extreme Programming Cookbook, *296 Pages*	Burke	225.00
8184042167	**Java Generics and Collections, *308 Pages***	**Naftalin**	**325.00**
817366434X	Java in a Nutshell: A Desktop Quick Reference, 4/ed, *1,000 Pgs*	Flanagan	600.00
9788184042665	**Java in a Nutshell, 5/ed, *1,266 Pages***	**Flanagan**	**650.00**
8184041187	**Java I/O, 2/ed, *740 Pages***	**Harold**	**550.00**
8173664404	Java Management Extensions, *318 Pages*	Perry	275.00
8173663211	Java Message Service, *300 Pages*	Monson-Haefel	225.00
817366353X	Java Network Programming, 3/ed, *770 Pages*	Harold	500.00

ISBN	Title	Author	Price
8173665117	Java NIO, *308 Pages*	Hitchens	275.00
8173665788	Java Performance Tuning, 2/ed, *600 Pages*	Shirazi	450.00
8173663904	Java Programming with Oracle JDBC, *504 Pages*	Bales	300.00
8173663815	Java RMI, *578 Pages*	Grosso	400.00
8173664129	Java Security, 2/ed, *624 Pages*	Oaks	500.00
9788173668227	Java Servlet & JSP Cookbook, *756 Pages*	Perry	500.00
8173662851	Java Servlet Programming 2/ed, *786 Pages*	Hunter	500.00
8173665680	Java Swing, 2/ed, *1,288 Pages*	Loy	750.00
9788173665929	Java Threads (Covers J2SE 5.0), 3/ed, *368 Pages*	Oaks	300.00
9788173663444	Java Web Services, *286 Pages*	Chappell	300.00
8173666695	Java Web Services in a Nutshell: A Desktop Quick Reference (Covers J2EE 1.4 & JWSDP), *696 Pages*	Topley	500.00
8173666709	JavaScript and DHTML Cookbook, *546 Pages*	Goodman	475.00
9788184041941	**JavaScript: The Definitive Guide, 5/ed, *1,032 Pages***	**Flanagan**	**750.00**
8173669031	JavaServer Faces, *614 Pages*	Bergsten	450.00
8173665303	JavaServer Pages (Covers JSP 2.0 & JSTL 1.1), 3/ed, *762 Pgs*	Bergsten	550.00
8173663831	JavaServer Pages Pocket Reference, *96 Pages*	Bergsten	65.00
8173669465	JBoss: A Developer's Notebook, *182 Pages*	Richards	200.00
8184040172	JBoss at Work: A Practical Guide, *318 Pages*	Marrs	325.00
8173666717	JDBC Pocket Reference, *160 Pages*	Bales	100.00
8173668604	JUnit Pocket Guide, *100 Pages*	Beck	100.00
8184041160	**JUNOS Cookbook, *682 Pages***	**Garrett**	**450.00**
059600768X	Just A Geek, *296 Pages*	Wheaton	700.00
817366515X	JXTA in a Nutshell: A Desktop Quick Reference, *422 Pages*	Oaks	225.00
8173665605	Kerberos: The Definitive Guide, *280 Pages*	Garman	275.00
8173669724	Killer Game Programming in Java, *986 Pages*	Davison	675.00
8184040261	Knoppix Pocket Reference, *104 Pages*	Rankin	100.00
8173666725	LDAP System Administration, *318 Pages*	Carter	300.00
9788184042863	**Learning C# 2005, 2/ed, *566 Pages***	**Liberty**	**450.00**
8173669635	Learning GNU Emacs, 3/ed, *544 Pages*	Cameron	450.00
8184040334	**Learning Java,3/ed (Book / CD-ROM) (Cover J2SE 5.0), *986 Pgs***	**Niemeyer**	**650.00**
8184042159	**Learning JavaScript (Covers Ajax & Dcom), *368 Pages***	**Powers**	**350.00**
8184042671	**Learning MySQL, *632 Pages***	**Tahaghoghi**	**525.00**
8173663912	Learning Oracle PL/SQL (Covers Oracle9i), *452 Pages*	Pribyl	325.00
9788184040043	Learning Perl 4/ed, *316 Pages*	Schwartz	300.00
8173667322	Learning PHP 5, *378 Pages*	Sklar	350.00
8184041535	**Learning PHP and MySQL, *390 Pages***	**Davis**	**325.00**
9788184043716	**Learning PHP and MySQL, 2/ed, *444 Pages***	**Davis**	**400.00**
8173667381	Learning Python (Covers Python 2.3), 2/ed, *630 Pages*	Lutz	525.00
9788184043341	**Learning Ruby, *272 Pages***	**Fitzgerald**	**300.00**
9788184040128	Learning SQL, *318 Pages*	Beaulieu	200.00
9788184043044	**Learning SQL on SQL Server 2005, *342 Pages***	**Bagui**	**350.00**
8173668051	Learning the Bash Shell, 3/ed, *362 Pages*	Newham	375.00
8173664447	Learning the Korn Shell, 2/ed, *438 Pages*	Rosenblett	325.00
9788173664236	Learning the UNIX Operating System, 5/ed, *174 Pages*	Peek	125.00
8173660611	Learning the vi Editor 6/ed, *352 Pages*	Lamb	250.00
8173666741	Learning UML, *304 Pages*	Si Alhir	150.00
9788184042689	**Learning UML 2.0, *300 Pages***	**Miles**	**275.00**
817366563X	Learning Visual Basic .NET, *326 Pages*	Liberty	250.00
9788184043495	**Learning WCF, *624 Pages***	**Bustamante**	**500.00**
8184040903	Learning Web Design: A Beginner's Guide to HTML, Graphics and Beyond, 2/ed, *484 Pages (with 16 Color Pages)*	Niederst	375.00
8173669422	Learning Windows Server 2003, *682 Pages*	Hassell	525.00

ISBN	Title	Author	Price
817366062X	lex & yacc 2/ed, *392 Pages*	Levine	225.00
8184041438	**Linux Annoyances for Geeks, *516 Pages***	**Jang**	**400.00**
8173668442	Linux Cookbook, *590 Pages*	Schroder	450.00
8184040164	Linux Desktop Pocket Guide, *202 Pages*	Brickner	150.00
8173663602	Linux Device Drivers, 2/ed, *650 Pages*	Rubini	450.00
9788173668494	**Linux Device Drivers (Covers Version 2.6.10 Linux Kernel), 3/ed, *646 Pages***	**Rubini**	**450.00**
8173669627	Linux in a Nutshell, 5/ed: A Desktop Quick Reference, *954 Pages*	Siever	500.00
8173669457	Linux in a Windows World, *504 Pages*	Smith	450.00
8173668507	Linux iptables Pocket Reference, *106 Pages*	Purdy	100.00
9788184043525	**Linux Kernel In A Nutshell, *216 Pages***	**Kroah**	**225.00**
8173662541	Linux Network Administrator's Guide, 2/ed, *510 Pages*	Kirch	400.00
8173664544	Linux Network Administrator's Guide, 3/ed, *372 Pages*	Kirch	350.00
8173668647	Linux Pocket Guide, *212 Pages*	Barrett	150.00
8173667187	Linux Security Cookbook, *340 Pages*	Barrett	325.00
9788184042887	**Linux Server Security, 2/ed, *556 Pages***	**Bauer**	**450.00**
817366675X	Linux Server Hacks: 100 Industrial - Strength Tips & Tools, *240 Pages*	Flickenger	225.00
8184040512	**Linux Server Hacks: Volume 2, *490 Pages***	**Hagen**	**400.00**
9788184043105	**Linux System Administration, *310 Pages***	**Adelstein**	**300.00**
9788184043815	**Linux System Programming, *404 Pages***	**Love**	**375.00**
8184040318	**Linux Multimedia Hacks, *342 Pages***	**Rankin**	**350.00**
8173668434	Linux Unwired, *322 Pages*	Weeks	300.00
8184041780	**LPI Linux Certification in a Nutshell, 2/ed, *996 Pages***	**Pritchard**	**650.00**
817366465X	Managing & Using MySQL, 2/ed, *448 Pages*	Reese	325.00
8173662746	Managing IMAP, *412 Pages*	Mullet	200.00
8173660271	Managing IP Networks with Cisco Routers, *352 Pages*	Ballew	200.00
8173663610	Managing NFS & NIS, 2/ed, *518 Pages*	Stern	400.00
8173669589	Managing Projects with GNU Make, 3/ed, *310 Pages*	Mecklenburg	325.00
8173665230	Managing RAID on Linux, *268 Pages*	Vadala	275.00
8173668655	Managing Security with Snort & IDS Tools, *296 Pages*	Cox Ph.D.	300.00
8173662800	Managing the Windows 2000 Registry, *564 Pages*	Robicheaux	325.00
0596007035	Mapping Hacks: Tips & Tools for Electronic Cartography, *574 Pages*	Erle	900.00
8173661162	Mastering Algorithms with C **(Book / DISK)**, *572 Pages*	Loudon	400.00
8173664455	Mastering FreeBSD and OpenBSD Security, *472 Pages*	Korff	425.00
8173664617	Mastering Oracle SQL (Covers Oracle Database10g), 2/ed, *504 Pages*	Mishra	400.00
8173666768	Mastering Perl for Bioinformatics, *406 Pages*	Tisdall	300.00
8173665087	Mastering Regular Expressions, 2/ed, *492 Pages*	Friedl	400.00
9788184043013	Mastering Regular Expressions, 3/ed, 556 Pages	Friedl	450.00
8173665702	Mastering Visual Studio .NET 2003, *420 Pages*	Flanders	375.00
8173667918	Maven: A Developer's Notebook, *232 Pages*	Massol	250.00
9788184042184	**MCSE Core Elective Exams in a Nutshell, *604 Pages***	**Bhardwaj**	**500.00**
8184041551	**MCSE Core Required Exams in a Nutshell, 3/ed, *750 Pages***	**Stanek**	**450.00**
8184040520	**Monad, *218 Pages***	**Oakley**	**225.00**
8173667497	Mono: A Developer's Notebook, *312 Pages*	Dumbill	325.00
9788184042801	**MySQL Cookbook, 2/ed, *990 Pages***	**DuBois**	**750.00**
817366806X	MySQL in a Nutshell, *358 Pages*	Dyer	325.00
8173666776	MySQL Pocket Reference, *94 Pages*	Reese	100.00
8184041403	**MySQL Stored Procedure Programming, *650 Pages***	**Harrison**	**450.00**
8173665249	NetBeans: The Definitive Guide, *662 Pages*	Boudreau	500.00
8173668809	Network Security Assessment, *398 Pages*	McNab	400.00
8173663521	Network Security Hacks: 100 Industrial-Strength Tips & Tools, *328 Pages*	Lockhart	325.00
9788184042740	**Network Security Hacks, 2/ed, *492 Pages***	**Lockhart**	**425.00**
8173668396	Network Security Tools: Writing, Hacking, and Modifying Security Tools , *350 Pages*	Dhanjani	350.00

ISBN	Title	Author	Price
8173663688	Network Troubleshooting Tools, *370 Pages*	Sloan	250.00
9788184043532	**Network Warrior, *614 Pages***	**Donahue**	**450.00**
8173667926	Nokia Smartphone Hacks: Tips & Tools for Your Smallest Computer, *418 Pages*	Yuan	400.00
8173667845	NUnit Pocket Reference, *100 Pages*	Hamilton	100.00
8173668264	Office 2003 XML, *596 Pages*	Lenz	450.00
9788184043303	**Office 2007 the Missing Manual, *890 Pages***	**Grover**	**550.00**
8184040296	Open Sources 2.0, *488 Pages*	DiBona	425.00
8173667721	Open Source for the Enterprise, *246 Pages*	Woods	250.00
8173667519	OpenOffice.org Writer **(Book / CD-ROM)**, *234 Pages*	Weber	250.00
8173667403	Optimizing Oracle Performance, *426 Pages*	Milsap	375.00
8173669287	Oracle Applications Server 10g Essentials, *292 Pages*	Greenwald	275.00
8173661170	Oracle Built-in Packages **(Book / DISK)**, *956 Pages*	Feuerstein	475.00
8173667071	Oracle Data Dictionary Pocket Reference, *150 Pages*	Kreines	125.00
8173660670	Oracle Database Administration: The Essential Reference, *552 Pages*	Kreines	325.00
817366417X	Oracle DBA Checklist Pocket Reference, *88 Pages*	RevealNet	65.00
8184040008	Oracle DBA Pocket Guide, *164 Pages*	Kreines	125.00
8173660689	Oracle Distributed Systems **(Book / DISK)**, *552 Pages*	Dye	325.00
8173664110	Oracle Essentials: Oracle9i, Oracle8i & Oracle8, 2/ed, *382 Pages*	Greenwald	250.00
817366935X	Oracle Essentials: Oracle Database 10g, 3/ed, *368 Pages*	Greenwald	275.00
817366580X	Oracle in a Nutshell: A Desktop Quick Reference, *934 Pages*	Greenwald	600.00
8173664560	Oracle Initialization Parameters Pocket Reference (Oracle Database 10g), *128 Pages*	Kreines	125.00
8173663629	Oracle PL/SQL Best Practices, *208 Pages*	Feuerstein	200.00
8173661189	Oracle PL/SQL Built-ins Pocket Reference, *78 Pages*	Feuerstein	60.00
8184040350	Oracle PL/SQL for DBAs, *466 Pages*	Feuerstein	350.00
818404254X	**Oracle PL/SQL Language Pocket Reference, 3/ed, *140 Pgs***	**Feuerstein**	**125.00**
8184040482	**Oracle PL/SQL Programming, 4/ed, *1,210 Pages***	**Feuerstein**	**600.00**
8173662401	Oracle PL/SQL Programming: A Developer's Workbook, *576 Pages*	Feuerstein	300.00
8173661197	Oracle PL/SQL Programming: Guide to Oracle8i Features **(Book / DISK)**, *264 Pages*	Feuerstein	235.00
8173668116	Oracle Regular Expression Pocket Reference, *74 Pages*	Burcham	75.00
8173661200	Oracle SAP Administration, *208 Pages*	Burleson	175.00
8173660298	Oracle Scripts **(Book / CD-ROM)**, *208 Pages*	Lomansky	250.00
8173660719	Oracle Security, *448 Pages*	Theriault	220.00
8173663637	Oracle SQL* Loader: The Definitive Guide, *278 Pages*	Gennick	175.00
8173669333	Oracle SQL*Plus Pocket Reference, 3/ed, *160 Pages*	Gennick	125.00
8173666067	Oracle SQL*Plus: The Definitive Guide, 2/ed, *592 Pages*	Gennick	400.00
8173662916	Oracle SQL: The Essential Reference, *424 Pages*	Kreines	200.00
8173661847	Oracle Utilities Pocket Reference, *136 Pages*	Mishra	100.00
8173661219	Oracle Web Applications: PL/SQL Developer's Intro, *264 Pages*	Odewahn	180.00
817366028X	Oracle8 Design Tips, *136 Pages*	Ensor	120.00
8173668027	PC Annoyances: How to Fix the Most Annoying Thingsabout your Personal Computer, *236 Pages*	Bass	225.00
9788184042528	PC Annoyances, 2/ed :How To Fix The Most Annoying Things About Your Personal Compter, Wind & More, *268 Pages*	Bass	300.00
8173667152	PC Hacks: 100 Industrial-Strength Tips & Tools, *316 Pages*	Aspinwall	300.00
8173669732	PC Hardware Annoyances: How to Fix the Most ANNOYING Things About Your Computer Hardware, *276 Pages*	Bigelow	275.00
817366532X	PC Hardware in a Nutshell: A Desktop Quick Reference, 3/ed, *848 Pages*	Thompson	325.00
8173668272	PC Pest Control, *296 Pages*	Gralla	300.00
818404139X	**PC's: The Missing Manual, *612 Pages***	**Rathbone**	**450.00**
8173667128	PDF Hacks: 100 Industrial-Strength Tips & Tools, *308 Pages*	Steward	300.00
8173664463	Perl & XML, *224 Pages*	Ray	175.00

ISBN	Title	Author	Price
8173661073	Perl 5 Pocket Reference, 3/ed, *96 Pages*	Vromans	70.00
8184042760	**Perl 6 and Parrot Essentials, 2/ed, *304 Pages***	**Randal**	**325.00**
8173668280	Perl Best Practices, *554 Pages*	Conway	425.00
9788173667336	Perl Cookbook, 2/ed, *976 Pages*	Christiansen	675.00
8184041381	**Perl Hacks, *310 Pages***	**Chromatic**	**325.00**
8173668043	Perl Template Toolkit, *600 Pages*	Chamberlain	525.00
8173668361	Perl Testing: A Developer's Notebook, *212 Pages*	Langworth	225.00
8173665710	PHP Cookbook, *638 Pages*	Sklar	550.00
9788184043006	PHP Cookbook, 2/ed, 842 Pages	Sklar	550.00
8184040814	**PHP Hacks: Tips & Tools for Creating Dynamic Web Sites, *468 Pages***	**Herrington**	**400.00**
8184040237	PHP in a Nutshell, *370 Pages*	Hudson	325.00
8184040253	PHPUnit Pocket Guide, *88 Pages*	Bergmann	100.00
817366871X	Postfix: The Definitive Guide, *288 Pages*	Dent	275.00
8173669805	Powerpoint 2003 Personal Trainer (Book / CD-ROM), (2 Color book) *242 Pages*	CustomGuide	425.00
9788184042566	**Powerpoint 2007: The Missing Manual, *502 Pages***	**Veer**	**450.00**
9788184042948	**PowerPoint 2007 For Starters: The Missing Manual, 325 Pgs**	**Vander**	**325.00**
8173660301	Practical C Programming 3/ed, *456 Pages*	Oualline	225.00
8173666822	Practical C++ Programming, 2/ed, *582 Pages*	Oualline	225.00
8184040059	Practical Development Environments, *340 Pages*	Doar	325.00
817366711X	Practical mod_perl, *932 Pages*	Bekman	675.00
8184040326	**Practical Perforce, *370 Pages***	**Wingerd**	**375.00**
8173663920	Practical PostgreSQL **(Book / CD-ROM)**, *642 Pgs*	Command Prompt Inc.	450.00
8173666733	Practical RDF, *360 Pages*	Powers	325.00
8173666830	Practical Unix & Internet Security, 3/ed, *994 Pages*	Garfinkel	650.00
8173664390	Practical VoIP Using VOCAL, *532 Pages*	Dang	450.00
8184040091	Prefactoring, *248 Pages*	Pugh	250.00
8184042108	**Process Improvement Essentials, *364 Pages***	**Persse, PhD**	**400.00**
8184040229	Producing Open Sources Software, *302 Pages*	Fogel	325.00
9788184043709	Programming Collective Intelligence Building Smart Web 2.0 Application, *374 Pages*	Segaram	375.00
9788184040340	Programming .NET Components, 2/ed (Covers .NET 2.0 & Visual Studio 2005), *656 Pages*	Lowy	425.00
8173667209	Programming .NET Security, *704 Pages*	Freeman	550.00
8173664382	Programming .NET Web Services, *500 Pages*	Ferrara	375.00
8173667411	Programming .NET Windows Applications (Covers .NET 1.1, & Visual Studio .NET 2003), *1,316 Pages*	Liberty	750.00
8184042086	**Programming Atlas, *418 Pages***	**Wenz**	**375.00**
8184040970	**Programming ASP.NET (Covers 2.0), 3/ed, *966 Pages***	**Liberty**	**600.00**
9788184043839	**Programming ASP.NET Ajax, *490 Pages***	**Wenz**	**400.00**
9788173669651	**Programming C# (Covers C# 2.0, .NET 2.0 & Visual Studio 2005), 4/ed, *680 Pages***	**Liberty**	**525.00**
817366076X	Programming Embedded Systems in C & C++, *198 Pages*	Barr	150.00
9788184042627	**Programming Embedded Systems with C and GNU Development Tools, 2/ed, *340 Pages***	**Barr**	**250.00**
8184041454	**Programming Excel with VBA and .NET, *1,128 Pages***	**Webb**	**750.00**
8173669694	Programming Flash Communication Server, *842 Pages*	Lesser	600.00
9788184043358	**Programming Flex 2, *518 Pages***	**Kazoun**	**425.00**
8173661278	Programming Internet E-mail, *384 Pages*	Wood	225.00
9788173668180	Programming Jakarta Struts 2/ed, *470 Pages*	Cavaness	400.00
8184040792	**Programming MapPoint in .NET (Book / CD-ROM), *400 Pages***	**Thota**	**350.00**
9788173662652	Programming Perl 3/ed, *1,116 Pages*	Wall	750.00
8173663114	Programming PHP, *530 Pages*	Lerdorf	350.00
9788184042719	**Programming PHP, 2/ed, *425 Pages***	**Lerdorf**	**425.00**

ISBN	Title	Author	Price
8173667500	Programming Python (Covers Python 2) **(Book / CD-ROM)**, 2/ed, *1,305 Pages*	Lutzf	750.00
9788184043792	**Programming Python, 3/ed**, *1582 Pages*	**Lutz**	**800.00**
8173667861	**Programming SQL Server 2005**, *600 Pages*	**Wildermuth**	**400.00**
8173662371	Programming the Perl DBI, *372 Pages*	Descartes	200.00
8173667063	Programming Visual Basic .NET 2003, 2/ed, *564 Pages*	Liberty	425.00
8184040377	**Programming Visual Basic 2005**, *580 Pages*	**Liberty**	**400.00**
9788184043051	**Progamming WCF Services**, **600 Pages**	**Lowy**	**500.00**
8173665737	Programming Web Services with Perl, *492 Pages*	Ray	400.00
8173662045	Programming Web Services with SOAP, *268 Pages*	Snell	200.00
817366207X	Programming Web Services with XML-RPC, *240 Pages*	St.Laurent	175.00
8173668175	Programming with QT (Covers Qt 3), 2/ed, *532 Pages*	Dalheimer	450.00
8184041500	**Project 2003 Personal** Trainer, (Book / CD-ROM), *246 Pgs*	**CustomGuide**	**300.00**
817366479X	Python Cookbook (Covers Python 2.3 & 2.4), 2/ed, *852 Pages*	Martelli	600.00
8173666857	Python in a Nutshell: A Desktop Quick Reference (Cover Python 2.2), *662 Pages*	Martelli	500.00
8173669708	Python Pocket Reference (Covers Python 2.4), 3/ed, *168 Pages*	Lutz	125.00
8173668485	qmail, *268 Pages*	Levine	275.00
9788184042962	**Rail Cookbook**, **600 Pages**	**Orsini**	**450.00**
817366689X	Real World Web Services, *230 Pages*	Iverson	225.00
9788184043327	**Restful Web Services**, *462 Pages*	**Richardson**	**400.00**
8184040865	**RFID Essentials**, *276 Pages*	**Glover**	**275.00**
8184041985	**The Relational Database Dictionary**, *126 Pages*	**Date**	**150.00**
8173667276	Regular Expression Pocket Reference, *112 Pages*	Stubblebine	100.00
9788184043761	Regular Expression Pocket Reference, 2/ed, *132 Pages*	Stubblebine	150.00
8184041373	**Repairing and Upgrading Your PC**, *462 Pages*	**Thompson**	**350.00**
8173669686	RT Essentials, *228 Pages*	Vincent	250.00
8184041802	**Ruby Cookbook**, *920 Pages*	**Carlson**	**650.00**
8184041993	**Ruby on Rails: Up and Running**, *196 Pages*	**Tate**	**225.00**
9780596007195	Revolution in the Valley, *324 Pages*	Hertzfeld	775.00
9788184043624	**Ruby Pocket Reference**, *182 Pages*	**Fitzgerald**	**150.00**
8173665206	Running Linux, 4/ed, *702 Pages*	Welsh	425.00
9788184042726	**Running Linux, 5/ed**, *986 Pages*	**Welsh**	**600.00**
8173667055	Samba Pocket Reference, 2/ed, *146 Pages*	Eckstein	125.00
8173664226	SAX2 (Simple API for XML), *248 Pages*	Brownell	175.00
8173667217	Secure Coding: Principles & Practices, *200 Pages*	Graff	225.00
8173667284	Secure Programming Cookbook for C and C++, *800 Pages*	Viega	600.00
9788184043754	**Security Power Tools**, *872 Pages*	**Burns**	**650.00**
9788184043617	**Securing Ajax Applications**, *266 Pages*	**Wells**	**275.00**
8173663262	Securing Windows NT/2000 Servers for the Internet, *200 Pages*	Norberg	125.00
8173669376	Securing Windows Server 2003, *456 Pages*	Danseglio	400.00
8184040083	Security and Usability, *748 Pages*	Cranor	550.00
817366840X	Security Warrior, *562 Pages*	Peikari	500.00
8173660786	sed & awk, 2/ed, *440 Pages*	Dougherty	300.00
817366918X	SELINUX NSA's Open Source Security Enhanced Linux, *264 Pages*	McCarty	275.00
8173665834	sendmail, 3/ed, *1,238 Pages*	Costales	850.00
817366823X	sendmail Cookbook, *418 Pages*	Hunt	400.00
8173666865	Sequence Analysis in a Nutshell: A Guide to Common Tools and Databases (Covers EMBOSS 2.5.0), *310 Pages*	Markel	275.00
9788184040449	SharePoint 2007, The Definitive Guide, *836 Pages*	Pyles	600.00
817366983X	SharePoint Office Pocket Guide, *94 Pages*	Webb	100.00
817366739X	SharePoint User's Guide, *158 Pages*	IDC	150.00
8184040679	**Skype Hacks: Tips & Tools for Cheap, Fun, Innovative Phone Service**, *354 Pages*	**Sheppard**	**350.00**

ISBN	Title	Author	Price
8173669503	Snort Cookbook, *296 Pages*	Orebaugh	300.00
9788184043693	SOA in Practice, *358 Pages*	Josuttis	375.00
8173669198	SpamAssassin (Covers 3.0), *232 Pages*	Schwartz	250.00
8173668191	Spidering Hacks: 100 Industrial - Strength Tips & Tools, *436 Pages*	Hemenway	350.00
9788173668371	Spring: A Developer's Notebook, *202 Pages*	Tate	200.00
9788184040685	**SQL Cookbook (Cover SQL Server, PostgreSQL,Oracle, MySQL, AND DB2), *640 Pages***	**Molinaro**	**475.00**
9788184042207	**SQL Hacks, *424 Pages***	**Cumming**	**400.00**
8173666520	SQL in a Nutshell (Covers SQL Server, DB2, MySQL, Oracle & PostgreSQL), 2/ed, *720 Pages*	Kline	450.00
8173667438	SQL Pocket Guide (Cover Oracle. DB2, SQL Server & MySQL), *170 Pages*	Gennick	125.00
9788173668241	SQL Tunning (Covers Oracle, DB2 & SQL Server), *356 Pages*	Tow	325.00
8173668418	Squid: The Definitive Guide, *472 Pages*	Wessels	450.00
9788184042795	**SSH The Secure Shell: The Definitive Guide, 2/ed, *680 Pages***	**Barrett**	**525.00**
9788184042634	**Statistics Hacks, *380 Pages***	**Frey**	**350.00**
8173668574	STL Pocket Reference, *136 Pages*	Lischner	100.00
8184041799	**SUSE Linux, *460 Pages***	**Brown**	**400.00**
8173664811	Swing Hacks, *554 Pages*	Marinacci	425.00
8173665311	Switching to VoIP, *514 Pages*	Wallingford	450.00
8173669511	SWT: A Developer's Notebook, *330 Pages*	Hatton	325.00
8173663254	T1: A Survival Guide, *312 Pages*	Gast	225.00
8184040539	**Talk is Cheap: Switching to Internet Telephones, *278 Pages***	**Gaskin**	**275.00**
817366093X	Tcl/Tk in a Nutshell: A Desktop Quick Reference, *480 Pages*	Raines	240.00
8173664676	TCP/IP Network Administration 3/ed, *756 Pages*	Hunt	500.00
8173666512	Test Driving Linux: From Windows to Linux in 60 Seconds (Book / CD-ROM), *372 Pages*	Brickner	350.00
818404030X	**Time Management for System Administrators, *238 Pages***	**Limoncelli**	**250.00**
8173666032	**TOAD Pocket Reference for Oracle, 2/ed, *136 Pages***	**McGrath**	**125.00**
8173666873	Tomcat: The Definitive Guide (Cover Tomcat 4), *336 Pages*	Brittain	300.00
8184040210	Twisted Network Programming Essentials, *210 Pages*	Fettig	275.00
8184041594	**Ubuntu Hacks, *462 Pages***	**Oxer**	**350.00**
9788184040029	UML 2.0 in a Nutshell, *246 Pages*	Pilone	200.00
9788184042993	UML 2.0 Pocket Reference, 150 Pages	Pilone	125.00
8173667225	UML Pocket Reference, *96 Pages*	Pilone	100.00
8184040768	**Understanding Linux Network Internals, *1,074 Pages***	**Benvenuti**	**600.00**
9788184043198	**Understanding MySQL Internals, *208 Pages***	**Pachey**	**300.00**
8184040830	**Understanding the Linux Kernel (Cover Version 2.6), 3/ed, *954 Pages***	**Bovet**	**550.00**
8184041608	**Unicode Explained, *692 Pages***	**Korpela**	**525.00**
817366627X	Unit Test Frameworks (Book / CD-ROM), *222 Pages*	Hamill	225.00
8184040601	**Unix in a Nutshell, 4/ed, *992 Pages***	**Robbins**	**450.00**
8173665656	Unix Power Tools, 3/ed, *1,162 Pages*	Powers	750.00
8173666202	Upgrading to PHP 5 (Covers MySQL 4.1), *358 Pages*	Trachtenberg	350.00
8173660948	Using & Managing PPP, *464 Pages*	Sun	240.00
8173665842	Using Samba, 2/ed, *570 Pages*	Eckstein	500.00
9788184043037	Using Samba, 3/ed, 464 Pages	Carter	450.00
817366594X	VB .NET Language Pocket Reference, *160 Pages*	Roman	125.00
8173666881	VBScript in a Nutshell: A Desktop Quick Reference, 2/e, *528 Pages*	Lomax	400.00
8173663300	VBScript Pocket Reference, *118 Pages*	Childs	60.00
8173668582	Version Control With Subversion, *332 Pages*	Collins - Sussman	350.00
8173662622	vi Editor Pocket Reference, *76 Pages*	Robbins	60.00
8173661340	Virtual Private Networks, 2/ed, *228 Pages*	Scott	150.00

ISBN	Title	Author	Price
8173666164	Visual Basic 2005: A Developer's Notebook, *272 Pages*	MacDonald	250.00
8184040911	Visual Basic 2005 in a Nutshell 3/ed, *766 Pages*	Patrick	500.00
8184040067	Visual Basic 2005 Jumpstart, *226 Pages*	Lee	225.00
8173669740	Visual C# 2005: A Developer's Notebook, *250 Pages*	Liberty	225.00
8184042094	Visual Basic 2005 Cookbook, *754 Pages*	Craig	575.00
8173660964	Visual Basic Controls in a Nutshell, *512 Pages*	Dictor	310.00
8184040695	**VOIP Hacks: Tips & Tools for Internet Telephony, *326 Pgs***	Wallingford	325.00
0596007337	We the Media: Grassroots Journalism by the People, for the People, *320 Pages*	Gillmor	775.00
9788173669057	Web Database Application with PHP & MySQL (Covers PEAR, PHP 5 & MySQL 4.1), 2/ed, *828 Pages*	Willaims	600.00
8173663750	Web Design in a Nutshell: A Desktop Quick Reference, 2/ed, *656 Pages*	Niederst	425.00
9788184040982	Web Design in a Nutshell: A Desktop Quick Reference, 3/ed, *826 Pages*	Niederst	450.00
8173664412	Web Performance Tuning, 2/ed, *488 Pages*	Killelea	350.00
8173665214	Web Privacy with P3P, *350 Pages*	Cranor	300.00
8173663947	Web Security, Privacy & Commerce, 2/ed, *768 Pages*	Garfinkel	500.00
8173667624	**Web Site Cookbook, *262 Pages***	**Addison**	**300.00**
8173663394	Web Services Essentials, *320 Pages*	Cerami	200.00
8173669678	Web Site Measurement Hacks: Tips & Tools to Help Optimize Your Online Business, *442 Pages*	Peterson	400.00
8173663092	WebLogic 8.1: The Definitive Guide, *860 Pages*	Mountjoy	600.00
8173661308	The Whole Internet: The Next Generation, *576 Pages*	Conner/Krol	425.00
8173661367	Win32 API Programming with Visual Basic **(Book / CD-ROM)**, *534 Pages*	Roman	400.00
8173663319	Windows 2000 Commands Pocket Reference, *122 Pages*	Frisch	60.00
9788184042603	**Windows Developers Power Tools, *1,322 Pages***	**Avery**	**750.00**
8173660883	Windows NT TCP/IP Network Administration, *512 Pages*	Hunt	250.00
8184040776	**Windows Server 2003 Security Cookbook, *522 Pages***	**Danseglio**	**475.00**
8173668833	Windows Server Hacks: 100 Industrial-Strength Tips & Tools , *328 Pages*	Tulloch	325.00
9788184042139	**Windows Vista: The Definitive Guide, *958 Pages***	**Stanek**	**600.00**
9788184042580	**Windows Vista: The Missing Manual, *860 Pages***	**Pogue**	**600.00**
9788184042979	**Windows Vista For Starters: The Missing Manual, *493 Pages***	**Pogue**	**325.00**
9788184042986	**Windows Vista In A Nutshell, *766 Pages***	**Gralla**	**500.00**
9788184043075	**Windows Vista Pocket Reference, *208 Pages***	**Gralla**	**150.00**
817366966X	Windows XP Cookbook, *690 Pages*	Allen	500.00
8173667454	Windows XP Hacks: 100 Industrial-Strength Tips & Tools, *294 Pgs*	Gralla	350.00
8173669643	Windows XP Personal Trainer **(Book / CD-ROM)**, *480 Pgs*	CustomGuide	550.00
8173666911	Windows XP Pocket Reference, *196 Pages*	Karp	125.00
8173667462	Wireless Hacks: 100 Industrial-Strength Tips & Tools, *424 Pages*	Flickenger	275.00
9788184043020	Wireless Hacks, 2/ed: Tips & Tools For Building, Extending & Securing Your Network 2/ed, *480 Pages*	Flickenger	425.00
9788184042931	Word 2007 For Starters: The Missing Manual, *372 Pages*	Grover	350.00
817366692X	Word Pocket Guide, *160 Pages*	Glenn	125.00
8173665354	Writing Excel Macros with VBA, 2/ed, *580 Pages*	Roman	450.00
8173660778	Writing Word Macros, *416 Pages*	Roman	275.00
818404142X	**XAML in a Nutshell, *316 Pages***	**MacVittie**	**300.00**
8173666156	XML Hacks: 100 Industrial-Strength Tips & Tools, *490 Pages*	Fitzgerald	425.00
8173668450	XML in a Nutshell (Covers XML 1.1 & XInclude), 3/ed, *724 Pages*	Harold	500.00
8173663343	XML Pocket Reference, 2/ed, *128 Pages*	Eckstein	100.00

ISBN	Title	Author	Price
9788184042641	**XML Pocket Reference, 3/ed,** *198 Pages*	**Laurent**	**125.00**
8173664900	XSLT 1.0 Pocket Reference, *188 Pages*	Lenz	150.00
8184040784	**XSLT Cookbook (Cover XSLT 1.0 & 2.0, 2/ed,** *786 Pages*	**Mangano**	**500.00**
9788184043181	**XQuery,** *528 Pages*	**Walmsley**	**500.00**
8184040075	Yahoo! Hacks: Tips & Tools for Living on the Web Frontier, *504 Pages*	Bausch	400.00
8184040881	**Zero Configuration Networking: The Definitive Guide,** *252 Pages*	**Cheshire**	**275.00**

US EDITION AVAILABLE AT INDIA SPECIAL PRICE:

ISBN	Title	Author	Price
0596102364	**Adobe Creative Suite 2 Workflow,** *634 Pages*	**Alspach**	**1,625.00**
0596006004	Adobe Encore DVD: In the Studio, *336 Pages*	Dixon	1,225.00
0596100973	**Adobe InDesign CS2 One-on-One (Book / CD-ROM),** *420 Pages*	**McClelland**	**1,375.00**
9780596529758	**Adobe Photoshop CS3 One-On-One (Book / DVD),** *544 Pages*	**McClelland**	**US$40.00**
0596100965	**Adobe Photoshop CS2 One-on-One (Book / DVD),** *512 Pages*	**McClelland**	**1,225.00**
0596001088	The Cathedral & The Bazaar: Musings On Linux and Open Source by an Accidental Revolutionary, Revised & Expanded, *256 Pages*	Raymond	525.00
059600849X	**Commercial Photoshop Retouching: In The Studio,** *410 Pages*	**Honiball**	**1,425.00**
0596008589	**Creating Photomontages with Photoshop: A Designer's Notebook,** *96 Pages*	**Collandre**	**800.00**
9780596008031	**Designing Interfaces,** *352 Pages*	**Tidwell**	**1,800.00**
9780596526801	**Devices of the Soul Batting for Our Selves in an Age of Machines,** *302 Pages*	**Talbott**	**US$18.00**
0596005474	Digital Photography: Expert Techniques (Covers Photoshop CS), *496 Pages*	Milburn	1,375.00
0596006667	Digital Photography Hacks: 100 Industrial - Strength Tips & Tools, *336 Pages*	Story	800.00
0596100159	Digital Photography Pocket Guide, 3/ed, *160 Pages*	Story	450.00
0596008414	**Digital Photography: The Missing Manual,** *432 Pages*	**Grover**	**1,200.00**
0596009461	Digital Video Hacks: Tips & Tools for Shooting, Editing & Sharing, *426 Pages*	Paul	800.00
0596005237	Digital Video Pocket Guide, *474 Pages*	Story	500.00
9780596006624	**Hackers & Painters: Big Ideas From the Computer Age,** *276 Pages*	**Graham**	**700.00**
0596008597	**Illustrations with Photoshop: A Designer's Notebook,** *96 Pages*	**Rodarmor**	**775.00**
0596100485	**InDesign Production Cookbook,** *224 Pages*	**Dabbs**	**1,200.00**
9780596527051	**Myths of Innovation,** *196 Pages*	**Berkun**	**US$20.00**
0596008600	**Photo Retouching with Photoshop: A Designer's Notebook,** *96 Pages*	**CLEC'H**	**775.00**
9780596100209	**Photoshop Blending Modes Cookbook for Digital Photographers,** *176 Pages*	**Beardsworth**	**1,025.00**
0596008511	**Photoshop CS2 Raw: Using Adobe Camera Raw, Bridge, and Photoshop to Get the Most Out of Your Digital Camera,** *206 Pages*	**Aaland**	**1,075.00**
0596100213	**Photoshop Filter Effects Encyclopedia,** *176 Pages*	**Pring**	**1,050.00**
0596100620	**Photoshop Fine Art Effects Cookbook,** *176 Pages*	**Beardsworth**	**1,050.00**
0596100221	**Photoshop Photo Effects Cookbook,** *176 Pages*	**Shelbourne**	**1,025.00**
0596100302	**Photoshop Retouching Cookbook for Digital Photographers,** *176 Pages*	**Huggins**	**1,025.00**
9780596101138	**Programming Windows Presentation Foundation,** *430 Pages*	**Sells**	**1,100.00**
9780596523701	**Stephen Johnson on Digital Photography,** *320 Pages*	**Johnson**	**1,500.00**
0596100833	**Windows Seat,** *152 Pages*	**Kost**	**1,600.00**

FORTHCOMING TITLES

November 2007

ISBN	Title	Author	Price
9788184043648	Mastering Perl, 358 Pages	Schwartz	350.00
0596100310	Digital Video Production Cookbook, *192 Pages*	Kenworthy	1,200.00
8184043171	Flash 8: The Missing Manual, *460 Pages*	Moore	500.00
8184043244	Fonts & Encodings, *992 Pages*	Haralambous	675.00
8184043198	Information Dashboard Design, *223 Pages*	Few	250.00
0596101686	Photoshop Workflow Setups, *207 Pages*	Tapp	1,170.00
0596527683	Practical Color Management: Eddie Tapp on Digital Photography, *168 Pages*	Tapp	1,170.00